# 3D Studio
# in Motion

## Basics Using Release 2.5

Stephen J. Ethier
Christine A. Ethier
*CADInnovations*

Prentice Hall
*Upper Saddle River, New Jersey* *Columbus, Ohio*

**Library of Congress Cataloging-in-Publication Data**

Ethier, Stephen J.
3D Studio MAX in motion: basics using Release 2.5 / Stephen J. Ethier, Christine A. Ethier.
p. cm.
Includes index.
ISBN 0-13-022549-5
1. Computer animation. 2. Three-dimensional display systems. 3. 3D Studio. I. Ethier, Christine A. II. Title.
TR897.7.E84 2000
006.6'93—dc21 99-31916
CIP

Cover art: Stephen J. Ethier
Editor: Stephen Helba
Assistant Editor: Michelle Churma
Production Supervision: Lisa Garboski, bookworks
Production Editor: Louise N. Sette
Design Coordinator: Karrie M. Converse-Jones
Text Designer: STELLARViSIONs
Cover Designer: Rod Harris
Production Manager: Deidra M. Schwartz
Marketing Manager: Chris Bracken

This book was set in Adobe Caslon by STELLARViSIONs and was printed and bound by Courier/Kendallville, Inc. The cover was printed by Phoenix Color Corp.



Printed in the United States of America

10 9 8 7 6 5 4 3 2 1

ISBN: 0-13-022549-5

Prentice-Hall International (UK) Limited, *London*
Prentice-Hall of Australia Pty. Limited, *Sydney*
Prentice-Hall of Canada, Inc., *Toronto*
Prentice-Hall Hispanoamericana, *S. A., Mexico*
Prentice-Hall of India Private Limited, *New Delhi*
Prentice-Hall of Japan, Inc., *Tokyo*
Prentice-Hall (Singapore) Pte. Ltd., *Singapore*
Editora Prentice-Hall do Brasil, Ltda., *Rio de Janeiro*

*To Tilley*

*an old and constant companion*

*and to*

*Nevan Dobson Barar*

*a brand new miracle*

*goodbye...*

*and hello*

*3D Studio MAX™ in Motion* is a text that commits to covering all the basics of the 3D Studio MAX program, which produces, with your help, realistic renderings of still images and animations. With a few skills and techniques at your fingertips, you will be impressed with the professional results you can accomplish. If you have half the fun reading the text and completing the labs that we had in writing them, you are in for a wonderful time. And, if what learning theorists say is true and you learn better when you can combine learning with pleasure, then picking up this book is just the first step to your newfound skill and expertise.

*3D Studio MAX™ in Motion* combines a theoretical approach with accompanying hands-on activities to instruct you on the reasons for your actions while you experience the actions. It is our hope that whether you are in a school setting, the business world, or your basement office, you can pick up the text and learn from it in a progressive fashion. It is designed to be a positive learning experience for the individual who knows just the basics about both computers and CAD, and an enriching experience for those who are experts in CAD but wish to add a new dimension.

## FEATURES OF OUR TEXT

- Practical Applications chapters in a variety of areas, including architectural, mechanical motion, and graphic arts
- An accompanying CD-ROM with a variety of features, including
    - A materials library
    - Bitmap images
    - Scenes (3D models)
    - Still renderings
    - Animation
- Questions and Assignments at the end of each chapter

- Lights...Camera...Action boxes introduce special tips and tricks that help you achieve your animation goals
- Tool icons throughout the text help you to follow the path to the correct command every time, even in an unknown land
- More than 1000 images create a vivid picture of each action and part of the process
- A full-color insert shows the results of the completed projects and other illustrations
- A tear-out Quick Chart shows all the shortcut keys
- An instructor's manual includes a test bank of true/false, multiple choice, matching, and fill-in-the-blank questions for each chapter

## ORGANIZATION OF THE TEXT

The text is divided into six parts, plus appendices, that explore all the basics of 3D Studio MAX. They include, in the following order:

- Introduction to Computer Animation
- Exploring 3D Studio MAX
- Preparing for 3D Modeling
- 3D Modeling
- Presentation
- Practical Applications

Each chapter begins with a section of theory and ends with a lab that complements and extends the theory presented in that chapter. The labs progress in complexity and simultaneously decrease hand-holding instruction.

## ACKNOWLEDGMENTS

Stephen Helba, Stephen Helba, Stephen Helba: as he plays, at the very least, the role of three people in the process, we thank him from the bottom of our hearts. Others who deserve much gratitude include Michelle Churma and Lisa Garboski and the entire contributing staff at Prentice Hall.

We also thank reviewers for their helpful comments: Wen M. Andrews, Sargeant Reynolds Community College; Adrian G. Baird, Ricks College; Donald K. Chastian, Black Hills State University; Michael Ehrlinger, Catonsville Community College; Earl M. Faulkner, ITT Technical Institute, Boise; Dennis Jorgensen, Bakersfield College; Kirk Narburgh, Syracuse University; and Jeenson Sheen, Norfolk State University.

# BRIEF CONTENTS

# CONTENTS

# PART TWO Exploring 3D Studio MAX 35

# PART FOUR 3D Modeling 177

PART
ONE

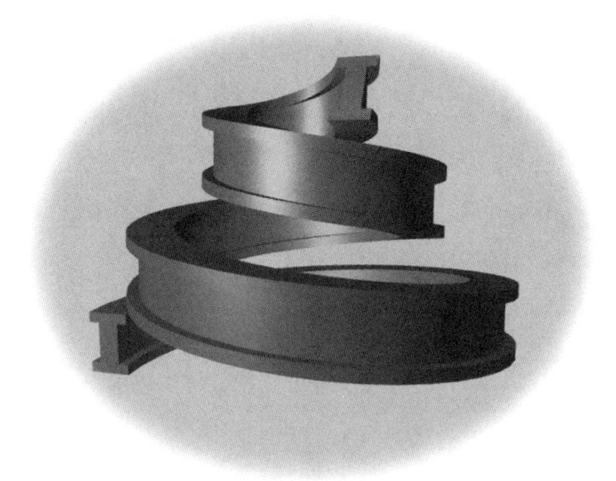

# Introduction to Computer Animation

# Introduction to Three-Dimensional Presentation

## 1.1 INTRODUCTION

Turning these initial pages is the beginning of your journey into the exciting realm of three-dimensional presentation. *3D Studio MAX in Motion*, as your guide on this adventure, will help you to become proficient in the use of Kinetix's (a division of Autodesk) 3D Studio MAX™ program, allowing you to create wonderful, realistic still images and animated presentations. Look at Figure 1.1 for a sample. If you are anything like us, you will be amazed at what you can do with this software technology. Whereas the sky was traditionally the limit, this program allows you to travel beyond, creating alien worlds populated by your imagination.

3D Studio MAX is a complete three-dimensional modeling, rendering, and animation program that runs within the Windows NT© or Windows 95© or above environment. Whatever your field or intended field, 3D Studio MAX has a place—from creating photorealistic static presentations of a mechanical part to dynamic flybys of a new architectural complex. Chapter 2 will pique your interest and whet your appetite, as you survey the techniques required to create those scenes. Then, the rest of the text will teach you how to use and apply 3D Studio MAX.

In this chapter we introduce the basics necessary for the creation of 3D presentations, including the 3D model-creation concepts themselves and an outline of model rendering. Also, we discuss the organization of the text.

For those of you who are impatient to get going, a character trait we share, Chapter 3 gives you a tour of 3D Studio MAX, showing how to interact with the program, and Chapter 4 allows you to create 3D objects, assemble them into a scene, render them, and animate them. You will experience the satisfaction of a 3D presentation before becoming expert in all the technical aspects.

The purpose of this text is to introduce you to the power of 3D Studio MAX through a logical, step-by-step process. You will learn the basics and how to apply

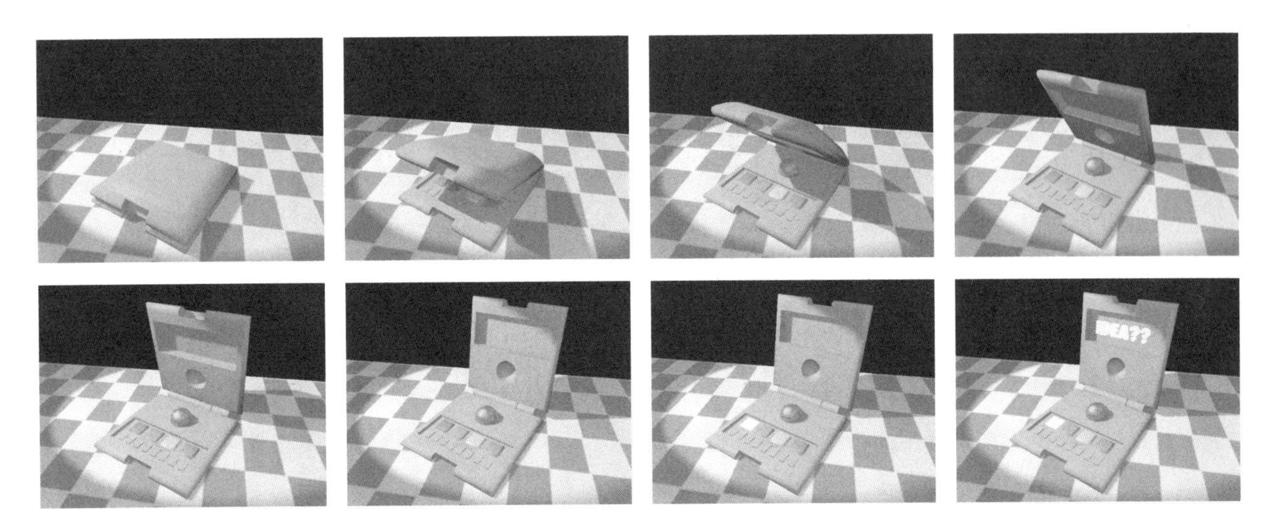

FIGURE 1.1
3D Studio MAX uses still frames to create an animation.

them. By the time you complete this text, you should have a firm grounding in three-dimensional presentation, including 3D modeling, rendering, and animation. There are millions of ways to use 3D Studio MAX. This text will give you the necessary start; where you go from there is up to you.

## 1.2 THREE-DIMENSIONAL CREATION CONCEPTS

Before using 3D Studio MAX, some basic concepts on model creation need to be reviewed. These concepts should make it easier to grasp the technical aspects of using 3D Studio MAX.

### Three Dimensions

To work with 3D Studio MAX, you must understand the concept of three dimensions in computer model creation. When creating in three dimensions, you are using three axes: X, Y, and Z. These axes control the shape, proportion, and position of the objects you create. Refer to Figure 1.2 for an illustration of a simple L-shaped object. The object is defined in 3D space by the Cartesian coordinate system. This system is based on an origin point of (0, 0, 0), where X, Y, and Z are all 0, and positive and negative X, Y, and Z axes run away from the origin. When looking at a top or plan view on the computer screen, the X axis runs from left to right horizontally across the screen, the Y axis runs vertically across the screen from top to bottom, and the Z axis runs away from the viewer and toward the viewer, seemingly retreating into the screen or coming out from the screen to touch the viewer. The L-shaped object is positioned within the three axes, and its shape and proportion are defined by its length, width, and height along the three axes.

### Model Building

In addition to reviewing the concept of three dimensionality, we must also review several of the terms used in building three-dimensional models. Later chapters introduce the processes and methods specific to these techniques.

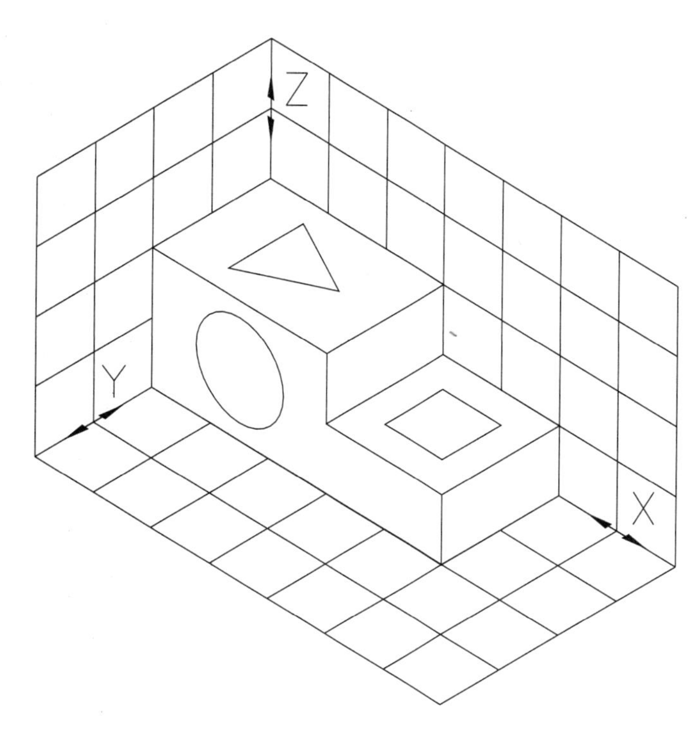


**FIGURE 1.2**
Three-dimensional axes.

### Construction Planes

All three-dimensional creation takes place on two-dimensional grid planes. Refer to Figure 1.3, showing the L shape in different views—top, front, left side, and user (isometric). Each view could be thought of as a plane. Creating and manipulating in 3D Studio MAX relies on identifying the grid plane upon which you are creating. By working in different views, you are, in effect, working on different grid planes. You will find out later how to create your own grid planes at any location in the 3D space.

### Model Structure

Complex objects in 3D Studio MAX are composed of several possible structures as shown in Figure 1.4. A *vertex*, which is a 2D or 3D location, is the simplest form.

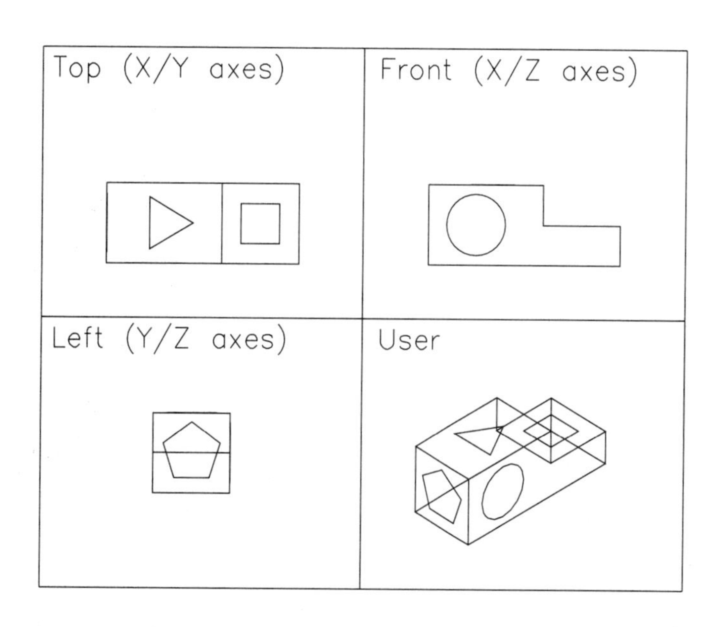


**FIGURE 1.3**
L-shape and plane relationships.

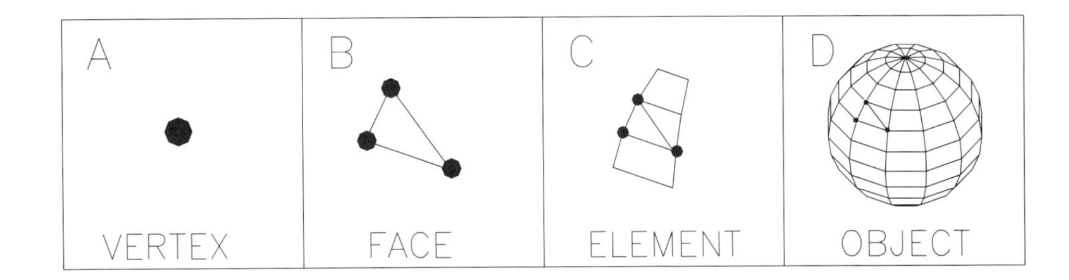


FIGURE 1.4
Model structure.

Next, a *face* is a surface plane defined by three vertices; it is used to cover an object. Even more complex, an *element* is several faces linked together to form part of an object. If two faces share the same edge and the same plane, the linking edge is usually not displayed and the surface may appear rectangular. Finally, an *object* is the compilation of many elements to form a complex shape.

Depending on your skill level within 3D Studio MAX, you can create from fully formed primitive objects such as boxes and spheres or specify each vertex to create a convoluted shape.

### Shapes

In 3D Studio MAX, shapes are defined as 2D splined polygons (two-dimensional closed profiles) used as the basis of complex 3D object creation. When open, they define paths used in the creation of 3D objects and animation sequences. Refer to Figure 1.5 to see two types of three-dimensional creation using a shape.

### Meshed Objects

The objects that are created in 3D Studio MAX are covered in a mesh of faces, explaining the term meshed object. Refer to part D of Figure 1.4. Once you have created an object, you can use various modifiers to manipulate any part of the object from vertices to faces and elements.

## MODEL DISPLAY

There are several ways that models can be displayed to facilitate their viewing and manipulation.

### Viewports

Viewports are used to display single or multiple views of an object or scene on the screen. Refer to Figure 1.3 again, which shows four viewports, each displaying a different view of the object or scene. There are common orthographic (straight) views, such as top and front or perspective views, showing how the human eye would

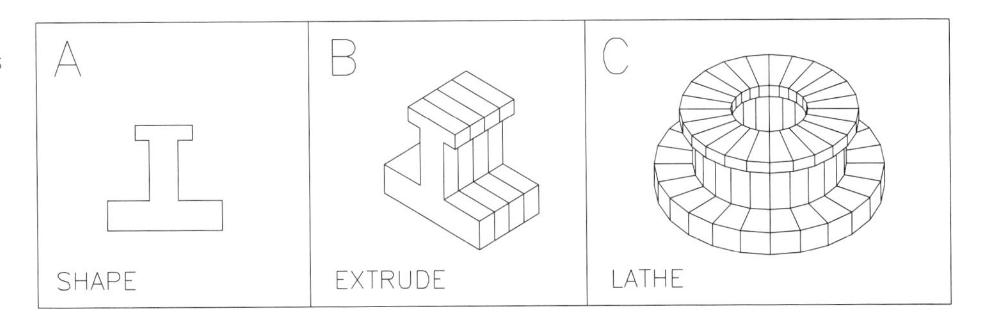


FIGURE 1.5
A shape and some of its uses.

observe the scene. You can create your own views, called *user* views, or create and place a camera to create a camera view.

### Wireframe (Backface Cull Off)

Wireframe display is the display of the object or scene with all edges visible. Refer to part A of Figure 1.6. This skeleton effect shows all the edges of an object and how they affect other objects.

### Wireframe—Hidden Line Removed (Backface Cull On)

Hidden line removed display is the display of the object with edges or lines that are obstructed from view, or hidden. Refer to part B of Figure 1.6. This display gives a more three-dimensional look to an object and makes it easier to identify separate objects. Only the backfaces of individual objects are hidden. You can still see objects behind each other.

### Bounding Box

The bounding box display is the display of the objects as individual boxes that enclose each complex object. Refer to parts A and C of Figure 1.6. Part A shows a scene composed of various complex objects. Part C portrays the same scene with the complex objects shown as simplified rectangular boxes. The purpose of this is to speed up the manipulation of complicated scenes. 3D Studio MAX refers to this form of display as *box*.

### Rendered Views

It is also possible to display rendered views of the scene with effects such as Facets and Smooth. Refer to parts D and E of Figure 1.6. These views can help to deter-

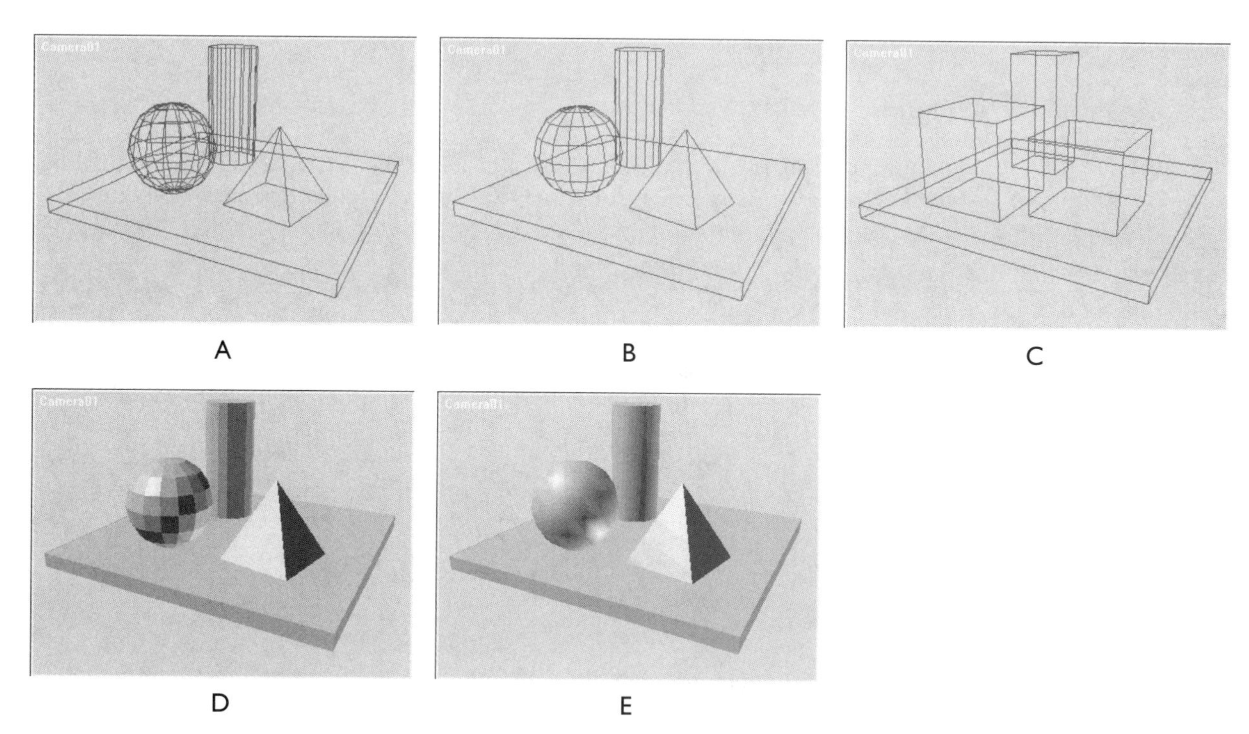


FIGURE 1.6
Display of 3D model.

mine positional relationships between objects. The drawback is that it can slow down the creation process by adding computer calculation time.

## 1.3 RENDERING

Rendering is the technique of taking a three-dimensional model and applying color, material, and light (or darkness) to its surfaces or faces. The resulting rendered image may be displayed on the screen or stored on disk in various formats. There are a variety of rendering levels including constant (faceted), phong, and metal.

### Color

The simplest way to render a model is to apply different colors to the various surfaces or objects. In this way each surface or object will stand out from the others. In the initial creation of a model, use color to differentiate the various objects in your scene in order to make it much easier to identify them for manipulation. Figure 1.7 shows the Color Selector dialog box.

#### RGB

The primary colors used in a 3D Studio MAX rendering are red, green, and blue (RGB). By adjusting the intensity value of each, you can create different colors. All three at 0 produce black, whereas all three at 255 produce white. By mixing, you can achieve any color you want.

#### HLS

You can also use three other setting types to control or create colors: hue, luminance, and saturation. Hue selects the color band, luminance sets the brightness or intensity of the color, and saturation sets the purity of the color (the higher the saturation, the less gray the color).

#### HBW

A new form of mixing colors for use in 3D Studio MAX is the mixing of hue, blackness, and whiteness. This represents a natural, pigment-based method of mix-

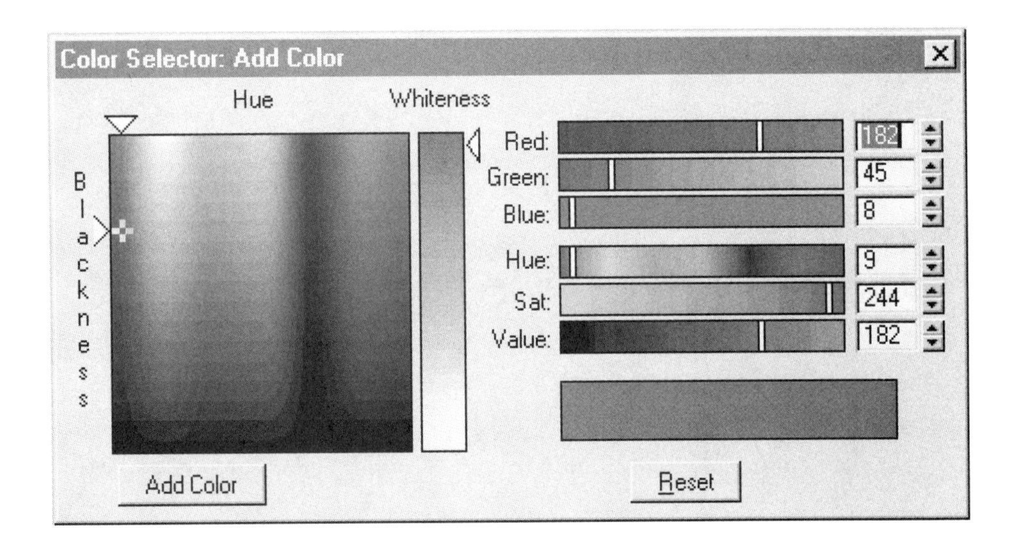


FIGURE 1.7 Color Selector dialog box.

ing color. Hue selects the pure color, which is made darker by adding black or lighter by adding white.

### Gamma

You may think the color red is red. However, when you use a variety of displays, such as computer monitors, televisions, and slides, you will see that the same red appears different in each method of display. The control of the display of colors is achieved through gamma correction.

Gamma affects the intensity of the low and middle tones of your display and your bitmap images. The level of gamma correction results in darker or brighter images. The gamma setting is separate from the contrast and brightness controls of your system's monitor. A gamma value of 1.0 corresponds to an "ideal" monitor. The value for computer monitors is commonly in the range of 1.5 to 2.0. For NTSC video (televisions and video tape), the setting is usually 2.2. You will learn how to set the gamma levels in Chapter 5.

## Material

To add realism to your model, you will need to add materials to the various surfaces and objects that make up the scene. This process creates the surface characteristics of a material and then assigns the material to the surface of an object. Some of the surface characteristics are color, behavior, and image mapping. Refer to Figure 1.8 for some illustrations of the application of bitmaps to a simple sphere.

### Surface Color

The surface color of an object changes depending on how light strikes it. Some of the object's surface is facing away from the light and is darker, some of the surface is in the direct beam of the light and is very bright, and some of the surface falls in between. Even though the object's surface may be one color, the color will appear different depending on its relationship to the light. The directly lit area shows the specular surface color, the darker area is ambient surface color, and the in-between area is diffuse surface color.

### Surface Behavior

A surface may behave in a variety of ways. It may be shiny or dull, transparent or opaque. It may even glow. These characteristics are considered surface behaviors. When you create or use materials, you will apply these behaviors to a material to force it to appear as you wish.

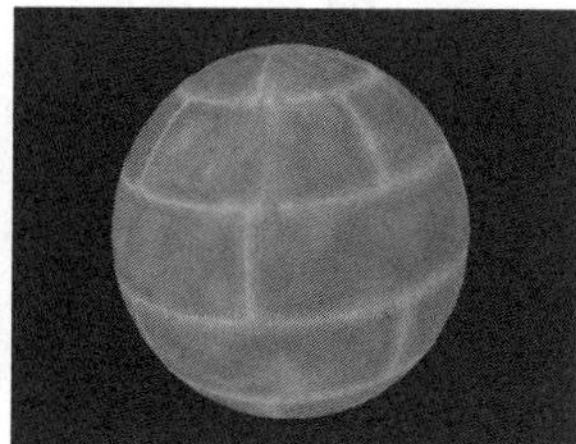

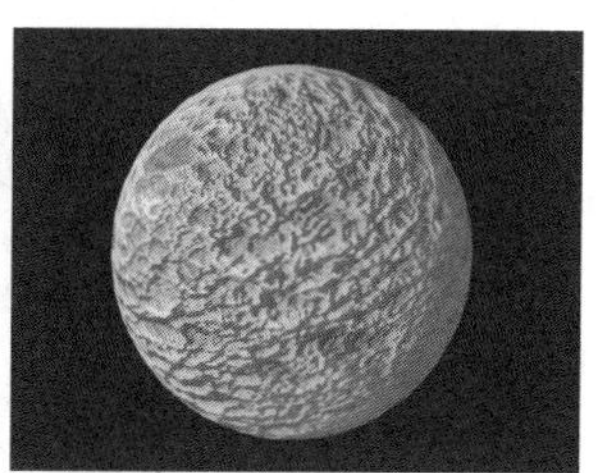

FIGURE 1.8
Bitmaps applied to a sphere.

### Image Mapping

Image mapping is the process of taking an already-produced electronic picture (referred to as a bitmap image) and applying it to a surface. This process allows you to produce a complex and realistic-looking surface without having to create a complex 3D model. There are different ways to apply a bitmap from texture maps, such as pasting, to reflection maps, where the image appears to be reflected on to the surface.

## Light

By lighting a model in various ways, its presentation is made more realistic. Displaying a range of tones on the surfaces, from light to dark, makes the objects jump out at you or recede into the background, enhancing the three-dimensional appearance. And finally, the application of shadows adds to the realism of the scene by recreating the visual experience that the human eye is accustomed to seeing in everyday life. Several lighting types, including ambient, omni, and spot, contribute to this realism.

### Ambient Light

Ambient light is used to control the overall brightness of a scene. When other light types are added to a scene, the ambient light will affect the contrast. A low ambient value increases contrast, whereas a high value decreases the contrast. You can also use a colored ambient light to tint an entire scene.

### Omni Light

Omni light is similar to light cast by a lightbulb or candle. The light radiates in all directions from the light source. Usually the intensity of an omni light decreases (called falloff, or attenuation) with the distance from the source, so that the brightest objects are those closest to the scene's light source. See Figure 1.9.

### Spotlight

A spotlight is a directional light source that casts a beam of light into a scene, such as a flashlight. It is used to cast shadows and can be used as a form of image projector. Refer to Figure 1.10.

FIGURE 1.9
Omni light rendering.

FIGURE 1.10
Spotlight rendering.

FIGURE 1.11
Constant rendering.

FIGURE 1.12
Phong rendering.

## Rendering and Material Shading Types

There are different levels of detail to which a material may be rendered, constant (faceted), phong, and metal. Each progressive setting increases not only the detail of the material rendering but also the time it takes to render.

### Constant (Faceted)

Constant, or faceted, rendering is basic rendering of color to surfaces. Individual faceted faces can be seen, and image maps can be applied. See Figure 1.11

### Phong

Phong rendering gives smoother surfaces to objects instead of the many-faceted surfaces of the constant type. Edges are blended to give a smooth appearance, and highlights are shown realistically. A new render type called Blinn is a subtle variation of Phong shading. It shows rounder highlights (See Figure 1.12).

### Metal

Metal rendering is similar to phong but is able to simulate accurately a metallic effect. Refer to Figure 1.13.

FIGURE 1.13
Metal rendering.

## 1.4 ANIMATION

When we are shown a series of pictures in rapid succession with minute scene changes in each picture, we perceive that motion is taking place. Animation is based on this perception.

### Cartoon Animation

In the case of cartoon animation, the illustrators draw a series of images, each slightly different from the last. For instance, if a cartoon character is throwing a ball, the character's arm is depicted in each frame in a more advanced throwing position, with the ball following suit. When the pictures are shown in quick succession, motion appears to be taking place, although in reality we are simply seeing a stream of still images.

### Film and Video Animation

Recording movement on film or video uses the same process as cartoon animation. A series of individual frames are captured on film or video tape. To show the action, the film or tape is played back quickly, running the individual frames into a series of smooth movements. When you use the pause button on your VCR, you are pausing on an individual frame.

### 3D Studio MAX Frames

3D Studio MAX uses the process outlined previously to create action. A series of still frames or images are created and then replayed in sequence. Refer again to Figure 1.1. This shows a series of frames in which an electronic box lid opens increasingly wider. In the second-to-last scene, the leftmost button lights up, and in the last frame the word IDEA! appears on the screen. A single file can store this series of images and can be replayed. With 3D Studio MAX, you can store a single frame such as a BMP or JPG file or the entire animation such as an AVI or FLC file. These formats are discussed in more detail in the chapters on rendering and animation.

### Replaying Animation Files

It is possible to view stills or animations on your computer through 3D Studio MAX or without entering 3D Studio MAX using the Windows Media Player. The Windows Media Player is supplied with Windows, and the appropriate driver for FLC and AVI files is supplied when you install 3D Studio MAX.

### Replay Speed

The speed of the display of the frames or images controls how the animation will be perceived and the speed at which the image changes controls the appearance of the motion. About 10 frames per second provides the illusion of motion; faster rates produce more fluid motion, and slower rates produce jerky movement and image flicker. Creating animations with different playback speeds deliberately creates these effects for various applications. The following are some sample frame rates:

| | |
|---|---|
| Cartoons | 12 or 24 frames per second |
| Motion pictures | 24 frames per second |
| NTSC television | 30 frames per second |

## 1.5 ORGANIZATION OF 3D STUDIO MAX IN MOTION

The purpose of this section is to explain the organization of this text. It is separated into five parts, each one categorized by both the nature of the information and the level of your expertise. Contained within each part are the relevant chapters, comprising the theory involved in the chosen topic and, in most cases, ending with a lab assignment.

### Lab Assignments

The lab assignments at the end of most of the chapters are written in a step-by-step approach. They reinforce the theory from the preceding chapter in a practical fashion.

#### Lab Icons

As you complete the labs, you will notice that there are icons placed at the beginning of certain steps. Their purpose is to help identify the icon tool required in the step adjacent to it. Using the tool may not be the first thing you do, but it will be required sometime during the step. Later, when you are more familiar with the icons, they will not be shown, and it will be up to you to remember their appearance.

### Insight Boxes

Throughout the text, you will find special boxes entitled "LIGHTS! CAMERA! ACTION!" These boxes present specific insights into the use of 3D Studio MAX.

### MAX IN MOTION Quick Chart

At the back of this text you will find a tear-out cardboard called the MAX IN MOTION Quick Chart. This chart contains tips on the use of various shortcut keys, such as the use of CTRL and ALT keys with other commands and the mouse. You may want to tear this out and place it in a visible spot near your computer screen.

### Part Descriptions

Brief descriptions of each part of the text follow. This walk through new territory will allow you to develop an early familiarity with the text.

***LIGHTS! CAMERA! ACTION!***

**Sample**

This is a sample LIGHTS! CAMERA! ACTION! box. These boxes give you insights into lighting techniques and camera placements that affect an animation sequence and tips for creating realistic 3D objects to populate your three-dimensional scenes. Also, these boxes explain scene setup and offer some guidelines to make your renderings more realistic and your animation flow more smoothly.

### Part 1: Introduction to Computer Animation

This first part introduces the concept of three-dimensional presentation and provides some real-life applications. In Chapter 1, we discuss the basic concepts of three-dimensional modeling, rendering, and animation. Then, in Chapter 2 you look at some applications of 3D Studio MAX in the realm of still presentations and animations.

### Part 2: Exploring 3D Studio MAX

This section moves quickly into the thick of things, with Chapter 3 demonstrating the feel of using 3D Studio MAX by moving about the various utilities. Chapter 4 then takes an overall look at 3D Studio MAX, including a final lab that travels from creation to rendered animation as an introduction to the complete process.

### Part 3: Preparing for 3D Modeling

Before you begin complex 3D dimensional creation, it is essential that you become familiar with the procedures and commands that allow movement through the 3D space created on the screen. In Chapter 5 you learn how to navigate the 3D world, such as establishing different views, and in Chapter 6 you learn the fundamentals of creation. Chapter 7 goes over the basics of editing.

### Part 4: 3D Modeling

This part is divided into three chapters and three stages. In Chapter 8 you learn to create with primitive 3D objects and 2D shapes as well as to apply modifiers to extrude, twist, or bend objects. Chapter 9 goes into more complex creation through the use of lofting and Boolean operations. Chapter 10 introduces some special creation techniques such as space warps, particle systems, and morphs.

### Part 5: Presentation

Now that you can create a 3D model and visually move about it on the screen, it is time to study the various aspects of presentation. In Chapter 11 you learn how to add cameras and lights and how to perform still renderings of your scenes. Chapter 12 deals with the creation and application of materials to your objects. Chapter 13 is about animation, where you will learn how to move your geometric objects and how to place the cameras and lights to create animated sequences. Chapter 14 introduces hierarchy linking and inverse kinematics, which are used to achieve realistic movement to linked objects.

### Part 6: Practical Applications

This is a special applications section that explains how to apply 3D Studio MAX to present your final products more effectively. Chapter 15 deals with creating rendered still images. In Chapter 16 you learn how to use the program to create architectural flybys, and Chapter 17 demonstrates methods of applying bitmaps using an art gallery as our medium. Robotic motion is demonstrated in Chapter 18, which relies on hierarchy linking and inverse kinematics.

### Appendices

This section outlines what is contained on the CD-ROM included with this text.

The CD-ROM also contains a material library and a bitmap image library that should be copied on to your computer's hard disk for easier access. There are also some 3D objects and scenes on the CD-ROM that can be copied into the scenes subdirectory on your hard disk. This procedure—and the reasons for it—are explained in the appendix.

This section also covers inputting and outputting external files and the use of video post.

## 1.6 SUMMARY

At the end of every chapter you will find a brief summary of the previous chapter and an introduction to the lab that follows. Chapter 1 provides a brief introduction to such things as model building, lighting, rendering, and the layout of the ensuing text. Get ready for some fun, because Chapter 2 provides you with real-life examples of animations.

## QUESTIONS AND ASSIGNMENTS

### QUESTIONS

This section, at the end of every chapter, asks questions about the material learned in the chapter.

1. As it pertains to model structure, define each of the following:
   a. Vertex
   b. Face
   c. Element
   d. Object
2. What are construction planes?
3. What is rendering?
4. List and explain the three different light sources.
5. Name the three levels of rendering. What are the characteristics of each?
6. Upon what human perception is animation based?

### ASSIGNMENTS

In the Assignments section, you are asked to extend your classroom learning. This extension may be accomplished by doing outside research, building on a lab already in the text, or coming up with something original.

1. Before looking at Chapter 2, make a list of disciplines you feel may make use of programs such as 3D Studio MAX.

CHAPTER 2

# Rendering and Animation Applications

## 2.1 INTRODUCTION

The wide variety of 3D Studio MAX uses makes it an exciting and burgeoning area, not to mention an area where experts are becoming more in demand. Although there are interesting opportunities in the more classic fields of engineering specialties, graphic arts, forensic laboratories, and even Hollywood are getting involved, opening up more romantic possibilities.

In architectural design, walkthroughs or flybys can be created for preliminary designs. The animated presentation can show the client what the structure will look like, inside and out, as if the client were walking through or around the building.

Similarly, in mechanical design, mechanical movement can be shown; gears rotate and robotic arms swing into motion. This application allows the designer or client to see how a particular piece of equipment will operate in an easily studied environment.

In the area of graphic design, the artist can create impressive and dynamic presentations of ideas and concepts from flying corporate logos to quick mock-ups of a video advertisement without the production overhead. Even computer game designers make use of 3D Studio MAX to create creatures and the virtual environments they inhabit.

In fact, these suggestions barely touch on the areas where 3D Studio MAX is being utilized. The program is currently being used by ballet and theater producers to orient their actors on stage without wasting valuable time and money; it is helping criminologists decide the course of events that culminated in a murder, thereby helping to solve the case; coaches use the program to teach ideal plays visually, before the players hit the field; air-traffic controllers use it to try to decide what went wrong upon approach and how to avoid the problem in the future; even historical researchers use it as they continue to ask what went on behind the grassy knoll. In much the same way as flight simulators were originally used to train pilots, 3D Studio MAX is found where it makes more sense—time sense, money sense, and safety sense—for the program to go before the actual people go or before real money is spent.

## 2.2 STILL IMAGES AND ANIMATED FLICS

The figures described next are still images taken from animations that are contained on the CD-ROM included with this book. Each numbered figure shows three frames from the associated animated file. At this point, you can flip through the images and read the text explaining concepts and ideas about the animations. You can then use the animation player included in 3D Studio MAX to view the associated animation files.

## 2.3 ANIMATION OF IDEAS

This section has only one animation, and it is used to start things off. Figure 2.1 shows three frames from the animation DESIGN.FLC. They illustrate the design process through the use of a traditional design table, with the addition of a nontraditional electronic box. The box controls what happens throughout the flic; as its screen and buttons change, so does the scene. Each segment builds on the next—from the idea through two-dimensional enhancement, three-dimensional projection, and finally an animated structure.

In this animation the camera does not move, but the objects in the scene move while the scene builds.

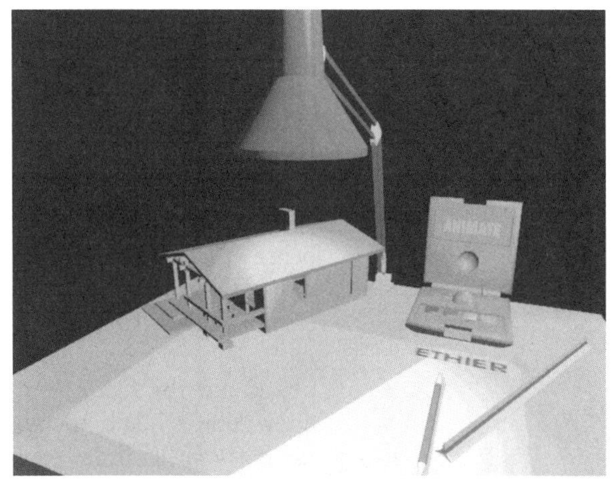


FIGURE 2.1
From idea to reality: DESIGN.FLC.

## 2.4 ARCHITECTURE

The following five animations show different aspects of architecture, inside and out with structural and civil terrain, demonstrating different ways to present ideas.

### Windows on the Fly (Figure 2.2 ANDWIND.FLI)

In this animation a truck delivers a shipment of windows. The windows fly from the truck and place themselves in their proper locations. As the animation progresses, you will see a computer, and on the computer is a drawing of the plan and window details. Even though this animation uses only lines to describe the objects, the ideas it presents are strongly stated.

### Furniture Disassembly (Figure 2.3 DRESSER.FLI)

This is fairly simple animation, but it delivers the idea of interior design. In this animation a piece of furniture is disassembled, with each component flying off in a different direction.

### Structural Erection (Figure 2.4 SD_STRUC.FLI)

This animation shows the structural components of a building being erected. The pieces assemble themselves while the camera moves about the scene giving different vantage points.

### Airport Tour (Figure 2.5 AIRPORT.FLI)

This animation uses a combination of the camera and you watching the motion of a passenger train going to an airport; then you are with the train moving along. You

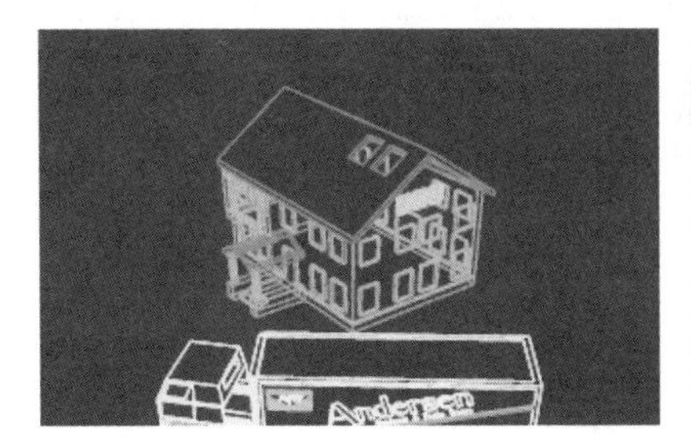

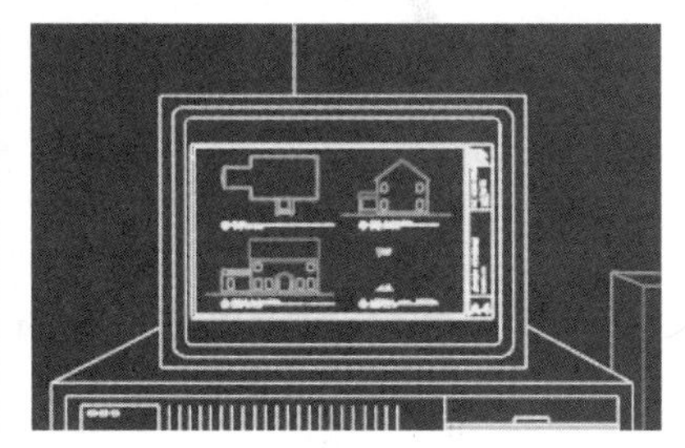

FIGURE 2.2
Windows on the fly: ANDWIND.FLI. (Supplied courtesy of Autodesk, Inc.)

FIGURE 2.3
Furniture disassembly: DRESSER.FLI. (Supplied courtesy of Autodesk, Inc.)

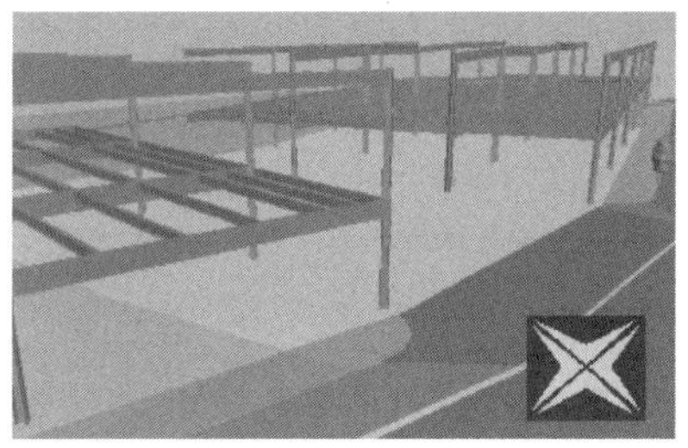
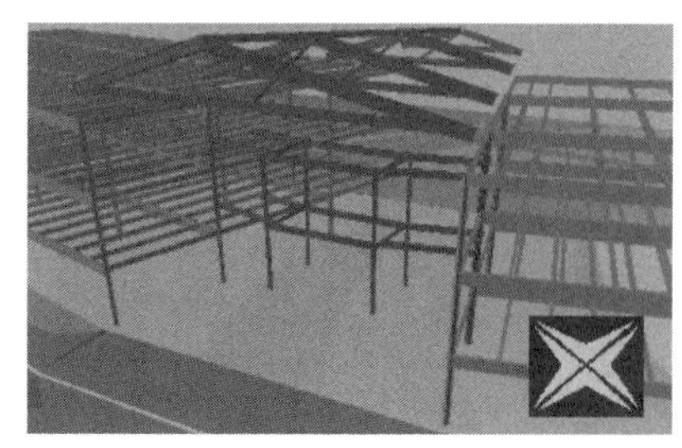

FIGURE 2.4
Structural erection: SD_STRUC.FLI. (Supplied courtesy of Autodesk, Inc.)

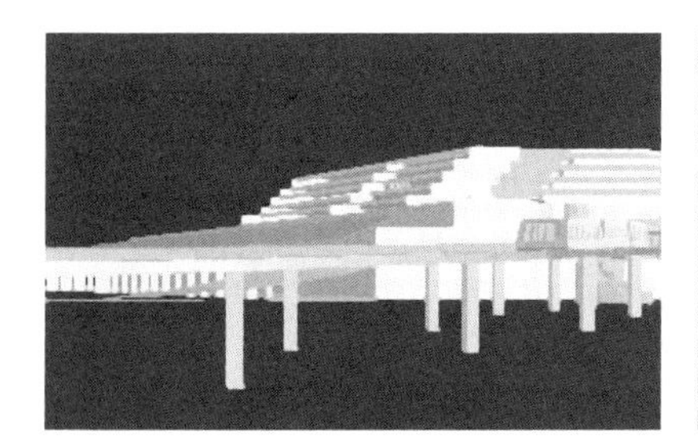

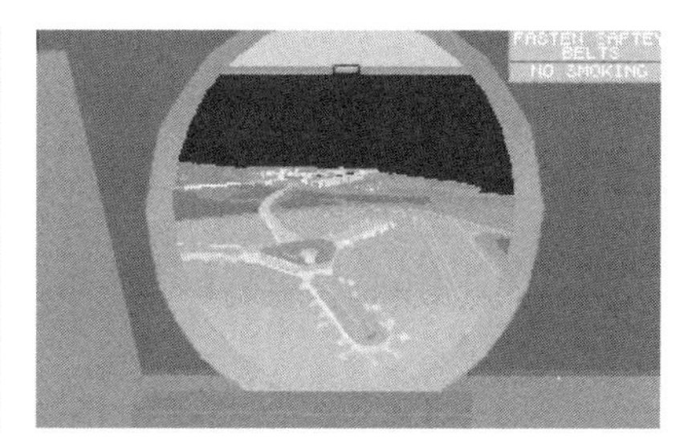


FIGURE 2.5
Airport tour: AIRPORT.FLI. (Supplied courtesy of Autodesk, Inc.)

travel through the airport, and finally board a plane and take off. Once more you are stationary while the scene moves—you watch out the window of the plane as it takes off and the airport is left behind.

### Terrain (Figure 2.6 LANDFILL.FLI)

This animation shows a simulated section of terrain and a river. During the animation the river's course is redirected, and sections of the terrain are excavated and filled. You can see the effects of different types of excavation or erosion and the effect of each on a river's course.

## 2.5 MOVEMENT AND ASSEMBLY

The sequence of animations in this section have mechanical motion in common. Although three-dimensional modeling and increasingly realistic rendering packages have added tremendously to the presentation possibilities in this field, animation adds an entirely new and effective element.

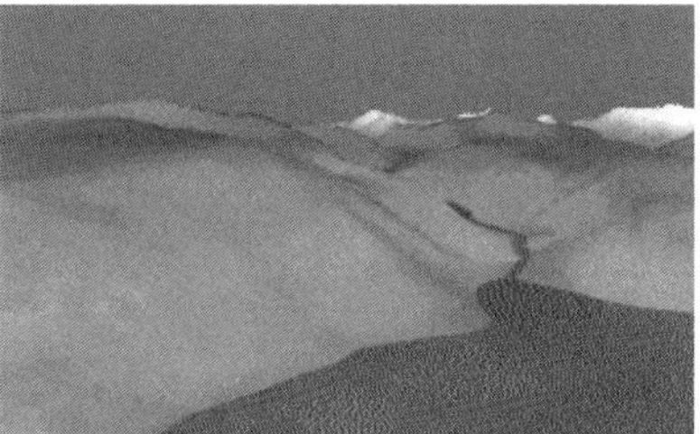
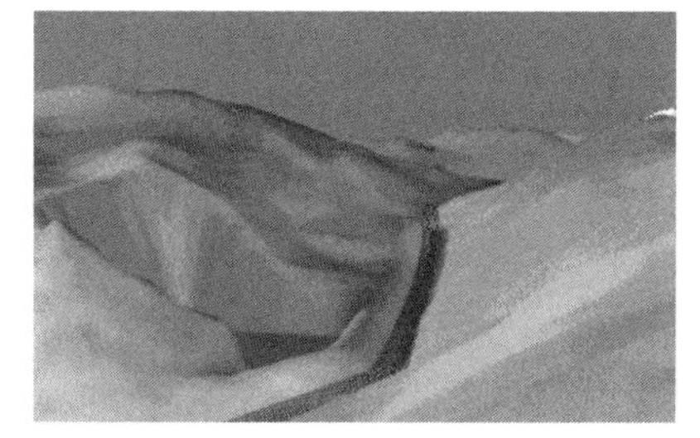

FIGURE 2.6
Terrain: LANDFILL.FLI. (Supplied courtesy of Autodesk, Inc.)

### **Motion** (Figure 2.7 BACKHOE.FLI)

Motion and linking are demonstrated in this animation of the movement of a backhoe. It shows how the various components of the arm interact with each other.

### **Robotics** (Figure 2.8 CHEMIST.FLI)

This animation demonstrates the repetitive action of robotic motion. An arm swings back and forth, taking samples from glass beakers as they move along an assembly line conveyor. While this is taking place, a handle moves back and forth and a piston moves in and out, demonstrating combined action in a scene.

### **Assembly Training** (Figure 2.9 FLASHLT2.FLI)

In this animation, a flashlight is assembled, turned on, and directed to shine on some text. This animation not only shows how animated sequences can be used to demonstrate the operation of equipment, but also details its assembly. This can be useful for training technicians or the general public to put together a series of components.

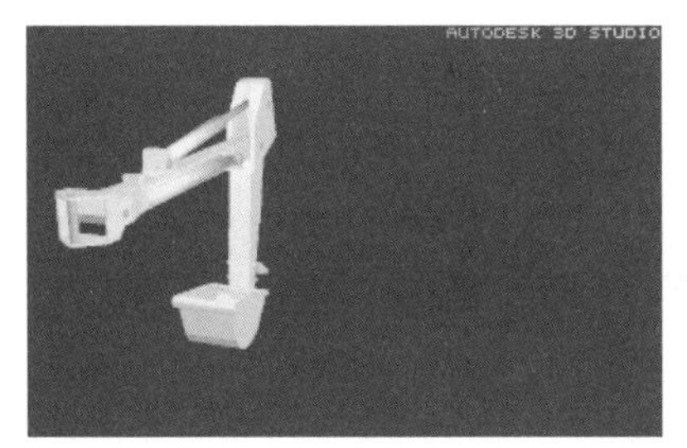

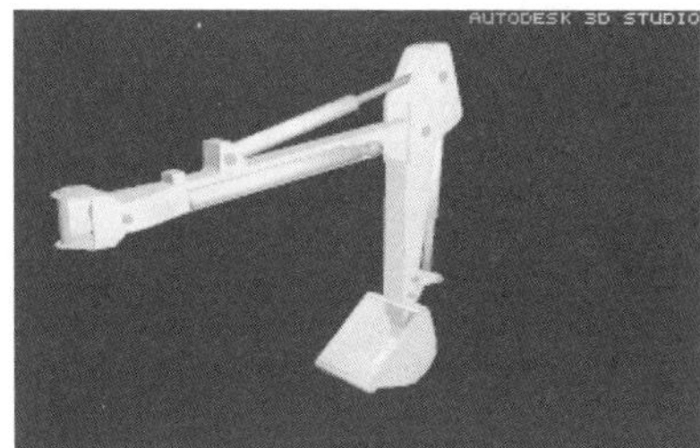

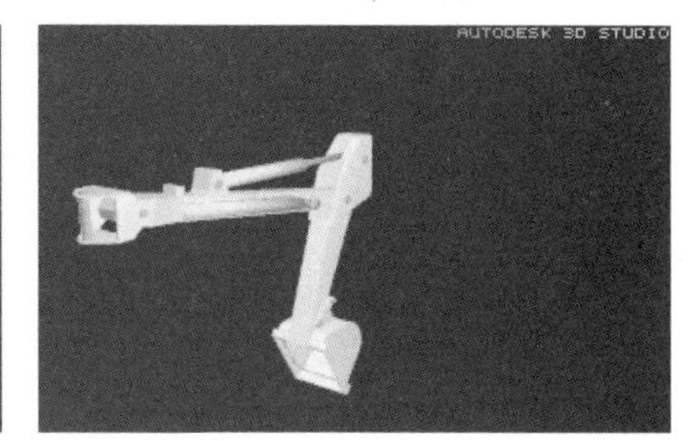


FIGURE 2.7
Motion: BACKHOE.FLI. (Supplied courtesy of Autodesk, Inc.)

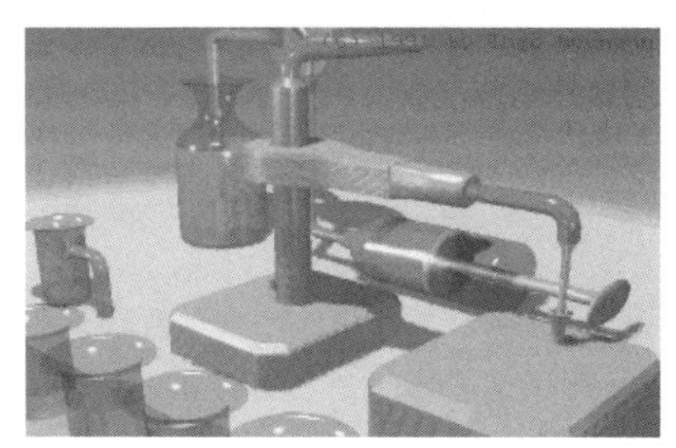

FIGURE 2.8
Robotics: CHEMIST.FLI. (Supplied courtesy of Autodesk, Inc.)

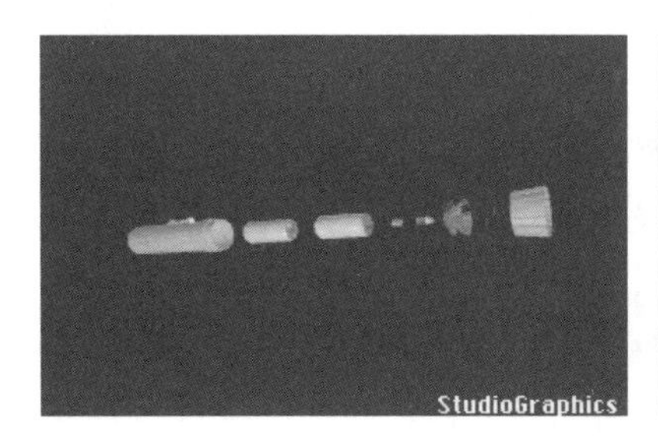

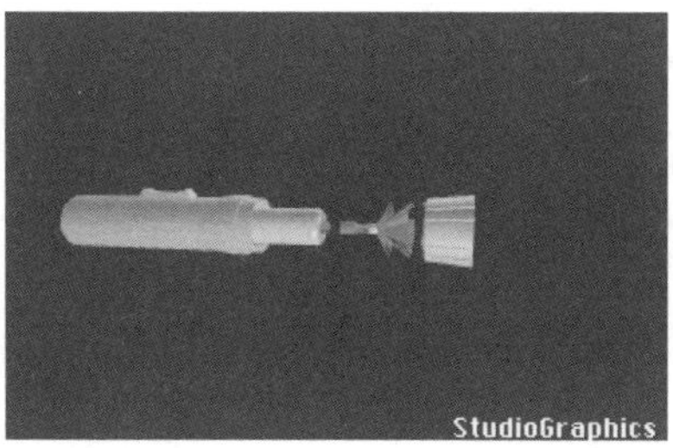

FIGURE 2.9
Assembly training: FLASHLT2.FLI. (Supplied courtesy of Autodesk, Inc.)

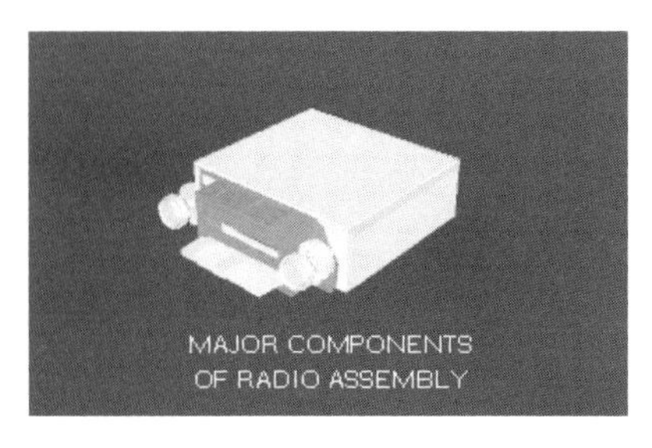

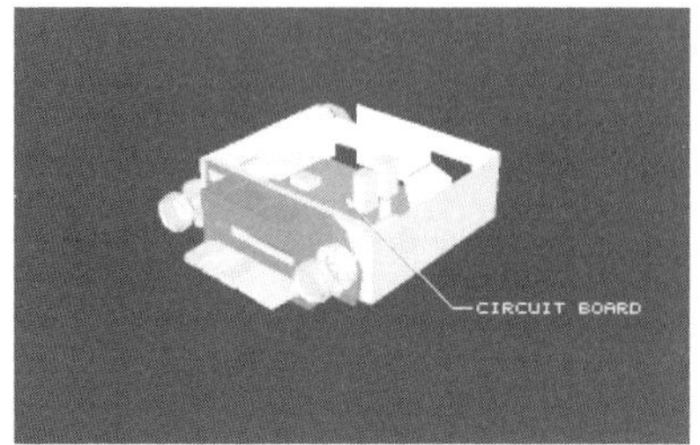

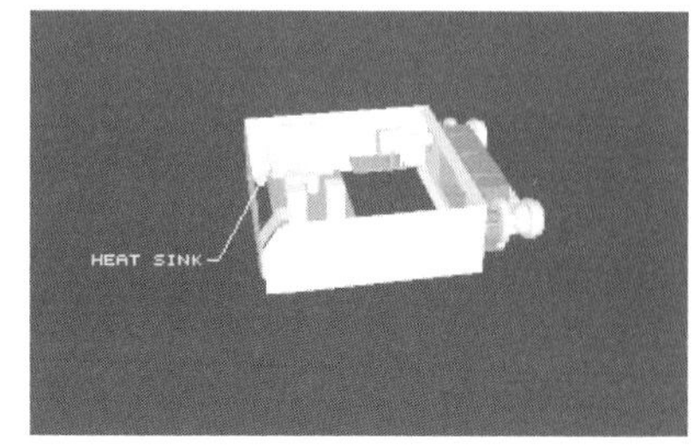


FIGURE 2.10
Equipment education: RADIO03.FLI. (Supplied courtesy of Autodesk, Inc.)

### Equipment Education (Figure 2.10 RADIO03.FLI)

This animation has similar benefits for assembly training, with the additional element of part identification. In this case, the sequence identifies various pieces of a radio; the text is added to explain what each component represents.

## 2.6 TRANSPORTATION

These next three animations use a transportation theme to convey their ideas. Two show the movement through the air, whereas the third uses truck transportation with some inventive and unconventional alterations.

### Helicopter and Bridge (Figure 2.11 BRIDGFLY.FLI)

This animation depicts a helicopter as it flies around a bridge. The helicopter moves and the camera follows it, demonstrating combined motion of objects and the camera. The camera breaks off at one point and zooms down the road on the bridge to meet the helicopter on the other side.

### Lone Helicopter (Figure 2.12 CHOPPER3.FLI)

Here a lone helicopter swings into the scene and swings out again. This shows a more detailed rendering of a helicopter and its movement against a stationary background.

### Robot and Truck Combined (Figure 2.13 ROBOTRK.FLI)

This humorous animation shows what a creative mind can come up with—the combination of a transport trailer and robot—ROBOTRUCK. The animation demonstrates the capabilities of the robotruck as it moves through traffic, unloads, and

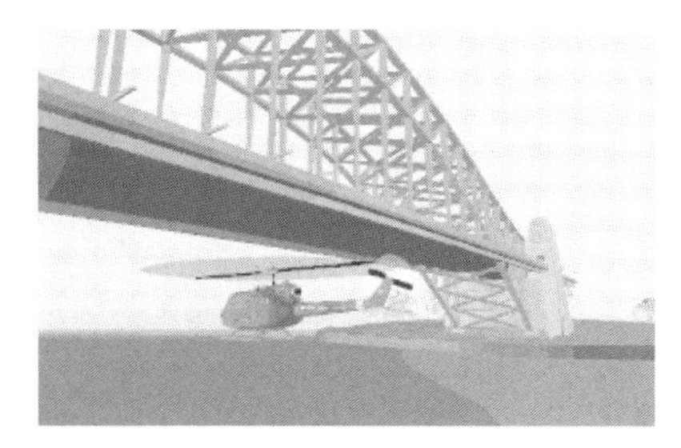

FIGURE 2.11
Helicopter and bridge: BRIDGFLY.FLI. (Supplied courtesy of Autodesk, Inc.)

FIGURE 2.12
Lone helicopter: CHOPPER3.FLI. (Supplied courtesy of Autodesk, Inc.)

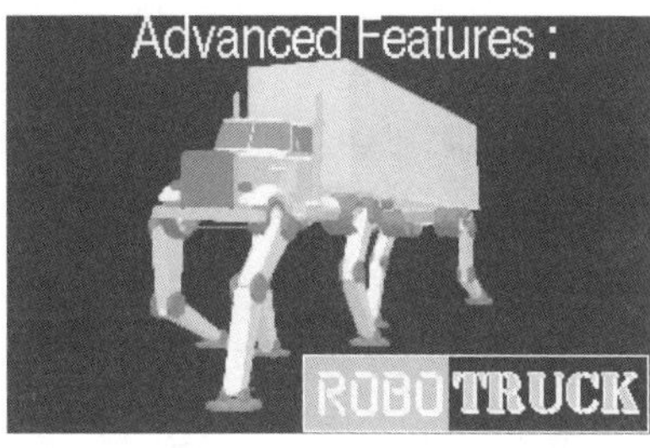

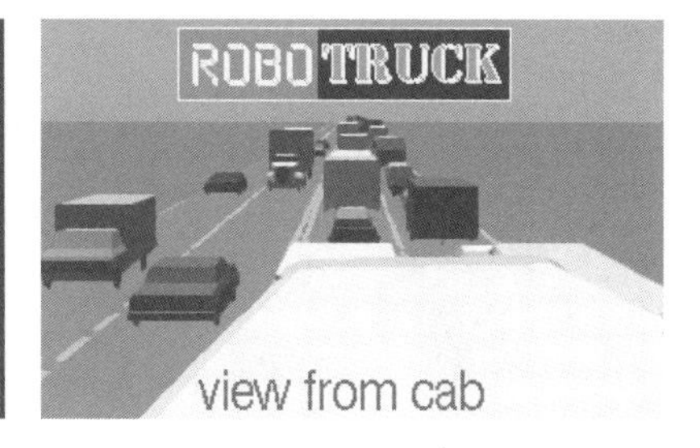


FIGURE 2.13
Robot and truck combined: ROBOTRK.FLI. (Supplied courtesy of Autodesk, Inc.)

avoids a nasty traffic ticket. Its appeal is grounded in the frustration all people feel as they try to move quickly from point A to point B.

## 2.7 HUMAN CHARACTERISTICS

The two animations in this section illustrate the use of 3D Studio MAX to demonstrate human anatomy and its movement. Unlike the situation with mechanical components, which have relatively few moving parts that tend to remain rigid, showcasing human movement offers a far greater challenge.

### Medical Visualization (Figure 2.14 VPHAND.FLI)

This animation starts with a hand rotating on the screen; as it rotates, the flesh disappears, revealing the bones underneath. This provides a taste of the benefits of using animation for medical training, showing various parts of the anatomy, in any state, to demonstrate the appearance, components, and interaction of bone, muscle, and tendon.

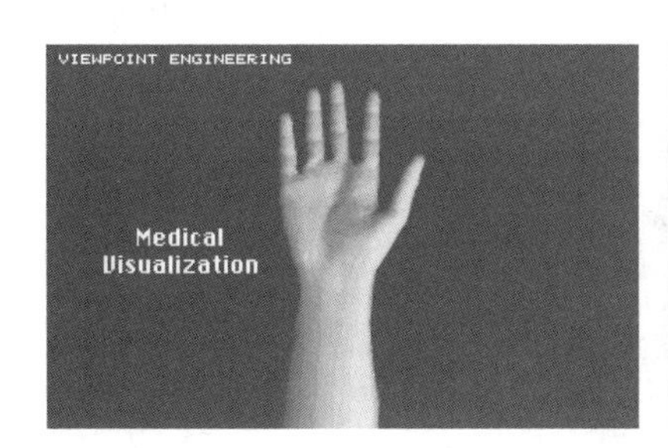

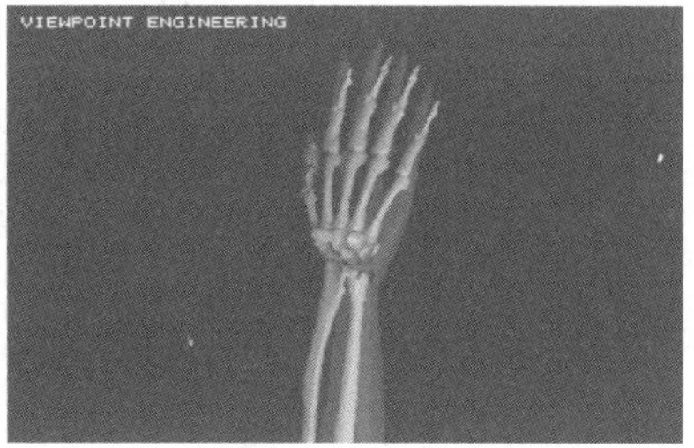

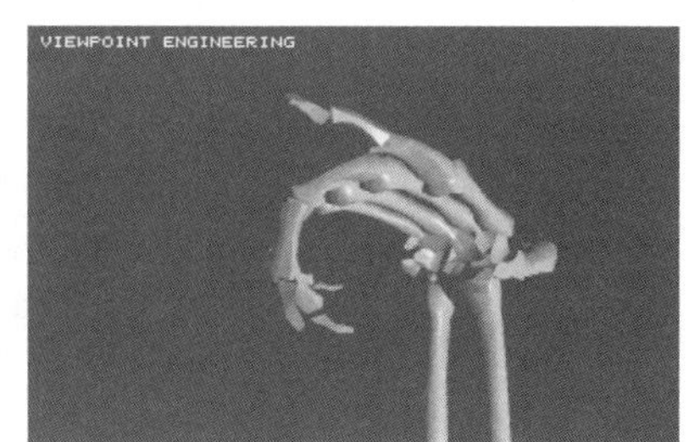


FIGURE 2.14
Medical visualization: VPHAND.FLI. (Supplied courtesy of Autodesk, Inc.)

FIGURE 2.15
Rocking form: ROCKER.FLC. (Supplied courtesy of Autodesk, Inc.)

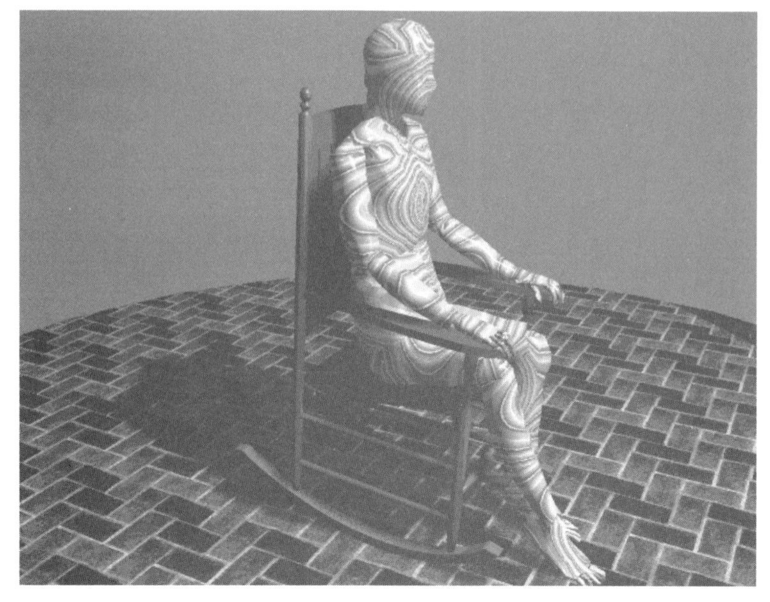

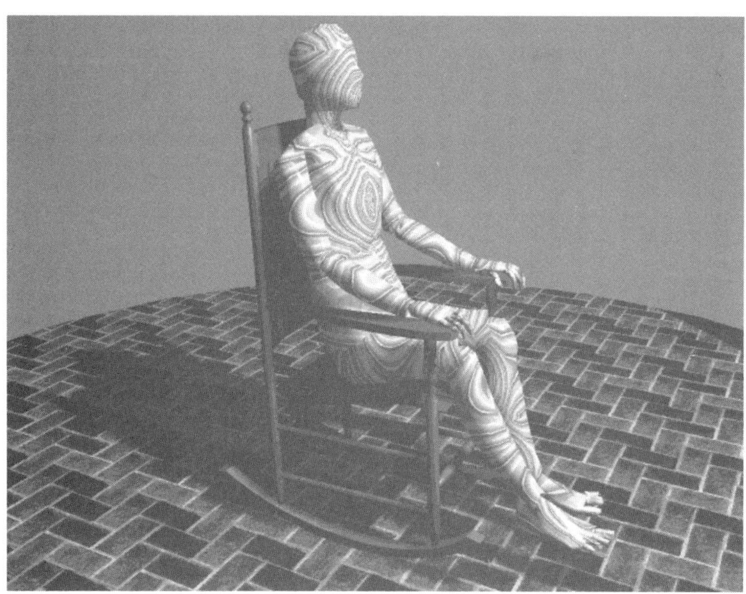

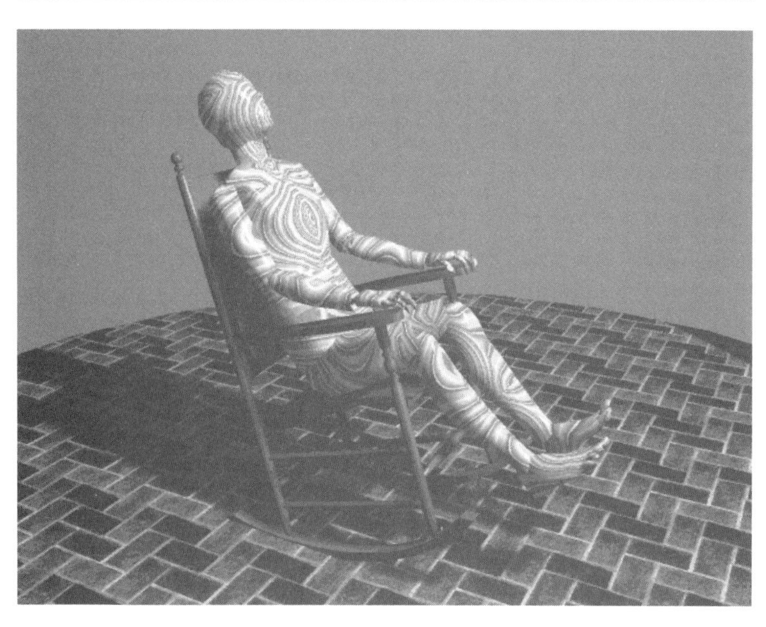

### Rocking Form (Figure 2.15 ROCKER.FLC)

As does the medical visualization, this animation shows a humanoid and the movement involved in rocking in a rocking chair. The head moves backward and forward as the feet and legs move to push the chair back and forth.

## 2.8 ANIMATIONS: CONCEPT ILLUSTRATION

The next animations are used to demonstrate different ideas or concepts. The first two use inanimate objects to mimic human movement and, consequently, human emotion. The last animation simply shows the lifelike movement possible using 3D Studio MAX.

### Chained by Life (Figure 2.16 CHAINED.FLI)

This clever animation attaches human characteristics to a previously inanimate table lamp. It also shows the effectiveness of the contrast between light and dark. We won't give away the ending of the short film, but it is poignant.

### An Excitable Lamp (Figure 2.17 LUXOPC.FLI)

The animated table lamp is back, and this time it is very excited at the thought of playing with a ball. But even innocent playfulness can have hazardous results, as you will find out when you watch the animation.

### A Deadly Predator (Figure 2.18 SHARK1.FLC)

Just when you though it was safe to play an animation, this animation shows fluidity of motion using the silent glide of a shark as it appears through murky water and swims right past your nose. It demonstrates the lifelike motion achievable with the 3D Studio MAX programs.

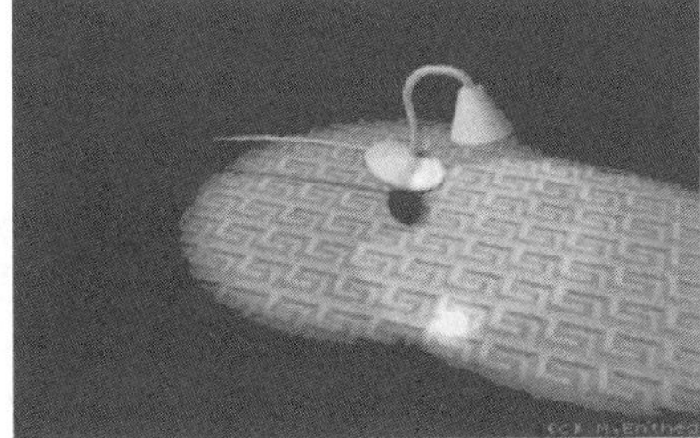

FIGURE 2.16
Chained by life: CHAINED.FLI. (Supplied courtesy of Autodesk, Inc.)

FIGURE 2.17
An excitable lamp: LUXOPC.FLI. (Supplied courtesy of Autodesk, Inc.)

FIGURE 2.18
A deadly predator: SHARK1.FLC. (Supplied courtesy of Autodesk, Inc.)

## 2.9 ADVERTISING AND SELLING

These next animations demonstrate the impact of using motion to deliver a message. Television advertising has recognized this potential for some time; now 3D Studio MAX allows you to animate the previously unanimatable as well as to bring animation within small-office capabilities.

### Screen Artists (Figure 2.19 MONITKEY.FLC)

This animation shows how an animation can be used to advertise, simply by catching your eye. Once you watch the screen for a while, look carefully at the keys of the keyboard.

### Sales Projections (Figure 2.20 SCISSPS.FLI)

This animations demonstrates how simple 3D objects can be used to effectively present an idea. In this case, it is the use of 3D cylinders that grow in height to represent sales projections.

## 2.10 GAMING

Using 3D Studio MAX to create gaming environments is a very effective application. In these two animations, new worlds are conceived, visualized, and brought to a virtual reality.

### Space Fighter (Figure 2.21 CYRUSHIP.FLI)

Here, a science fiction theme shows the possibilities of using 3D Studio MAX to create animated effects for electronic gaming. A spaceship-fighter craft takes off from

FIGURE 2.19
Screen artists: MONITKEY.FLC. (Supplied courtesy of Autodesk, Inc.)

FIGURE 2.20
Sales projections: SCISSPS.FLI. (Supplied courtesy of Autodesk, Inc.)

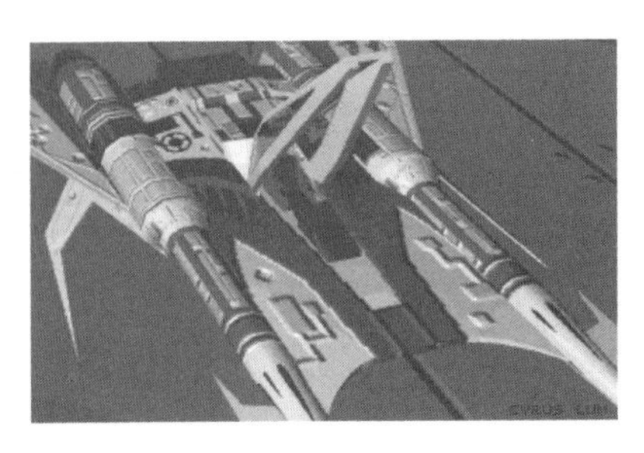

FIGURE 2.21
Space fighter: CYRUSHIP.FLI. (Supplied courtesy of Autodesk, Inc.)

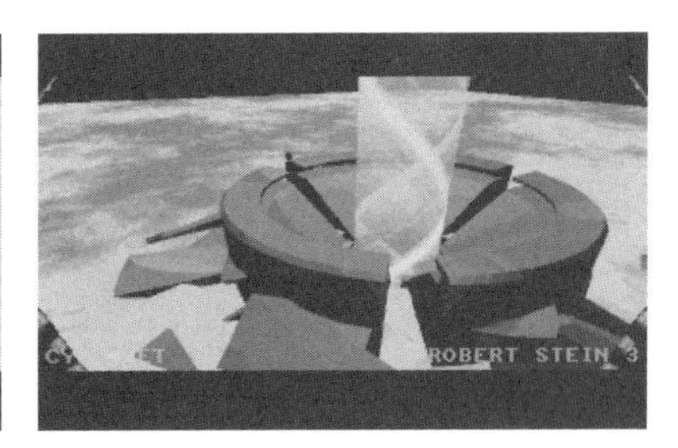


FIGURE 2.22
Cybernet: CYCART_1.FLI. (Supplied courtesy of Autodesk, Inc.)

inside its base and zooms off through an access port. Pay particular attention to the swaying motion of the craft and its reflection in the mirrorlike surface of the deck.

### Cybernet (Figure 2.22 CYCART_1.FLI)

This surreal sequence shows the fascinating possibilities of using 3D Studio MAX to create a different world. In this one, an unusual craft moves though an equally unusual world. Notice the transition when the camera swings from outside the craft to inside, providing a new perspective on the scene.

## 2.11 ACCIDENTS

The use of animations to demonstrate accidents is a cost-effective way to repeat a disaster without the cost of the labor and equipment needed for its re-creation. Also, it allows those studying the accident an endless series of possible scenarios and repetitions of them as they collect the necessary data to solve the mystery.

### Airplane Crash (Figure 2.23 AIRCRASH.FLI)

In this animation, an airplane makes its approach to a runway, sways, and touches one of its wings on the runway, causing it to disintegrate on impact.

### Car Accident (Figure 2.24 VPACCIDN.FLI)

This animation shows a car passing through an intersection without stopping at the stop sign. A car traveling in the other direction cannot stop in time, hits the first car, and causes both to spin out of control.

FIGURE 2.23
Airplane crash: AIRCRASH.FLI. (Supplied courtesy of Autodesk, Inc.)

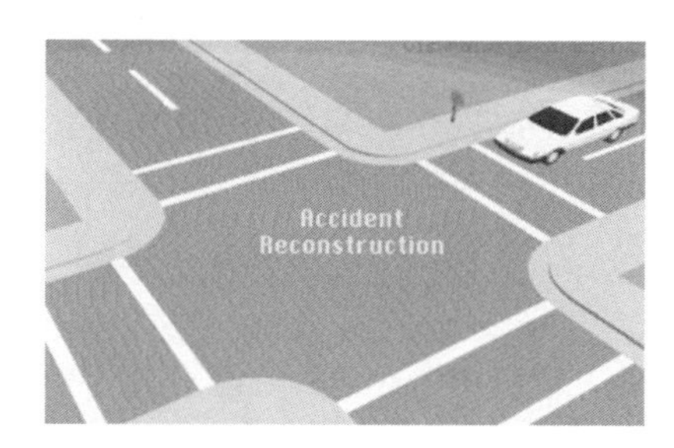

FIGURE 2.24
Car accident: VPACCIDN.FLI. (Supplied courtesy of Autodesk, Inc.)

## 2.12 SPECIAL EFFECTS

This section of animations illustrates the special routines and effects it is possible to achieve, in addition to the animated properties of objects as they move about a scene.

### Apple Squash (Figure 2.25 APPLE.FLI)

This animation demonstrates the special effect of applying a squash to an object while it is moving. In this case, an apple falls onto a wooden desk. When the apple touches the desk, it starts to deform as it squashes flat. Of course, this wouldn't take place in reality, but isn't that the fun part of special effects?

### Deformation (Figure 2.26 DROP_IT.FLI)

This demonstration shows the possible deformation of a flat surface.

FIGURE 2.25
Apple squash: APPLE.FLI. (Supplied courtesy of Autodesk, Inc.)

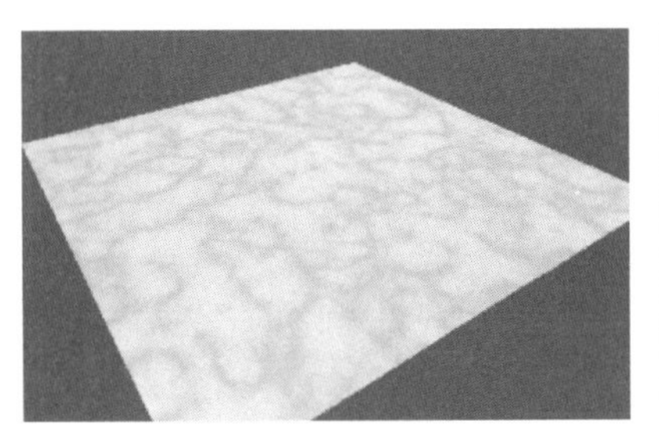
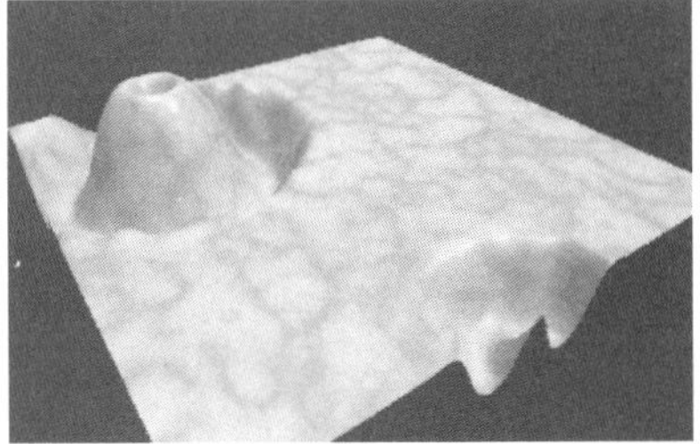
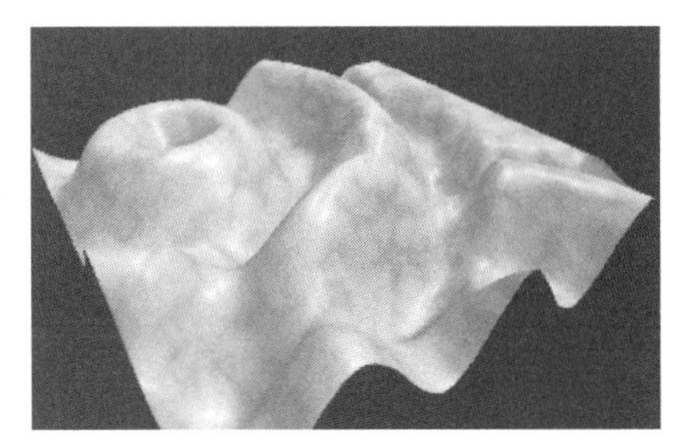

FIGURE 2.26
Deformation: DROP_IT.FLI. (Supplied courtesy of Autodesk, Inc.)

### Reflection and Squash (Figure 2.27 REFLECT.FLI)

Here, the possibility of automatic reflection is illustrated. The extremely reflective surfaces of two balls mirror each other as they move up and down. As with the apple animation, the ability to squash objects is also shown.

### Wave Motion (Figure 2.28 MANTA.FLC)

In this animation, a plug-in routine adds a ripple or wave effect to the body of a stylized manta ray. This situation shows how effectively plug-in routines save time in the creation of complex movement.

### Morphing and Water (Figure 2.29 NEWFAC01.FLI)

This animation shows how morphing (translating geometry from one form to another) can be used to create the effect of an animated column of water. By having the water morph into different shapes in subsequent frames, the illusion of a solid moving column of water is achieved.

### Watery Sphere (Figure 2.30 ORB.FLC)

In this animation, a globe of liquid sits nestled among some vegetation. A drop falls into the globe, causing a ripple to pass over the surface, defying gravity.

FIGURE 2.27
Reflection and squash: REFLECT.FLI. (Supplied courtesy of Autodesk, Inc.)

Figure 2.28
Wave motion: MANTA.FLC. (Supplied courtesy of Autodesk, Inc.)

Figure 2.29
Morphing and water: NEWFAC01.FLI. (Supplied courtesy of Autodesk, Inc.)

FIGURE 2.30
Watery sphere: ORB.FLC. (Supplied courtesy of Autodesk, Inc.)

## 2.13 SUMMARY

This is an exciting point in the exploration of 3D Studio MAX, but it can also be a frustrating one. It takes some time for animators to reach the skill level that allows them to complete their creations. However, you will reach that point with a willingness to learn the background information required. The important thing to remember is that you have started the journey that leads to the end showcased in Chapter 2. Now, let's get closer still by delving into the next section.

# QUESTIONS AND ASSIGNMENTS

## QUESTIONS

1. Suggest some other possible uses for 3D Studio MAX. Be specific.
2. Why does animation make expressing ideas more effective?

## ASSIGNMENTS

1. Interview someone who uses 3D Studio MAX at work.
2. Find some examples of 3D animation in the world around you.

PART TWO

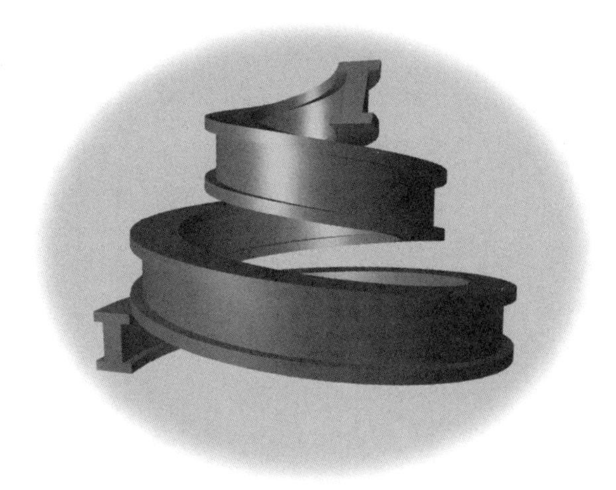

# Exploring 3D Studio MAX

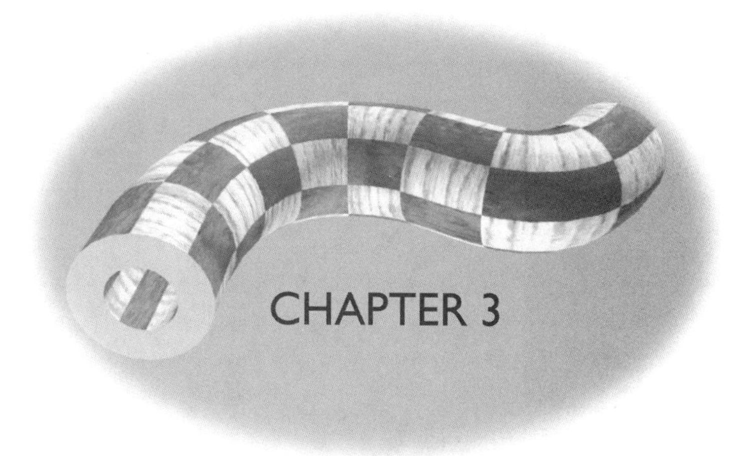


# Interacting with 3D Studio MAX

## 3.1 INTRODUCTION

3D Studio MAX can create either rendered still images or an animation by assembling these rendered stills into a movie file. To accomplish either of these, 3D Studio MAX can be broken down into logical steps, which include creating geometry, covering it with materials, preparing a scene, and producing a still rendering or animation. This text focuses on each of these steps successively in order to make your learning easier and more intuitive.

To use 3D Studio MAX, you must be able to navigate the program itself, become familiar with the screens and menus, and learn the various functions performed by the mouse buttons. You will not be learning what all the commands do at this point but rather gaining an understanding of how to get to them and activate them. If you are familiar with the use of the Windows operating system, then you may already be accustomed to the operation of some of the 3D Studio MAX features. However, the 3D Studio MAX screen has been designed to make the best use of available space. As such you will find some new menu features, such as rollouts, that need to be mastered to utilize the program fully.

The purpose of this chapter is to introduce 3D Studio MAX and become familiar with moving throughout the program. Here you will learn the layout of the screen, how to access the commands, and how to manipulate the files associated with 3D Studio MAX.

## 3.2 REVIEWING THE SCREEN

Once you have launched the 3D Studio MAX program, you are presented with the screen shown in Figure 3.1. The window is divided into eight main areas: viewports,

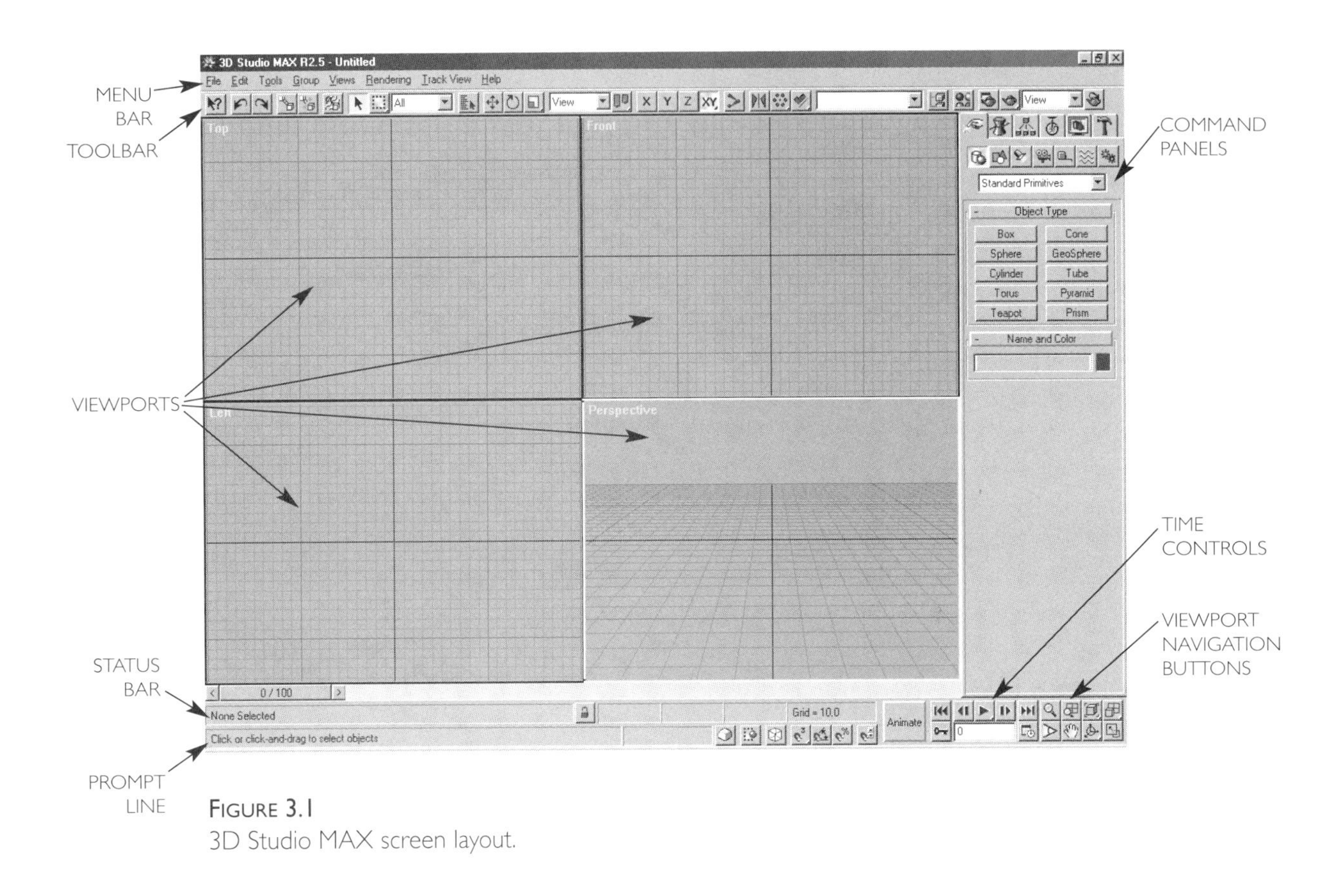


FIGURE 3.1
3D Studio MAX screen layout.

menu bar, toolbar, viewport navigation buttons, time controls, command panels, status bar, and prompt line. The following is a brief description of each area so that, later on when you learn more of the specifics, you will already be familiar with their location.

## Viewports

As you might imagine from a graphics-oriented program, the majority of the area is taken up with the graphics viewport area. You can display from one to four viewports, with each viewport displaying a different view of the model. Refer to Figure 3.2 for the Viewport Configuration dialog box, from which you can decide the viewport layout. You will learn how to do this in Chapter 5. Remember that only one model or scene can be worked on at one time and that the viewports display different views of the same model or scene.

**LIGHTS! CAMERA! ACTION!**

Launching 3D Studio MAX

3D Studio MAX is a single document application and, as such, you can launch and run only one copy at a time.

FIGURE 3.2
Viewport Configuration dialog.

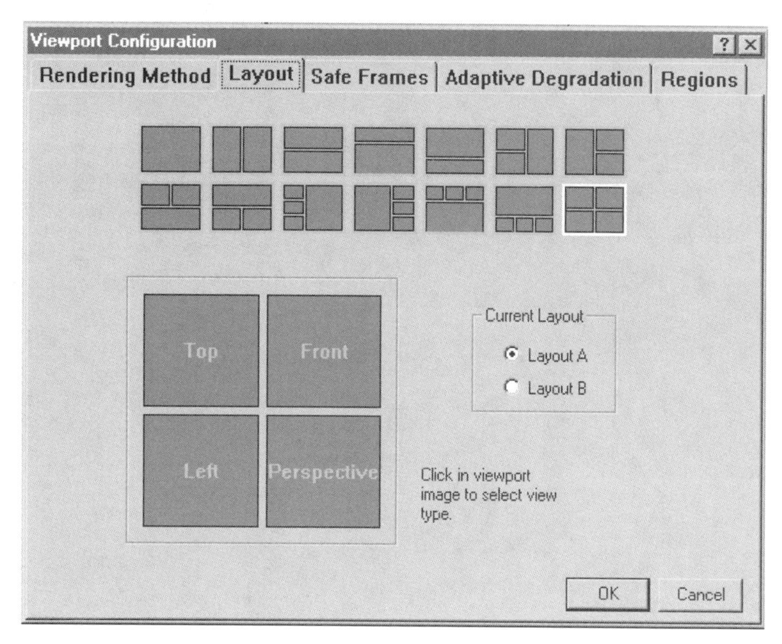


## Menu Bar

The menu bar lies at the top of the screen and has many of the 3D Studio MAX commands grouped together in the standard Windows pull-down menu format. Some of these commands are similar to most Windows programs, such as New, Open, and Save As, whereas others are specific to 3D Studio MAX. Refer to Figure 3.3, which shows the various menus open so that you can see the commands under each. To open a menu, simply move the cursor over the menu heading and pick it.

Note the commands that are gray. This signifies that the command cannot be accessed. This usually happens when you have not yet performed a procedure required by the command. Observe the Undo command under the Edit menu. If you have not performed any command yet, there is nothing to undo; so it is gray.

### *LIGHTS! CAMERA! ACTION!*

#### Redrawing the Screen

Sometimes a viewport will seem to be missing pieces of geometry even though the geometry is still there. To redraw all the viewports to show their proper condition, use the number 1 key at the top of the alphanumeric keyboard. Another solution is to activate the viewport by right-clicking on it.

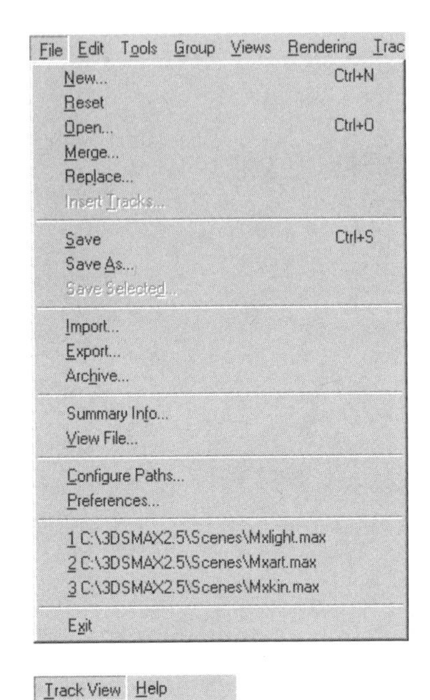


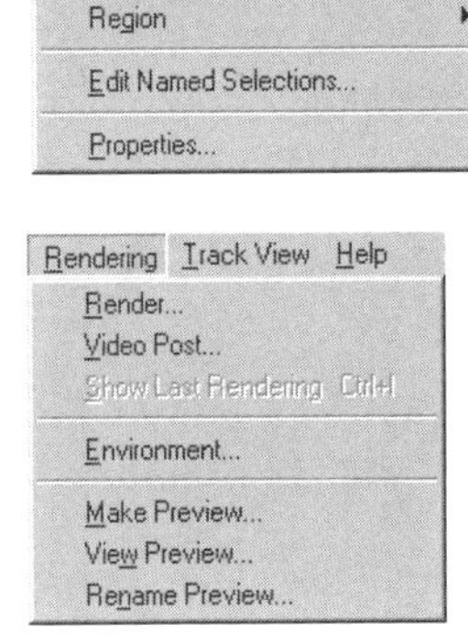


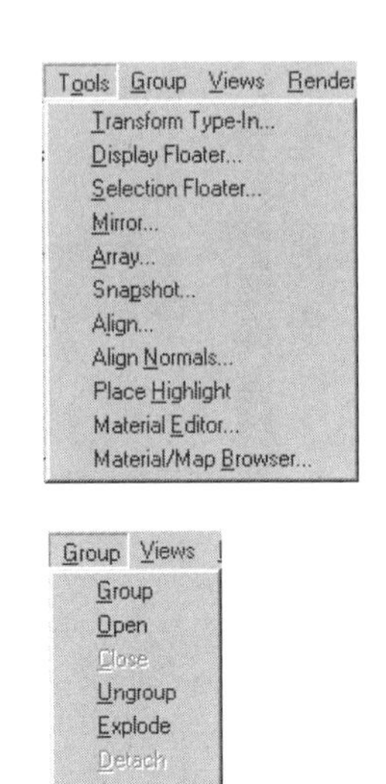


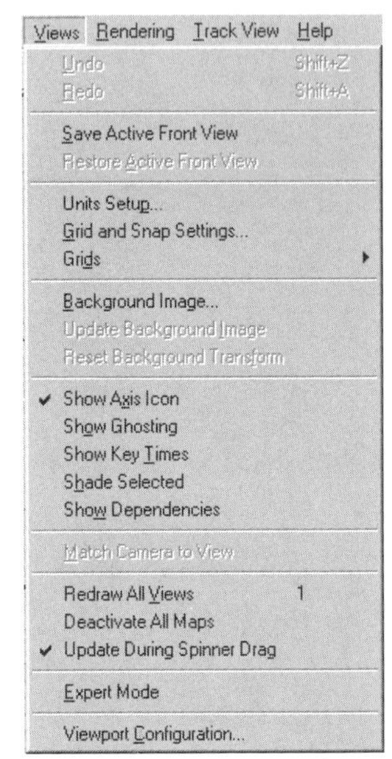


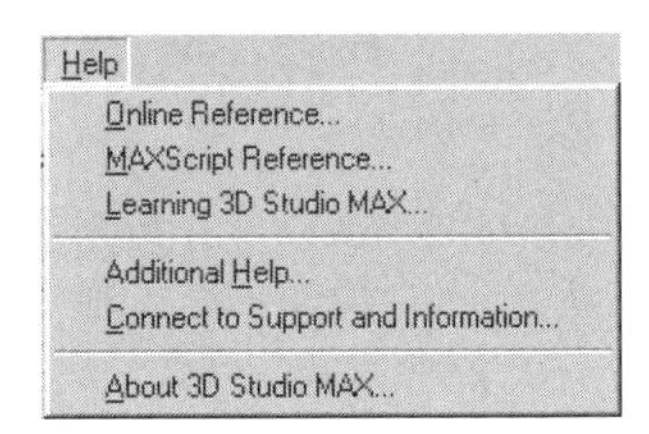


FIGURE 3.3
Various pull-down menus.

## Toolbar

The toolbar lies under the pull-down menu and contains various icon buttons used to select and transform geometry as well to set up materials and render. To use an icon button, move the cursor over the button and pick it.

If you rest the cursor on the icon without picking, a line of text will appear describing the icon. This is called a *tooltip*.

Some of the icons have a small black triangle in the lower-right corner. This means that the icon button has a flyout containing more icon buttons. If you pick and hold down on this type of button, a series of buttons will fly out. You then can slide the cursor over the other buttons, while still holding down on the pick button. When you release the button, the button you are on will be activated.

There are also drop-down lists used to display a list of possible selections when you pick on the list. The following is a description of the different icons and lists located in the toolbar.

### Help

Displays the 3DS MAX help system.

### Undo and Redo

Used to Undo or Redo the previous edit commands.

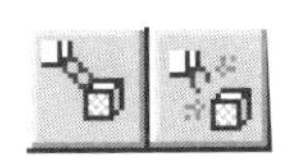

### Hierarchical Linking

Used to create and break hierarchical links between objects.

### Bind to Space Warp

Used to bind objects to a space warp.

**Selection Controls**
Provides different ways of selecting objects. The first icon is the pick object icon used to select an object.

**Transforms**
Provides different ways of transforming objects: move, rotate, and scale. You select objects with these buttons.

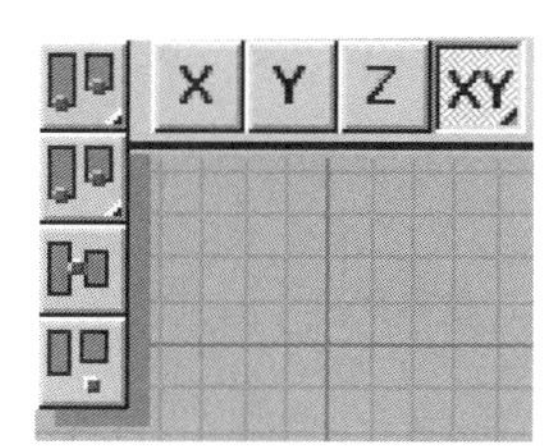


**Transform Managers**
Controls how objects are transformed by applying constraints such as uniform scaling or locking axis movement.

**Inverse Kinematics (IK)**
Toggles on and off the use of inverse kinematics. Best to keep this off (not pressed) at the beginning.

**Mirror**
Used to create mirror copies of selected objects.

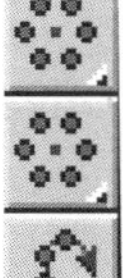

**Array Flyout**
Used to create array and snapshot copies of selected objects.

**Align Flyout**
Used to align objects with different objects or normals.

**Named Selection lists**
Used to name a selection set or select a previously named one.

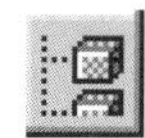

**Track View**
Displays a dialog used to track objects, to discover how they were created, and to see their animations.

**Material Editor**
Displays the material editor dialog used to create and apply materials.

**Rendering Controls**
Icons and lists used to control the rendering of your scene. The first button displays the render dialog.

### Viewport Navigation Buttons

The viewport navigation buttons are located in the bottom right corner of the screen and are used to control the display inside a viewport. With these buttons you can zoom in or out and pan around a viewport. The top four buttons are Zoom, Zoom All, Zoom Extents, and Zoom Extents All. All refers to all viewports. The bottom four buttons are Zoom Region, Pan, Arc Rotate, and Minimize/Maximize Viewport. The standard viewport navigation buttons are used on the orthographic, user, and perspective viewports. This group of buttons will change if you are manipulating the display of a camera or light viewport.

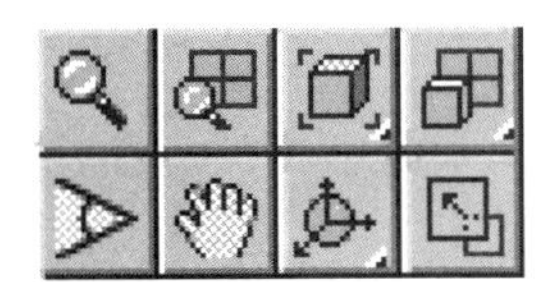
Standard viewport navigation buttons

### Time Controls

The time control buttons are at the bottom of the screen and are used to create and control an animation.

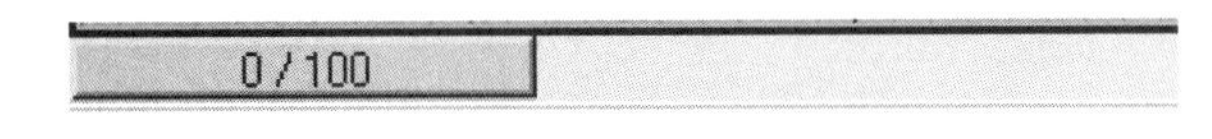


**Time Slider**
Used to indicate or set the currently active frame in an animation.

**Animate**
Used to toggle on (red) or off (grey) the animation mode. It is best to leave this off at the beginning.

**Others**
Used to control the playing or movement through an animation.

### Command Panels

There are six nested command panels located at the right of the screen. Each one is selected by picking on the appropriate tab. Only one can be displayed at a time. Refer to Figure 3.4 for the display of a sample command panel.

**Create**
Displays controls for creating objects.

**Modify**
Displays controls for modifying object parameters.

**Hierarchy**
Displays controls for adjusting object linking and pivot points.

**Motion**
Displays controls used to assign and edit transform controllers and object motion paths.

**Display**
Displays controls used to set display preferences.

FIGURE 3.4
Sample command panel.

**Utilities**

Provides access to third party developers' plug-ins.

## Status Bar and Prompt Line

The status bar and prompt line display information on the current state of an active command as well as a constant coordinate readout. At the right end of the line you will find special toggle icons to control selections, precision, and display properties. The following lists specific information on the two areas.

### Status Bar

The status bar displays information about the current selection, such as "None Selected" as shown in Figure 3.5.

Notice the lock icon, which is used to temporarily lock in the currently selected items. This allows you to pick anywhere in a viewport to pick and drag without losing the contents of the selection set.

The coordinate readouts display the X,Y, and Z locations of the cursor in world coordinates. If you are transforming an object, such as by using move or rotate, the coordinate readout displays the offset from the original position.

Grid = 10.0

There is also a box displaying the status of the grid scale, which is important when positioning an object precisely.

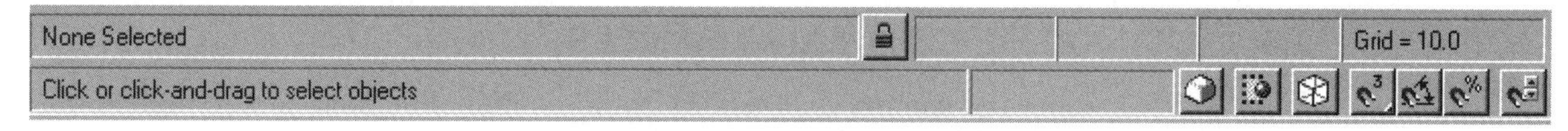


FIGURE 3.5
Status bar and prompt line.

### Prompt Line

The prompt line displays the current command state, such as "Click or click and drag to select objects."

The plug-in keyboard shortcut toggle icon is used to switch between 3D Studio MAX's standard keyboard shortcuts and plug-in keyboard shortcuts that have been added.

It also contains toggle icons to control the method of region selection. When the toggle is popped out, a region selection box (or circle or fence) selects objects that cross the box as well as those enclosed in the box. If the toggle is pushed in, objects are selected if they are totally enclosed by the region.

The degradation override button toggles on or off adaptive display degradation. Adaptive display degradation happens when you drag a complex object into a scene and its display reverts to a simplified version, such as a box.

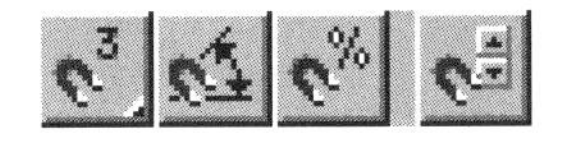

Snap controls allow precise movement of the cursor. These are explained in more detail in Chapter 6.

## 3.3 USING THE INPUT DEVICE

The mouse is the primary method of selection and manipulation within 3D Studio MAX. The left button on the mouse is referred to as the *pick button*, used for selecting most commands and objects on the screen. When you are asked to pick, select, or choose, it usually means to move the cursor to the desired location and press the left mouse button. The right button is used for special features and is simply called a right-click. For instance, if you place your cursor over the name label on a viewport and right-click it, the properties menu for the viewport will appear. This works for objects as well. Finally, the right button will cancel most commands or actions. As you go through the text, the special functions of the left and right mouse buttons will be revealed. You can also refer to the MAX IN MOTION Quick Chart tear-out card at the end of the text.

Sometimes you will be asked to double-click on an item or object. Double-clicking means that you move the cursor over the item and press the left mouse button twice, in rapid succession.

You may also be asked to click and drag. To click and drag, move the cursor to the desired location, press the left mouse button, and hold it down while you drag the cursor to a new location. When you move the cursor over objects in your scene, the name of the object will appear. This can help during selection.

The cursor can change appearance, depending on what action is being performed. These changes are used to give you an indicator of the type of action. For instance, if the cursor is an arrow, it indicates that it is in command pick mode; if it is a thin-lined cross, it is in coordinate location pick mode; and if it is a stubby thick cross, it is in object pick mode. You should become used to the appearance of the cursor so that it can communicate this information to you visually.

## 3.4 USING THE COMMAND PANELS

When using the command panels, knowing their specific behavioral characteristics will help with their use. They are called rollouts, spinners, special methods for entering numbers, and panning hand.

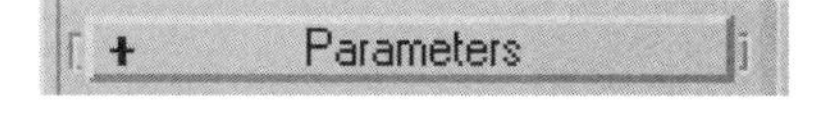


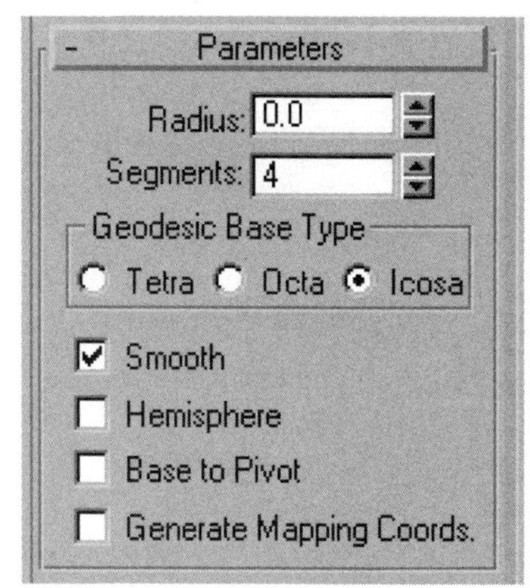


FIGURE 3.6
Rollouts.

## Rollouts

Rollouts are areas in the command panels and dialogs that you can collapse (roll in) or expand (roll out). This ability makes it easier to manage the screen space as you expand only the panels with which you are concerned. Refer to Figure 3.6, which shows a collapsed and an expanded rollout. The plus (+) sign indicates that the roll-out is collapsed and can be expanded by picking the title bar. The menu's (-) sign indicates that the rollout is expanded and can be collapsed by picking the title bar.

## Spinners

FIGURE 3.7
Numeric entry field.

Spinners are a special way of incrementally entering values by moving the cursor. Figure 3.7 shows a numeric entry field. To enter a number, pick inside the box and type the number, pick the up and down arrows to raise or lower the current value, or use the spinner feature.

To use the spinner feature, move the cursor over the up and down arrows and click and drag by holding down on the left button as you move the cursor up or down. The value in the numeric field box will increase or decrease, depending on whether you move up or down. Release the button when you have arrived at the desired value.

## Enter Numbers

When numbers are entered in a numeric field, they are usually absolute values. However, if you place an R before the value, the value becomes a relative value, which means it is added to the current value. For instance, if the number in the numeric field is 6 and you enter R4, the resulting value in the numeric field is 10. You can also enter negative R numbers, such as R–3. This has the effect of subtracting the R value from the current value.

**LIGHTS! CAMERA! ACTION!**

If you hold down on the Ctrl key while clicking and dragging, it increases the rate at which the numeric value increments increase. Conversely, holding down on the Alt key while clicking and dragging decreases the rate at which the numeric value increases.

### Panning Hand

It is possible to increase the size of command panels or dialogs so that they will not fit entirely on the screen. To get around this, 3D Studio MAX has what is called the *panning hand*. If the panel or dialog is too large, some portion will be scrolled off the screen area. To access these portions, move the cursor to an empty area in the panel or dialog and click and hold. The cursor turns into a hand that lets you move the panel or dialog area up or down. Release the button when you see the area you want.

## 3.5 USING DIALOGS

Dialogs are rectangular areas of information or data that appear over the screen area and look very much like small application windows. Figure 3.8 illustrates the Track View dialog. They appear when you select a command or option that requires you to see or manipulate the data contained in a dialog. You can move a dialog around the screen by clicking and dragging on its title bar. There are two types of dialogs in 3D Studio MAX: modeless and modal.

### Modeless Dialogs

Modeless dialogs look like Figure 3.8; they allow you to work inside them or outside them while they are still visible. To close a modeless dialog, pick on the X in the upper-right corner.

### Modal Dialogs

Modal dialogs look like Figure 3.9. With these dialogs, you observe the data, manipulate the data as needed, and then close them by picking the OK button or the Cancel button if you do not want to make changes. You cannot work outside a modal dialog while it is visible. You must exit from it first.

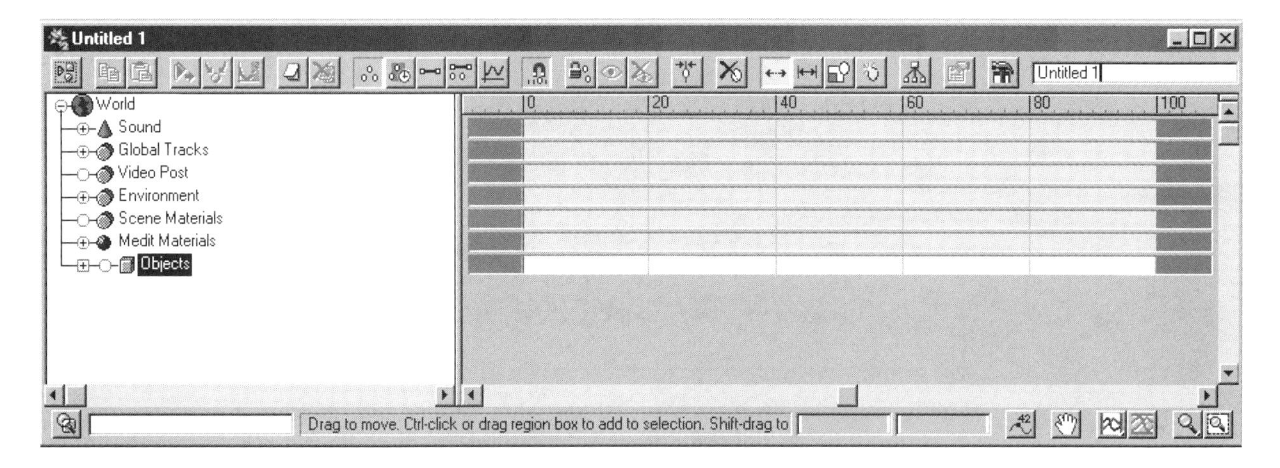


FIGURE 3.8
Track View is a modeless dialog.

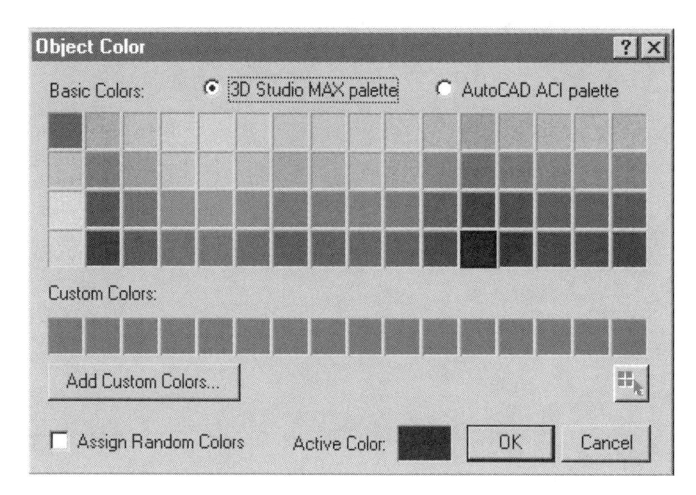


FIGURE 3.9
Object Color is a modal dialog.

## 3.6 HANDLING FILES

### Saving Scenes

The creation you do in 3D Studio MAX takes place in what are called *scenes*. Scenes can be saved as files so that you can open them whenever you want to continue. To save the current scene, choose the File/Save pull-down menu item. If it is the first time you saved the scene, you will be presented with the Save As dialog shown in Figure 3.10. This allows you to choose a name and location for the file although by default it will be saved in the Scenes subdirectory of the 3D MAX directory. The file name will contain the suffix .MAX, identifying it as a 3D Studio MAX scene file. If you choose File/Save again, the command will save the file automatically, using the file name and location you supplied earlier. You can use the File/Save As pull-down menu item if you wish to save the scene under a new name.

### New Scenes

You can start a new scene by choosing the File/New or File/Reset pull-down menu item. The File/New choice creates a new scene using the same program settings as the previous scene. The File/Reset choice creates a new scene using the 3DS MAX start-up defaults.

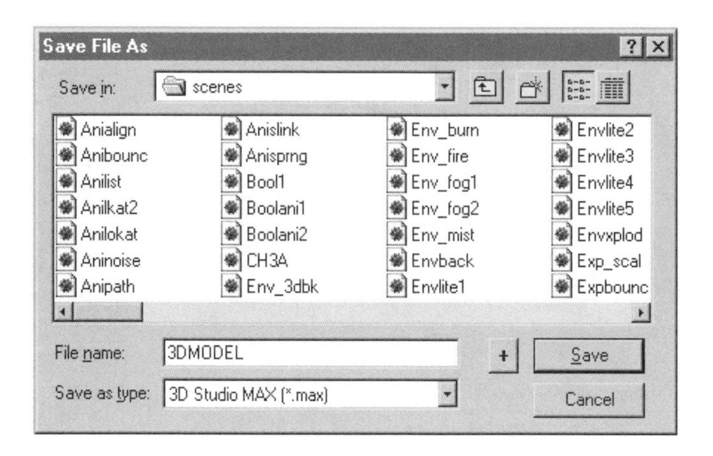


FIGURE 3.10
Save File As dialog.

FIGURE 3.11
Open File dialog.

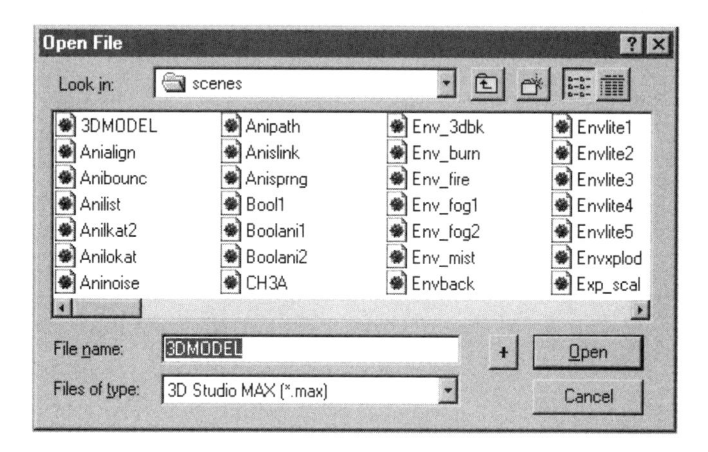


## Opening Scenes

To open 3D Studio MAX scenes that have already been saved, select the File/Open pull-down menu item. This will display the Open File dialog as shown in Figure 3.11. It usually defaults to the Scenes subdirectory of the 3D MAX directory located on the drive on which you installed 3D Studio MAX. The scene files have the extension .MAX. If you locate a file bearing that prefix, it is probably a scene file. There are previously created scenes on the CD-ROM that accompanies this book. Refer to Appendix A if you wish to view some of them at this point.

## Merging Scenes

You merge a previously saved scene file with a currently opened one by using the File/Merge pull-down menu item. This can be useful when you want to take objects from one scene into another. When you use this command, you are presented with the Merge File dialog, as shown in Figure 3.12. When you have selected the file to merge, you are then presented with the Merge dialog, as shown in Figure 3.13. Use this box to pick the items you want to bring into the current scene. You can pick one, several, or all, depending on your needs.

## File Types and Locations

3D Studio MAX makes use of several different file types in the creation, rendering, and animation of a scene. Each file type has a different application. Some are

FIGURE 3.12
Merge File dialog.

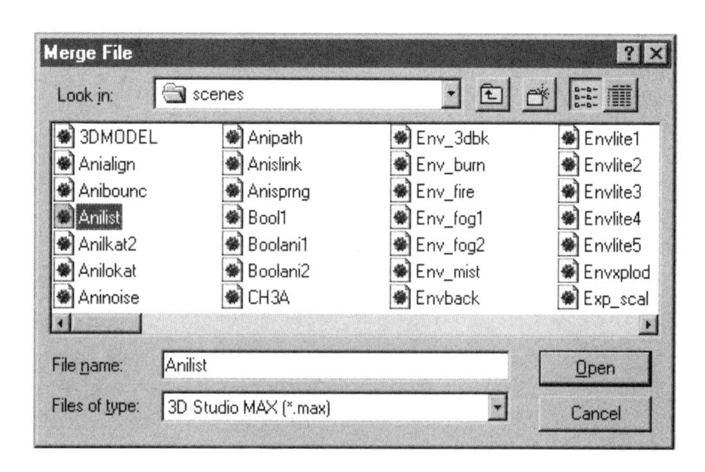

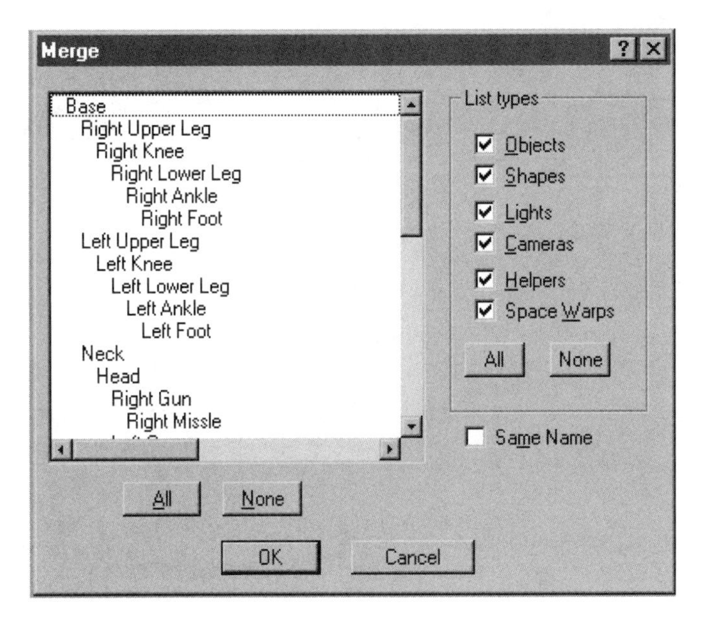


FIGURE 3.13
Merge dialog.

meshes that represent objects; some are images that represent renderings. There are even sound files to add sound to your animations. To help to keep things organized, the different file types are stored in individual subdirectories. Figure 3.14 shows the Configure Paths dialog. It is used to establish where the different files will be stored. To access this dialog, select the File/Configure Paths pull-down menu.

## Viewing Files

3D Studio MAX is capable of viewing several different file types. Refer to Figure 3.15 for the View File dialog. This dialog is accessed through the File/View pull-down menu item. If you select a static (single frame) file for display, it is shown in the 3DS MAX Virtual Frame Buffer (VFB), as shown in Figure 3.16. If you select an

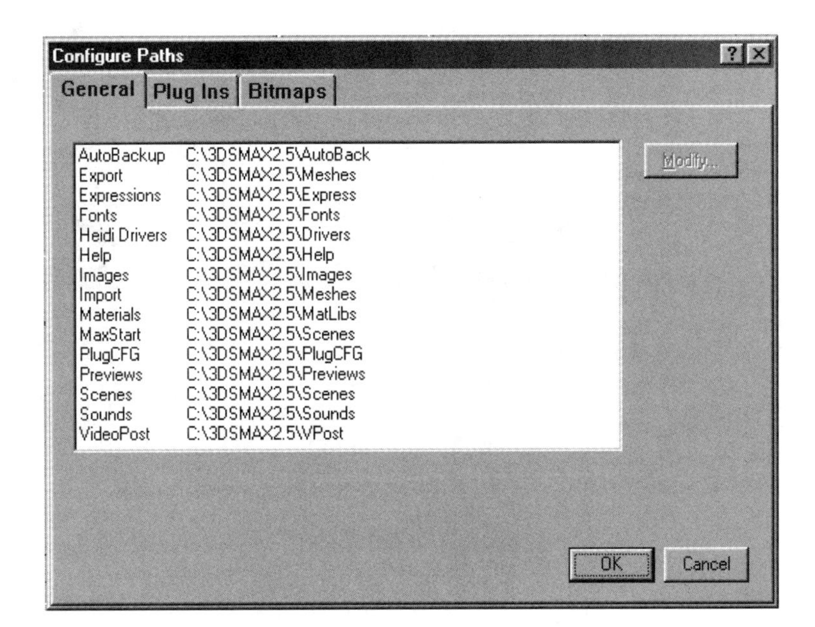


FIGURE 3.14
Configure Paths dialog.

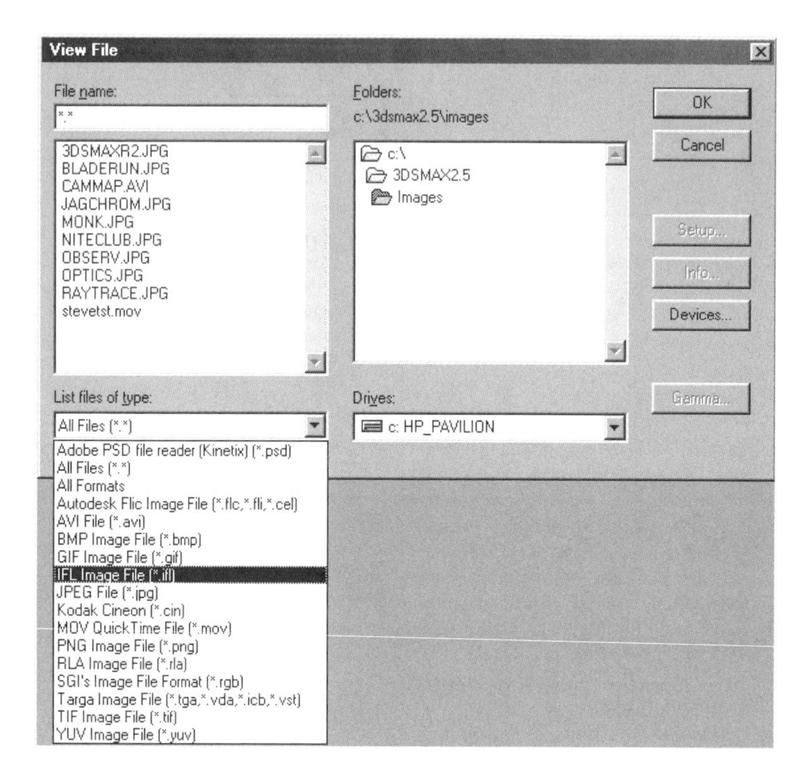


FIGURE 3.15
View File dialog.

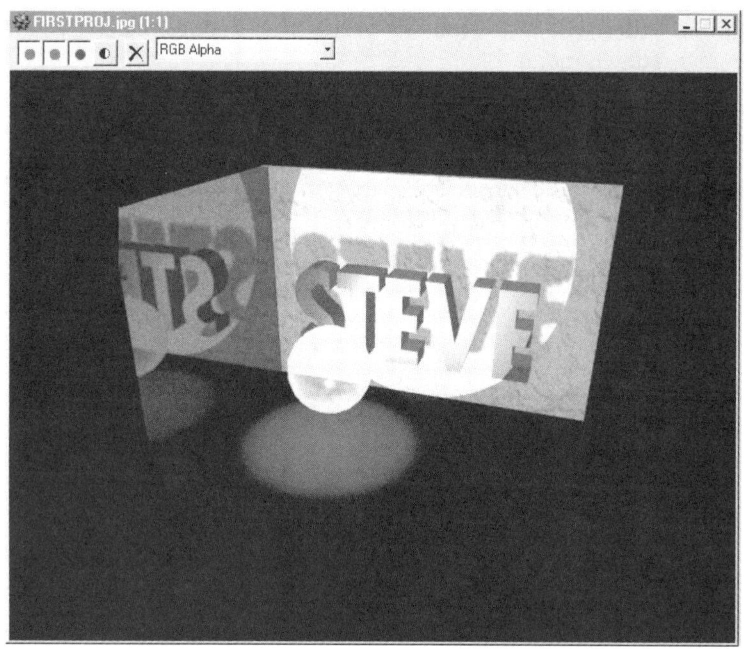


FIGURE 3.16
Virtual Frame Buffer.

animation file, it will be displayed using the Windows Media Player. Figure 3.17 shows the Media Player window.

## Scene Status

There are times when you will want to see a summary of the scene you have been working on. If you select the File/Summary Info pull-down menu item, you will be presented with the Scene Info dialog, as shown in Figure 3.18. This dialog gives you a variety of information on the currently opened scene.

FIGURE 3.17
Media Player window.

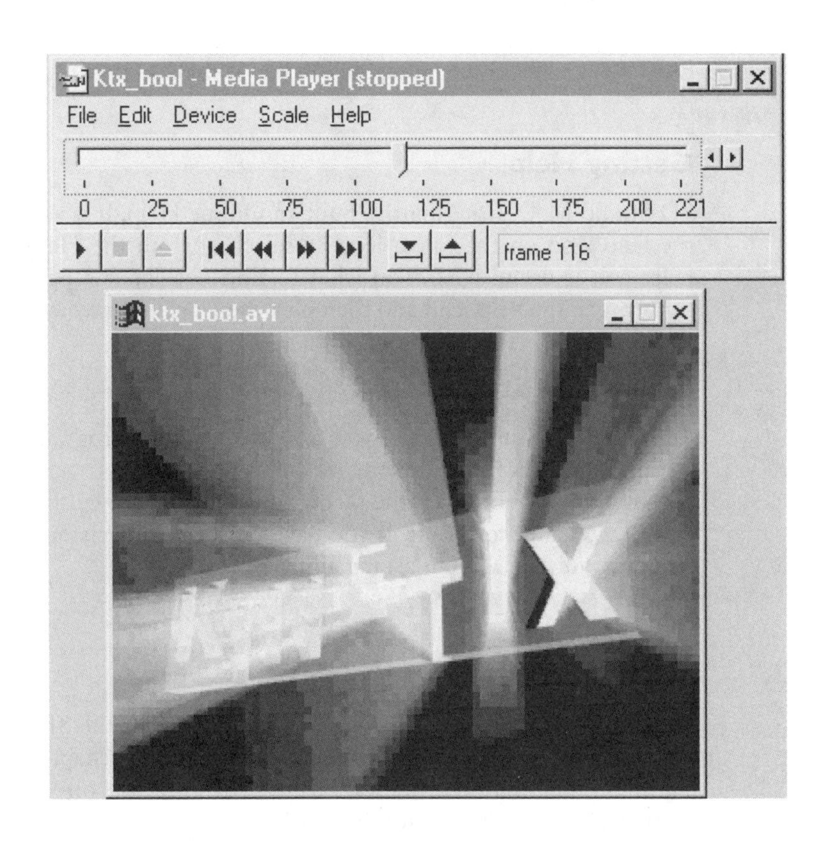


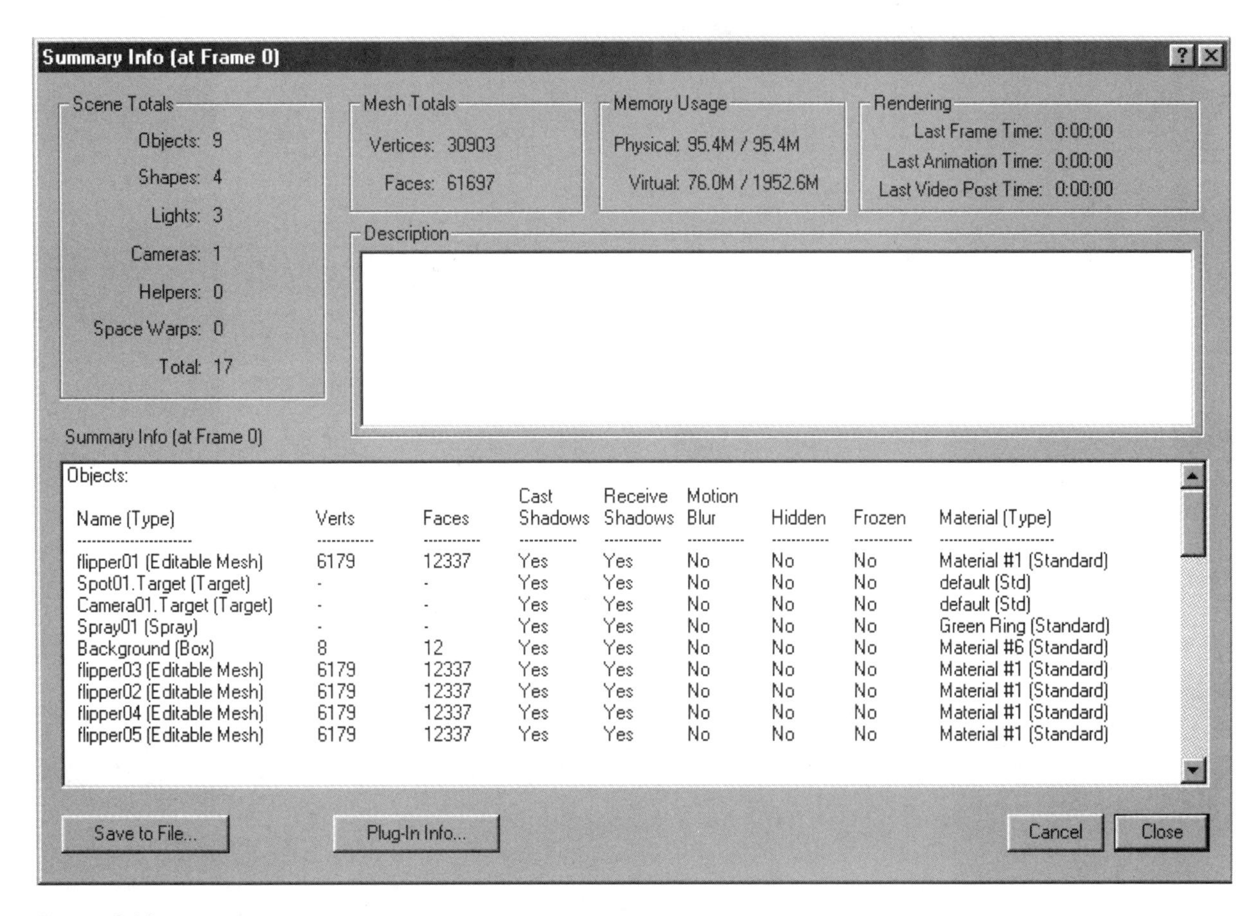


FIGURE 3.18
Scene Info dialog.

### Getting Help

3D Studio MAX has extensive built-in Online Help. It is accessible by either picking the help icon on the menu icon or selecting from the Help pull-down menu. The help icon is useful when you what to find out about a particular icon button. You simply pick the help icon and then pick the icon about which you want to know.

### Closing 3D Studio MAX

To close 3D Studio MAX, you need to exit the program. To do this select the File/Exit pull-down menu item.

If you have not saved the scene on which you are currently working, you will be given the chance to save it. If you have not made any changes since the last save, the program will exit without asking any questions.

## 3.7 SUMMARY

Now that you have been introduced to the layout of the 3D Studio MAX program, it's time to test the waters. Remember to reread this chapter if you need a refresher course on the location of the various commands in the on-screen environment. Now, go ahead and get you feet wet with the following lab.

## LAB 3.A

## Moving Around the 3D Studio MAX Environment

### Purpose

This lab will familiarize you with the 3D Studio MAX environment. You will load the program and move about the different parts of it, testing some of the features in order to become comfortable with using the various menus and screens. In Chapter 4, you will get a more detailed look at creating your own scene.

### Objectives

You will be able to

- Load and quit the program.
- Access commands from the pull-down menus and command panels.
- Use the various icon buttons.
- Load and save scene files.
- Use the Help icon feature.
- Create some simple geometry.
- Use the cursor and keyboard for data entry.

### Procedure

#### LOADING 3D STUDIO MAX

1. Look for the 3D Studio MAX icon in your Windows program menu or locate a shortcut icon. Once you have found it, double-click on it. After a few moments the program will load and display a screen similar to Figure 3.19. By default, the graphics screen is usually divided into four viewports. Later you will learn how to create you own configuration.

   *Note:* The 3D Studio MAX program requires a special hardware key. If the key is not available to the program, the program will automatically stop.

#### MOVING ABOUT THE VIEWPORTS

2. Whenever you are about to begin a project within 3D Studio MAX, choose File Reset so that all the settings are returned to their normal starting positions. This can help if someone using the machine before you has saved undesired settings. Move your cursor about the center graphics screen. You should notice that one viewport has a bold white border. This signifies that it is the currently active viewport. Thus, the cursor has control over that particular viewport.

   Move the cursor within that viewport. A coordinate readout should appear at the bottom of the screen in the status bar. As you move the cursor in the active viewport, two of the possible three coordinates will change.

   Move your cursor into one of the other viewports and right-click (press the right button of the mouse) on the screen. That viewport will now become the active viewport. Note the bold white border and watch the coordinate readout as you move the cursor.

   Each viewport has its name in the top left-hand corner. Each viewport controls the movement of the particular axis and the plane on which your creation will take place. By switching viewports, you will switch to the desired working plane.

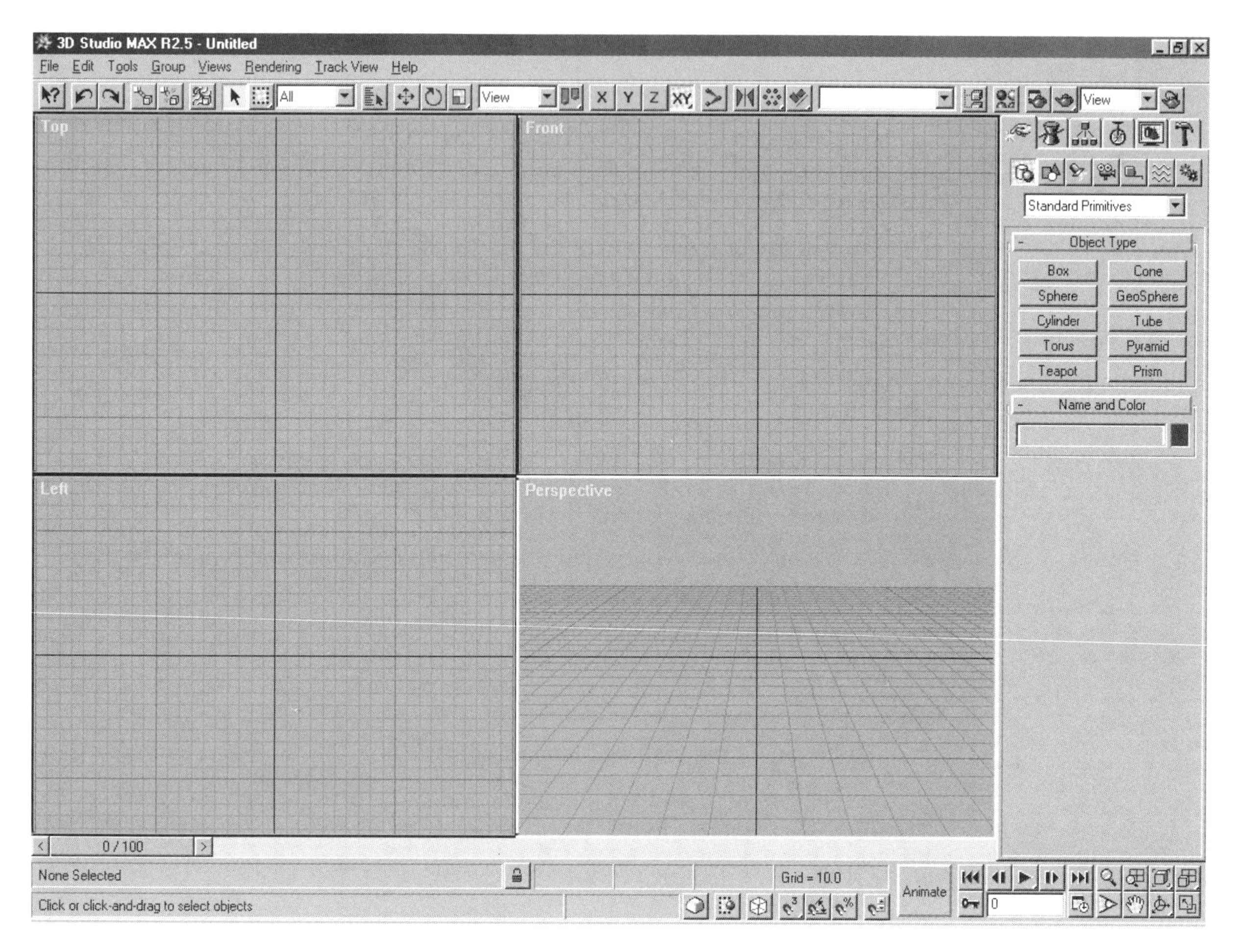


FIGURE 3.19
The 3D Studio MAX screen.

## MOVING ABOUT PULL-DOWN MENUS

3. Move your cursor up into the line area of the pull-down menu area. Move your cursor over the menu item File and pick it. A menu list should be pulled down onto the screen. This list displays the menu items under the File category.

   Move the cursor down into the menu list but do not pick anything yet. Note how items are highlighted as you drag the cursor over the list. That is how you will identify the item you want to select. As you move through the items, the prompt line at the bottom of the screen with give you some more information about the highlighted command.

   Also notice how the Save Selected menu item is greyed out. This means that it cannot be selected yet. The 3D Studio MAX program knows that you are in a new file and have not selected any objects to save. If you had selected some objects, the Save Selected item would be black, allowing you to select it.

4. Move your cursor away from the pull-down menu and pick an empty portion of the screen. This will close the pull-down menu when you don't want to pick an item. Right-click in the Perspective viewport to make it active. Pick on the Views pull-down menu and select Viewport Configuration from the list. The Viewport Configuration dialog will appear. Under the Render level heading, make sure the Wireframe radio button is on (black dot). Then pick OK to close the dialog. Explore the other pull-down menus to familiarize yourself with other item locations.

## MOVING ABOUT COMMAND PANELS

5. Move the cursor over to the right of the screen, where the command panels are located. Move the cursor over the command panel tab for Modify and pick (*pick* means to place the cursor over the item and then press the left mouse button) the tab. The Modify command panel will appear, as shown in Figure 3.20.

6. Now pick the Create command panel tab. The Create command panel should appear over the Modify panel, as shown in Figure 3.21. Command panels overlap each other, depending on the tab that you pick.

7. Pick Geometry in the Create command panel. It may have already been highlighted, depending on the state of the program. Look over the lower part of the panel. There should be a list of the standard primitive objects, such as Box and Cylinder.

   Pick the Torus button. The Create panel should now be displaying the options for creating a torus, as shown in Figure 3.22.

   Move your cursor into a blank area among the torus options. The cursor should change to look like a hand. This is to let you slide the torus creation options up or down to access more of its options.

   With the hand displayed, press the left mouse button and move the cursor up and down. The panel should slide up and down with the cursor movement. Release the button to stop the motion. Make sure that the primitive objects list is visible. You may need to use the panning hand again.

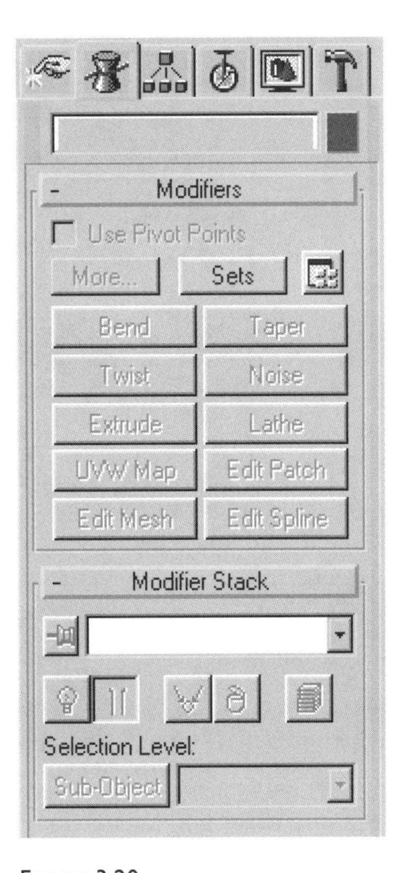


FIGURE 3.20
Modify command panel.

FIGURE 3.21
Create command panel.

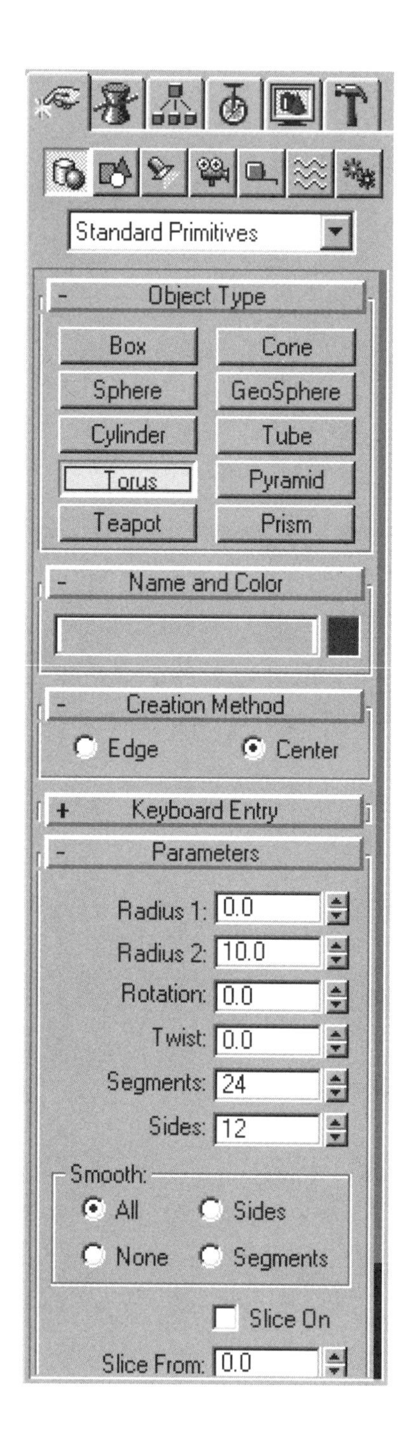


FIGURE 3.22
Torus creation options.

## CREATING SOME SIMPLE GEOMETRY

8. Right-click in the Top viewport to make certain it is active; this is the plane on which we'll create.

9. Press the S key on the keyboard to turn the Snap option on. This helps to create and place objects with accuracy. The icon should look pressed in.
10. By default the cursor will snap to the grid intersections when the snap option is on. To check the type of snap that is currently set, right-click on the icon and a dialog will appear showing the different snap options. Note that the Grid Points box is checked. Pick the X to close.

11. Move the cursor about the screen. If the Torus command is still active, you should notice that the cursor will snap to the intersection of the grid lines (grid points) and a small blue box will appear. This represents the grid point snap. If no command is active, the cursor will move freely.

12. Move to the pull-down menu heading Edit, pick it, and then pick on the Hold menu item. This command temporarily stores the current working environment so that it may be recalled if you make a mistake. It is used in combination with the Fetch command to restore a previous Hold file.

13. While still in the Create panel, pick on the Box button. Observe the prompt line at the bottom of the screen. It should now read:

    Click and drag to begin the creation process

    The prompt is telling you to pick a coordinate location on the screen to start one corner of the box. One way to create an object is by using the cursor. Instead, you will use the keyboard to enter the values.

    Move your cursor onto the +Keyboard entry button in the Box creation options to the rollout keyboard entry and pick the button. The panel should look like Figure 3.23.

    You can now enter the coordinates for the center of the box, the X, Y, Z coordinate for the bottom of the box, and its length, width, and height in the numeric entry boxes. Do so with the following values:

    X: 0 Y: 0 Z: 0
    Length: 200 Width: 200 Height: 30

    Once you have entered the values, then pick the Create button. A white rectangular box should appear in the Top, Front, and Right viewports. Some of the box may be obscured in the perspective viewport.

    It is important to give the object a name. By default it is assigned a name and a number, as in Box01. Pick in the box that contains the object name and change it to PLATFORM. The name box can be found under the Name and Color rollout in the Create command panel. You cannot assign a name until the object is created.

    Your screen should now look something like Figure 3.24.

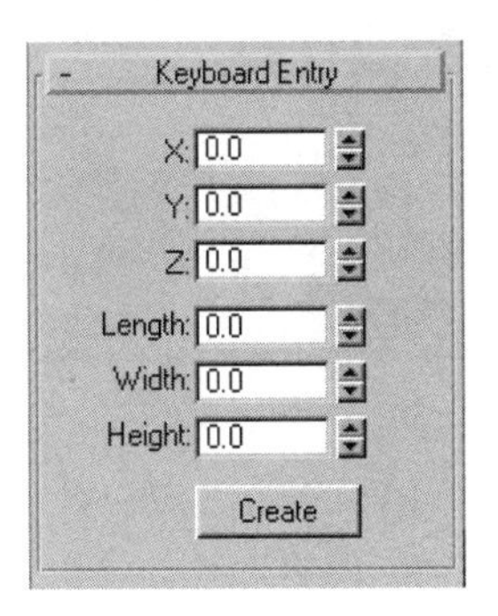


FIGURE 3.23
Keyboard entry rollout for box creation.

14. If you are not happy with the box you created, you can remove it quickly by picking the Fetch button in the Edit pull-down menu. This will "fetch" the contents stored when you picked the Hold menu item. You should get in the habit of using the Hold button just before you attempt something of which you are unsure. Then, if anything goes wrong you can return to the previous state with the Fetch button. There are also Undo and Redo commands in the Edit pull-down menu that can be used to undo or redo the previous commands.

    For this step in the lab, pick on the Fetch button to see the results. A dialog box appears to give you a chance to change your mind. Select Yes to continue the fetch sequence. The 3D box disappears, because it was created after you pressed the Hold button. Create the box again using step 13.

15. Pick on the Hold button to store the box temporarily.

16. Pick the File pull-down menu heading and then pick the Save As item. The Save As File dialog should appear; make sure you are saving to the proper subdirectory. It usually defaults to the Scenes subdirectory. Enter CH3A as the file name and OK it. A file called CH3A.MAX will be created, and the dialog box will disappear.

17. With the Create panel still open, pick the Cylinder button. As with the box, you will need to enter the various parameters to define the cylinder. Roll out the keyboard entry and enter the following data:

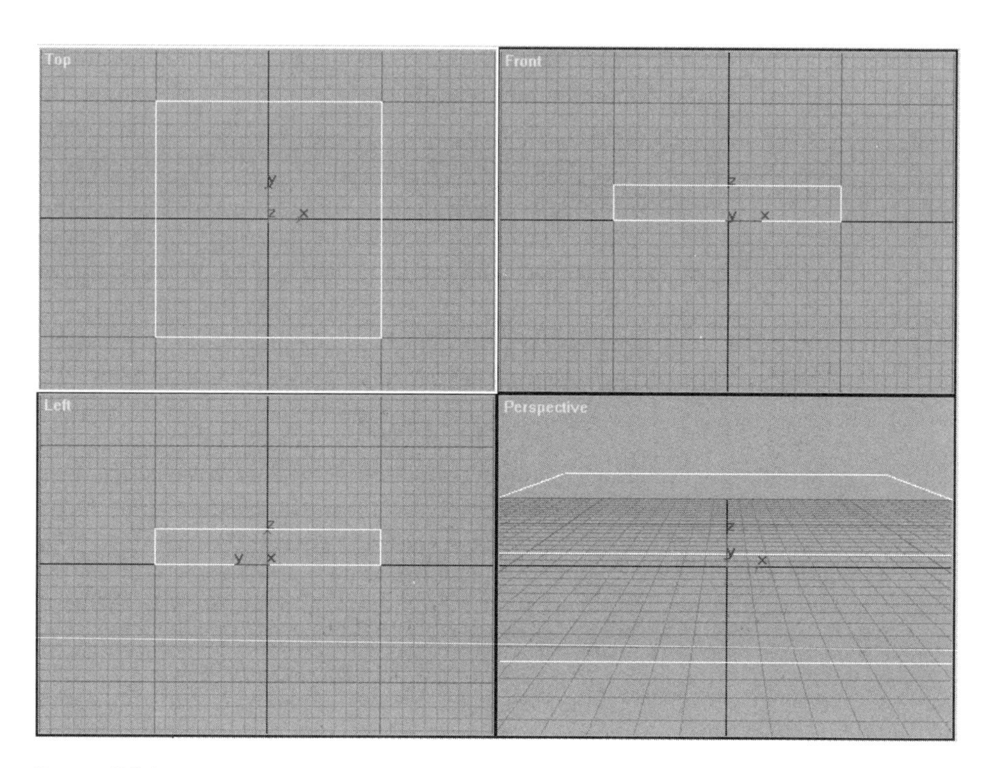


FIGURE 3.24
Viewports displaying the newly created three-dimensional box.

X: 0 Y: 0 Z: 30
Radius: 40 Height: 100

Before you create the cylinder, you need to make sure that the Smooth box is checked. It usually is but you must confirm it. With the Keyboard Entry rolled out, you may need to use the pan hand to access it.

Pick the Create button; the new object CAN should be created, and it should be sitting on top of the platform, as shown in Figure 3.25. Pick the Name box and enter CAN as its name.

## USING ZOOM ICONS

18. The Perspective viewport still doesn't show much of the model. The view is too close. Activate the Perspective viewport by right-clicking in it and then pick the Zoom Extents icon button in the lower-right corner of the screen to reduce or magnify the view so all the objects in the scene fit on the screen.

19. You'll notice that the PLATFORM is still slightly out of the scene. Use the Zoom icon button to reduce or magnify the perspective view.

    Make sure the Perspective viewport is active, turn on the Zoom icon, pick and hold in the Perspective viewport, and slide the cursor up and down. The view should get larger or smaller as you move the cursor. When both the CAN and PLATFORM are visible, release the button. See Figure 3.26.

20. Make the Front viewport active and pick on the Region Zoom icon. It has a rectangular dashed box representing a window. You are now prompted to pick one corner of the window and then the opposite corner. Make a window close around the CAN in the Front viewport. The image of the model should fill the screen. The Region Zoom provides a closer view of your work.

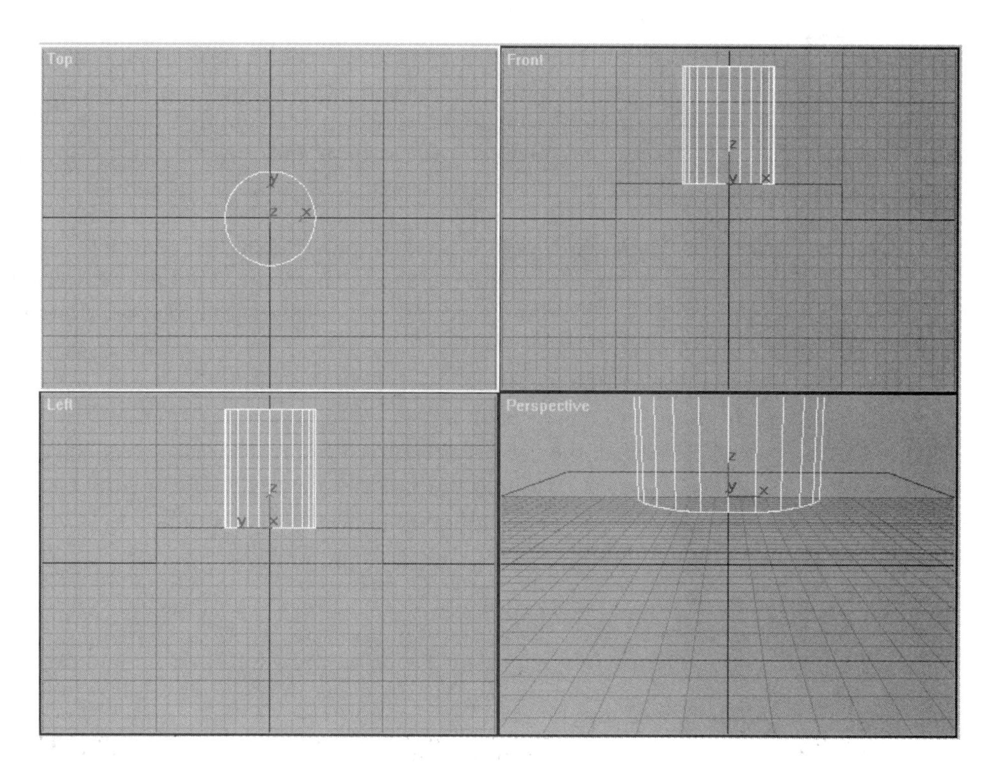


FIGURE 3.25
Creation of a cylinder.

## CHANGING VIEWS

21. Activate the Left viewport. Press the R key and see that the Left viewport has now changed to the Right viewport. You can change the view in any viewport by simply activating the viewport and pressing the appropriate letter associated with the view. Return the view to the Left viewport and Zoom Extents.

22. Activate the Perspective viewport. Press the W key. The Perspective viewport should now fill the screen, making it easier to see the detail at a larger scale. Now press W again and the four viewports reappear. You can switch back and forth with the W key at any time.

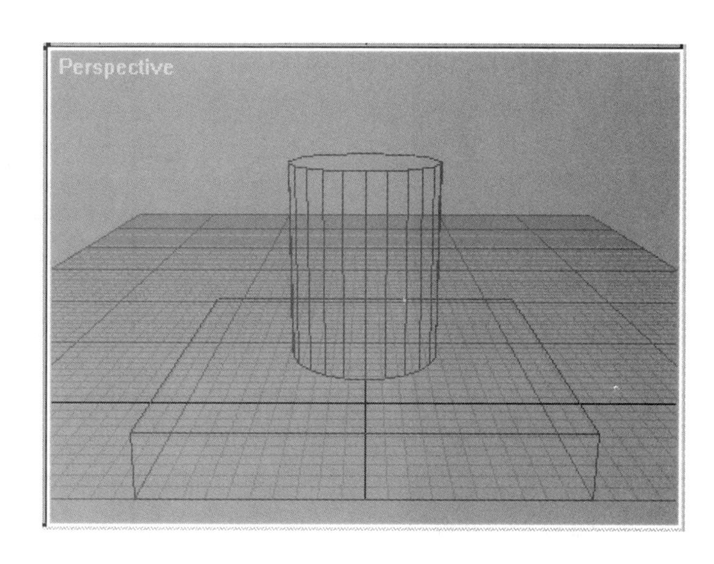


FIGURE 3.26
Adjusting the perspective view.

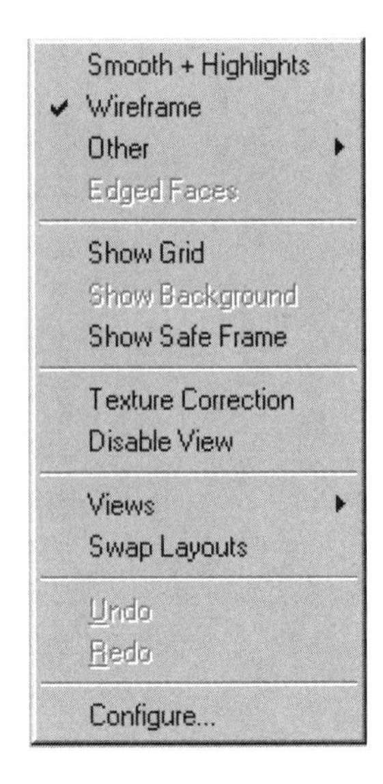


23. With the Perspective viewport still active, move your cursor over the Perspective label and right-click on it. A small menu should appear. This menu controls the properties of the active viewport. Note that the item Wireframe is checked. Pick the Smooth+Highlight item and observe the perspective viewport. A simple form of rendering has been applied to the objects in the viewport. See Figure 3.27. This can be useful when you want a more concrete view in one or all of the viewports. However, it is usually easier in construction to use a wireframe view so that you can see the objects that may be hidden behind others.

    Return the perspective viewport to display wireframe.

## TRANSFORMING THE CYLINDER

24. Pick the Edit/Hold pull-down menu item to store the current model temporarily in case of a mistake. Redraw all viewports using the 1 key on the top of the keyboard. Nothing may happen, depending on the state of the viewports. The redraw refreshes the views by erasing ghost objects or pieces and redrawing the actual objects. You should do this periodically to make sure you have an actual picture of your scene.

25. Right-click on the Front viewport to activate it and then use the Zoom Extents icon button to make sure you can see all the objects in that viewport.

26. Transforming is the act of moving, rotating, or scaling. You are going to rotate the CAN and then move it. First pick on the Select and Rotate transform icon in the middle of the icon bar at the top of the screen. *Note:* Because you can select with all the transforms, the Select portion of the transform will be omitted from the command description; for instance, the Select and Rotate transform will be referred to as just the Rotate transform.

    Move the cursor over the CAN in the front view and pause. Note how the name of the object appears. This can help when selecting an object in a crowded scene. With the cursor over the CAN, pick and hold down on the mouse button. Note how the cursor shows the rotate icon and that the CAN turned white. This is telling you that you are using the rotate transform on the CAN object.

    While still holding down on the button, slide the cursor up and down and see how the object rotates in each viewport. It rotates about its own pivot point. Every object has its own local coordinate system. It is represented by the X-Y-Z axes tripod shown on the object. Now, look at the status line and coordinate readout. It has changed to angular readout as you move up and down. The value

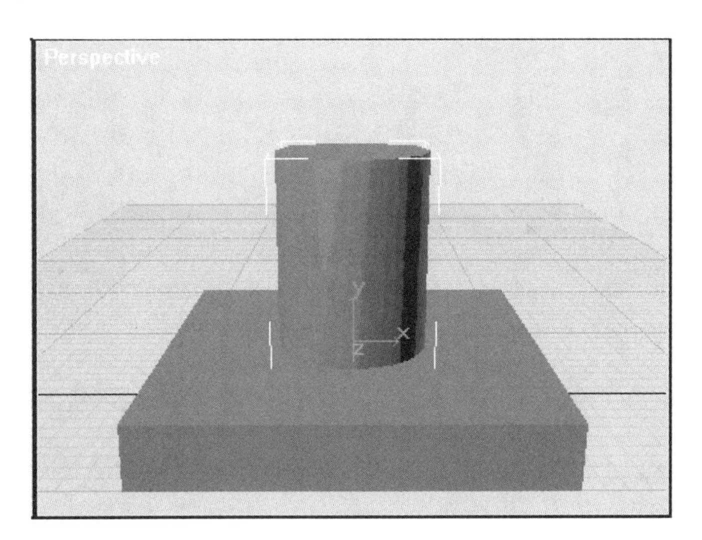


FIGURE 3.27
Simple rendering in perspective viewport.

is in the Z axis, because that is the axis around which you are rotating. Also note the value of the angles. They are shown to at least two decimal places and move in random increments. This is because you have not set any accuracy to the angular movement. We'll do that in a moment. For now just rotate the CAN to any position by moving the cursor and then releasing the button.

27. Now pick the Edit/Fetch menu item, respond with yes, and see what happens. The CAN was restored to its original position. This is because you used the Hold command before performing the rotate transform.

28. Use the Transform Rotate command again to rotate the CAN. As before, the position is not critical. Once you have done this, select the Edit/Undo menu item. This command will undo (or backstep) the last editing you did. It is similar to the Hold command but does not save the scene. It removes only that last command. Use the Hold command before any major changes, and use the Undo command whenever you want to undo any minor changes.

29. Next you are going to perform an accurate rotation. Pick on the Angle Snap Toggle icon at the bottom of the screen so that it is pushed in, meaning that it is turned on. This controls the angular movement of the cursor. By default it is set to every 5 degrees. Later on you will learn how to set it.

30. Pick on the Rotate transform icon to make sure it is on (if it is green, it is on) and then pick and hold the CAN in the Front viewport. Move the cursor up and down and observe the angular readout. It should be moving in 5-degree intervals if the angular snap has been turned on.

    Rotate the CAN counterclockwise (to the left) so that it lies flat and the angular degree reads Z:90 and then let go of the button. The CAN should now be rotated so that it lies horizontally and within the PLATFORM. Refer to Figure 3.28.

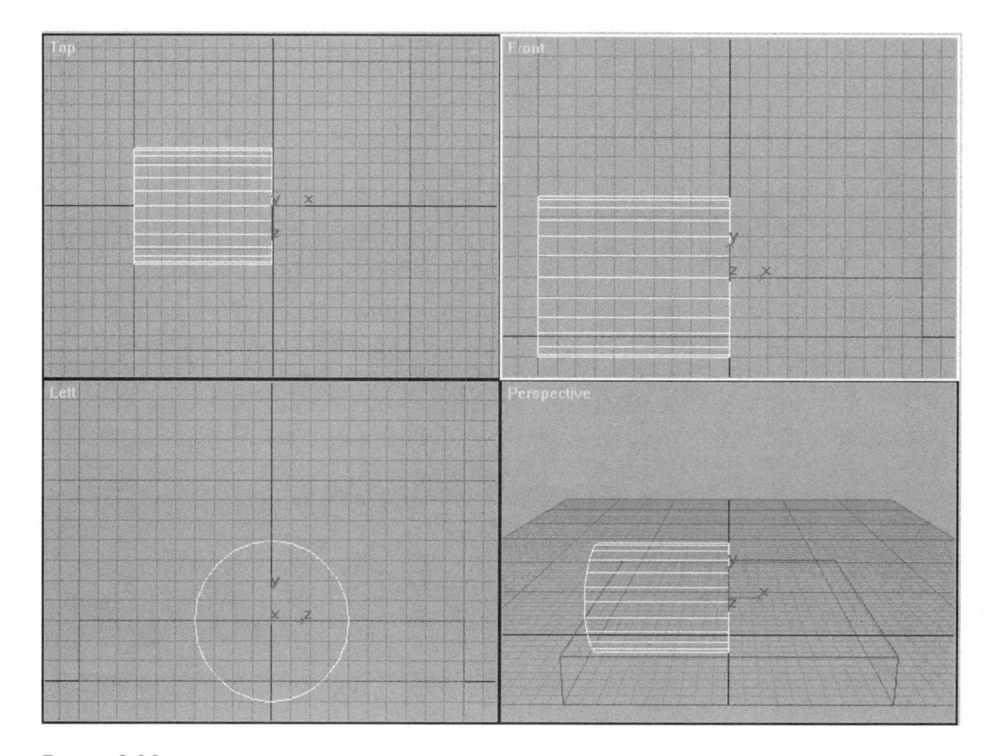


FIGURE 3.28
Rotating the CAN.

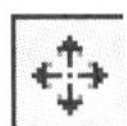

31. Make sure the CAN is still white by picking on it without moving the cursor (in the Front viewport). Use the Zoom Extents button once more just to ensure that you are seeing the entire scene.

    Now pick on the Move transform icon button to turn it on. Move your cursor so that it lies at the top/left of the CAN object. The point should be near the intersection of two grid lines (approximately 100,0,69) but still be in the form of the move icon. Pick and hold on the CAN and slide the cursor upward. It should be moving in 10-unit intervals along the Y axis, because you turned on snap in steps 10 and 11. Move the CAN upward so that it sits on top of the PLATFORM (the coordinates should read 0,40,0) and release the button. See Figure 3.29.

## SAVING AND OPENING YOUR SCENE

32. Select the File/Save As pull-down menu item. You should be presented with the Save File As dialog. Make sure you are in the proper subdirectory to save your file. The default is the Scene subdirectory of the 3D MAX directory. Enter CH3A as the file name and pick the SAVE button to save the scene file.
33. Select the File/New pull-down menu item. You should be presented with a New dialog. Make sure the New All is marked and then pick the OK button. Your objects should disappear as a completely new scene is created. Normally you would start a new scene at this point. Instead you are going to bring back your previous scene.
34. Select the File/Open pull-down menu item. Make sure you are in the subdirectory that contains your file; highlight your file, CH3A, and then pick the Open button. Your scene with the PLATFORM and CAN should appear just as you saved it.

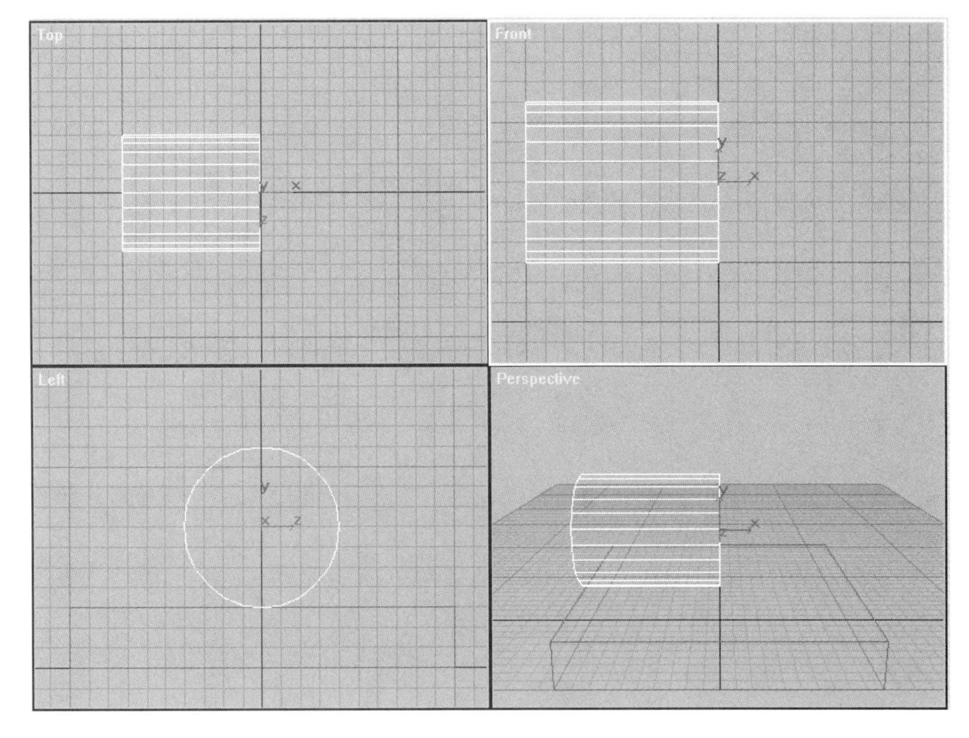


FIGURE 3.29
Moving the CAN.

35. Go through the other command panel items and experiment, adding and transforming until you become more comfortable with this new environment. To delete an object, use the Select icon, pick on the object to turn it white, and then press the Delete key on the keyboard.

36. If you have modified the model, save it under a different name. When you have finished your experimentation, use the Exit menu item found in the File pull-down menu. This will cause you to exit from the 3D Studio MAX program. You should now be familiar with moving around the various menus, understand how to enter coordinates on the keyboard, and be able to use the cursor to create some three-dimensional geometry.

## QUESTIONS AND ASSIGNMENTS

### ? QUESTIONS

1. What function do viewports serve?
2. What is a flyout and how does it work?
3. Explain rollouts and how they operate.
4. Explain how the spinner function operates.
5. What is the purpose of the R key when entering numbers?
6. What function does the numeric key 1 perform?
7. What is the difference between modeless and modal dialogs?
8. What is the file extension that appears on a scene that has been saved?
9. Explain the two methods of obtaining help within the program.

### ASSIGNMENTS

1. For this assignment you are going on a searching expedition for various commands and icon tool buttons. The purpose is to make you more familiar with using the program. Find and identify the following:
   a. *Place Highlight* tool button (*Hint:* It is contained in a flyout.)
   b. *Helpers* button (*Hint:* It is contained in the Create command panel.)
   c. *Show Home Grid* pull-down menu command (*Hint:* It is a submenu contained off the main pull-down menus.)
   d. *Hide by Category* rollout (*Hint:* It is contained within a command panel.)

2. Create a box of any size. Pick on the Select objects button and then pick on the box to make sure it is selected. Normally an object is selected when it is created, but picking the box makes certain it is. Open the Display command panel. Look over the panel and locate the Edges Only box. It is accessible when an object is selected. It is normally checked. Uncheck the box by picking it, and watch what happens to the box. Note the extra lines. Every object is composed of triangles, but to clean up the display, the objects are showing edges only, controlled by the Edges Only box. Check the Edges Only box to return the display of the box to its default status.

2. Using the Create command panel, create a Geosphere and a Sphere. The size and position do not matter. Can you see the difference between the two?

3. Load your file CH3A and experiment with transform buttons, such as Move. Move the Cylinder about the screen; make use of the transform managers to control the movement of the cursor. By default, movement is usually restricted to the XY plane. First, restrict the cylinder's movement so that the cylinder can move only in the X axis and then in the Y. Refer to Section 3.2 (Reviewing the Screen) to locate the transform managers. Do not save this file as CH3A once you have modified it. If you want to save it, save it under a new name, such as CH3B.

# The Fast Lane

## 4.1 INTRODUCTION

As the name of this chapter implies, you are about to move quickly through the different elements that comprise the 3D Studio MAX program. It will be a fast ride, giving you an all-encompassing overview of creating and modifying objects, adding cameras and lights, choosing materials, rendering, and, finally, animation.

The purpose of this chapter is to provide an overview, or a look at the big picture. This will make your understanding of the details, explained in later chapters, that much easier.

The lab at the end of this chapter will expose you to creation, materials, rendering, and animation.

## 4.2 THE SCENE

All your creation and manipulation takes place in a scene in which you form objects and place them in the desired layout. The material properties added in the scene make them look more realistic, lights create shadow and highlights, and the correct camera placement provides the most effective viewpoint. Once the scene is complete, you can render a single, static frame to get a photorealistic picture or take the objects contained in your scene and animate them. The starting point, however, is the objects you create.

### Object-Orientated Design

Because object behavior is governed by the object's assigned properties, it is the objects and their properties that, in effect, control what may happen within a scene. These properties vary, depending on the object type, which in turn depends on the plug-in (external programs) software available. Some plug-ins accompany 3D Studio MAX; others can be purchased from third-party developers.

The following list contains the basic object types that can be created within 3D Studio MAX:

**Standard Primitives**
Parametric objects for creating standard-shaped primitive objects such as boxes or spheres. Parametric design is the process of supplying varying data, such as length, width, and height, to create a variety of forms. Primitives are building blocks that can be used as the basis for final complex objects such as table legs, room floors, and planetary bodies.

**Shapes**
2D or 3D spline curves. These curves can be open or closed. When closed they define outlines used to loft (sweep) a complex 3D form or to create flat, meshed objects. When open, they can define paths that are used for loft direction or for animated motion paths that objects follow.

**Lofts**
Compound objects created by sweeping (pushing) profile objects along a path. The profile can be any shape, closed or open. The path, another shape, may be straight, curved, or extremely convoluted like a helix. The resulting object can be simple or complex, defined by the profile and path combined.

**Patch Grids**
A surface object referred to as a Bezier surface patch. Think of it as a paper shape. It has no thickness, but you can rotate and bend it at any angle and, by welding the surfaces together, you can create a three-dimensional object.

**Meshes**
Collection of vertices connected by triangular faces to form an object.

**Morphs**
Compound objects used to cause an object to change shape over time. Usually two objects are used, with the first object changing into the second object over time. Note that the two objects must contain the same number of vertices for successful morphing.

**Booleans**
Compound objects created by the action of Boolean operations such as union (adding together) and subtraction (taking one from the other) of two objects.

**Particles**
Objects that emit 2D and 3D particles to simulate rain or other similar effects.

**Lights**
Three types of lights, omni, spot, and directional, are used to light a scene, cast shadows, project images, and create other effects.

**Cameras**
Objects that behave as real-life cameras, allowing you to set the camera lens and field of vision. These are used to view movement or they move themselves.

**Helpers**
Objects that are used to define 3D points, measure distances and angles, and create working grid planes.

**Space Warps**
Special objects that are used to influence other objects that come within a space warp's boundary. A space warp can deform or move objects that move over them.

## 4.3 WORKING PLANES AND VIEWING

Working with 3D Studio MAX's world involves understanding how objects relate to one another and how they are positioned. There are two spatial coordinate systems within 3D Studio MAX. These two systems are called *object space* and *world space.*

### Object Space

Object space is a coordinate system based on the object itself. Each object created has its own vertices, placement modifiers, mapping coordinates, and materials, and these are located in reference to the object's *object space.*

Figure 4.1 shows an object's pivot-point axes and bounding box. The pivot point, defined in object space, governs the object's movement and modification. The bounding box is a rectangular box that defines the dimensional extent or limit of the object.

### World Space

World space is 3D Studio MAX's universal three-dimensional coordinate system used to keep track of all objects in a scene. The Home Grid, discussed next, is based on world space and is used as the initial ground working plane. Figure 4.2 indicates that the world axis sits in the center of the Home Grid. Every object is positioned in world space. Consequently, world space is fixed and cannot be moved or rotated.

### Home Grid

The Home Grid is three coordinate planes (working planes) aligned to the world space coordinates. Figure 4.3 shows the intersection of the three planes. Each plane is a combination of two of the three axes, creating XY, XZ, and YZ planes. They intersect at the 0,0,0 point in world space. This means that the XY plane sits on the 0Z axis, the XZ plane sits on the 0Y axis, and the YZ plane sits on the 0X axis. When you create, the object is positioned on one of the planes. You are also able to create your own construction planes with *grid objects.*

### Grid Objects

Grid objects are helper objects; their sole purpose is to create construction planes in any scene location. You can position them anywhere in world space and are not forced to match the fixed Home Grid. Refer to Figure 4.4 for a representation of a grid object.

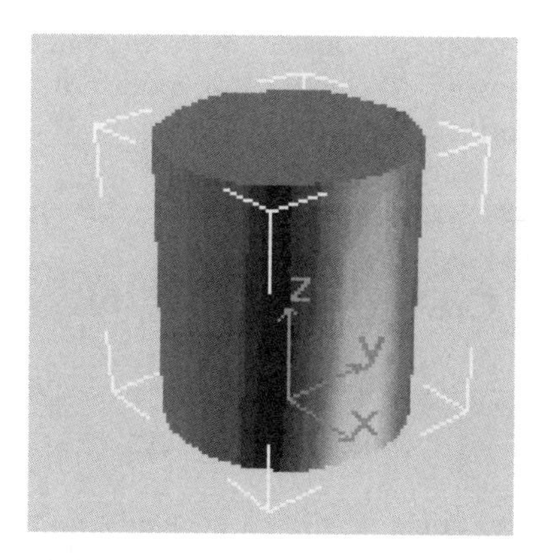


FIGURE 4.1
An object showing a pivot point and bounding box.

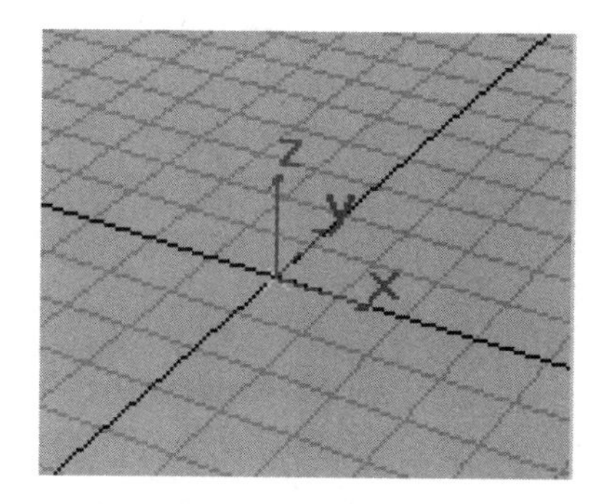


FIGURE 4.2
World space axis icon.

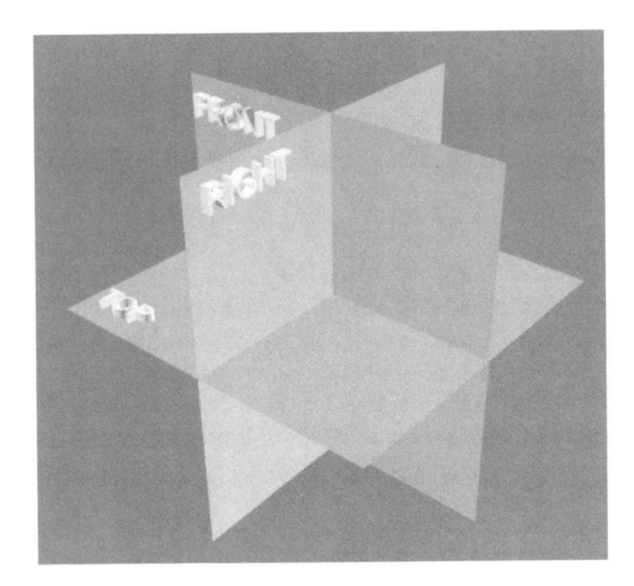


FIGURE 4.3
Intersection of three working planes.

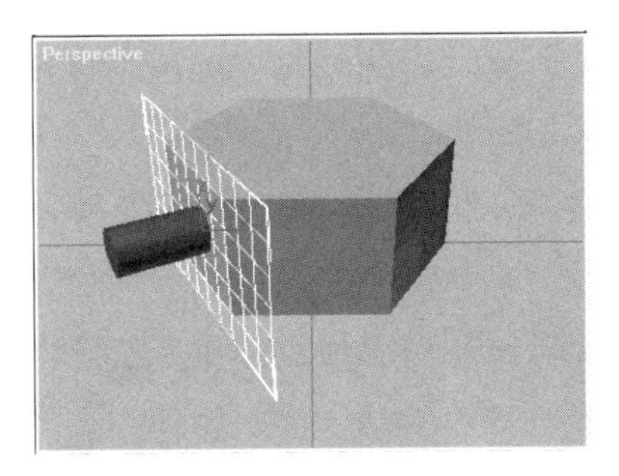


FIGURE 4.4
Grid helper object used as a construction plane.

### Viewports

Viewports behave as the windows to a scene and control the planes upon which you construct. The standard orthographic viewports that align with the Home Grid, such as front, top, and right side, are the default method of creation. When you activate such a viewport, you are drawing on one of these three views.

Perspective, user, camera, light, and grid object viewports are available, in addition to the standard viewports. A grid object viewport can be used for creation, whereas the others are used mainly to get a clearer view of the 3D scene.

## 4.4 MODELING AND EDITING

When first you create an object, it is called a *master object* and is controlled by an initial set of creation parameters. Take a box, for instance. Initially the box is defined by its length, width, height, the number of segments along each of those shape descriptors, and the original position and orientation of its pivot point. The object is also assigned surface properties. Once an object has been created, you can edit it by transforming it (such as by moving or rotating) or modify it (such as by changing the length or surface properties).

***LIGHTS! CAMERA! ACTION!*** 

#### Naming Objects

Every object you create should be given a unique name so that you can identify it. You give an object its name when you create it by filling in the Name parameter box. However, the object must be created (must be in the scene) before you can enter its name in the box.

## Creation Parameters

Creation parameters are the initial values used to describe the shape, size, and position of an object. Figure 4.5 shows the creation command panel and the creation parameters. They can be altered during the creation process but only until you generate another object. Remember to give a unique name to every object you create.

## Pivot Point

The *pivot point* defines the object's local coordinate system (object space) and the object's location in world space. It is also used as the center of rotation and scaling. Figure 4.6 shows the tripod axis of the pivot point. It is possible to modify the orientation of this pivot point using the hierarchy command panel. This process is discussed later.

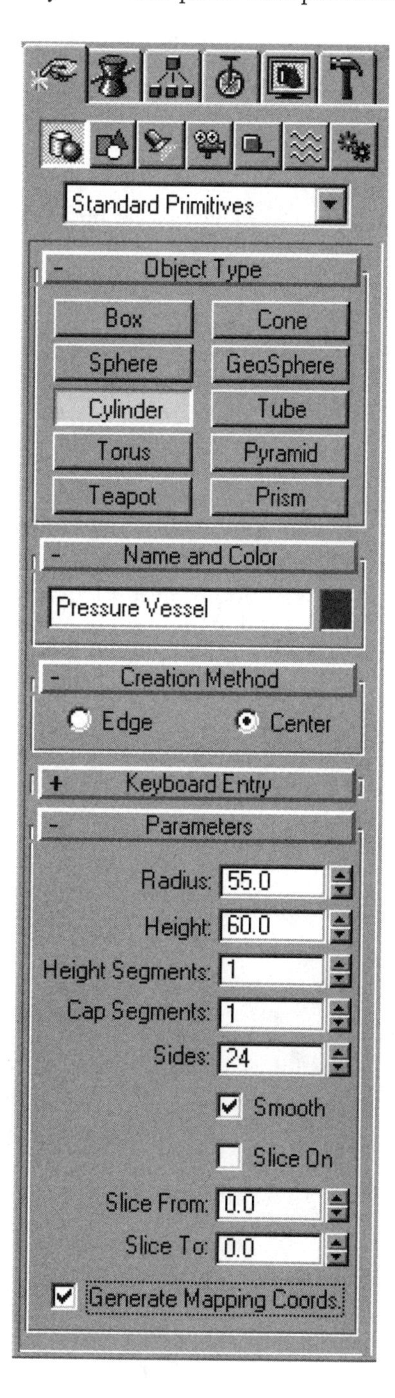


FIGURE 4.5
Creation command panel showing creation parameters.

FIGURE 4.6
Shaded display showing bounding box and pivot point.

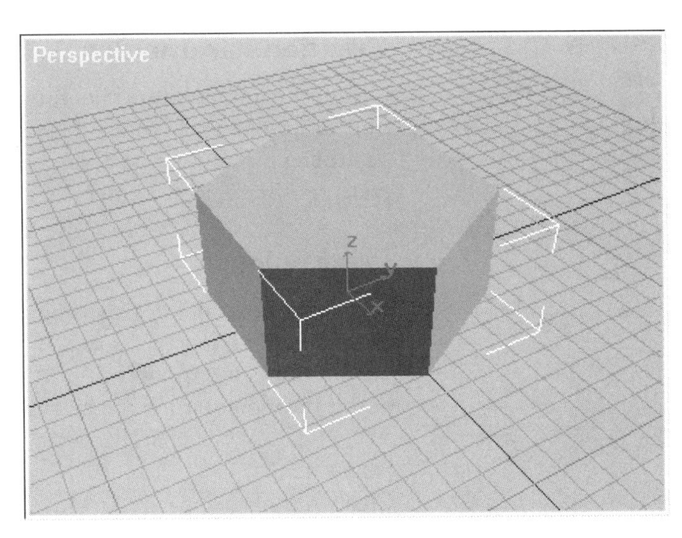


## Bounding Box

The *bounding box* defines the dimensional extents, or limits, of the object. It will appear as the corners of a rectangular box when the object is displayed in a shaded mode or as a complete box when the object is displayed in box mode. See Figure 4.6. Note the rectangular shape that represents the bounding box.

## Surface Properties

Every geometric object you create has a set of surface properties. These are called face normals, smoothing groups, and mapping coordinates.

A *face normal* is a vector that defines the direction in which a face is pointing. Remember that a face has two sides. The face normal decides which side of a face is visible. During the usual creation of objects, the face normals usually face outward and do not need modification. Figure 4.7 shows the vectors pointing outward on an object. However, imported objects from other programs may have their normals reversed. You can modify the entire object's face normals or adjust individual ones. This is accomplished within the modify panel and is explained in more detail in Chapter 7.

*Smoothing groups* affect pairs of faces joined at an edge. When an object is rendered, sometimes you want to see an edge and sometimes you want the edge to be

FIGURE 4.7
Face normals pointing outward.

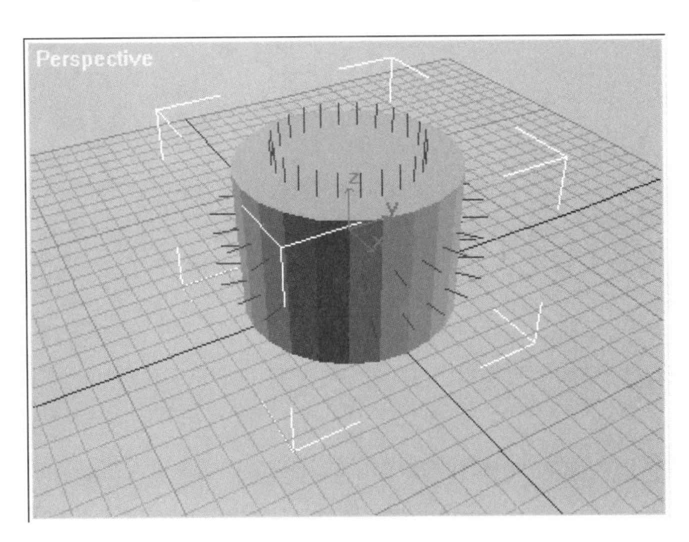

smoothly blended. Each face is assigned a smoothing group. If two adjacent faces have the same smoothing group, they will be blended. If they do not share the same smoothing group, the edge between them will be defined. During the creation of objects you can turn smoothing on or off; once an object is created you can modify the object's smoothing groups. Refer again to Figure 4.5, which shows the creation panel. Near the bottom of the panel is a box to check for automatic smoothing.

Mapping coordinates are used to tell 3D Studio MAX how to apply mapped materials to an object. If an object is going to have mapped materials applied, it needs mapping coordinates. When you initially create an object you can automatically apply mapping coordinates to it. You can also modify a previously created object so that it has mapping coordinates or adjust existing ones. Refer again to Figure 4.5. At the bottom of the creation panel there is a box for the automatic application of mapping coordinates.

*Note:* If an object has mapping coordinates, it takes longer to render. As a rule of thumb, don't using mapping coordinates if an object is not going to have bitmap image material applied to it.

## Selecting Objects

Whenever you want to change an object, whether you're deleting, moving, or modifying, you need to be able to select it. There are several ways to go about this.

To simply select an object or objects, activate the Select Object icon on the toolbar at the top of screen. Then, if you want to select a single object, move over an object and the cursor changes to a thick stubby cross. This change tells you that you can pick that object to select it. If you pick an object that hasn't yet been selected, it will turn white, letting you know you have selected it. If you pick in open space, any selected objects will be unselected.

To select several objects at once, activate the Select Object icon, pick and hold in open space, drag the cursor to form a window around the objects to be selected, and release the button. All the objects will be added to the selection set.

*Note:* There are special options for this that are explained in Chapter 6.

If you want to select objects one after another or add to those already picked, hold down the CTRL key while picking objects. They will be added to the selection set.

If you want to remove one or more objects from a selection set, hold down the ALT key as you pick previously selected objects. They will be removed from the selection set.

Once you have picked your objects, you can lock your selection using the lock icon on the status bar at the bottom of the screen. When this is active, no more objects can be selected or unselected. If you turn the lock icon off, you can select and unselect objects as normal.

**LIGHTS! CAMERA! ACTION!**

### Object Selection by Name

If you want to select a single object or group of objects by name, use the Select by Name tool. This brings up a list of named objects from which you can select.

## Object Modifiers

Once you select an object or objects, you can then open the Modify command panel, as shown in Figure 4.8. At the top of the modifier panel is the name of the object, which you can change. There will be no name if you have selected more than one object. Below this is the list of modifiers. Here you can pick on a particular modifier and use it to make changes to the object. When you make a modifier change, it goes in the modifier stack. This stack is shown as a pull-down list in the middle of the panel. To review the different modifiers you have used on an object, select the modifier from the stack. Before you make any modifier changes, the only item in the modifier stack is the original object itself. This modifier is used to modify creation parameters, such as length and width.

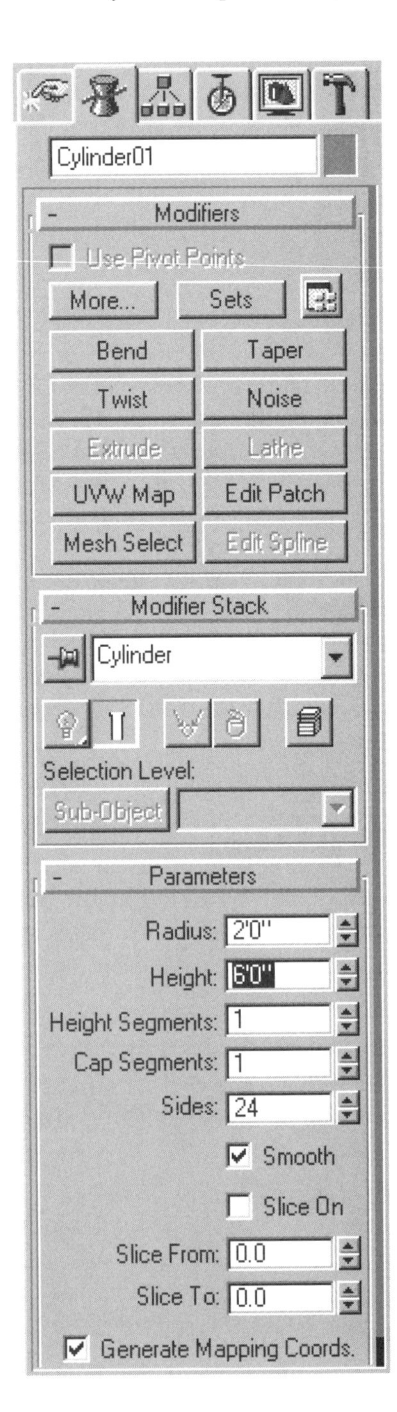


FIGURE 4.8
Modify panel.

## Object Transforms

Transforms affect position, rotation, and scale changes and are activated with the transform tool icon buttons on the toolbar. The transform tools have the added feature of a built-in select option. To use them you do not have to have previously picked the object. You can pick on the tool and then pick on the object to transform.

## Object Clones

There are several ways to make clones with 3D Studio MAX—Shift-Clone, Array, Mirror, and Snapshot. Clones are similar to copies, but there are some differences, which we explain.

The Shift-Clone method of making clones involves holding down the Shift key while performing a Transform. For instance, if you want to make a clone of an object and move it to a new location, you activate the Move tool, hold down on the Shift key, and pick the object. As you move the cursor away, a clone of the object will travel with it.

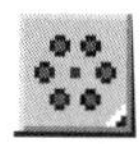

The Array method creates repeated clones and allows you to control all three transforms: position, rotation, and scale. Figure 4.9 illustrates the original object, the Array dialog, and the final arrayed clones.

The Mirror method creates a clone in mirror position to the original object. The Mirror command has the added ability of being able to transform the original into the mirror image instead of cloning. Figure 4.10 shows the Mirror dialog.

The Snapshot method clones an animated object over time. This is explained in more detail in Chapter 12.

## Copies versus Instances or References

When you make a clone of an object, you have three choices for the type of clone: copy, instance, and reference.

A *copy* is a new, independent, master object that has all the characteristics of the original but is not tied to the original in any way.

An *instance* is bound to the original object's creation parameters and object modifiers. If you change the creation length of the original, the instance clone will change to match it. The instance is separate from the original with regard to transforms, space warps, and object properties such as materials. Thus, you can move the instance or change its materials separately from the original. Remember that if you make a change to the creation parameters or modifiers of any instance clone, you will make the change to all the instance clones of the original object.

A *reference* is the same as an instance, except that a reference can have its own object modifiers as well as being controlled by the original object's modifiers.

## Undo: Edit, View

To undo a change to a scene, either use the Undo icon button or the Edit/Undo pull-down menu item. This will work for most changes in 3D Studio MAX. For extra insurance make sure you use the Edit/Hold pull-down menu items discussed earlier.

There is also an Undo for reversing the changes made to a viewport. This command can be found under the View pull-down menu.

For both the Edit/Undo and View/Undo, there are Redos. Redo reverses the effect of the Undo.

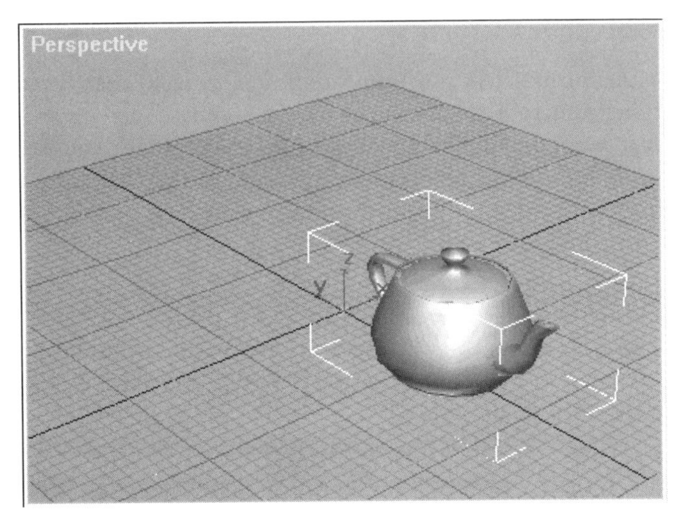


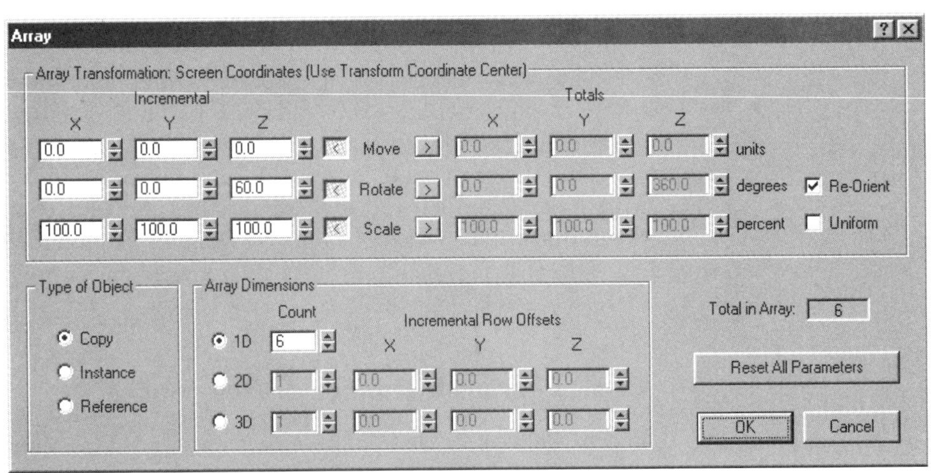

FIGURE 4.9
Original object, the Array dialog, and the final arrayed clones.

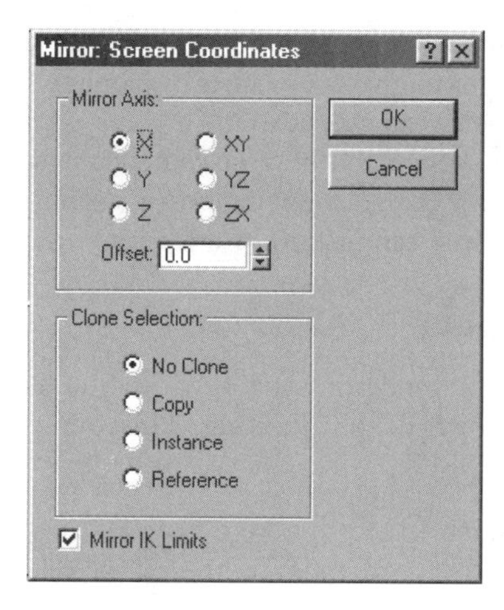


FIGURE 4.10
Mirror dialog.

## 4.5 CAMERAS AND LIGHTS

This section introduces camera and light objects. Cameras are used to display a view that can be altered as you would alter a camera lens. Lights are used to give light to a scene and enhance the visibility and realism. There are different camera and light types for different effects. This section gives an overview, while Chapter 11 goes over these types in more detail.

### Cameras

*Cameras* are objects that can simulate still-image or motion picture viewing. 3D Studio MAX's cameras have features that mimic real-life cameras. The first is the lens size, which controls the focal length and the field of view (FOV). You can select from stock (preset) lens sizes or create your own custom sizes. Small lens sizes give a wide-angle FOV, whereas large lens sizes give a small, magnified (zoomed-in) FOV. Figure 4.11 shows two views of the same object using different lens sizes.

There are two types of cameras you can place in your scene, target and free. Target cameras are usually used for fixed camera placement while the target moves. Free cameras are used when the camera itself will be animated.

Because cameras are objects, you will find the camera button in the Creation command panel. When you pick it, you will be presented with the camera options, allowing you to pick either target or free. Once you pick the type, you will be pre-

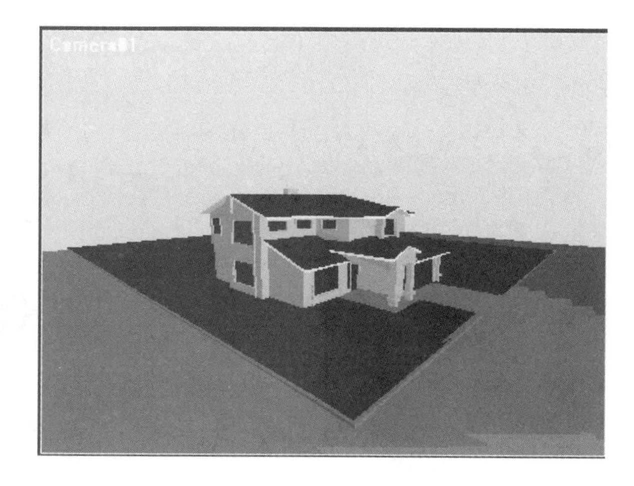


FIGURE 4.11
Two views with different lens sizes.

sented with the camera type's creation parameters, as shown in Figure 4.12. Don't forget to give your camera a name to help you keep track of it. You can transform and modify cameras as well.

When you have placed a camera you can activate one of the viewports and display a camera view by pressing C on the keyboard. If you have more than one camera, you can pick one from a list.

## Lights

If you render a scene in which you have not placed any lights, 3D Studio MAX uses its own default lighting. This way you can render even before you have mastered

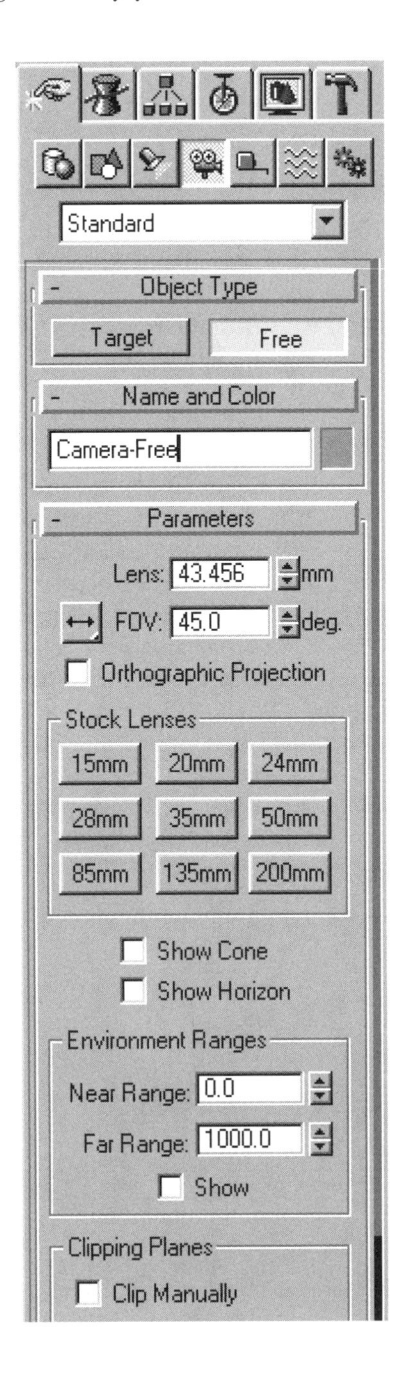


FIGURE 4.12 Camera creation parameters.

lighting. As soon as you place a light, default lighting is turned off, and the scene relies on your expertise. You may be shocked the first time a well-lit scene suddenly changes drastically when you add your first light. However, the key to a realistic scene lies in its lighting. Many of these techniques are discussed in Chapter 10. Here you will get just a taste.

3D Studio MAX has different light types to light a scene in virtually anyway you wish: ambient, omni, and directional lights, target and free spotlights.

Ambient light in 3D Studio MAX simulates background light or light that reflects from objects. It can be used to increase or decrease the overall lighting of a scene. The ambient light value can be adjusted by selecting the Rendering/Environment pull-down menu item. Normally it is set to black, providing the greatest contrast available to the scene.

Omni light radiates light equally in all directions, like a lightbulb. However, omni lights cannot cast shadows. Omni lights are useful for lighting a scene with no necessary direction for the light source. See Figure 4.13, part A.

Because it casts parallel light rays, directional light is used to simulate the sun. It can cast shadows and project bitmap images. When you place a directional light, you direct its beam by using the rotate transform. See Figure 4.13, part B.

Spotlights cast a focused beam of light similar to a flashlight, theater spot, or automobile headlight. There are two types, target and free. Their placement and directional behavior are similar to target and free cameras. As in the case of directional light, they cast shadows and project bitmap images. See Figure 4.13, part C.

## 4.6 RENDERING AND MATERIALS

Rendering and materials work hand in hand because the choice of materials controls the generation of a realistically rendered scene. This section introduces you to the concept of materials and how to apply them. Once you have assigned materials to an object, it's time to render.

### Materials

Materials are the properties of an object. According to which properties are assigned, objects can reflect or absorb light and can have pictures upon their surfaces.

The selection, creation, and application of materials happens in the Material Editor dialog. To access this dialog, pick on the Material Editor icon button near the right end of the tool bar. Figure 4.14 illustrates the Material Editor dialog. When you first open this dialog, it shows six standard materials that bear six different colors and have no bitmaps associated with them. To assign one of these materials to an object in your scene, pick one of the six sample display boxes, identify the object to which you wish to apply the material, and then pick the Assign Material to Selection button.

There are many premade materials available, stored in the material library. To access the library, pick the Get Material button. This displays the Material/Map Browser dialog, as shown in Figure 4.15. If you pick the Material Library box in the Browse From area of the dialog, you will have access to all the materials that are contained in the currently opened material library. Figure 4.15 shows some of the material listings in the default material library, 3DSMAX.MAT. You can scroll through the various materials and then double-click on the one you want. It will be placed in the sample display box that was currently active, replacing whatever material was previously displayed. You can then assign that material to a selected object or objects. You must remember that you need to assign a mapping coordinate property to an object if it is going to have a material that makes use of bitmaps. Note that you assign mapping coordinates during creation, as mentioned in Section 4.4 under Surface Properties.

FIGURE 4.13
Directional and omni lights and spotlights.

A

B

C

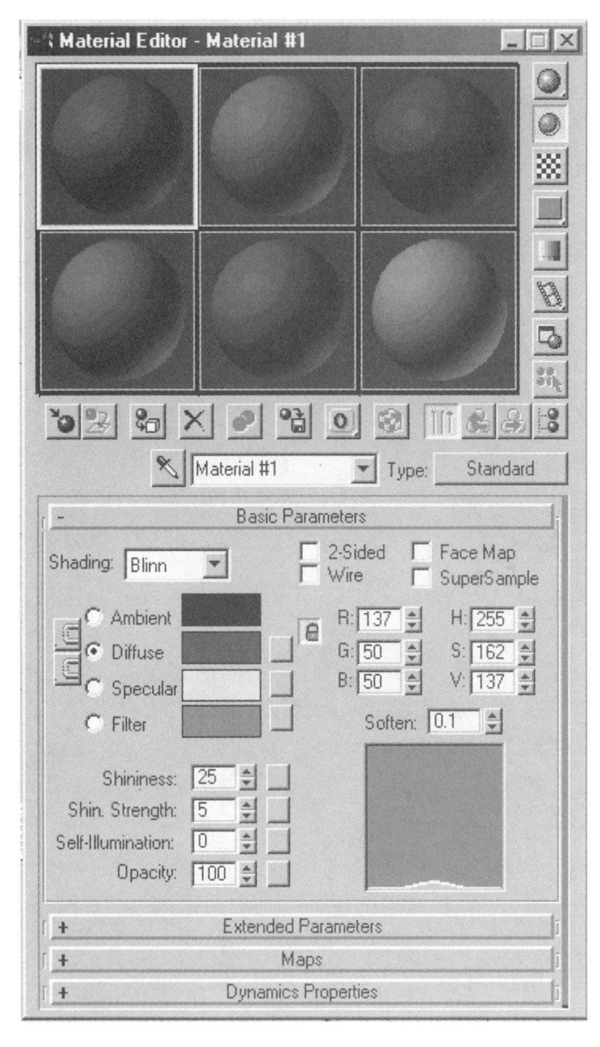

FIGURE 4.14
Material Editor dialog.

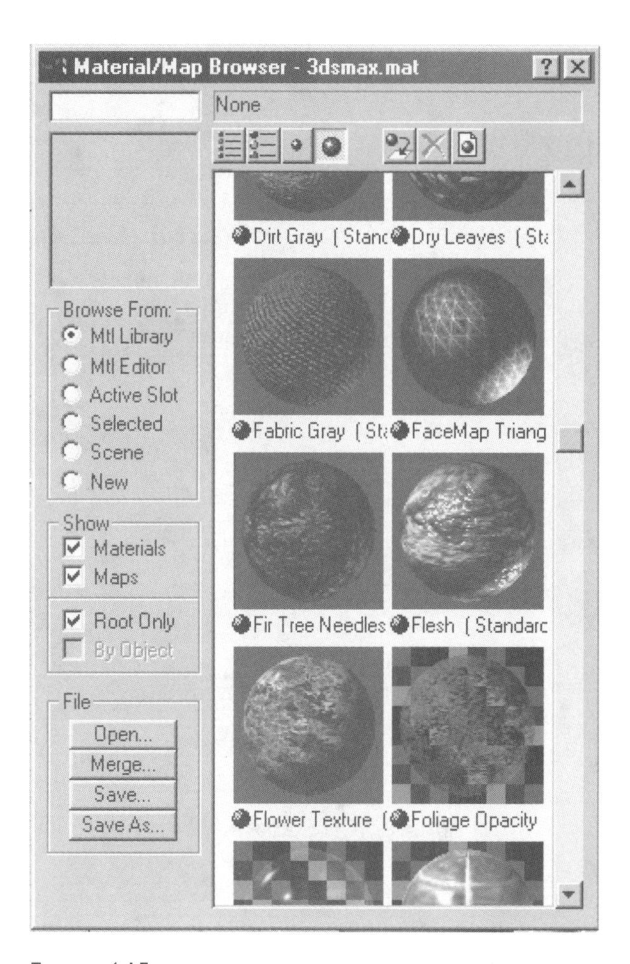


FIGURE 4.15
Material/Map Browser dialog.

You can also create your own custom materials using the Material Editor, as explained in Chapter 12.

## Rendering

Although you can render at any time, your scene will be more realistic once you have added lights and assigned materials to your objects. To render, pick either the Render Scene or Quick Render icon buttons at the right end of the tool bar.

The Render Scene button will bring up the Render Scene dialog, as shown in Figure 4.16. Here you can control different options that will affect the final rendering. Review the figure, noting such areas as Time Output and Output Size.

Time Output is used to control whether a single frame, part of an animation, or the entire animation is rendered. Output Size controls the size, in pixels, of the rendered image. Once you have chosen your settings, then pick on the Render button at the bottom of the dialog. A separate window will open and the rendering will take place in this window. See Figure 4.17.

The Quick Render button will perform a rendering using previously set options in the Render Scene dialog. This button is useful when you want to render a scene without changing any settings.

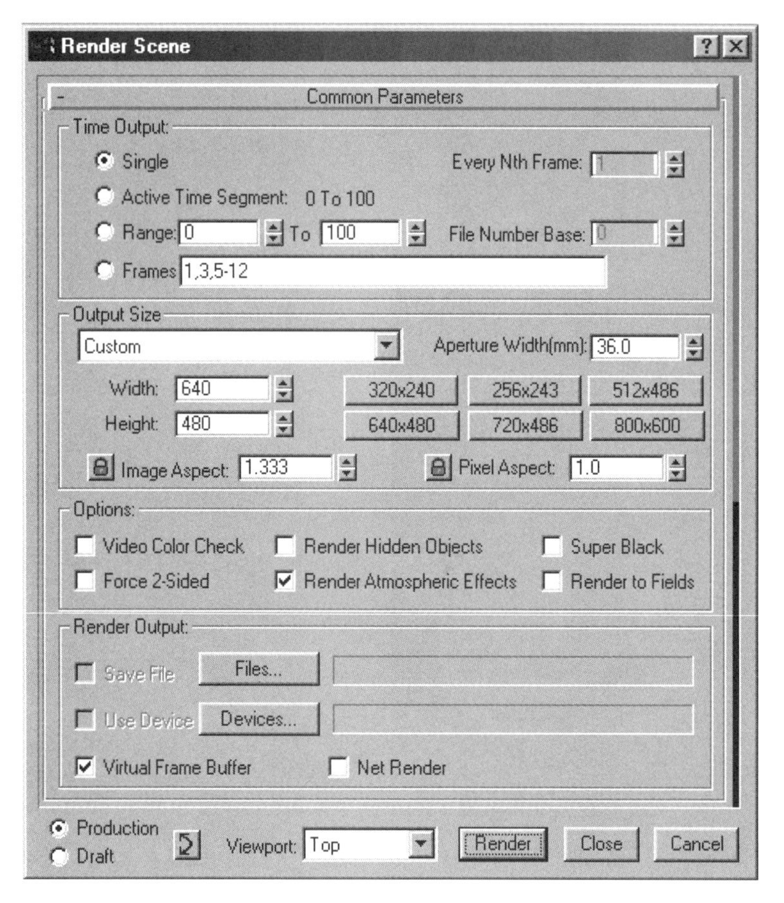


Figure 4.16
Render Scene dialog.

Figure 4.17
Rendered window.

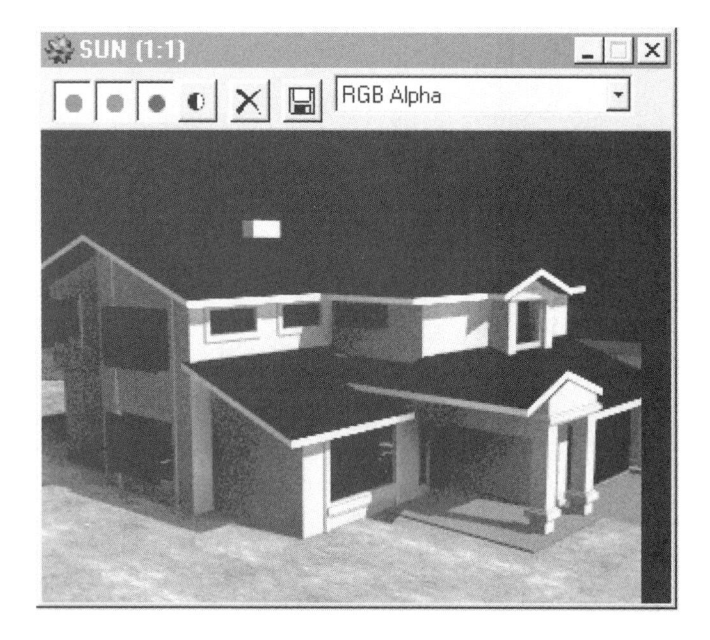

### LIGHTS! CAMERA! ACTION! 

#### Saving Rendering Time

A useful technique for saving time when rendering stills and animations is to render at a lower resolution when testing lights and cameras. Once you are happy with the overall results, render the still or animation with a higher resolution.

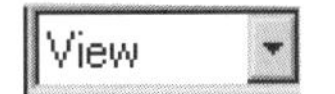


Near the end of the tool bar, just after the Render Scene and Quick Render buttons, is the Render Type pull-down list. Use this list to select the areas of the scene you wish to render: View, Selected, Region, and Blowup.

## 4.7 ANIMATION

Animation is the act of imparting motion or activity. Almost any object in your scene can be animated, as long as that object is altered in some way, such as movement or shape, over a period of time. Within 3D Studio MAX, these changes occur over frames. Each frame can contain a different change to a scene. When the frames are played one after another, animation occurs. A frame can be a frame of the scene or a unit of time.

### Key Frames

To make the animation process even easier, there are special frames you can use as key frames. For instance, suppose an object sits in a certain position in frame 1 and you want the object to slide across the scene, coming to rest in another position in frame 8. Instead of moving the object in each frame from 2 to 8, you go to frame 8 and move the object to its new position. Frame 8 is a key frame. 3D Studio MAX knows that you want the object to move from its position in frame 1 to its new position in frame 8. It then creates the movements in the frames from 2 to 7 automatically. Figure 4.18 shows

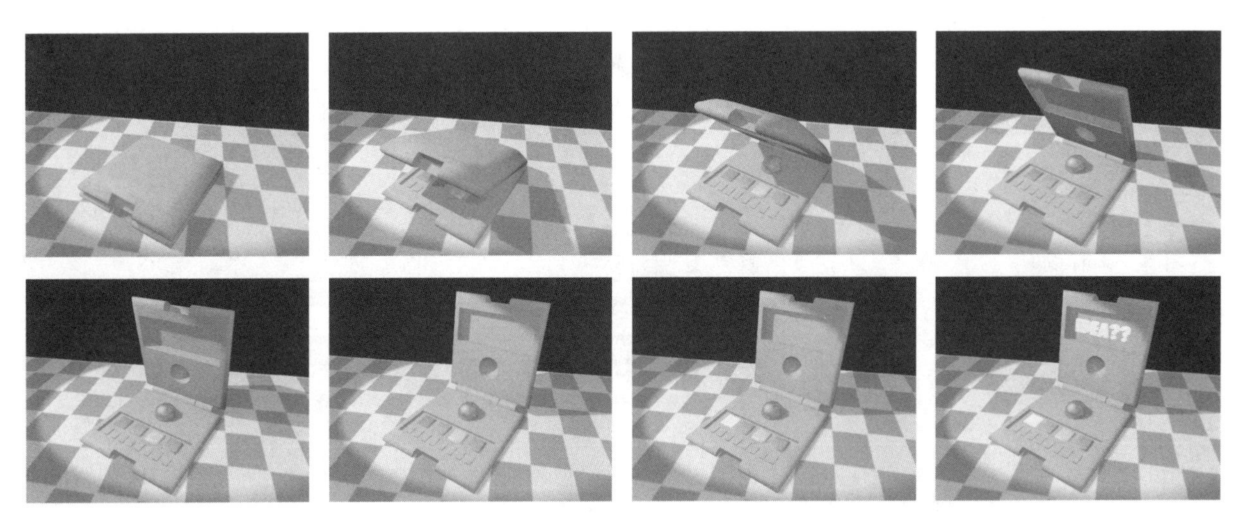

FIGURE 4.18
Rendered frames.

a rendering of frames 1 to 8. This animation shows an electronic panel opening and the word IDEA?? appearing on its screen. Frame 1 shows the instrument closed, frame 6 shows the panel fully open, frame 7 shows the leftmost button lit up, and frame 8 shows the word "IDEA??" appearing on the panel's display screen.

### Tracks

The movements or transformations that take place through an animation are recorded as keys on tracks. Every object, including cameras and lights, has tracks. When you add a key frame or make some changes to an existing key, the change is recorded on the object's track. The track represents the length of the animation in frames. You use tracks to make changes to keys. Figure 4.19 shows the Track View dialog. Note the list on the left of the dialog. It is called the hierarchy list and contains all the objects in the scene. Each object can be broken down into the various properties associated with it. Along the right is the window that contains the tracks associated with each object property. The tracks provide a visual indicator showing when a particular property is acted upon during the animation, and the oval dots indicate the frame in which an action occurs. The track view dialog is modeless, which means it can stay visible while you work on your scene. To display the dialog, pick the Track View button on the right along the tool bar.

### Animate button

To make a change that will be animated, use the large Animate button at the bottom of the screen. When it is on (red), any transform or change to an animatable parameter will create a key. The basic procedure for animating is as follows:

1. Select the desired frame/time using the time slider at the bottom of the screen. Do not use frame 0. Frame 0 is used to contain the original parameters of the objects in your scene.
2. Turn on the Animate button (red).
3. Select the object or objects and perform the change, and a key will be created or modified.

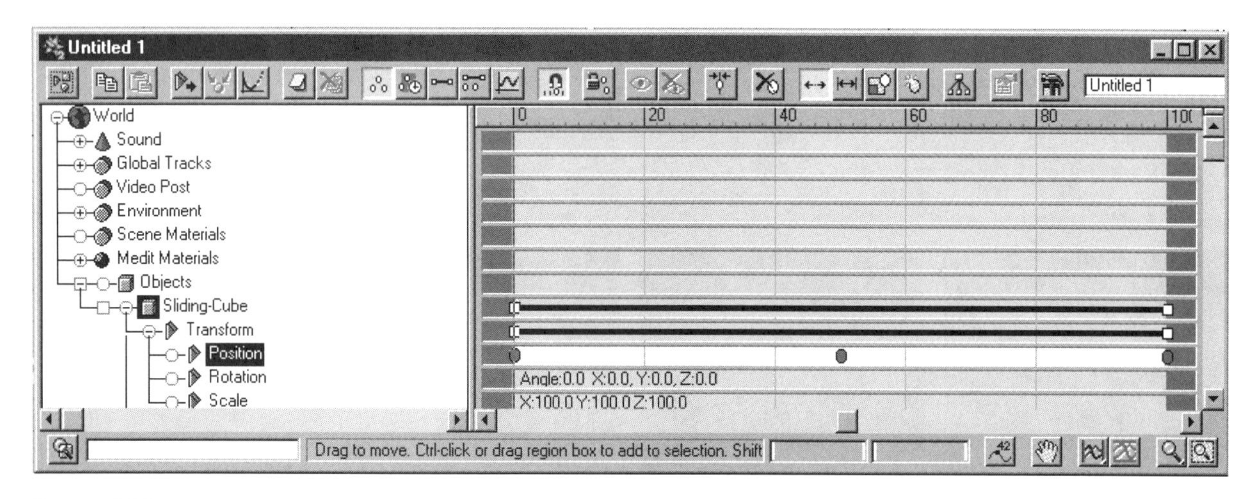


FIGURE 4.19
Track View dialog.

## Animation Tools

The following describes some of the animation tools available to you. Chapter 13 gives more on these tools.

### Animation Tools

**Go to Start**
Moves you to the beginning of the active time segment.

**Previous Frame**
Moves you backward one time increment.

**Next Frame**
Moves forward one time increment.

**Go to End**
Moves to the end of the active time segment.

**Play Animation**
Plays the animation for the active time segment.

**Stop Animation**
Stops animation playback.

**Key Mode Toggle**
When active, jumps the Previous Frame and Next Frame buttons to the nearest key frame.

**Time Configuration**
Displays the Time Configuration dialog, as shown in Figure 4.20. The dialog is used to set the time display format and the number of frames or time units in an animation.

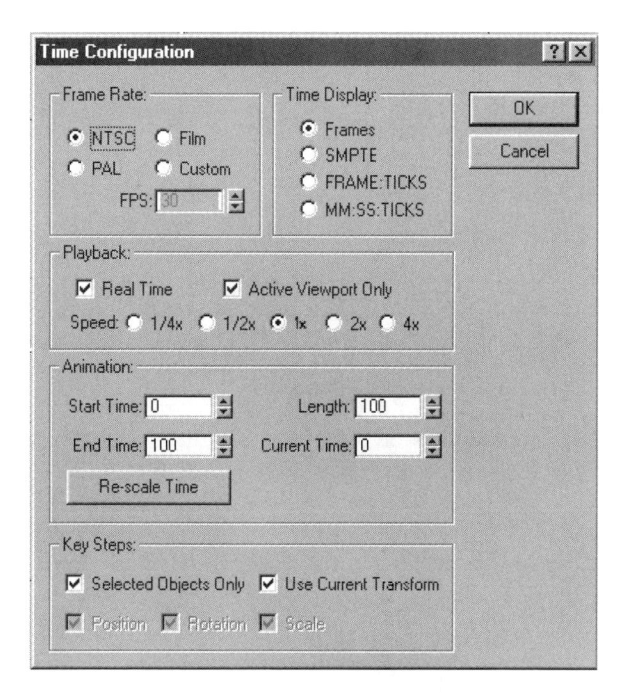


FIGURE 4.20
Time Configuration dialog.

### Hierarchical Linking

When you have objects whose movement affects other objects, you must link them in some way. Think of your arm: you have a hand, a lower arm, and an upper arm. When you move that arm, the upper arm swings up at the shoulder, and the lower arm and hand obviously move with it. They are physically linked together. This principle remains true in 3D Studio MAX; you decide which objects are linked together and under what parameters. This is refered to as *hierarchical linking* and is described in more detail in Chapter 14.

## 4.8 SUMMARY

If your head is spinning, take a deep breath and relax. You can review the previous material any time you wish. Besides, that whirlwind tour isn't the last exposure you'll have to these important concepts. However, you now have enough information to perform the following lab with a little guidance; after this first taste of 3D Studio MAX's abilities, you're bound to be hooked. The parts following this chapter will give you the information you need in greater detail. For now, let's tackle the lab.

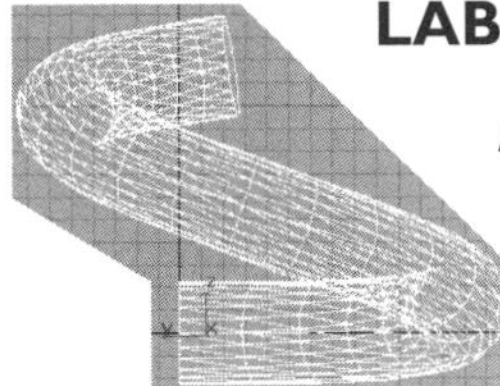

# LAB 4.A

## An All-encompassing Look

### Purpose

This lab introduces the various aspects of the 3D Studio MAX program.

You are going to create an animated scene that contains three boxes to form two walls and a floor that come together in a corner, your name in three dimensions, a spotlight, and a camera. In addition you will create a glowing sphere that will contain an omni light and will move through the scene. Figure 4.21 shows a rendered still of one of the frames.

*Note:* This is a long exercise covering many of the features of 3D Studio MAX; be prepared to spend the time to complete it, to save your work periodically, and to leave and return to it.

### Objectives

You will be able to

- Create spline text and extrude the text into a three-dimensional object.
- Create simple geometry and assemble the scene.
- Animate the ball.
- Create a camera.
- Apply mapping coordinates to objects.
- Assign materials to objects.
- Render a still image.
- Render an animated sequence.
- Use various processes to test animated sequences.

### Procedure

#### SETTING UP THE PROJECT

With any project you need to establish some starting settings. These settings are usually standard for any project, and you should become familiar with checking them before you start any creation.

FIGURE 4.21 Rendered still of first animation.

1. You are going to recall a previously created scene to get you started. Some objects have already been created and you are going to add to them. This file should have been copied into the SCENES subdirectory of 3D Studio MAX. If the file is not there, it may still be on the CD-ROM that came with this book. Refer to Appendix A on installing files.

   Select the File/Open pull-down menu. Make sure you are in the Scenes subdirectory of 3D Studio MAX. Locate the file called MXSTART.MAX, highlight it, and pick the Open button. The screen should look similar to Figure 4.22. There should be a wall, a floor, and a floating ball below the floor.

   Save your file as CH4A.MAX.

2. When you start a new scene, you normally have to establish the units, grid, and snap settings. However, when you recall a previously saved scene, the units, grid, and snap are saved with it. Check to see what they are set to.

   Select the Views/Unit Setup pull-down menu item. The Units Setup dialog box will appear as shown in Figure 4.23A. Note that the US Standard is set to Feet w/Fractional Inches at 1/8 of an inch increments. Don't change any of these settings. Pick OK to exit the box.

   Select the Views/Grid and Snap Settings pull-down menu item. The Grid and Snap Settings dialog box will appear. Usually the Snaps panel is visible as shown in Figure 4.23B. Note the various of types of snaps. The Grid Points item should be the only one checked. This means that, when snap is turned on, the

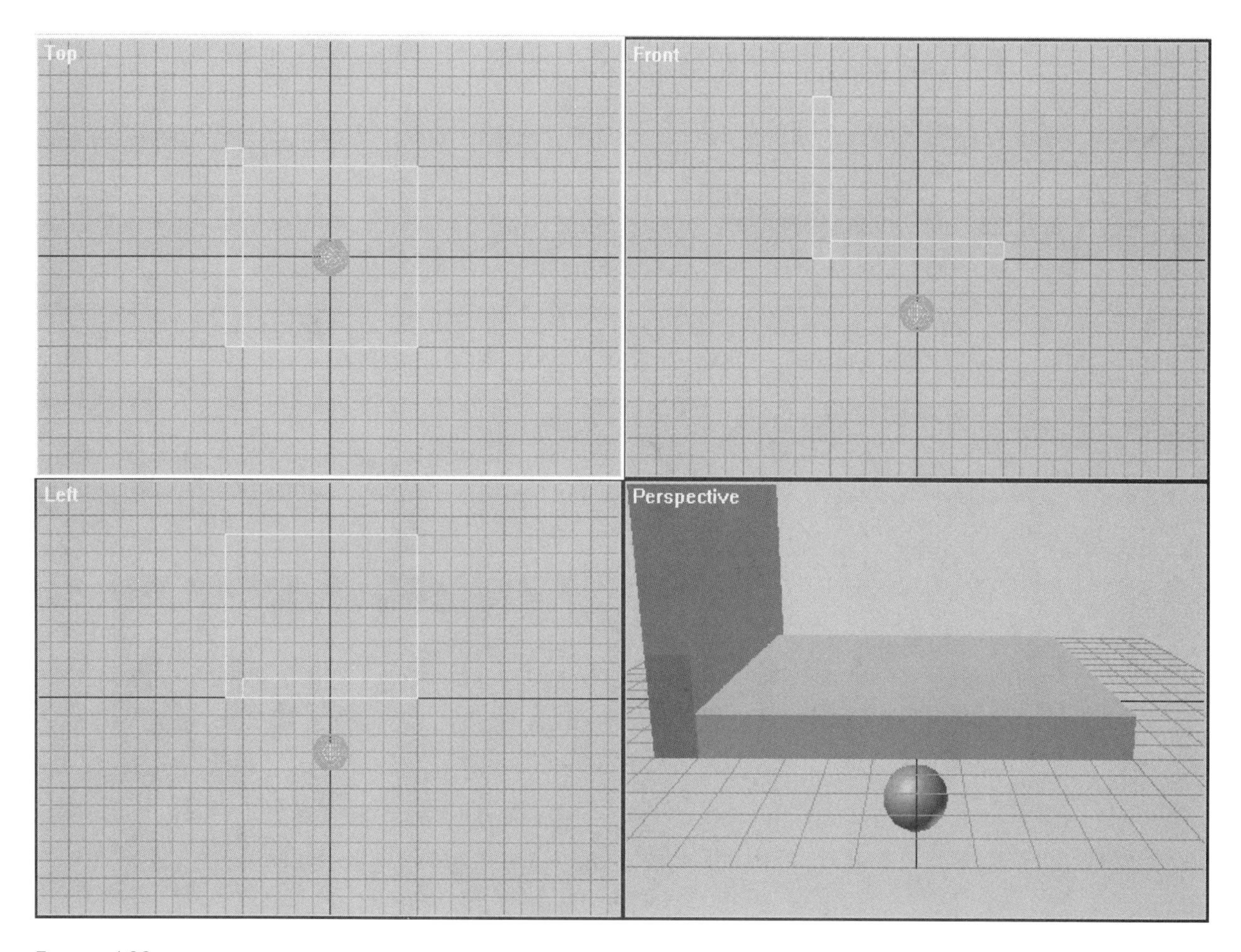


FIGURE 4.22
The initial scene.

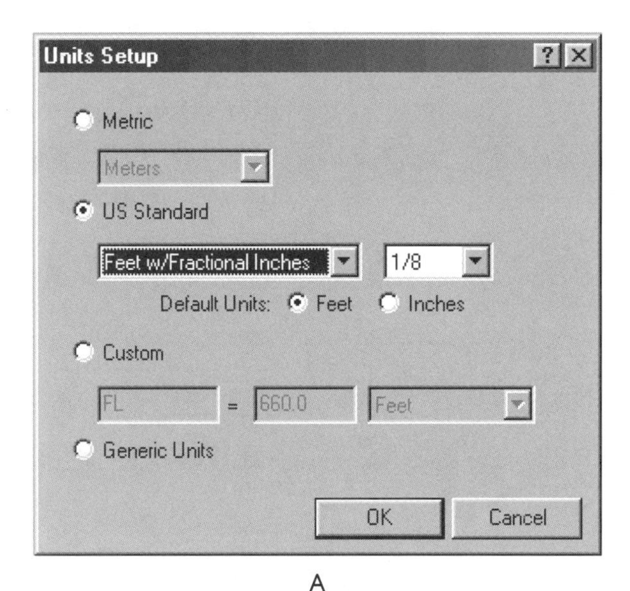


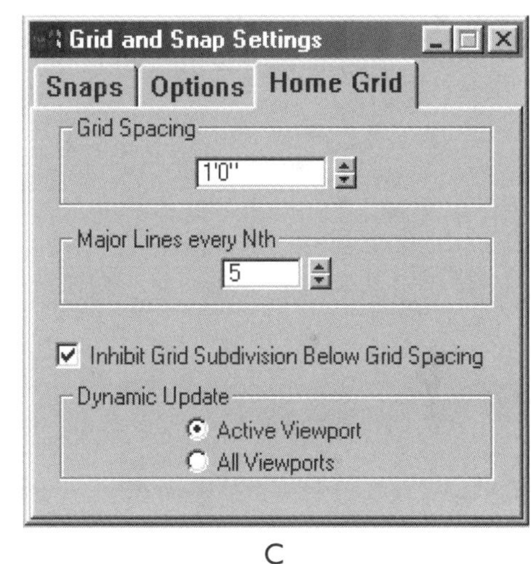


FIGURE 4.23
Units, Snaps, and Home Grid dialogs.

cursor will automatically snap to the grid intersection points as you move the cursor within a viewport.

Select the Home Grid tab to display the Home Grid settings as shown in Figure 4.23C. This controls the grid lines displayed in any of the viewports. This can help with the placement of objects. The grid spacing should be set to 1'0" and the major lines set to 5. Pick OK to close the dialog box.

3. Check the state of various icon buttons. Activate the Top viewport. Refer to Figure 4.24 for the state of the Toolbar buttons and the Prompt Line buttons. Match your buttons to the figures.

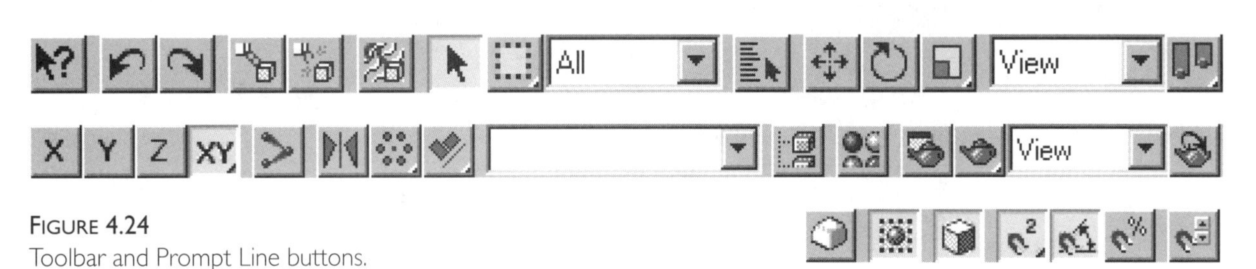


FIGURE 4.24
Toolbar and Prompt Line buttons.

The following should be the current state of the Prompt Line buttons:

| BUTTON | STATE | PURPOSE |
|---|---|---|
| Region Selection | Window Selection | Limit selection of objects totally contained within a window. |
| 2D Snap | ON | Limit cursor movement to 2D. The 2D tool is a flyout. |
| Angle Snap | ON | Limit angular movement to set intervals. |

4. Establish the display state of the various viewports. Activate the viewport and right-click on the viewport label.

| VIEWPORT | DISPLAY STATE |
|---|---|
| Top | Wire-Frame (default) |
| Front | Wire-Frame (default) |
| Left | Wire-Frame (default) |
| Perspective | Smooth+Highlight |

5. Right-click on the Top viewport to activate it.

   Remember to use the Hold button before you perform any command you are unsure of. If something doesn't work, you can always use the Fetch button to restore the geometry to its pre-Hold state.

## CREATION OF SIMPLE OBJECTS

You are going to create some simple geometry to set the stage for your animated rendering. Figure 4.25 shows three thin, rectangular boxes that represent the floor, rear, and left walls of the scene.

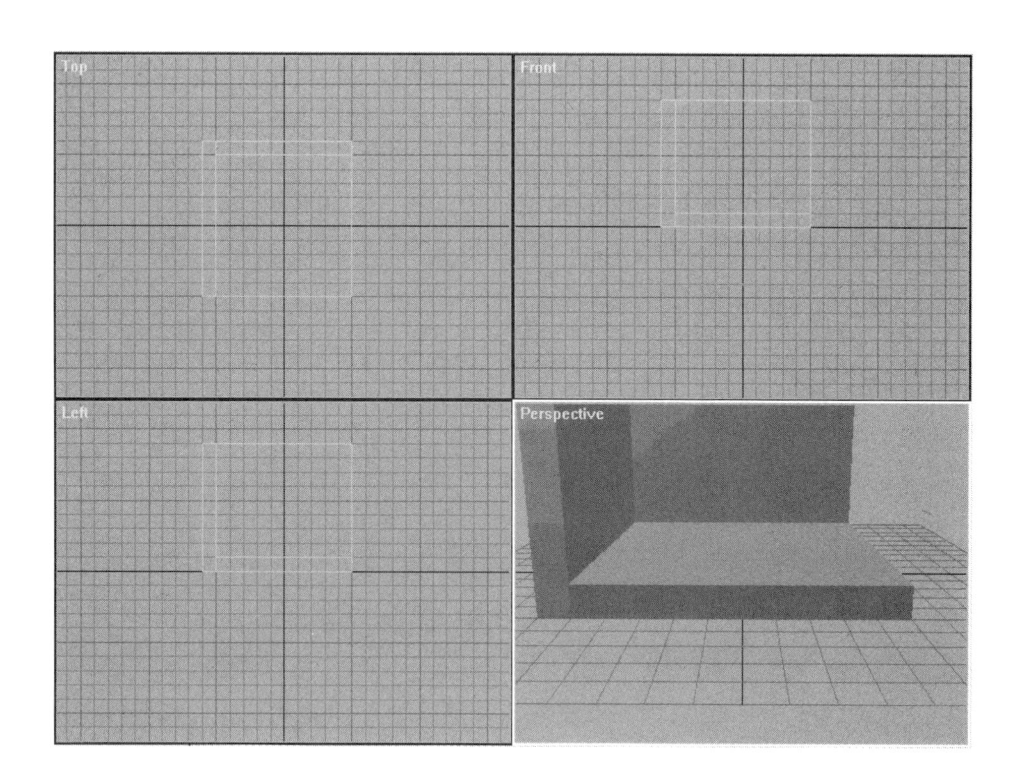


FIGURE 4.25
Walls and floor constructed.

6. With the Top viewport active, open the Create Command Panel and create the rear wall using the Box option with the following coordinates. When grid snap is on, you must only be near the desired coordinate, and the cursor will snap to the intersection when you pick. Make sure Generate Mapping Coordinates is checked for the wall object and that each wall is created using a different color. The following is the procedure for creating an object by picking and dragging in a viewport.

   a. Activate the Top viewport.
   b. Select the Create command panel tab and pick the Box button.
   c. Move the cursor into the Top viewport and move the cursor until the coordinates are close to the desired first corner. Pick that location and the program will automatically snap to the intersection of the grid lines closest to that spot. Hold down on the pick button.
   d. Drag your cursor until the coordinates are close to the values for the second corner and then release the button. The program will again snap to the intersection of the two grid lines.
   e. Move your cursor upward to set the value for the height of the box. Once the height parameter box reads the value you desire, pick that location. If you like, you can set the value by picking in the height box and entering the value.

      1st Box
      Corner 1: X: -5' Y: 5' Corner 2: X: 5' Y: 6'
      Length: 1' Width: 10' Height: 9'
      Object Name: REAR-WALL
      (You won't be able to name an object until it is created.)

   If you forgot to turn on Generate Mapping Coordinates when you created the boxes, you can use the Modify command panel to make the change to each box.

   Figure 4.25 shows the outcome.

7. Although the ball was created earlier, we'll check its parameters using the Modify panel.

   Using the Select tool, pick the ball in the Top viewport so that it's highlighted. Open the Modify panel. It should look similar to Figure 4.26. Review the ball's parameters. Note that it has the Generate Mapping Coords box checked. As a beginner, you will want to make sure that this box is checked for all the primitive objects you create. It will make the application of materials much easier.

8. Use the Zoom Extents All button and make sure the Front viewport is active. Save this project as CH4A.MAX (Chapter 4, Lab A).

## CREATING YOUR NAME USING A SPLINE SHAPE

To create your name, you will have to use a spline shape.

9. Select the Shapes button on the Create command panel and then pick the Text box. The command panel will then display the various options used to control the creation of text spline shapes. Make sure that the text object uses a new color. The following are some of the options to set:

   Object name = NAME
   Font = ARIAL BOLD
   Size = 2'
   Text = STEVE (Enter your first name. Use the short form of your name or a nickname if your name exceeds the six-letter maximum.)

FIGURE 4.26
BALL creation parameters.

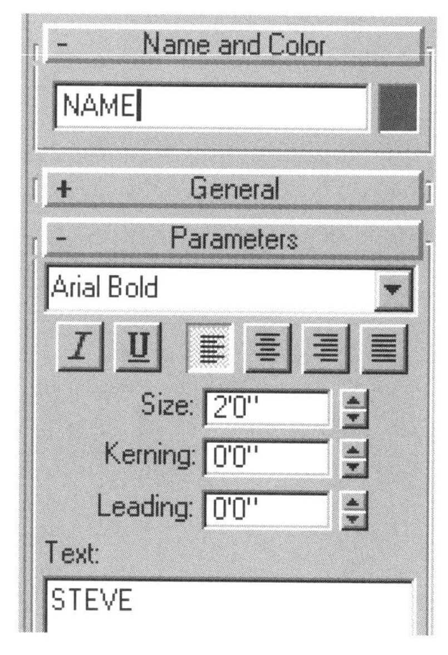


FIGURE 4.27
Creation command panel showing settings for creating a text shape.

Figure 4.27 illustrates the command panel.

10. Make sure the Front viewport is active and then pick close to the following coordinates to center the text:

    X: 0 Y: 0 Z: 5'

## TRANSFORMING THE TEXT

11. Refer to the other viewports for the position of the text. You are going to move the text back toward the REAR-WALL. Activate the Top viewport and pick on the Select object button. Pick the edge of the text to select it (it should turn white).

12. Lock your selection by pushing in the Lock Selection Set button. This makes sure that your transformation will affect only the text and no other objects accidentally.

13. Pick on the Move transform button and then move your cursor in the top view so that it is in the center of the text. The coordinates should be close to X: 0, Y: 0, and Z: 0. Pick this position and hold down on the pick button. Move the cursor toward the REAR-WALL until it is 2 ft away from it.

    The coordinates should be X: 0, Y: 3', Z: 0.

## MODIFYING THE TEXT

14. You are now going to modify the text so that it has a thickness of 1 ft. Select the Modify tab in the command panel. Because the selection of the text is locked, the Modify panel already displays the properties of the text shape.

15. Pick on the Extrude button. The panel should change to display the properties associated with extrusion. Make sure that Generate Mapping Coordinates is checked and then enter 1 ft for the amount of the extrusion. When you enter the amount, the text should change to reflect this value. Figure 4.28 shows your scene.
16. Pick on the Lock Selection Set button to unlock the NAME object.

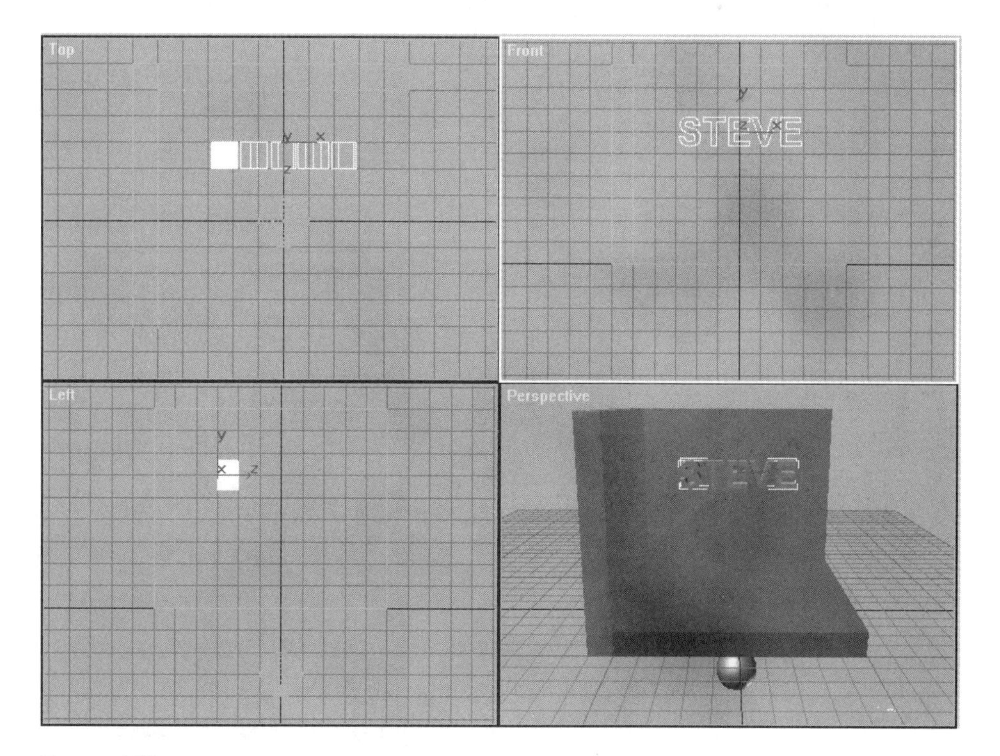


FIGURE 4.28
The completed scene.

## ADDING A CAMERA

Now it's time to create a more interesting view using a camera.

17. Activate the Top viewport and use the Zoom button. Pick the Top viewport and hold down the pick button. Slide the cursor downward to reduce the magnification in the Top viewport. Keep dragging until the FLOOR is reduced to a quarter of the size of the viewport and then release the button.

18. Pick the Create tab and pick the Cameras button. Finally, pick the Target button and you will be presented with the target camera options. Figure 4.29 shows the desired settings.
19. First you are going to place the Camera. Move the cursor into the Top viewport so that the coordinates read close to X: 10', Y: -12', Z: 0 and pick and hold this location for the camera. As you move the cursor with the button still held, a camera icon will appear and let you drag the cursor to the location of the target. Drag the cursor until the coordinates read X: -4', Y: 4', Z: 0 and then release the button.
20. Use the Zoom Extents All button so that you can see the Camera and target in the three orthographic viewports. Note how it is laying at ground level. You are going to have to move the camera upward.
21. Activate the Front viewport. Select the camera object and lock it. Then pick on the Move transform button and pick and hold in the center of the camera in the Front viewport. Slide the cursor upward until the coordinates read X: 0, Y: 11', Z: 0. This should place the camera 2 ft above the top of the 9-ft-high walls pointing downward on a slope.
22. Unlock the Lock Selection Set button and activate the Perspective viewport. Now press C on the keyboard, and the perspective view should be replaced with

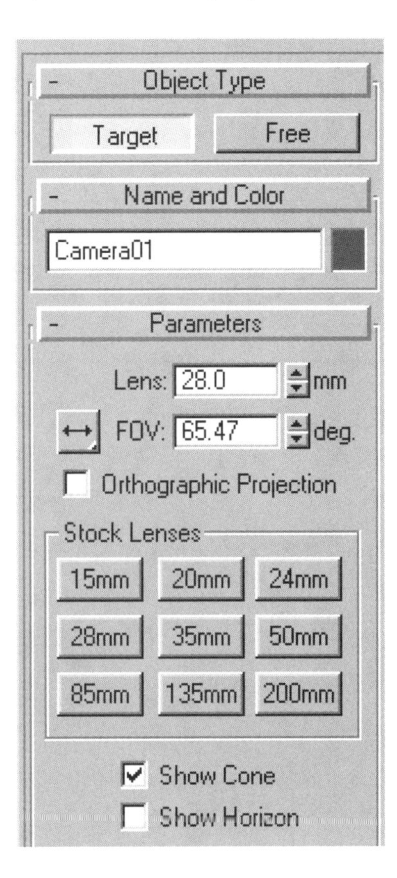


FIGURE 4.29
Target camera settings.

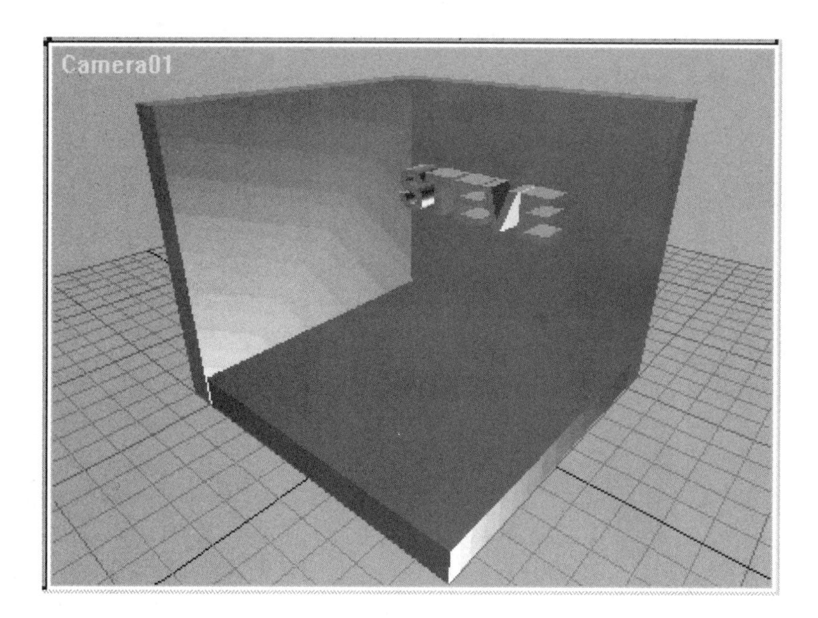


FIGURE 4.30
Camera view.

the new camera view. The view should look similar to Figure 4.30. If it does not, try moving the camera and target around in the Front and Top viewports and watch the view change in the Camera viewport. Try to match Figure 4.30 as closely as possible.

23. Lights have already been added to the scene but they are hidden from view. You are going to make them visible and then hide them again.

    Open the Display Command Panel as shown in Figure 4.31. Note that the box next to Lights is checked under the Hide by Category section. This hides them from display. You will find the practice of hiding objects useful when you have many lights and cameras in a scene.

FIGURE 4.31
Display command panel.

Un-check the box and observe the various viewports. You should be able to see a small cone and lines projecting from it. This is a spotlight shining on your name and the wall.

24. Using the Select icon, select the small cone that represents the spotlight and open the Modify panel. It should look similar to Figure 4.32. Note the various settings such as attenuation, which controls the size of the cone of light and also note that the Cast Shadows box is checked so that the light will cast shadows of the objects it shines upon. You may have to use the panning hand to see all the settings.

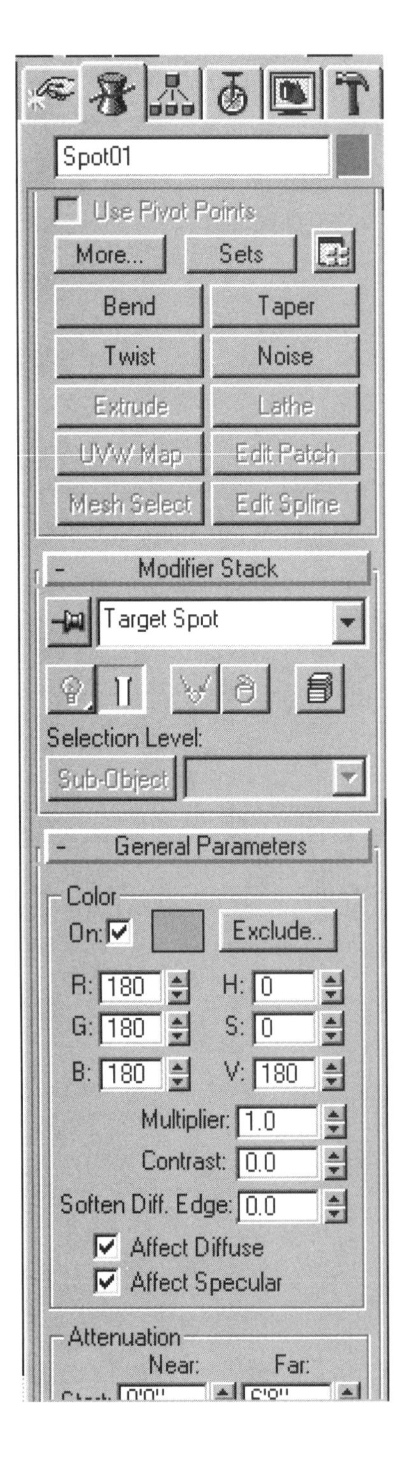

FIGURE 4.32 Settings for the spotlight.

25. Open the Display Command Panel again and check the Lights box so that the light icons are hidden from view.

## TEST RENDERING

Although materials are not yet assigned to your objects, a test rendering at this point will show what the scene looks like before materials are added.

26. Pick on the Render Scene button and refer to Figure 4.33 for the settings in the Render dialog. You may have to use the panning hand to see all the settings. Once you have checked the settings, pick on the Render button and, in a few

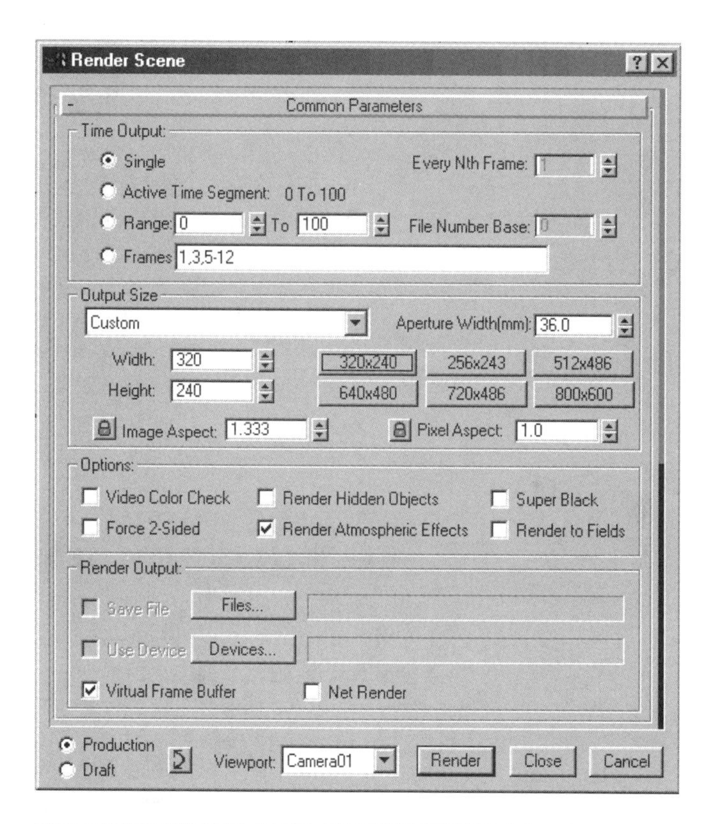


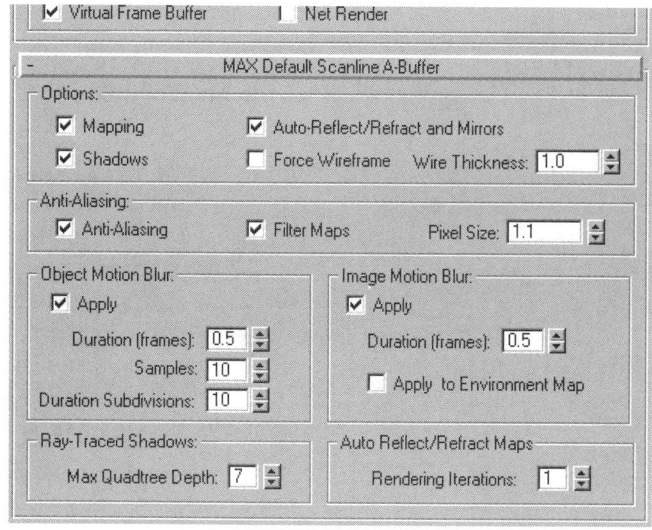


FIGURE 4.33
Render dialog settings.

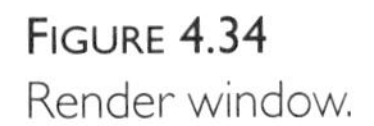

FIGURE 4.34
Render window.

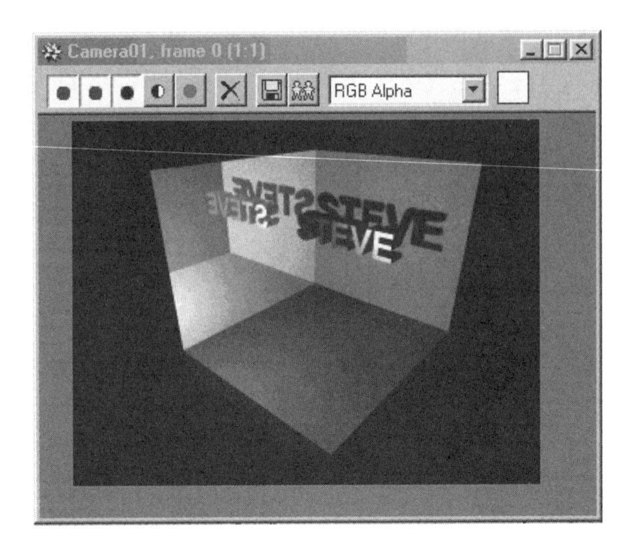


moments, a render window will appear. It should look similar to Figure 4.34. Note the shadow of your name cast on the REAR-WALL by the spotlight. Also note the mirror reflecting on the left wall. A material was added to the surface of the wall to make it reflective. Soon you are going to add some materials to other objects in this scene for some practice. The different light types available in 3D Studio MAX can create some very interesting effects; this is just one. Also note that the ball is nowhere to be seen, because it is hidden under the floor. Soon you will be animating the ball so that it shoots through the floor and then disappears through the mirror.

## ASSIGNING MATERIALS AND APPLYING MAPPING COORDINATE MATERIALS

To assign various materials to the objects you have created, use the material library on the CD-ROM included with this text. The file is called MOTION2.MAT. If you followed the directions in Appendix A, you have copied it from the CD-ROM onto your workstation.

To assign materials to the objects in this lab, you need to apply mapping coordinates to the objects. Most of the objects had mapping coordinates automatically applied when they were created. The only special case was the LEFT-WALL. The LEFT-WALL was modified so that the mirror material is applied only to one face of the wall. First, however, you will apply materials to the other objects in the scene.

27. Pick the Material Editor button and the Material Editor dialog will appear. Pick the first of the six sample boxes at the top of the dialog to activate it.

28. Pick the Get Material button and the Material/Map Browser will appear. Check the Browse From: Material Library box and the Show: Materials box. Next, pick the File: Open button and you will be presented with the Open Material Library dialog. Enter the proper drive and subdirectory for the MOTION2.MAT library location. It will be either on your hard drive if it was copied or on the CD-ROM.

    Once you have found it, highlight and OPEN it. The Material/Map Browser should be listing the materials contained in the library. Scroll through the list until you find the material called FLOOR. Double-click on it and the FLOOR material should appear in the first sample box. The FLOOR material is a parquet wood check.

Repeat the procedure for three more sample windows, placing a new material in each one. Figure 4.35 shows an illustration of the Material Editor dialog. The following is a list of the materials for this scene:

| | |
|---|---|
| Sample 1 = | FLOOR |
| Sample 2 = | WALL |
| Sample 3 = | GLASS-GLOW |
| Sample 4 = | GOLD-LETTER |

29. Now it's time to assign the materials to the objects in the scene. Activate the Camera viewport and, using the Select Object button, pick on the FLOOR object to select it. Once it has been selected, pick on the Material Editor sample window that contains the floor material.

30. Now pick the Assign Material to Selection button in the Material Editor dialog box. The FLOOR material has now been assigned to the FLOOR object. Try a test rendering again to see the results. You should see a checkered wood material covering the floor. This is just a taste of what the addition of materials can do.

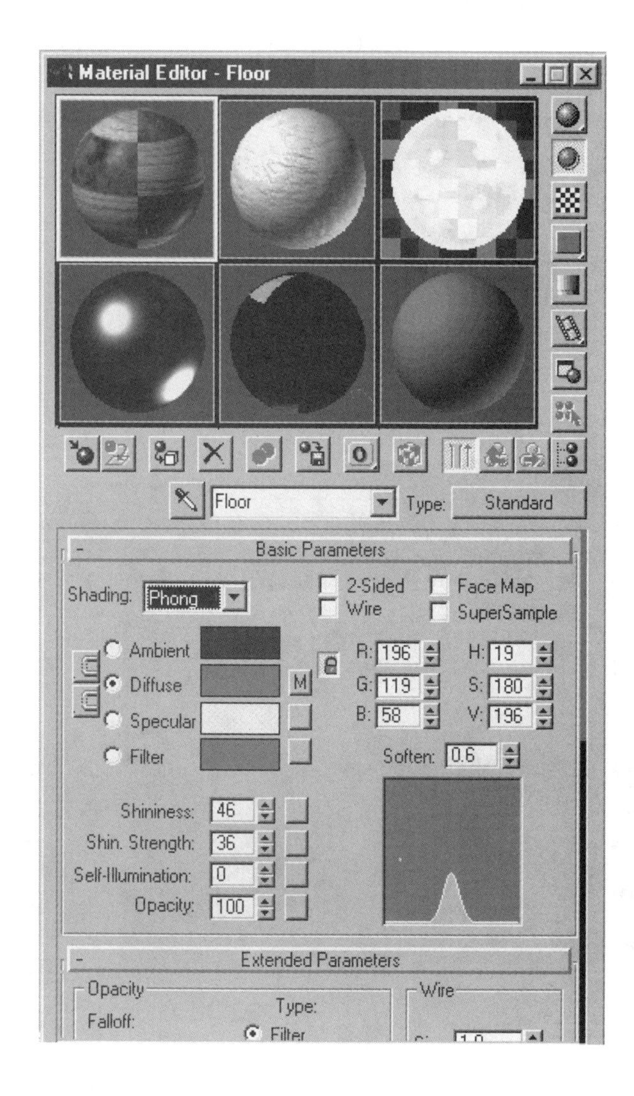


FIGURE 4.35
Material Editor dialog.

31. Repeat the procedure to assign materials to the rest of the objects in the scene, except for the LEFT-WALL. The following is a list of the objects and their materials:

| **Object** | **Material** | |
|---|---|---|
| REAR-WALL | WALL | |
| BALL | GLASS-GLOW | (You will have to select the BALL in another viewport) |
| NAME | GOLD-LETTER | |

32. Use the Quick Render Scene button this time. It performs the rendering using the last settings without asking any questions. If all went well, your render should look like Figure 4.36. Does that give you some idea of the power of materials to add realism to a scene?

## ANIMATING THE BALL AND LIGHT

The next step is animating the ball and light so that it moves upward though the floor, stops, and then moves to the left through the mirror.

33. The first step of animation is to establish the number of frames comprising the animation. For this project, there are going to be 40 frames. Pick on the Time Configuration button. You should see a dialog similar to Figure 4.37. Make sure your settings match the figure.

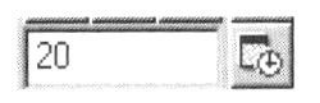


34. Pick the Frame Number field box, the white window that displays the number 0, next to the Time Configuration button and enter 20. This will place you at frame 20 in the animation.

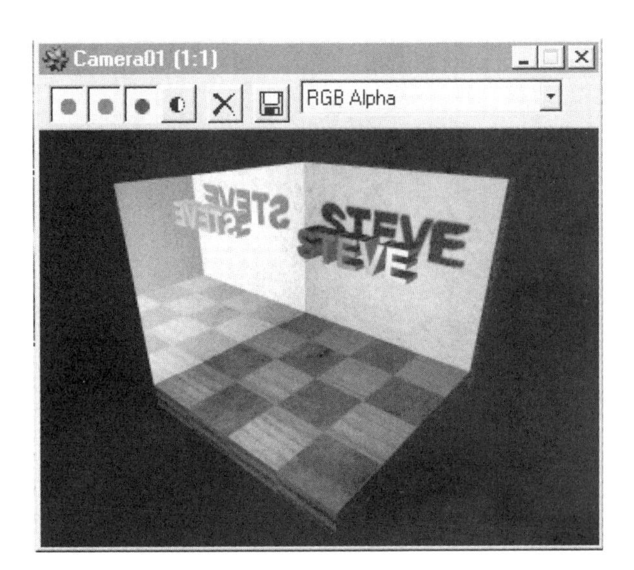


FIGURE 4.36
Rendering with materials assigned.

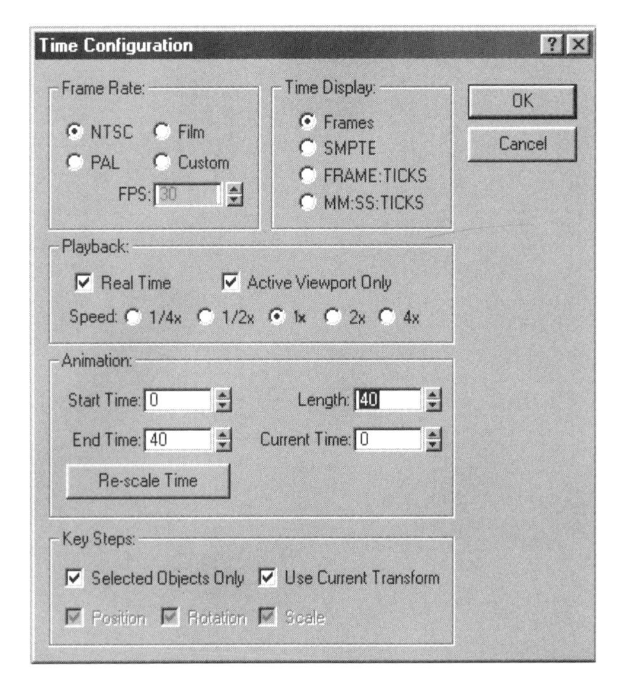


FIGURE 4.37
Time Configuration dialog.

35. Pick the Animate button so that it turns red. This signifies that any changes you make to your scene will be animated; be careful when this button is on. Also note that the active viewport has a red border. This is just another indicator that animation is turned on.

36. Activate the Front viewport and, using the Move transform button, pick the BALL to select it. Lock it. Move the cursor in the Front viewport so that it is on the center of the BALL; pick and hold. Drag the BALL upward until the coordinates read X: 0, Y: 8', Z: 0. This should place the BALL 4 ft above the FLOOR in frame 20. What this means is that the BALL will travel from under the FLOOR in Frame 1 to 4 ft above the FLOOR in frame 20. It is as simple as that.

37. Now let's move the BALL in frame 40. Pick in the Frame Number field box again and enter 40.

38. With the Move transform still active, pick in the center of the BALL in the Front viewport and drag it to the left until the coordinates read X: -10', Y: 0, Z: 0. This should place the BALL 4 ft behind the LEFT-WALL. Turn off the Animate button.

## TESTING THE ANIMATION

There are several ways to check your animation. Let's try them.

39. First, make sure the Camera viewport is active and use the Select Object button to select the BALL. Next, make the trajectory path visible by selecting the Display tab in the Command Panel. Make sure the Trajectory box is checked and check the Lights and Cameras boxes so that they are hidden and not cluttering the scene. Figure 4.38 shows the trajectory path of the ball. Note the path is curved. 3D Studio MAX automatically attempts to smooth the flow of a path. Later on you will learn how to adjust the parameters of the path.

    Turn off the trajectory path by unchecking the trajectory box.

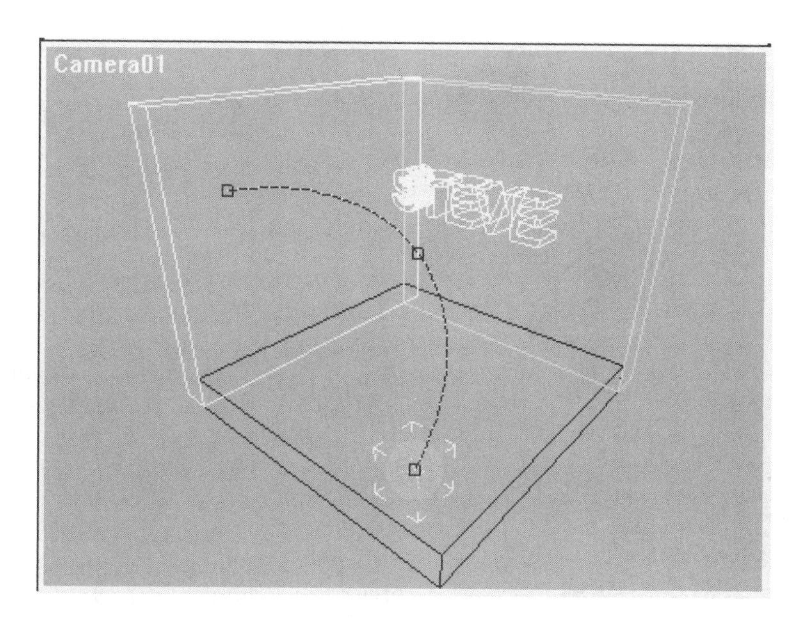


FIGURE 4.38
BALL trajectory path.

40. Pick the Play button and the BALL should travel along its path in the Camera viewport. You can activate any of the viewports, one at a time, and watch the movement of the BALL. Use the Stop button anytime to stop the BALL's travel.

41. The second way to check your animation is to use the Make Preview command located in the Rendering pull-down menu. With the Camera viewport active, select the Make Preview command. Refer to Figure 4.39. Press the Create button to accept the default settings. After the preview is rendered, the Media Player is displayed, allowing you to play the preview. Although it is low resolution and does not show the materials, it does display how the objects will interact with each other. You can see how the ball appears through the floor and travels out through the left wall. There is an omni light traveling with the ball.

    Stop the preview when you are satisfied. If you want to see the preview again, select the View Preview command. A file is created when you make the preview that can be replayed. When you create another preview, the previous one is overwritten with the new preview.

    Save your project.

42. Now let's make a test rendering. You will make a rendered animation with a 320 × 200 resolution, which is quicker than a higher resolution. Once you are happy with the outcome, you can render at a higher resolution.

    Activate the Camera viewport and select the Render Scene button. Refer to Figure 4.40 for the dialog box settings. Pick the Files button to give your animation a name. This will save the animation to a file that you can play at any time. For the file type, pick Autodesk Flic Image File and use GLOW1.FLC for this animation (or use the .AVI extension). Refer to Figure 4.41. Once you have set the file name, OK it and then check Medium for the Palette Method; OK this. In the Render Scene dialog, pick the Render button and the rendering will take place for each frame. This may take substantial time, depending on your machine. A Pentium II 350 Mhz with 96 Mb of

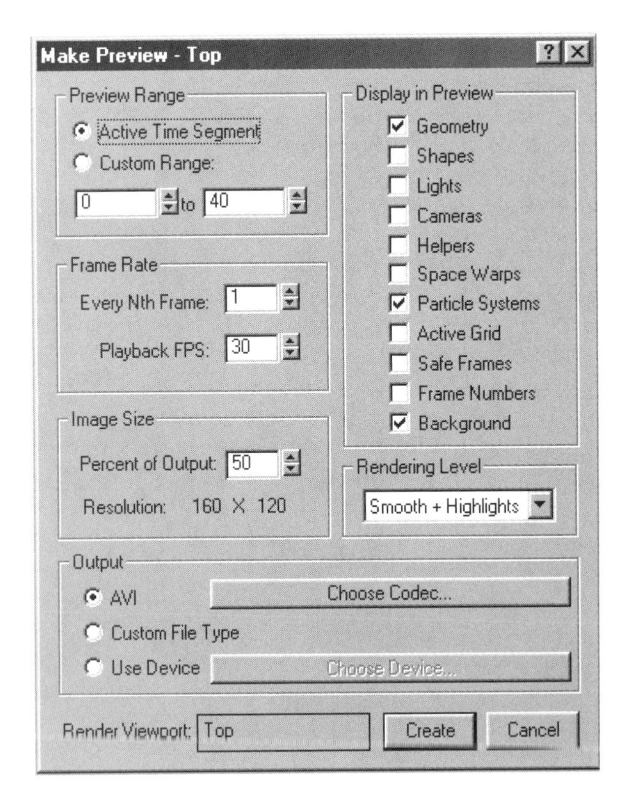


FIGURE 4.39
Make Preview dialog box.

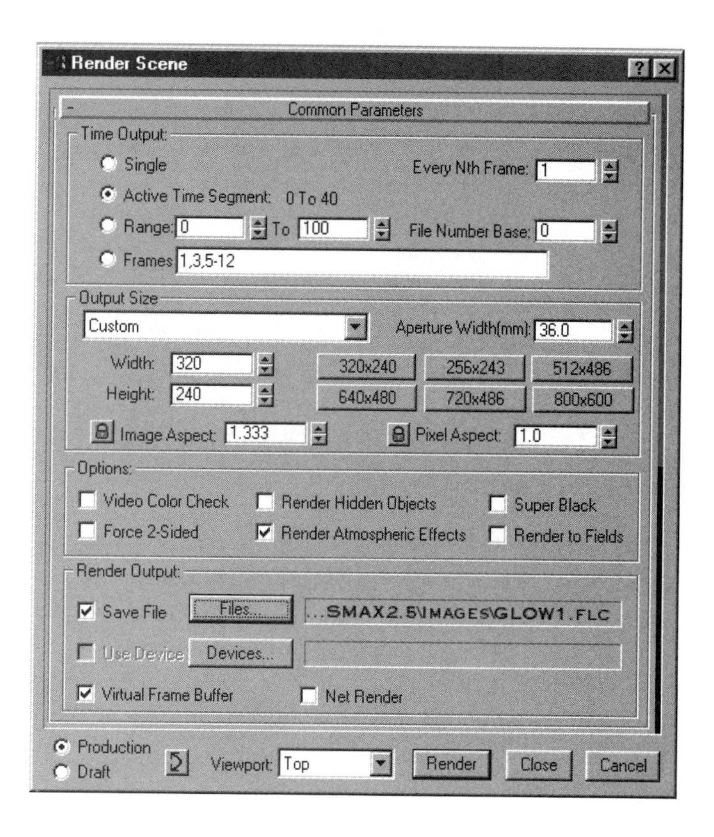


FIGURE 4.40
Render Scene dialog.

RAM takes about 3 minutes. When the rendering is done, you will have a file named GLOW1.FLC (or GLOW1.AVI).

43. Select the File/View File pull-down menu command and find your animation. If you can't remember the file path, return to the Render Scene dialog and make note of it. Remember that its extension is FLC or AVI. Double-click on it. After a few moments the Media Player will appear, allowing you to play your first animation.

    You should be able to see your name lit up with the spotlight, and its shadow will be cast upon the rear wall. The ball should appear, glowing, casting its own light as it moves through the scene.

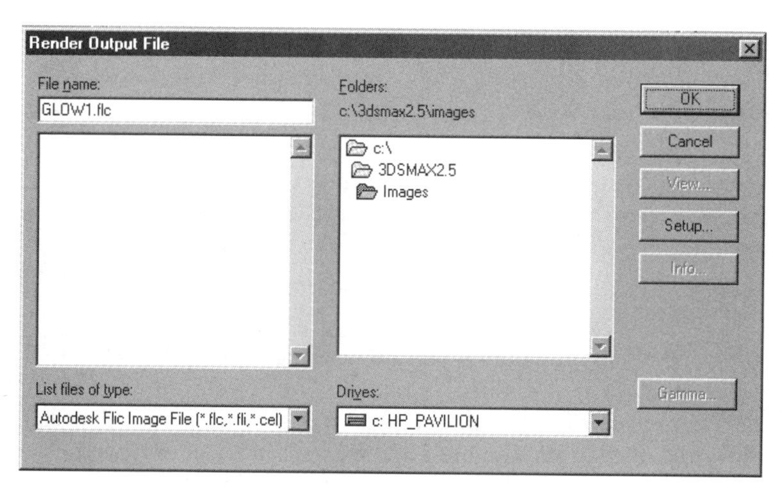


FIGURE 4.41
Render Output File dialog.

### FINAL ANIMATION RENDERING

44. You will make a final rendered animation with a 640 × 480 resolution. You can use higher resolution if you want, but 640 × 480 gives better detail than 320 × 200 without dramatically increasing the time to render. Note that the rendering time does increase rapidly when the resolution is increased.

    Select the Render Scene button and pick on the 640 x 480. Change the file name to GLOW2.FLC so that you won't overwrite your lower resolution file. A Pentium II 350 Mhz with 96 Mb of RAM takes about 10 minutes.

    Repeat step 43 to see your new, higher resolution animation. Remember to select the GLOW2.FLC file this time.

    You have just created your first animation. This should prepare you for the next section of the text, which explores the details of moving and working in a 3D world.

## QUESTIONS AND ASSIGNMENTS

### QUESTIONS

1. Explain the relationship between Home Grid and World Space.
2. What are Grid Objects?
3. Explain the pivot point's function.
4. What is the bounding box?
5. How would you select several objects at once?
6. What function does the Lock icon button perform?
7. Explain the difference between a *copy*, an *instance*, and a *reference clone.*
8. What two types of Cameras are there?
9. What light type is used to simulate the sun?
10. What dialog is used to manipulate materials and how do you get access to it?
11. What are key frames?
12. Explain the basis of hierarchical linking.

### ASSIGNMENTS

1. Create several different types of objects, such as a sphere, box, and cone. Select each one in turn and locate their pivot point/axis tripod. Now select them all using the window feature of the Select Object icon button. Where is the pivot point now? When you select a group of objects, the pivot point will be the three-dimensional center of the group.
2. Use the objects created in assignment 1 or create new ones. Using the Select Object button, select one object. Right-click on the same object (move the cursor over the object and press on the right mouse button). A short menu will appear, listing various commands that you can perform on the object. If more than one object is selected, the commands will apply to the entire group. From the list, select the properties command; you will be presented with its properties. Do the

same for each individual object, noting the different properties; then do the same for a selected group. What is omitted from the properties when you pick more than one object?

3. Create a single object such as the teapot and then use the Shift-Clone method for creating a copy of the teapot. Experiment with the Array and Mirror methods of creating clones. Don't worry if you have difficulty with the array or mirror; they are explained in more detail in Chapter 7.
4. Open the CH4A lab. Use the Modifier command panel to make changes to the camera. Try adjusting the lens size and observing the different results. The smaller the lens size, the larger the field of view. If you save the scene, give it a new name, such as CH4B.
5. Open the CH4A lab. Use the Modifier command panel to make changes to the spotlight. Uncheck the Overshoot button and render a single frame of the scene. What was the difference? Try rendering the entire animation with the overshoot box unchecked. Experiment with lights by adjusting the existing spotlight and adding others. If you save the scene, give it a new name, such as CH4C.

PART THREE

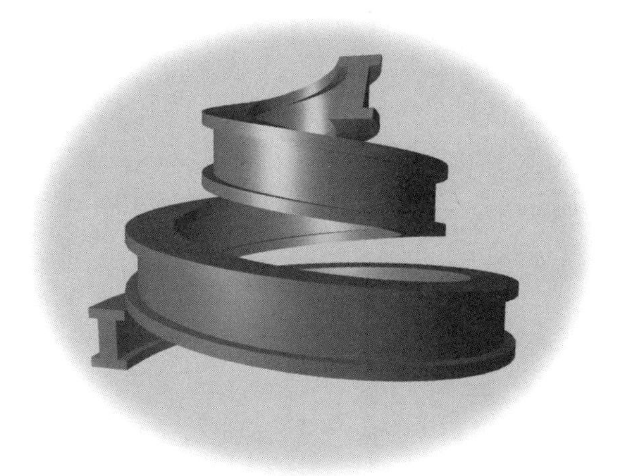

# Preparing for 3D Modeling

# Moving About the 3D World

## 5.1 INTRODUCTION

To create effective 3D worlds using 3D Studio MAX, it is important first to know how to move around those 3D worlds. This chapter deals with the concepts and techniques needed to view your 3D world from any position, configure multiple views, view your model in different forms, and manage basic navigation methods. Knowing how to move around the 3D world will make creation much easier.

## 5.2 VIEWING CONCEPTS

All creation and viewing of the 3D model takes place inside viewports; you can have several viewports displayed at one time, as in the default, or you can display a single maximized viewport filling the screen. In either case a single scene is being worked on and each viewport displays a certain viewpoint of that scene. Having several viewports on the screen at one time allows you to observe different locations in your scene or look from various vantage points in the scene. When you make changes in one viewport, the other viewports will update to reflect the change. It is also possible to disable viewports so that they are not updated automatically; this procedure is explained later in this section.

### Viewport Properties

Each viewport has its own set of properties. These are initially established when the viewport layout is created, which is explained in the next section. However, you can alter many of these properties as you work by right-clicking on the viewport label. The following is a brief description of the items contained in the viewport property menu:

## LIGHTS! CAMERA! ACTION!

### Activating Viewports

Normally you should use your right mouse button to activate a viewport. Although you can use your left button to activate a viewport, using the left button may also cause the current command to be activated as well. For instance, if you left-click to activate a viewport while selecting objects, the currently selected objects will be unselected unless they are locked.

**Smooth+Highlight**
Renders objects in the viewport with smooth shading and displays specular highlights.

**Wireframe**
Draws objects in the viewport as wireframes with no shading applied.

**Other**
Gives you more methods by which to render a viewport.

**Edge Faces**
Superimposes edges on top of objects in rendered viewports.

**Show Grid**
Toggles on or off the display of the grid in the viewport.

**Show Background**
Toggles on or off the display of a background image assigned in the Views/Background Image pull-down menu item.

**Show Safe Frame**
Shows the safe frame, a colored rectangle that provides a guide to help avoid rendering portions of your image that might be blocked in the final output. What lies within the rectangle will be shown during rendering.

**Texture Correction**
Corrects the display of textures that are displayed in a viewport.

**Disable View**
Temporarily stops the automatic updating of changes to a viewport.

**Views**
Allows you to select the viewpoint for the viewport.

**Swap Layouts**
Switches between the two viewport layouts A and B.

**Undo**
Undoes changes to the viewport display.

**Redo**
Repeats the last change to a viewport if the Undo command was used.

**Configure**
Performs detailed changes to the active viewport or all the viewports.

## LIGHTS! CAMERA! ACTION!

### Viewport Properties

Right-clicking on a viewport label is a quick way to access some (but not all) of a viewport's properties or options.

## Perspective View

We view our world perspectively. Objects that are farther and farther away from us appear smaller and smaller, until they are so small they appear as a dot or vanish completely. This point is commonly referred to as the *vanishing point.* A common view displayed in a viewport is a perspective view. This view provides an easy way of interpreting a scene because it closely mimics what we would see with our own eyes. See Figure 5.1

However, perspective viewing is quite hard for construction purposes. It is very difficult to determine different sizes and positions of objects if this perception is based on their distance from us. To alleviate this problem, orthographic views are used.

## Orthographic and Axonometric View

Ortho is from the Greek for straight, and graphic means picture or drawing. An orthographic view is a two-dimensional depiction done as if the edges or lines of an object are projected straight, or parallel to the viewer. Only two dimensions, such as width or height, are visible at one time. In this way you can view an object in proper proportion no matter how close or far you are from the object. All the other objects around it stay in proportion regardless of their proximity. Orthographic views make it easy to tell if corners are straight or if objects line up. Typically, engineering drawings or architectural plans are drawn orthographically. See Figure 5.2.

There are six standard orthographic views: top, bottom, front, back, left, and right.

FIGURE 5.1
Perspective viewport.

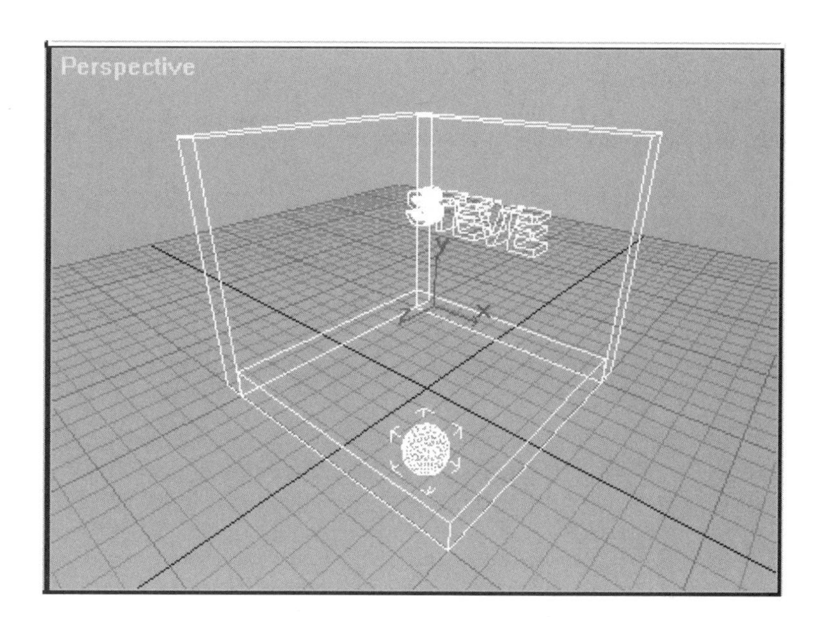

**LIGHTS! CAMERA! ACTION!** 

### Perspective and Camera Views

The view generated by a camera is a form of perspective view, but it has special properties that allow more control of the actual view. Once you are comfortable with placing cameras, you may never need to use a perspective view.

With axonometric views, which are based on orthographic views, the object is projected straight toward the viewer. However, usually with axonometric views, referred to as user views in 3D Studio MAX, the object is turned so that three dimensions of the object can be seen.

## User View

When you rotate the viewpoint in an orthographic viewport, it becomes an axonometric viewpoint and is then labeled as a User viewport. See Figure 5.3. To rotate a viewpoint in an orthographic viewport, activate the viewport; then pick the Arc Rotate icon button in the viewport navigation area in the lower right. This is explained in detail in Section 5.6.

## Grid View

You can display a view parallel to a construction grid, which is useful when you create your own grid that lies in a different plane than the Home Grid. Figure 5.4 shows a viewport view aligned to a construction grid and not the Home Grid.

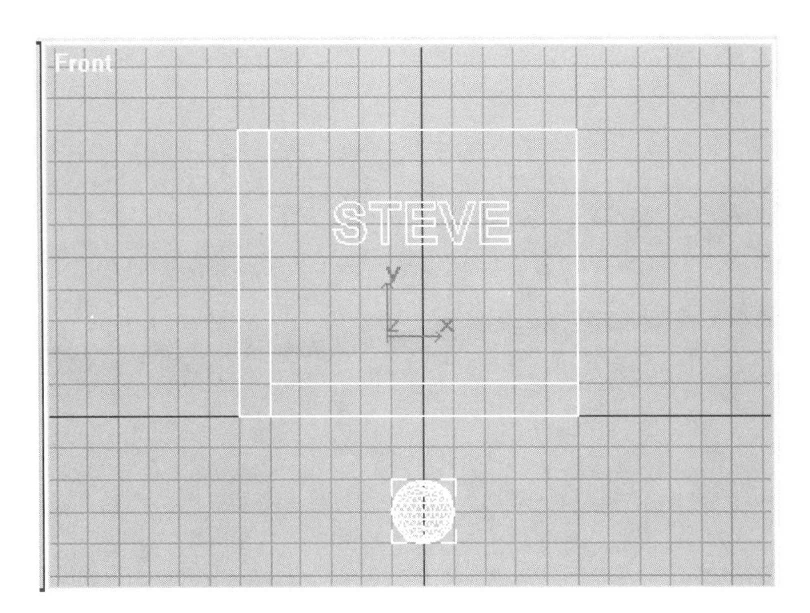


FIGURE 5.2
Orthographic viewport.

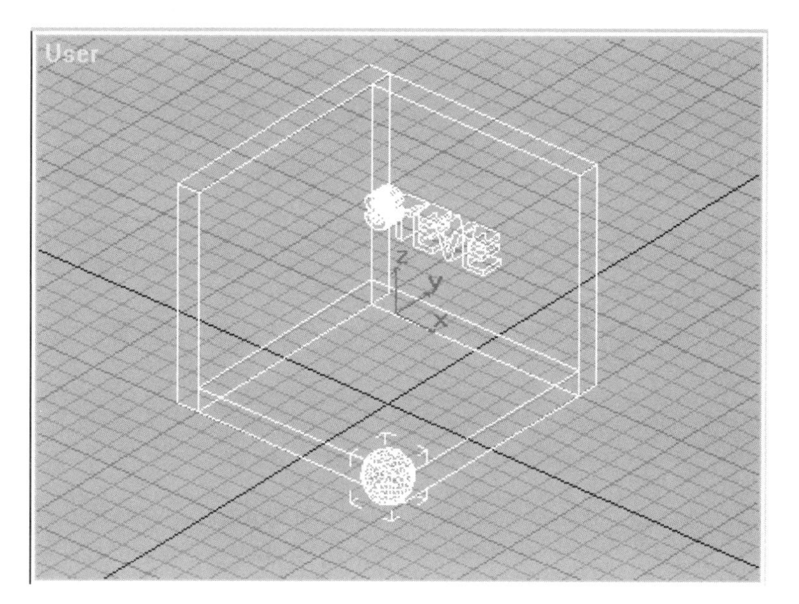


FIGURE 5.3
User (axonometric) viewport.

## Shape View

Shape view is a special type of view and can be set by using the Viewport Properties menu (accessed by right-clicking on the viewport label). This view aligns itself to the extents of a selected shape and its local XY axis.

## Changing Views

You can change a viewport view in several ways. The easiest way uses shortcut keys. Each type of view has a key associated with it. Pressing the key in an active viewport switches the view. The following list gives the shortcut keys.

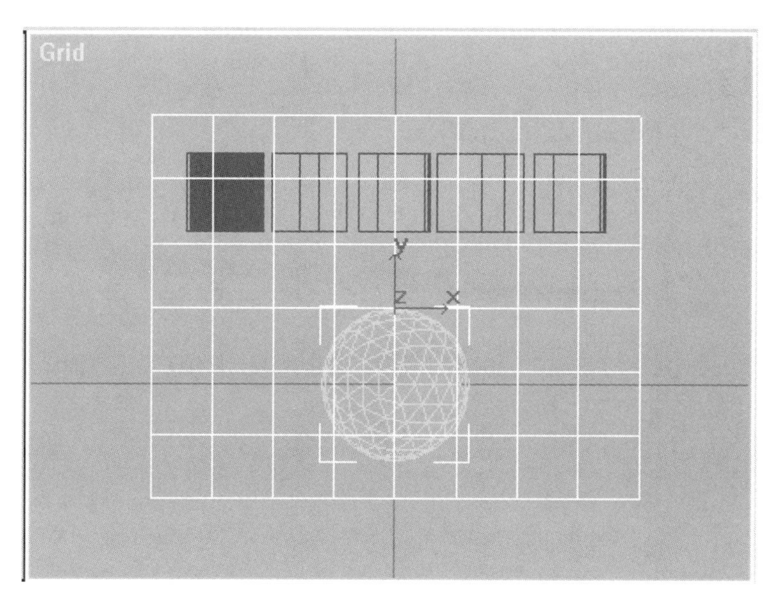


FIGURE 5.4
Viewport view aligned to a construction grid.

| Key | View Type | |
|---|---|---|
| T | Top view | |
| B | Bottom view | |
| F | Front view | |
| K | Back view | |
| L | Left view | |
| R | Right view | |
| C | Camera view | |
| $ | Spotlight view | |
| P | Perspective view | |
| U | User view | |
| G | Grid view | |
| E | Track view | |
| None | Shape view | Set by using the menu. |

You can also use the menu method to select a view. Right-click on the viewport label and select Views from the pop-up menu. From the extended list you can pick the view you want displayed.

## Saving a View

You can save and restore an active view, which is useful when you want to make several viewpoint changes to a viewport view and then return to a previous view. To save an active view, select the Views/Save Active View pull-down menu item. The view will be stored in a temporary buffer. To restore a previously saved view, select the Views/Restore Active View pull-down menu item.

## Disable View

Normally, when you make a change in one viewport the change is automatically reflected in the other viewports. However, there are times when a scene is so complex that you do not want all the viewports dynamically changing at the same time. To alleviate this problem, you can disable different viewports. If you right-click on the viewport label, you can select Disable View from the menu or you can use the shortcut key D. Both methods toggle the disable function on or off. The word disable will appear as part of the viewport label, and the word Inactive will appear in an inactive disabled viewport.

## Maximizing a View

You can switch between the current viewport configuration and full-screen view of the current viewport. This can be useful when you want to display a more detailed

**LIGHTS! CAMERA! ACTION!** 

### Saving a View

Remember that only one view can be saved at a time using the Views/Save Active View pull-down menu item. When you use the command again, the last view saved will be lost.

view of a current viewport. To switch back and forth, activate the viewport and then press the Min/Max toggle button located in the lower-right part of the screen.

### Redraw

During the scene-creation process, extraneous geometry or objects will be left visible on the screen. Although 3D Studio MAX normally cleans them up automatically, there are times when they are left behind. To manually clean up all the screens, select the Views/Redraw All Views pull-down menu item or press the shortcut key 1.

## 5.3 VIEWPORT CONFIGURATION

Not only can you control what is inside viewports, you can also control the layout and properties of the viewports themselves. This is referred to as viewport configuration. You can get access to viewport configuration by selecting from the Views pull-down menu or the Viewport menu (right-clicking on the viewport label). You are then presented with the Viewport Configuration dialog. Contained within the dialog are five panels that give you access to different viewport configuration options. What follows is the explanation of the five panels.

### Rendering Method

There are many methods for displaying a scene inside a viewport. The Render Method panel, as shown in Figure 5.5, controls how objects are shown. The following are the descriptions of the five areas contained within the panel.

#### Rendering Level

The Rendering Level area controls the level of object rendering in the viewport. It goes from the simplest, Bounding Box, to the most complex, Smooth+Highlights. The more complex the level, the slower the display of objects will be. 3D Studio

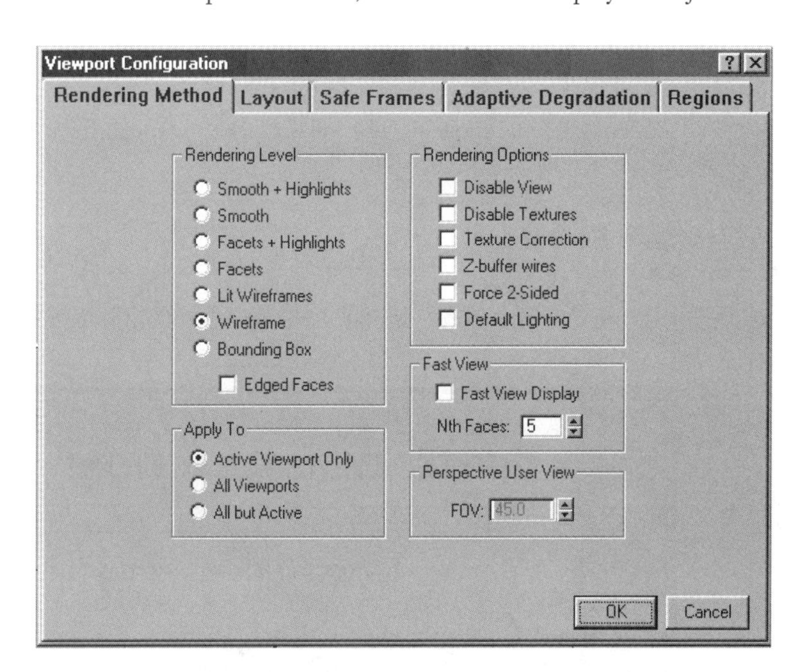


FIGURE 5.5
Render Method panel.

MAX can automatically switch from a higher level to a lower level to increase display speed. This automatic process is referred to as Adaptive Degradation, which is explained later in this section.

### Apply To

The Apply To area controls which viewports are affected by the changes you make in the other areas.

### Rendering Options

The Rendering Options area controls the render options that are available with different rendering levels. Disable Textures can be useful for speeding up rendering by turning off the rendering of complex textures. Turning on Z-Buffer Wires can correct occasional problems of objects overlapping each other, while slowing down rendering. The Default Light option can be useful when you have not adjusted your lights to their proper levels. This option will light the scene with "fake" light until you are ready to use your lights.

### Fast View

The Fast View setting will increase display speed by only showing a reduced number of faces of objects. The objects will look like pieces are missing but you can still get an idea of what form the objects have while increasing display speed for testing animated sequences. You can control the number of visible faces.

### Perspective User View

The Perspective User view setting controls the Field of View (FOV) angle for a perspective viewport. The larger the angle, the wider the view and the smaller the objects appear.

## Layout

There are 14 different viewport layouts available, as shown in Figure 5.6. You also have two separate layouts, A and B. Once you have identified the desired layout using the icons in the upper portion of the panel, you can click inside the lower viewport image to change the contents.

## Safe Frames

This panel is used to control the boundaries of the safe frames. See Figure 5.7. There are three main areas of display, Live Area, Action Safe, and Title Safe; the last two

***LIGHTS! CAMERA! ACTION!*** 

### Swapping Viewport Layouts

To switch between viewport layouts while you are working, right-click on the viewport label and then select Swap Layouts from the menu.

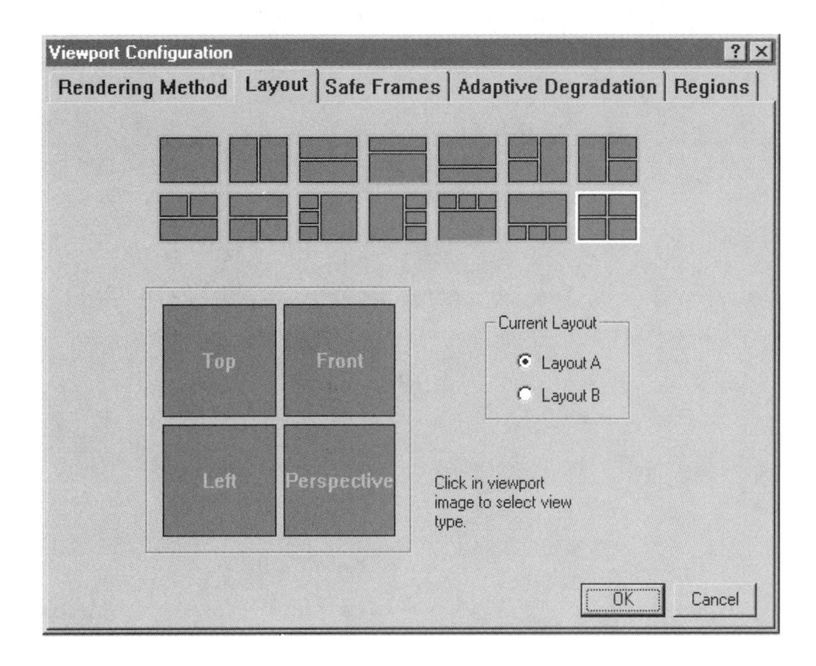


FIGURE 5.6
Layout panel.

are safe frames. When Safe frames are displayed, each boundary is in a different color: Yellow (Live), Green (Action), and Cyan (Title). The Live area is the area that will actually be rendered, regardless of the size or aspect ratio of the viewport. The Action area is the area in which it's safe to include your rendered action. The Title area is the area in which it's safe to include titles or other information. When used correctly, this area is smaller than the Action frame.

## Adaptive Degradation

As mentioned earlier, adaptive degradation is used to automatically adjust the level (or complexity) of rendered objects. See Figure 5.8. The process is simple. In the Rendering Method panel, you select the highest level of rendering you want; in the Adaptive Degradation panel you set the lowest rendering level you will accept. When different

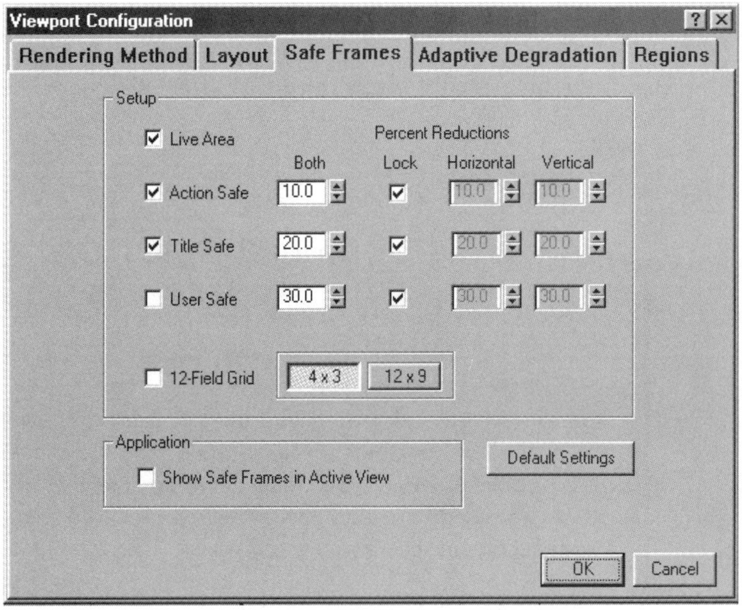

FIGURE 5.7
Safe Frames panel.

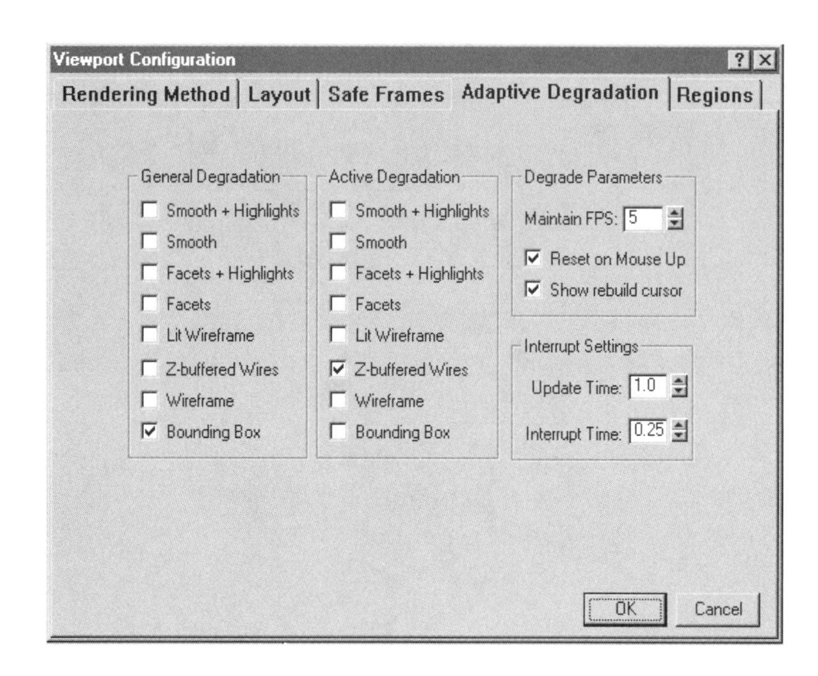


FIGURE 5.8
Adaptive Degradation panel.

action takes place in the viewports, the program will try to display the highest level of rendering you set but will then go to a lower level if the display slows down. You can set multiple levels of degradation, but this can cause jumpy display while the program switches between the various levels. There are four areas to this panel:

**General Degradation**
Controls how inactive viewports degrade.

**Active Degradation**
Controls how the active viewport degrades.

**Degrade Parameters**
Controls the number of frames per second (FPT) the program should try to maintain.

**Interrupt Settings**
Controls the update time that the program waits between updates and the interrupt time, used to check the mouse status. Both are measured in seconds.

***LIGHTS! CAMERA! ACTION!***

### Adaptive Degradation Override

You can override adaptive degradation by using the Degradation Override button at the bottom of the screen. If the button shows a wireframe box, the display of objects will degrade, depending on speed of movement. If the button shows a shaded box, then objects will be rendered at the desired level despite the reduction in speed.

### Regions

The Regions panel controls the default-selection rectangle sizes for Render Region and Render Blowup. The rectangular selection region appears when you render with Blowup or Region selected in the Render Modifier List.

## 5.4 DISPLAY OF OBJECTS

There is a separate command panel to control the display of objects. The following is a description of the various areas contained within the panel. See Figure 5.9.

### Display Color

The Display Color area controls whether an object is rendered in its creation color or its material color.

FIGURE 5.9
Display command panel.

## Hide by Category

The Hide by Category area is used to hide types or categories of objects from the display. This can help unclutter a scene for viewing. For example, once you have placed a camera, you may not want to see its icon in other viewports. You can then hide all the camera icons by checking the appropriate box.

## Hide

The Hide by Selection area is used to hide selected objects.

## Freeze

The Freeze area allows you to freeze selected objects. When an object is frozen, it turns grey and is protected from being selected. In this way you will not inadvertently modify the object.

## Display Properties

The Display Properties area is used to reduce the geometric complexity of objects, resulting in faster computer response time and less cluttered views. The object(s) must be selected first to use the options. The following is a brief description of each:

**Display as Box**
Displays objects as boxes only.

**Backface Cull**
Removes the display of faces hidden by an object.

**Edges Only**
Displays only the edges of an object and not all the internal polygonal facets.

**Vertex Ticks**
Displays tick marks at the vertexes of objects.

**Trajectory**
Displays the animation paths associated with the object.

**Vertex Colors**
Highlights the vertex by color.

***LIGHTS! CAMERA! ACTION!***

### Double Hide

It is possible to hide an object by selection and then hide it again using Hide by Category. As a result, you will have to unhide with both options to make the object reappear.

### Link Display

This area controls the identification of linked objects. Display Links shows a wireframe display of links affecting the selected object. Link Replaces Object replaces the selected object with a wireframe representation of the link. If both linked objects are selected, link lines will be drawn showing the connection.

## 5.6 VIEW NAVIGATION

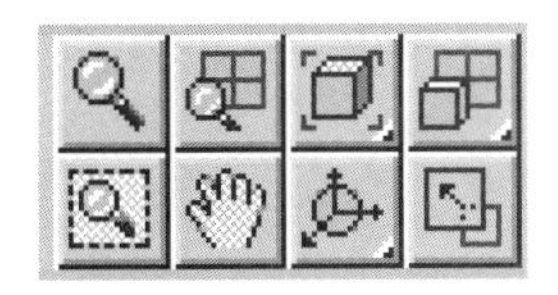

FIGURE 5.10
View navigation buttons.

3D Studio MAX has placed the standard view navigation buttons in the lower right corner of the screen for easy access. They are used to control and manipulate the viewpoint in a viewport and perform three basic functions: view magnification, view position, and view rotation. Typically they look like Figure 5.10, but they can change when a perspective, camera, or spotlight viewport is active. The following explains the various navigation buttons, except for camera and spotlight, which are explained in Chapter 11.

### Magnification

One of the most common desires when creating in 3D space is to be able to increase or reduce the magnification of a view. You may need to look closer for detail or move back to get the big picture. The process of increasing and decreasing magnification is referred to as Zooming, as in Zooming in and Zooming out.

#### Zoom and Zoom All

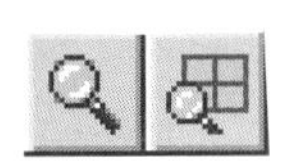

The Zoom and Zoom All buttons increase or decrease magnification by picking and dragging in the active viewport. If you want to Zoom In or Zoom Out at 2X intervals, use the Shift+Grey Plus (+) or Shift+Grey Minus (–) shortcut keys.

#### Zoom Extents and Zoom Extents Selected

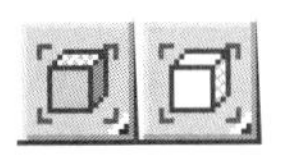

The Zoom Extents and Zoom Extents Selected buttons magnify the view in a viewport to display either the extents of all the objects created or the extents of selected objects. The shortcut key for Zoom Extents is Alt+Ctrl+Z.

#### Zoom Extents All

The Zoom Extents All button will perform a zoom extents in all viewports at once. Hold down the CTRL key during the process to stop zooming in the perspective view. The shortcut key for Zoom Extents All is Shift+Ctrl+Z.

#### Zoom Region

The Zoom Region button is used to zoom in on a region or window that you define by picking and dragging in the active viewport. This is an efficient way to look more closely at a specific area of a scene. This icon changes into the FOV button when used in a perspective viewport. The shortcut key for Zoom Region is Ctrl+W.

#### Field of View

The Field of View button is visible when the active viewport is displaying a perspective view. It is used to increase or decrease the Field of View (FOV), thereby showing

## LIGHTS! CAMERA! ACTION!

### Zoom into a Specific Area in a Perspective Viewport

A fast and easy way to zoom in on a particular area in a perspective viewport is to activate the perspective viewport, press U to change it to a User viewport, use the Region Zoom command to zoom in on a particular area, and then press P to return it to a Perspective view.

more or less of the overall scene. To use the function, activate the Perspective viewport, pick the FOV button, and then pick and drag in the viewport. Upward drag decreases FOV, whereas downward drag increases FOV. If you increase the FOV too much, the display can become distorted, as if you were using a fish-eye lens on a camera.

### Panning

The Pan button is used to move (slide) your view parallel to the current viewport plane. To use, pick the Pan button and pick and drag in the desired viewport. The Pan shortcut key is Ctrl+P.

## Rotating a View

If you want to replace a view in a viewport with a user view, activate the viewport, press U, and then use the Arc Rotate icon button. The following are the two methods of using arc rotate and their associated icon buttons.

**Arc Rotate**
Uses the center of the current viewport as the center of the rotation.

**Arc Rotate Selected**
Uses the center of currently selected objects as the center of rotation.

### Rotate Options

When you select either of the Arc Rotate buttons, you are presented with the arc rotation arcball. Figure 5.11 shows a circle with handles placed at the four quadrants. The direction in which rotation takes place depends on where the cursor is placed on or around the arcball. As you move the cursor around the arcball, the cursor will change form showing how the rotation will be controlled. When the cursor changes to the desired rotation type, pick and drag the cursor to affect rotation. The following are the various rotate options.

**Freely Rotate**
Picking and dragging inside the arcball gives rotation in the horizontal and vertical planes simultaneously.

**Roll a View**
Picking and dragging outside the arcball gives rotation about the current depth axis.

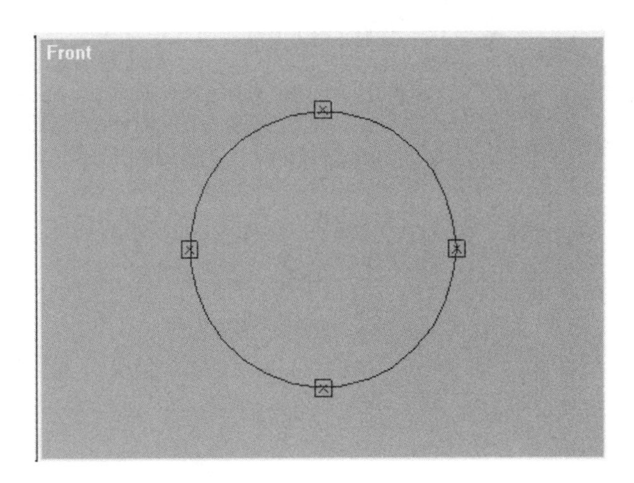


FIGURE 5.11
Arc rotation arcball.

**Rotate Vertically**
Picking on the top and bottom handles (tabs) gives vertical rotation.

**Rotate Horizontally**
Picking on the left or right handles (tabs) gives horizontal rotation.

### Shortcut Keys

There are several shortcut keys that can be used with arc rotate.

**Ctrl R**
Turns on the current mode of arc rotate.

**Left arrow**
Left horizontal view rotate.

**Right arrow**
Right horizontal view rotate.

**Up arrow**
Upward vertical view rotate.

**Down arrow**
Downward vertical view rotate.

**Shift+Left or Right arrow**
Rolls the view.

## Camera and Spotlight Views

Camera and spotlight viewports have special view navigation buttons associated with them. The buttons not only alter the view but also modify the properties of the camera or spotlight objects. These are explained in detail in Chapter 11.

## Undo for Views

The undo feature reverses changes to views, allowing you to restore the previous viewpoint. To access this feature, select the Views/Undo pull-down menu item. If you mistakenly undo a view, reverse the process by selecting the Views/Redo pull-down menu item. The shortcut keys are Shift+Z for View Undo and Shift+A for View Redo.

## 5.7 SUMMARY

This chapter has given you the tools to move freely about your 3D world. Mastering these techniques early is essential for allowing you the freedom to see your world from different viewpoints, making creation that much easier. The following lab reinforces these techniques by letting you test each one in a simulated environment.

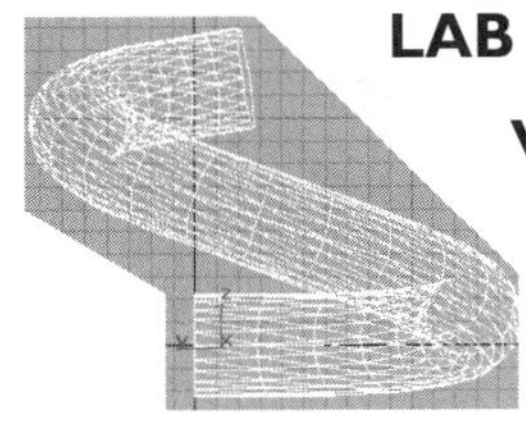

# LAB 5.A

## View Navigation

### Purpose

This lab practices the techniques needed to navigate your 3D world. Using the scene you created in Lab 4.A, you are going manipulate the views and viewports so that you have a clear understanding of the various viewing features.

### Objectives

You will be able to

- Modify viewport properties.
- Change view types in various viewports.
- Save and restore a view.
- Perform viewport configurations.
- Alter the display of different objects, such as hiding and freezing.
- Practice the use of Zoom, Pan, and Arc Rotate view navigation buttons.

### Procedure

#### SETTING UP THE PROJECT

With any project you need to establish some initial settings. These settings are usually standard for any project, and you should become familiar with checking them before you start any creation.

1. First, select the Reset command from the File pull-down menu. This ensures that there are no active settings from a previous session.
2. Use the File/Open pull-down menu item to recall your file from Lab 4.A (file name CH4A.MAX).
3. Most of your settings are already set from use in the previous lab. However, you will need to check some of them so that you start this lab correctly.

   Units = feet and fractional inches
   Snap = Grid Points (Figure 5.12, part A)
   Options = no change but check that it matches Figure 5.12, part B
   Grid = 1 ft (Figure 5.12, part C)

4. Check the states of various icon buttons. Activate the TOP viewport. Figure 5.13 shows the state of the Toolbar buttons and the Prompt line buttons. Match your buttons to the figures.

   The following should be the current state of the prompt line buttons:

| BUTTON | STATE | PURPOSE |
|---|---|---|
| Region Selection | Window Selection | Limits selection of objects totally contained within a window. |
| 2D Snap | ON | Limits cursor movement to 2D. |
| Angle Snap | ON | Limits angular movement to set intervals. |

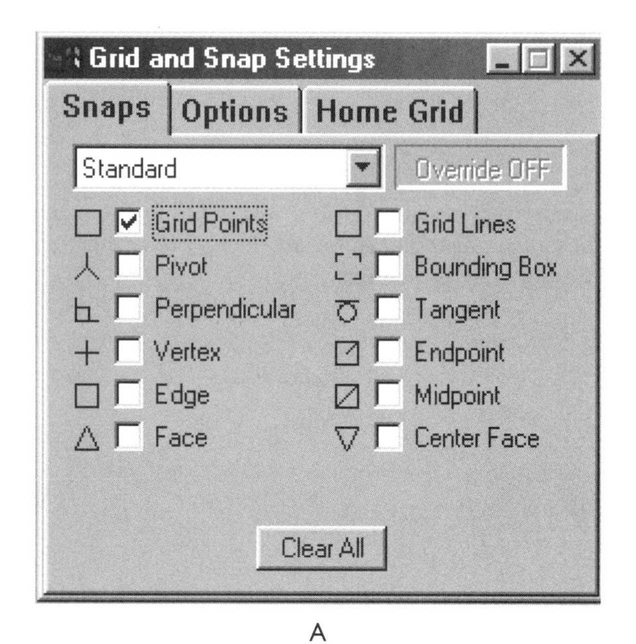


A

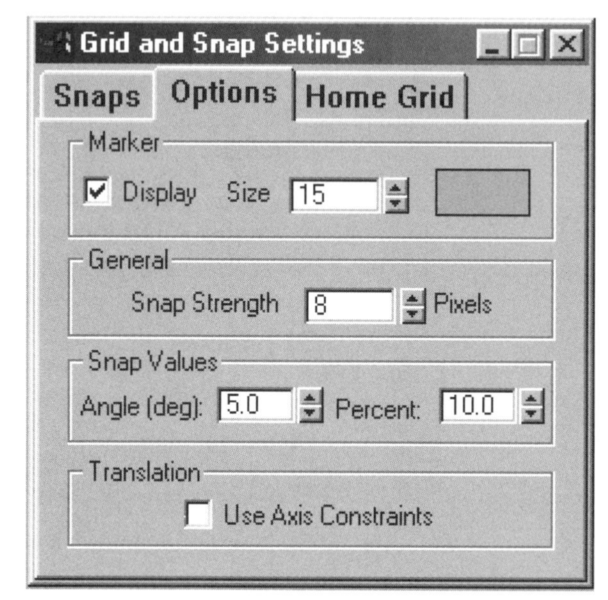


B

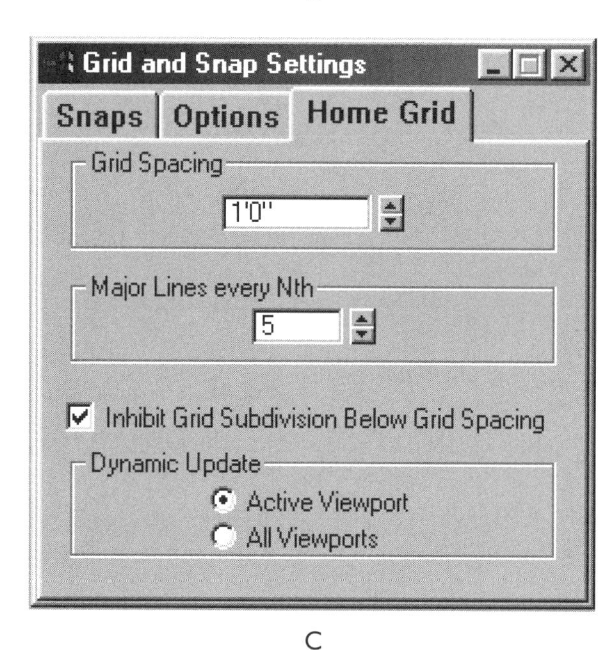


C

FIGURE 5.12
Snap, Options, and Home Grid dialogs.

FIGURE 5.13
Toolbar and Prompt Line buttons.

5. Use the Zoom Extents All button to display all the objects in all the viewports.

## VIEWPORT PROPERTIES

6. Establish the display state of the various viewports. Activate each viewport in turn and right-click on the viewport label.

| VIEWPORT | DISPLAY STATE |
|---|---|
| Top | Wire-Frame (default) |
| Front | Wire-Frame (default) |
| Left | Wire-Frame (default) |
| Camera01 | Wire-Frame |

7. Turn the Home Grid off in the camera viewport by right-clicking on the camera viewport label and selecting Show Grid from the menu. The grid should disappear from the perspective viewport.
8. Disable the view in the top viewport by right-clicking on the Top viewport label and selecting Disable View from the menu. Note how the label changed to include *Disabled.* Activate a different viewport and observe what happens to the top viewport. The word INACTIVE appears in its center. The inactive viewport will not show any changes until it is activated or the disable is turned off. Figure 5.14 shows the inactive viewport.
9. You are going to perform a temporary move in the Front viewport. First, make sure you are in frame 0 by either moving the frame slider back to frame 0 or picking in the frame box and enter the number 0. Next, use the Edit/Hold command to temporarily store the scene.

   Now, use the Move transform and move the BALL from its current location to the upper right of the Front viewport. Watch the other viewports as you perform the move. You can see the BALL move in the other viewports except for the Top viewport, which is inactive.

   Activate the Top viewport and see that it updates to show the new location of the BALL.

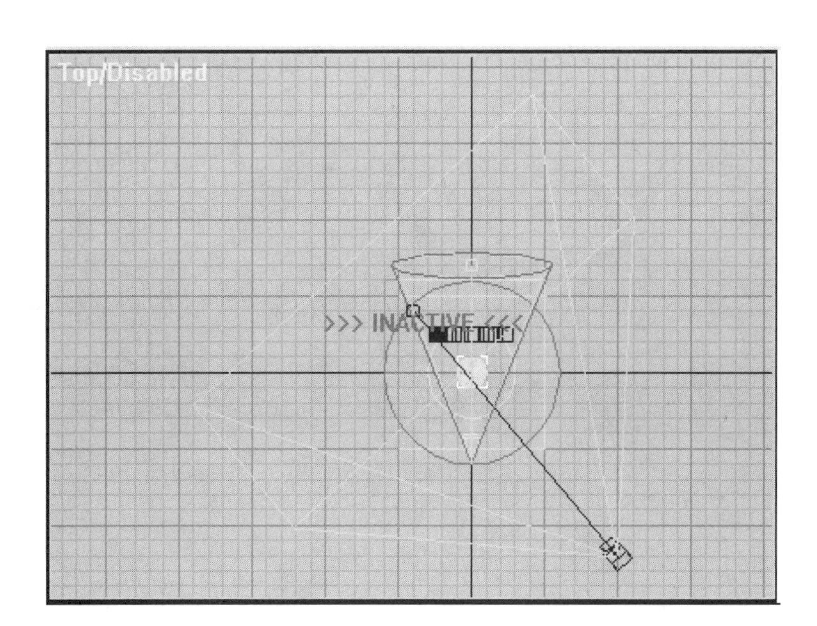


FIGURE 5.14
Inactive viewport.

10. Select the Edit/Fetch pull-down menu item and answer Yes to restore the previous hold. The BALL should move back to its original position.

11. Turn Disable View off in the Top viewport by right-clicking on the Top viewport label and selecting Disable View menu item. The word Disable should disappear from the label on the viewport.

## CHANGING VIEW TYPES

12. Activate the Left viewport and then press the R key. The viewport view should change to Right.

13. Activate the Front viewport and press the K key. The viewport view should change to the Back. Figure 5.15 shows the changed views.

14. Restore the Left and Front views to their original displays.

## SAVING AND RESTORING A VIEW

15. Activate the Top viewport and select the Views/Save Active View pull-down menu item.

16. Pick the Region Zoom button and window in on the BALL so that it fills the screen.

17. To restore the previously saved active view, select the Views/Restore Active View pull-down menu item. The Top viewport should have returned to its previous state before you zoomed in using the Region Zoom button.

## VIEWPORT CONFIGURATIONS

18. You are going to create your own viewport configuration.

    Select the Views/Viewport Configuration pull-down menu item. From the displayed dialog, pick the Layout tab. The Layout panel should now be dis-

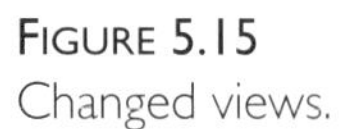

FIGURE 5.15
Changed views.

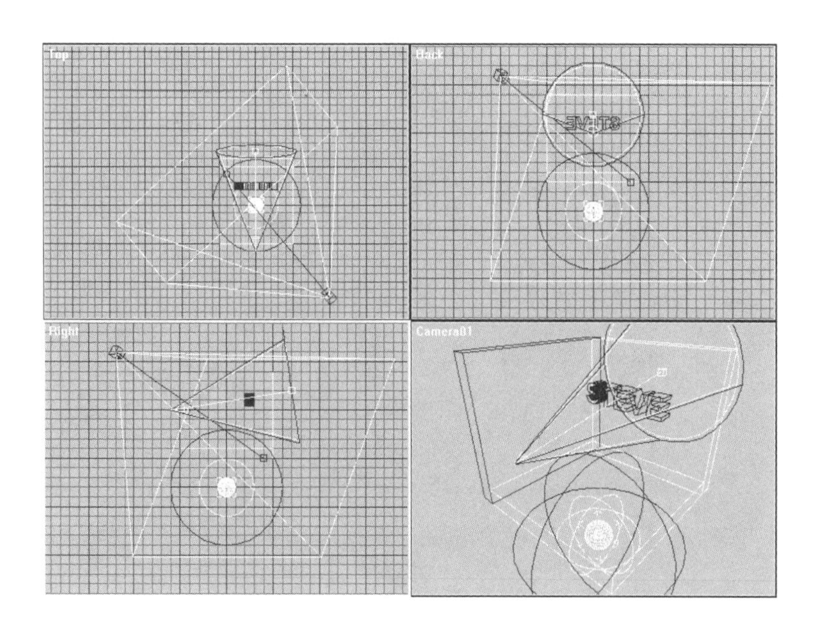

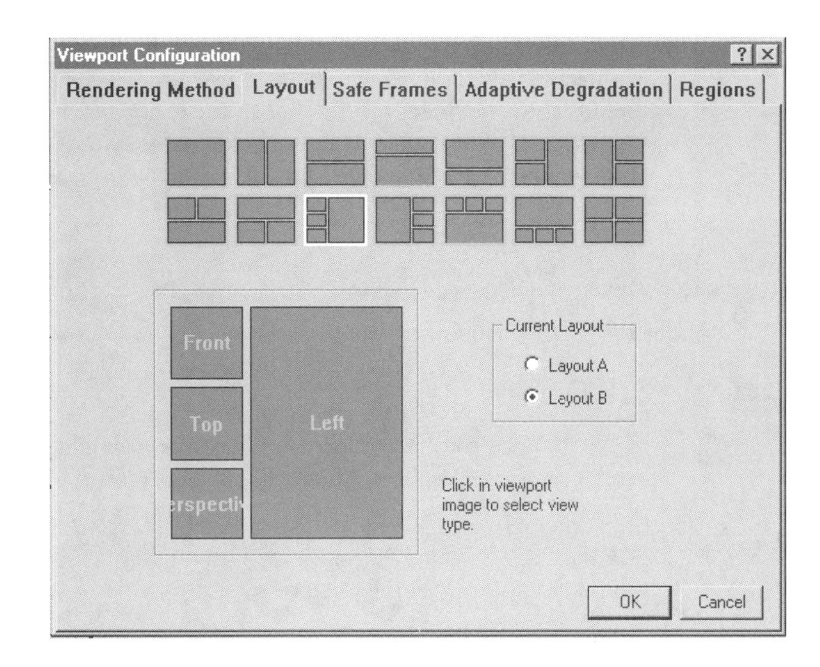


FIGURE 5.16
Layout panel.

played. Pick on the Layout B box. The configuration should change in the panel. Move your cursor into the top icons and pick the one that has three small viewports running along the left and one large one on the right. See Figure 5.16.

Move your cursor into the lower display, which shows the current viewport configuration. Pick on the Track viewport and change it to Front.

OK the dialog to see the results. The new viewport layout B should replace the original layout A.

19. You are going to change the Rendering Level for all the viewports. Select the Views/Viewport Configuration again. Pick on the Rendering Method tab. The Rendering Method panel should appear.

    In the Apply To area, pick the All Viewports box to check it.

    In the Rendering Level, pick the Smooth+Highlights box. See Figure 5.17. OK the dialog to see the results. The objects in all the viewports should be rendered.

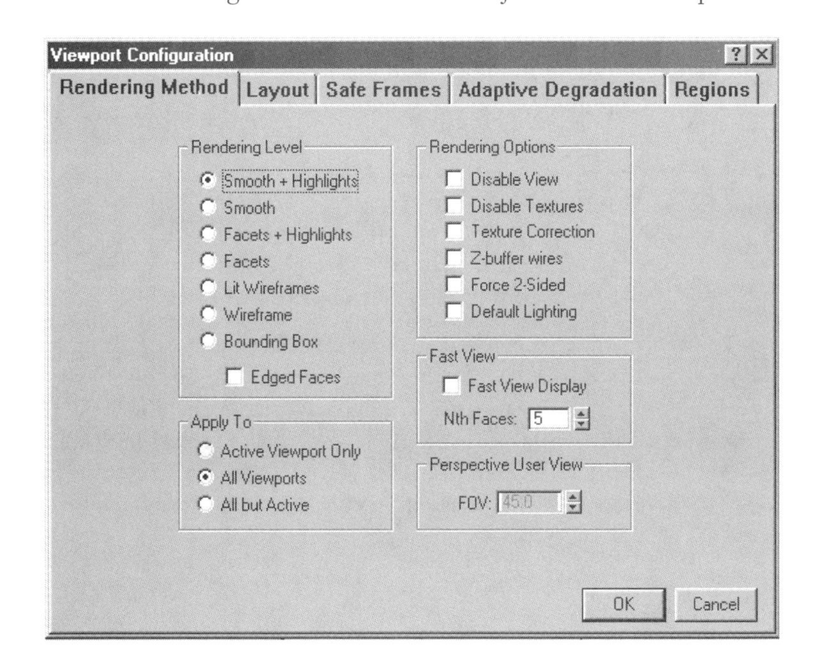


FIGURE 5.17
Rendering Method panel.

20. Now you are going to swap back and forth between viewport layouts A and B. Right-click on any viewport label and select the Swap Layouts. The screen should return to the layout A. Perform the command again to swap layouts so B appears again. You can easily have two different layouts for different types of creation or editing and switch between them at any time.
21. Return the viewport layout to A.

## DISPLAY OF OBJECTS

22. You are going to hide the camera by category. Select the Display command panel tab. Locate the Hide by Category area and pick the Cameras box, so that it is checked. Once you have done this, the camera should disappear from the scene in all viewports. Even if it is hidden, it still operates.
23. Using the Select Object button, pick on the BALL so that it is selected. Now, pick the Hide Selected button in the Display command panel. The BALL should disappear in all the viewports.
24. To make the BALL reappear, pick on the Unhide by Name button. You are presented with a dialog that lists the names of the hidden objects. Because you have hidden only the BALL, it is the only object in the list. Pick the name BALL to highlight it and then pick the Unhide button. The BALL should reappear.
25. Now, pick the NAME to select it. From the Display command panel, pick the Freeze rollout button and then pick on the Freeze Selected button. The NAME should turn grey. Once it has turned grey, try to select it in a number of ways, such as picking it or making a window around it. You will find that it cannot be selected. That is the purpose of the Freeze display option—to inhibit the selection of objects to protect them from accidental modification.
26. To unfreeze the NAME, pick on the Unfreeze by Hit button. Drag the cursor over the NAME and pick it. The name will return to its original color, showing that it is unfrozen.

## VIEW NAVIGATION BUTTONS

27. Activate the Front viewport and then use the Region Zoom button to zoom in on the NAME.

28. Use the Pan button to pan in the Front viewport until the BALL appears. You will need to pick the buttom of the Front viewport using the Pan hand and then drag upward. It may take several times for the BALL to appear. If you get lost, use the Zoom Extents button and start over.

29. Activate the Top viewport and select the BALL so that it turns white. Then, pick the Zoom Extents Selected button. The button may be hidden under the Zoom Extents button, so you may have to hold down on the Zoom Extents button until it flies out; then you can drag the cursor upward to highlight the Zoom Extents Selected button. If you do it correctly, the BALL should fill the Top viewport. If it does not, try again until it does.

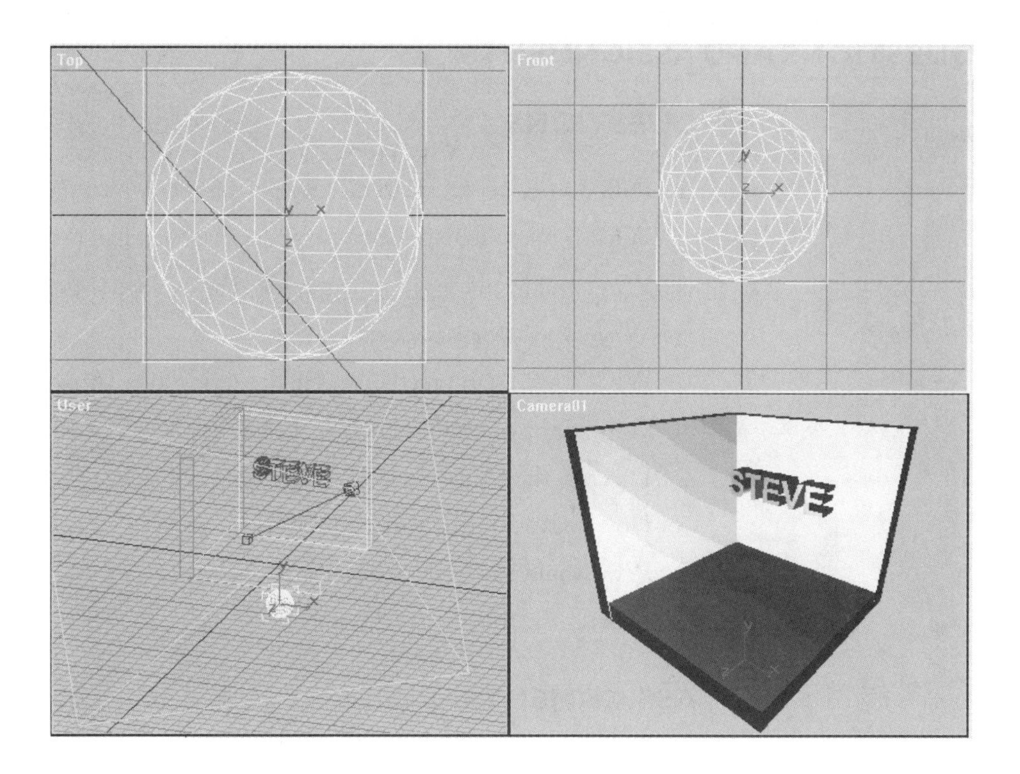


FIGURE 5.18
Rotating the view horizontally and vertically.

30. Now you are going to practice rotating a view. Activate the Left viewport and then pick the Arc Rotate button. This button will only show on the screen if you are *not* in the camera viewport. The arcball should appear in the Left viewport. Move the cursor around the arcball, inside and out, and watch the behavior of the cursor. It will change, depending on its position around the arcball.

    Move the cursor so that it lies within the left handle box on the arcball. The cursor will change to the horizontal rotate icon. Pick in the box and hold. Drag the cursor horizontally back and forth in the Left viewport. Release the pick button when you have turned the view somewhat.

    Move the cursor so that it lies within the top handle box on the arcball and pick and hold. Drag the cursor upward and downward and watch the result. Release the pick button when you have turned the view somewhat.

## UNDO FOR VIEWS

31. Select the Views/Undo View Rotate pull-down menu item. The vertical rotate has been undone. Select the Views/Undo View Rotate pull-down menu item again. The horizontal rotate has been undone. If all went well the Left view should be back where it was. If it is not, press the L key to force the Left view to be displayed in the viewport. Figure 5.18 shows the results of rotating horizontally and vertically.
32. Save the file as CH5A.MAX.

## QUESTIONS AND ASSIGNMENTS

### QUESTIONS

1. How do you get access to the viewport property menu?
2. What is the difference between a perspective and an orthographic view?
3. Why would you use an orthographic view over a perspective view?
4. What type of view is a user view?
5. What is the easiest method to change a view type in a viewport?
6. Why might you want to disable a view?
7. Describe the rendering levels displayable in a viewport.
8. How does adaptive degradation work?
9. Why would you want to freeze an object?
10. What is the function of the arcball?

### ASSIGNMENTS

1. Open the CH5A.MAX file. Experiment with the Arc Rotate command to show four different axonometric views in each of the four viewports. If desired, save the file as CH5B.MAX.
2. Open the CH5A.MAX file. Experiment with the Zoom button to practice zooming in and out. Also try the shortcut keys Ctrl+Grey Plus (zoom in) and Ctrl+Grey minus (zoom out).
3. Open the CH5A.MAX file. Change one of the viewports into a perspective view. Activate the Perspective viewport and experiment with the Field of View button. Keep widening the FOV and observe the results. What happens to the grid and the objects?
4. Open the CH5A.MAX file. Experiment with all the options of the Arc Rotate and Arc Rotate Selected buttons, especially the Freely Rotate and Roll a View options.

# Basics of Creation

## 6.1 INTRODUCTION

In this chapter you learn about the basic techniques necessary to create the objects that comprise a 3D world and the precise tools that make these procedures more user-friendly. These new techniques enhance what you already know about creation from earlier chapters and provide more detail about the Creation command panel. Further explanation of units and grids is given, as is the application of the snap settings. Special helper objects, whose power you will see in later chapters, are introduced.

## 6.2 CONSTRUCTION PLANES

Before we explain the Creation command panel, we must review construction planes. Construction planes control the orientation of objects when they are created. Think of construction planes as the ground upon which you build your objects. When you build something, it must have a starting frame of reference; the construction plane is that frame of reference. The plane itself can have a variety of orientations from representing the ground to the sky.

The Home Grid is a method of using construction planes. As detailed in Chapter 4, the Home Grid is a combination of three intersecting coordinate planes in world space. Each plane is a combination of two of the three axes, creating XY, XZ, and YZ planes. Because the planes intersect at 0,0,0, the third axis for each plane is at 0, with the positive direction running toward the viewer and the negative going away. The standard orthographic views, such as top and front, are aligned to those planes. When you activate a viewport that contains one of the orthographic views, you are working on one of the Home Grid planes and, by definition, on a construction plane. See Figure 6.1.

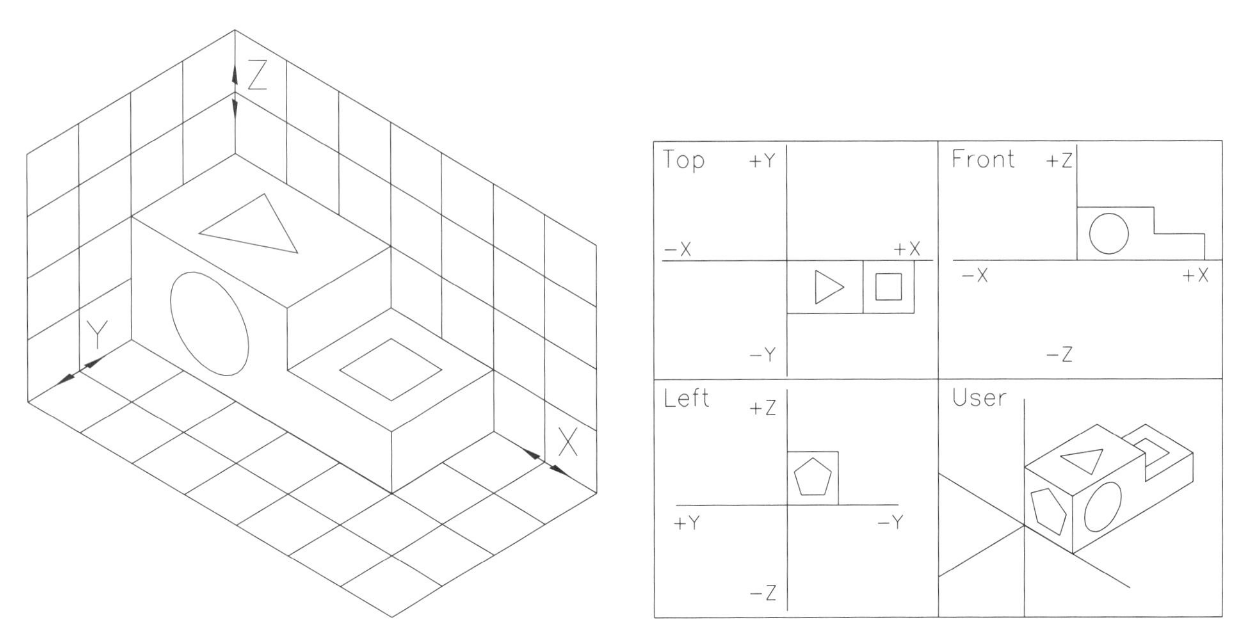


FIGURE 6.1
Construction planes and X, Y, and Z axes.

You can also create your own construction planes by using a Helper Grid. This grid object, similar to a Home Grid plane, can be created any size and oriented in any position. With the use of helper grids, you can create objects on any plane in 3D space. The Helper Grid is explained in Section 6.4.

## 6.3 CREATION BASICS

As we explained in Chapter 4, all creation and manipulation takes place in a scene where you form objects and place them in the desired layout. And as we further explained, there are a variety of objects you can create, from simple boxes and cylinders to compound objects and space warps. All these objects are created using similar techniques and require an understanding of the Creation command panel.

The purpose of this section is to explain those basic techniques so that you may apply them to whatever objects you wish to create.

### Primitives versus Complex Objects

When you activate the Creation command panel, you can see that there are seven basic categories of objects, represented by seven buttons:

Geometric

Shapes

Lights

Cameras

Helpers

Space Warps

Systems

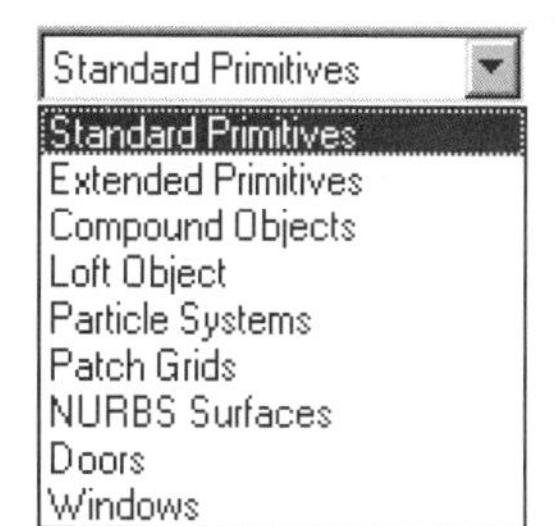


FIGURE 6.2
Standard Primitives object subcategory drop-down.

Under the Geometric category you will find a subcategory drop-down list, from which you can select the type of geometric object you want to create (see Figure 6.2). The following is a list of some of those objects and a brief explanation of their characteristics:

**Standard Primitives**
3D geometric objects such as Box and Cylinder.

**Loft Objects**
Super objects that use shapes along a path to form a 3D object.

**Patch Grids**
2D surfaces.

**Compound Objects**
Complex objects created using Boolean and Morphing operations.

**Particle Systems**
Animated objects to simulate rain, snow, dust, and other small objects.

The details of creating models using these objects are explained in coming chapters.

## Object Type

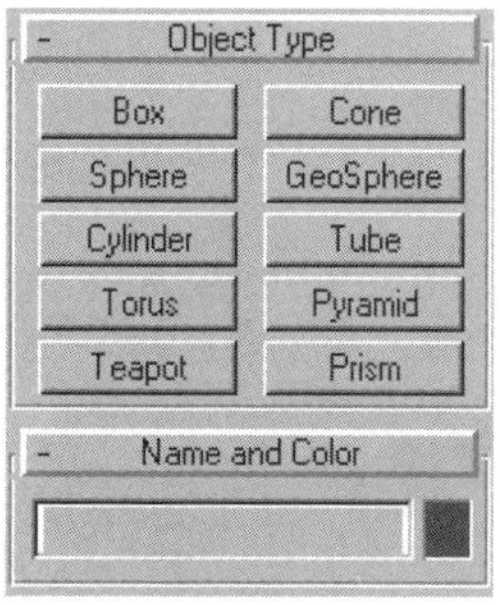

This rollout of the Creation command panel allows you to select the different types of objects that fall under a specific geometric type. Figure 6.3 shows the various possible objects that can be created under the Standard Primitives category. The object type you select from this rollout will control the parameters that will be called for.

FIGURE 6.3
Object type buttons.

## Name and Color

The Name and Color rollout is used to establish an initial color for an object and the object's unique name. Refer to the bottom of Figure 6.3. If you pick on the color box, you will be presented with an Object Color dialog, as shown in Figure 6.4. From this dialog you can choose the color for the object or check the Assign Random Colors box and have the program assign the colors for you.

Depending on the creation procedure, you will often find that you cannot assign an object name until the object has been created in the scene. Once the object has been placed, the box for entering the name becomes accessible. You should enter a name for the object at that point before leaving the command panel or creating another object.

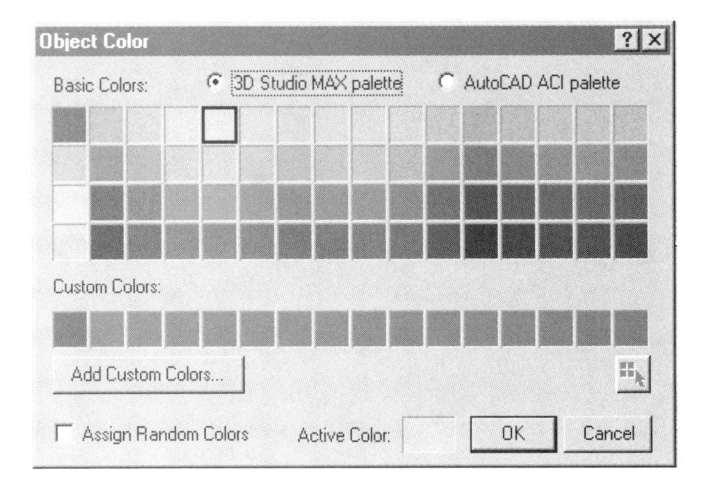


FIGURE 6.4
Object Color dialog.

If you do not enter a name, the program will come up with its own unique name for objects; although this takes the work out of your hands, you will have better control in selecting objects if you assign a name that you will remember later on.

## Creation Method

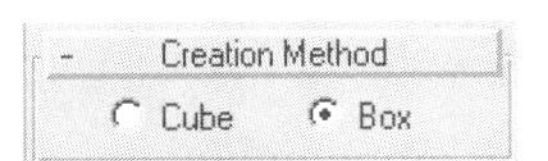


FIGURE 6.5
Creation Method rollout.

The Creation Method rollout, as shown in Figure 6.5, is used to control either the starting point for creation, as in the center or edge, or the definition of a basic shape, as in a cube or box.

## Keyboard Entry

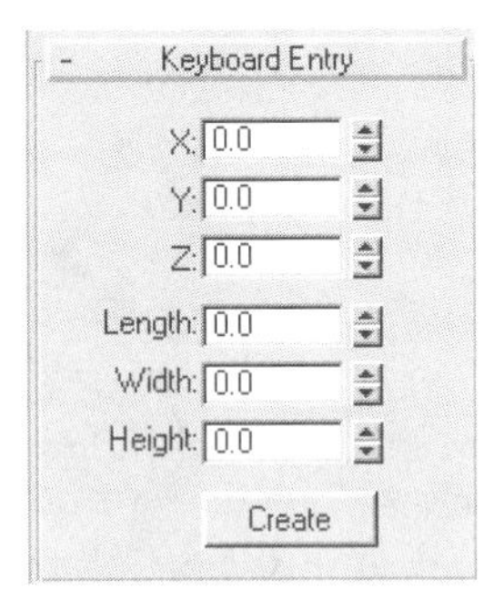


FIGURE 6.6
Keyboard Entry rollout.

The Keyboard Entry rollout allows you to give precise sizes and positions to the objects you create. See Figure 6.6. Most objects will allow you to use keyboard entry, with the exception of the Hedra primitive. The following is a list of some Standard Primitives and their keyboard entry parameters.

| PRIMITIVE | XYZ POINT | PARAMETERS |
|---|---|---|
| Box | Center of Base | Length, Width, Height |
| Sphere | Center | Radius |
| Cylinder | Center of Base | Radius, Height |
| Torus | Center | Radius 1, Radius 2 |

***LIGHTS! CAMERA! ACTION!***

### Assigning Colors

You should try to give different colors to different categories of objects. Remember, color is another tool that may enhance the presentation of an idea or just aid in the ease of construction. However, if you want to have color assigned automatically, check the Assign Random Colors box in the Object Color Dialog. The dialog is shown in Figure 6.4.

| | | |
|---|---|---|
| Tube | Center of Base | Radius 1, Radius 2, Height |
| Cone | Center of Base | Radius 1, Radius 2, Height |
| Teapot | Center of Base | Radius |

Remember, you can use the mouse to pick and drag in a viewport to establish the location and sizes of objects instead of using the keyboard entry method.

### Parameters

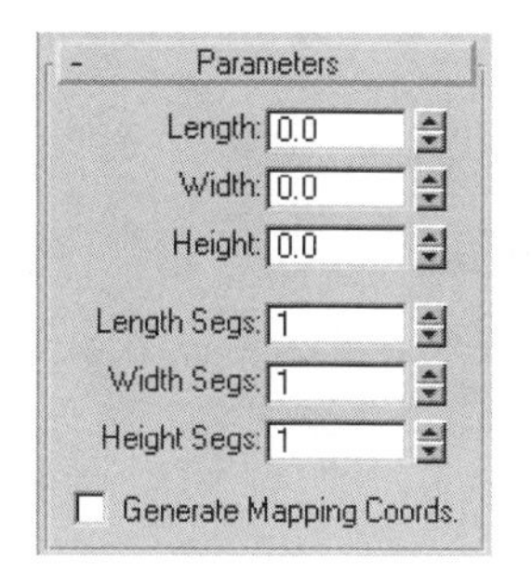


FIGURE 6.7
Parameters rollout.

The Parameters rollout gives a complete set of creation parameters for the specific object you are creating. See Figure 6.7. The list of parameters will change, depending on the complexity of the object. For instance, parameters such as width and height will change automatically and dynamically as you use the mouse to create the object by picking and dragging in a viewport.

#### Slice

The Slice parameter is a special parameter that can be applied to any circular primitive except the sphere. It basically removes a slice of the primitive, much like a slice of pie. You define whether it is on or off, the From point (in degrees), and the To point (in degrees). See Figure 6.8. This parameter, like the others, can even be animated.

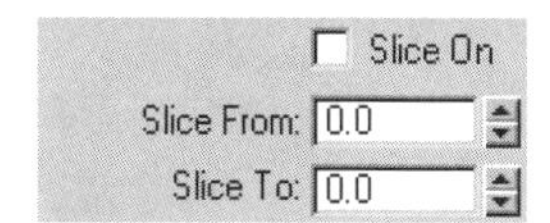


FIGURE 6.8
Slice parameter.

### Applying Mapping Coordinates During Creation

Mapping coordinates are used to tell 3D Studio MAX how to apply mapped materials to an object. Most objects that you create can have mapping coordinates automatically assigned to them. This assignment can be a great time saver. Instead of going through the mapping procedure, the program does it for you. It most cases, you should make sure the Generate Mapping Coordinates box is checked. If you forget to assign mapping coordinates, you can use the Modify command panel to assign them after creation. For more details on mapping coordinates, refer to Section 12.7.

### Facets versus Smoothing

Another parameter that can be assigned to objects with curved portions is the Smooth option. All objects are created with facets, which are the faces that comprise the shape. But often you don't want to see each individual face edge; you want, instead, the transition between edges to appear smooth. This is the purpose of the Smooth option. For most objects, such as cylinders or cones, make sure the Smooth option is checked.

***LIGHTS! CAMERA! ACTION!*** 

Object Parameters

Once an object is created and before you start another, you can make adjustments to the object's parameters. These affect the currently created object.

### Creation Procedure

The following lists the basic procedure for creating an object. This procedure will help you to relate to the various areas of the Creation command panel.

1. Pick the Create tab.
2. Pick the Geometric button.
3. Choose a subcategory from the drop-down list.
4. Pick the object type.
5. Set the object color or use random color assign.
6. Choose the creation method.
7. Adjust the creation parameters, such as Smooth and Mapping.
8. Create the object by using the pick-and-drag method or by using keyboard entry.
9. Fine-tune the creation parameters as necessary. Use navigation controls such as Zoom and Pan while making adjustments.
10. Enter a unique name for the object.
11. Leave the Creation command panel or create another object.

## 6.4 PRECISION TOOLS

There are several tools that you can use to create and edit an object. The following describes their purposes.

### Units

Units are used to establish real-world measurements in the worlds you create. It may be easier to create without worrying about units; however, when it is time to relate your creation to other creations, you will have no common ground without units. It is better to establish working units for every project you do so that you will have a frame of reference.

**LIGHTS! CAMERA! ACTION!** 

#### Creating Objects You Can't See

It is possible to create an object that is so small you cannot see it. This often happens when you are in the Creation command panel and you inadvertently pick and release in one of the viewports. This action automatically creates a very small object at that point and you should delete it by pressing the Delete key. Because it was the last object created, it should be removed. However, if another object is deleted, use the Edit/Undo pull-down menu item to get it back.

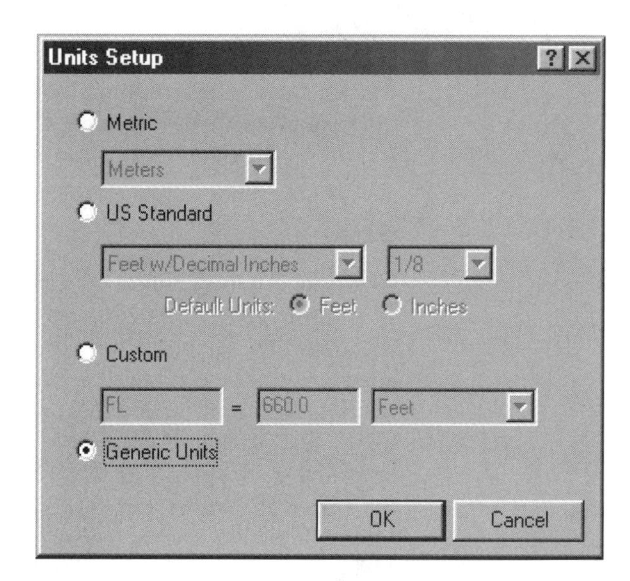


FIGURE 6.9
Units Setup dialog.

Remember that the labs in Chapters 4 and 5 started by setting up the units for the projects. To define the current working units, select the Views/Units Setup, and you will be presented with a dialog box similar to Figure 6.9. Within the dialog you can work in Metric, US standard, or Custom units of measure. The Generic Units are the system units used internally by 3D Studio MAX. One system unit is defined as 1.000 in. You can change this unit value, but is highly recommended that you do not.

## Snap Settings

Snap settings provide a precise method for creating, moving, scaling, and rotating objects. When activated they force the cursor to move at certain intervals or automatically snap to specific objects.

Snaps are accessed in two ways: The first way is to use the snap buttons that lie on the status line; the second is to use the Snap panel of the Grid and Snap Settings. The snap buttons turn on and off certain snap modes, whereas the panel controls the major settings. The snap button must be on (pushed in) for the snap to be active. Figure 6.10 shows the panel; the following text gives the description of the snaps and their settings. The Options panel is used to change the color of the snap markers, the strength, and the snap values for angle and percent.

FIGURE 6.10
Snap and Options Panels

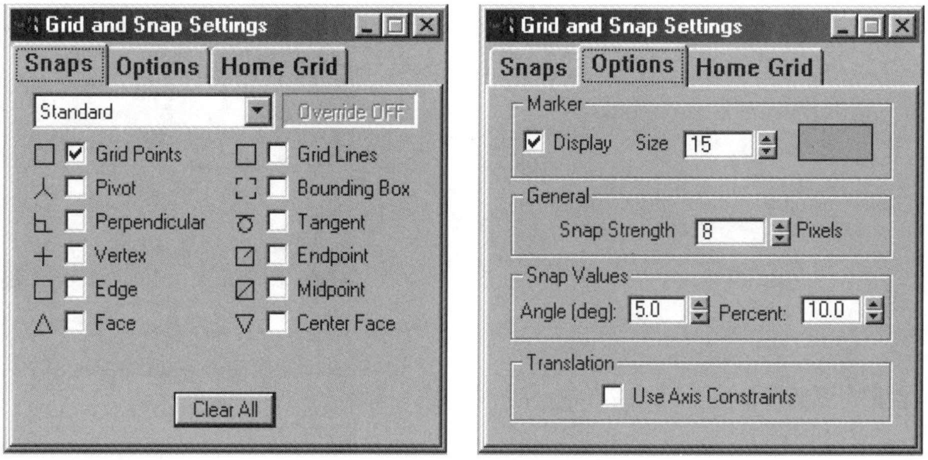

### Snap Strength

The snap strength determines how close the cursor needs to be to a snap point before the snap takes place. The larger the value, the greater the distance between the object and the cursor can be and yet still allow a snap to take place.

## Grids

Grids are a two-dimensional array of lines that intersect to form a screen of lines. This screen gives you a visual method of measuring distance and size and also allows you to set the snap settings so that the cursor can snap either to lines or to their intersection. There are two types of grids, the Home Grid and the Helper Grid.

The Home Grid is the program's basic reference system and is tied to world space. The spacing of the Home Grid lines is controlled by the Grid and Snap Settings dialog shown in Figure 6.11. To set the Home Grid, select Grid and Snap Settings from the Views pull-down menu. Here you can set the Grid Spacing and the Major lines. For instance, you could set the Grid Spacing to every inch and the Major lines to every twelfth line to indicate foot markings. Then you can easily see feet for large spaces and also see inches for fine tuning. The Home Grid is described further in Section 4.3.

The Helper Grid is actually an object that you create. You can create this object in any position and move and rotate it into position. It is explained in more detail in the section on Helpers.

There are three spacial interaction buttons or boxes—2D, 2.5D, and 3D. The snap button needs to be *pushed in* on the status line to use the geometry snaps.

**2D**

The cursor will snap only to the active plane, including the grid or objects that lie on the plane.

**2.5D**

The cursor behaves as with 2D but will snap to vertices or edges of the projection of an object. This means the program calculates the projection of the vertex of an object until it touches the plane.

**3D**

The cursor will snap to any geometry in 3D space.

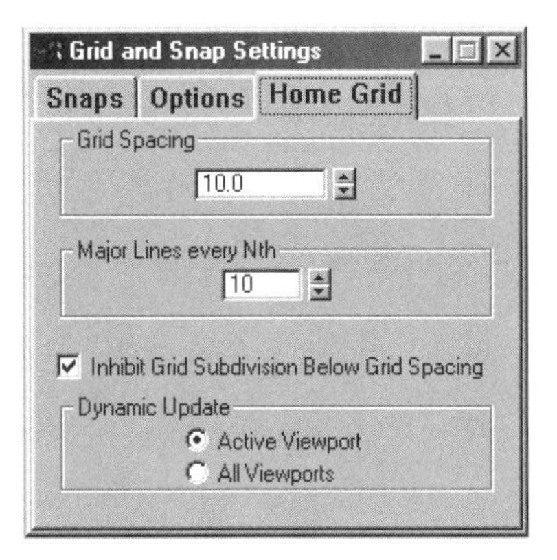


FIGURE 6.11
Home Grid panel.

### Snap Values

This area of the Options panel controls angular snap values and the percent snap increment for scaling. To use these snaps, the appropriate button needs to be on.

Angle Snap

Percent Snap

### Spinner Snap

The Spinner Snap button is used to control the numeric increments for spinner fields. When the button is on, the spinner fields will increase or decrease in increments previously set. To set the spinner increment value, right-click on the Spinner Snap button.

## Helpers

Helpers are objects that assist you in creating your 3D world. There are six different helpers, each with a different role. There are accessed from the Helper button under the Creation command panel.

### Dummy

A Dummy helper object is a wireframe cube with a pivot point at its geometric center. Its main purpose is to be used as a parent object, to which other objects are linked. In this way you can move, rotate, or scale the dummy parent object and the other linked objects will change with it. It is often used for animation. By animating the dummy, you animate the linked objects as well.

### Tape

The Tape helper object provides an on-screen *tape measure* for determining distances. When used, the object has a tape icon on one end of a line and a target at the other. The line represents the measured length. Either end of the tape can be snapped, aligned, or linked to objects in your scene.

You can measure a distance by placing the tape icon at one point and dragging the target to the other and reading the value in the Length field.

To set a distance, check the Specify Length parameter, set the distance, and then create the tape. You can reorient the tape as required.

### Point

The Point helper object is a single point that contains a pivot point. It can be linked to other objects and used as a new pivot-point location. In this way you can have a pivot point anywhere on an object, not just at its creation point. You can adjust the display of the point's axis tripod, changing the lengths of the axis lines for better visibility.

### Grid

The Grid helper object is a 2D object that is used as a custom construction grid. You can create a grid object anywhere in 3D space and adjust the spacing of the grid lines. This type of mobile grid can take the place of the Home Grid that is fixed.

When the grid object is created, it is shown as a rectangle with two intersecting lines in the middle. Its grid spacing isn't seen until the grid is activated.

Once you have created a grid object, it needs to be activated to be used as a construction plane. To do this simply select the grid object (turning it white) and right-click on it. Select the Activate Grid item from the menu, the Home Grid will disappear and the active grid object will change to display the grid spacing you set during its creation.

To reactivate the Home Grid, go through the same procedure, except select the Activate Home Grid item.

Remember, you can use transforms to move and rotate a grid object, but you should not scale a grid object. Using a scale transform will alter the grid spacing you set during creation, making it unreliable. If you must change parameters such as size, use the Modify command panel.

### Protractor

The Protractor helper is used to measure the angle between two objects you select.

### Compass

The Compass helper is used when a sunlight system, an advanced method of animating a sun in a scene, is created. Normally you wouldn't create a stand alone compass.

## 6.5 SUMMARY

Creation takes place on construction planes. You make use of the Home Grid for the six standard orthographic construction planes and use helper grids to create your own custom construction planes. The Creation command panel provides access to seven basic categories of objects, which are further divided into object types. When creating objects, always give the objects unique names and assign different colors to different object categories. To make creation easier and more precise, there are several types of tools, including units, grids, snap settings, and helper objects. This grounding in creation theory and the practice in the next lab will give you the insight to go on to create more complex objects in later chapters.

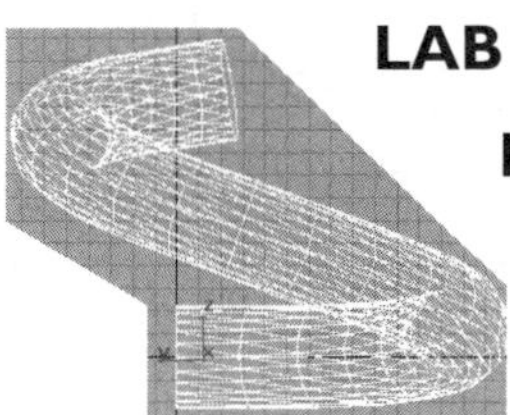

# LAB 6.A

## Basics of Creation

### Purpose

This lab practices the techniques used in the creation of objects in your 3D world. You will learn to effectively create on different construction planes of the Home Grid and create your own construction planes using Helper Grids.

### Objectives

You will be able to

- Set up the units, grid, and snap settings for a project.
- Switch between construction planes.
- Create in positive and negative directions.
- Use the screen and keyboard to enter creation parameters.
- Snap to grid intersections.
- Create custom construction planes using a Helper Grid object.

### Procedure

#### SETTING UP THE PROJECT

With any project you need to establish some starting settings. These settings are usually standard for any project, and you should become familiar with checking them before you start any creation.

1. First, select the Reset command from the File pull-down menu. This ensures that there are no active settings from a previous session. Then, establish the units in which you intend to work. Select Units Setup from the Views pull-down menu. You will be presented with a dialog similar to Figure 6.12. Modify the settings to match the figure. You are going to work in decimal units.

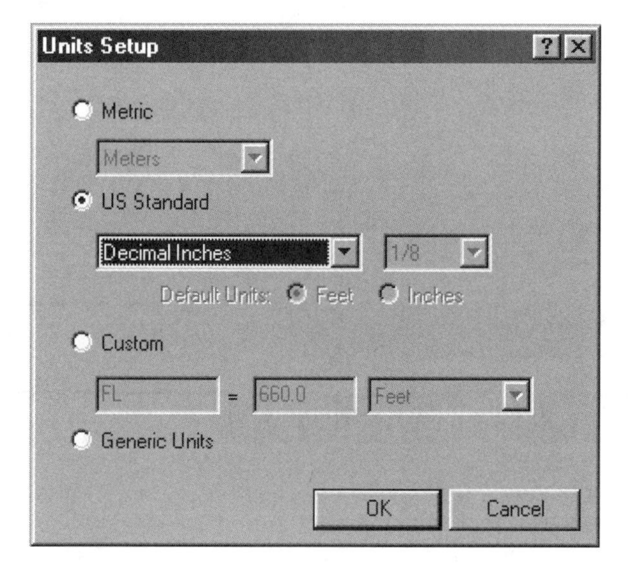


FIGURE 6.12
Units Setup dialog.

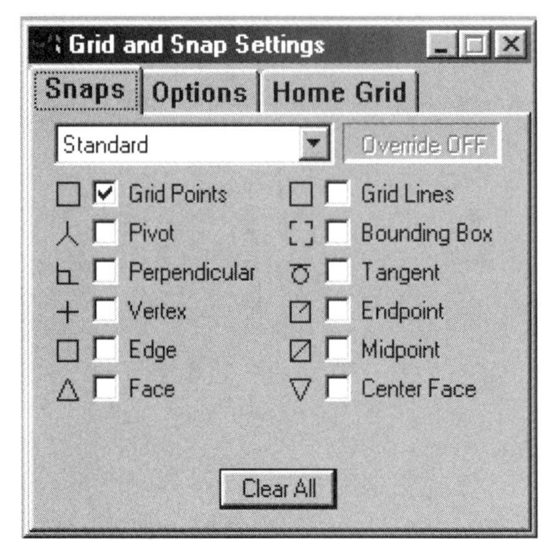


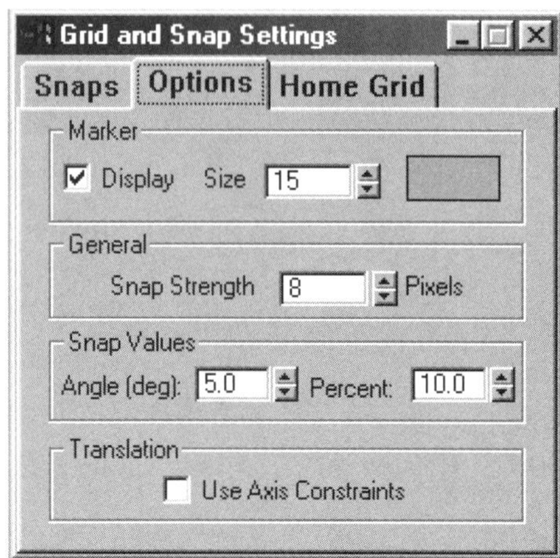


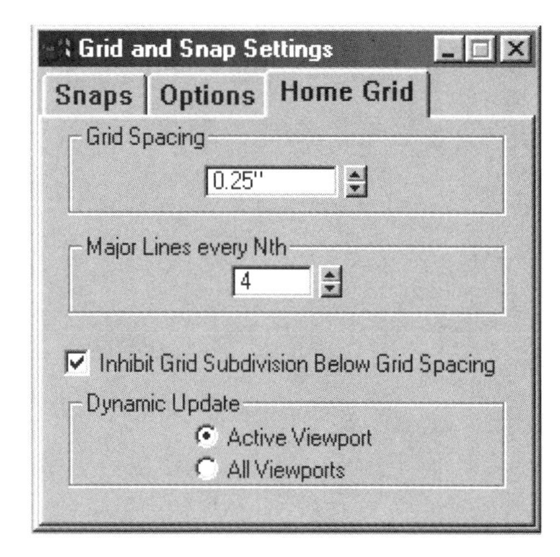


FIGURE 6.13
Snap, Options, and Home Grid dialogs.

2. Establish an initial grid and initial snap settings. These will control the display of grid guidelines and the cursor movement on the screen. Select the Grid and Snap Settings from the Views pull-down menu. You are going to set the grid to 1/4 of an inch and set the snap to grid intersection only.

   Figure 6.13 shows the settings for the Home Grid and the Snap. Match your dialogs to the figures. When the snap is set to grid intersection, you don't have to be exact when you are picking coordinates. As long as you are close to the intersection point of two grid lines, the cursor will snap to that point when you pick.

3. Check the state of various icon buttons. Activate the TOP viewport. Figure 6.14 shows the state of the Toolbar buttons and the Prompt line buttons. Match your buttons to the figures.

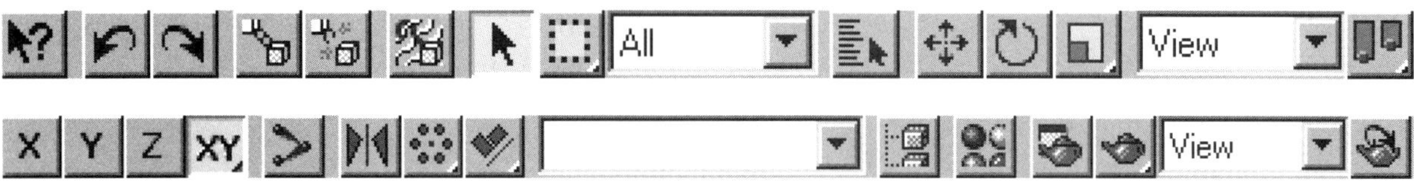

FIGURE 6.14
Toolbar and Prompt line buttons.

The following should be the current states of the Prompt line buttons:

| BUTTON | STATE | PURPOSE |
|---|---|---|
| Region Selection | Window Selection | Limits selection of objects totally contained within a window. |
| 2D Snap | ON | Limits cursor movement to 2D. |
| Angle Snap | ON | Limits angular movement to set intervals. |

4. Establish the display state of the various viewports. Activate the viewport and right-click on the viewport label.

| VIEWPORT | DISPLAY STATE |
|---|---|
| Top | Wire-Frame (default) |
| Front | Wire-Frame (default) |
| Left | Wire-Frame (default) |
| Perspective | Wire-Frame |

5. Right-click on the Left viewport to activate it and right-click on its label. Turn off Show Grid so that the Home Grid is not shown in that viewport.

   Remember to use the Hold button before you perform any command you are unsure of. If something does not work, you can always use the Fetch button to restore the geometry to its pre-Hold state.

## CREATING A 3D WORKING ENVELOPE

6. You are going to create a three-dimensional envelope that will represent your working envelope. It is used to give you an idea of the size of the space in which you are working. It can be used to keep track of the objects you create and to ensure they are created inside the working 3D envelope.

   Open the Create command panel and the geometric section. Ensure that the drop-down box displays Standard Primitives. Activate the Top viewport.

7. From the Creation panel pick the Box object type. You are going to use the keyboard entry to create a box that will represent the 3D envelope. Open the Keyboard rollout and enter the following values:

   X: 0  Y: 0  Z: 0
   Length: 12  Width: 12  Height: 12

   Select the create button, and a small box should be created on the screen. This box represents the 12 in. cube that will be your 3D Working Envelope. Be sure to change the object name to 3DENV and set the object color before you move on. Use dark blue as the object color.

8. Use the Zoom Extents All button to fill the viewports with the 3DENV object.

9. You are going to change the display of the cube so that you can see all its edges, even the rear ones. This will give you a better feel for the three-dimensional space.

   Open the Display command panel and make sure the cube has been selected (turned white). Turn off Backface Cull. This will let you see all the edges of the 3D Working Envelope. Your screen should look similar to Figure 6.15.

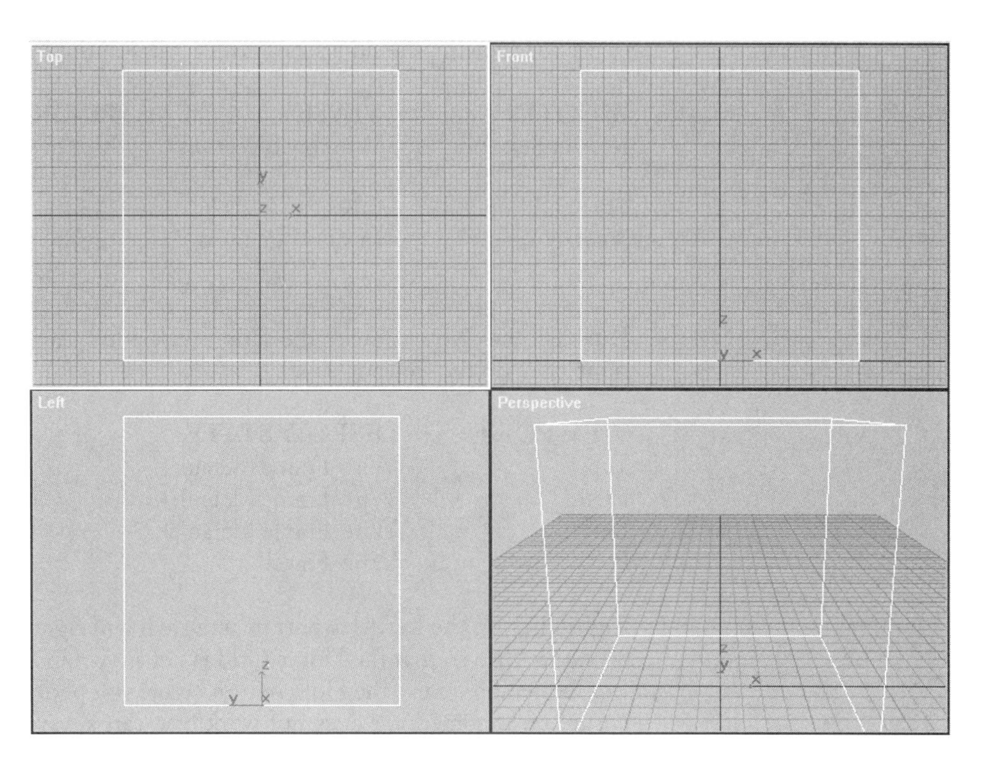


FIGURE 6.15
3D Working Envelope.

## CREATING ON CONSTRUCTION PLANES

10. You are going to create several objects on the different construction planes of the Home Grid in positive and negative directions.

    Make sure the Top viewport is active and open the Creation command panel. Select the Box object type button.

11. This time you are going to use the click-and-drag method to create a box that will be used as a platform. Move the cursor into the Top viewport and place it close to the coordinates -4,-4,0 (read on the status line). Click, hold, and drag the cursor toward the upper right until the coordinates read close to 4,4,0; release the button.

    Now slowly drag the cursor downward and watch the parameters in the creation panel. The Height value will change as you drag the cursor. It should be negative. If it is not, drag the cursor down some more until it is. Look at the viewports. Observe how the new box height is going down below the bottom of the 3D working envelope.

    Now drag the cursor upward until the Height value reads +2 and then press the pick button on the mouse. The height is now fixed at 2.

    *Note*: When you are using the Click and Drag option to place coordinate locations, the cursor will automatically snap to the grid intersections upon picking a location. This is because you set and activated that particular snap in step 1. This way, you just have to be near the intersection point when you pick.

    Change the name of the box to PLATFORM and its color to green. Refer to Figure 6.16, showing PLATFORM. You have created an 8-in.-square by 2-in.-high platform.

12. You are now going to create a plate object that is on its edge on the platform.

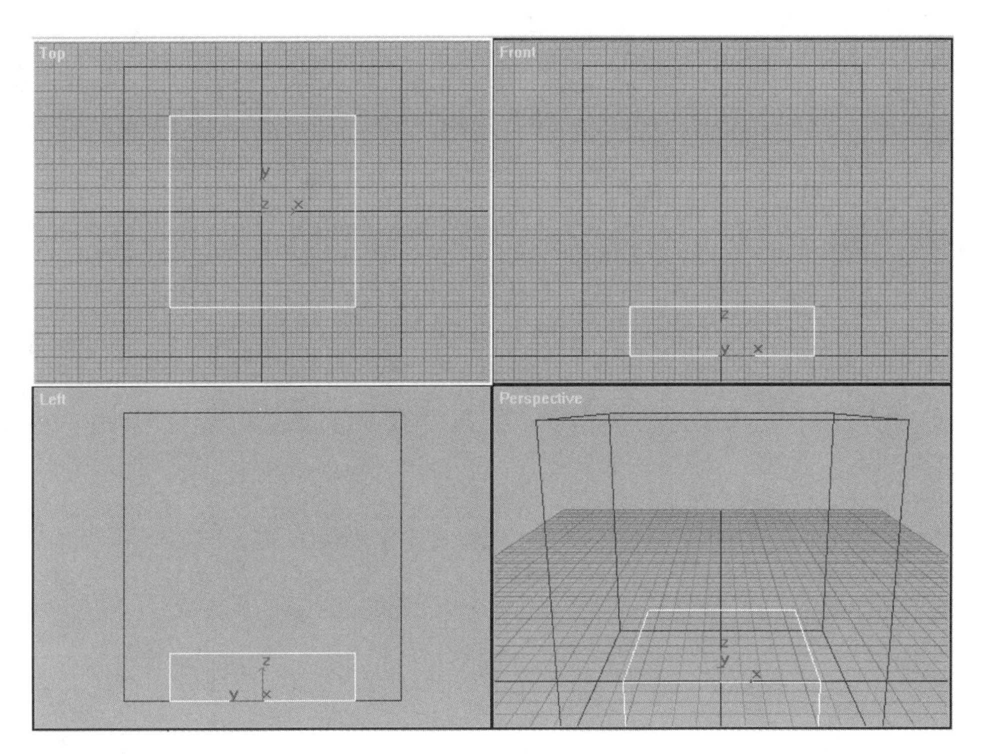


FIGURE 6.16
PLATFORM.

Activate the Front viewport and then select the Cylinder button on the Creation panel. In the Parameters section, set the number of sides to 24 and make sure Smooth is on.

Use the Click and Drag option, move the cursor close to 0,0,5, and pick, hold, and drag the cursor until the radius in the parameters box reads close to 3; release the button. Now, slowly drag the cursor downward until the height parameter reads -1; pick that location. Change the object name to PLATE and the color to light blue (cyan).

13. Refer to each of your viewports and Figure 6.17. Observe where the plate was created. By using the Front viewport, the creation of the cylinder took place in the X and Z world space axes, and its height was in the Y world space axis. You can see by switching viewports that you are switching to different construction planes on the Home Grid. The Home Grid's planes are tied to the world space planes.

14. Now you are going to attempt to create a teapot object that sits upright on top of the platform using the Click and Drag method.

    Activate the Top viewport and select the Teapot object type button. Move the cursor close to -2,-2,0 in the Top viewport. Click, hold, and drag in the Top viewport. Observe where the teapot is being created. Drag until the radius is 1.25 and release the button. Notice that the teapot was created at the bottom of the platform, because that is where the construction plane of the Home Grid is located. Figure 6.18 shows that the teapot is not on top of the platform.

15. Delete the teapot.

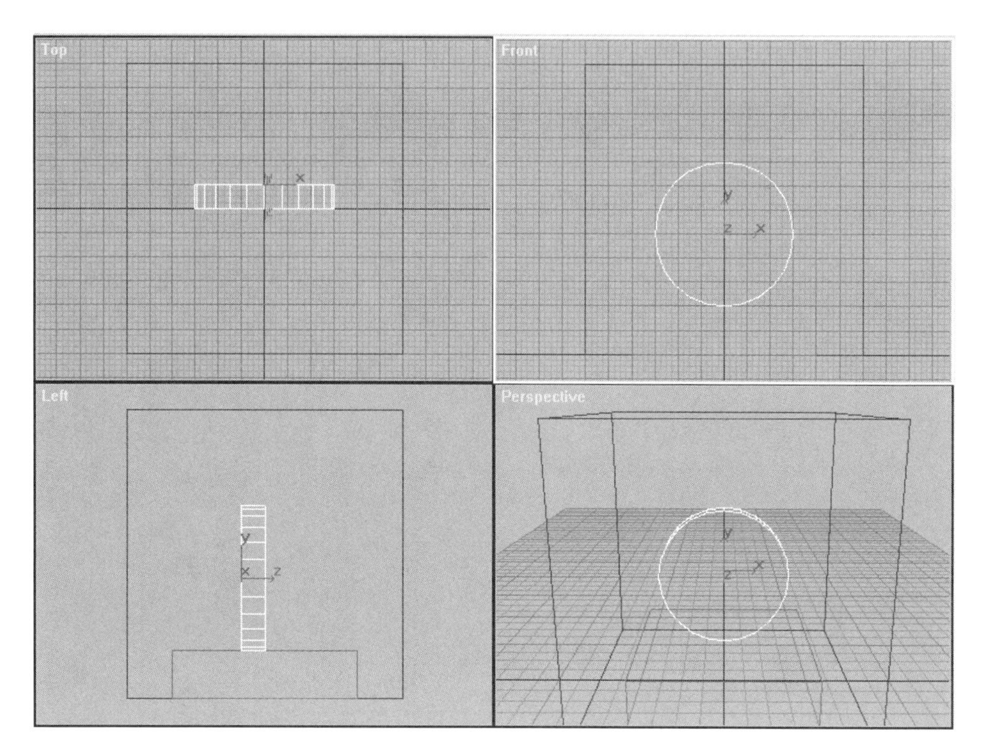


FIGURE 6.17
Addition of upright plate.

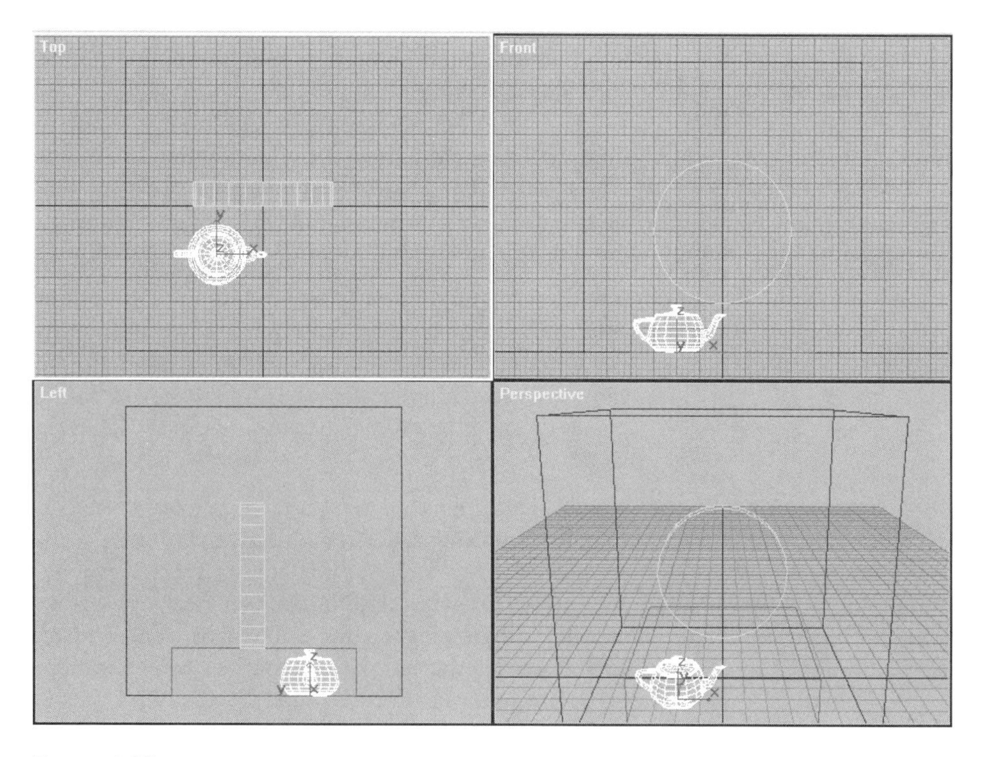


FIGURE 6.18
Teapot sitting at bottom of platform.

## CREATING A CUSTOM CONSTRUCTION PLANE

16. Activate the Top viewport and select the Helper object category. From the types of helper objects, select the Grid button.

    Move the cursor close to -4,-4,0 in the Top viewport; click, hold, and drag until the coordinates are close to 0,0,0; release the button. Change the object name to TOP-PLANE and set its color to yellow. Set the Grid Spacing to 0.5.

    Like the teapot, the helper grid object was created at the bottom of the platform. You are going to move it upward.

17. The Helper Grid should have been automatically selected after creation. If it is not, use the Select Object button to select it.

18. Once the Helper Grid has been selected, Lock it.

19. Activate the Front viewport and use Region Zoom to display a closeup view of the corner of the platform, as shown in Figure 6.19. Select the Move transform and move the cursor to the left bottom corner of the platform, where the edge of the help grid is located. Click and drag the grid upward until it is in line with the top of the platform. It should look similar to Figure 6.20.

20. Turn off Lock and Zoom Extents in the Front viewport.

## CREATION ON A CUSTOM CONSTRUCTION PLANE

21. To use a Helper Grid object you must activate the Top viewport. Select the grid and right-click on it. From the menu, select Activate Grid. The screen should look similar to Figure 6.21. The grid spacing of 0.5 can now be seen.

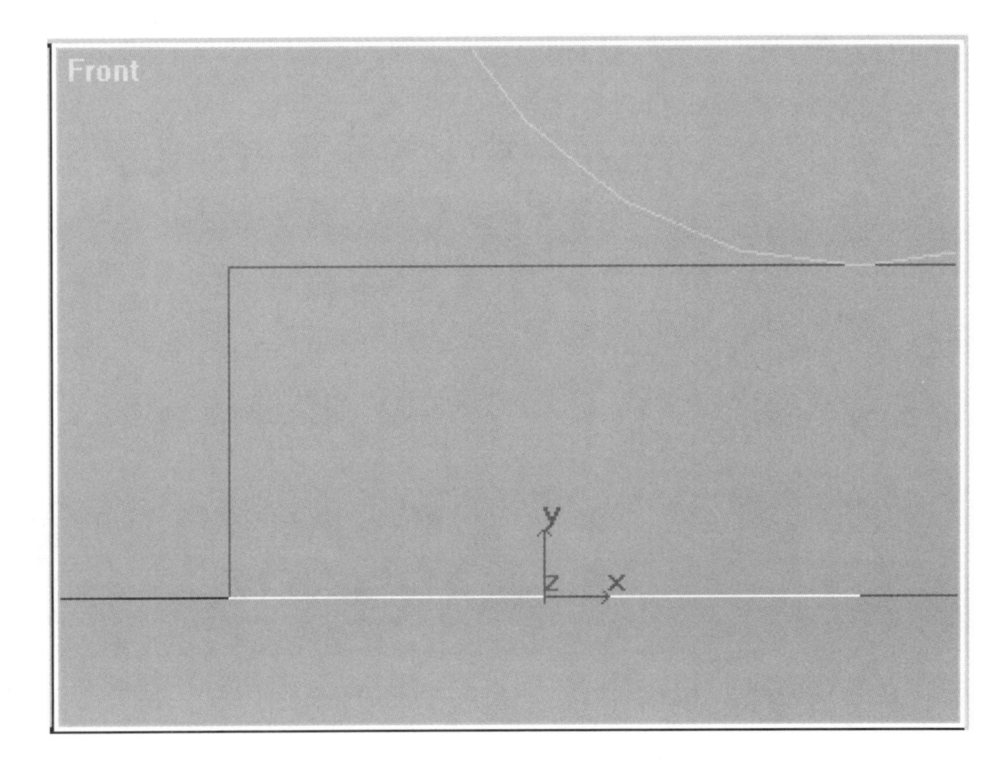


FIGURE 6.19
Closeup of the platform (with grid turned off for clarity).

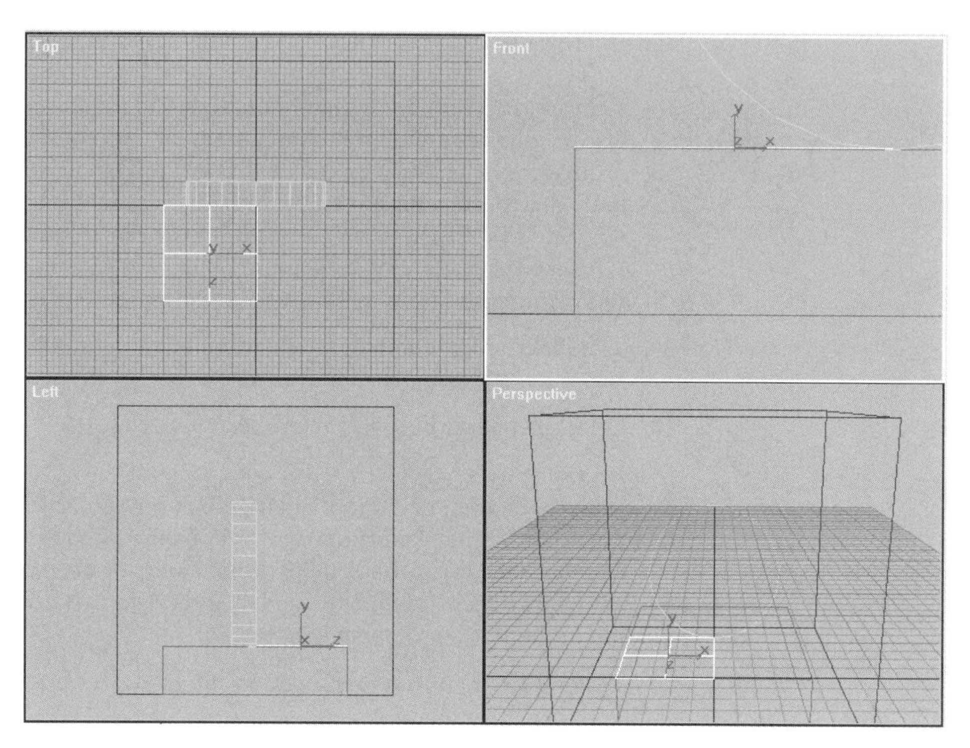


FIGURE 6.20
Helper Grid moved to the top of the platform (grid turned off in the Front viewport for clarity).

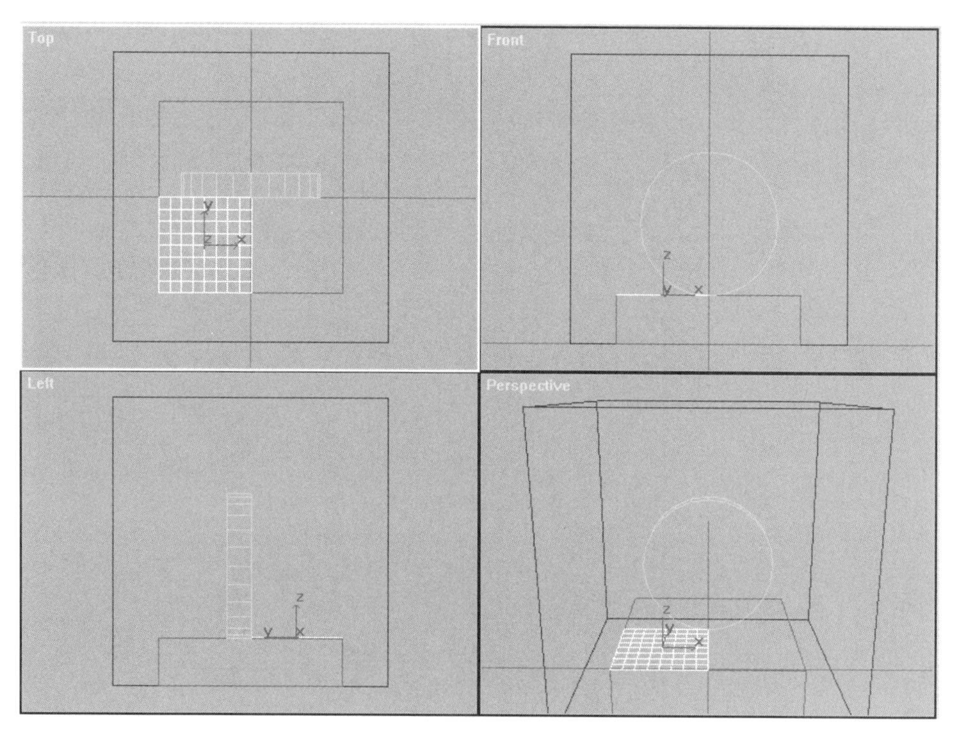


FIGURE 6.21
Activated Helper Grid object.

22. Activate the Top viewport, open the Creation command panel, and select the Geometry category. Pick the Teapot button.

    Move the cursor to the center of the Helper Grid, approximately -2,-2,0. Click, hold, and drag until the parameter radius is 1.5; release the button. Change the name of the object to POT and its color to red.

    Refer to your screen and Figure 6.22. The teapot has now been created on the level of the Helper Grid object. While the grid is active, all creation will take place on that level.
23. Activate the Home Grid by selecting the helper grid, right-clicking on it, and selecting Activate Home Grid. The Helper Grid should turn back to its original display and the Home Grid should appear.
24. Save the scene file as CH6A.

## WHY YOU MIGHT HIDE AN OBJECT

25. Activate the perspective viewport and use the Render Scene button. Render the scene at 640 × 480 for a quick render. All you should be able to see is the 3D working envelope.
26. Now you are going to hide the 3DENV object. Select it and open the Display command panel. From the panel pick the Hide Selected button, and the box should disappear.
27. Now re-render the scene using the Quick Render button. The 3DENV is gone and you can see the other objects. This is why you might want to hide objects from time to time—to stop them from obstructing a scene.
28. With the Display panel still open, use the UnHide All button, and the box should reappear in the viewports. Re-render if you wish to double check.

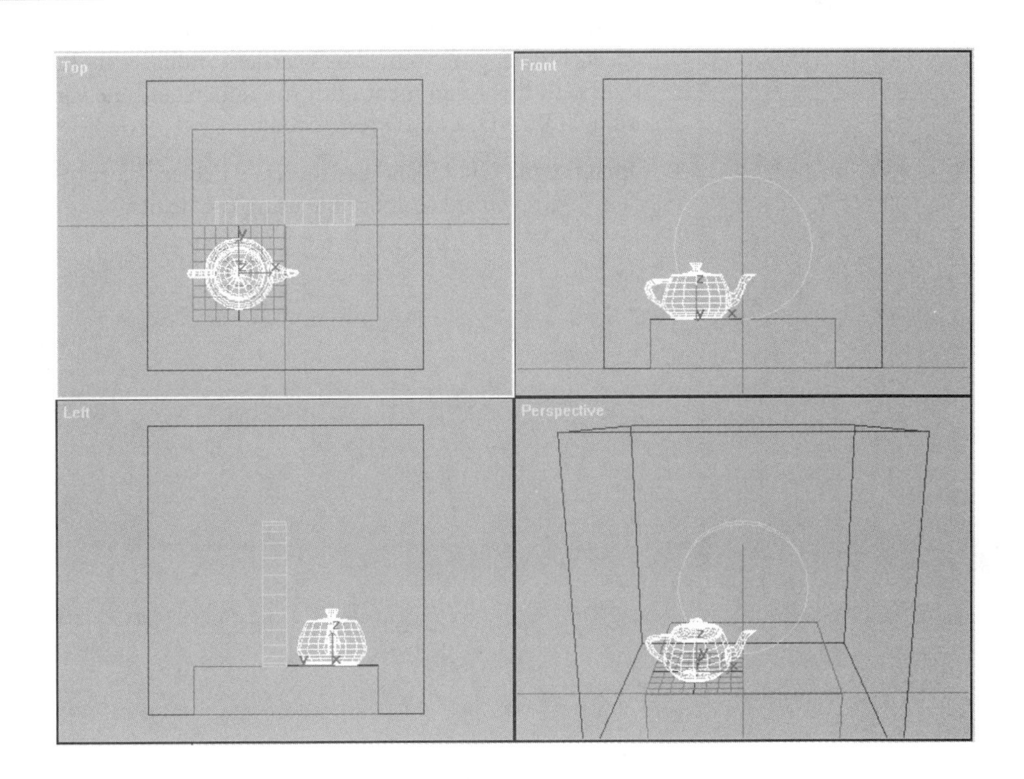


**FIGURE 6.22**
Teapot created on Helper Grid construction plane.

## QUESTIONS AND ASSIGNMENTS

### ? QUESTIONS

1. What function does the Home Grid serve?
2. List the seven basic categories of objects that can be created.
3. Why is it important to assign your own name to objects?
4. Explain *keyboard entry*.
5. What is the function of the Slice parameter?
6. What is the purpose of units?
7. What are the two types of grids?
8. Explain the purpose of snaps and their settings.
9. List and explain the six helper objects.

### ASSIGNMENTS

1. To demonstrate the positive and negative areas of all three axes, create eight different colored spheres that lie in the eight different areas of the Home Grid:

   +Z,+X,+Y +Z,–X,–Y +Z,+X,–Y +Z,–X,+Y<br>
   –Z,+X,+Y –Z,–X,–Y –Z,+X,–Y –Z,–X,+Y

2. Experiment with the keyboard entry to create the seven primitive objects: box, sphere, cylinder, torus, tube, cone, and teapot. Create them all in one file, with different colors, and assign unique names.
3. Experiment with the snap priority by creating a box and trying to create other objects by snapping to the box's vertices and faces in 2D, 2.5D, and 3D. Continue with this assignment until you understand the various snaps and the effect of the 2D, 2.5D, and 3D restrictions.
4. Open the file CH4A and use the Tape helper object to check various measurements until you are comfortable using the helper.

# Basics of Editing

## 7.1 INTRODUCTION

In this chapter you learn the basics of editing the objects in your 3D world, including the various methods for selecting and combining objects. The techniques used in transformations and modifications are reviewed and, once you are familiar with these editing tools, you will have a firm grounding to continue to create and edit more complex worlds.

## 7.2 SELECTION BASICS

To edit an object, whether you are transforming it to a new location or modifying its parameters, you need to be able to select it. Regardless of the procedure used to select the object, you will know the object has been selected because the object or its bounding box turns white. As well, you can select more than one object to edit by using selection tools such as window selection or selecting by name. Selecting more that one object is usually referred to as defining a selection set. The next section explains the various methods used to select objects.

### Selecting Objects

There are several buttons that can be used to select objects. The most obvious is the Select Object button. The other buttons that can select objects are the transform buttons; however, they serve a dual function of both selecting and transforming and are explained in Section 7.4.

### Single Objects

Once the Select Object button has been activated, move your cursor over an object (the cursor will change to a thick, stubby cross) and pick it to select it, turning it

**LIGHTS! CAMERA! ACTION!** 

**Frozen Objects**

If an object is frozen, you will not be able to select it.

white. If you try to pick another object or pick an empty portion of a viewport, the first selection will be de-selected.

### Multiple-Single Selection

If you want to keep the first object while selecting another, hold down the Ctrl key while picking. It will add or remove objects from the selection set. You can also use the Alt key to remove objects from the selection set.

### Multiple-Region Selection

To select several objects at once, use the Region-Selection option. Activate the Select Object button, pick and hold in open space, drag the cursor to form a window around the objects to be selected, and release the button. All the objects will be added to the selection set. Hold down the Ctrl key while making a window to add objects to the current selection set. There are two suboptions to this mode, which are controlled by the Region-Selection button at the bottom of the screen. If the button is convex, then the crossing option is active. If the button is concave, then the window option is active.

The Crossing option selects objects that are within the region and crossing the boundaries of the region.

The Window option selects only objects that lie within the region.

You can also control the shape of the region window with the use of buttons that lie at the top of the screen. The following are the buttons and their functions. Note that these buttons are flyouts connected to each other.

The Rectangular region option forms a region with a rectangular shape.

The Circular region option forms a region with a circular shape.

The Fence Region option allows you to create an irregular region by picking points to form the boundary shape.

### Locking a Selection

You can lock a selection set with the Lock Selection Set button at the bottom of the screen. This can be useful when you want to make sure that a single object or group of objects stays selected while you perform a function.

### Selection Filter

When you have many different types of objects making up your scene, it can be difficult to select the object you desire. The Selection Filter drop-down list that lies at the top of the screen allows you to choose the type of objects to be included in the selection set. Once this filter has been set, only the type of object with the defined characteristics will be able to be selected.

### Select by Name

It is often simpler to select objects by their names instead of by trying to pick each one. To pick from a list of named objects, select the Select by Name button or select the Edit/Select By/Name pull-down menu item. You will be presented with a dialog similar to Figure 7.1. Highlight the name of the object to select and then pick the Select button at the bottom of the dialog. Use the Ctrl or Shift keys to highlight several names.

### Named Selection Sets Drop-down

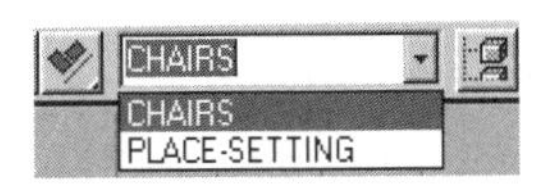


You can assign names to a selection set for later retrieval. To do this, create a selection set and then add the name to the Named Selection field in the toolbar. It lies between the Align and Track View buttons and starts out empty. Once a name has been added to the list, you can highlight it any time you want to reselect the objects contained within a previously named selection set. Remember to press Enter to lock the name in the list when entering a new name. If you want to remove a name from the list, highlight it and then select the Edit/Remove Named Selections pull-down menu item.

### Select by Color

By assigning specific colors to different categories of objects, you can easily select all of them for editing with the Select By Color command. This command can be found in the Edit/Select By pull-down menu. When activated, the cursor will change to

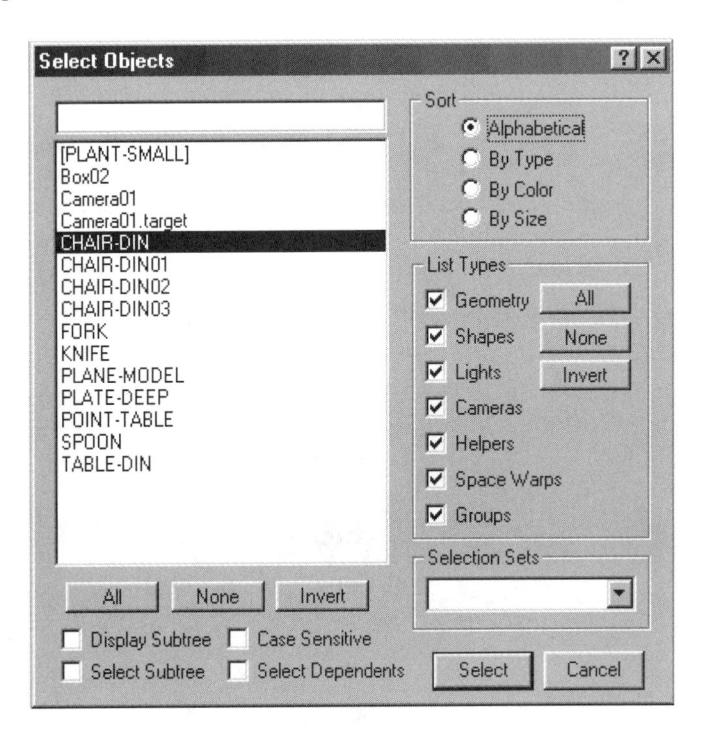


FIGURE 7.1
Select Objects dialog.

display the color-select mode. You need only pick on an object of the desired color and all the objects of that color will be selected.

### Edit Menu

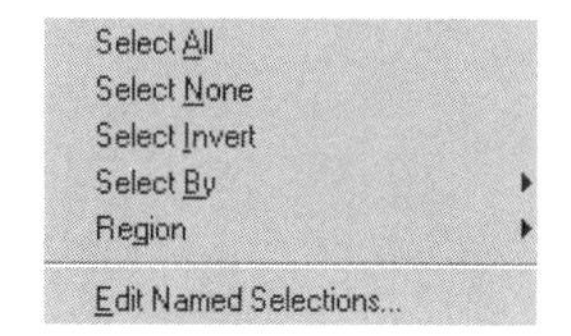


Refer to the Edit pull-down menu for a list of the various selection modes.

## 7.3 COMBINING OBJECTS

There will be times when you want to combine several objects in order that they be treated as a single object. There are two methods of doing this, grouping and attaching.

### Groups

Grouping lets you combine two or more objects into a single grouped object. The grouped object is given a unique name and can be treated as a standard object. In this way you can modify or transform a whole group of objects. Also, you can modify individual objects in the group by temporarily opening the group.

#### Defining a Group

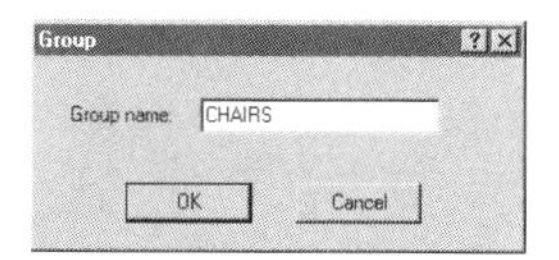


FIGURE 7.2
Group dialog.

To define a group of objects, select the objects and then choose the Group/Group pull-down menu item. You will be presented with the Group dialog, as shown in Figure 7.2, within which you enter a unique name for the group. From then on, when you select one object from the group, all the objects in the group are selected and acted upon.

#### Opening a Group

To edit a single object in the group, you can temporarily open the group for individual access. To do this, select the group and choose the Group/Open pull-down menu item. A pink dummy object appears, and the objects within the group are now accessible. Once you are done, use the Group/Close pull-down menu item to re-form the group.

#### Dissolving a Group

If you want to remove the objects permanently from a group, select the group and then either choose the Group/Ungroup pull-down menu item to dissolve one level in a nested group or select the Group/Explode pull-down menu item to dissolve all the nested groups.

### Attached Objects

To attach objects to each other, you need to use the Modify command panel. The following is the procedure:

1. Open the Modify command panel.
2. Select the parent object.

3. Apply an Edit Mesh to the parent object.
4. Turn off the Sub-Object selection button.
5. Pick the Attach button on the Edit Object rollout and pick on an object you want to join to the parent. Both will appear white, with the second joined to the first.

When you attach one object to another, it is a permanent part of the first object. You can detach parts of the objects, but it can be difficult to remove an entire object. So use the attach modifier with caution. It can be less troublesome to use a group instead.

## 7.4 TRANSFORMING AND CLONING

Transforming is the adjustment of an object's position, orientation, or size, whereas cloning is the act of duplicating an object. This duplication may occur during the act of transforming an object.

There are three transform buttons, Move, Rotate, and Scale, and each has the dual function of selecting objects prior to transforming them. However, because the previous text dealt with *selection*, only the transform aspects of the command are explained next.

### Move

The Move transform is used to reposition objects in the 3D world. You can preselect objects using the Select Object tool or use the Move tool to select the object. Once the object has been selected, you drag the object into its new position. There are some factors that can limit movement, such as the viewport axes, the transform coordinate system, and the axis constraints. Because these factors control all the transforms, they are explained following the descriptions of the three transforms.

### Rotate

The Rotate transform is used to change the rotation or orientation of objects in the 3D world. The plane in which the rotation takes place is controlled by the active viewport and any axis constraints you may have active. The pivot point used in the rotation is set by the transform center, explained later in this section. To control the degree of rotation, set the angle snap value by right-clicking on the Angle Snap button on the status line at the bottom of the screen. Don't forget to turn the Angle Snap button on.

### Scale

The Scale transform is used to change the size of objects by percentage. A value under 100% reduces the size of an object, whereas a value over 100% increases the

**LIGHTS! CAMERA! ACTION!**

**Transform Will Not Work**

If you find that a transform will not work, such as when you cannot move an object, check to see what axis constraints are in effect. These constraints will limit transforms along specific axes.

size. To control the percentage of scaling, set the percent value by right-clicking on the percent snap on the status line. Don't forget to turn the Percent Snap button on. There are three forms of scale contained in the scale flyout. The following is a description of each.

**Uniform scale**
This option is used to scale the objects equally in all three axes. The center of the scale is determined by the Transform Center tool, which is explained later.

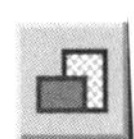

**Nonuniform scale**
This option is used to scale the object differently along the three axes. The scaling is controlled by the axis constraints. The Transform Coordinate system controls the direction of scaling and the Transform Center tool determines the center from which scaling takes place.

**Squash**
This option is used to scale along one axis and in the opposite direction in the other axis. The Axis Constraint tool controls the axis of the scale and is explained later.

## Transform Type-In

There is a command for typing in values for the three transforms, which is called the Transform Type-In. It is accessed from the Edit menu. To use it, you select the objects, pick the desired transform, and then select Transform Type-In from the Tools pull-down menu. A dialog for the particular transform will appear. You can then type in the various values for the transforms. Figure 7.3 shows the three dialogs for the three transforms. The absolute fields show the current location, rotation, or scale of the selected objects. You can change any of these absolute values or you can enter offset values. The offset value will be added to the current absolute value to arrive at a new absolute value.

## Viewport Axes

Remember that the viewport you select to perform a transform has its own set of two axes. These axes can affect and limit the direction of any transform.

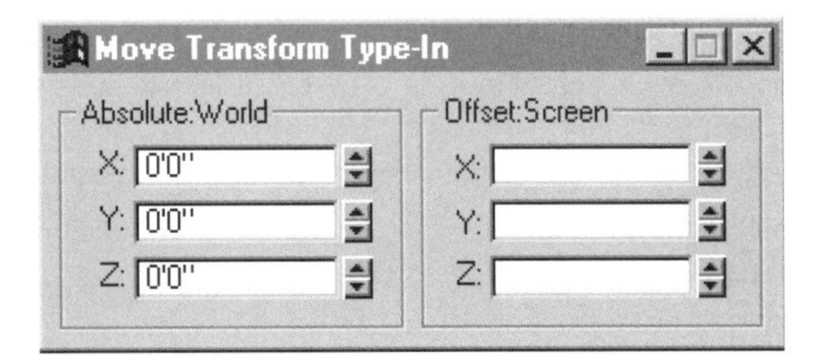


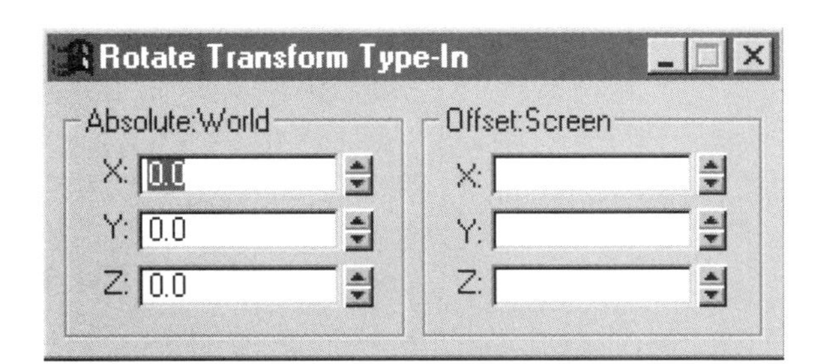


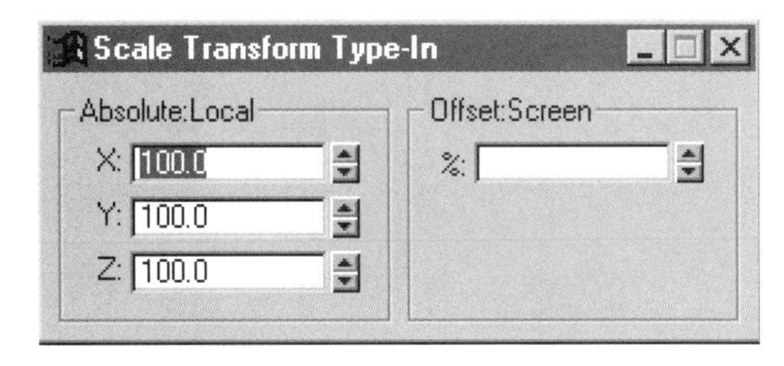


FIGURE 7.3
Transform Type-In for Move, Rotate, and Scale.

## Transform Coordinate System

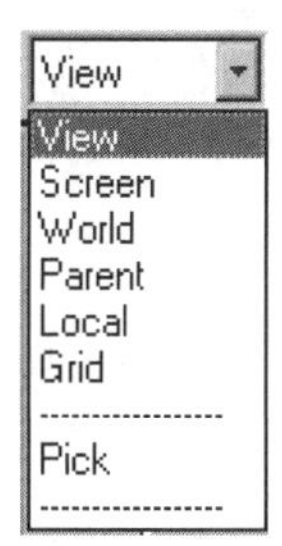


You can set the type of coordinate system to be used when a transform is to take place. By default it is usually set to View, so that the axes match the active viewport. The following is a description of the possible coordinate systems:

**View**
A hybrid of the World and Screen coordinate systems. If you activate an orthographic viewport, the Screen coordinate system is used. If you activate a user, perspective, or camera viewport, the World coordinate system is used.

**Screen**
Uses the active viewport screen as the coordinate system. The X axis runs horizontally, and the Y axis runs vertically. The Z axis is depth and the positive direction is toward the viewer (you).

**World**
Uses the World coordinate system, whose axes never change orientation. Viewing the model from the top shows the X axis running from left to right (horizontal), the Y axis running from top to bottom (vertical), and the Z axis providing depth, with the positive axis toward the viewer.

**Parent**
Uses the coordinate system of the parent of the selected object.

**Local**
Uses the coordinate system of the selected object.

**Pick**
Uses the coordinate system of another object in the scene.

**Grid**
Uses the coordinate system of the active grid, which may be the Home Grid or a Helper Grid object.

## Transform Axis Constraints

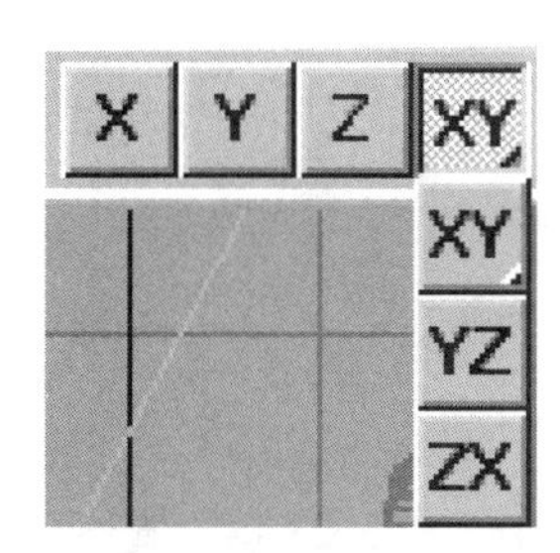


The axis-constraint tools are used to limit the transforms to specified axes. The tool button that is visible is the form of constraint. You can constrain the axis to XY, YZ, or ZX or a single axis, such as: X, Y, or Z, using the single-axis tool.

For instance, if you pick the YZ tool and use the Move transform, the movement is limited to the Y and Z axes. If you then pick the single Y tool button, then movement is constrained (limited) to the Y axis.

## Transform Center

When performing transforms such as scale and rotation, there is a pivot point used for the transform. It is referred to as the *transform center*. You can select different locations for this center. The tools are contained in a flyout in the toolbar and are described next. The tool button that is visible at the time of the transform is the active tool.

**Pivot point**
Transforms occur about the center of the object's pivot point.

**Selection center**
Transforms occur about the center of a bounding box surrounding the current selection set.

**Transform coordinate center**
Transforms occur about the center of the active transform coordinate system.

## Transform Cloning

If you hold down on the Shift key while performing a transform, a clone is created, leaving the original in its previous form.

### Array Cloning

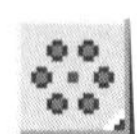

Array cloning is used to create precise clones in a linear or circular pattern. The array is relative to the current viewport settings for the coordinate system and transform center. The following is the basic procedure for creating an array.

1. Select the object or objects to be arrayed.
2. Choose the coordinate system and transform center.
3. Pick the Array tool button.
4. Set the array parameters in the dialog and pick the OK button to create the array.

**Linear array**

To create a linear array, reset the dialog settings and enter a value in only one axis (positive or negative). The value is the distance moved between objects. The center of the array is controlled by the transform center. Figure 7.4 shows the original object, the dialog settings, and the outcome.

FIGURE 7.4
Linear array.

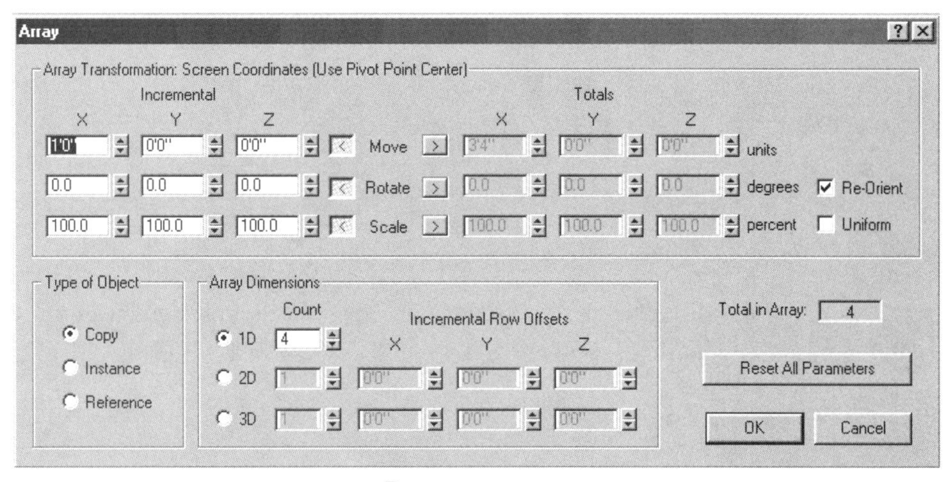


DIALOG SETTINGS

ORIGINAL OBJECT

OUTCOME

**Circular array**

To create a circular array, reset the dialog settings and enter a value in the axis about which you want to rotate. The value is the angle rotated between the objects around the transform center. If you use the transform coordinate center, you can use the transform coordinate system to pick a point object as the pivot point. This is illustrated in the lab at the end of this chapter. Figure 7.5 shows the original object, the dialog settings, and the outcome.

**Spiral array**

To create a spiral, set the values as you would with a circular array and then give a distance along the axis about which you are rotating. Figure 7.6 shows the original object, the dialog settings, and the outcome.

## Mirror Cloning

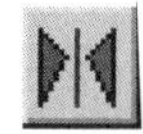

Mirror cloning creates a clone that is a mirror image of the original. To create a mirror clone, create a selection set and pick the Mirror tool. A dialog box is used to set the parameters. The mirror axis sets one of six possible axes for the mirror operation. The Offset moves the mirrored object along the mirror axis. Figure 7.7 shows the original object, the dialog settings, and the outcome.

FIGURE 7.5
Circular array.

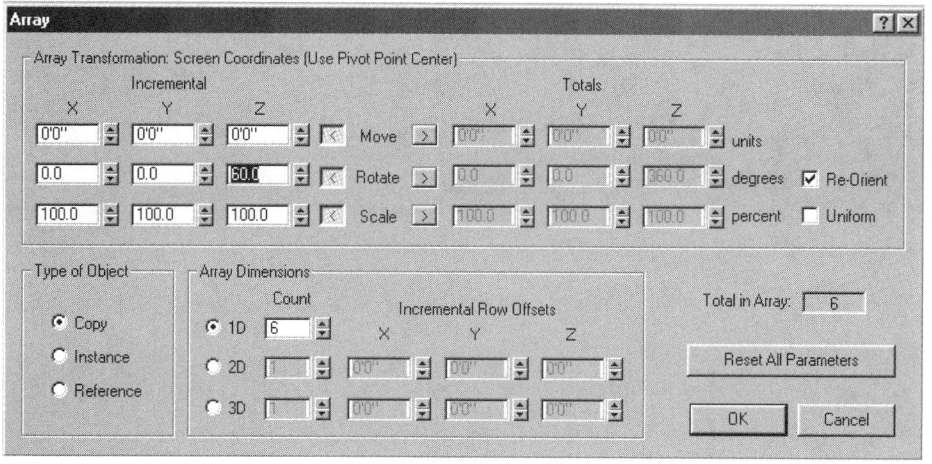


DIALOG SETTINGS

ORIGINAL OBJECT

OUTCOME

FIGURE 7.6
Spiral array.

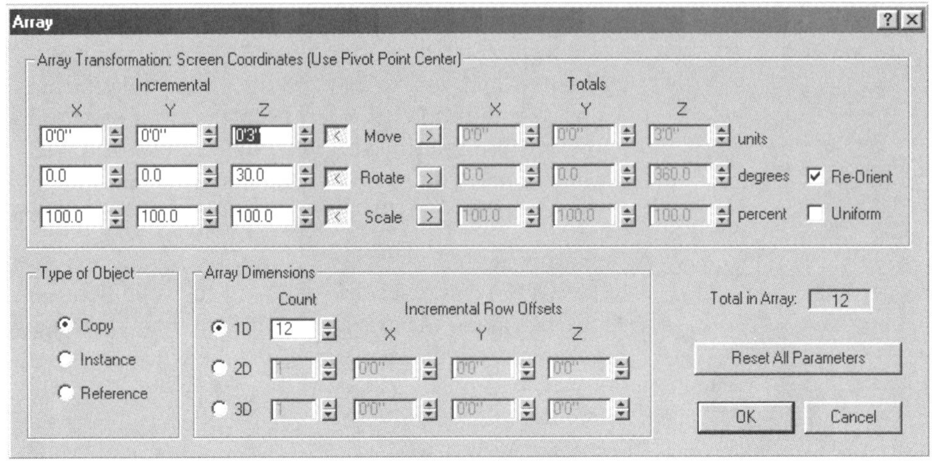


DIALOG SETTINGS

ORIGINAL OBJECT

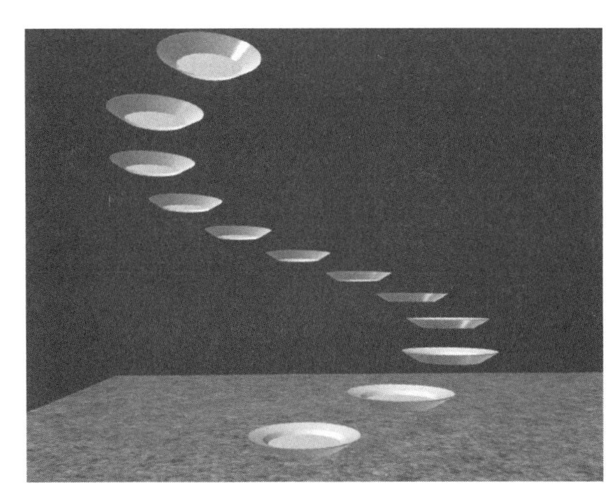

OUTCOME

### Snapshot Cloning

Snapshot cloning is used to clone an object along an animation path. You can make a single clone at any frame or multiple clones spaced over a selected number of frames.

## 7.5 ALIGN OPTIONS

Align options let you match the position and orientation of objects to one another. The process involves a source object and a target object. The source object is the object you want to move, and you select it to start the process. The target object is used as the center of alignment and is selected last.

There are three align options, Align, Align Normals, and Place Highlights.

**Align**

Aligns one object with another while allowing you to align with one or more axes of the target object. Figure 7.8 shows the original objects and the outcome of align.

FIGURE 7.7
Mirror cloning.

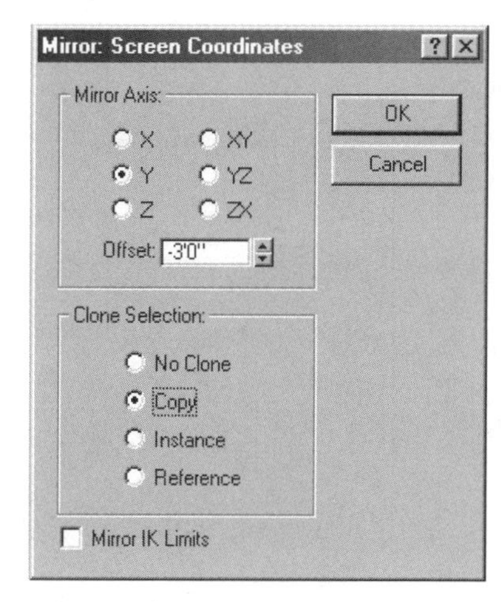


DIALOG SETTINGS

ORIGINAL OBJECT

OUTCOME

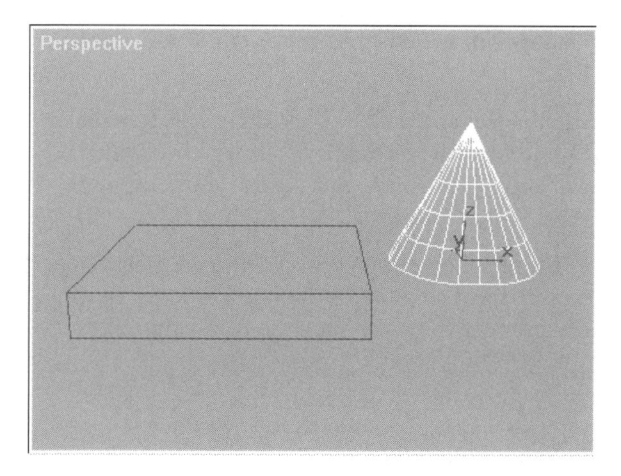


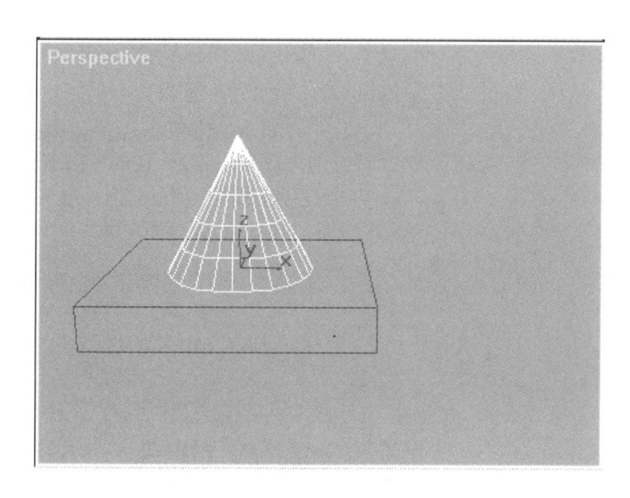


FIGURE 7.8
Using Align.

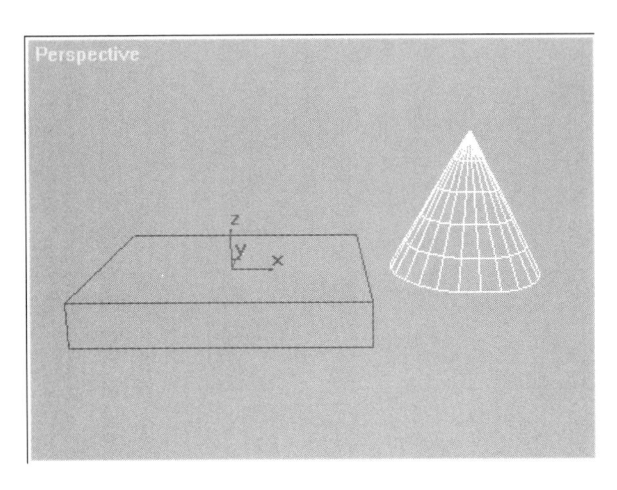


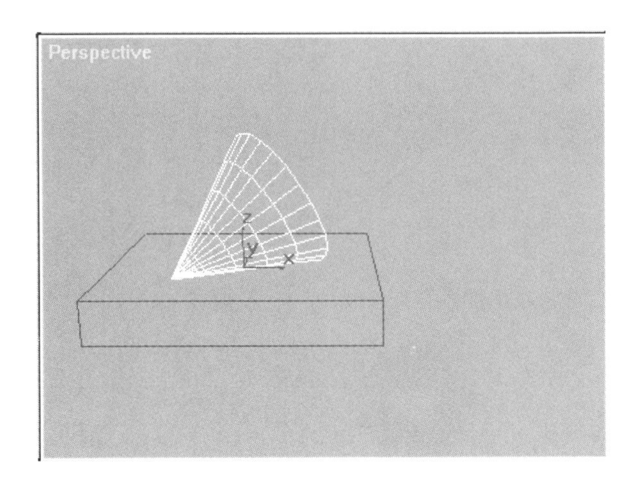


FIGURE 7.9
Using Align Normals.

**Align Normals**
Aligns a face normal on one object with the face normal of another. Figure 7.9 shows the original objects and the outcome of align normals.

**Place Highlights**
Aligns a light, camera, or other object with a specified point on an object.

**Camera**
Camera aligns a camera to a face normal.

**View**
View aligns the local axis of an object with the current viewport plane.

### Align Procedure

The following is the basic procedure for aligning an object with another object:

1. Select the source object. This is the object that will be moved.
2. Pick the Align tool. The align cursor appears attached to the crosshair.

3. Move the crosshair over the target object and pick it. The Align Selection dialog appears, as shown in Figure 7.10. Review the dialog. You can establish which point on the Current Object will align with which point on the Target Object. Then you can pick which axis to use, X, Y, and/or Z.
4. Before you pick Apply to effect the change, you can observe the movement in the viewports. You may have to drag the dialog out of the way for better viewing. Once you have established the alignment you want, pick the Apply button.

## 7.6 MODIFYING

Once an object has been created, it can be modified in a variety of ways, from adjusting the standard creation parameters such as height and width to the application of object modifiers that can bend and twist an object. This section explains the basics of the Modify command panel so that you can go on to modify your world of objects in any way imaginable.

## Modify Command Panel

The Modify command panel, shown in Figure 7.11, is broken into different areas that are used to perform different modification functions upon a selected object. These functions change, depending on the type of object selected and the type of modification to be performed. The following is a description of the areas contained within the panel.

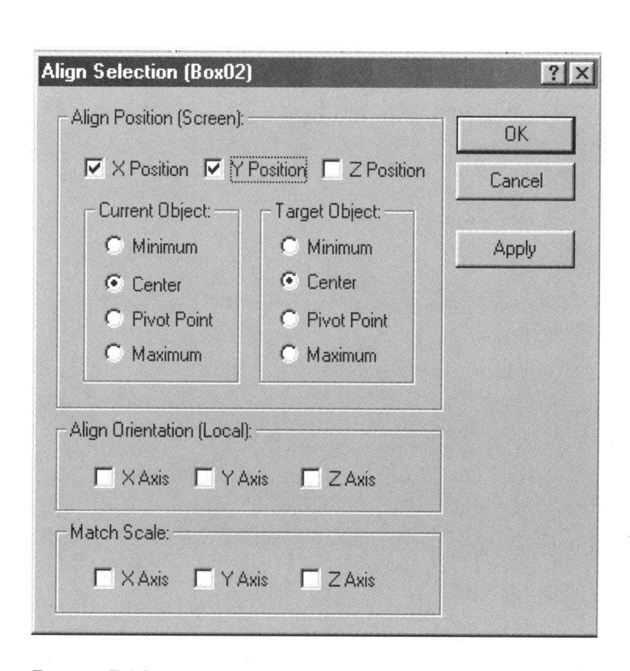


FIGURE 7.10
Align Selection dialog.

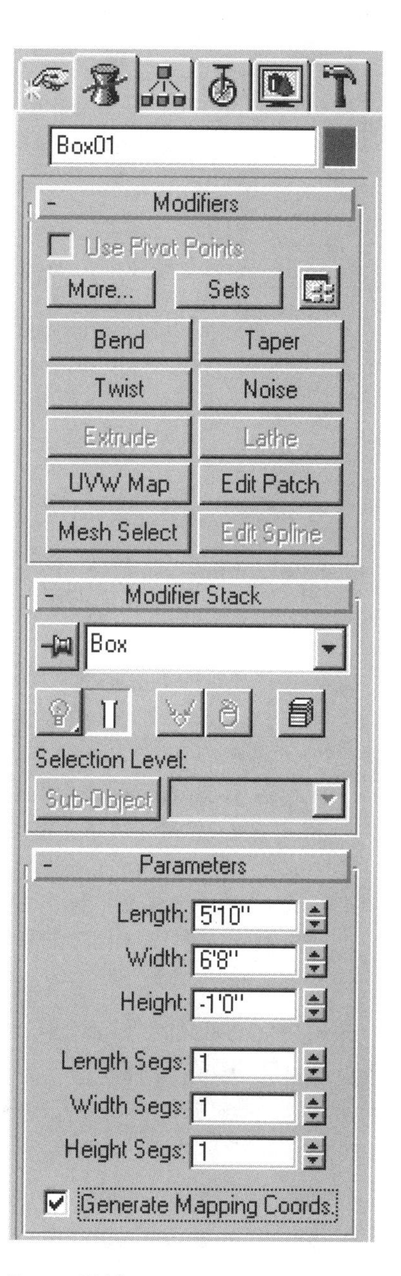


FIGURE 7.11
Modify command panel.

## Name and Color

The first items in the panel are the name and color of the object selected. You can change either one. If you have selected multiple objects, the name area will be greyed out, which indicates that it cannot be changed.

## Object Modifiers

There are up to 16 different modifier buttons available in this area. If you pick on one of the buttons, that modifier will be added to the modifier stack. The modifier stack is a list of the different modifiers applied to an object. In this way you apply several different modifiers to the same object. The list of modifiers is referred to as the *modifier stack.*

There are other modifiers available other than the 16 that are visible. To get access to the other modifiers, pick the More button. The Sets button is used to choose from a drop-down list of customized modifier button sets. You can customize the modifier button sets by picking on the Custom Set tool that is next to the Sets button.

## Modifier Stack Options

When you use an object modifier, the modifier is added to the stack list. To make adjustments to a modifier in the list, you can select it from the drop-down list. The bottom most item on the list is the standard creation parameters of the object and is identified by the object type, such as cylinder. Beside the stack drop-down list is the Pin Stack button. Its purpose is to lock the stack.

A series of buttons follow this area:

**Active/Inactive**
Turns off the current modifier without deleting it.

**Show End Result**
Shows the effect of the entire stack on the selected object.

**Make Unique**
Makes an instance modifier unique to a selected object.

**Remove Modifier**
Deletes the current modifier from the stack.

**Edit Stack**
Edits the order of modifiers in the stack.

## Selection Level Controls

Below the modifier stack buttons are the Selection Level controls. This area is used to edit objects and modifiers at the subobject level. An object is composed of faces, edges, and vertices. These items are subobjects. If you want to edit these components, then you need to select them from the Selection Level drop-down list after you have highlighted the Edit Mesh parameter item from the modifier stack or picked the Edit Mesh button. When you have selected the subobject type, you can select the actual object type on the object itself. For instance, if you pick face as the subobject, you can then pick the particular face you want to modify on the object. Remember

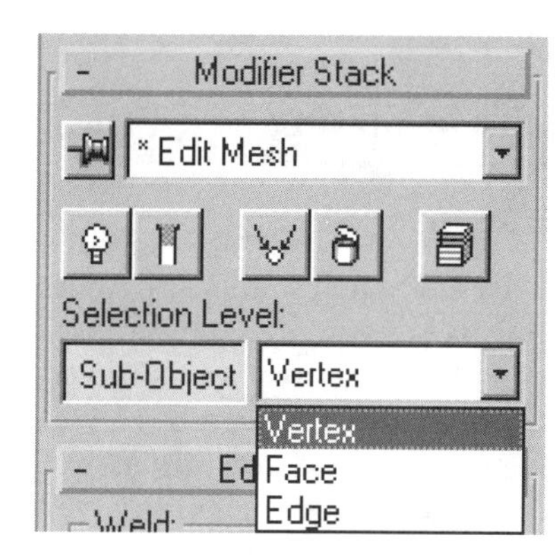


FIGURE 7.12
Sub-Object selection level.

the Sub-Object button must be on (pushed in) for you to alter objects at the subobject level. Figure 7.12 shows the subobject selection level.

### Object Parameters Rollout

The last area in the Modify panel is the Parameters rollout. This rollout is sometimes named the Edit rollout, depending on the modifier with which you are working. Within this area you alter the different parameters based on the current item in the modifier stack. The parameters present will change, depending on the current modifier.

## 7.7 SUMMARY

Creation is only one part of forming 3D worlds; you can also alter those objects that compose your world. Editing can be broken down into several areas; the first is selection. To edit an object or several objects you must be conversant in the various methods of selection. Once you have selected an object, you can transform it by repositioning, rotating, or scaling. Also, once an object has been created, you are not bound by the initial creation parameters. You can change the standard parameters or you can alter the object's form by, for instance, bending and twisting. Finally, you can reorient objects in relation to other objects with alignment tools. In fact, you have access to diverse editing tools, allowing you to alter your world even after the creation process has started.

# LAB 7.A

## Basics of Editing

### Purpose

This lab practices the techniques used in the editing of objects in your 3D world. In this lab you are going to use a scene file that has already been created. It contains a dining area with various pieces of furniture and other objects. The objects are in disarray, and it will be your job to put them in order. This will involve moving, scaling, and rotating as well as cloning. You will use various selection techniques and axis constraints.

This precreated file is contained on the CD-ROM included with this textbook. The file is called MXEDIT.MAX.

### Objectives

You will be able to

- Use the CTRL key to select objects.
- Select objects by name and color.
- Use the move, rotate, and scale transforms.
- Use transform axis constraints.
- Clone objects.
- Use arrays to create multiple objects.

### Procedure

#### SETTING UP THE PROJECT

With any project you need to establish some starting settings. These settings are usually standard for all projects, and you should become familiar with checking them before you start any creation.

1. Normally you would set your units. However, with this project you are using the precreated file MXEDIT.MAX. The units have already been established for this file. The file may have been copied onto your computer's drive or it may be still on the CD-ROM. If it has not been copied onto your computer, refer to Appendix A on installing the files.

   Open the file called MXEDIT.MAX and immediately save the file as CH7A.MAX. This way you retain the original file if you need to refer to it again. Remember to periodically save your scene, so that if something happens, you won't lose your work.
2. Review the initial grid and snap settings. These will control the display of grid guidelines and the cursor movement on the screen. Select the Grid and Snap settings from the Views pull-down menu. Figure 7.13 shows the settings for the Home Grid and the Snap. Match your dialogs to the figure.
3. Check the state of various icon buttons. Activate the TOP viewport. Figure 7.14 shows the state of the Toolbar buttons and the Prompt Line buttons. Match your buttons to the figures.

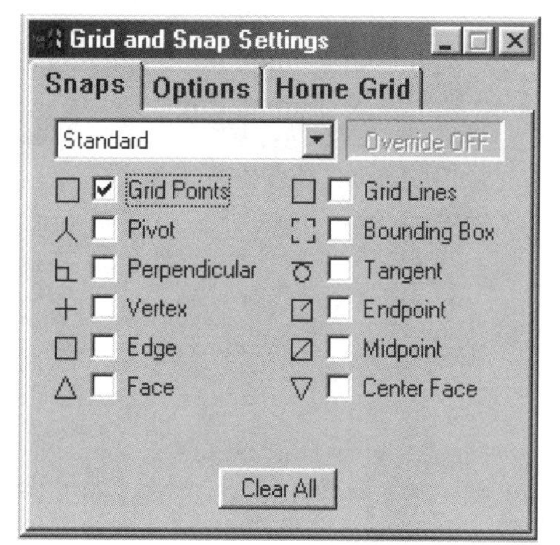


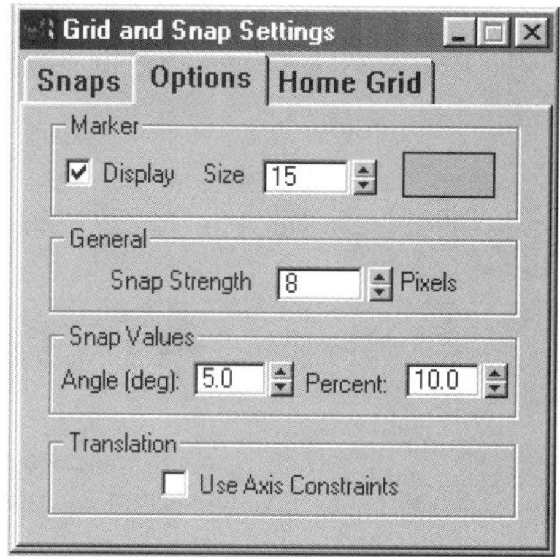


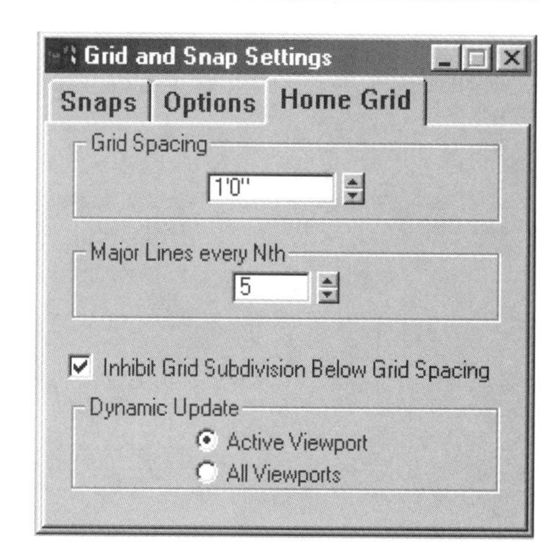


FIGURE 7.13
Home Grid and Snap dialogs.

The following should be the current state of the prompt line buttons:

| BUTTON | STATE | PURPOSE |
|---|---|---|
| Region Selection | Window Selection | Limits selection of objects totally contained within a window. |
| 2D Snap | OFF | Allows unlimited cursor movement in 2D. |
| Angle Snap | ON | Limits angular movement to set intervals. |
| Percent Snap | ON | Limits percent scaling to set intervals. |

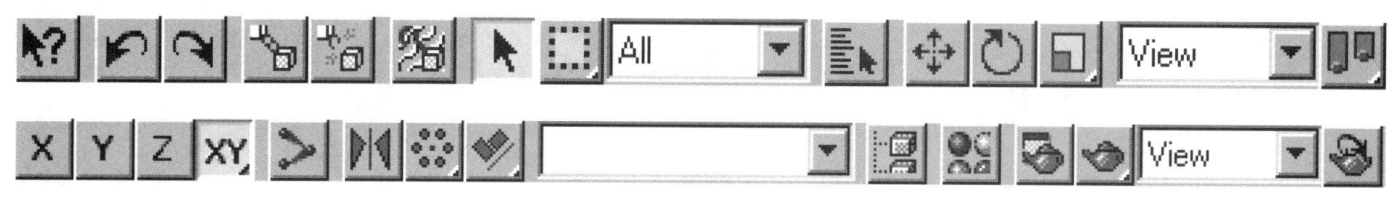

FIGURE 7.14
Toolbar and Prompt Line buttons.

4. Establish the display state of the various viewports. Activate the viewport and right-click on the viewport label.

| VIEWPORT | DISPLAY STATE |
|---|---|
| Top | Wireframe (default) |
| Front | Wireframe (default) |
| Left | Wireframe (default) |
| Perspective | Smooth+Highlight |

5. Right-click on the Left viewport to activate it.

Remember to use the Hold button before you perform any command you are unsure of. If something doesn't work, you can always use the Fetch button to restore the geometry to its pre-Hold state.

## TEST RENDERING OF THE SCENE

6. The first step is to perform a test render of the camera view. Activate the camera viewport and then pick the Render Scene tool. Figure 7.15 shows the settings and render. The resulting rendering should look like the "before" image shown in Figure 7.16A. When you are done with your editing, the final rendered scene should look like the "after" image shown in Figure 7.16B. Look back and forth between your rendering and the final image. Notice the changes such as the chairs in proper position, the model-airplane scaled down to a smaller size, and the additional place settings. These are the tasks you are going to perform.

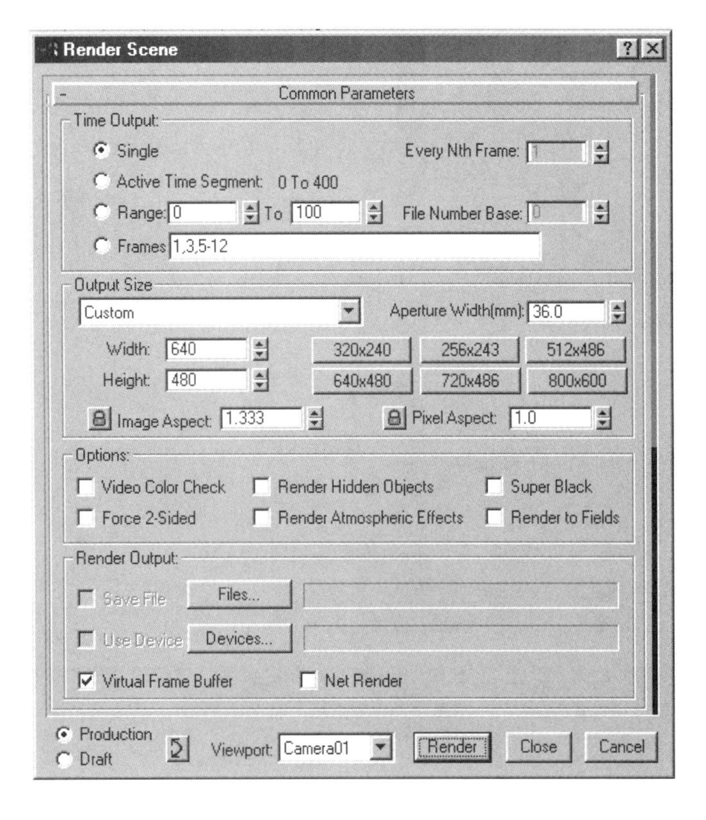


FIGURE 7.15
Render Scene dialog.

A BEFORE

B AFTER

FIGURE 7.16
Before and after rendered scenes.

## UNIFORM SCALING AND MOVING THE MODEL PLANE

7. In this scene the model airplane was made intentionally too large. You are going to scale it down. Make sure the Left viewport is active and use the Region Zoom tool to give you a closer look at the model airplane. Once you have zoomed in, the view should look similar to Figure 7.17.

8. Using the Select Object tool, select the model airplane and then lock the selection.

9. Pick the Uniform Scale transform tool and click and drag on the model in the Left viewport. Hold down on the button and drag downward. Observe the coordinate readout on the status line. It now shows scaling percentage in all three axes (uniform scaling). Drag the cursor until the readout shows 60% in the three axes. This means that the model will be 60% of its original size. Release the button. Notice how the plane is now off the tabletop.

10. Pick the Move transform and click and drag on the model again in the Left viewport. Drag the plane down until its wheels and tail rest on the tabletop. Figure 7.18 shows the reduced size and the placement on the tabletop.

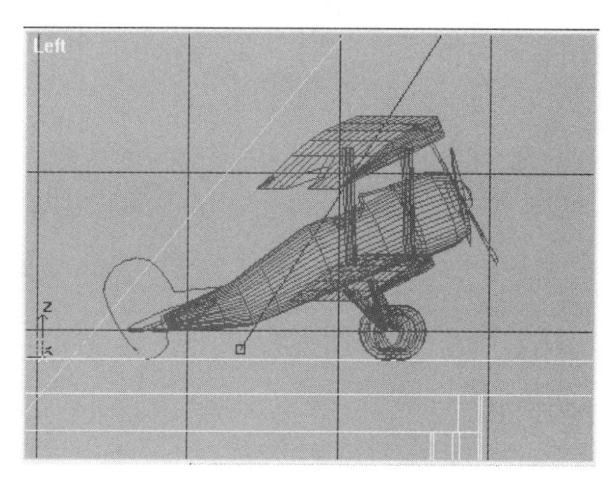


FIGURE 7.17
A closer look at the model airplane.

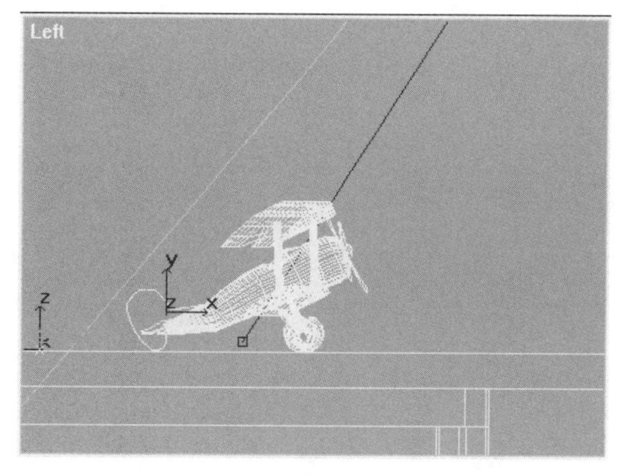


FIGURE 7.18
Model airplane scaled down and resting on tabletop.

11. With the Move transform still active, activate the Top viewport. Click and drag the model airplane to the bottom left corner of the table. Figure 7.16 shows its approximate location.

    Unlock the selection.

## CLONING THE FORK

12. In the scene you are working on now there is only one dinner fork. You are going to create a clone of that fork and scale it down to make it a salad fork.

    Activate the Top viewport and use Region Zoom to get a closer view of the dinner fork. Use the Select Object tool to select the fork and then Lock the selection. The view should be similar to Figure 7.19.

13. Select the Move transform tool and then, while holding down the shift key, click, hold, and drag on the fork. Drag the new copy of the fork slowly downward so that it is beside the original fork and release the button. A dialog will appear asking for the type of clone (pick the default *copy*) and the name of the new object (use the default of FORK01). OK this dialog, and the cloned fork should appear.

## NONUNIFORM SCALING OF THE FORK

14. You now need to scale down the clone fork so that it represents a salad fork. For this you are going to use the Non-Uniform Scale transform. This transform will allow you to scale the fork in the X and Y axes and leave the Z axis; thus, the fork will retain its thickness but become a smaller fork.

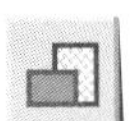

    Select the Non-Uniform Scale transform. You will receive a warning about using nonuniform scaling. Don't worry about this. Answer Yes to continue with the scaling. Click, hold, and drag on the fork. Watch the percentage scale on the status line but only in the X and Y axes and not in the Z. Drag the cursor until the percentages read 90% and then release the button. The view should look similar to Figure 7.20.

    Unlock the selection.

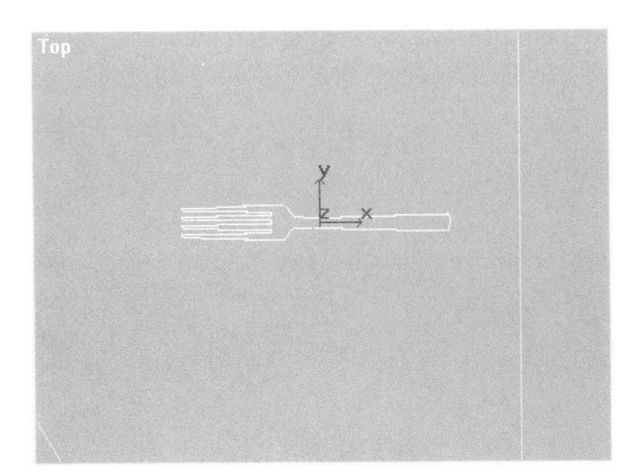


FIGURE 7.19
Closeup of the fork.

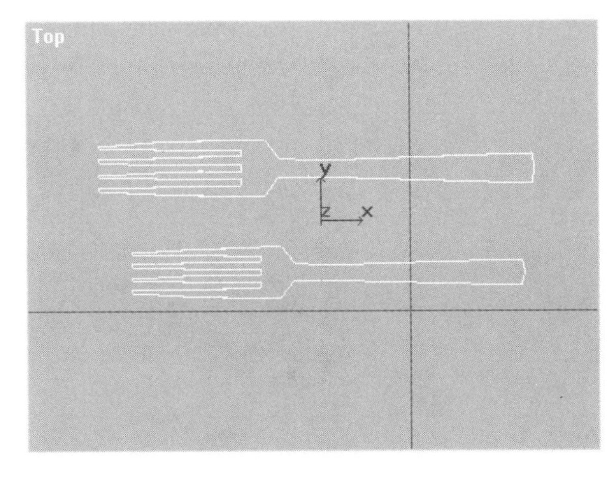


FIGURE 7.20
Cloned and scaled fork.

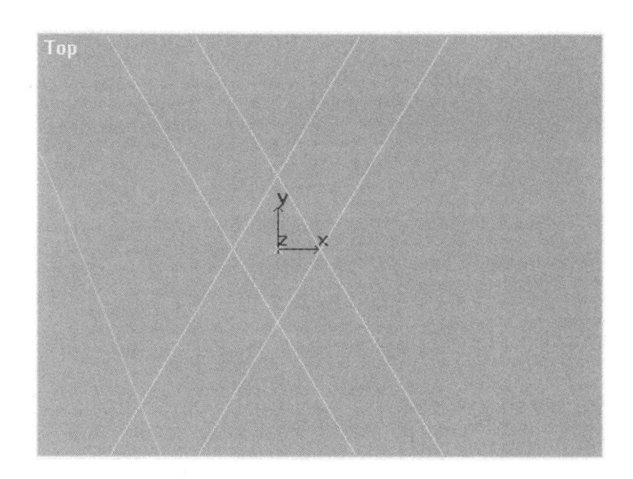


FIGURE 7.21
Close-up of table showing the helper point object.

## ARRAY CLONING THE TABLE SETTING

15. Now you have the complete place setting, you need to make three more copies for the other places. To do this you will use the Array tool and a helper point object that lies in the center of the tabletop.

    First you will need to change the reference coordinate system. It is used to establish pivot or reference points. To make it easier, the helper point object has already been added. Activate the Top viewport, Zoom Extents, and then use the Zoom Region command and zoom in close to the center of tabletop. See Figure 7.21.

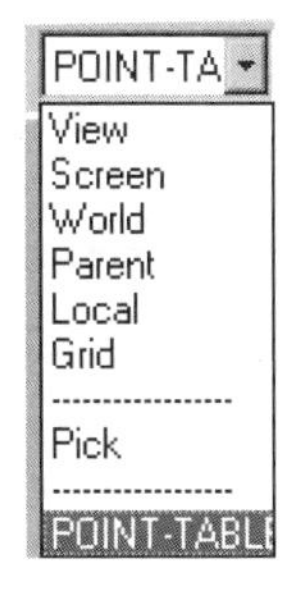


16. Open the Reference Coordinate System drop-down list and select the Pick item. Now pick the point object that lies in the center of the tabletop. The Reference Coordinate System list should now be displaying the words POINT-TABLE. This means that the point object called POINT-TABLE will now be used as the reference point.

17. Use the Zoom tool to zoom out until you can see the entire table.

18. You are going to select the plate and cutlery by color. Select the Edit/Select By/Color pull-down menu item. The cursor will change to display a rainbow symbol. Move the cursor until it is over the plate and then pick the plate. Because the plate and cutlery are all the same color, all were selected.

    Lock the selection.

19. Select the Use Transform Coordinate Center tool from the flyout in the toolbar. This ensures that the point will be used as the center for the array.

20. Select the Array tool, and a dialog should appear. Match the settings shown in Figure 7.22. The two specific areas are the rotation in Z axis, which should be 90°, and the number of copies, which should be 4. The angle means that the selection set will be rotated 90° for each copy. The number of copies includes the original, so there are 4 copies in all. Once you have made the settings, OK the dialog and 3 more table settings should appear, as shown in Figure 7.23.

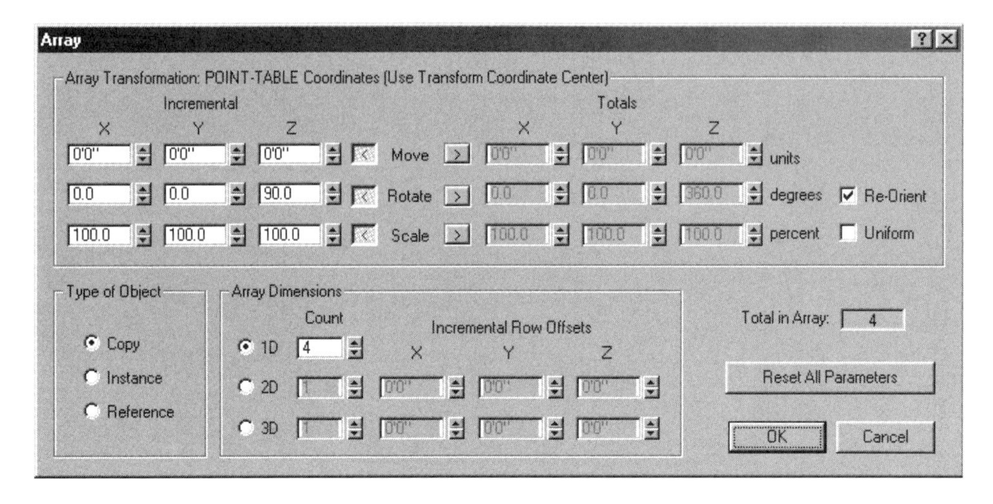


FIGURE 7.22
Array dialog.

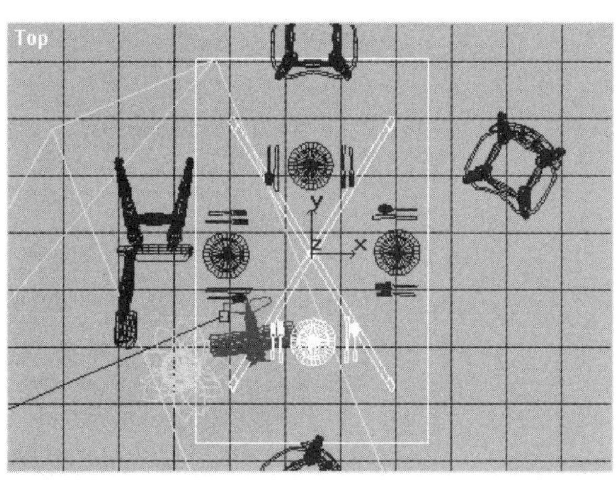


FIGURE 7.23
Arrayed table settings.

## MOVING THE SETTINGS INTO POSITION

21. Notice how the last place setting is still selected. Lock this selection. You are going to move it down, nearer the edge of the table.

    Pick (push in) the Restrict to Y axis constraint button. This will limit the movement of the place setting to the Y axis only.

    Select the Move transform and click and drag until the place setting is close to the edge of the table. Unlock the selection after the move.

22. Now you going to move the upper place setting into its proper position.

    Use the Region zoom to get a closer view of the edge of the table and the place settings. The view should look similar to Figure 7.24.

23. Using the Select Object tool, pick the plate to select it. Now, hold down the Ctrl key and pick the spoon, knife, and two forks. Because you are using the Ctrl key, each of the newly picked objects will be added to the selection set with the plate.

24. With the movement still restricted to the Y axis, click and drag the place setting and move it near the table edge.

    Unlock the selection set.

## MOVING THE PLANT

25. Now you are going to move the plant up onto the table top. You're going to be left on your own to do this except for selecting the plant. First, use the Zoom Extents All tool, so that you can see the entire scene in every viewport.

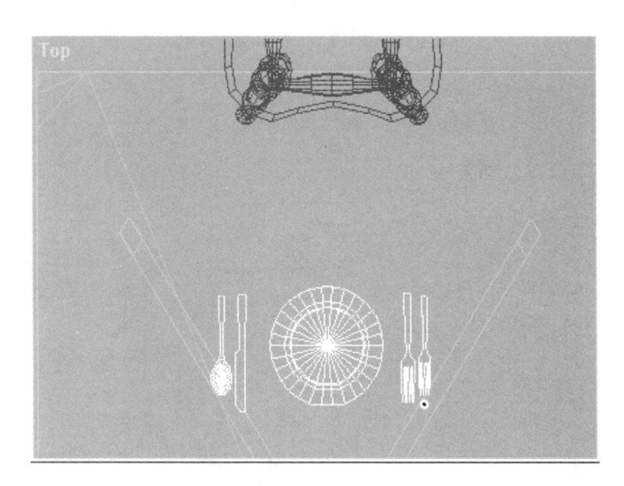


FIGURE 7.24
Enlarged view of place setting and table edge.

26. Pick the Select by Name tool, and a dialog will be presented to you. If the place setting is still highlighted (selected), pick the None button.

    Now look over the list of named objects in the scene. Find and highlight [PLANT-SMALL]. The reason that PLANT-SMALL is in brackets is that it is made up of a group of objects—the leaves, the pot, and the dirt. This is one application of making groups. If you select the group and move it, all the items in the group move. Once you have highlighted [PLANT-SMALL], pick the Select button. The group of objects that make the plant should now be selected.

    Lock the selection.

27. Now you are on your own. Use the Move transform in different viewports to get the plant up onto the table and in the upper corner. Refer to the image in Part B of Figure 7.16 for the approximate placement.

## ROTATING AND MOVING THE CHAIRS

28. Three of the four chairs need to be placed in their proper positions in front of the place settings. You will need to use the Rotate and Move transforms to get them in the right place. Again you're on your own. Here is a hint: As with moving the plant, you need to switch to different viewports to rotate the chairs in different planes. Remember to use the Hold button if you are unsure of the outcome of a command. In this way you can restore the previous arrangement by using the Fetch button.

    Figure 7.25 shows the approximate locations of the chairs.

29. Save your scene.

FIGURE 7.25
Render Scene dialog settings.

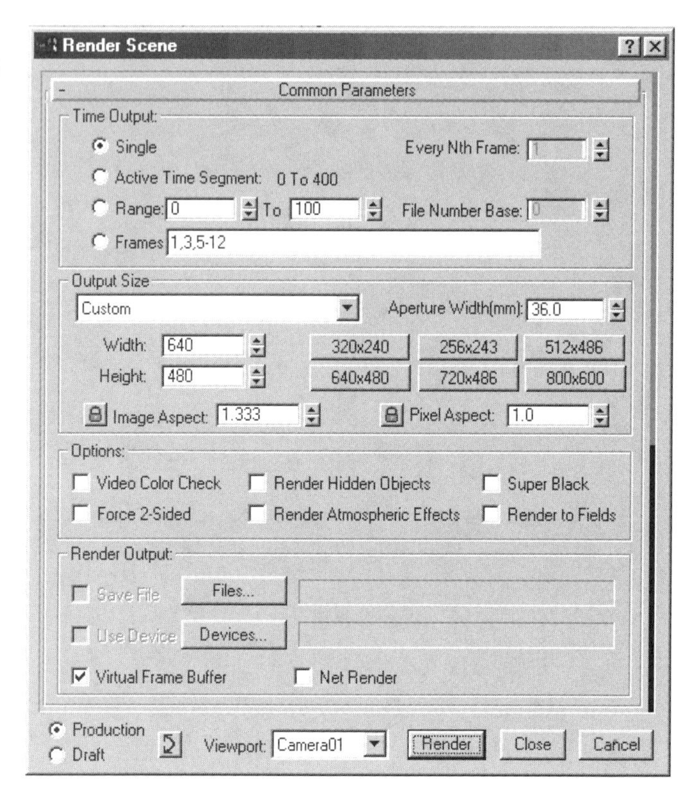


FIGURE 7.26
Final rendering of edited scene.

## FINAL RENDERING OF THE EDITED SCENE

30. Now that you have edited the scene, it's time to see a rendered view of the outcome. Select the Render Scene tool and refer to Figure 7.26 for the settings. The final rendering should be similar to Figure 7.25.

## QUESTIONS AND ASSIGNMENTS

### QUESTIONS

1. What is the selection set?
2. What do you use to add objects to the current selection set?
3. What is region selection?
4. Why would you lock a selection set?
5. Explain the two methods of combining objects. Why would you choose one method over the other?
6. Explain the three transforms.
7. What tool do you use to limit transforms to certain axes?
8. What is the Transform Center?
9. Explain the three methods of array cloning.
10. What function does the Modify command panel serve?
11. Explain the modifier stack.

## ASSIGNMENTS

1. Open the scene CH7A.MAX from this chapter's lab. Experiment with the selection options to select objects in various ways, such as Region Selection and Select By Color. Try the Ctrl and Alt keys to see how they can be used to add and remove objects from the selection set. If you want to save the modified file, save it as CH7B.MAX.
2. Open the scene CH7A.MAX from this chapter's lab. Experiment with the grouping of objects. First try transforming portions of the plant. Because it is a group already, you will have to temporarily open the group to transform individual options. Remember to close it again when you are finished. Try grouping other objects, such as the place settings, so that each setting moves as one. Save the modified scene as CH7C.MAX.
3. Open the scene CH7A.MAX from this chapter's lab. Experiment with different forms of cloning. Create more chairs and place settings to go around the table. Create a fleet of model airplanes using the spiral array clone. Save the new scene as CH7D.MAX.
4. Open a new scene and create some basic objects such as boxes and cones. Experiment with the Modify command panel to apply modifiers to the objects. Try bending, twisting, and tapering the different objects. Save the scene as CH7E.MAX

PART FOUR

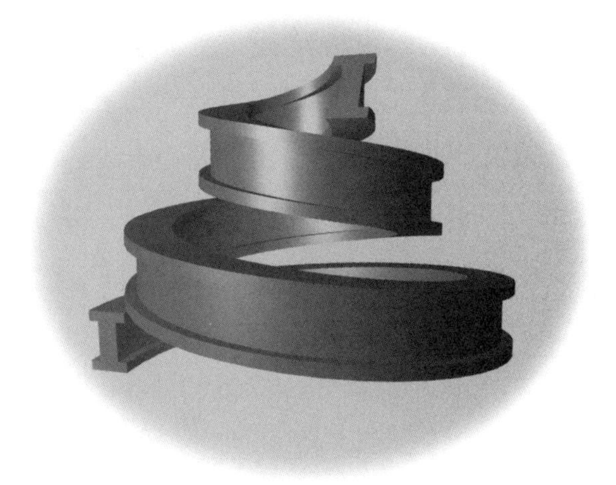

# 3D Modeling

# Basic Modeling: Primitives, Shapes, and Shape and Geometric Modifiers

## 8.1 INTRODUCTION

This chapter deals with basic modeling. You will be shown the techniques needed to create the various primitive objects such as boxes and cylinders, as well as the two-dimensional surface patches. You will learn about spline shapes and how to turn them into three-dimensional objects through the extrude and lathe modifiers. You will also be introduced to geometric modifiers that can be used to bend and twist an object.

## 8.2 PRIMITIVES AND PATCHES

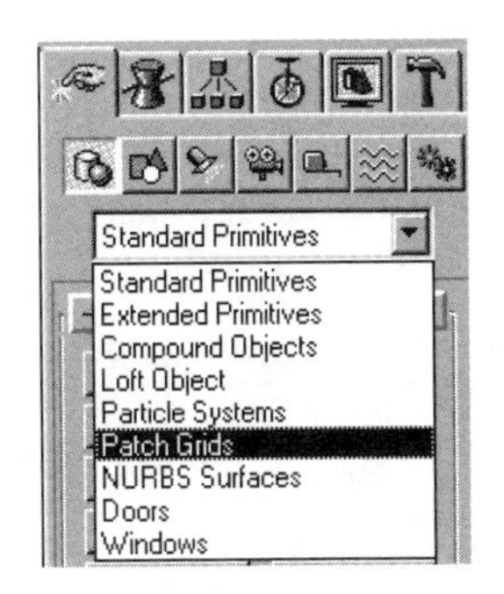


This section is about the creation of parametric primitives and patches that are basic building blocks. Parametric means that you can have a standard object and by changing its parameters you can have a new object. That is just what these primitives can do. You can initially create them using one set of parameters and then modifiy them into something with a different set of parameters. The result is that you can have an endless variety of objects from several basic forms. Some of the three-dimensional primitive object types are box, cylinder, tube, cone, sphere, torus, and teapot. There are also Standard Primitives Extended. These are more advanced primitives in specific shapes such as Hedras and OilTanks. The two-dimensional patches are Tri Patch and Quad Patch. This section reviews the common creation elements and explains the particulars about each primitive and patch form. Figure 8.1 illustrates some of the basic primitives and patches.

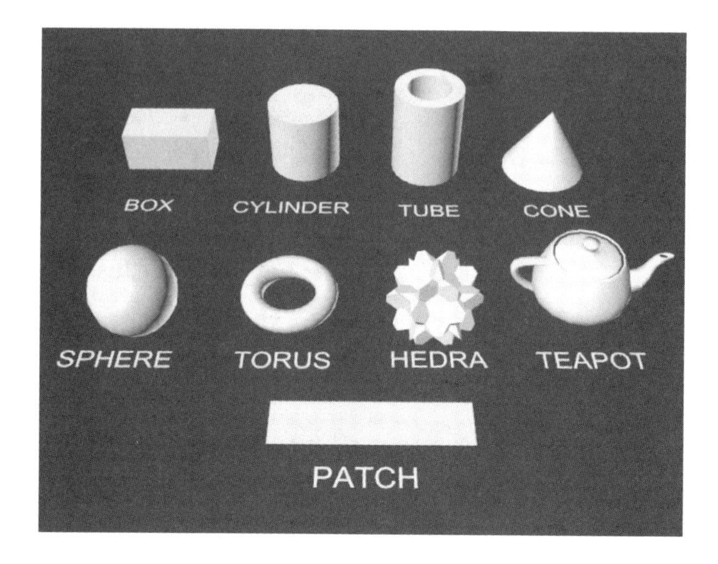


FIGURE 8.1
Basic primitives and patches.

## Common Creation Elements

There are some common elements to all primitive objects or primitive object shape categories.

### Segments

Every object is composed of faces, and these faces represent one or several segments. Think of a box with six sides. These sides could be thought of as six segments. However, you could also divide each side up into two or more segments. This increased number of segments allows a variety of modifications later on. Those segments can be altered by changing size, shape, or position to arrive at very complex shapes. Figure 8.2 shows a cylinder on the left with only one segment running along its length. Now observe the cylinder next to it, with eight segments running along its length and the same cylinder on the right with modifiers applied to it. The result is a complex shape from a basic cylindrical form. Objects with only one segment running along an axis cannot have certain modifiers, such as bend, applied along the limited axis.

### Smoothing and Sides

Each of the circular primitives have *Smooth* and *Number of Sides* parameters. The Smooth parameter is used to make a circular object smooth at its diameter. When the parameter is checked, the program renders the object with a smooth transition between the edges.

The number of sides controls how cylindrical an object looks. For instance, you could create a cylinder with only six sides with Smooth on. From the side the cylinder would look smooth and curved. However, if observed from above or at an angle,

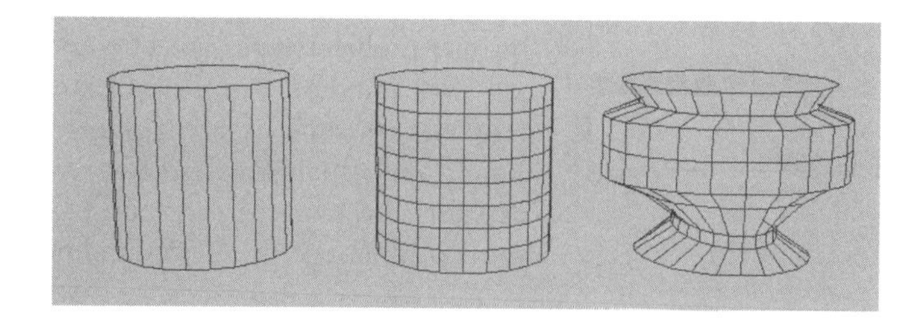

FIGURE 8.2
Segments and their effect on modification.

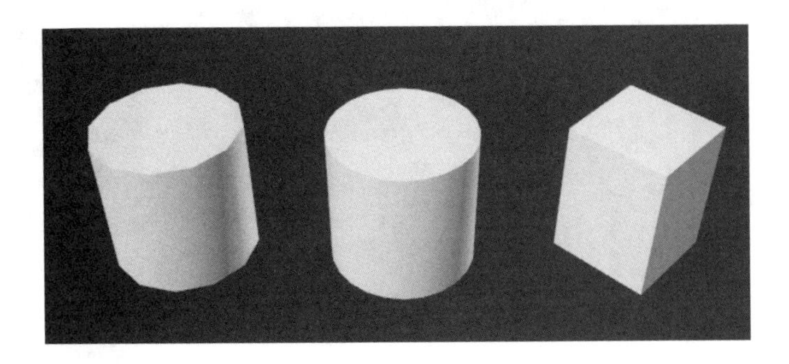

FIGURE 8.3
Effects of Smooth and Number of Sides parameters on creation and rendering.

the six edges would be noticeable. Increase the number of sides if you want the object to look more rounded from an edge view.

When smoothing is turned off, the edges between faces are defined and noticeable. This can be useful when you want to create faceted objects such as prisms and pyramids from circular objects such as cylinders and cones. When smooth is off and the number of sides is small, polygonal forms are created. Figure 8.3 shows the Smooth parameter on with a 12-sided and 24-sided cylinder and the Smooth parameter off to create a 6-sided.

### Circular Objects Creation and Slice

When you create circular objects, you can specify either the edge or center creation method. With the Edge option, you identify the two outside edges of the object to create it. With the Center option, you identify the center of the object and then the radius.

Another option particular to circular objects is the Slice option, which is used to create circular objects with pie-shaped slices removed. With the slice option, there are three parameters, Slice On, Slice From, and Slice To. Slice On is a toggle to engage slicing or not. Slice From specifies the start point of the slice removal. It is set in degrees around the Z axis. Slice To specifies the endpoint of the slice removal. Both values can be either positive, negative, or a combination. Figure 8.4 shows some sliced circular objects.

## Box

The simplest of the three-dimensional objects is the box. You have a choice of using the box method of creation, which allows you to set all three dimensions independently, or using the cube method, which holds a uniform three-dimensional shape, allowing you to set the overall size. If you want to create a box with a square base but nonuniform height, hold down on the Ctrl key as you drag the base of the box. It will match the length to width but let you set any height. Figure 8.5 shows a typical box creation.

## Cylinder

The next three-dimensional primitive is the cylinder. The parameters for a cylinder allow you to set the number of segments for the height and the cap. The cap is either

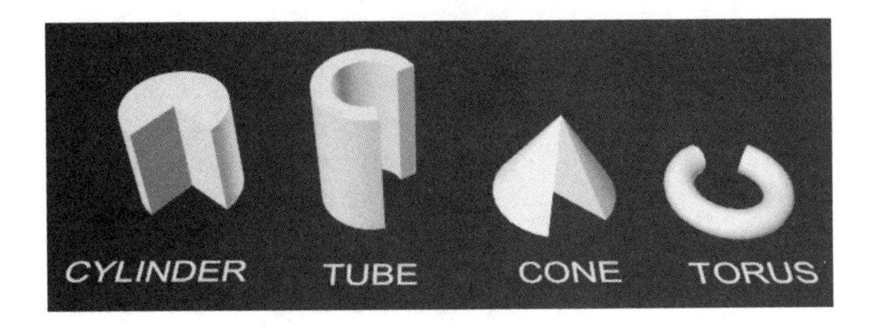


FIGURE 8.4
Sliced circular objects.

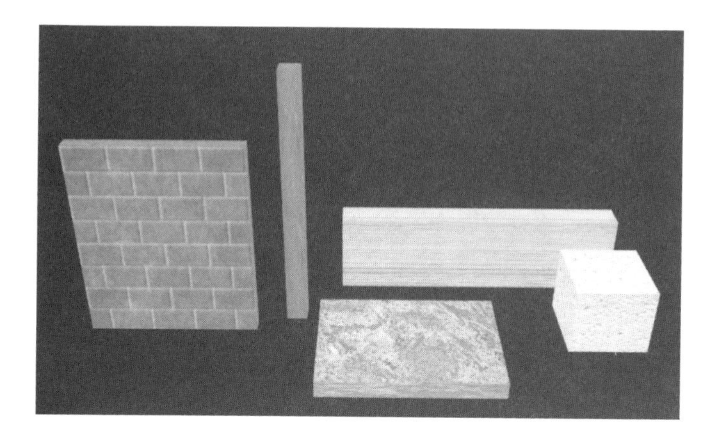

FIGURE 8.5
Boxes in different shapes.

end of the cylinder. By setting the number of sides, you can create a smooth cylindrical shape. If the number of sides is reduced to 3, for instance, and the Smooth option is turned off, a prism-type object is created. See Figure 8.6.

### Tube

The tube is basically the same as the cylinder except for the addition of a hole through the cylinder. Like the cylinder, the tube can be cylindrical or prismatic. See Figure 8.7.

### Cone

The Cone object can create both round cones and angular pyramids, either upright or inverted. The object can also be truncated. See Figure 8.8. The following are the steps for creating a cone:

1. Select the Cone button.
2. Drag and release to define the radius for the base.
3. Move up or down to define the height and click to set it.
4. Move to define the radius of the other end of the cone. Set the radius of the cone to 0 for a point or a greater value to create a truncated cone. Click to set the radius.

As with the cylinder or tube, reducing the number of sides and turning off Smooth allows you to create a pyramidal form.

**LIGHTS! CAMERA! ACTION!** 

Number of Sides

Remember that the increased number of sides for a cylinder increases the complexity of the objects and increases rendering time. Always set the number of sides to be as small as you can and still get the results you desire. If the object will always be far away from the viewer, it may not need a large number of sides.

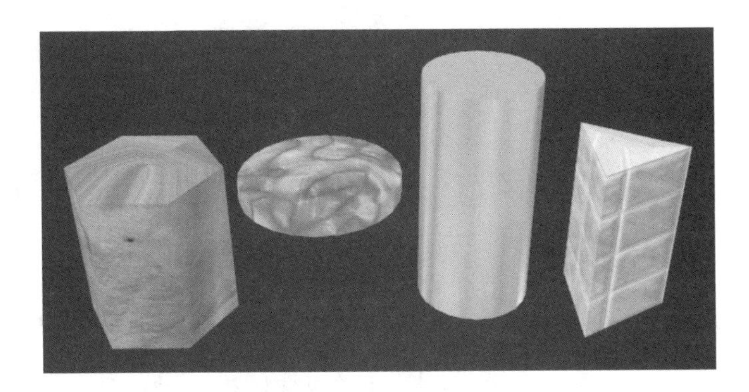
FIGURE 8.6
Cylinders and prism.

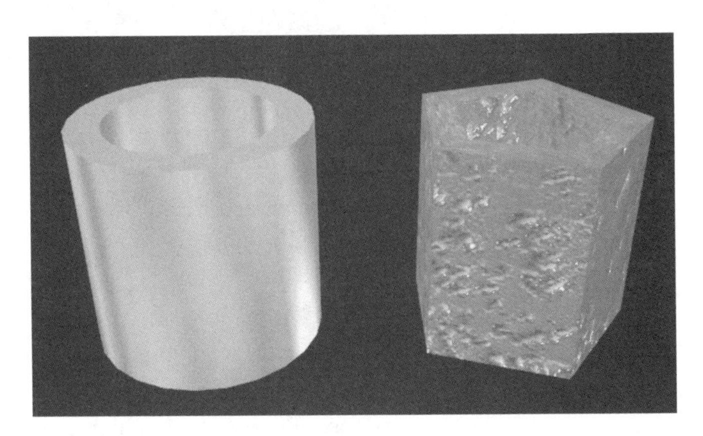
FIGURE 8.7
Tubes in circular and prismatic form.

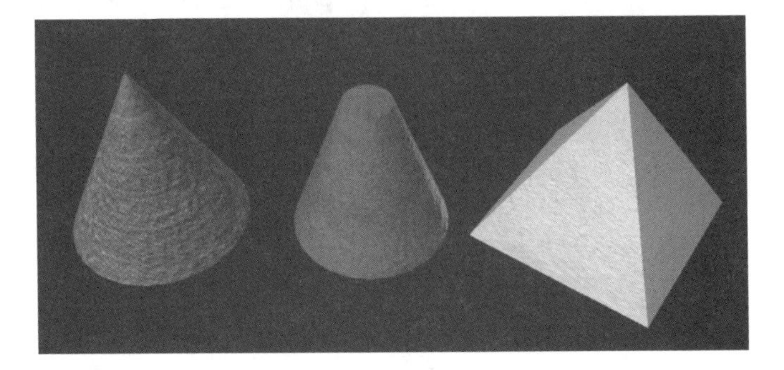
FIGURE 8.8
The cone in circular and pyramidal form.

## Sphere/Geosphere

The sphere or geosphere creation can take several forms, depending on the creation parameters. The default creates a spherical shape. The hemisphere option lets you set a value between 0 and 1. A value of 0 produces a full sphere. As the value approaches 1, a greater portion of the sphere is cut off. The Chop option is the default, and it reduces the number of vertices and face as the sphere is cut smaller. The Squash option is used when you want to maintain the number of vertices and faces as you cut the sphere smaller. This is useful when you want to use morphing on the sphere. (Morphing is explained in Chapter 10.) Reducing the number of sides of a sphere can create a crystal. See Figure 8.9.

## Torus

The Torus command creates a circular ring shape that looks like a donut. There are two radii: The first establishes the radius from the center of the overall body to the cross-sectional circle; the second radius defines the size of the cross-sectional circle.

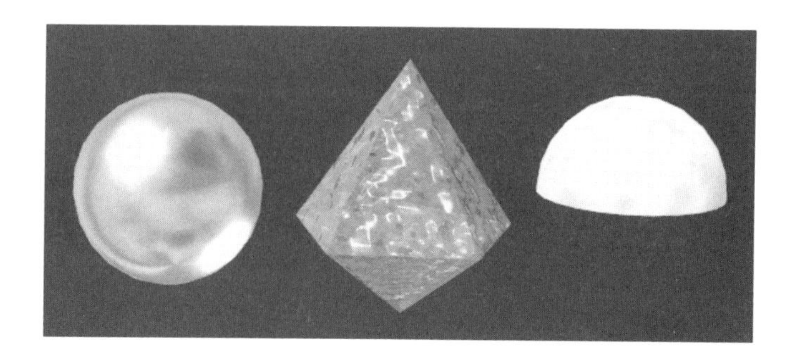

FIGURE 8.9
The sphere in different forms.

When you enter the values with keyboard entry, you set the two radii. When you use the drag method, you first establish the outside of the shape and then drag inward to define the size of the cross section. There are several options specific to the torus: Smooth, Rotation, and Twist. There are three levels of smooth for a torus, All, Sides, or None. Rotation is an angular value that rotates the faces around the cross-sectional circle. Twist, angular as well, causes the cross sections to be progressively rotated about the circle until the last section is rotated to match the twist angle. You should use increments of 360° to avoid constriction in the first segment of a closed torus. Figure 8.10 shows the effects of the smooth options and twisting.

## Teapot

The Teapot command creates the classic three-dimensional teapot object. You can create the complete teapot or individual parts. The usefulness of the teapot object is its convoluted nature, which makes it well suited for testing mappings of different material types. Figure 8.11 shows the teapot and its parts.

## Hedra

The Hedra is one of the extended primitives. The Hedra command creates a polyhedron that is a three-dimensional solid whose face comprises polygons—triangles, squares, pentagons. There are five family types: tetra, cube/octa, dodec/icos, star1, and star2. Figure 8.12 shows a sample of each family type.

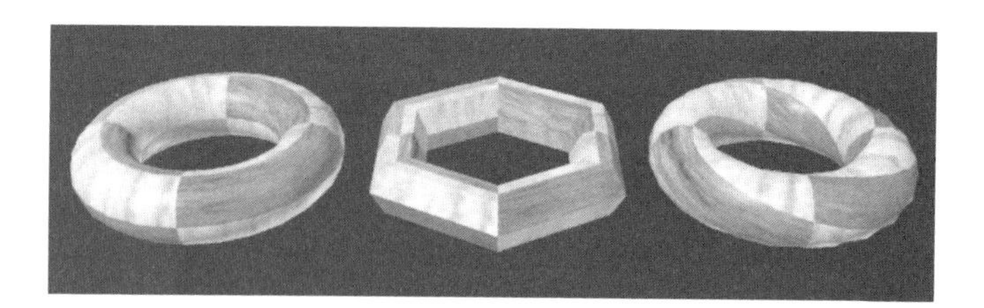

FIGURE 8.10
Different forms of a torus.

FIGURE 8.11
The teapot and its parts.

FIGURE 8.12
The family of polyhedra.

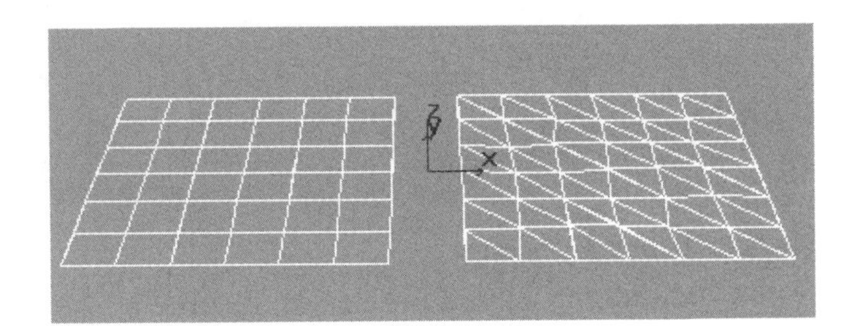

FIGURE 8.13
Quad and Tri patches.

### Patches

Patches are two-dimensional objects in the form of a grid of faces. There are two types, Quad and Tri Patch. They are used as building materials to create custom-shaped objects either by attaching them to each other or attaching them to existing objects. See Figure 8.13.

Quad Patch creates a flat grid with 36 visible rectangular facets, with each rectangular facet divided by a hidden line, for a total of 72 triangular faces.

Tri Patch creates a flat grid with 72 triangular faces.

## 8.3 SHAPES

A shape is initially a two-dimensional object created with the use of a spline. It is just an outline made up of line segments and vertices. The segments can be straight or curved. A spline on its own will not render; however, once the two-dimensional shape has been created, it can be turned into a two-dimensional object with the Edit Mesh modifier or it can extruded, revolved (using lathe), or lofted into a three-dimensional shape. Figure 8.14 shows some two- and three-dimensional spline shapes and what they can be turned into.

### Common Spline Controls

The two common controls for most spline creation are the spline's interpolation and its creation method.

#### Interpolation

Interpolation controls how the spline is created. Each spline is made up of smaller straight lines (steps). The number of steps between each vertex can be set from 0 to

FIGURE 8.14
Spline shapes and the 2D and 3D objects created from them.

100. There are also two options that can be applied to the steps, Adaptive and Optimized. Adaptive automatically sets the number of steps for each spline to produce a smooth curve, while giving zero steps to straight segments. When Adaptive is unchecked, interpolation uses the step value you set and the Optimized option. Optimized removes unneeded steps from straight segments.

Normally you would use the Adaptive option for most creation and the Optimized method for splines used in morphing, because morphing requires exact control over the number of vertices.

### Creation Method

Most of the splines have two creation methods, edge and center. With the edge method, you establish one outer edge point first and then the opposite one. With the center method, you establish the center first and then one of the outer edges.

### Creation of Splines

The following describes the particular techniques in the creation of the different spline types. Figure 8.15 illustrates the various spline shapes.

### Line

The Line spline uses Initial Type and Drag Type to define the spline. Initial Type can be either Corner or Smooth; corner produces a sharp point at the vertex, whereas smooth produces a nonadjustable curve through the vertex.

The Drag Type sets the type of vertex you get when you drag a vertex location.

To create Line splines, simply pick the points using the left button and right-click when you are finished. If you hold down on the pick button at each point and drag, you can form Bezier curves with the line segments. This is useful for creating curved splines.

### Rectangle

A rectangle spline is created by specifying the length and width.

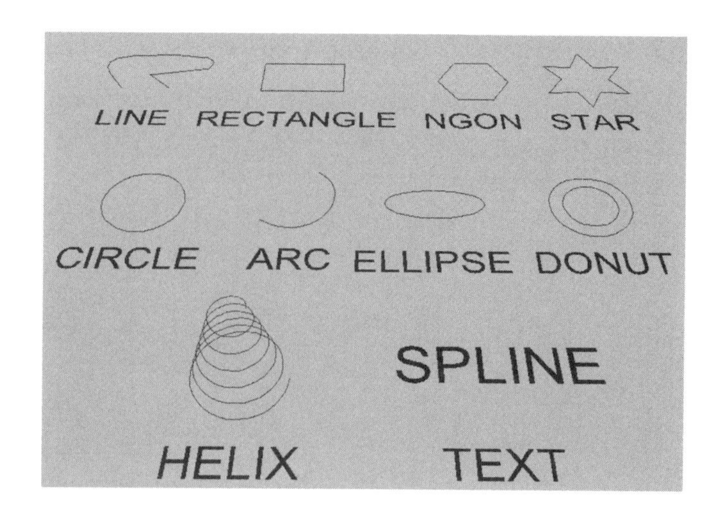


FIGURE 8.15
Various spline shapes.

### Ngon

The Ngon is used to create a closed, flat-sided or circular spline with any number of sides. If the Circular option is checked, a circle shape is created regardless of the number of sides.

### Star

You can set the number of points a star shape will have as well as applying a distortion value to rotate the outer star points.

### Circle

The circle shape is created by specifying a radius.

### Arc

You can create an arc spline by specifying the End-End-Middle or Center-End-End. Once it has been created, you can apply the Pie Slice option to close the arc forming the shape of a slice of pie.

### Ellipse

An ellipse shape is created by specifying the length and width and then establishing the minor and major axes. If you hold down the Ctrl key during drag creation, the ellipse is constrained to the shape of a circle.

### Donut

You can create a donut shape by specifying inner and outer radii.

### Helix

A helix is a spring shape. The spline is created by following a circular path and moving in the Z direction at the same time. You can set two different radii for start and end as well as the height, number of turns, and bias. The bias forces the turns to accumulate at one end of the helix. A value of −1 forces the turns toward the start and a value of 1 forces the turns toward the end.

### Text

The Text command creates text splines using any font installed on your system. Some fonts work better than others, depending on their type. Once you have picked the font and set the text size (height), you enter the text in the Text edit box. Once this is done you pick in the appropriate viewport to see the text. If you hold down on the button while doing so, you can drag the text into position.

### Section

The Section command will create a spline in the form of a section profile based on an imaginary cutting plane that you place on an object.

## 8.4 SHAPE MODIFIERS

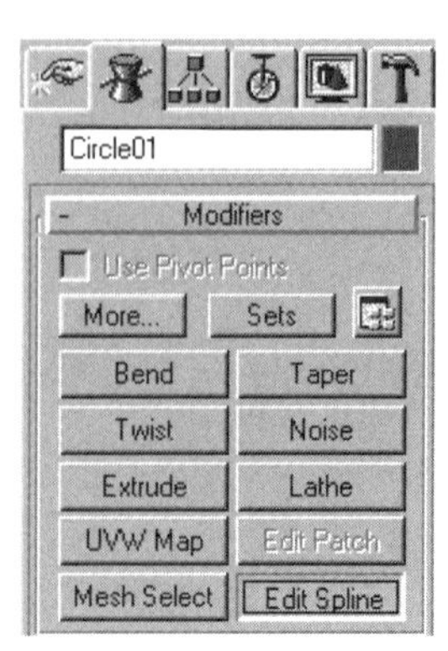


Shape modifiers are used to exclusively make changes to spline shapes. There are three basic shape modifiers, Edit Spline, Extrude, and Lathe. The second two are used to turn a two-dimensional shape into a three-dimensional object. Even though it is possible to work with more than one shape at a time, working with one at a time gives more predictable results. The following is a description of each of the spline modifiers and the Edit Mesh modifier that has a special effect on spline shapes.

### Edit Spline

The Edit Spline modifier is used to select and change entire splines, their segments, or vertices within a shape.

Once you have selected a shape to modify, you can specify the subobject level, such as spline, segment, or vertex. With the subobject level specified, submodifiers for that component are displayed. The following are the submodifiers for each sublevel.

#### SPLINE

**Close**
Adds a segment to an open spline to create a closed shape.

**Outline**
Creates an outline shape around the selected spline.

**Boolean**
Allows you to union (add), subtract, or intersect two splines to create a third unique spline shape.

**Mirror**
Creates a mirror move or mirror copy of a spline.

**Detach**
Detaches splines to make an independent shape.

**Delete**
Deletes the selected spline.

#### SEGMENT

**Break**
Breaks a segment at the picked point. You can then move each segment end separately.

**Refine**
Inserts a vertex at the picked point without changing the shape of the segment.

**Detach**
Detaches the selected segment.

**Delete**
Deletes the selected segment.

#### VERTEX

**Connect**
Connects one end of an open spline to the other by picking on one vertex and dragging to the other.

**Break**
Splits a spline at a vertex location.

**Refine**
Adds a vertex at the picked location.

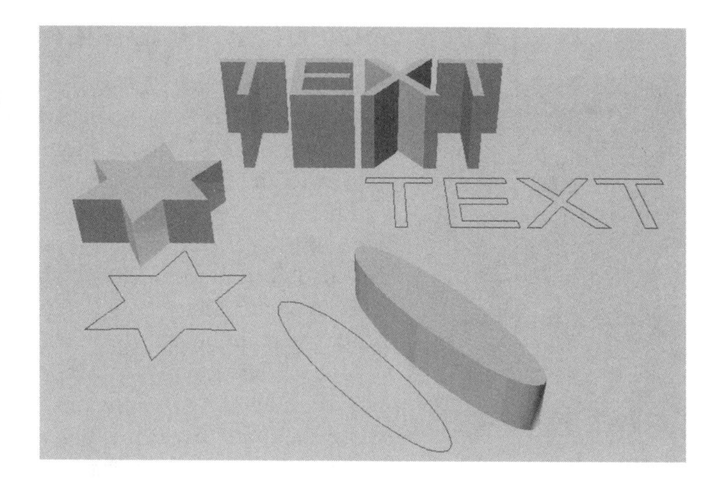


FIGURE 8.16
Extruding splines to form three-dimensional objects.

**Insert**
Adds a vertex at the picked location and allows you to drag the mouse to set the location and curve direction.

**Make First**
Establishes which vertex will be identified as the *first vertex*. This is important for lofting and path creation.

**Weld**
Welds two vertices together to make one.

**Delete**
Removes a vertex and associated segments.

## Extrude

The Extrude modifier will create a three-dimensional object from a selected shape by setting the Amount (thickness) value. Figure 8.16 shows a spline and the resulting extrusion. You can also specify if you want a 3D object to be capped or not. There are two output methods, Patch and Mesh. Use mesh for a standard surface and patch if you want to edit the extrusion surface.

## Lathe

The Lathe modifier creates a three-dimensional object from a selected shape by revolving the shape around a selected direction axis. See Figure 8.17. The Align options move the lathe axis. You can manually adjust the axis by using the subobject level and applying a transform such as Move.

## Mesh Select

The Mesh Select modifier will edit a mesh and turn a closed spline shape into a two-dimensional meshed object that can be rendered.

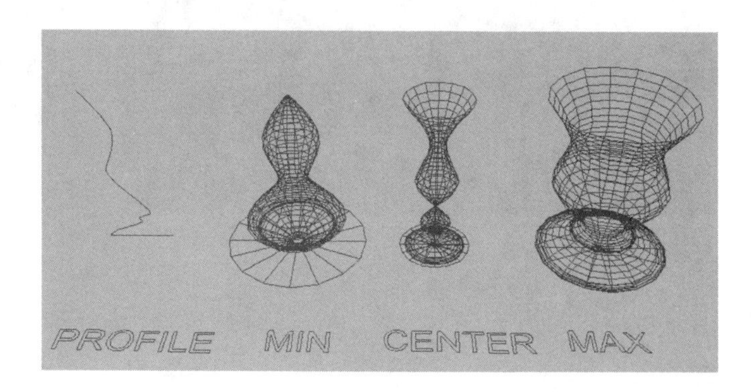


FIGURE 8.17
Using Lathe to form a three-dimensional object through revolution.

## 8.5 GEOMETRIC MODIFIERS

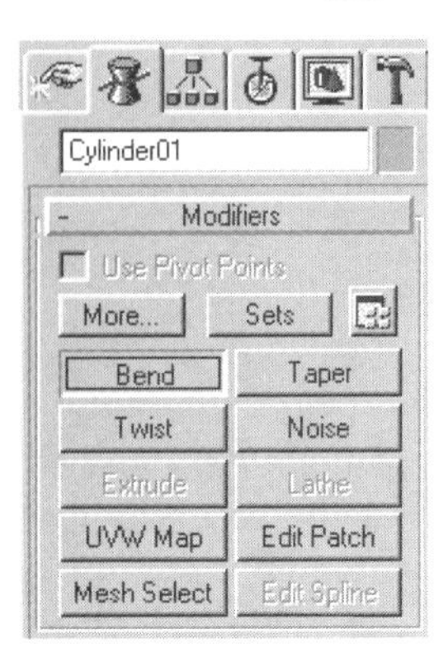


Geometric modifiers can be applied to objects to create more complex shapes. This section explains six basic geometric modifiers. Figure 8.18 illustrates some of the various geometric modifiers. It should be noted that you apply more than one geometric modifier to an object to achieve a complex modification.

There is also a special sublevel modifier, called a Gizmo, that applies to each geometric modifier. A Gizmo represents the envelope of the modifier around the selected object. If you select the Gizmo sublevel, you can use transforms on it to rotate, move, or scale. This has the effect of changing the orientation or size of the modifier as it applies to the object.

One application of this would be to control the direction of a wave modifier over a surface patch. Once the wave has been applied, you can select its Gizmo sublevel and use the rotate transform to change the direction of the wave over the object.

The following is a description of the six basic geometric modifiers.

### Bend

Bend produces a uniform bend in a selected object. You can control the bend angle and direction, the axis the bend will take place in and the limits. Limits are distances above and below the modifier's center that are affected by the bend.

A ORIGINAL

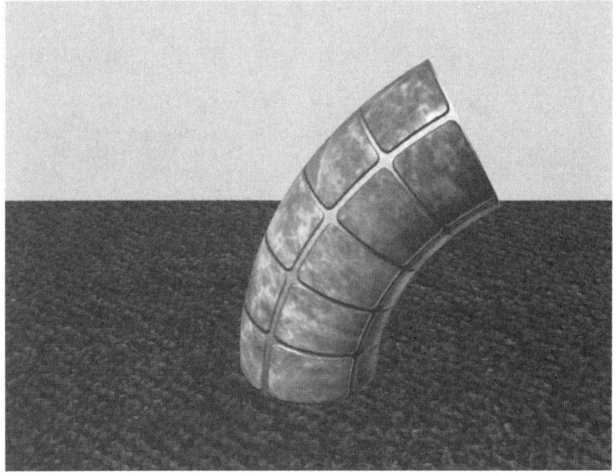

B BEND

C TAPER

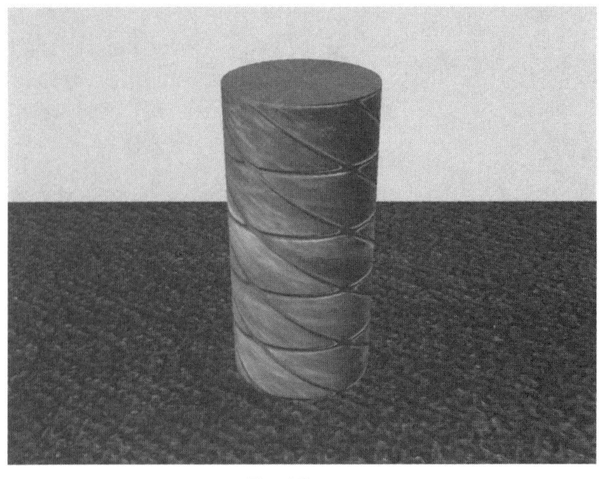

D TWIST

FIGURE 8.18
Geometric modifiers.

### Taper

Taper produces a tapered contour by scaling one end of an object's geometry. You can set the amount of the taper and apply a curve. As with the bend, you can control the limit of the taper.

### Twist

Twist applies a corkscrew effect to an object. The object is twisted about a selected axis and by a number of degrees.

### Skew

The skew modifier tilts the object off center while maintaining parallel planes.

### Wave

Wave applies a wave effect to an object. This modifier works best with broad, flat objects with many segments, such as surface patches. There are two amplitudes with which to work to control the vertical heights of the wave; the wave length controls the number of waves over a distance, and the phase setting moves the peaks along the

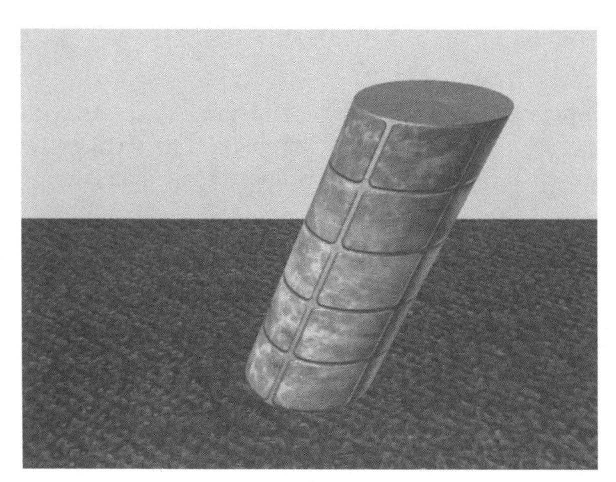

E SKEW

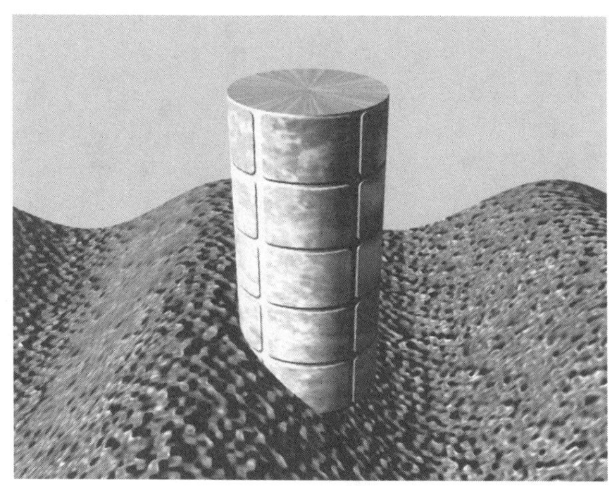

F WAVE

G RIPPLE

H NOISE

## LIGHTS! CAMERA! ACTION! 

### Segments and Geometric Modifiers

To achieve some of the desired effects using geometric modifiers, the object being modified may require many segments. This is especially true for wave, ripple, and noise modifiers. You may have to add 20 or more additional segments to a surface patch to get the desired effect. You can usually tell that there are not enough segments if the surface displacement looks jagged when it should be smooth. If this happens, increase the number of segments used to create the object.

object, particularly effective when animated to simulate the swells of ocean waves. The decay increases or decreases the amplitude near the center or edges, and the value increases amplitude near the center and flattens the wave at the edges; small values can have a large effect.

### Ripple

The ripple modifier applies a ripple effect over the surface of the object. As with wave, this works best with broad, flat objects with many segments. The settings are similar to the wave modifier; however, although the wave is linear, the ripple is more localized, causing bubbling effects.

### Noise

The noise modifier modulates the position of an object's vertices along any combination of the three axes. It can be very useful in creating terrain automatically with the use of the fractal option.

## 8.6 SUMMARY

You now have reviewed the basic building blocks, from primitive objects to geometric modifiers. With these tools at your disposal you are well on your way to the modeling of a variety of environments. Many objects can be created using these basic tools, from wooden boards to convoluted vases or bubbling broths. Experimentation is the best test—taking a basic shape, applying a variety of modifiers, and observing the results. It is up to your imagination to choose which modeling tools to apply and then to observe the results.

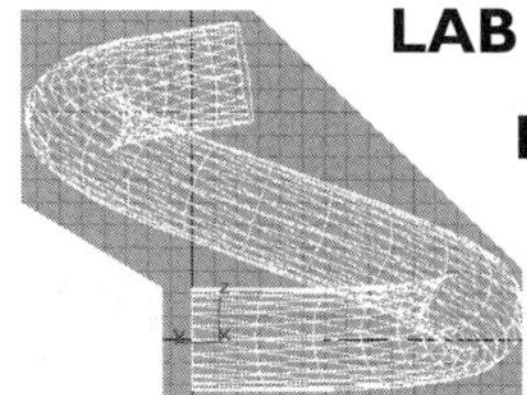

# LAB 8.A

## Basic Modeling

### Purpose

This lab practices the techniques used in basic modeling to form your 3D world. In it you create primitive objects and apply geometric modifiers, as well as create spline shapes and extrude and lathe them into three-dimensional objects.

### Objectives

You will be able to

- Set up the units, grid, and, snap settings for a project.
- Create primitives.
- Create surface patches.
- Apply geometric modifiers to primitives and surface patches.
- Create spline shapes.
- Apply shape modifiers to spline shapes to create 3D objects.

### Procedure

#### SETTING UP THE PROJECT

With any project you need to establish some starting settings. These settings are usually standard for all projects and you should become familiar with checking them before you start any creation. Because you have used these settings for the previous labs, it's time to start setting them on your own.

1. Activate the Top viewport and set or check the following settings:

Units = decimal inches
Grid = every 1 in. and major lines every 10 in.
Snap = Set snap to grid points

| | |
|---|---|
| Buttons | Region Selection = Window<br>2D Snap = On<br>Angle Snap = On |
| Viewports | Standard Top, Front, Left, Perspective; all wireframe except for Perspective, which should be set to Smooth+Highlight. |

Remember to use the Hold button before you perform any command you are unsure of. If something doesn't work, you can always use the Fetch button to restore the geometry to its pre-Hold state.

#### PRIMITIVE CREATION

With this lab, the size of the objects created will not be important. As long as the proportional shape matches the associated figure in the text, you will be okay.

2. Create a box, as shown in Figure 8.19, with Generate Mapping Coords. turned on. The box requires 10 segments along its length, width, and height and is named TWISTER.

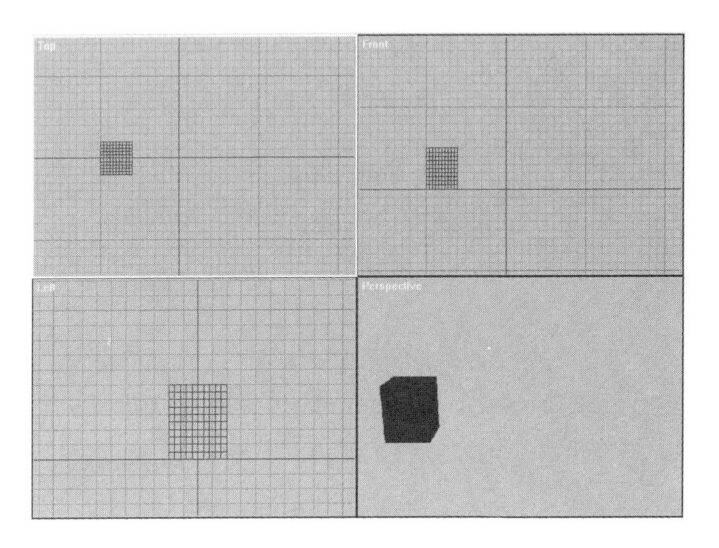

FIGURE 8.19
Placement of TWISTER box.

3. Figure 8.20 shows the cone you are about to create. Now follow the procedure listed next:
   a. Select the Cone creation button.
   b. Pick in the center of the Top viewport, hold down, and drag to define the radius of the cone. Once you have the desired radius, release the button.
   c. Move the cursor upward to define the height of the cone. Click the pick button when the cone is the desired height.
   d. Move the cursor up and down and observe the shape of the cone. Move the cursor upward until there is a point at the top of the cone. Click to set it.
   e. Turn on Generate Mapping Coords.
   f. Give the cone the name DROOP.
4. Create a tube, as shown in Figure 8.21. Follow this procedure:
   a. Select the Tube creation button.
   b. Pick the Top viewport to establish the center of the tube, hold down on the button, and drag to set the radius of the outside of the tube and release the button.
   c. Move the cursor to set the inside radius of the tube and click to set it.
   d. Turn on Generate Mapping Coords. and set height and cap segments to 10.
   e. Give the tube the name VOLCANO.

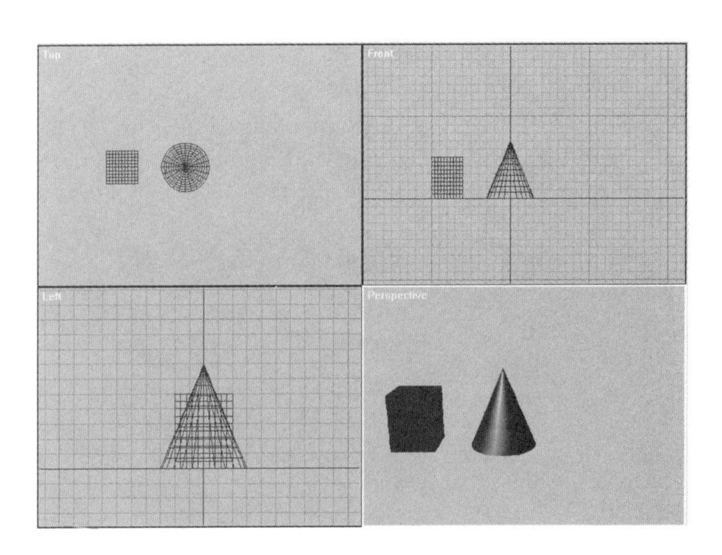

FIGURE 8.20
Placement of DROOP cone.

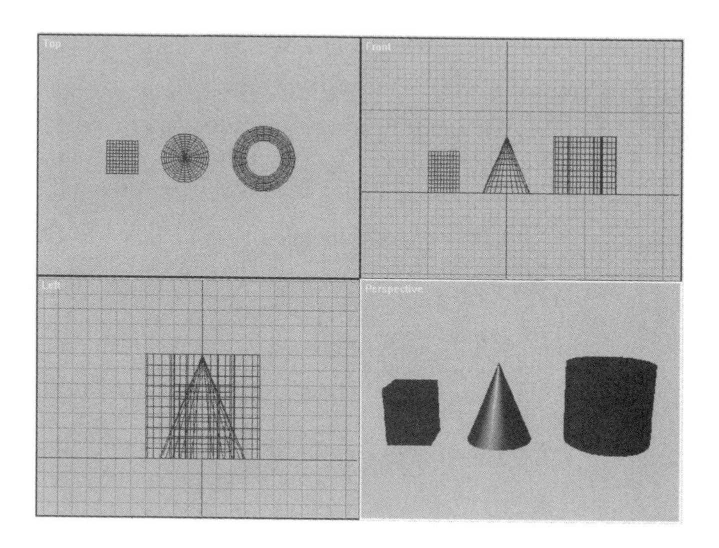

FIGURE 8.21
Placement of the tube VOLCANO.

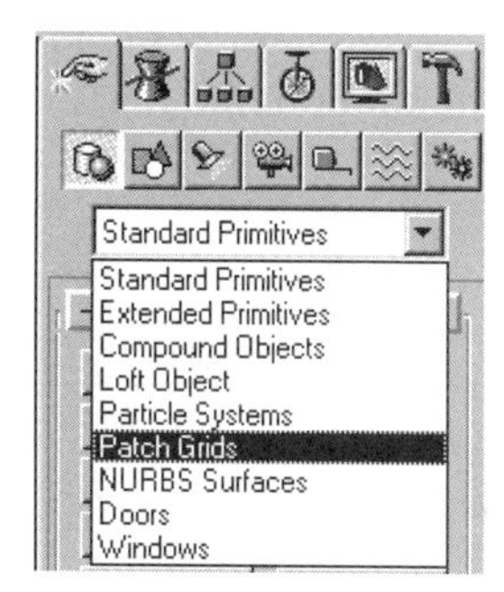


5. You are now going to create a surface patch that covers an area that the other objects will sit on. Figure 8.22 shows the extents of the patch.

   To do this you, first select Patch Grids from the drop-down list and then follow this procedure:

   a. Pick the Quad Patch button.
   b. Pick the lower-left start corner of the patch in the Top viewport, drag to the upper-right corner, and click to set.
   c. Increase the number of length and width segments from 1 to 5. You will need the extra segments when you apply the geometric modifiers.
   d. Turn on Generate Mapping Coords.
   e. Give the patch the name HILLS.

6. Use the Zoom Extents All button to see the entire scene and save the file as CH8A.MAX.

## GEOMETRY MODIFIERS

Now you are going to apply some geometric modifiers to objects you just created. The box will be twisted, the cone bent, and the tube tapered.

7. Activate the Front viewport and select the TWISTER object using the Object Selection. Lock the selection.

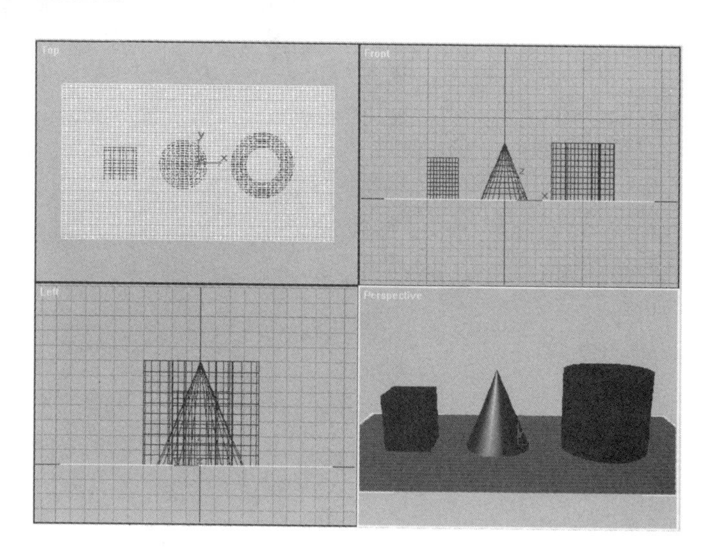

FIGURE 8.22
Placement of the patch HILLS.

8. Open the Modify command panel.
9. Pick the Twist modifier button and refer to Part A of Figure 8.23 for the settings. You are going to twist the box 360° from top to bottom. See Part B of Figure 8.23 for the results. *Note:* This wouldn't work if you had not increased the number of segments along the surfaces of the box.
10. Unlock TWISTER; select DROOP and lock it.
11. With the Modify command panel still open, select the Bend modifier button. You are going to bend the cone so that it looks like it's drooping. See Part A of Figure 8.24 for the settings and Part B for the results.
12. Unlock DROOP; select VOLCANO and lock it.
13. With the Modify command panel still open, select the Taper modifier button. You are going to taper the tube to form a conical shape. See Part A of Figure 8.25 for the settings and Part B for the results.
14. Unlock VOLCANO; select HILLS and lock it.
15. With the Modify command panel still open, select the Noise modifier button. You are going to apply random movement of an object's vertices to create hills. See Part A of Figure 8.26 for the settings and Part B for the results.
16. Unlock HILLS; select VOLCANO and lock it.
17. Let's apply some noise to the VOLCANO to see the effect. Select the Noise modifier button and refer to Part A of Figure 8.27 for the settings and Part B for the results. As you can now see, you can create unlimited shapes by starting with initial primitives and applying modifiers.
18. Save the file as CH8A.MAX.

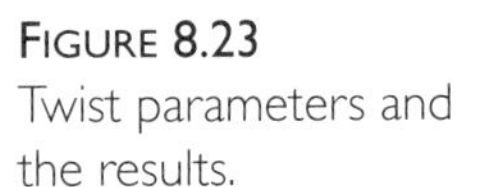
FIGURE 8.23
Twist parameters and the results.

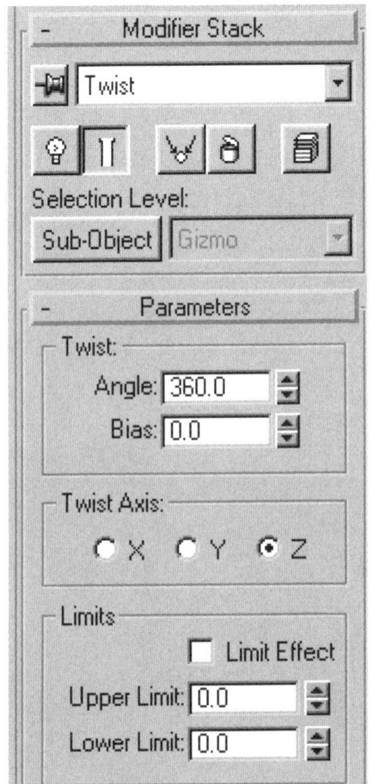


A

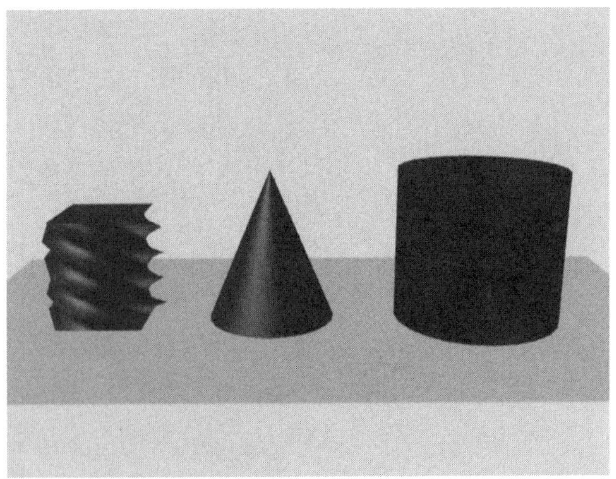

B

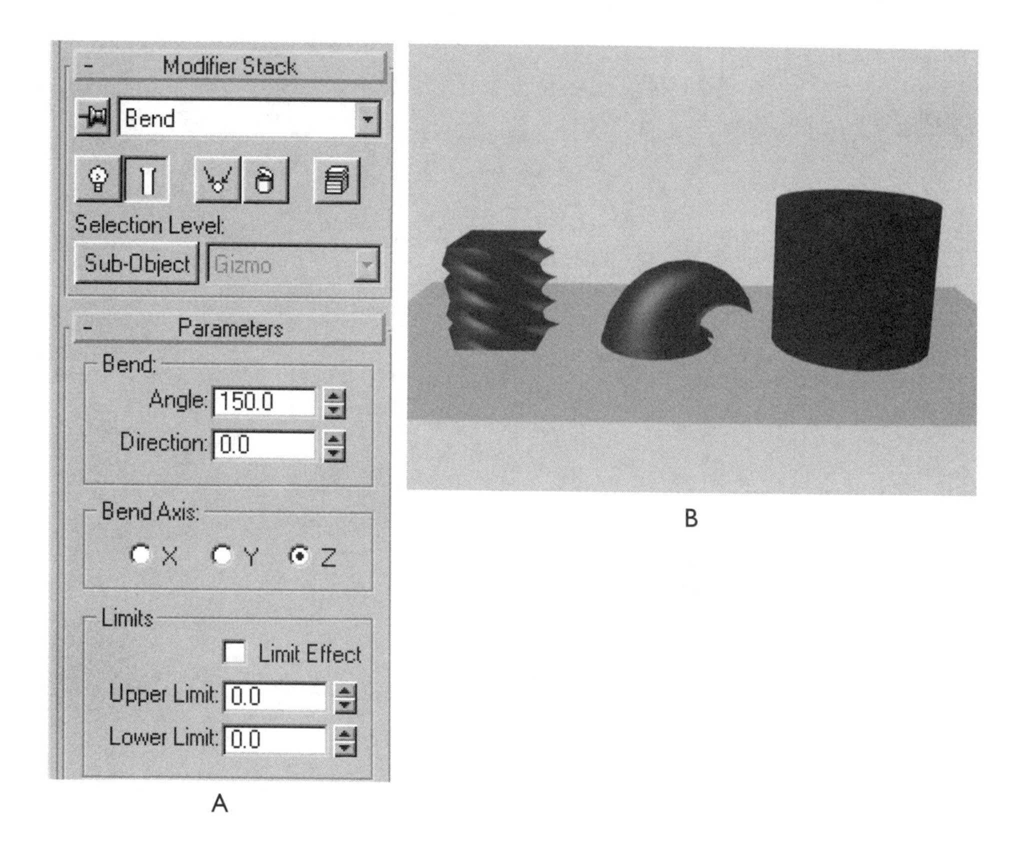


FIGURE 8.24
Bend parameters and the results.

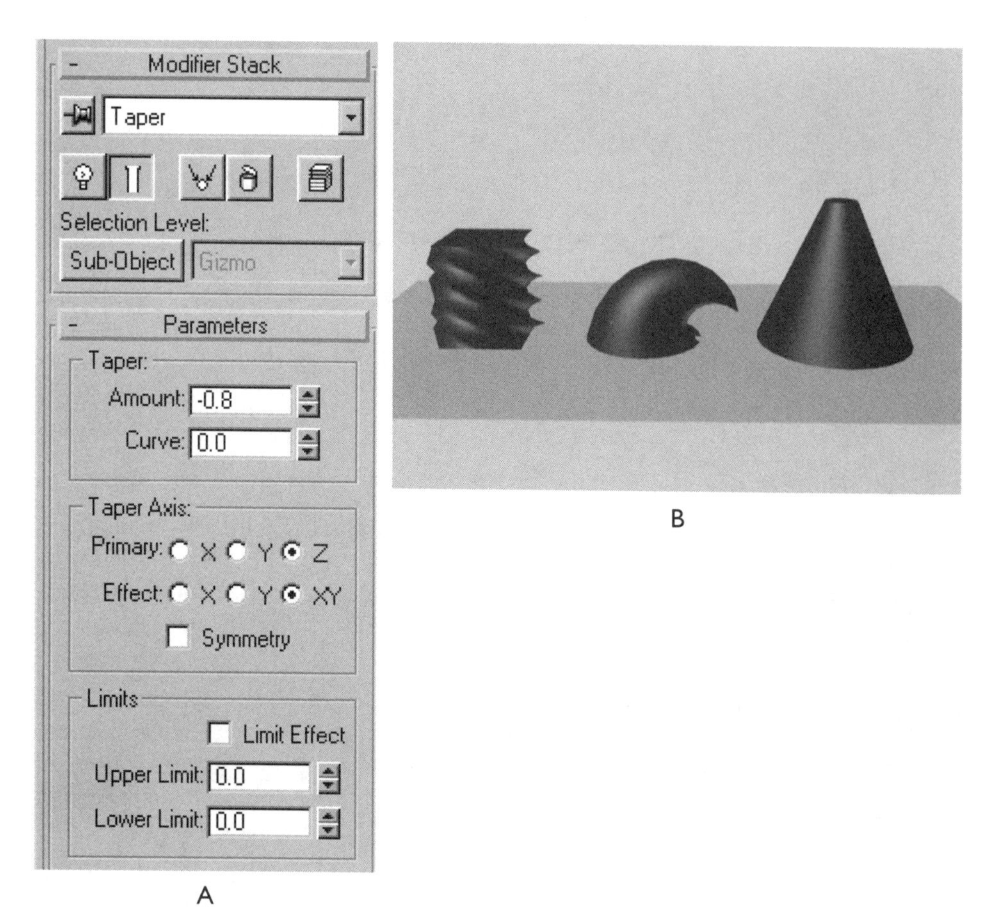


FIGURE 8.25
Taper parameters and the results.

FIGURE 8.26
Noise parameters and the results.

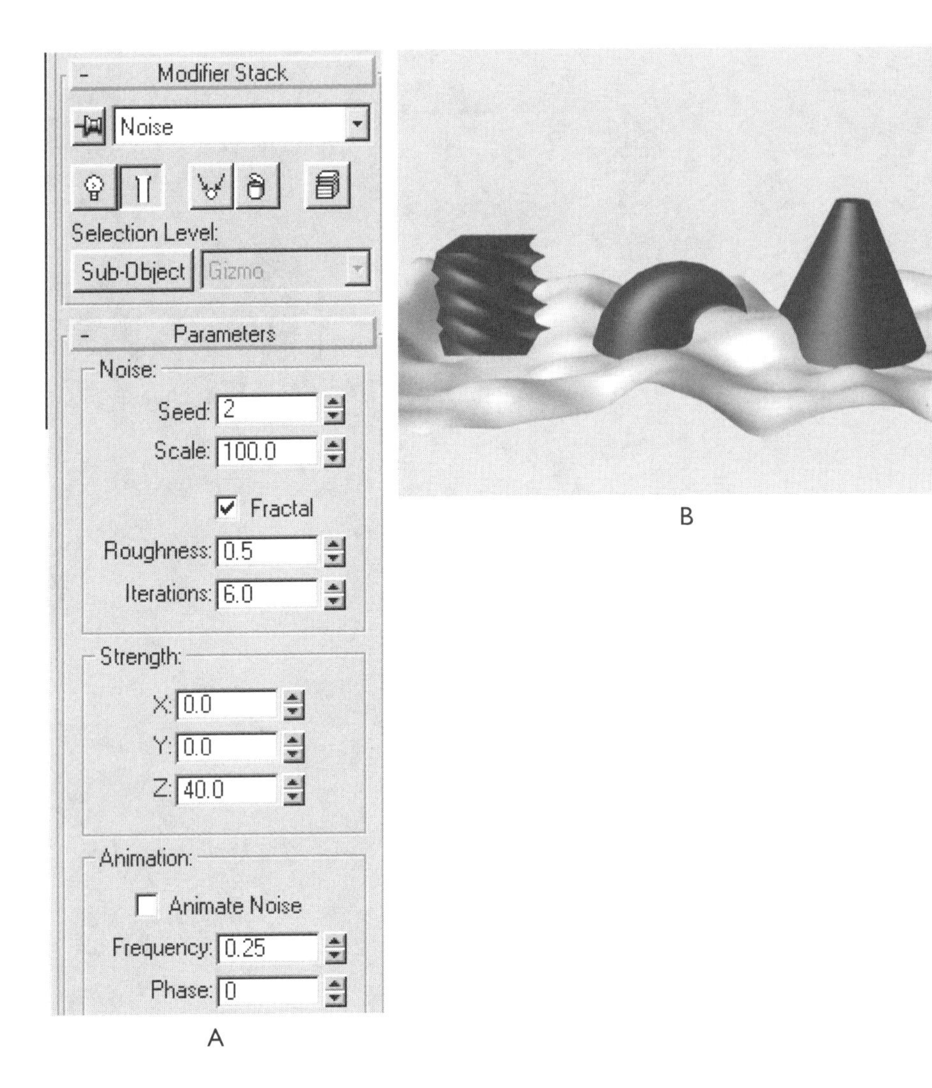


## CREATING SPLINE SHAPES

You are going to create three spline shapes: a box, a star, and a profile with lines. Once these are created, you are going to apply shape modifiers to turn them into three-dimensional objects. Like the primitive objects you created previously, size is not important as long as the shape is proportional to the figures.

19. Start a new scene by selecting the File/New pull-down menu item. Select New All.
20. Pick the Shapes button from the Creation command panel.

21. Activate the Top viewport and select the Rectangle button. See Figure 8.28 for the position and size of the rectangle. Pick in the top viewport to position the lower-left corner of the rectangle shape and drag toward the upper right until the desired shape is formed; release the cursor. Give the rectangle shape the name CURVEIT.
22. Select the Star shape button. Figure 8.29 shows the position and size of the star. Pick the top viewport to establish the center of the star shape and drag to form the outer radius; release to set. Move the cursor to set the radius of the inner points of the star and pick when you have the desired shape. Give the star shape the name EXTRUDEIT.
23. Now you are going to draw a profile, as shown in Figure 8.30, to create half a balloon. To do this you will need to use the pick and drag feature to form curves. You will have to practice this until you feel comfortable.

**FIGURE 8.27**
Noise parameters applied to the VOLCANO and the results.

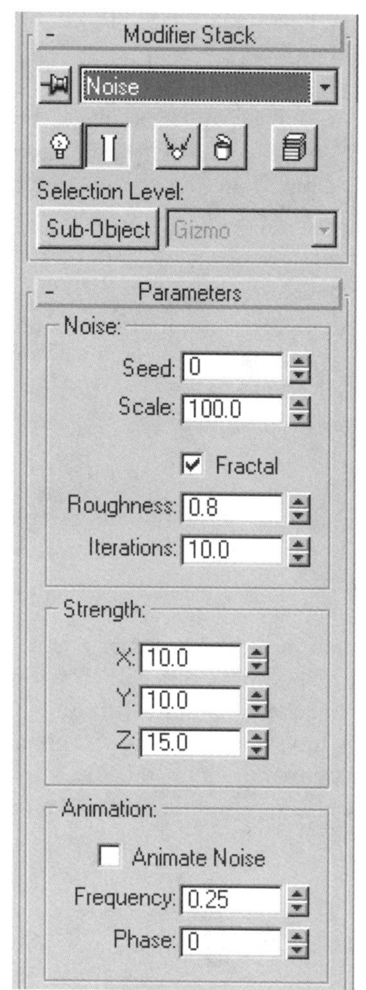


A

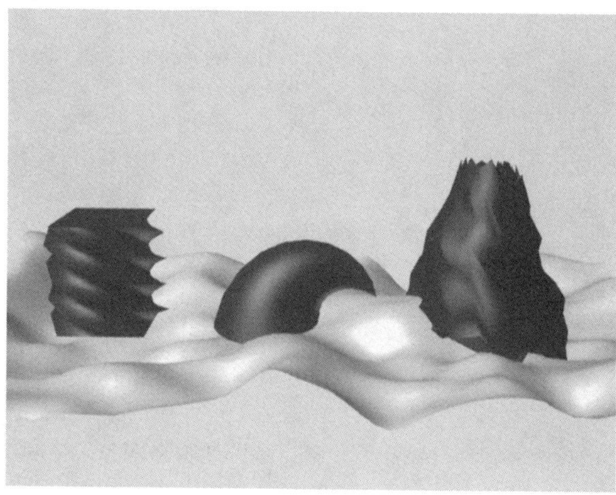

B

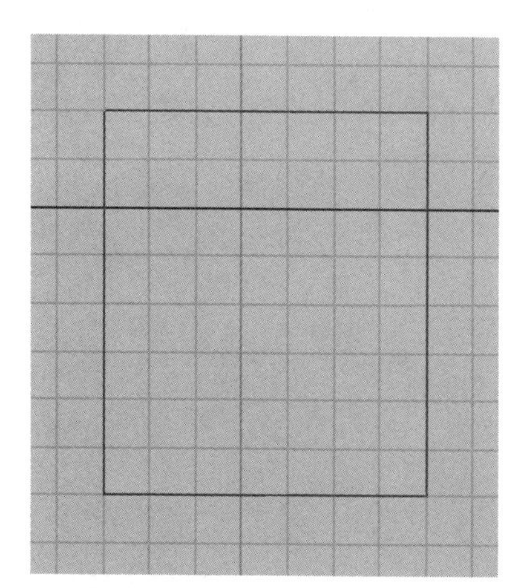

**FIGURE 8.28**
Rectangle spline shape.

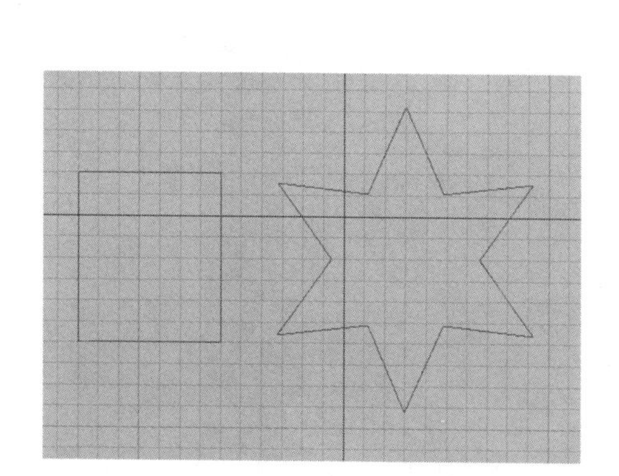

**FIGURE 8.29**
Star spline shape.

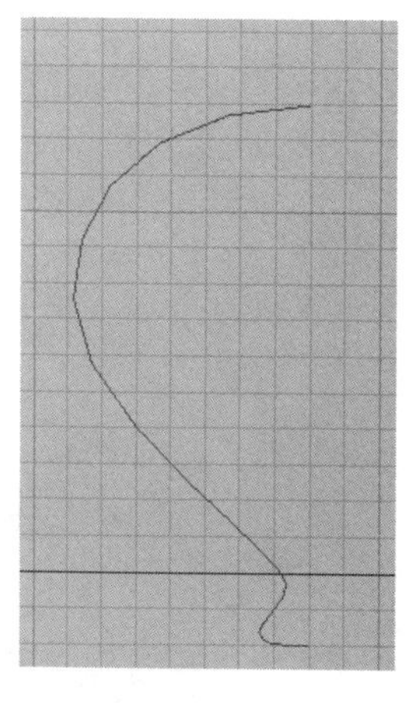

**FIGURE 8.30**
Shape profile.

To start, activate the Front viewport and select the Line shape button to create the shape. Then pick at the top point of the profile, hold down on the button, drag horizontally to the right, lift up on the button and drag the cursor downward. Observe how a curve is formed. Try this a couple of times before you attempt to create the balloon profile. *Note:* Right-click to stop the creation of the spline lines.

Once you are comfortable, draw the profile as shown in Figure 8.30. Give the profile shape the name LATHEIT.

## SHAPE MODIFIER

You are now going to apply various shape modifiers to the shapes you just created. The rectangle is going to be edited to create a curve, the star is going to be extruded to create a three-dimensional star, and the profile shape is going to be lathed (revolved) to create a cylindrical three-dimensional shape.

24. Select CURVEIT shape.
25. Open the Modify command panel. Now you will be able to select the Edit Spline modifier button. This will be used to modify the profile shape. Pick the pop-up list under the modifier stack button and pick rectangle from the list.

    The subobject selection level defaults to Vertex. Change it to Segment.

    Select the Move transform button and pick the top line segment of the rectangle in the Top viewport. It should turn red to signify that it is selected. Pick and drag the line until the shape looks similar to Figure 8.31. As you can see, you can manipulate a shape by modifying its basic components.

    Stay in the Modify command panel and select the Mesh Select modifier to turn the shape into a 2D object. This will allow it to be rendered even though it is only two-dimensional.

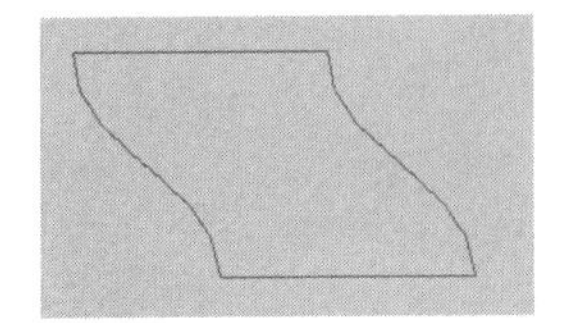

FIGURE 8.31
Applying an Edit Spline modifier to a shape.

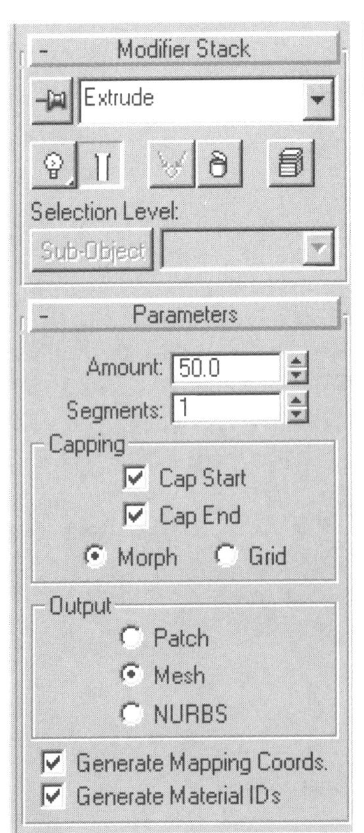


A

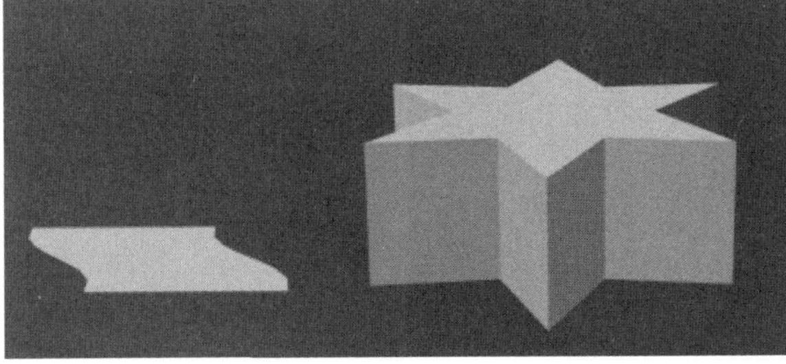

B

FIGURE 8.32
Extrude parameters and the results.

26. Open the Creation command panel to exit from the Modify command panel and select the EXTRUDEIT shape. You need to do this to close the Edit Spline sub-object level modification. You are going to extrude the star shape into a three-dimensional object.
27. Open the Modify command panel and select the Extrude modifier. See Part A of Figure 8.32 for the settings and Part B for the results.
28. Activate the Front viewport and select the profile LATHEIT. You are going to create a cylindrical object by revolving (lathing) the profile.
29. Select the Lathe modifier from the Modify command panel. Refer to Part A of Figure 8.33 for the settings and Part B for the results. You will need to pick the Max button to get the right size and shape.
30. Save the file as CH8B.MAX.

    With the use of shapes, you can create a variety of profiles and then you can apply the shape modifiers to create three-dimensional objects.

FIGURE 8.33
Lathe parameters and the results.

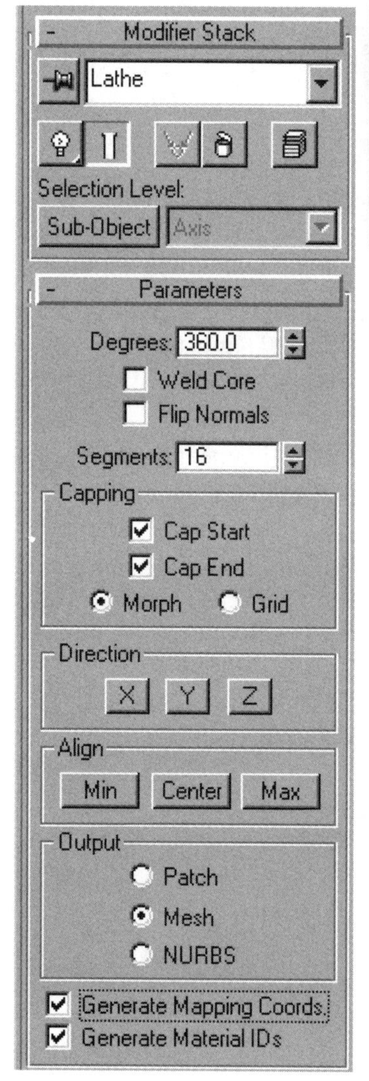


A

B

## QUESTIONS AND ASSIGNMENTS

### QUESTIONS

1. Why would you want to add additional segments to an object?
2. If you created an object with the cylinder command, why would you want to turn smoothing off?
3. What function does the slice option serve?
4. How would you create a pyramid object?
5. Why would you want to create a teapot object?
6. What is a shape?
7. What shape command creates a spring shape?
8. Explain the function of the shape modifiers Extrude and Lathe.
9. Explain the procedure to create a flat object that could be rendered.
10. What geometric modifier would you use to create a corkscrew effect?
11. What geometric modifier would you use to create the movement of a flag?

### ASSIGNMENTS

1. Create a new scene called CH8C.MAX. In the scene create each of the eight primitive shapes so that you can try the different creation parameters for each object.
2. Create a new scene called CH8D.MAX. In the scene create seven identical three-dimensional boxes with 10 segments for length, width, and height. Apply a different geometric modifier to each box so that you can see how the same object behaves under different modifiers.
3. Using the objects created in Assignment 2, assign several geometric modifiers, such as bend and twist, to the same object so that you can see the effect of multiple modifiers.
4. Create a text shape such as your name, apply the Extrude modifier, and then round the edges of the letters with the use of the MeshSmooth modifier with a strength of 0.1 and the Smooth Results turned on.

# CHAPTER 9

# Advanced Modeling: Lofting and Boolean Operations

## 9.1 INTRODUCTION

This chapter deals with more complex modeling that involves a combining of two or more objects to create the final result. The first type, called lofting, involves using a combination of spline shapes and a spline path to create the final complex object. The second type, called Boolean operations, involves the combining of two three-dimensional objects to create the final complex object.

## 9.2 LOFTING CONCEPTS

The term *lofting* comes from ancient times when wooden ships were built. The builders assembled a series of wooden cross sections of the hull shape, held together with lofts. The process of hoisting the cross sections into lofts became known as lofting. This is exactly what you do in the 3D Studio MAX. You place cross-sectional shapes along a path.

### Cross Section and Path Relationship

To understand creation using lofting techniques, you must understand how the cross section and path interact during lofting. Refer to Part A of Figure 9.1. The cross-section shape is used to define the perimeter shape of the exterior shell of the final 3D object. See Part B of Figure 9.1. The path is used to define the path the closed shape will travel. The path may twist and turn in any direction, as shown in Part C of Figure 9.1. During the lofting process the cross section is copied along the path at certain intervals—the vertices and step locations. See Part D of Figure 9.1. Using these cross sections as a guide, a mesh skin is wrapped around to form the 3D object.

The path and cross sections are created using the shape commands, and practically any open or closed 2D or 3D shape can be used. However, there are a few limitations: nested and text shapes cannot be used as paths and intersecting shapes should not be used because the final outcome can be unpredictable.

You can also use more than one cross-sectional shape placed along the path. These are placed at path levels. Each level can hold a totally different cross-sectional shape. The result is a complexly contoured 3D object.

## Loft Density

The number of faces used to create lofted objects is referred to as the loft density. The density is controlled by the number of vertices used to create the shapes and the skin parameters used during the lofting procedure. The density affects a number of factors in the final 3D object:

- The more dense the surfaces, the more accurately the curves and bends are represented.
- The more dense the surfaces, the easier it is to deform.
- The more dense the surfaces, the better the render.
- The less dense the surfaces, the faster rendering takes place.

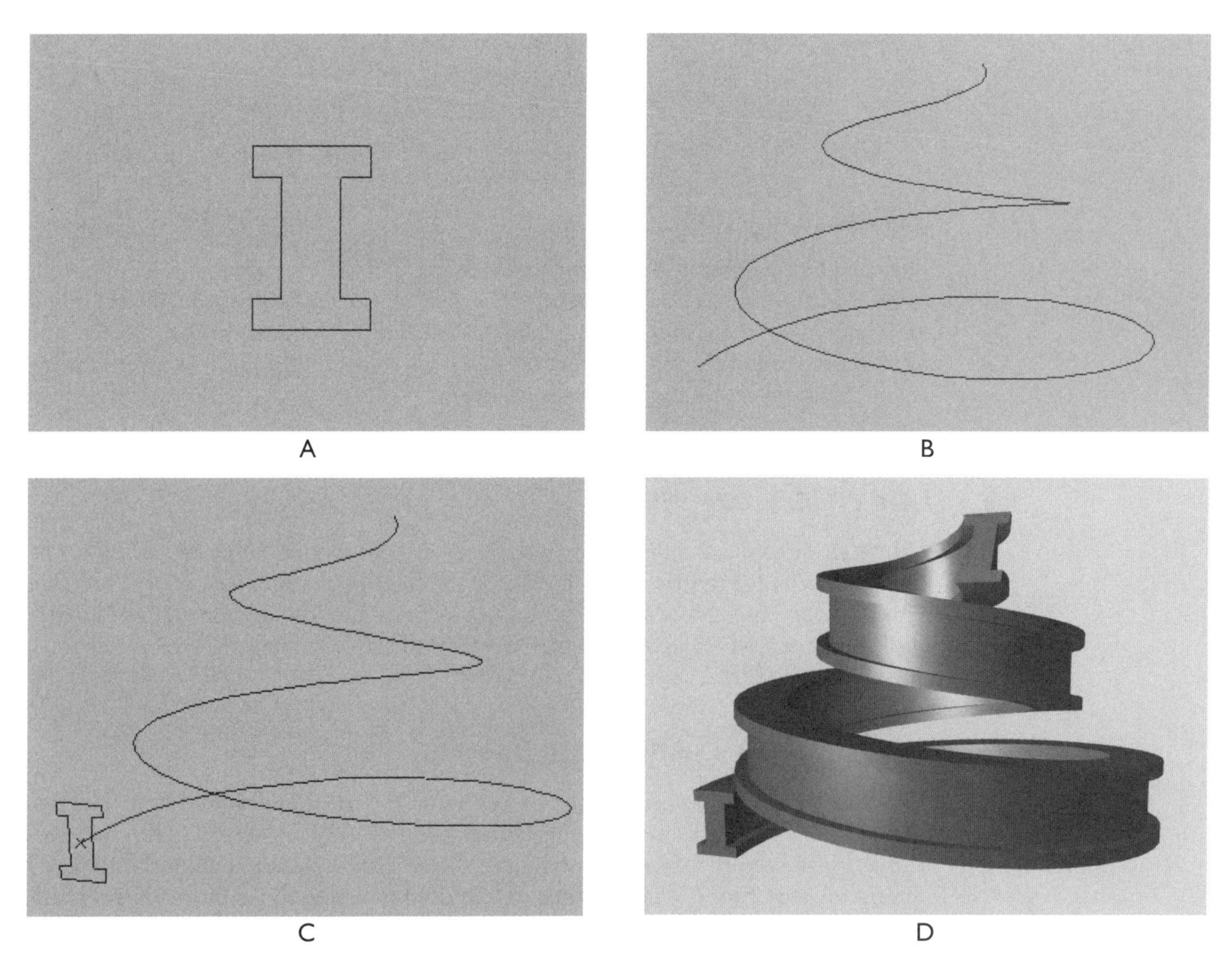


FIGURE 9.1
Relation of the cross section to the path.

## 9.3 LOFTING CREATION PANEL

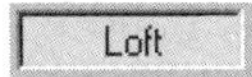


Lofting is controlled through the lofting parameters in the Creation panel. See Figure 9.2. Through the use of the various parameters, the final 3D object is achieved.

### Lofting Procedure

1. Select a shape for either the path or the cross-sectional shape (Figure 9.1A).
2. Pick the Geometry button in the Create panel and choose the Loft Object from the category list.
3. Pick Loft in the Object Type rollout.
4. Use the Get Path option if you first selected a cross-sectional shape (Figure 9.1B) or use the Get Shape option if you first selected a path shape. Choose Move, Copy, or Instance and then pick the shape (path or cross-sectional shape).
5. Set the other parameters: Surface, Skin, Path, Deformation.
6. The lofted object is created (Figure 9.1D).

The following sections refer to each parameter and what it controls in the lofting process.

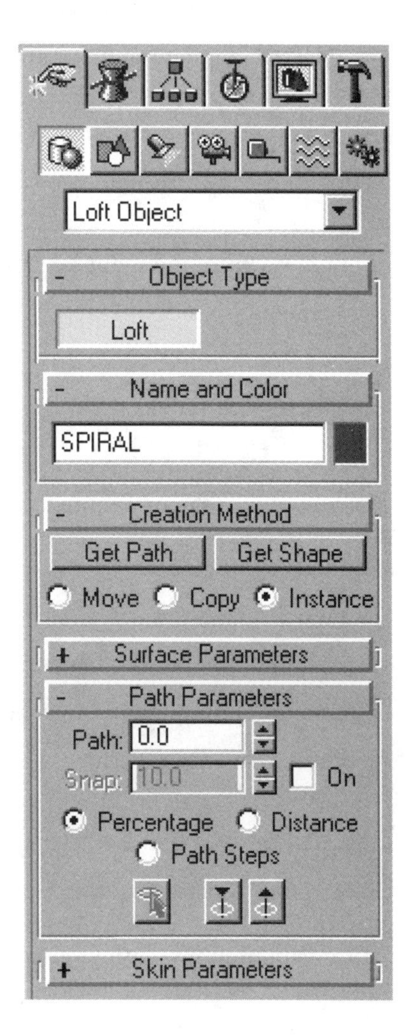


FIGURE 9.2
Lofting parameters.

## 9.4 CREATION METHOD

These parameters control the selection and placement of the path and the cross-sectional shapes.

### Get Path

Use this method if you want to move the path to meet the cross-sectional shape. In this way you can create a cross-sectional shape exactly where you want it and have the path move to it.

The new path position will be governed by the following:

- The first vertex on the path is located at the first shape's pivot point.
- The tangent to the first vertex on the path is aligned with the positive Z axis of the first shape.
- The local Z axis of the path is aligned with the local Y axis of the first shape.

The following is the procedure for using the Get Path option:

1. Select a shape as the first cross-sectional shape.
2. Pick the Geometry button in the Create panel and choose Loft Object from the category list.
3. Pick Loft in the Object Type rollout.
4. Pick the Get Path option in the Creation Method rollout.
5. Choose Move, Copy, or Instance.

   **Move**
   The shape becomes part of the loft.

   **Copy**
   A copy of the shape becomes part of the loft.

   **Instance**
   An instance of the shape becomes part of the loft.

6. Pick a shape for the path. The cursor will change to the Get Path cursor when you drag it over a valid shape.

The following is the procedure for replacing a path in an existing loft:

1. Select a loft object.
2. Pick the Modify panel and choose Loft in the Modifier Stack.
3. Pick Get Path in the Creation Method rollout.
4. Choose Move, Copy, or Instance.
5. Pick a shape for the path.

### Get Shape (Cross Section)

Use the Get Shape option if you want the shape to move to the location of the selected path. This is used when you want to place several different shapes along the path at various levels. Path levels are explained in Section 9.7 under Path Parameters.

The new shape position will be governed by the following:

- The pivot point of the shape, located on the path at the current path level.
- The positive Z axis of the shape, aligned with the tangent to the path at the current path level.
- The local Y axis of the shape, aligned with the local Z axis of the path.

The following is the procedure for using the Get Shape option:

1. Select a valid shape as the path.
2. Pick the Geometry button in the Create panel and choose the Loft Object from the category list.
3. Pick Loft in the Object Type rollout.
4. Pick Get Shape in the Creation Method rollout.
5. Choose Move, Copy, or Instance.
6. Pick a shape. *Note:* If you use the Ctrl key while selecting, the shape will flip orientation along the Z axis.

## 9.5 SURFACE PARAMETERS

The Surface Parameter's area controls the application of smoothing to the lofted object and the mapping of coordinates used for material rendering.

### Smoothing

The Smooth Length setting causes smooth transitions between edges along the length of the loft. The Smooth Width option causes smooth transitions between the edges around the perimeter of the lofted cross-sectional shapes. Refer to Figure 9.3. Remem-

FIGURE 9.3
Loft smoothing.

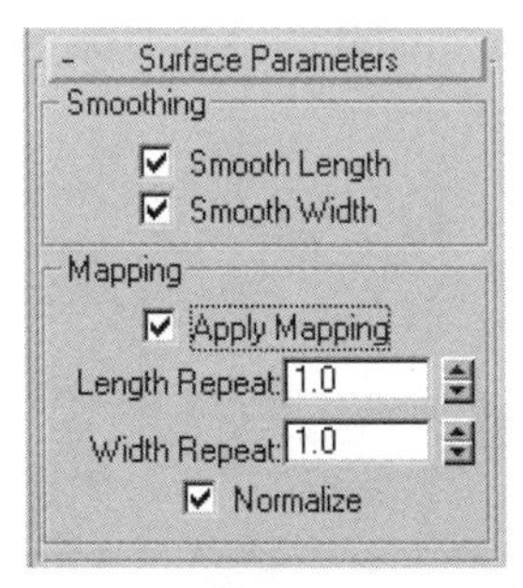


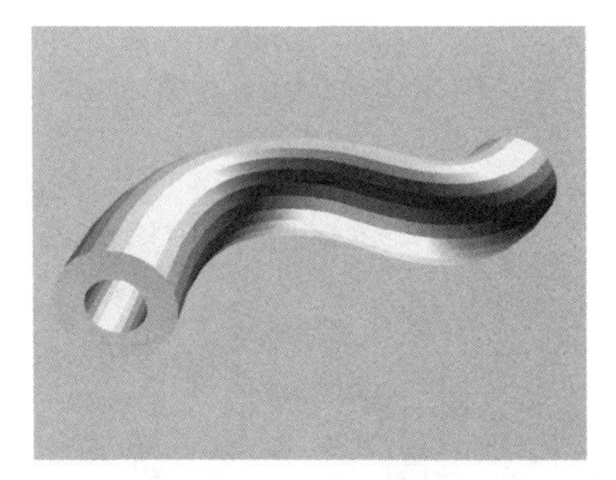

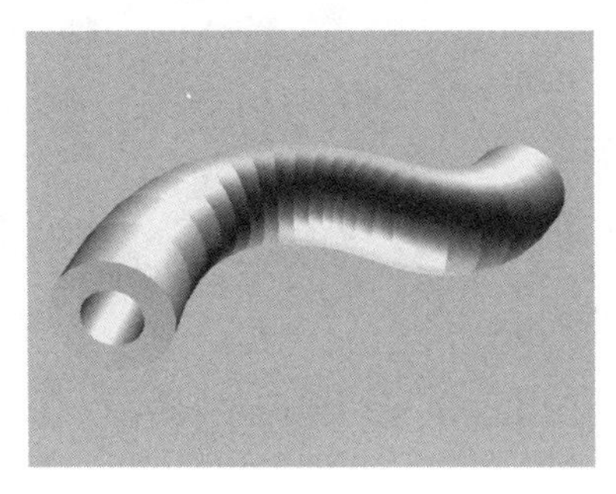

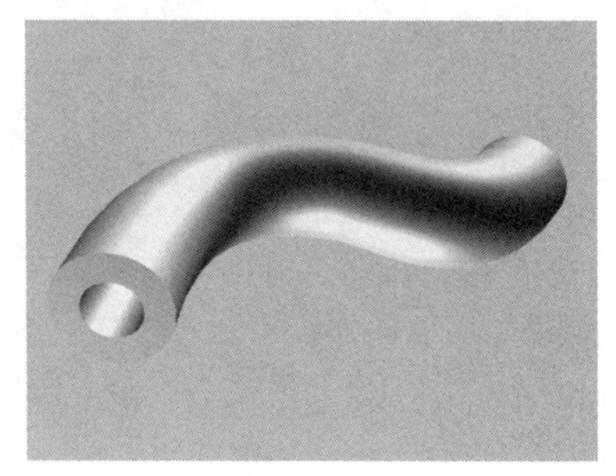

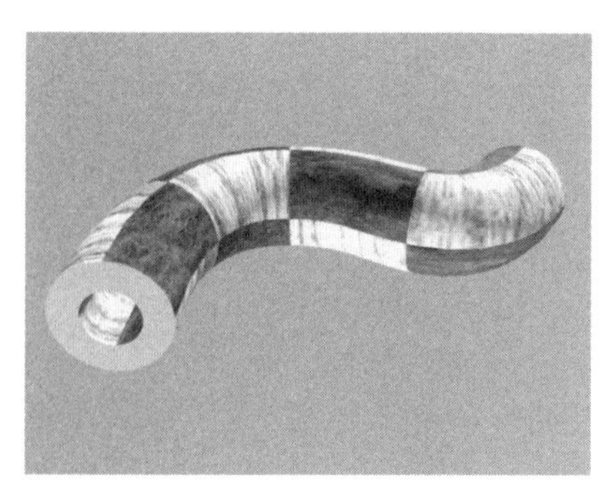

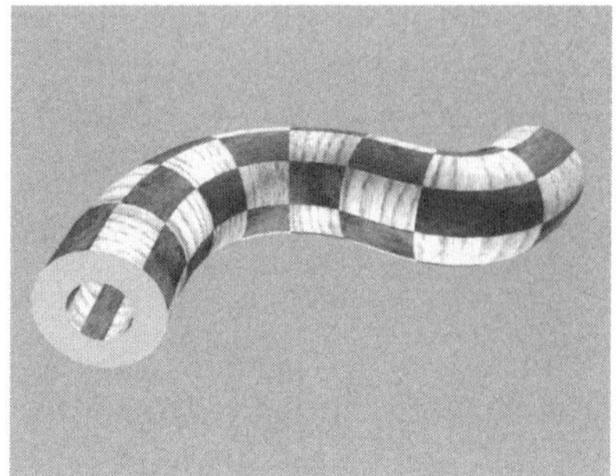

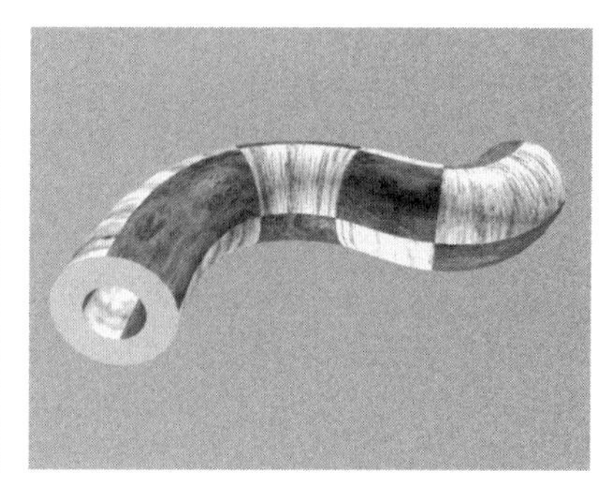

FIGURE 9.4
Loft material mapping.

ber that you will need a number of faces or steps to achieve satisfactory smoothing. Too few faces or steps will cause the object to look jagged or faceted.

### Mapping

The Apply Mapping option causes the application of lofted mapping coordinates over the lofted surface, whereas the Length Repeat option sets how many times a map will be repeated along the length of the path. The Width Repeat option sets how many times a map is repeated around the perimeter of the cross-section shapes; finally, the Normalize option causes the mapping to be spread out evenly along the path. If it is unchecked, mapping is applied to each major division or vertex spacing. See Figure 9.4.

## 9.6 SKIN PARAMETERS

Skin parameters control how the skin or surfaces are applied and displayed. See Figure 9.5 and the following descriptions.

### Capping

The capping options are used to place a cap to close either the start or end of the path. You can use a morph cap if you intend to morph the lofted object or a grid cap if you intend to apply modifiers.

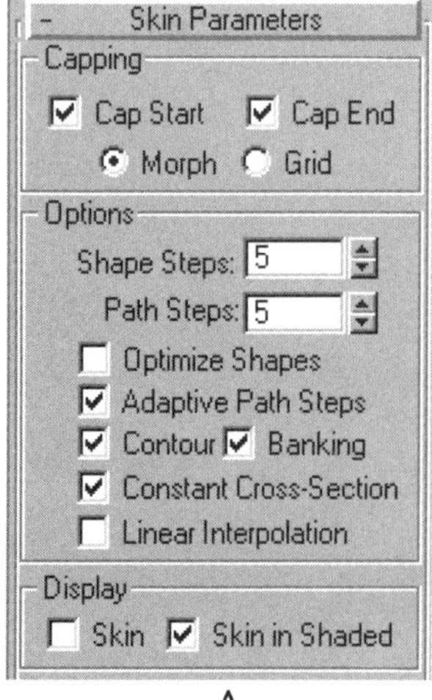


A

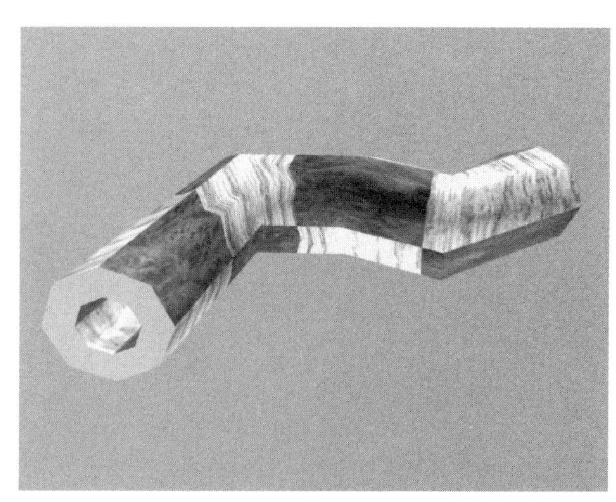

B

FIGURE 9.5
Too few shape and path steps.

## Options

The options area controls how the surfaces are created along the path.

**Shapes Steps**
Sets the number of steps used to define the perimeter of the cross-section shapes. If the Optimize Shapes box is checked, the number of Shape Steps is ignored for straight sections.

**Path Steps**
Sets the number of steps used along the length of the path. If Adaptive Path Steps is checked, the program analyzes loft and adapts the number of path divisions to generate the best skin. See Part B of Figure 9.5 for the effects of too few steps.

**Contour setting**
Causes the shapes to be aligned with the tangent to the path, giving you a consistent shape through a convoluted path.

**Bank setting**
Causes the shapes to rotate about the path.

**Linear Interpolation**
Causes the generated skin to have straight edges between each shape along the path. When it is unchecked, the skin will be smooth along the path.

## Display

The Display options are used to control the display of the skin in the different views. If Skin is checked, the loft's skin is displayed in all views using any shading level. If Skin in Shaded is checked, the loft's skin is always displayed in shaded views, regardless of the Skin setting.

# 9.7 PATH PARAMETERS

Path parameters control the application of different cross-sectional shapes to the same path. Each different shape is placed on a different level along the path. See Figure 9.6.

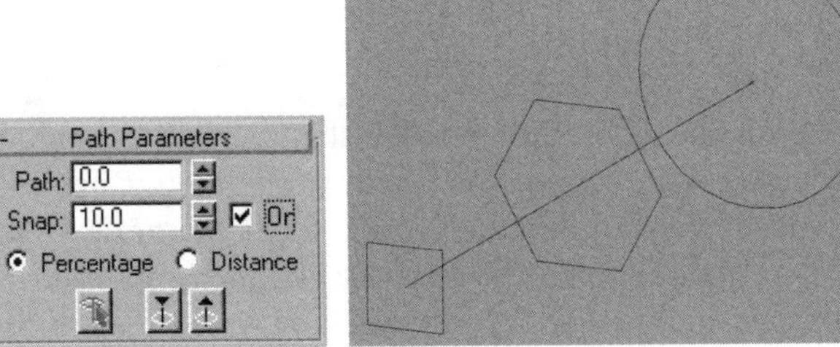


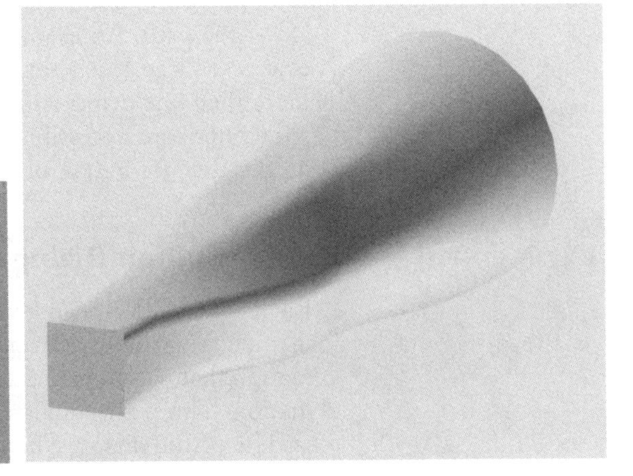

FIGURE 9.6
Path with cross-sectional shapes at different levels.

### Path

The Path setting sets the path level on which the shape will be placed. Set the path level value and then use the Get Shape button to get a shape for that level. The value may be a percentage or a distance, governed by the button that is checked. When you set a path level that contains a shape already, the shape will be highlighted by turning green.

### Snap

For precise location of levels, turn on the Snap and set the snap values. This will place a snap level at set intervals. You can set the amount of the intervals in percent of distance.

### Percentage/Distance

The Percentage and Distance buttons establish if the levels and snaps values are a measured distance or a percentage of the total path length.

### Shape Buttons

The shape buttons are used to navigate the path levels.

The Pick Shape button is used to set the current level at any shape on the path by picking the shape.

The Previous Shape button jumps the path level from its current location to the previous shape along the path.

The Next Shape button jumps the path level from its current location to the next shape along the path.

## 9.8 DEFORMATION CURVES

Deformation is the process of applying modification to a shape as its profile travels along the path. An example of this is scaling. You can start a shape at one size and change its size along the path, increasing or decreasing it as it goes. You can apply more than one deformation at a time to create some interesting results. Deformation parameters are accessible from the Modify panel once you have selected a lofted object. Refer to Part A of Figure 9.7.

### Deformation Dialog

Each deformation is controlled with the deformation dialog that displays a graph. By manipulating the graph line (deformation curve), you control the amount of deformation that occurs over the length of the path. Figure 9.7 illustrates the Scale Deformation. The path is illustrated by a thick grey line that travels horizontally in the middle of the dialog. The deformation curve travels on either side of the path line.

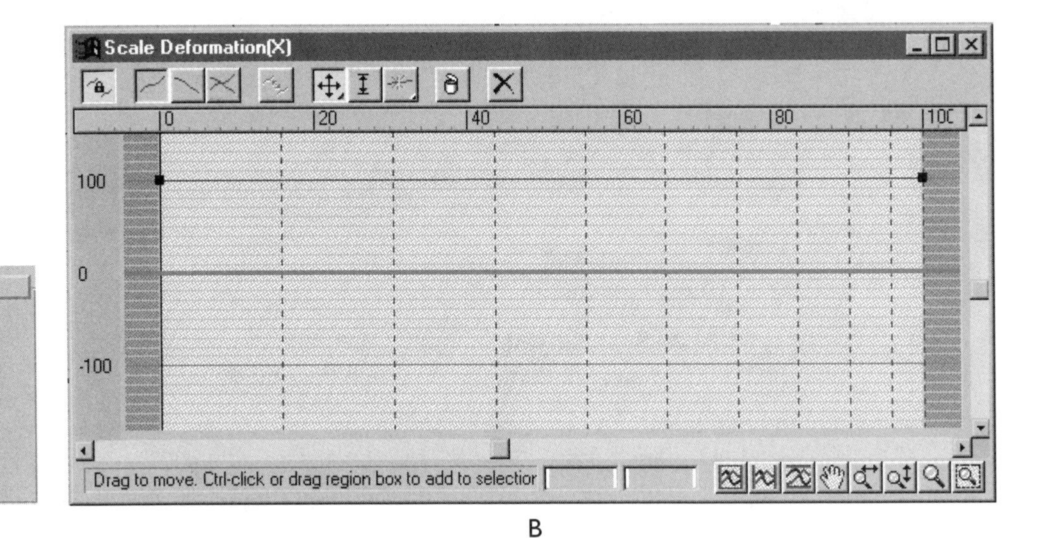


FIGURE 9.7
Deformations buttons and the Scale Deformation dialog.

Control points are placed at intervals along the curve line. By moving the control points (black boxes), you control the amount of deviation. Inserting more Control Points allows more adjustment along the path.

## Navigation Buttons

The following is a description of each of the buttons contained in the deformation dialog.

### Zoom

**Zoom Extents**
Displays entire deformation curve.

**Zoom Horizontal Extents**
Changes magnification along path length to display entire path.

**Zoom Vertical Extents**
Changes view magnification along the deformation values (vertical) to display entire deformation curve.

**Pan**
Drag in the view to move in any direction.

**Zoom Horizontally**
Drag to change magnification along path.

**Zoom Vertically**
Drag to change magnification along deformation values.

**Zoom**
Drag to change magnification along path and deformation values.

**Zoom Region**
Drag region to magnify area.

## Axes Curves

**Make Symmetrical**
Makes one axis, X or Y, match the other.

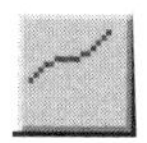

**Display X Axis**
Displays only the X axis deformation curve, shown in red.

**Display Y Axis**
Displays only the Y axis deformation curve, shown in green.

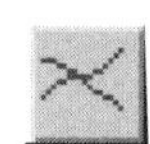

**Display XY Axis**
Displays deformation curves of both axes.

**Swap Curves**
Changes the X axis to the Y axis and the Y axis to the X axis.

## Control Points

**Move**
Changes the amount (vertical) and position (horizontal).

**Move Vertical**
Changes the amount (vertical).

**Move Horizontal**
Changes the position (horizontal).

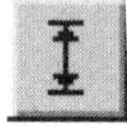

**Scale**
Scales the value of selected control points by dragging.

**Insert Corner Point**
Pick anywhere on the deformation curve to insert a corner (sharp) control point.

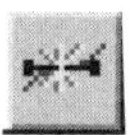

**Insert Bezier Point**
Pick anywhere on the deformation curve to insert a Bezier (curve) control point.

**Delete Control Point**
Select one or more control points and use the pick button to delete.

**Reset Curve**
Deletes all but end control points.

**Change Type**
Right-clicking any selected control point brings up menu to allow you to change the control point type.

## Types of Deformations

### Scale

Scaling increases or decreases the size of the shape along the path based on percentages. At 100% the object does not change. Less than 100% reduces the size, whereas greater than 100% increases the size. A negative scale makes a mirror image. You can scale in either or both the X and Y axes. See Figure 9.8.

### Twist

Twist creates a spiral effect and uses rotation angles to cause the effect. At 0° there is no rotation. Positive values cause counterclockwise rotation, whereas negative values cause clockwise rotation. See Figure 9.9.

### Teeter

Teeter rotates shapes about their local X and Y axes and uses rotation angles. You can apply rotation in either or both the X and Y axes. See Figure 9.10.

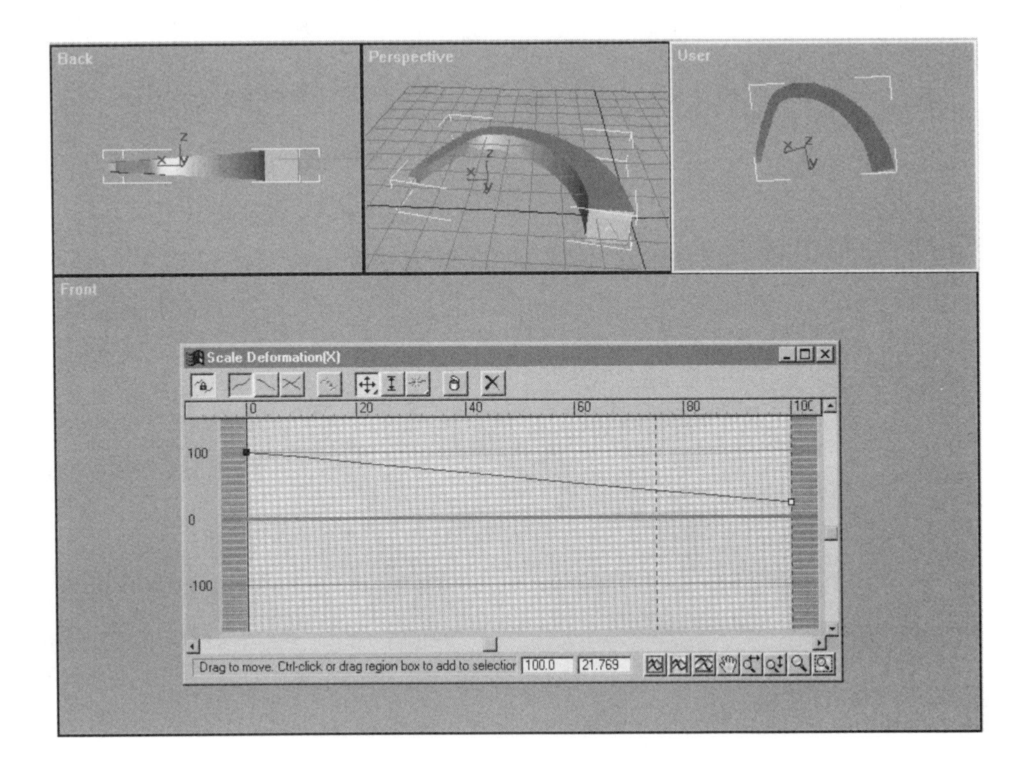


FIGURE 9.8
Scale deformation.

## Bevel

Bevel is used to remove the sharp edges on either end of the lofted object. The amount of bevel is set in units. At 0 units no change takes place. Positive values reduce the shape, and negative values increase the shape. See Figure 9.11.

## Fit

Fit is a special type of scale deformation that uses two fit curves to define the X and Y axes' profile of the lofted object. Instead of creating a scale curve, you use an already created spline shape for the X axis scaling and a spline shape for the Y axis scaling, and these are applied to a cross-sectional shape. Then, the previously lofted cross-sectional shape is scaled in the X and Y axes using the predrawing X and Y fit curve splines. See Figure 9.12.

There are several rules that apply to fit curves:

- Each axis curve must be a single spline. There can be no nested or separated spline shapes.
- Curves must be closed.
- Curves should not contain undercuts.
- Curves cannot extend past their first or last control point in the direction of the path.

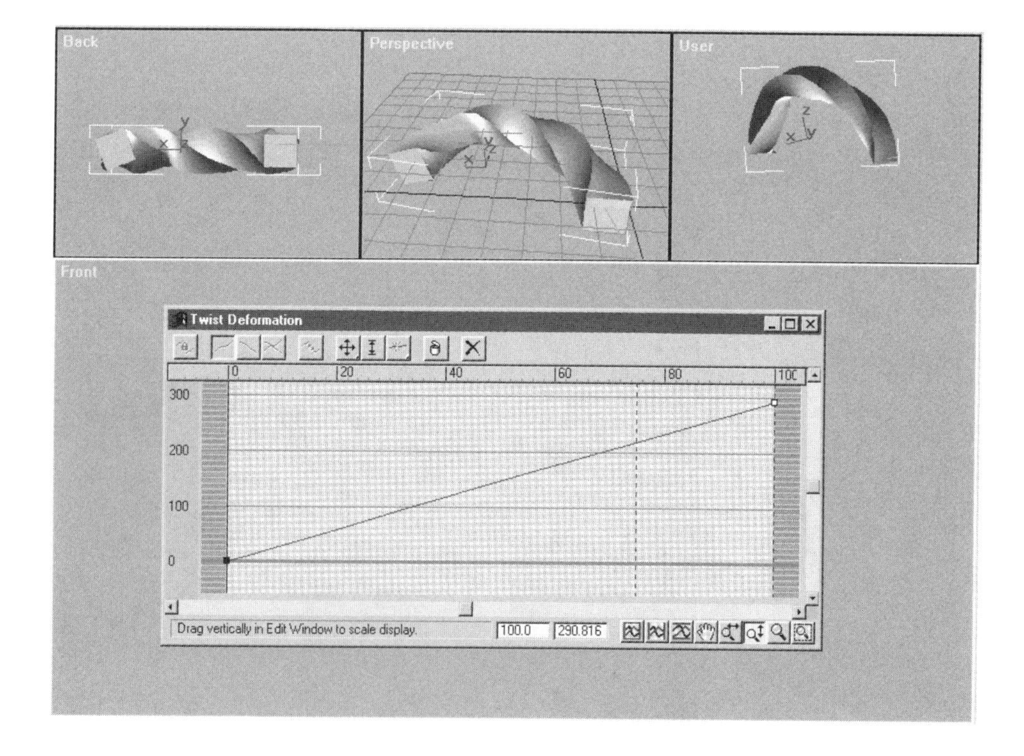


FIGURE 9.9
Twist deformation.

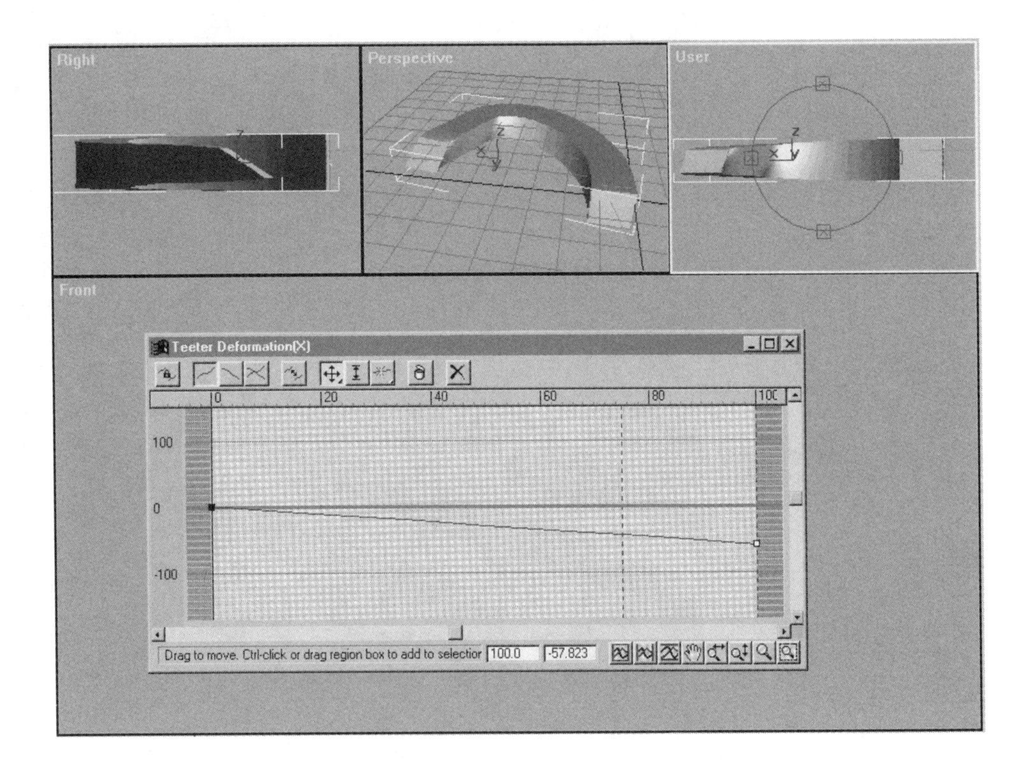


FIGURE 9.10
Teeter deformation.

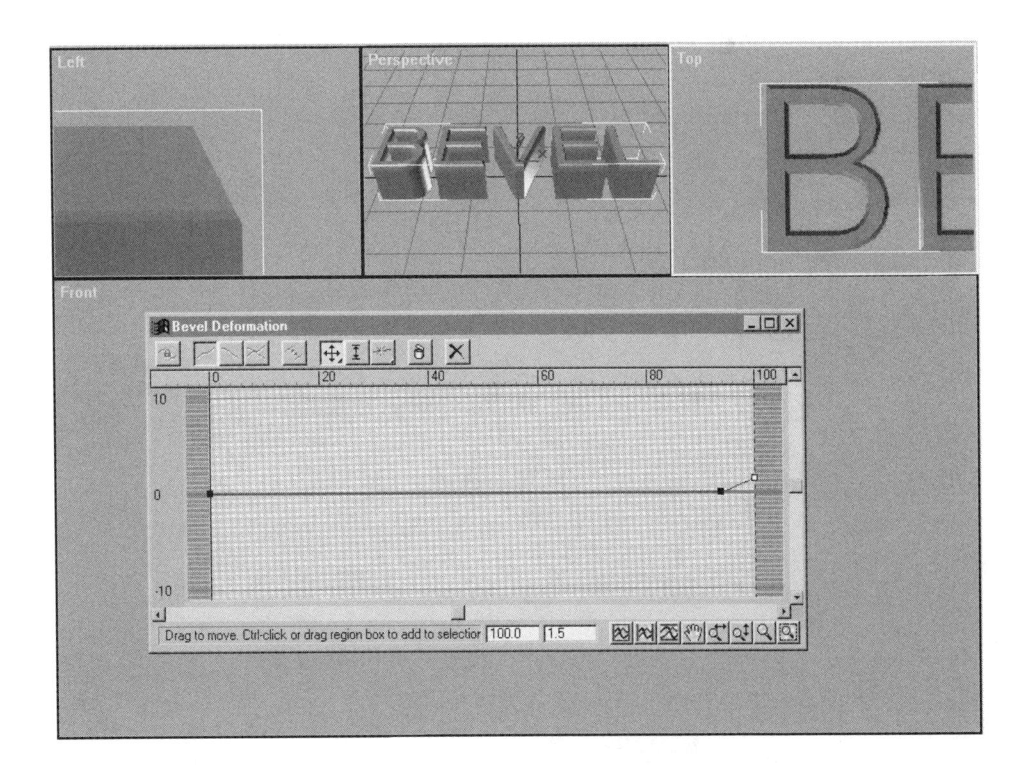


FIGURE 9.11
Bevel deformation.

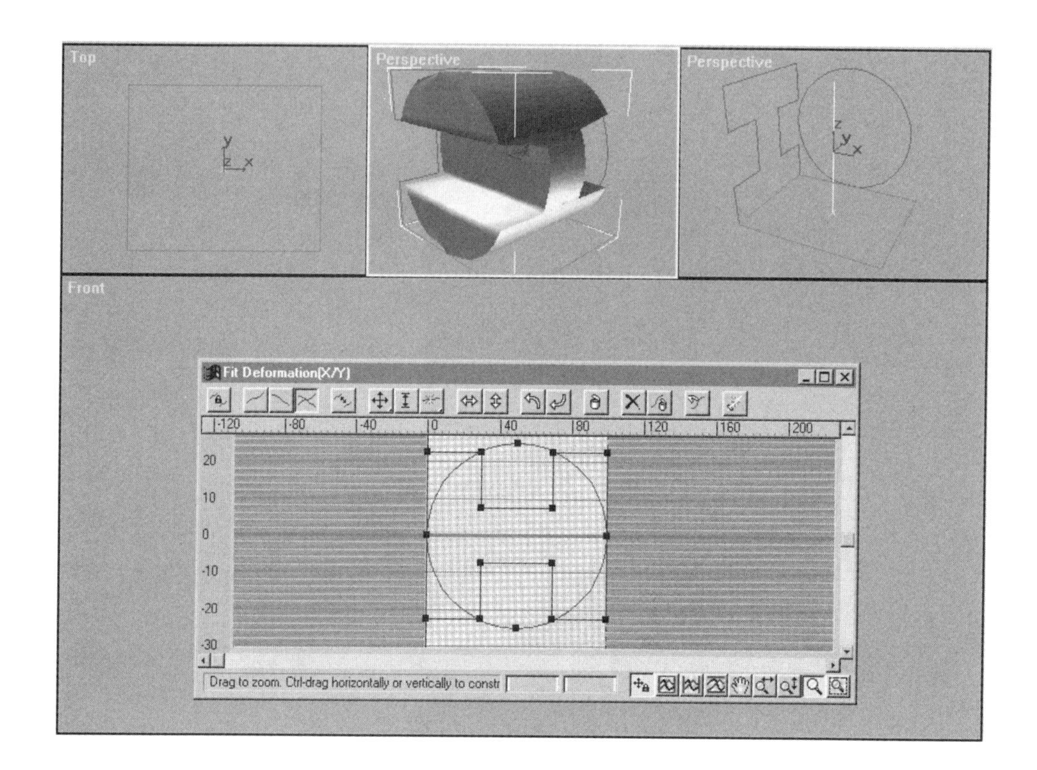


FIGURE 9.12
Fit deformation.

To get a shape to be used as a fit curve, use the Get Shape button in the Fit Deformation dialog.

To get individual fit curves for each axis, use the following procedure:

Turn off Make Symmetrical.

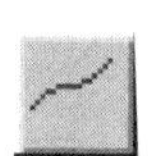

Pick the X or Y axis button to activate that axis curve.

Pick the Get Shape button and pick a shape in the scene.

## 9.9 BOOLEAN OPERATIONS

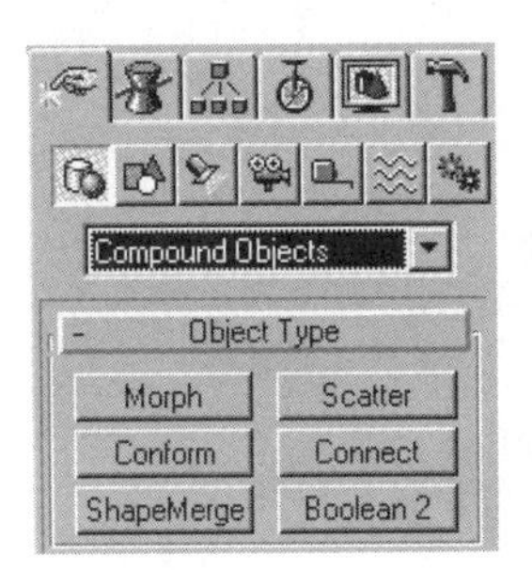


Whereas Lofting makes use of two 2D shapes to create the final 3D object, Boolean 2 operations make use of two original 3D objects to create the final Boolean object. Access to Boolean 2 operations is found under Compound objects in the Creation panel.

### Concept

The concept is quite simple, even though the actual mathematical operations in the background are quite complex. There are three types of Boolean operations: Union, Subtraction, and Intersection. Union creates an object that contains the volume of both original objects, whereas subtraction creates an object that contains the volume of the first original object with the intersection volume of the second original object subtracted from it. Intersection creates an object that contains only the volume that was common between the two original intersection objects. See Figure 9.13.

The two original objects are referred to as Operands: Operand A and Operand B. Operand A is the first object that you select. It is turned into the final Boolean object. With Operand B you have the option of using a copy, instance, move, or reference of the original object. The Move option uses the original object, and it is added to Operand A to create the final Boolean object.

### Display

There are several ways to display the Boolean operations as they occur. Refer to Figure 9.14.

**Results**
This option shows the result of the Boolean operations, hiding the display of the two original operands.

**Operands**
This option displays the two operands instead of the final Boolean object. It is useful if you want to modify the original operands.

***LIGHTS! CAMERA! ACTION!*** 

Boolean Operands

Boolean objects can be used as well as operands to create a new, more complex Boolean object.

FIGURE 9.13
Boolean operations.

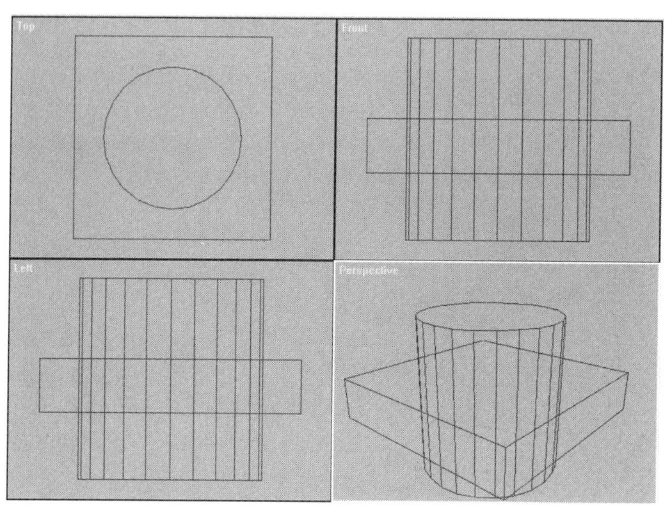


A ORIGINAL

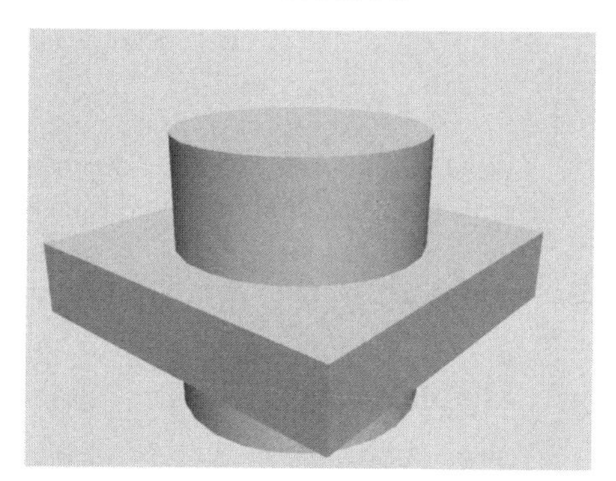

B UNION

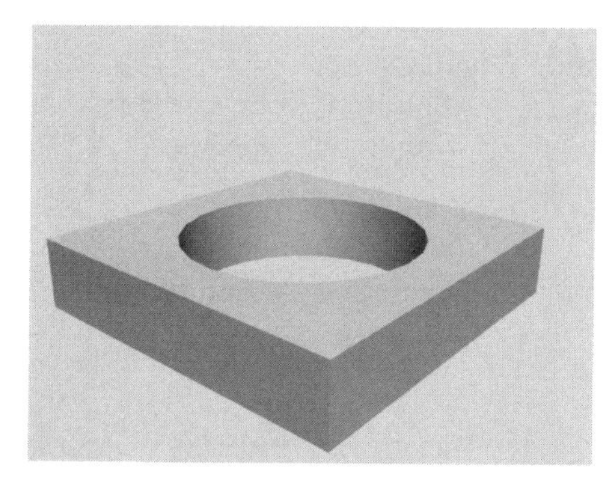

C SUBTRACTION

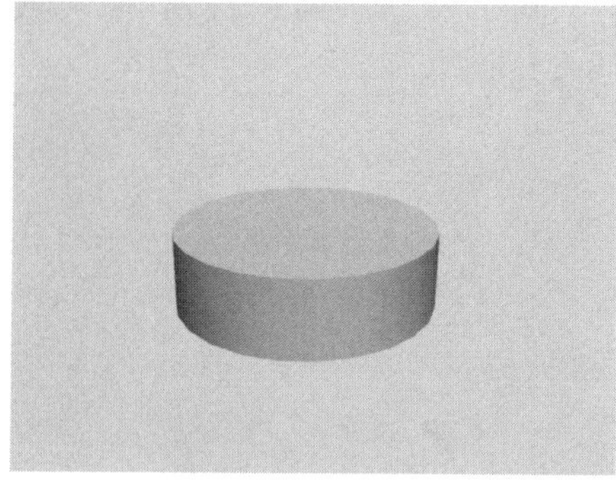

D INTERSECTION

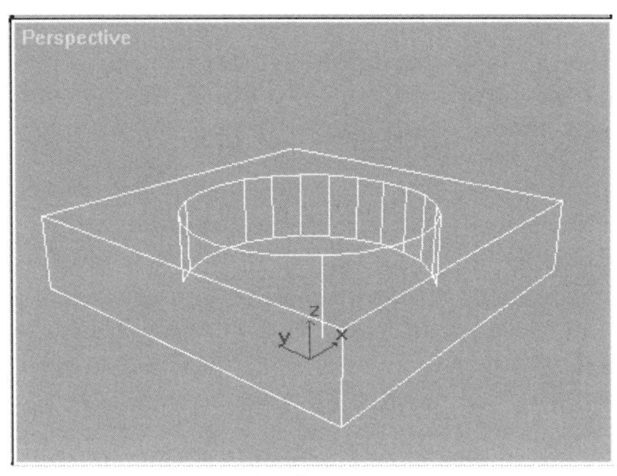


A RESULTS

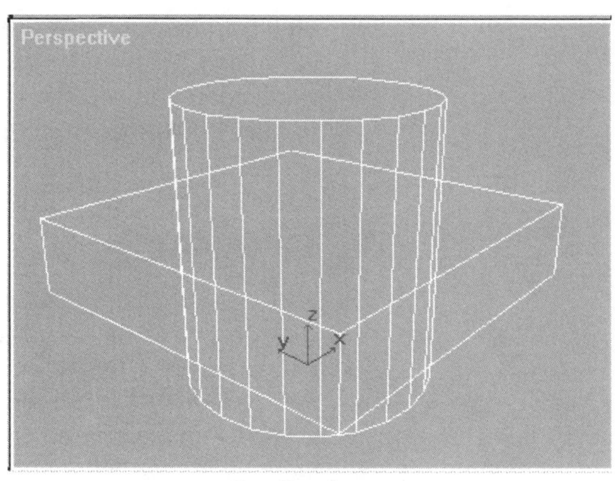


B OPERANDS

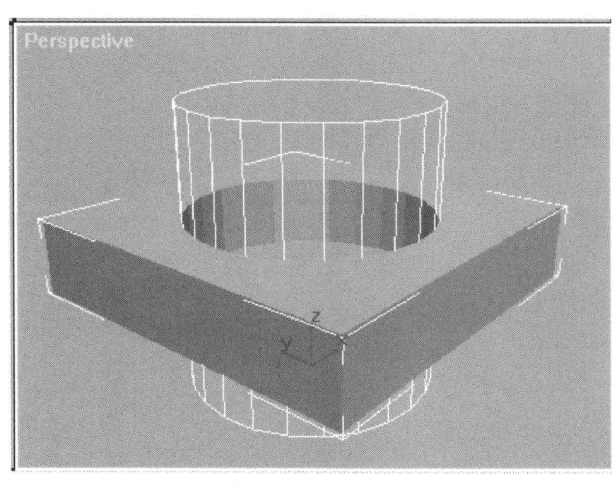


C HIDDEN OPS

FIGURE 9.14
Display of Boolean objects.

**Show Hidden Ops**

Displays the operands as wireframe and the Boolean object shaded in a shaded viewport. This is useful when you want to see both the operands and the Boolean object. Remember this works only in shaded viewports, and the Results box must be checked.

## Update Options

Whenever an operand is modified, the Boolean object is updated. However, in a complex animated scene this can cause a slowdown in performance. To alleviate this

**LIGHTS! CAMERA! ACTION!**

### Overlapping Objects

You should not use Boolean operations on objects that do not overlap. The function will still work; however, the results are unpredictable.

problem, there are several options: Always, When Selected, When Rendering, Manually, and Optimize Result. The Manually option updates the Boolean when you pick the Update button; the Optimize Result option removes coplanar faces when it updates Boolean geometry and should normally be checked.

## 9.10 SUMMARY

Lofting can make the creation of convoluted objects a simple process of creating a cross-sectional shape and a path for the shape to follow. Learning how to use the lofting process effectively allows you to create much more complex objects than either the Extrude or Lathe modifier permits. Application of deformation curves can add greatly to the lofting process by allowing the cross-sectional shape to be altered as it moves along the path.

Boolean operations give you the ability to combine the volumes of two separate three-dimensional objects in different ways to create a final complex shape.

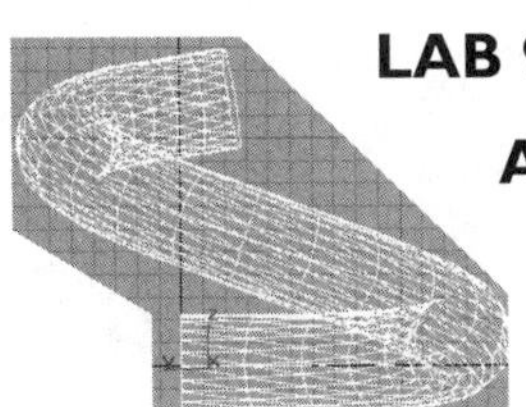

# LAB 9.A

## Advanced Modeling

### Purpose

During this lab you will learn how to create three-dimensional objects using the lofting process. This involves the creation of two-dimensional shapes to create cross sections and paths. Also, you will practice Boolean operations that involve the combining of two three-dimensional objects to create a new complex object.

### Objectives

You will be able to

- Create a two-dimensional cross-sectional shape.
- Create a three-dimensional path.
- Create a three-dimensional object using lofting.
- Apply deformation curves to a lofted object.
- Create a complex three-dimensional object by using Boolean operations.

### Procedure

1. Start a new file and establish the usual startup settings. Refer to Lab 8.A if you need to. Make sure that the Top and Perspective viewports are set to display Smooth and Highlight. The other two viewports should be set to Wireframe.

#### CREATING TWO-DIMENSIONAL CROSS SECTIONS

2. The first step in lofting is to create the cross-section shape that will be placed on the path. See Figure 9.15. Activate the Front viewport and use a circle spline to create the two-dimensional object shown in the figure. For this lab, the center point of the spline should be at 0,0,0 and the circle's radius should be approximately 20. The cross-sectional shape can be as complex as you require. It can be nested or open. However, it is best not to crisscross spline lines.

#### CREATING A PATH

3. The next step is to create the path that the cross-sectional shape will follow. See Figure 9.16. Activate the Top viewport and use a helix spline to create the path shown in the figure. First, click on the center and drag until you reach an outer radius (radius 1) of approximately 80. Release the pick button and drag to set a height of approximately 110. Pick to set the height, and then drag and pick to set the inner radius (radius 2) to approximately 50.

#### SELECTING THE LOFTING SHAPE AND PATH

4. In this step you will use the cross section (circle) as the primary object and later move the path to it. Use the Select Object button and pick the cross section.

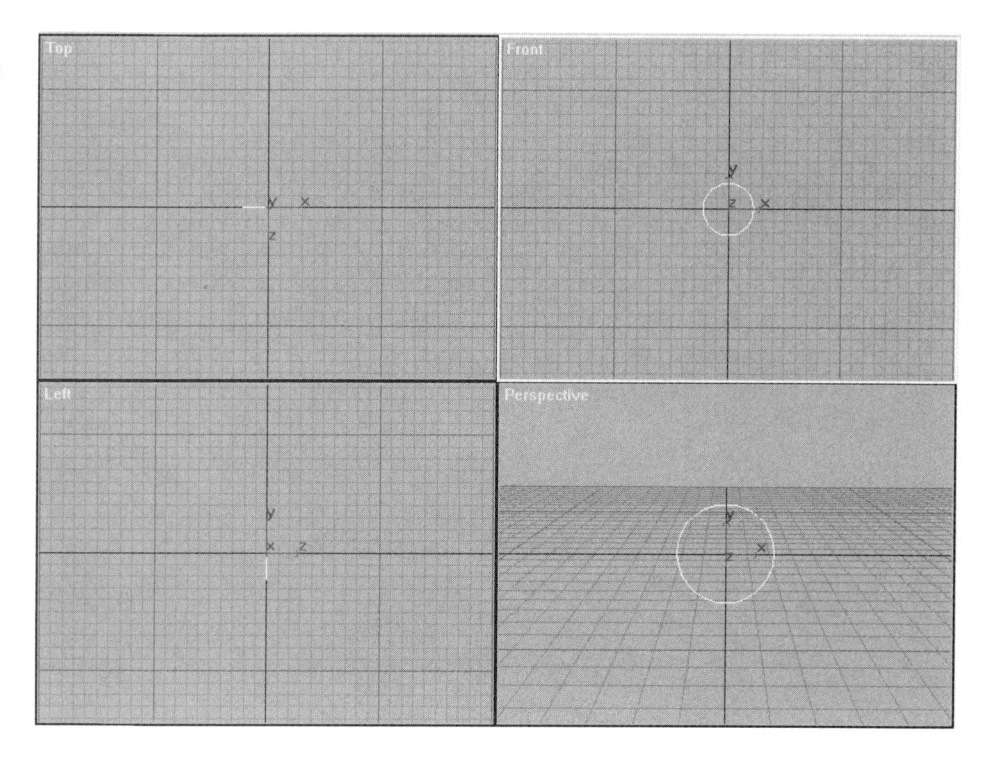


FIGURE 9.15
Spline shape to be used as the cross section.

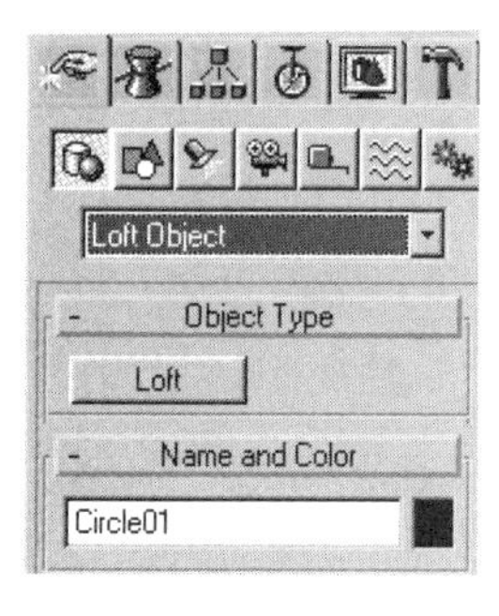


5. Open the Creation panel, pick the Geometry button, and choose Loft Object from the category list. Now, pick Loft from the Object Type rollout.

6. Check the Move box and then pick the Get Path option. You will now be prompted to pick the path shape. You should notice that the cursor changes to the Get Path cursor when you drag the cursor over a valid path shape. Pick the path. It should have moved to the shape, as shown in Figure 9.17. Use Zoom Extents All to see the lofted object in all the viewports.

   Once you have selected a shape and a path, it is time to review the lofting parameters.

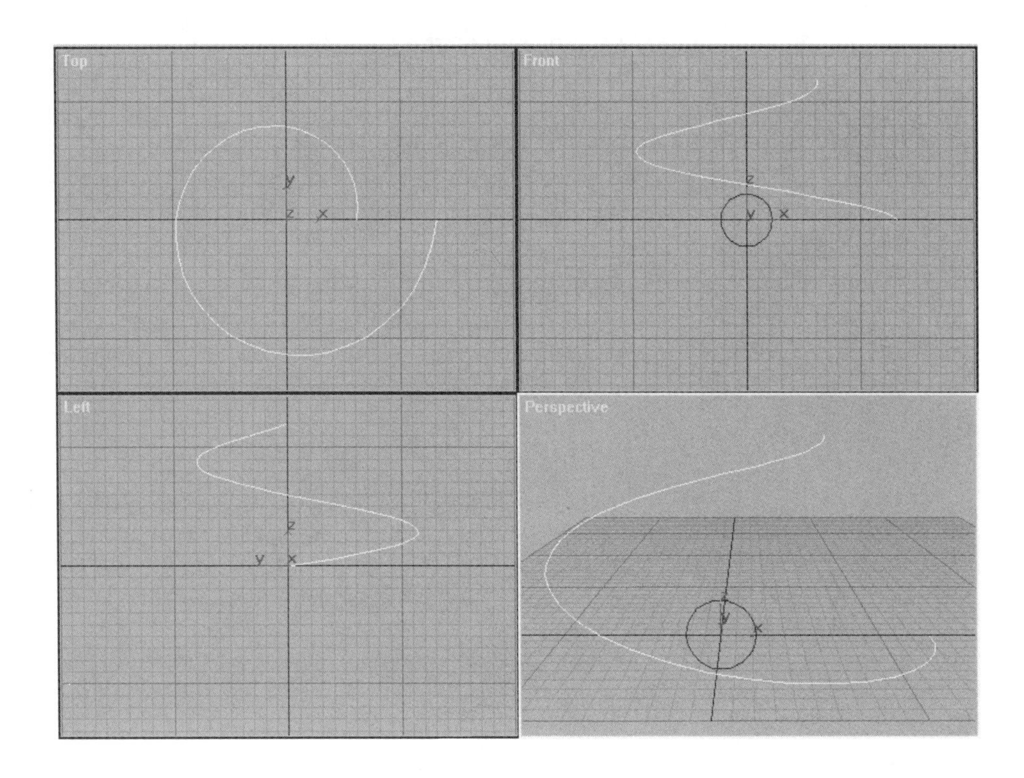


FIGURE 9.16
Spline path.

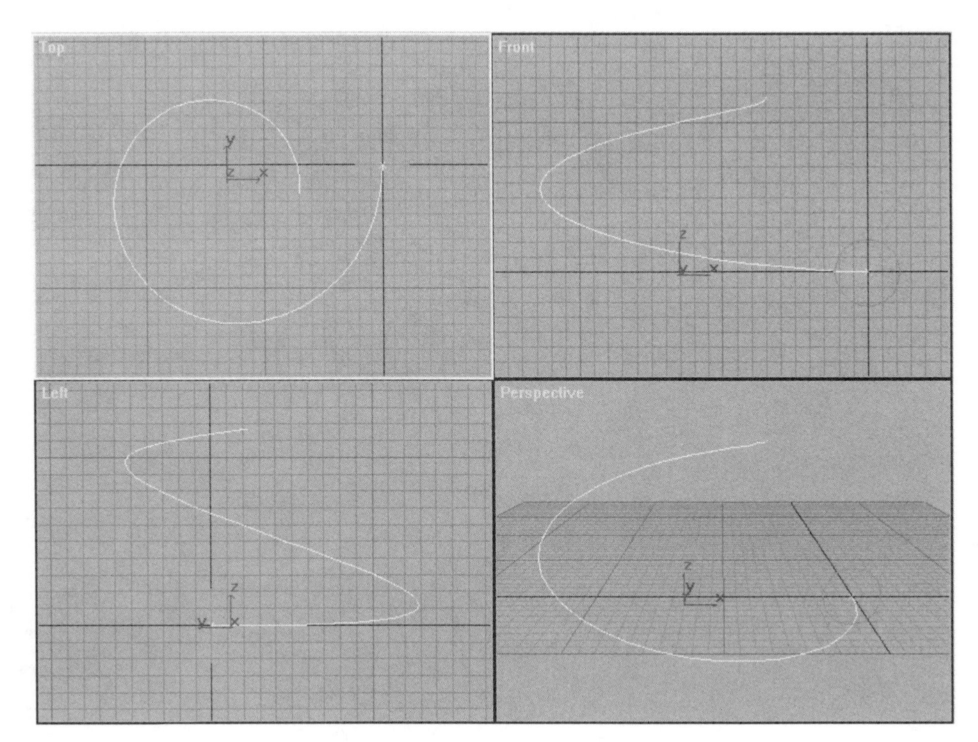


FIGURE 9.17
Path meeting the shape.

## SURFACE PARAMETERS

7. For this project make sure that Smooth Length and Smooth Width boxes are checked. This will ensure that the surface will be smooth over the entire lofted object.

## SKIN PARAMETERS

8. Make sure that the Skin and Skin in Shaded boxes are checked in the Display area and note how the skin is shown in the various views. Now, uncheck the Skin box and note the results. Only the path and shape are shown in the Wireframe viewports. Check the box again. Refer to Figure 9.18.

9. Cap both ends of the object using a grid.

10. To create very smooth profiles and contours along the path, you need to increase the number of steps. First set the Shapes Steps to 2 and the Path Steps to 2 and observe the results. The loft should look like Figure 9.19, very jagged. Now increase the Shapes Steps and Path Steps to 10; the loft should be very smooth.

11. Check the Adaptive Path box so that the program analyzes your loft and adapts the number of path divisions to generate the best skin.

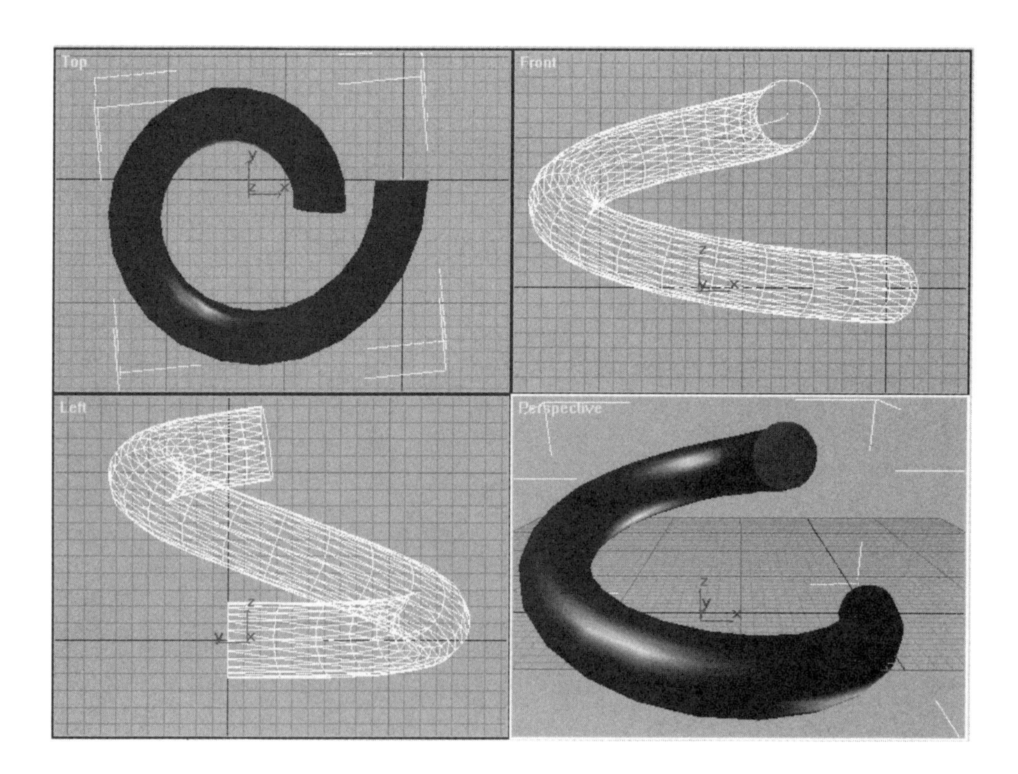


FIGURE 9.18
The skin displayed in the viewports.

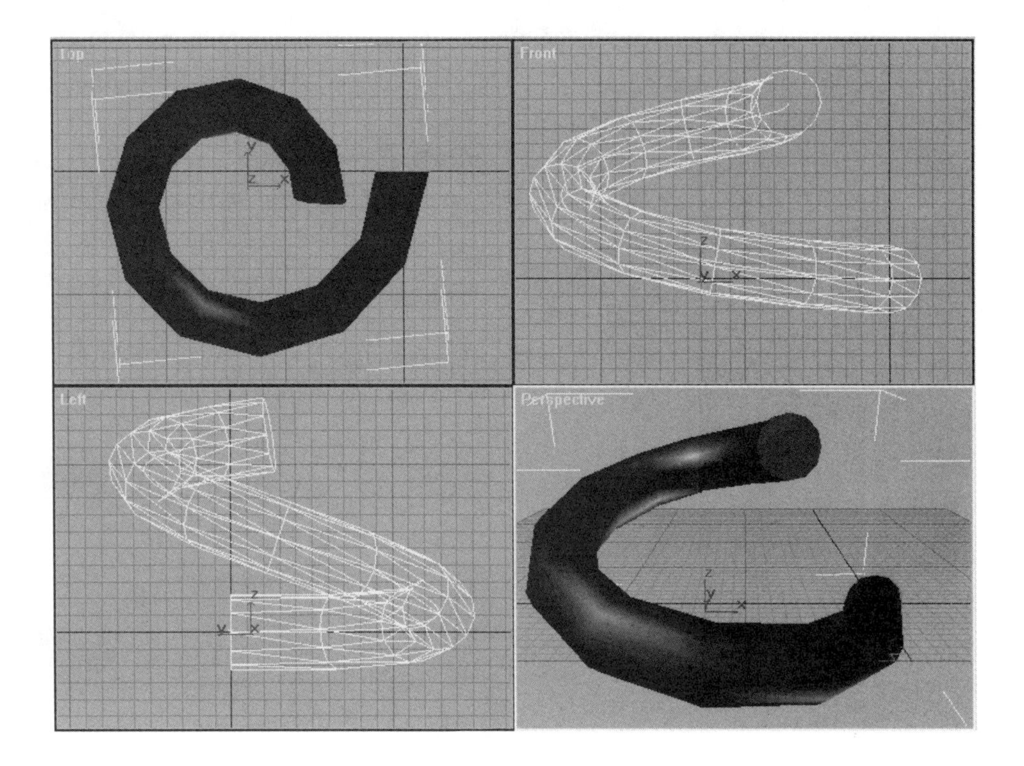


FIGURE 9.19
The loft with too few steps.

12. Uncheck the Contour box to turn off contour and observe the results. Your loft should look similar to Figure 9.20. Check the Contour box again so that the cross-sectional shape is aligned to the path, giving a consistent shape through the helical path.

## PATH PARAMETERS

13. Because you are using only one shape on the path, you will not need to make any changes to the path parameters.

## DEFORMATION CURVES

Now you are going to apply a deformation curve to the lofted object to further enhance it. The simplest plan will be to change the scale of the shape so that it starts out large and becomes smaller at the other end. Deformation curves are modifications of the standard loft and are adjusted from the Modify panel.

14. Make sure the loft is selected and then open the Modify panel. Pan to the bottom of the panel and you will see the Deformations roll-out. Open the rollout to see the various parameters, such as Scale and Fit.

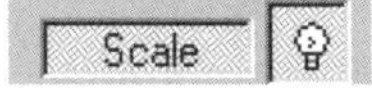


15. Pick the Scale deformation button and the Scale dialog should appear, looking similar to Figure 9.21. The thick grey line in the middle represents the path. The two ver-

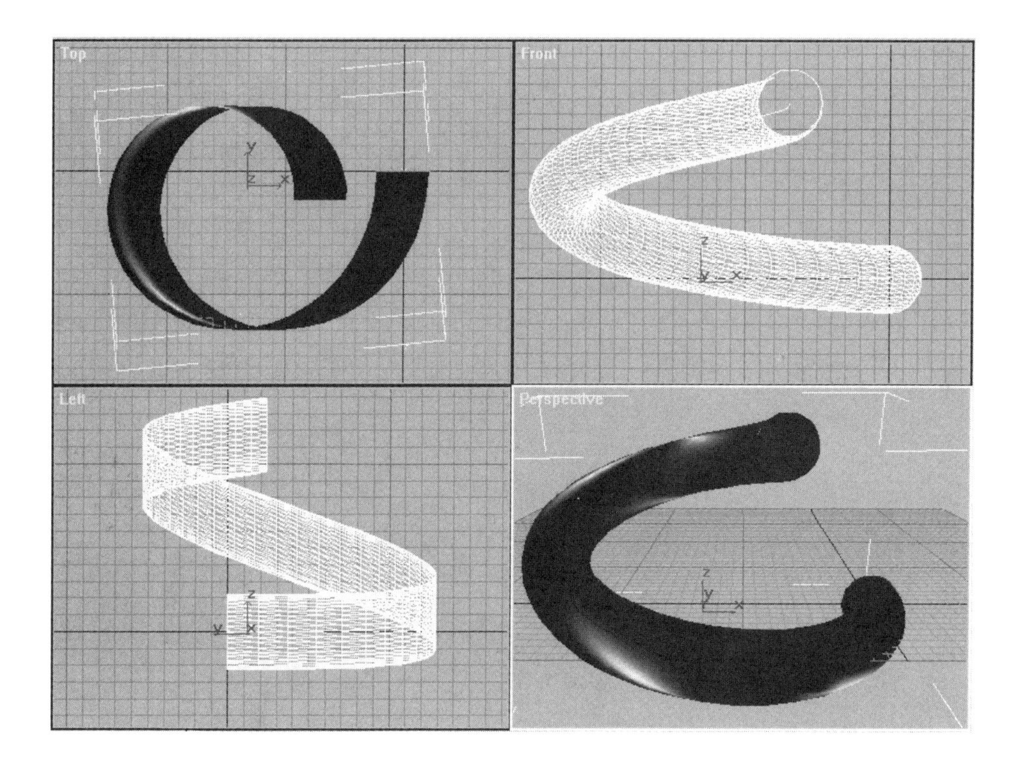


FIGURE 9.20
The loft with contour turned off.

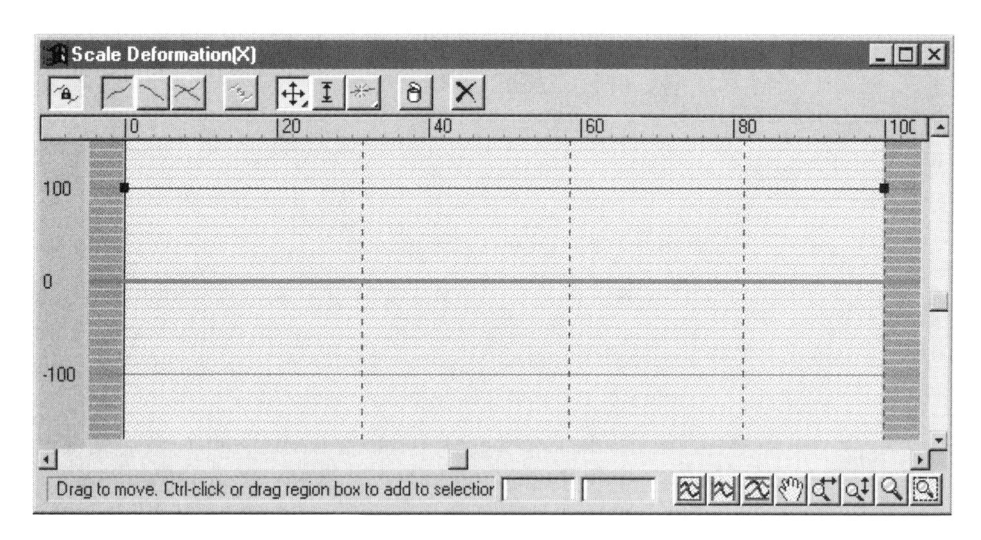


FIGURE 9.21
Scale deformation dialog.

tical grey bars at either end are the scale control points. You are going to move the control points. Figure 9.22 shows how the curve will look after you have modified it.

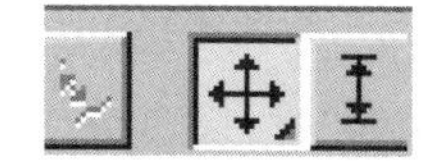

16. Pick on the Move button to depress it, turning it on. Now, move the cursor over the right control point; pick it and drag it until it looks similar to Figure 9.22; then release the pick button.
17. Close the dialog and look at the perspective viewport. Note how the cross section changes size from the start to the finish. Figure 9.23 should be similar to your screen.
18. Save the scene file as CH9A.MAX.

Lofting is a straightforward process that creates a complex object by having a cross-sectional shape follow a path.

## Boolean Operations

You are going to start a new scene and create some simple objects to test Boolean operations.

19. Start a new scene using settings similar to Step 1 of this lab.
20. Refer to Figure 9.24 and create the spherical objects shown. The size is not important, but the objects need to overlap, as shown in the figure.
21. Select the Hold menu item from the Edit pull-down menu. This will hold the current state of the objects so that you can return to them in later steps.
22. Using the Select Object tool, select the left sphere to highlight it.

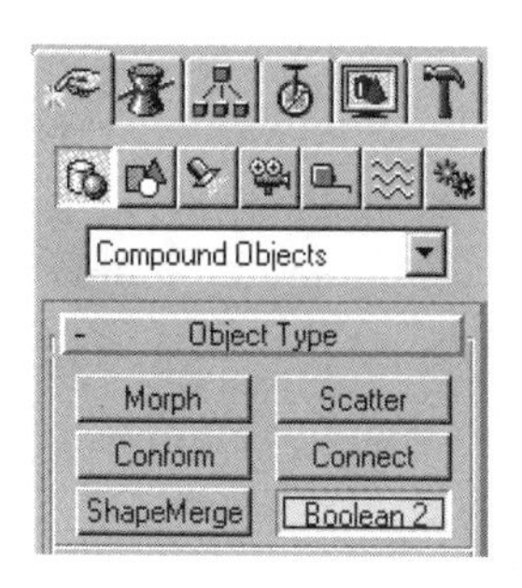


23. Open the Creation panel, pick the Geometry button, and choose Compound Objects from the category list. Now, pick the Boolean 2 button.

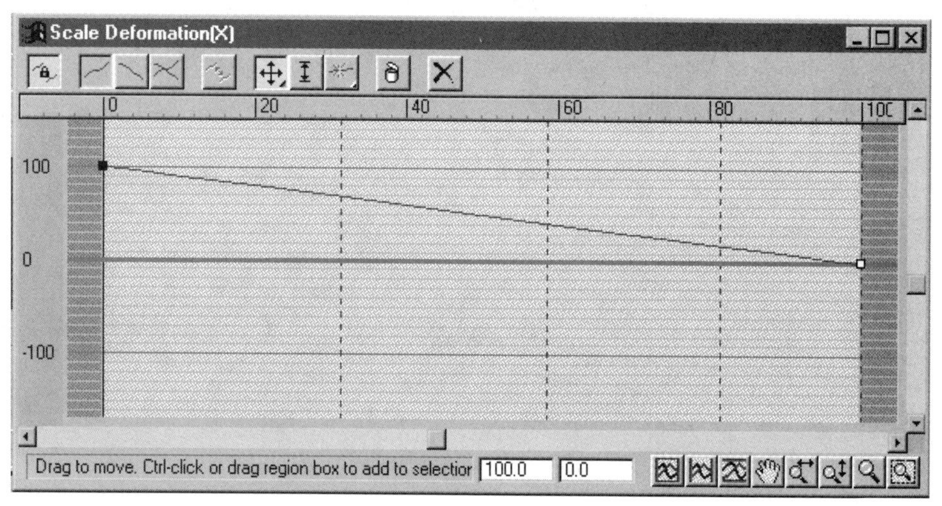


FIGURE 9.22
Moving the control point to change the scale deformation curve.

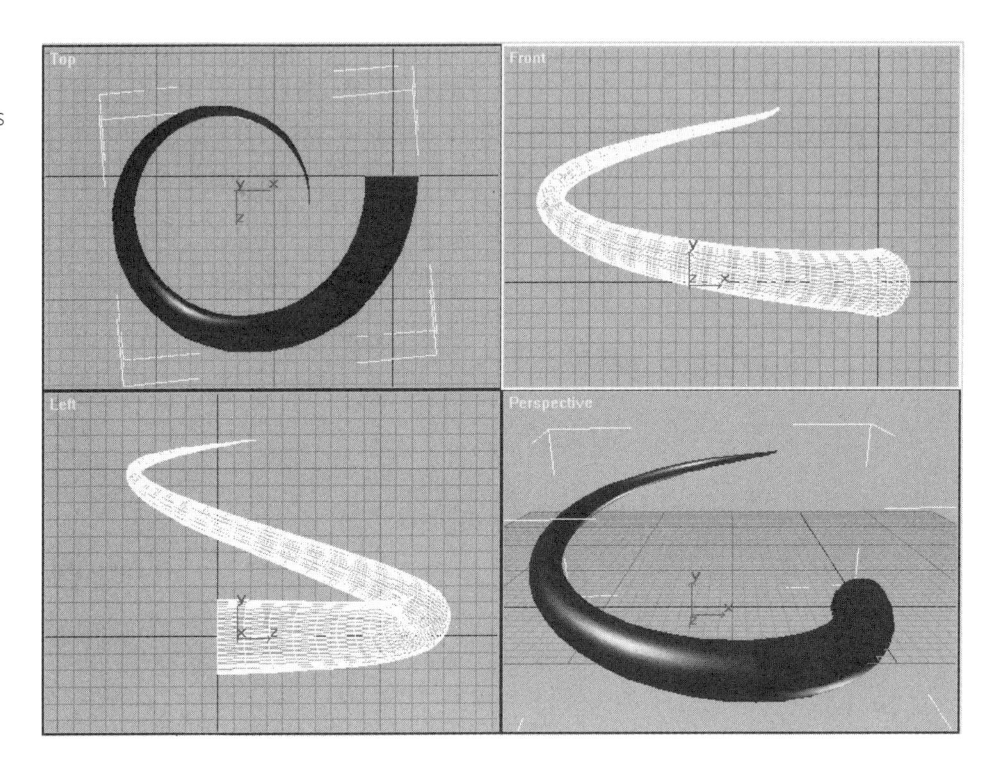


FIGURE 9.23
The lofted object after the scale deformation is applied.

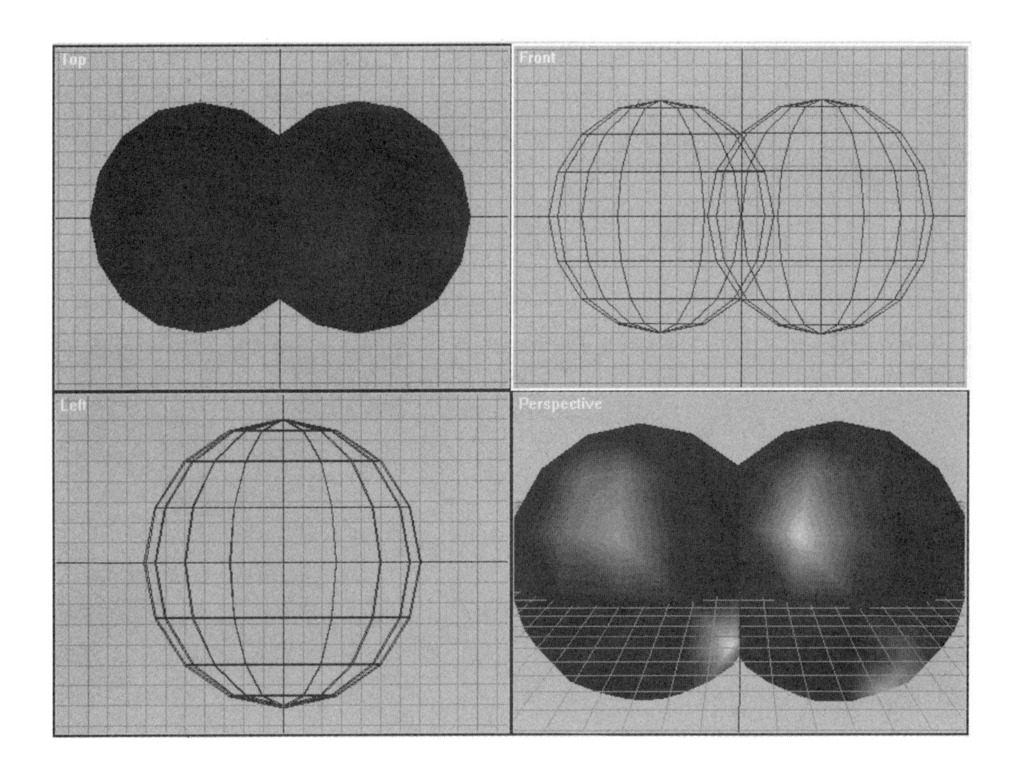


FIGURE 9.24
Two overlapping spherical objects.

24. Check the Display parameters to make certain that the Results box is checked.

## UNION

25. Pick the Union button to turn it on. This is used to add two objects together.
26. Pick the Move button, select the Pick Operand B button, and pick the object on the right. The two objects are now added together, as shown in Figure 9.25. It is sometimes hard to tell, but look in the Front viewport. You should see fewer wireframe lines where the two objects' volumes overlap. This is because they do not overlap now but are one single object.

## SUBTRACTION

27. Now, pick the Subtract (A – B) box. This causes Operand B to be subtracted from Operand A. The results should be similar to Figure 9.26.

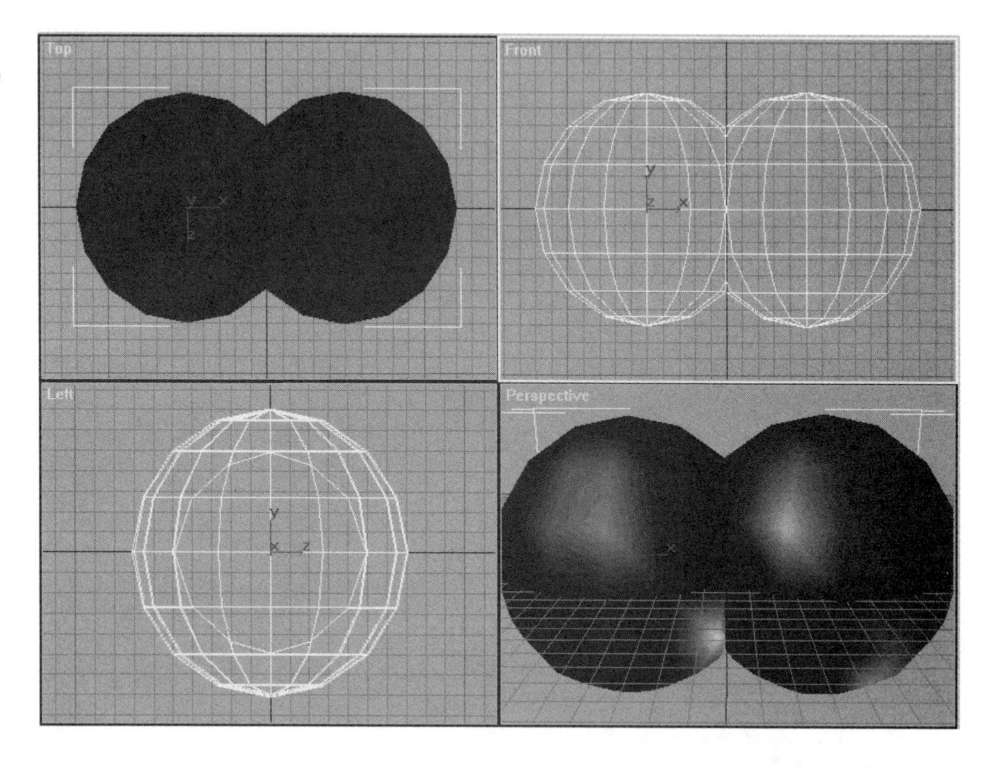


FIGURE 9.25
Joining two objects with the union Boolean.

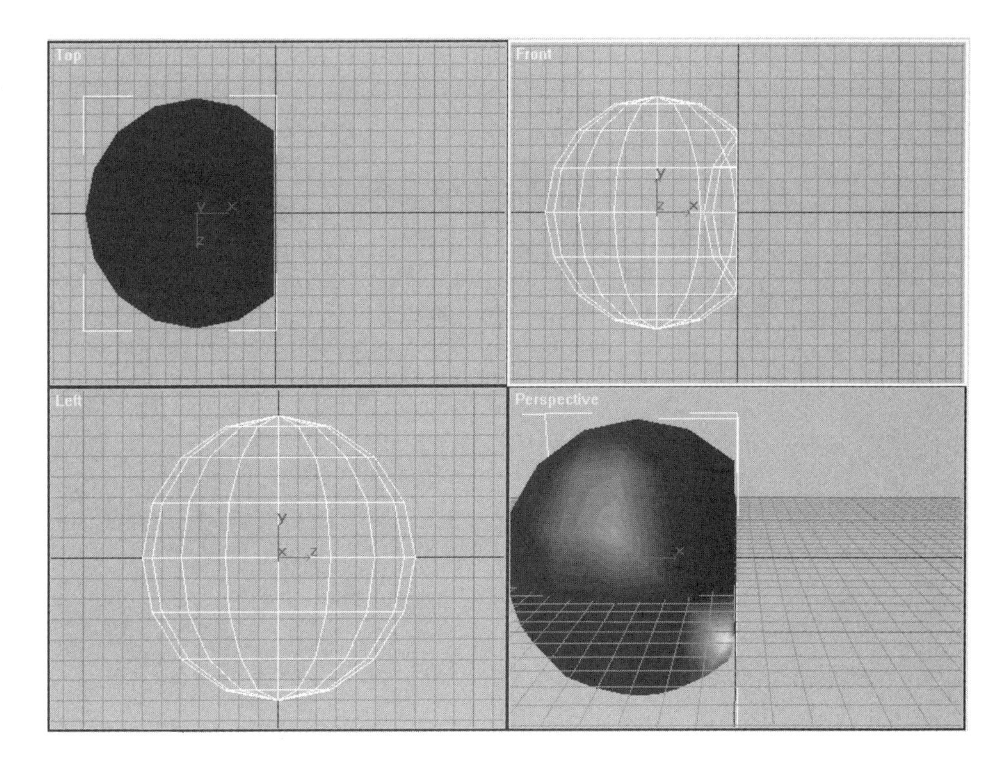


FIGURE 9.26
Subtracting one object from another.

## INTERSECTION

28. Finally, pick the Intersection box. The result is the intersecting volume of the two objects, as shown in Figure 9.27.

29. Use the Fetch command to return the two objects to their separate original states and save the file as CH9B.MAX. This way you can go back to it any time and test out the Boolean operations again.

    *Note:* If you exit from the Boolean operations, the commands will not work in succession. If you do this, go back to your original by fetching, and then continue from that point again through union, subtraction, and intersection.

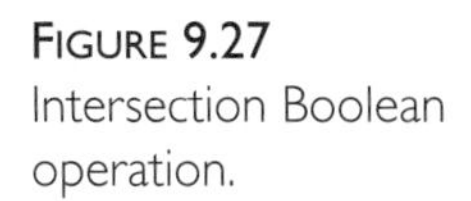

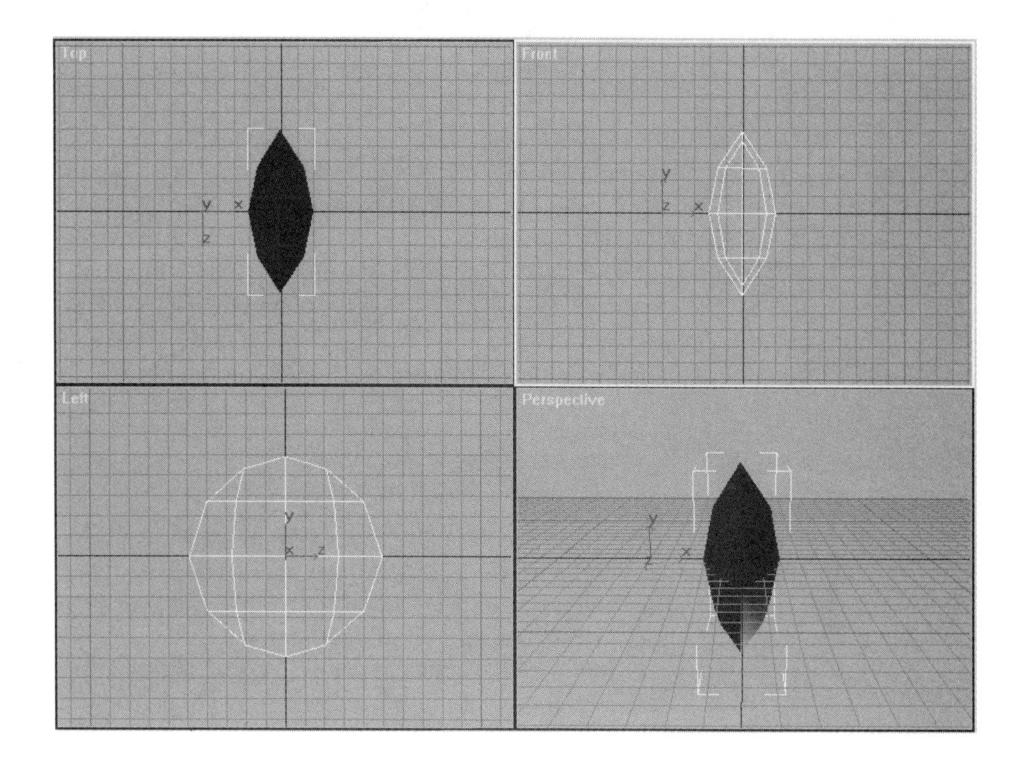


FIGURE 9.27
Intersection Boolean operation.

## QUESTIONS AND ASSIGNMENTS

### QUESTIONS

1. How was the term lofting derived?
2. What functions do the cross-sectional shape and the path shape perform?
3. What is loft density?
4. Explain the difference between the Get Path and the Get Shape creation method.
5. Explain the difference between Smooth Length and Smooth Width surface parameters.
6. Explain the difference between Length Repeat and Width Repeat to apply mapping to a lofted object.
7. What function does the Optimize Shapes skin parameter perform?
8. What function do the Path, Snap, and Percentage/Distance options of the Path parameters perform?
9. What are Boolean operations?

## ASSIGNMENTS

1. Experiment with using the Get Path and Get Shape options of the Lofting Creation Method.
   a. Create a cross-sectional shape in the Front viewport.
   b. Then create a path in the Top viewport that starts at the cross-sectional shape but travels negatively (down) along the Z axis. Use the Get Path option to align the path with the cross-sectional shape. Observe the results. How did the path move? Did it turn to point in the positive direction?
   c. Create a new path in the Top viewport. This time the path should start at the cross-sectional shape but travel in a positive Z direction. Use the Get Path option to align the path with the cross-sectional shape. Did this path move differently than the first one?
   d. Save the file as CH9C.MAX

2. Experiment with multiple cross-sectional shapes along a path.
   a. Create three distinctly different cross-sectional shapes and one path.
   b. Select one of the cross-sectional shapes as the first, and use the Get Path option to align the path to the first shape.
   c. In the Path parameters, turn Snap and Percentage on. Set the Path value to 50% and press Enter. This will move the path level to the middle of the path.
   d. Use the Get Shape option to get the second shape placed in the middle of the path.
   e. Set the Path value to 100%. This will move the path level to the end of the path.
   f. Use the Get Shape option to place the third shape at the end of the path.
   g. Set the Perspective viewport to display Smooth+Highlight and observe the results.
   h. Experiment with different shapes along the path.
   i. Save the file as CH9D.MAX.

3. Experiment with deformation curves.
   a. Create a simple cross-sectional shape, such as a box or circle.
   b. Create a simple path, such as a straight line.
   c. Loft the cross section along the path.
   d. Select the loft object and use the Modify Panel to get access to the Deformations rollout.
   e. First, use the Scale deformation and insert several control points along the curve. Move the various control points and observe the results of the loft. Turn off the Scale deformation by turning off the lightbulb button before going to the next step.
   f. Second, use the Teeter deformation and cause the cross-sectional shape to rotate as it moves along the path.
   g. Third, with Teeter still turned on, turn on the Scale by turning on the lightbulb. This has the effect of applying both Scale and Teeter to the same loft.
   h. Try adding other deformations.
   i. Save the file as CH9E.MAX.

4. Experiment with Boolean operations.
   a. Create some standard geometric 3D objects such as cones and spheres and use the three Boolean operations to union, subtract, and intersect the overlapping volumes.
   b. Create some lofted 3D objects and overlap them. Then, use Boolean operations to join them to create single complex objects.

# Special Modeling: Space Warps, Particle Systems, and Morphs

## 10.1 INTRODUCTION

In this chapter you will be introduced to three special types of modeling: space warps, particle systems, and morphs.

Space warps are objects that alter the appearance of other objects by doing such things as exploding or rippling them. Some are used during animations, and others work on nonanimated objects.

On the other hand, particle systems are objects that generate noneditable subobjects called *particles*. These particles can simulate snow, rain, and other small, numerous objects and are always used during animated sequences.

Finally, morphs are objects that change from a seed object to a target object over an animated sequence.

The details of animation are explained in Chapter 13; however, some information is given here so that you may understand the operation of these special creation methods that require animation.

## 10.2 SPACE WARPS

Space warps are similar to modifiers in that they alter or modify the appearance of objects or affect the motion of objects over time and space. The difference is that their influence is over world space and not object space. Space warps cannot be rendered but appear as wireframe in the viewports. Once you have created a space warp object, you then can bind one or more objects to the space warp object. There are three types of space warps: Geometric/Deformation, Modifier Based, and Particles and Dynamics.

## Using Space Warps

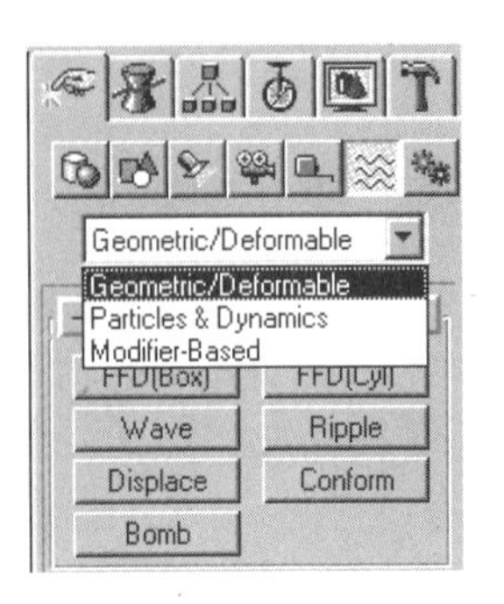


Space warps are found in the geometry section of the Creation command panel.

The procedure for using a space warp is as follows:

1. Create a space warp.
2. Adjust the space warp's parameters.
3. Bind objects to the space warp.
4. Transform the space warp as required. The effects of transforming a space warp directly affect the bound objects.

The distance an object is away from the space warp or its spacial orientation to the warp can change the warp's effect. During animation, moving an object through its bound space warp can cause various effects.

Because a space warp is an object, you can use transforms on it to move, rotate, and scale the warp to affect its influence.

You can bind objects to more than one space warp causing more complex effects.

## Binding and Unbinding Space Warps

To bind an object to a space warp, simply select the binding tool, pick on the object or particle system, and drag the icon to the space warp. To unbind an object, select it and delete the warp from the object's modifier stack.

If you delete a warp object, the bindings to the other objects are removed as well.

## Geometric/Deformation

Geometric/Deformation is used to deform the geometry of bound objects. There are different types of deformations and they are used for different applications. Some of the common types are bomb, ripple, and wave. The following is a more detailed description of some space warps and their options:

**Bomb**

The bomb space warp causes a geometric object's face to separate and expand over time resulting in an explosive effect. Refer to Figure 10.1. This occurs during an animated sequence. The closer the object is to the bomb space warp, the stronger the effect. The bomb space warp appears as a small wireframe pyramid.

The strength option sets how far the faces are scattered. The gravity option causes faces to either explode in place (0), fall (greater than 0), or rise (less than 0). The detonation option sets the frame number in which the explosion will take place.

**Ripple**

The ripple space warp creates concentric ripples through world space. It is useful when you want to apply a ripple effect to a large number of objects, as in raindrops falling on a pond's surface. Refer to Figure 10.2. The amplitude options set the strength of the ripples in the Y and X axes.

**Wave**

The wave space warp creates linear waves through world space and has parameters similar to ripple space warp. Refer to Figure 10.2.

Original with no Map

Diffuse Mapping

Specular Mapping

Shininess Mapping

Shininess Strength Mapping

Self-Illumination Mapping

Opacity Mapping

Filter Color Mapping

Bump Mapping

Reflection Mapping

Refraction Mapping

Material Creation in Chapter 12

**Natural Outdoor Lighting ● Chapter 11**

**Artificial Lighting ● Chapter 11**

Omni Lighting • Chapter 11

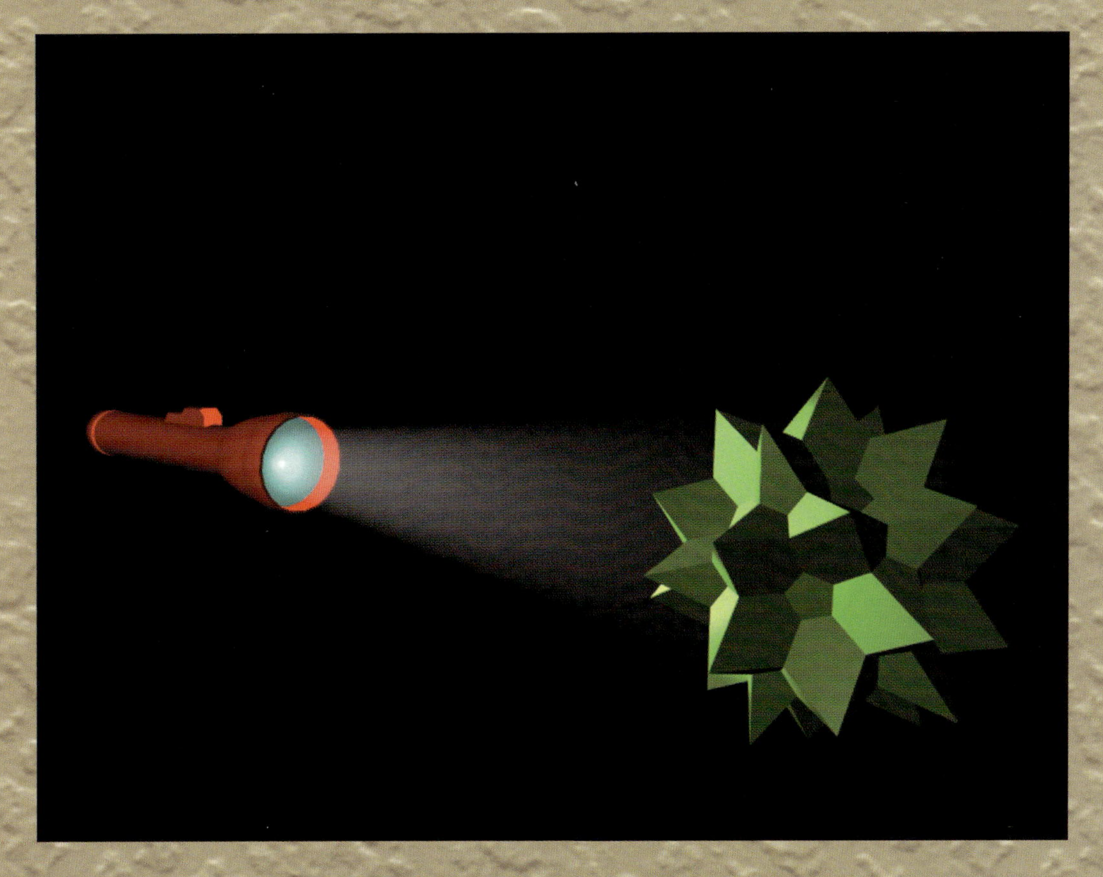

Spotlight Lighting • Chapter 11

Lab 11: Using the Camera, Lights, and Rendering ● Chapter 11

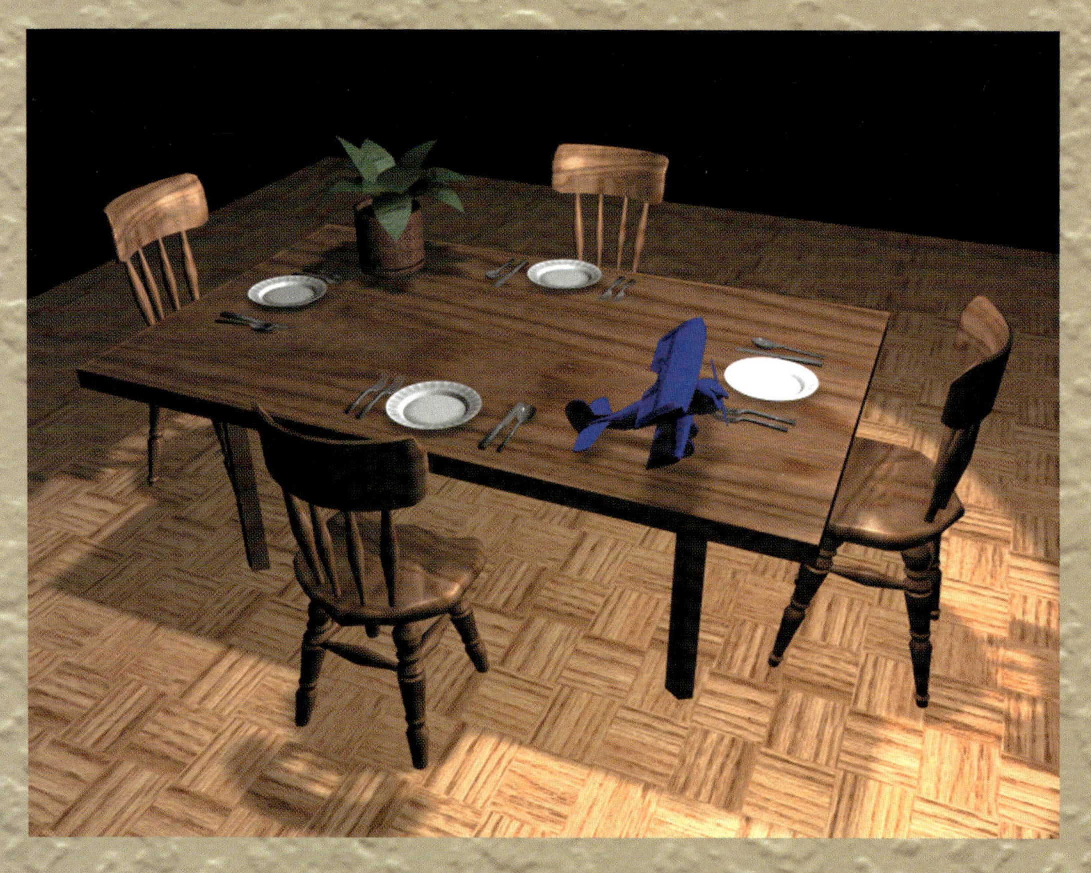

Basics of Editing ● Chapter 7

Different Surface Finishes ● Chapter 12

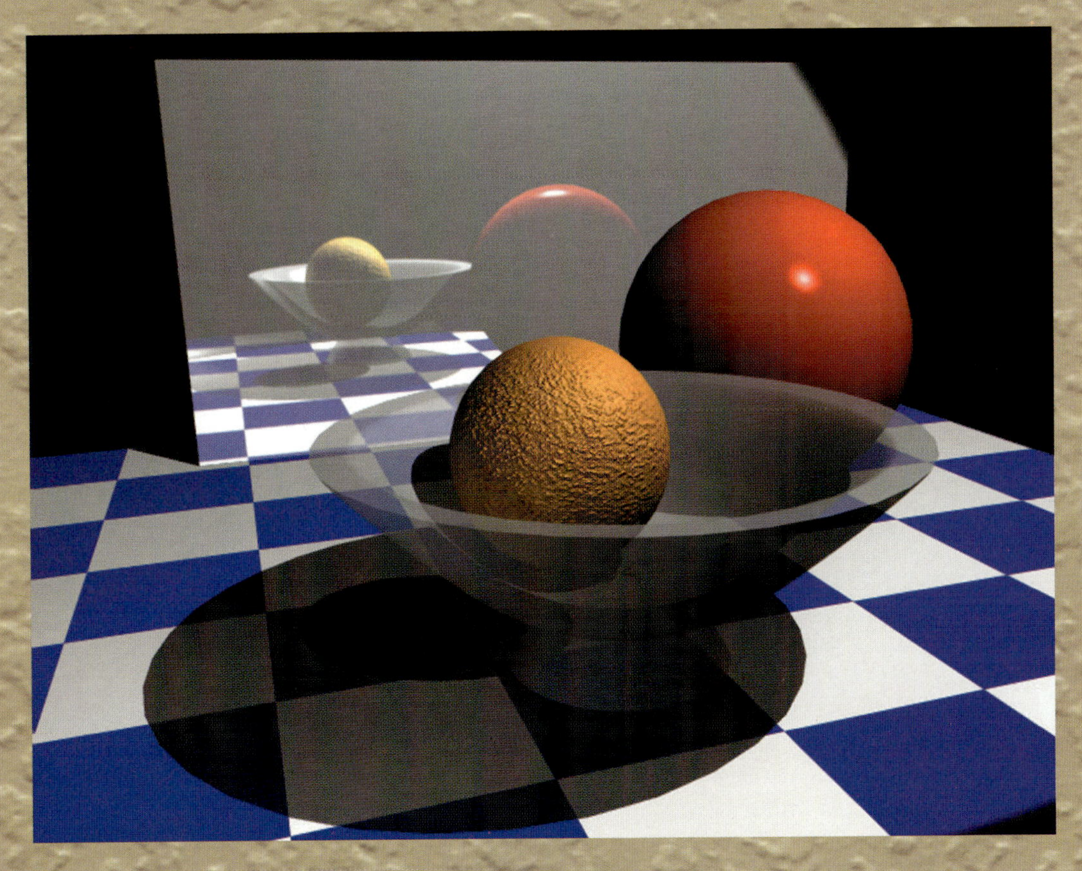

Lab 12: Material Creation and Application ● Chapter 12

Animation ● Chapter 13

Lab 13: Animation Basics ● Chapter 13

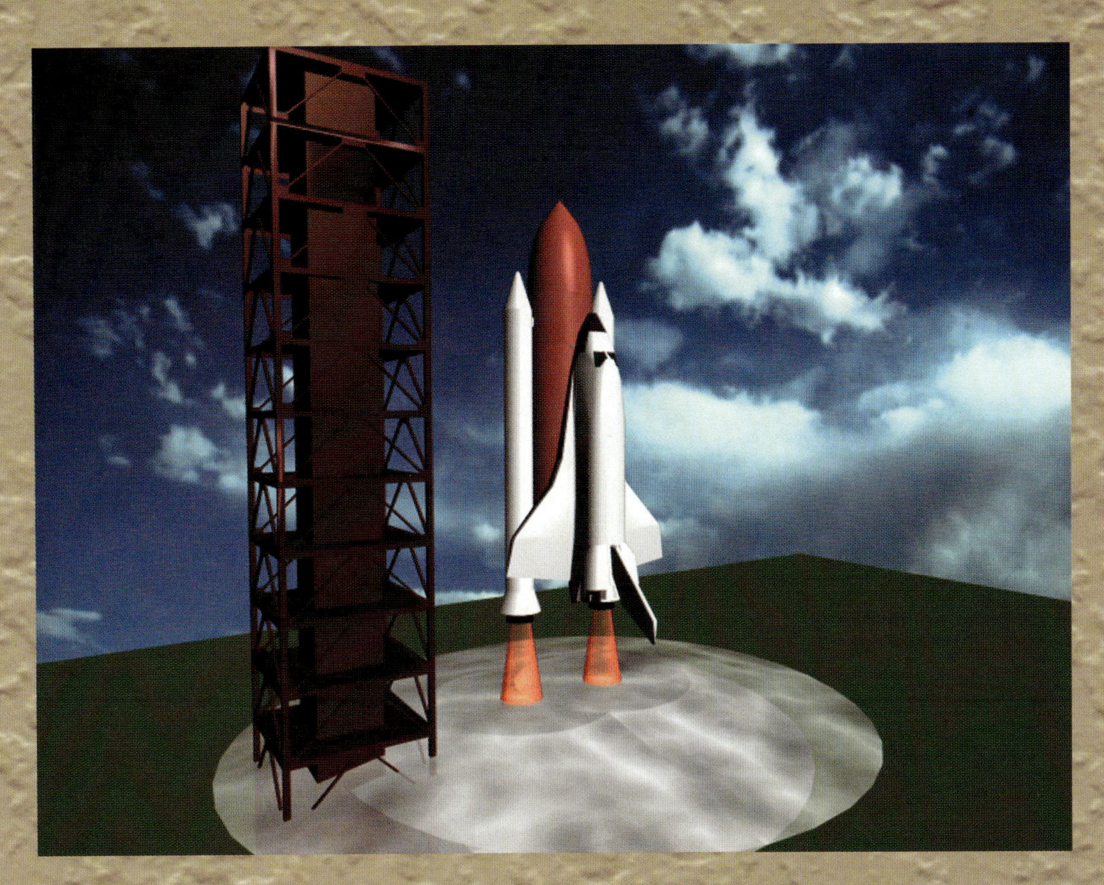

Lab 14: Hierarchy Linking • Chapter 14

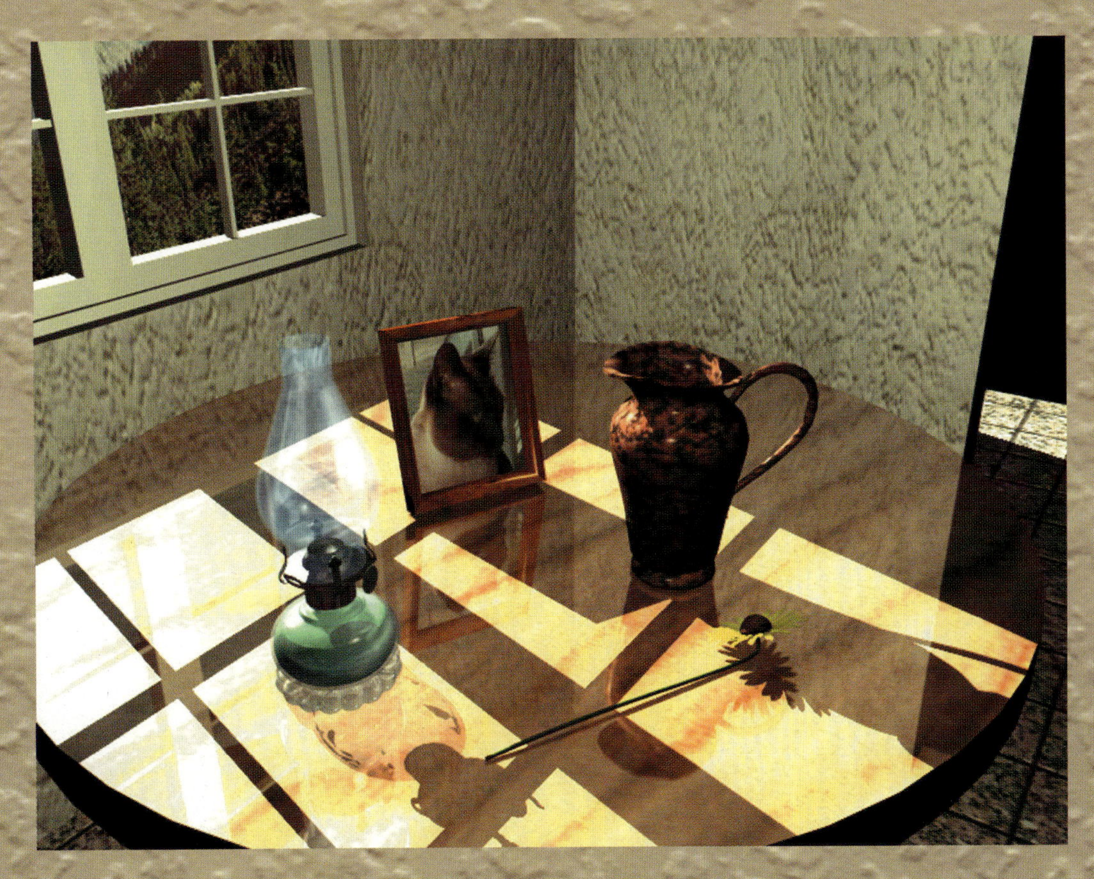

Working with Light and Shadow • Chapter 15

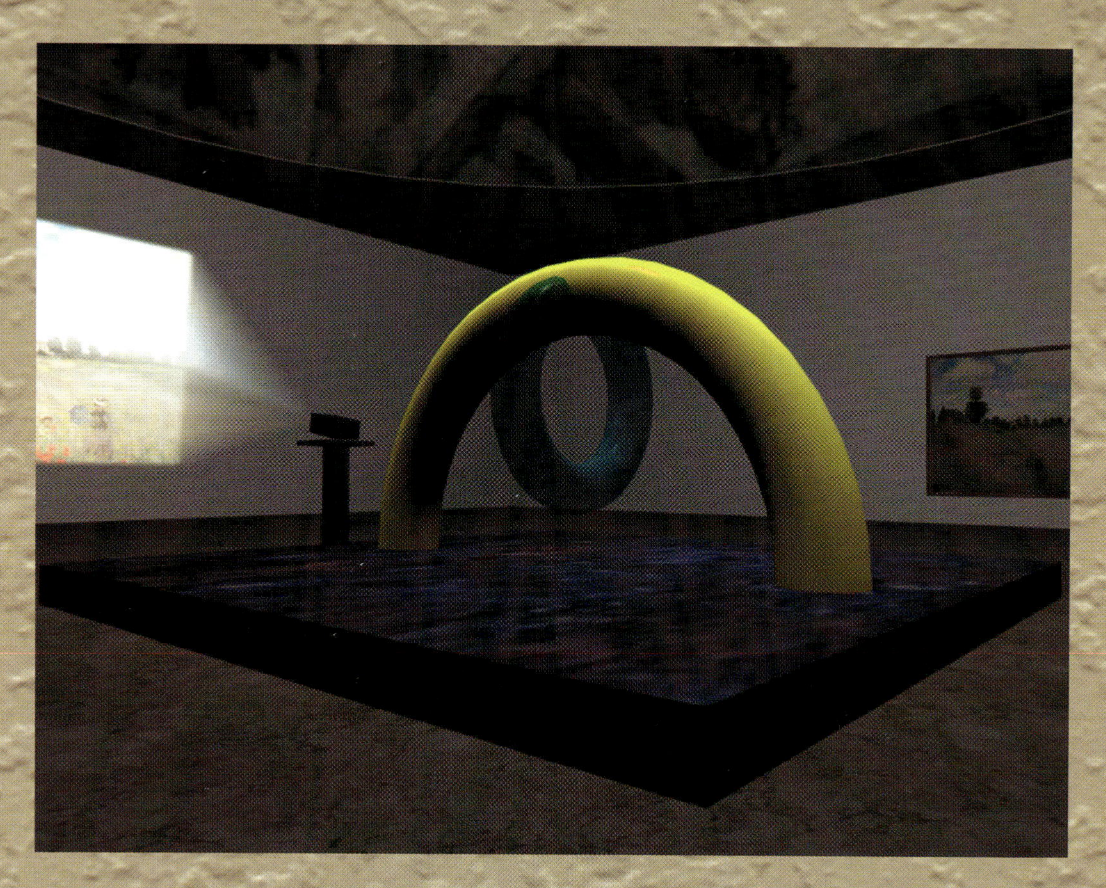

**Artist's Exhibition ● Chapter 17**

**Mechanical Motion ● Chapter 18**

FIGURE 10.1
Bomb space warp.

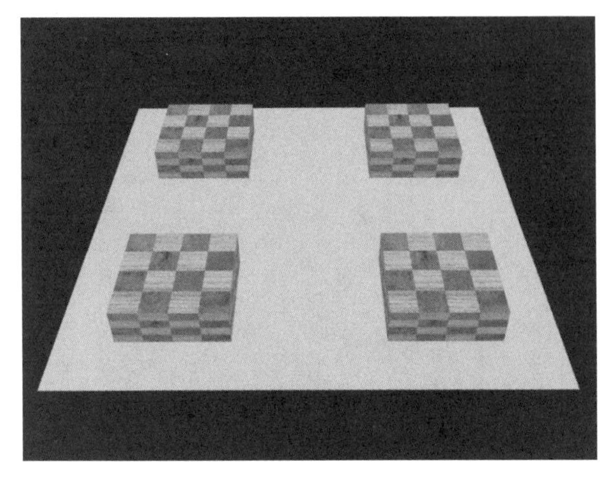

A Original

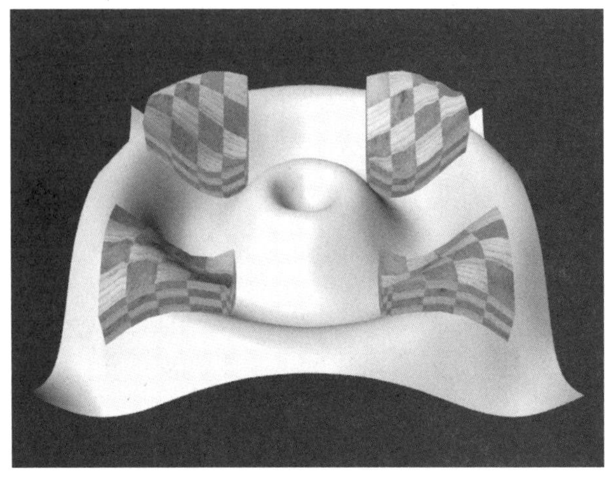

B Ripple

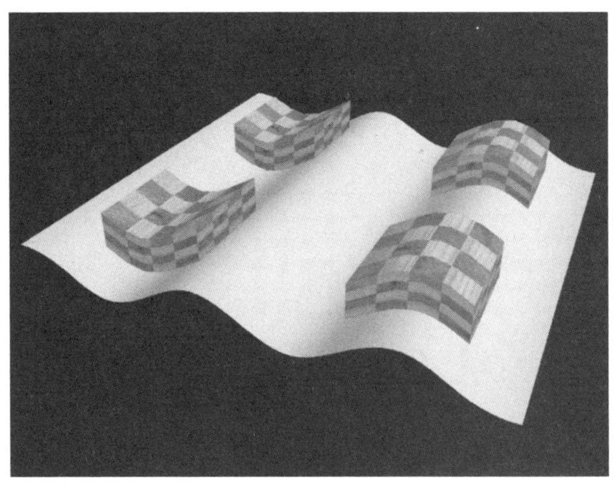

C Wave

Figure 10.2
Ripple and wave space warp.

### Modifier-based

These types of modifiers act similarly to regular modifiers such as bend or taper, but apply to deformation in world space. Some of the common types are bend, twist, taper, and skew.

### Particles and Dynamics

Particles and Dynamics space warps are used to affect the motion of bound particle objects. Particles are multiple objects created with particle systems, explained in section 10.3. Some of the common particle space warps are Gravity, Deflector, and Wind. The following is a more detailed description of some space warps and options:

**Gravity**

The gravity space warp pulls particles toward the area of the space warp. Refer to Figure 10.3. The strength option sets how strong the gravity is. A value of 0 is null gravity, a value greater than 0 increases gravity, while a value less than 0 causes a repelling effect, or negative gravity.

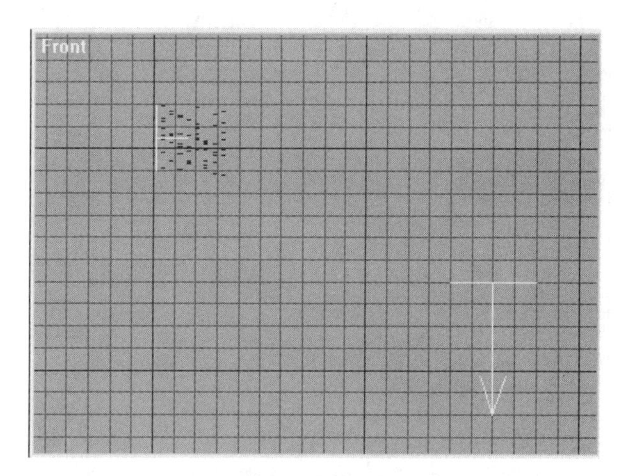


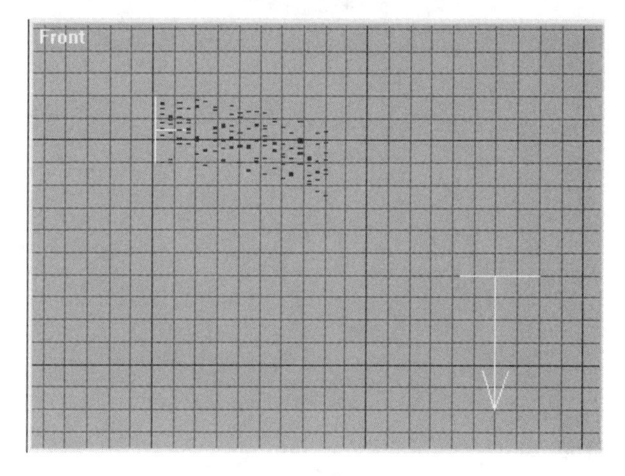


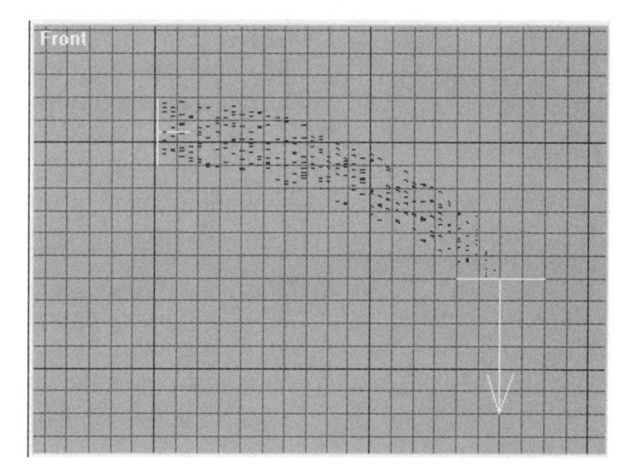


FIGURE 10.3
Gravity space warp.

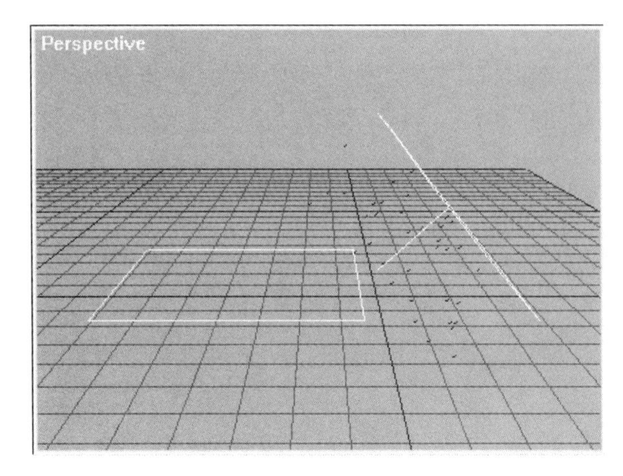


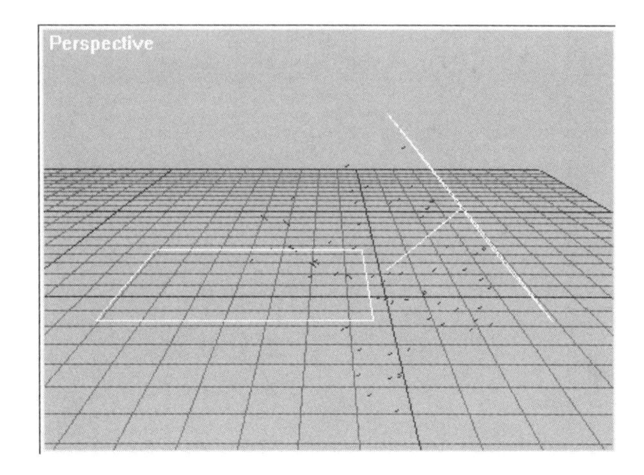


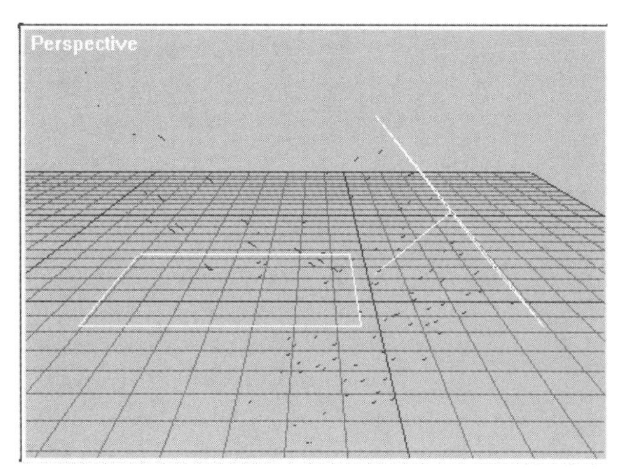


FIGURE 10.4
Deflector space warp.

### Deflector

The deflector space warp causes particles to bounce off the deflector. This space warp appears as a wireframe rectangle. Refer to Figure 10.4. The bounce option sets the speed at which the particles bounce off the deflector. A value of 0 causes no bounce, between 0 and 1 causes the particles to bounce at a speed less than their initial speed, a value of 1 maintains the same speed, and value greater than 1 causes the particles to bounce off at a greater speed.

### Wind

The wind space warp simulates the effect of windblown particles. Refer to Figure 10.5. The effect blows in the direction its icon points. A strength value greater than 0 increases the wind effect, and less than 0 causes suction. Turbulence causes the particles to change course randomly.

## 10.3 PARTICLE SYSTEMS

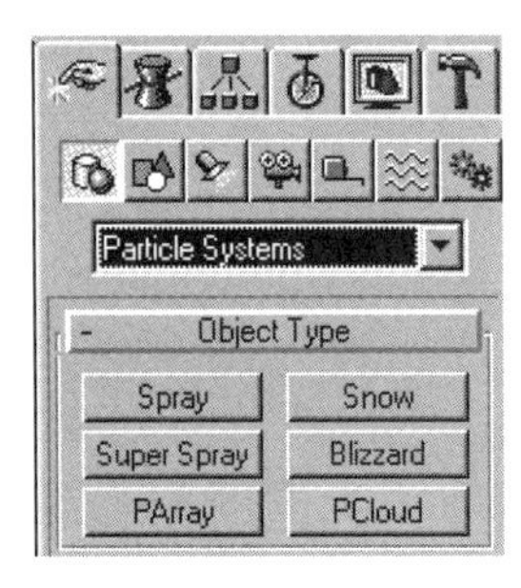


Particle systems are used to create multiple objects that move over time. They are used to simulate rain, snow, blowing sand, or anything that involves numerous small objects. There are a number of particle systems but the two simplest particle systems to use are spray and snow. Refer to Figures 10.6 and 10.7. Spray can be used to create rain while Snow creates snow, naturally. Once you have become familiar with these, you can experiment with the other more complex particle systems. The other systems give you more control and, in doing so, have more variables to master.

*Note*: You can apply material maps to the particles for added effect. The binding of space warps creates realistic weather conditions.

FIGURE 10.5
Rain particle system showing wind space warp with a deflector space warp added.

## Common Parameters for Spray and Snow

Some parameters are common to spray and snow particle systems.

**Emitter Width and Length parameter**
Controls the area over which the particle system will generate particles. It is represented by a rectangle with a vector line extending from it. The direction the vector is pointing shows the direction the particles will be moving. You can transform the particle system object to point the vector line in any direction.

**Timing parameters**
Controls the life of the particles. The Start value indicates the frame in which the particle show is created. The Life value indicates the life of the particle in frames. The Birth Rate sets the number of new particles to be created per frame. When the Constant box is checked, the birth rate equals the maximum sustainable rate.

## Spray Particle System

Spray simulates water drops. See Figure 10.6. The following are the parameters:

FIGURE 10.6
Rendering using spray particle system.

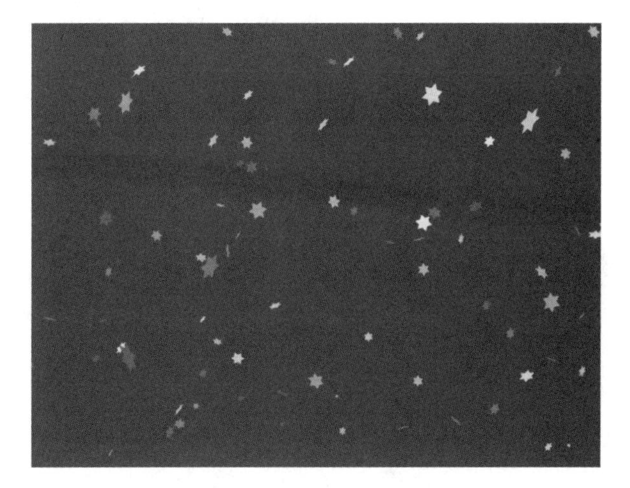

FIGURE 10.7
Rendering using snow particle system.

**Viewport Count**
Sets the maximum number of particles displayed in viewports at any given frame.

**Render Count**
Sets the maximum number of particles displayed in a single frame when you render.

**Drop Size**
Sets the size of the particles.

**Speed**
Sets the initial velocity of particles. This can be altered with the use of space warps such as gravity.

**Variation**
Varies the initial speed and direction of particles.

**Drops, Dots, or Ticks**
Sets the way the particles are displayed in viewports but has no effect on rendering.

**Render Tetrahedron**
Renders particles as long tetrahedrons that simulate a long raindrop.

**Render Facing**
Renders particles as square faces. You can apply material maps to these faces.

## Snow Particle System

Snow simulates falling snow or confetti. See Figure 10.7. Most of its parameters are the same as for spray. The following are unique:

**Tumble**
Causes the flakes to rotate at random if the value is 0 to 1.

**Tumble Rate**
Sets the speed at which the flakes rotate.

**Render Six Point**
Renders each particle as a six-point star.

**Render Triangle**
Renders each particle as a triangle.

## Super Spray and Blizzard

These two particle systems are similar to spray and snow but are much more advanced. They allow more control over the size and shape of the particles. You can choose between standard shapes, metaball particles, or instance geometry. Metaballs are used to provide close-up views of a liquid particle system. Instance geometry is used when you want your particles to be duplicates of another object in your scene.

The blizzard particle system can be used to create rain or snow and has a similar emitter to spray or snow.

The superspray particle system uses a cylinder as the emitter. The particles emit from a single point. Using the spread options under Basic Parameters/Particle Formation causes the particles to spread out after they are emitted.

### PArray and Pcloud

These two particle systems can use an object in the scene as an emitter to emit the particles. PArray can be used to create complex explosions. Pcloud is used when you want create a "group" of particles that fills a specific volume.

## 10.4 MORPHS

Morphing is the process of changing one shape into another over time. See Figure 10.8. In 3D Studio MAX, two or more objects with the same number of vertices are changed from one to another by moving the vertices of the seed object to match the location of the target object.

### Vertices and Mesh Objects

The key to successful morphing is that both objects, seed and target, must have the same number of vertices and be mesh objects. Lofted objects are commonly used as morphs. Making certain that Adaptive and Optimize parameters of lofting, extrude, or lathe modifiers are turned off will help to assure that you have the same number of vertices. Objects can also be modified so that the number of vertices can be reduced or increased.

### Morphing Procedure

The procedure to create morphs is as follows:

1. Create a seed and a target object that are meshed and have the same number of vertices.

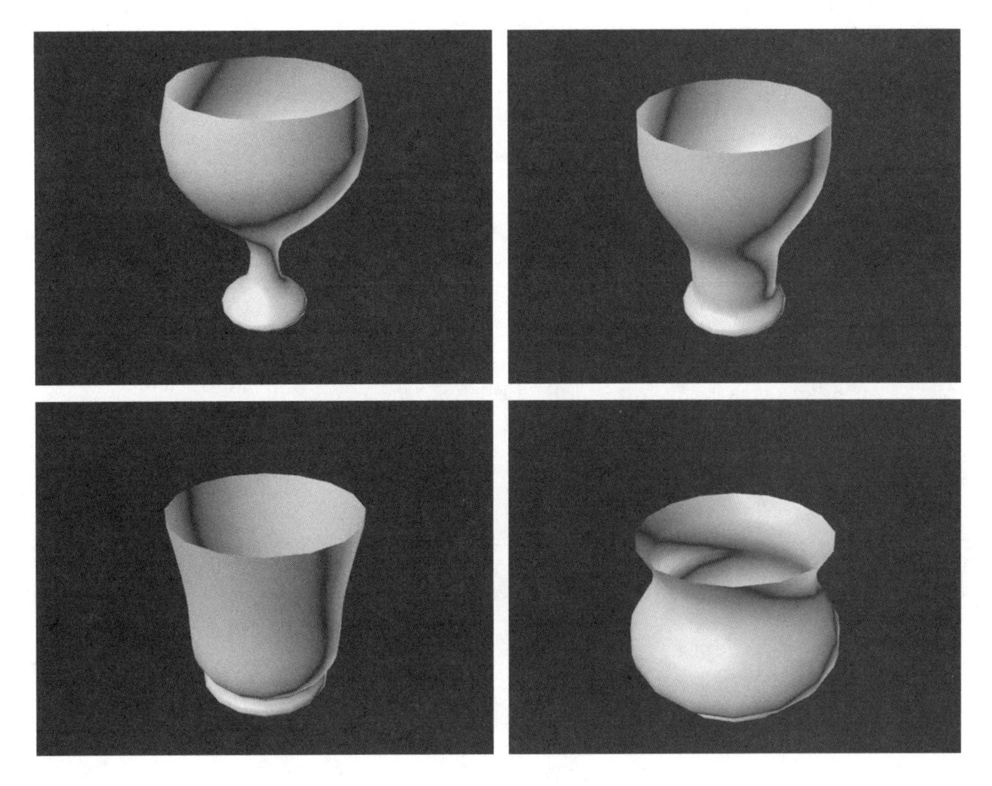

FIGURE 10.8
Morphing one object to another.

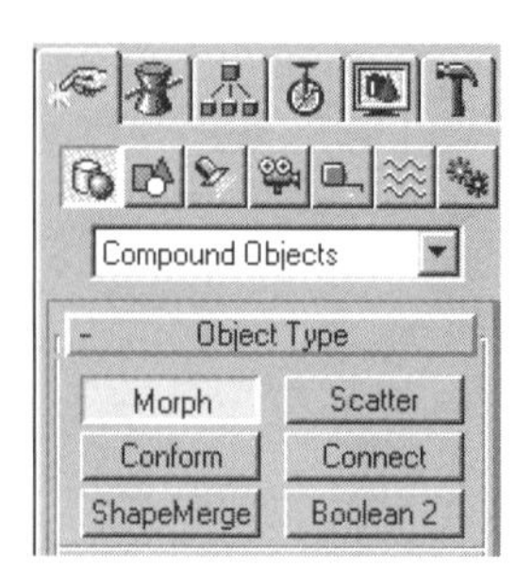


2. Select the seed (originating object).
3. In the Create panel, pick the Geometry button and Choose Compound Objects from the object category drop-down list.
4. Pick the Morph button and the seed object is turned into a morph object. *Note*: You will not be able to pick a target object unless it has the same number of vertices as the seed object.
5. Set the clone method by choosing either Reference, Move, Copy, or Instance and then select the target objects at the appropriate key frames. You can use one or more target objects, each at different frames.
6. Run the animation and the seed object will change (morph) into the target object at the appropriate frame.

## 10.5 SUMMARY

This chapter has shown three special ways to create objects: space warps, particle systems, and morphs. Space warps are used to modify existing objects in order to alter their appearances and are useful when you want to alter many objects at one time. Particle systems are used to create a multitude of small moving particles to simulate rain or other small objects, and morphs are used to change one object into another over time. Most of these require animation to fully see their effects; however, it is important that you understand their functions so that you can apply them as the need arises.

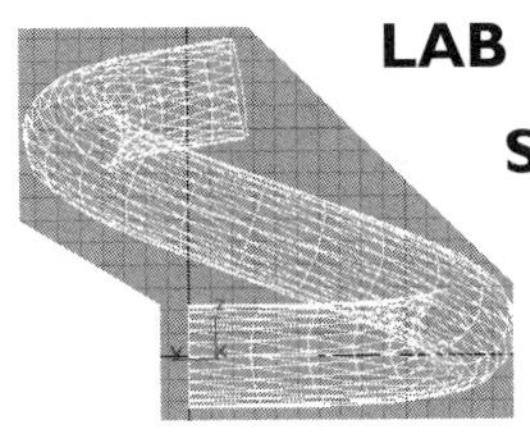

# LAB 10.A

## Special Modeling

### Purpose

During this lab you will be introduced to the three special modeling techniques of space warps, particle systems, and morphs. Most of these require animation. Thus, you will also be introduced to some animation techniques as well.

### Objectives

You will be able to

- Create a space warp and bind an object to it.
- Create a particle system and see it animated over time.
- Create a morph from seed and target objects.
- See the results of morphing over time.

### Procedure

1. Start a new file and establish the usual startup settings. Refer to Lab 8.A if you need to. Make sure that the Perspective viewport is set to display Smooth and Highlight. The other three viewports should be set to Wireframe. This will be the standard viewport setting for the entire lab.

### Space Warps

You are going to create a simple object and then bind it to a space warp. This requires some animation to see the effect, which will be explained.

2. Create a sphere in the middle of the top viewport, as shown in Figure 10.9.
3. Pick the Space Warp button from the Create command panel.
4. On the Object Type rollout, pick the Bomb space warp button.

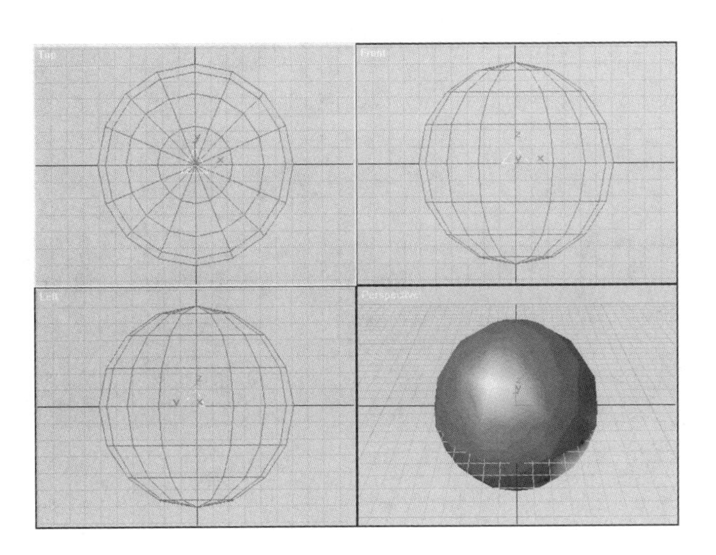

FIGURE 10.9
Sphere.

5. Pick in the center of the sphere in the Top viewport. A small wireframe pyramid will appear. This is the Bomb space warp object and is also shown in Figure 10.10.
6. Zoom in close to the Bomb space warp object so that it nearly fills the top viewport. You should still be able to see some of the lines of the sphere.

7. Pick the Bind to Space Warp tool. Pick the Sphere and drag the icon until it touches the Bomb space warp object (pryamid). This will bind the sphere to the bomb.

8. To test the space warp, activate the Perspective viewport. Pick the Play Animation button, and you should see the ball explode off the screen. By default there are 100 frames in the scene. This makes it easy for you to test the animation without having to know much about animation now.

9. Press the Stop Animation button and pick the text box that is right below the animation buttons. This contains the current frame number. Enter 50 in this box, which is the middle frame of the animation.
10. Now use the Zoom Extents button to show the extents of the explosion in frame 50. You do this to see more of the explosion during animation.
11. Press the Play Animation button. You should be able to see more of the effect now. Space warps are simple but effective. Figure 10.10 shows some sequence frames in the animation.
12. Save this scene as CH10A.MAX.

## PARTICLE SYSTEMS

You are going to create a particle system from rain and then bind it to a wind space warp to give the effect of rain on a windy day.

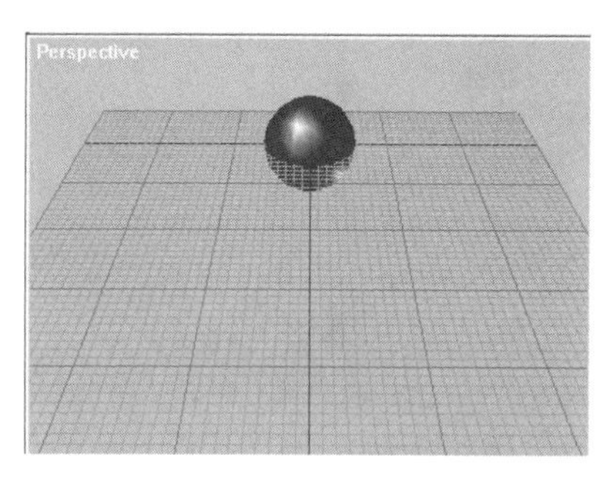


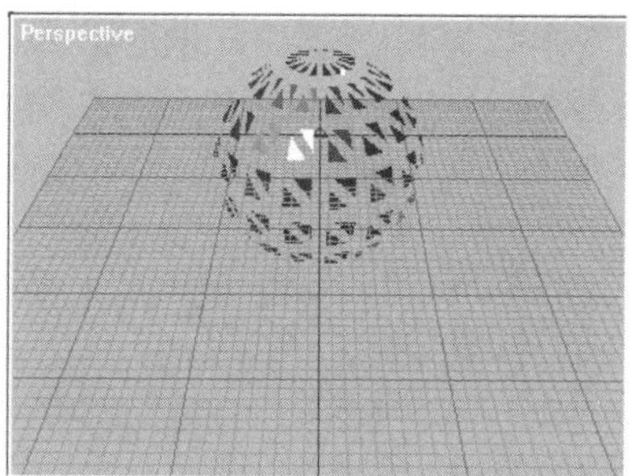


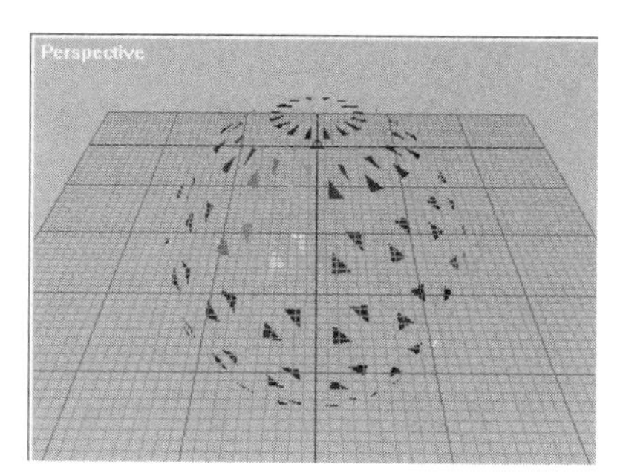


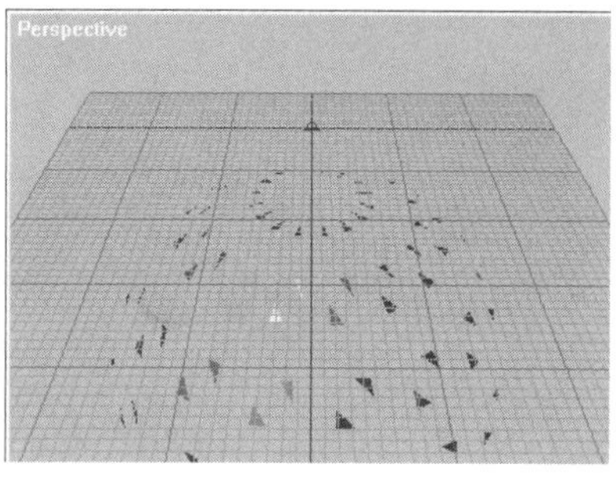


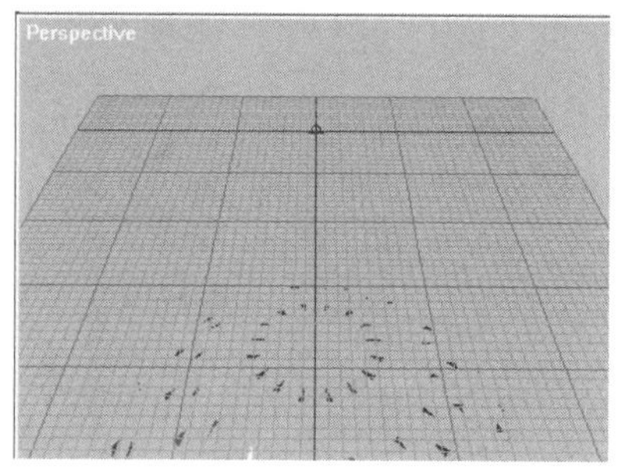


FIGURE 10.10
Several frames in the bomb animation.

13. Start a new scene.

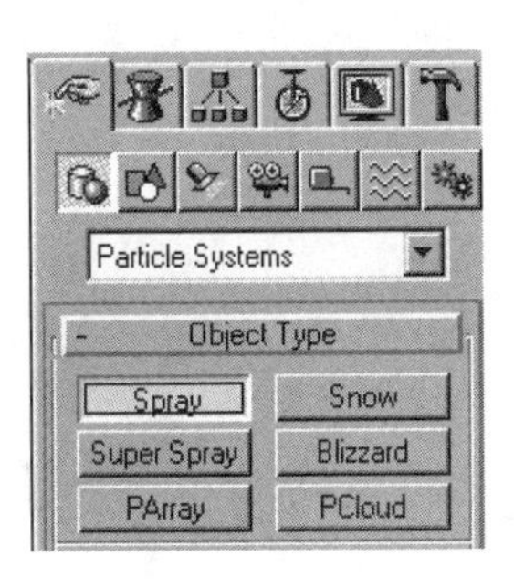


14. With the Geometry button active in the Create command panel, select Particle System from the object category drop-down list.
15. Pick the Spray button.
16. Pick and drag in the Top viewport to create an emitter similar to that shown in Figure 10.11.
17. See Figure 10.12 for the parameters of the spray particle system.
18. Activate the Perspective viewport and move to frame 100. Press the Zoom Extents button.
19. Play the animation. You should be able to see white specks being created and falling downward. Stop the animation and return to frame 0.
20. Now you are going to add some wind.
21. Activate the Left viewport.
22. Pick the Space Warp button from the Create command panel and pick the Wind button from the Object Type rollout.

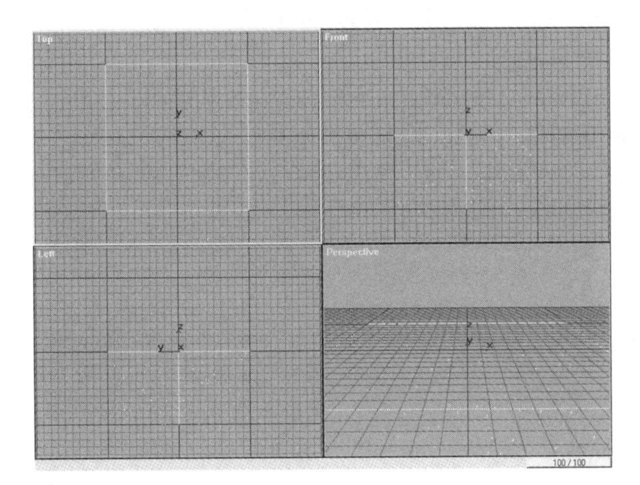

FIGURE 10.11
Spray emitter.

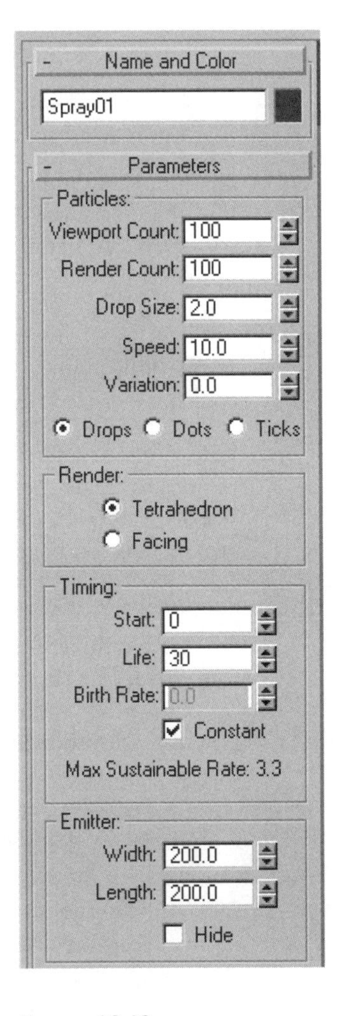


FIGURE 10.12
Spray parameters.

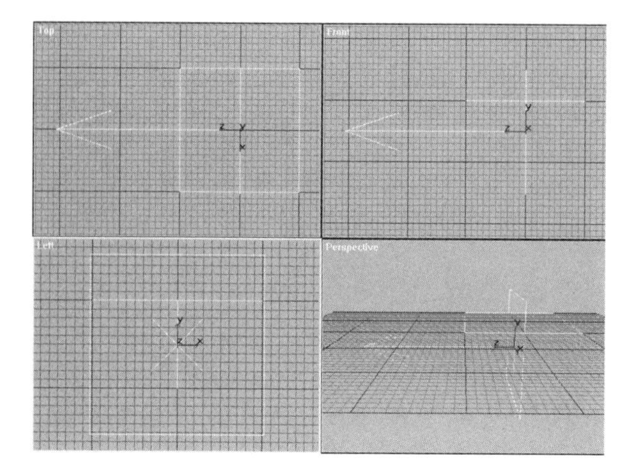

FIGURE 10.13
Wind space warp bound to a spray particle system to simulate blown rain.

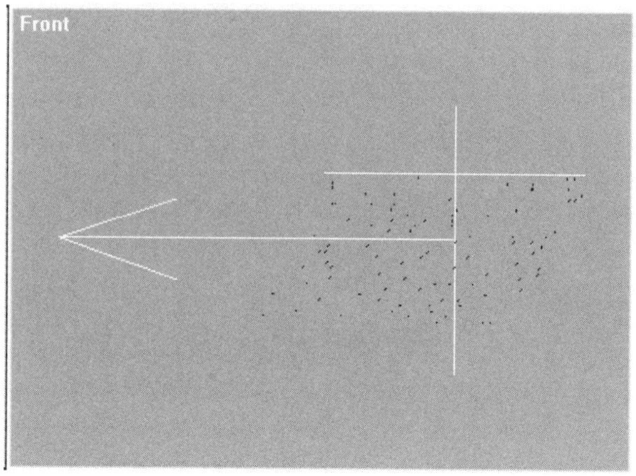

FIGURE 10.14
Front viewport showing frame 50.

23. In the Front viewport, create the wind space warp by picking its lower-left corner and dragging to its upper-right corner. Use Zoom Extents All; Figure 10.13 shows what it should look like.
24. Using the Bind to Space Warp tool, pick on the particle system object and drag to the wind space warp. This will bind the spray to the wind.
25. Activate the Perspective viewport and play the animation again. You should be able to see the wind blowing the rain sideways. This combination of wind and spray can be very effective. Figure 10.14 shows the front viewport of frame 50.
26. Save the scene as CH10B.MAX.

## MORPHS

Now you are going to create a simple morph. The key to effective morphing is that both the seed and the target objects must have the same number of vertices. The use of lofts to create morph shapes is particularly useful because you can control the number of vertices. In this part of the lab you are going to create three lofts: a cylinder and two rectangular boxes. You will then morph one into the other and back again.

27. Start a new scene.
28. Create three lofts, as shown in Figure 10.15, using two identical rectangles and a circle. The size is not important as long as the three objects are proportional to each other and have the same loft parameters. The following is the typical procedure for producing a loft, just to refresh your memory:
    a. Create a spline shape (rectangle) for the cross section.
    b. Create a spline shape (line) for the path.
    c. Select the cross section (rectangle).
    d. Pick the Geometry button in the Create panel and choose the Loft Object from the category list.
    e. Pick Loft in the Object Type rollout.
    f. Choose Copy, and then use the Get Path button. Pick the path (line).
    g. Adjust the parameters. Under Skin Parameters check the following:

       Capping is on and set to Morph.

Shape Steps and Path Steps are set to 5.

Optimize Shapes and Adaptive Path Steps are off.

The shape and path steps must match between the two objects that are going to be morphed so that they have the same number of vertices.

29. The process of morphing takes place over a series of frames in 3D Studio MAX. Pick the text box that is right below the animation buttons. This contains the current frame number. Enter 50 in this box. That is the middle frame of the animation. This is where you are going to have the first box change into the cylinder.
30. Select the Hold menu item from the Edit pull-down menu. This will protect your objects in case something goes wrong in the creation of the morph. If something does go wrong, you can always use the Fetch command to return to this state in the lab.

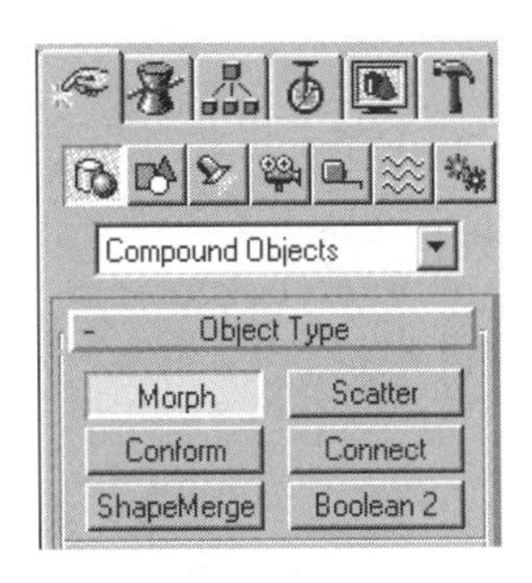


31. Activate the Perspective viewport and select the first box. Pick the Geometry button in the Create panel and choose the Compound Objects from the category list. Pick Morph in the Object Type rollout. As soon as you do this, the loft object becomes a morph object.

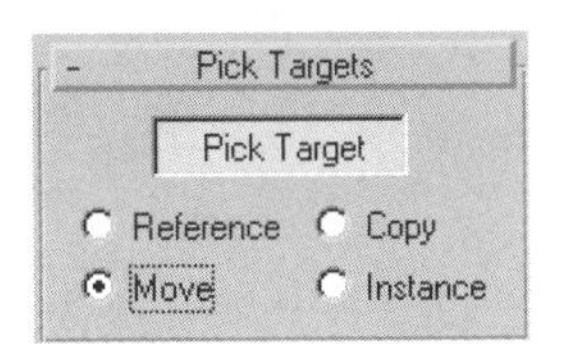


32. Under the Pick Targets rollout, turn on the Move option and then press the Pick Target button, turning it on (green). Move your cursor over the cylinder and pick it. The first box should disappear and be replaced with the cylinder. This is because the box will have morphed into the cylinder at frame 50 of the animation, the frame you are on. Refer to Figure 10.16 to see what the Perspective viewport should look like.
33. Pick in the text box that is right below the animation buttons. This contains the current frame number. Enter 100 in this box, which is the last frame of the animation. This is where you are going to have the cylinder change into the second box.

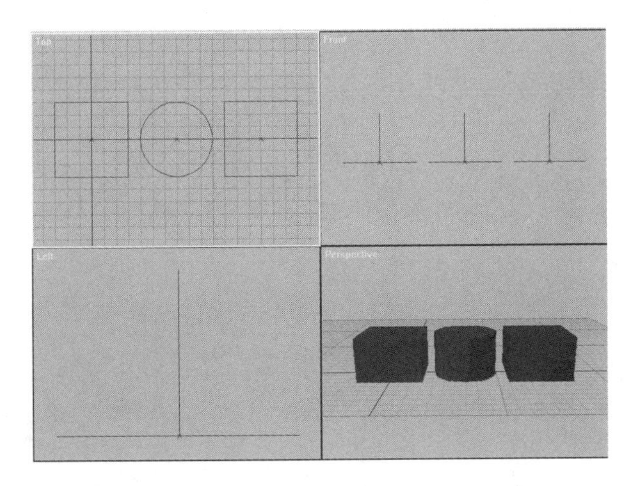

FIGURE 10.15
Three lofted objects to be used to morph.

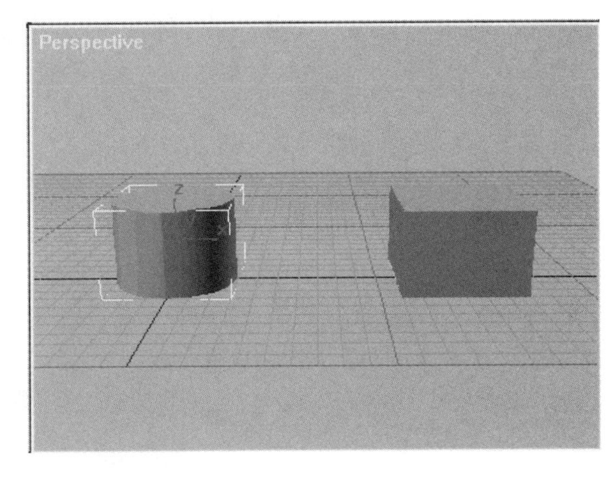


FIGURE 10.16
Cylinder replaces box.

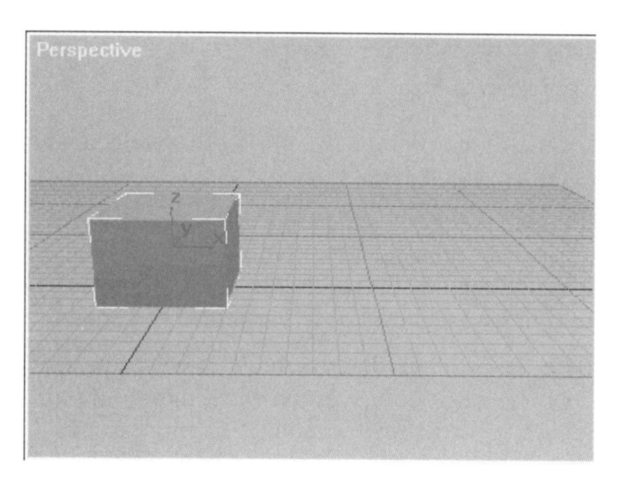


FIGURE 10.17
Box replaces cylinder.

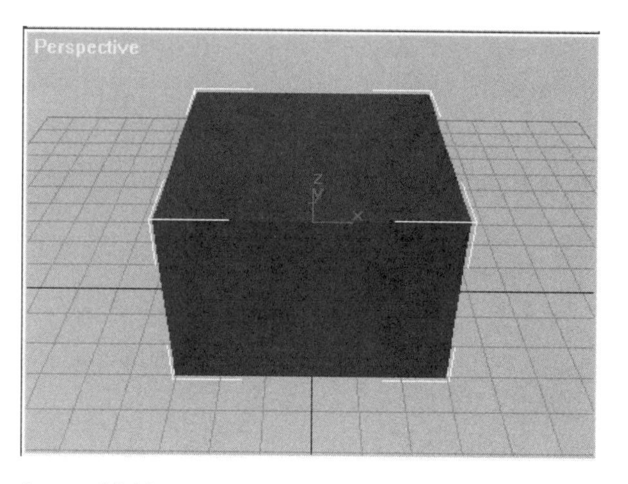


FIGURE 10.18
Perspective view showing box orientation.

34. While still in the Morph creation panel and with the Move and Pick Target still active, pick the second box. The cylinder should now disappear and be replaced by the second box. This is because the cylinder will have morphed into the box at frame 100 of the animation, the frame you are on. Figure 10.17 shows what the perspective viewport should look like.
35. Use the Zoom Extents on the Perspective viewport to center the final box. Follow this with the Zoom to reduce the display so that you can see the box and then use the Arc Rotate to turn the view to see more of the top of the box. Finally, use Pan to center the object in the viewport. Figure 10.18 shows the perspective view position.
36. With the Perspective viewport active, pick the Play Animation button and you should see the box change into the cylinder and back again. Press the Stop button when you have seen enough. Figure 10.19 shows a series of frames.
37. Save the scene as CH10C.MAX.

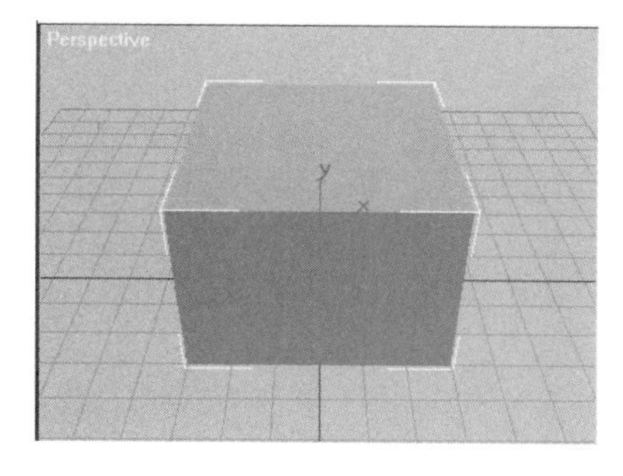

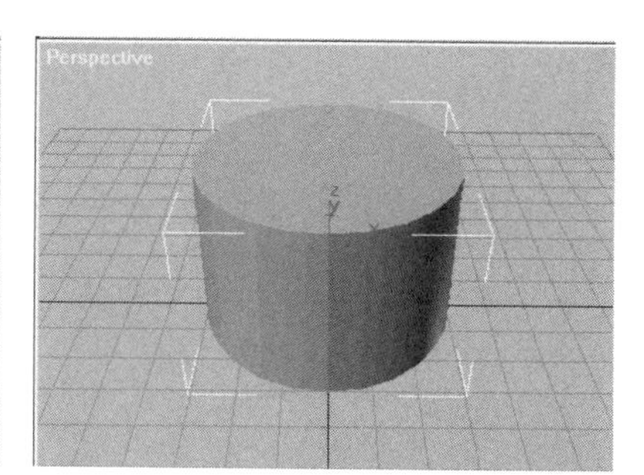

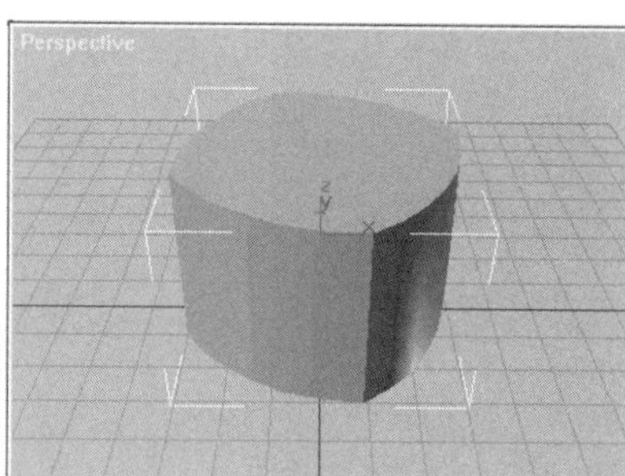

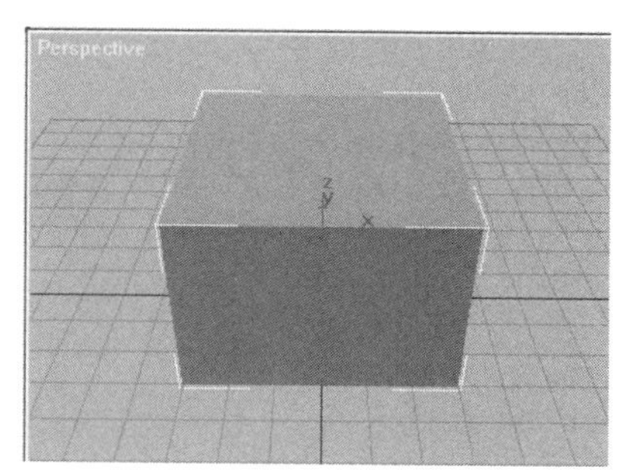

FIGURE 10.19
A series of frames showing the morph from a box to a cylinder and back to a box.

## QUESTIONS AND ASSIGNMENTS

### ? QUESTIONS

1. How are space warps similar to modifers?
2. How are space warps different than modifiers?
3. List the three types of space warps.
4. Briefly outline the procedure for applying a space warp.
5. What are the two simplest particle systems?
6. What is the relationship of the emitter to the particle system?
7. What are morphs?
8. What is the most important factor in achieving a successful morph?
9. Briefly outline the procedure for creating a morph.

### ASSIGNMENTS

1. Experiment with the bomb space warp on more than one object.
   a. Start a new scene and create four boxes arranged in a circle. Each box should have five segments in its height, width, and depth.
   b. Create a bomb space warp in the middle of the Top viewport. The bomb should have a strength of 10. It should be in the middle of the four boxes. You will have to move the space warp upward in the Front or Left viewport until it is in the middle of the boxes.
   c. Bind each box in turn to the bomb space warp object.
   d. Pick the Play Animation button. Notice how each box explodes. The effect of the bomb is radial.
   e. You may have to use Zoom extents in frame 50 to see the effect better.
   f. Play the animation in each viewport to see the effect of the bomb space warp.
   g. Save the scene as CH10D.MAX.
2. Experiment with the Deflector space warp to cause particles to bounce.
   a. Open the scene CH10B.MAX that contains the wind and the rain.
   b. Create a deflector space warp that lies under the falling rain, near the lower reaches of the rain. Bind the rain to this space warp and play the animation. You should be able to see the rain bounce as it hits the deflector space warp. This simulates rain bouncing off pavement.
   c. Save the scene as CH10E.MAX.
3. Experiment with the Gravity space warp to cause particles to curve downward to create a fountain effect.
   a. Start a new scene and create a spray particle system that has the particles pointing and flowing upward.
   b. Create a gravity space warp that is spherical and has a strength of -1. Bind the spray particle system to it.
   c. Play the animation and the particles should flow upward and spread out. If the spherical gravity were set to 1, the spray would turn inward. You want it outward (-1).

d. Create a second gravity space warp that is planar and is larger than the spray affected by the spherical gravity. It should have a strength greater than the spherical gravity. Give this one a strength of 2.
e. Play the animation again and the spray should flow upward, flow outward, and then fall to the ground. This simulates the water flowing from a fountain.

4. Experiment with a combination of a snow particle system and spherical wind to create a whirling snow storm.

5. Experiment with morphing and lofting.
   a. Start a new scene and create two identical lofts.
   b. Adjust the parameters of the second loft such as applying some deformation curves, so that the second loft doesn't resemble the first.
   c. Then create a morph where the first loft changes into the second. Remember both objects must have the same number of vertices.

PART FIVE

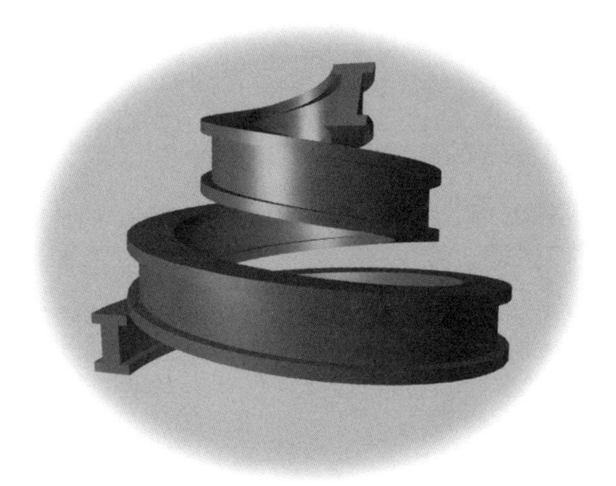

# Presentation

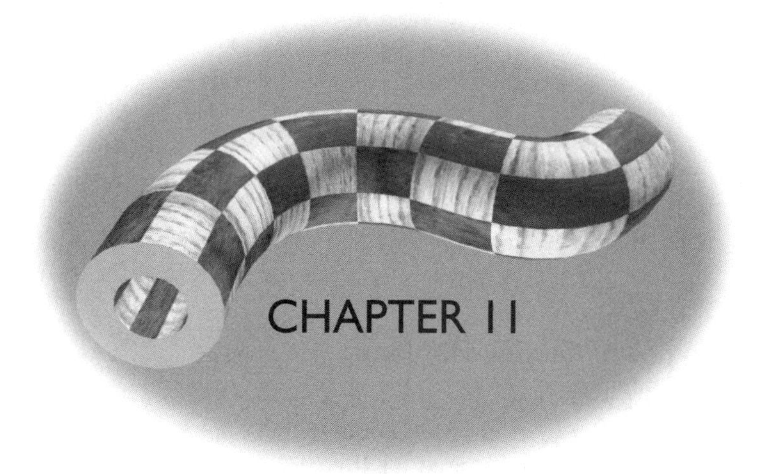


# A Brighter Outlook: Cameras, Lights, and Rendering

## 11.1 INTRODUCTION

Chapter 11 reviews 3D scene presentation. You will learn techniques for placing and modifying the cameras in your scene to produce a view over which you have more control and that resembles how the human eye perceives the world. The chapter also discusses the various light types and their use. Finally, this section reviews the scene-rendering procedure.

## 11.2 CAMERA BASICS

Up to this point, you have viewed your scenes using axonometric (orthographic) and perspective viewports. This type of viewing is extremely important in the model-building stage. With orthographic views, it is easy to tell if the model was created correctly, because the lines that create the model are parallel to each other. Perspective views are important because they offer a view of the model closer to the manner in which the human eye sees it. However, to achieve more control over the view, especially in the animation stage, a camera view is a necessity.

To create a camera view, you must first create a camera object with various parameters, and to understand how a camera object behaves, you must first understand the terms *focal length* and *field of view*. In a true camera the focal length represents the distance between the lens and the film in the camera. The focal length is usually referred to as the lens size and is measured in millimeters (mm). A 50-mm lens shows the view that an unaided, human eye would see. A lens with a value greater than 50 mm is referred to as a *telephoto*, or *zoom*, *lens* and is used to bring objects that are far away visually closer. A lens with a value less than 50 mm is referred to as a *wide-angle lens*. This type of lens is used to view a wider area of the scene. Figure 11.1 shows the three lens types.

The field of view (FOV) defines how much of an available view can be seen. It is measured in degrees along the horizon. The lens (focal length) and FOV depend on each other. The larger the lens size, the smaller the FOV and vice versa. When placing a camera object, you can set either the lens size or the FOV.

## Types of Camera Objects

There are two types of camera objects: the Target Camera and the Free Camera. A Target Camera is used to view the area around a selected target. This type of camera is easily placed and is used for still (unanimated) positions, which means the camera remains fixed in position and the scene moves around it.

A Free Camera is used to view an area in the direction the camera is pointing. This view is useful when you want to animate the camera along a path. As a further feature, a Free Camera can bank as it moves along a path, whereas a Target Camera cannot.

A 28 MM

B 50 MM

C 135 MM

FIGURE 11.1
Lenses: (A) 28-mm (wide-angle), (B) 50-mm (standard), and (C) 135-mm (zoom).

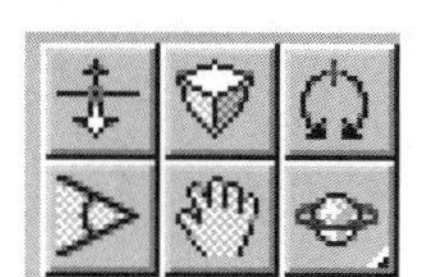

FIGURE 11.2
Camera Navigation buttons.

### Using the Camera View and Camera Navigation Buttons

To activate a camera view, simply activate any viewport and then either right-click on the viewport label, select Views, and choose one of the created cameras or use the shortcut key C and pick the previously created camera from a list.

Once you have activated a camera viewport, the navigation buttons in the lower right of the screen change. Figure 11.2 shows the Camera Navigation buttons. The following is a description of each of the new buttons:

**Dolly**
Moves the camera backward or forward along its own line of sight. This has no effect on the lens size or FOV, but it does change the area seen in the viewport.

**Perspective**
Dollies the camera and changes the FOV so that the same area is seen regardless of the distance moved. This process can cause a distorted view, depending on how close you move to objects, because of the decrease in lens size.

**Roll**
Rotates the camera about its own line-of-sight axis.

**FOV**
Changes the FOV without moving the location of the camera (which, in effect, changes the lens size).

**Truck**
Moves the camera and target perpendicular to the line of sight. It has the effect of sliding the camera around.

**Orbit and Pan**
A flyout that contains Orbit and Pan. Orbit rotates the camera about its target and Pan rotates the target about its camera. If you hold down the CTRL key as you drag the cursor, the movement will be constrained to either vertical or horizontal, depending on the direction first moved.

### Animating Cameras

Because cameras are objects, you can animate them just as you would any object in your scene. The techniques for animation, which is in itself a complex subject, is discussed in Chapter 13.

## 11.3 PLACING AND MODIFYING CAMERAS

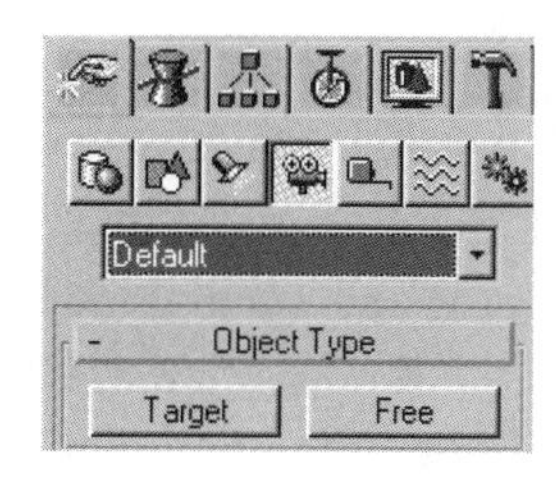


Cameras are objects; as such, they are created using the Creation command panel. Once you have selected the Camera icon, you must identify whether you are going to place a Target Camera or a Free Camera. The placement of each is slightly different because of their individual characteristics.

### LIGHTS! CAMERA! ACTION!

#### Display of Camera and Light Icons

Sometimes the Camera or Light icons can clutter a scene and make it hard to work on. Hide the Camera icon by opening the Display control panel and checking the Camera box in the Hide by Category rollout. Use the same procedure for lights.

## Target Camera

To place the Target Camera, you pick and drag. The initial pick location places the camera; as you drag you relocate the target. The camera swings to follow the target. When you have reached the desired location of the target, release the pick button. At this point, set the desired parameters, as shown in Figure 11.3. Some key parameters are Lens/FOV and Show Cone. It can be very useful to be able see the FOV cone as part of the camera object. In this way you can see how much of an area a particular lens *views*.

## Free Camera

To place the Free Camera, you simply pick in a viewport. The camera's viewing direction (line of sight) is initially perpendicular to the plane of the viewport, and the camera points in the negative Z direction. Once the camera is located, you can use Move and Rotate transforms to alter its location and orientation. See Figure 11.3 for the Camera parameters. Figure 11.4 shows the Target and Free Camera icons.

## Transforms

Transforms can be used to move or rotate the camera to change its placement and orientation. If the camera is a Target Camera, you can select either the target or the camera icon and then transform either one.

## Modify Command Panel

Because cameras are objects, you can employ the same methods used to modify other objects to modify cameras. Use the Modify command panel to alter any of the parameters associated with the camera.

## Clipping Planes

One special feature of either camera type is the ability to set clipping planes. Clipping planes exclude geometry not wanted for a particular view. When you activate the Clip Manually box, you can set either or both the Near and Far Clip. The Near Clip will exclude any objects that are nearer to the camera than the set Near Clip distance. The Far Clip will exclude any objects that are farther away from the camera than the set Far Clip distance.

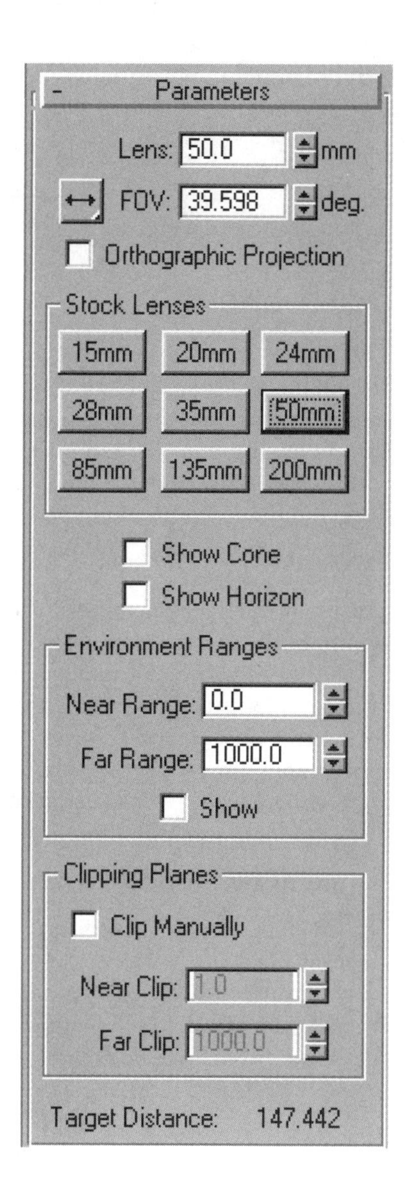


FIGURE 11.3
Camera parameters.

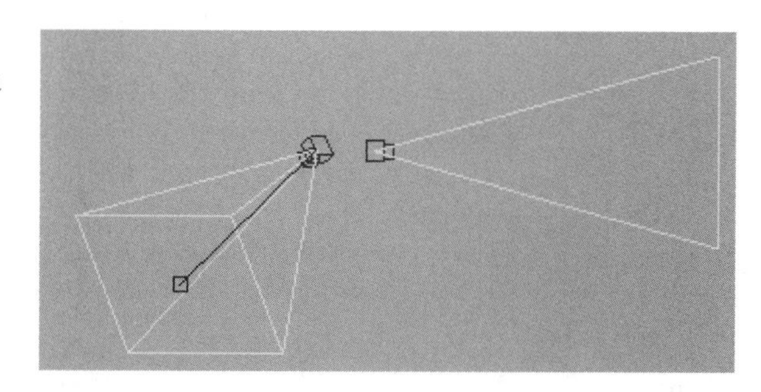

FIGURE 11.4
Target and Free Camera icons.

### Environment Ranges

The environment range parameter of a camera is similar to the Clipping plane, but it adds atmospheric effects such as fog. These effects are explained in Section 11.7, "Rendering."

## 11.4 LIGHT BASICS

The key to effective rendering is the selection and placement of lights. Before we discuss the placement of lights, we should review the characteristics of light. As with cameras, lights are objects and have certain parameters that control their behavior. The following is a discussion of light characteristics and how they are achieved within 3D Studio MAX.

### Intensity

The intensity of a light represents how strong light is or how much light will be radiated from the light source (light object).

In 3D Studio MAX intensity is measured by the light object's HSV (Hue, Saturation, Value). At a V value of 255 the light is the brightest; at a value of 0 the light is completely dark (or off). There is also a special parameter called the Multiplier. It should normally be kept at 1 but can be used for special effects by multiplying the HSV either positively (adds light) or negatively (removes light).

### Angle of Incidence

The angle at which light strikes a surface controls how bright the surface will be. The angle of incidence is the angle at which the light rays strike a surface. If the light strikes a surface at 90° (perpendicular), then the surface receives the maximum light. Anything less than 90°, the intensity of illumination decreases.

Where you place your lights and the direction in which they point affects the intensity of the light striking a surface.

### Attenuation

Light intensity diminishes over distance; the farther objects are away from the light source, the less light they receive. This is referred to as *attenuation.*

Only certain light types support attenuation, and those that can support it can have their attenuation activated or deactivated. When off, the light does not diminish with distance. There are two separate types of attenuation: near and far. Near is used when you want the light to fade in. The light will have a value of 0 at the start distance and increase to full when it reaches the end distance. Near is used for special effects whereas far is used when you want the light to fade out. This is the way light normally behaves. The light is at full intensity at the start distance, while it starts to fade to 0 when it reaches the end distance.

### Color of Light

Light is rarely perfectly white in the real world: sunsets can be reddish-orange; moonlight can be blue. Using colored light can produce a variety of natural and exotic effects.

In 3D Studio MAX you can adjust a light object's color by setting its hue. The following table lists some various light sources and their hue ratings as established by 3D Studio MAX. To use these hue numbers, you must set the Value to full (255) and adjust the saturation to meet your needs.

| Light Source | Hue |
|---|---|
| Overcast daylight | 130 |
| Noontime sunlight | 58 |
| White fluorescent | 27 |
| Tungsten/halogen | 20 |
| Incandescent, 100 W | 16 |
| Incandescent, 25 W | 12 |
| Sunlight at sunset | 7 |
| Candle flame | 5 |

## Shadows and Light

When light strikes an object, shadows are usually cast unless the light is all around the object.

In 3D Studio MAX, each light object can have shadow casting on or off. If it is set to off, the light passes through the object as if it weren't there. Normally, to enhance real-life visual effects, you leave shadow casting on.

There are also two different shadow casting procedures: Shadow Maps and Ray-Traced Shadows. Shadow Map shadows can have softer edges, whereas Ray-Traced shadows are more accurate but always have sharp, distinct edges. Figure 11.5 shows the difference between Shadow Map and Ray-Traced shadows.

## Natural versus Artificial Light

Natural light is the light from the sun. Because of the distance the sun is from the earth, its light rays are practically parallel when they strike the earth.

To perform this effect within 3D Studio MAX, a particular light type—called *directional* light—is used. Using a directional light source with its HSV numbers set to 45, 80, 255 simulates a clear, sunny day. You may also want to use Ray-Traced shadows to create sharp shadows. Figure 11.6 shows a brightly lit outdoor scene.

Artificial light usually requires multiple sources of light to light a scene effectively. There should be one dominant light source, referred to as the *key light*. Often a spotlight is used for key lighting. Depending on the effect, this light is usually placed in front of the main subject, above it and slightly to one side or the other, pointing toward the area of emphasis. In addition to the key light, there may be one or more

A

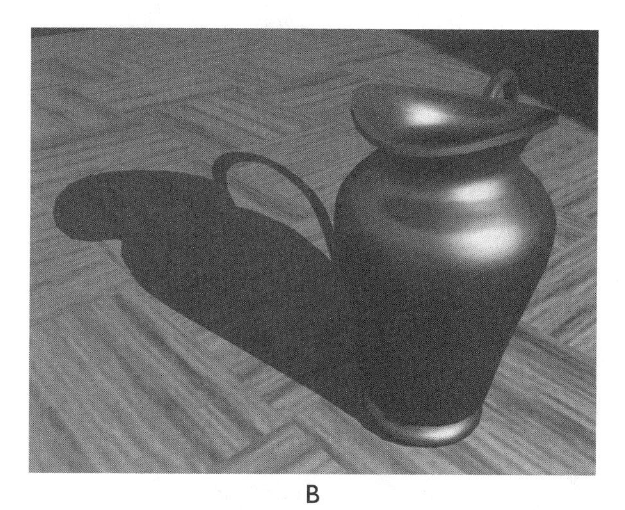

B

FIGURE 11.5
(A) Shadow Map and (B) Ray-Traced shadows.

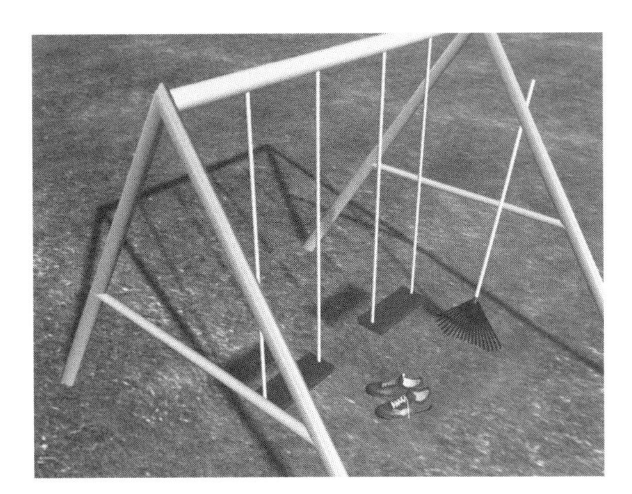

FIGURE 11.6
Natural outdoor lighting.

FIGURE 11.7
Artificial lighting using key and fill lighting.

backup lights, referred to as *fill light*. Usually omni lights are used for this purpose. The combination of key and fill lights is used to emphasize the scene or specific objects in the scene. This emphasis is accomplished by the contrast of light and dark and brings out the three-dimensionality of the objects in the scene. Figure 11.7 shows key light and the addition of fill light.

## Light Types

There are several different light types used within 3D Studio MAX to achieve a multitude of lighting conditions. The following is a list of the different light types available in 3D Studio MAX and their descriptions.

**Ambient**

Ambient light represents the light that is all around the scene. In real life, light is reflected off various surfaces, causing the overall area to be lit up. Currently this cannot be accomplished within 3D Studio MAX. However, it can be simulated with the use of the Ambient Light setting. You can increase or decrease the overall intensity of light in a scene or even change the color of the ambient light. These adjustments can be made by choosing the Rendering/Environment pull-down menu item and then picking the Ambient Light box. You then can change the color of the ambient light or its intensity by changing the Value setting of the HSV.

Remember, the higher the ambient light intensity, the lower the contrast between light and dark. Conversely, the lower the ambient light intensity, the greater the contrast. Figure 11.8 shows the effect of increasing ambient light.

**Omni**

Omni light is a form of radiant lighting. The light is cast all around the light source, similar to a lightbulb or a candle. See Figure 11.9. As mentioned before, it can be used for fill lighting to accent subjects in the scene. In 3D Studio MAX, omni lights can now cast shadows.

**Directional**

Directional light projects parallel rays. Its main purpose is to simulate the sun's rays. See Figure 11.6.

**Spotlight**

A spotlight is used to project a focused beam of light similar to an automobile headlight, flashlight, or stage lighting. Because the light can be focused, you have

FIGURE 11.8
Ambient light at different intensities.

control over the size of the cone of projected light. This cone has two parts: hotspot and falloff. Hotspot is the brightest area and falloff is where the light intensity becomes zero. The area between the hotspot and falloff is where the light intensity diminishes. Figure 11.10 shows a flashlight with a spotlight. In this figure the volume light, or atmospheric light effect, was added to make the beam of light show.

FIGURE 11.9
Omni light simulating a lamp.

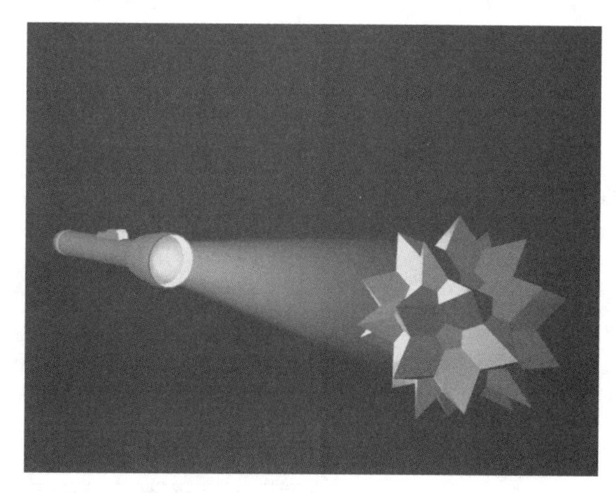

FIGURE 11.10
Spotlight simulating a flashlight beam.

There are two types of spotlights: target and free. Their behavior is similar to Target and Free Cameras.

## Spotlight Navigation Buttons

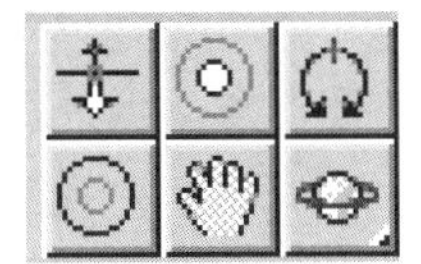

FIGURE 11.11
Spotlight Navigation buttons.

You can display a spotlight view in a viewport. This can be a convenient way to adjust a spotlight's parameters by seeing the scene through the *eye* of the spotlight. To switch a viewport to a spotlight view, activate the viewport and press the $ shortcut key. When you activate a spotlight viewport, the Navigation buttons will change to allow adjustment of the spotlight, as shown in Figure 11.11. The following is a description of those buttons.

**Dolly**
Moves the spotlight backward or forward along its own projection axis.

**Hotspot**
Increases or decreases the hotspot angle. Holding down the Ctrl key while dragging adjusts the hotspot and falloff.

**Roll**
Rotates the spotlight around its projection axes. It is only apparent when using a rectangular beam.

**Falloff**
Increases or decreases the falloff angle.

**Truck**
Moves the spotlight parallel to its projection axis.

**Orbit and Pan**
Rotates the spotlight. Orbit rotates the spotlight about its target; Pan rotates the target about its spotlight.

## Animating Lights

Because lights are objects, you can animate them just as you would any object in your scene. The techniques for animation are discussed in Chapter 13.

**LIGHTS! CAMERA! ACTION!**

### Spotlight Simulating an Omni Light

To simulate an omni light with a spotlight, a special parameter, called Overshoot, needs to be turned on. With the Overshoot turned on, shadows are cast within the normal cone of the spotlight; in addition, shadowless light is cast all around the scene, similar to an omni light.

## 11.5 PLACING AND MODIFYING LIGHTS

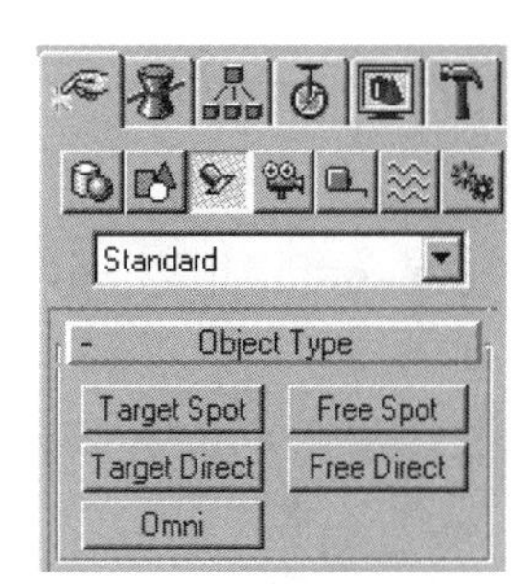


To place a light you must select the Light icon from the Creation command panel. You are then presented with the different light types from which to choose. Each one has its own placement method. The following describes those methods.

### Omni Light

Because omni lights cast light in all directions, you simply have to place the light in the desired viewport. Once it is in place, you must adjust its parameters and then use the Move transform to position it in the desired location. Figure 11.12 shows the Omni light parameters.

### Free Direct Light

When you place the directional light, it is pointing toward the negative Z axis of the viewport plane. As in the case of the Free Camera object, you will need to use the Move and Rotate transforms to orient the directional light so that it is positioned and pointing in the proper direction. This light has a parameter that allows you to

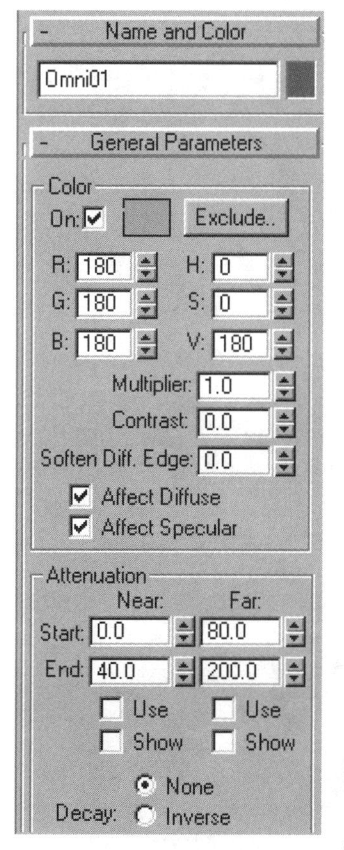


FIGURE 11.12
Omni light parameters.

choose the shape of its beam of light as either a circle or a rectangle. Figure 11.13 shows the directional light parameters.

### Target Direct

Target Direct allows you to direct the light by specifying the location of the light and the target location (toward where the light will point).

### Target Spotlight

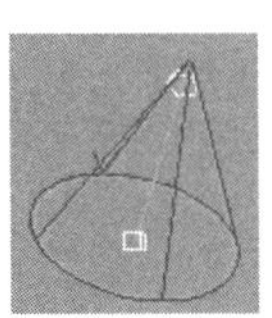

Target spotlights require a location for the spotlight and its target. To place a Target spotlight, pick and drag. The first pick locates the spotlight; then you drag to position the target. Remember that spotlights have hotspot and falloff parameters to adjust to get the desired effect. You can use the Move transform to reposition either the target or the spotlight. Figure 11.14 shows the spotlight parameters.

### Free Spotlight

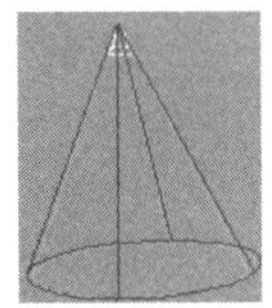

Free spotlights are similar to free directional lights in that they are first placed in a viewport and then their orientation is adjusted using the Move and Rotate transforms. Their initial projection direction is along the negative Z axis. Like Free Cameras, free spotlights are used when you want to animate the spotlight to move along a path.

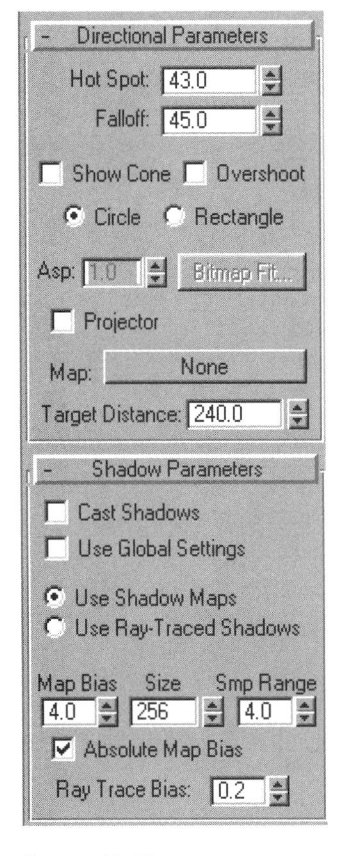


FIGURE 11.13
Directional light parameters (lower portion).

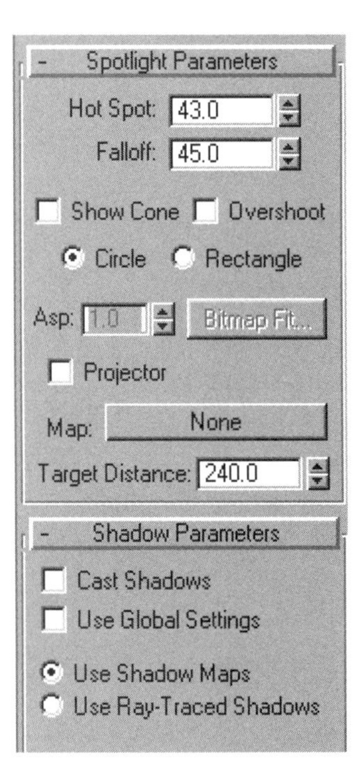


FIGURE 11.14
Spotlight parameters (lower portion).

**LIGHTS! CAMERA! ACTION!** 

**Selecting the Target of the Target Spotlight or Target Camera**

To make it easier to select the Target icon, which can be small, select the Spotlight icon first, right-click on it, and choose Select Target from the pop-up menu. Then use the Alt key to deselect the Camera icon. This also works for Target Cameras.

### Transforms and the Modify Command Panel

You can change the position of any light object using the Move and Rotate transforms and you can change the parameters using the Modify command panel.

## 11.6 LIGHT SPECIALTIES

This section reviews some of the special functions that can be performed in relation to lights.

### Excluding Objects from Lights

It is possible to select objects that will be excluded from a light. This can be useful when a light is too strong on a particular object but right for the rest of the scene. To exclude objects from or include them in a light source, pick the Exclude/Include button from the light's General Parameters rollout. Identify whether you want to Exclude/Include objects from Illumination, Shadow Casting, or Both. Then highlight the objects in the list and transfer them to either the exclude or include side using the arrow buttons.

### Shadows

As mentioned earlier, there are two types of shadows: shadow maps and ray-traced. With shadow maps there are three controlling parameters: Map Bias, Size, and Smp Range. Map Bias (0 to 1000) moves the shadow toward or away from shadow-casting objects. This is sometimes necessary to correct shadow errors. Size (0 to 10,000) is used to refine the shadow. The higher the value, the finer the shadow but the longer the rendering time. Smp (Sample) Range (0 to 20.0) affects how soft the edge of the shadow will be. The suggested range is between 2 and 5. Large sample values soften the edge but can produce streaking. To reduce streaking, increase size or bias. Low sample values produce coarse edges that can be reduced by increasing map size.

If the ray-traced setting is used, the Ray Trace Bias is the only controlling parameter.

You can also exclude shadows from individual objects in the scene by turning off Receive Shadows for the desired object in the Object Properties parameters.

### Projecting Images

Both directional lights and spotlights can be used to project images onto a scene similar to a slide or movie projector. The projections will appear only in a rendered scene.

To use a projected image, turn on Projector in the Directional parameters and then assign an image map from the materials library. To use a specific image you must first assign it to a material using the material editor. Use of the material editor is explained in Chapter 12. Omni lights can be used as projectors. However, because they are radial light and not directional, the projected images can give unusual effects.

## 11.7 RENDERING

The outcome of all your model creation is a static or several animated images. The Render area is where this all takes place. It should be noted at this time that to see the full effect of rendering you should assign materials to the objects in your scene. Assigning of materials and rendering were introduced in Chapter 4. Here you will learn more of details of rendering; in Chapter 12 you will learn more about the creation and application of materials.

### Types

There are different portions of your scene that you can render: View, Selected, Region, and Blowup. View renders the active viewport, whereas Selected renders only selected objects. Region renders a region (windowed area) within a viewport, and Blowup renders a region but increases the rendered image to fill the render screen.

You would normally choose the type of render to be performed before rendering.

### Render Scene Dialog

Once you have chosen the type of render to perform, you can pick either the Render Scene tool or the Quick Render tool. The Quick Render performs a rendering using the last established settings. The Render Scene brings up the Render dialog allowing you to make adjustments. Figure 11.15 illustrates the Render Dialog.

The following is a description of each area of the Render dialog.

#### Time Output

The Time Output area controls the number of frames rendered. You can indicate whether you want a Single frame used to create a still image or an Active Time Segment to render the entire animation sequence. You can also specify a Range of frames to render or indicate a selection of different frames. Finally, if you specify an Active Time Segment, you can also specify Every Nth Frame. You enter the number *n* and every *n*th frame is rendered.

#### Output Size

The Output Size area controls the size of the rendered image in pixels (picture elements). It is useful to render a small image for test cases, such as lighting and materials. This will save rendering time. Once you are satisfied, you can render a larger size.

#### Options

The Options area contains a variety of methods for activating rendering options.

> *Video Color Check* causes pixels that are beyond the safe video threshold to be rendered as black. This is useful for checking renderings that will be transferred to video.

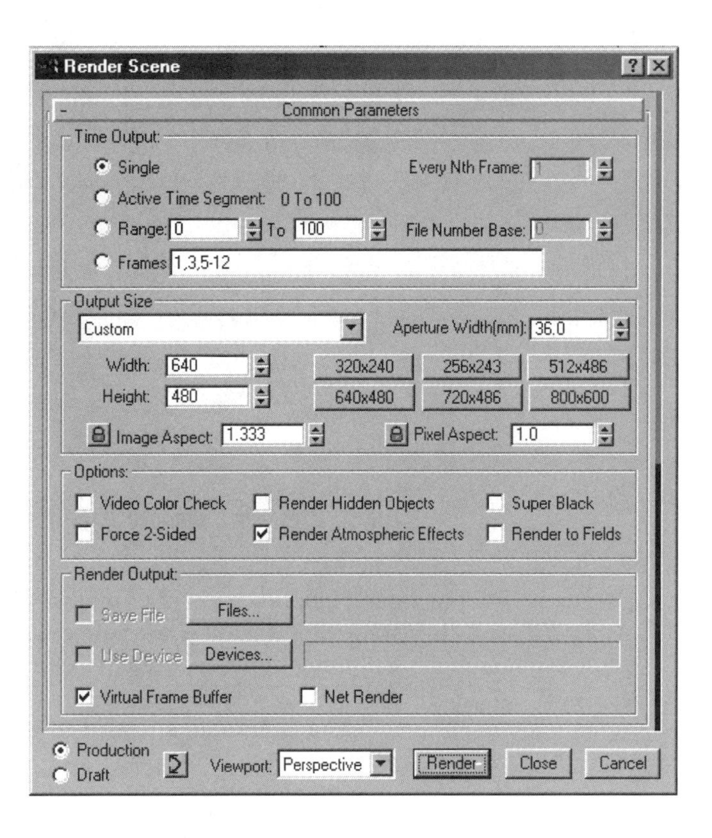


FIGURE 11.15
Render dialog.

*Force 2-Sided* renders all objects as two-sided, regardless of the material assigned to them. This can be used to render a scene containing objects for which both sides of a face are visible.

*Render Hidden Objects* causes all objects to render, even those hidden behind others.

*Render Atmospheric Effects* causes effects such as fog and volume light to be shown in the rendering. This is explained at the end of this section.

*Super Black* is used to cause dark shadows to be rendered with a slightly higher intensity than the "super black" background.

*Render to Fields* causes each frame to be rendered first with the even and odd scan lines. This is used when rendering to video. If you see a frame that is first made up of horizontal lines and then is filled in, Render to Fields has been checked. Normally it should be off (unchecked).

## Render Output

The Render Output area controls where the rendered image will be shown or stored. You can save it to a file. If it is a single frame you can save it to still image file types such as .BMP, .JPG, .TGA. If you are saving an animation, you can save it to animated file types such as .AVI or .FLC. It is also possible to save an entire animation as individual frames if you specify a single frame file format such as .BMP. You can also save to a specific device if it has been installed on your system.

The Virtual Frame Buffer is used to display the image on the screen regardless of where it is going to be stored. You may want to turn this off when sending the image to a file or device to save some rendering time.

The Net Render is used when rendering using a network system.

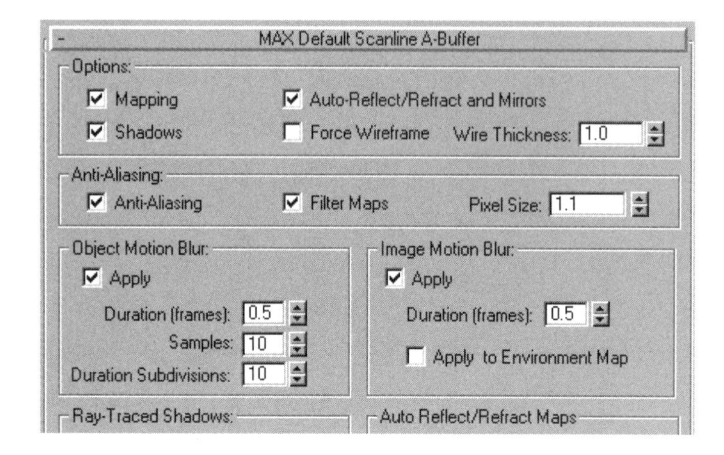


FIGURE 11.16
Max Default Scanline A-Buffer rollout.

### MAX Default Scanline A-Buffer

The MAX Default Scanline A-Buffer controls settings specific to the chosen renderer shipped with 3D Studio MAX. If you have others plugged into your system, you will have access to those renderers as well. See Figure 11.16. The following are the options for the standard 3D Studio MAX system.

The *Options* area is used to turn off or on different rendering elements, such as shadows and mapping.

The *Anti-Aliasing* area controls anti-aliasing and map filtering.

The *Motion Blur* area blurs objects in motion simulating very fast speeds with a slow shutter speed on the camera.

The *Ray-Traced Shadows* area controls global settings for ray-traced shadows instead of individual settings for each light. Here each light has the possibility of using its own ray-traced settings or the global ones.

### Atmosphere and Background Images

When rendering, you can add background images to any scene as well as adding atmospheric effects such as fog. If you open the Environment dialog by choosing Environment from the Rendering pull-down menu, you have access to these settings.

## 11.10 SUMMARY

To generate presentation images, whether single or animated, you must understand how to create a view using a camera object. The view can use different camera lenses or FOVs to zoom in close to an object or give a wide-angled view of the entire scene.

To create an image with a true, three-dimensional feel to it, it is necessary to have contrast between light and dark. This requires the placement of different types of light objects to create the desired effect, whether it is the sun using a direction light object or a car's headlight using a spotlight object.

Because both cameras and lights are objects, they can be modified using transforms and the Modify command panel. They can also be animated, which is explained in Chapter 13.

The outcome of modeling is the final, rendered single object or an entire animation sequence. These results can be created at various image sizes, such as 320 × 240 or 640 × 480, using a variety of visual effects.

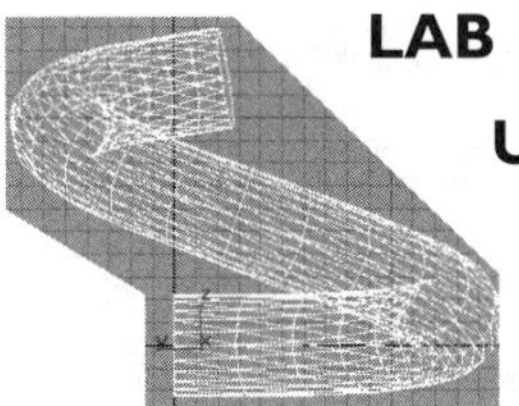

# LAB 11.A

## Using the Camera, Lights, and Rendering

### Purpose

This lab provides practice in the placement of cameras to test the effect of various lenses. You will also place various light types in order to understand the different properties associated with each. Finally, you will use Render to relate the use of the camera and lights to create the desired presentation image.

This lab requires the use of a scene that has already been created. It is called MXPRES.MAX and is contained on the CD-ROM included with this textbook.

### Objectives

You will be able to

- Create camera objects.
- Edit the camera objects to alter their position and parameters.
- Create light objects.
- Edit the light objects to alter their position and parameters.
- Use Render to test various cameras and lights.
- Create saved rendered images at variable resolutions.

### Procedure

1. In this lab you are going to use a scene that has already been created.
   Open the file called MXPRES.MAX and immediately save the file as CH11A.MAX. This way you retain the original file if you need to refer to it again. Remember to periodically save your scene so that if something happens you won't lose your work.
2. The following should be the current state of the prompt line buttons:

| BUTTON | STATE | PURPOSE |
|---|---|---|
| Region Selection | Window Selection | Limits selection of objects totally contained within a window. |
| 2D Snap | OFF | Allows unlimited cursor movement in 2D. |
| Angle Snap | ON | Limits angular movement to set intervals. |
| Percent Snap | ON | Limits percent scaling to set intervals. |

### TEST RENDERING

To start things off, you will do a test rendering of the perspective viewport using a 320 × 240 screen so that the rendering is quick but still clear enough to see the effects of the default lighting and the current view.

*Note*: Before performing any form of rendering, it is advisable to save your scene first. Strange things can happen when rendering, such as running out of disk space.

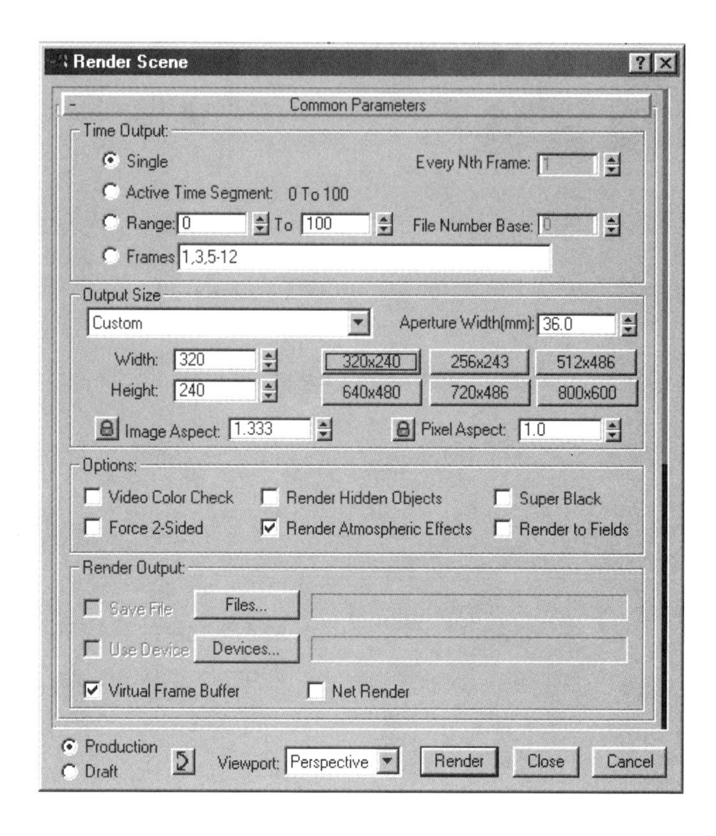


FIGURE 11.17
Render dialog settings.

3. Activate the Perspective viewport, pick the Render Scene tool, and check Figure 11.17 for the settings. Note that the output size is 320 × 240 and under Options, Render Atmospheric Effects has been turned off (unchecked). Virtual Frame Buffer needs to be checked to see the image on the screen. Once you have checked and adjusted the settings, pick the Render button; the results should be similar to Figure 11.18.

   When you have finished looking at the rendered image, close the Render window.

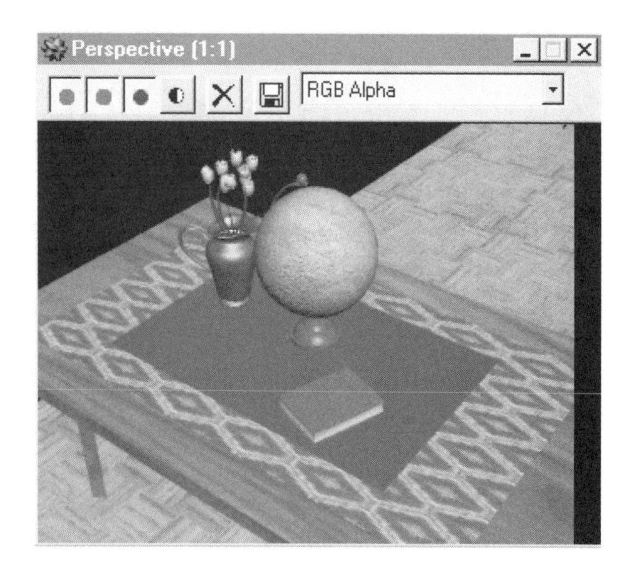


FIGURE 11.18
The initial rendered scene.

## CREATING A CAMERA

The next steps of this lab involve creating a camera and activating a camera viewport. Then you will adjust the lens to see the effect of varying lens sizes.

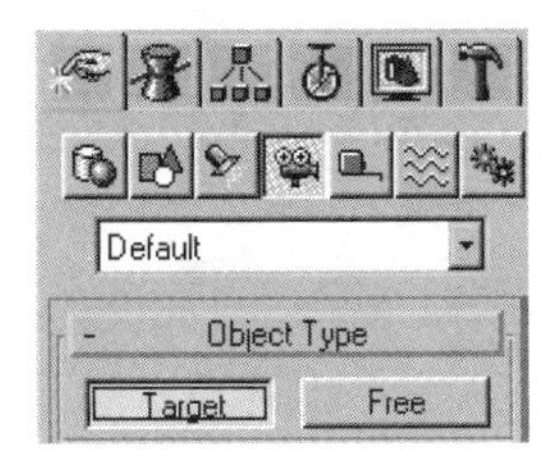


4. Open the Create command panel and pick the Camera button. You are now presented with the choice of a Target Camera or a Free Camera. Because you are not going to be animating the camera in this lab, a Free Camera is not required.
5. Select the Target Camera button. Refer to Figure 11.19 to place the camera in the Top viewport and drag the target to the desired location.
6. Review Figure 11.20, which shows the parameters for the camera you just created. Make sure your parameters match.
7. Observe the other viewports and note where the camera and target lie. Also note that the camera and target are in line with each other horizontally in the Front and Left viewports. The camera and target are created parallel to the active viewport during creation. You are going to change that in a moment.

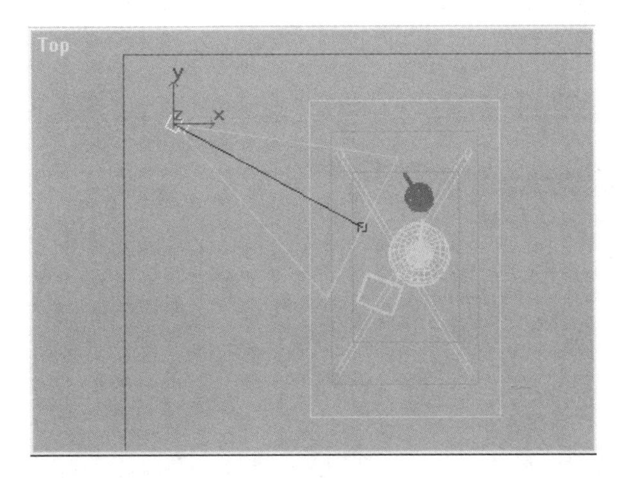


FIGURE 11.19
Top viewport showing placement of camera and target.

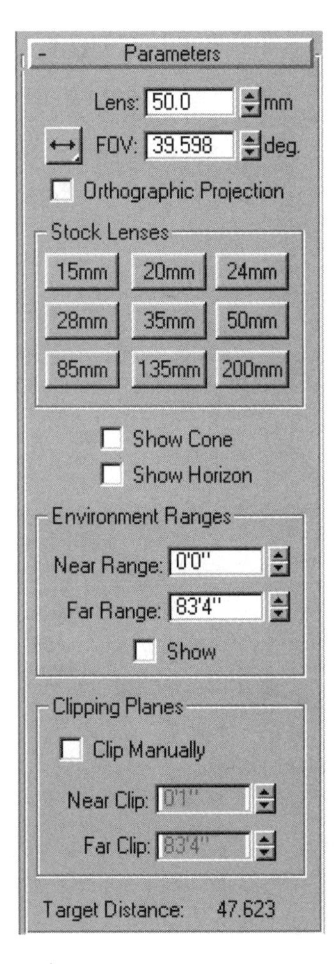


FIGURE 11.20
Camera parameters.

FIGURE 11.21
Position of camera.

## DISPLAYING A CAMERA VIEW

8. Activate the Perspective viewport and then press C to display the Camera view there. Note that the camera view is horizontal. This matches the in-line position of the camera and target, as shown in the other views.

## USING TRANSFORMS TO REPOSITION THE CAMERA

9. Use the Select Object tool, select the Camera icon, and lock it.
10. Activate the Left viewport and pick the Move transform.
11. Pick on the Camera icon and drag it upward. Watch the Camera viewport as you do it. Note that the view changes as you drag the camera. Drag the camera until it is in a position similar to that of Figure 11.21.
12. Unlock the camera icon.
13. With the Move transform still selected, pick on the target box of the camera. The camera's target should now be the only item selected. Lock it.
14. As before, make sure the Left viewport is active.
15. This time pick and drag the camera's target and watch the Camera viewport. See the effect. Now, position the target similar to Figure 11.22.

FIGURE 11.22
Position of target and new camera view.

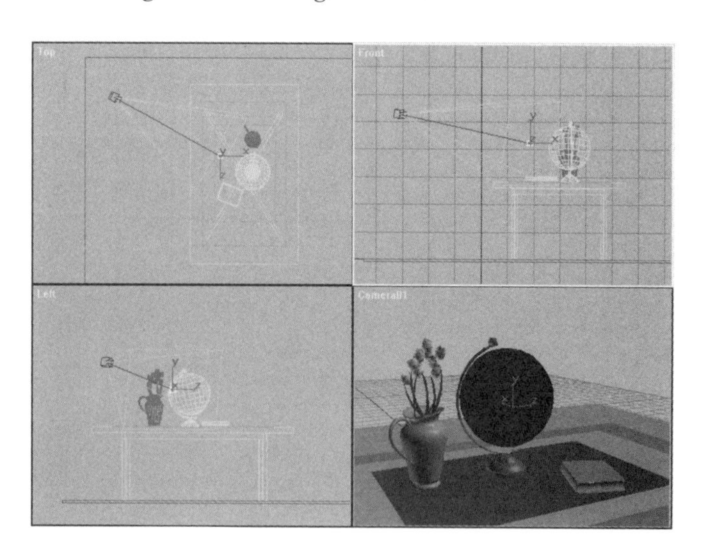

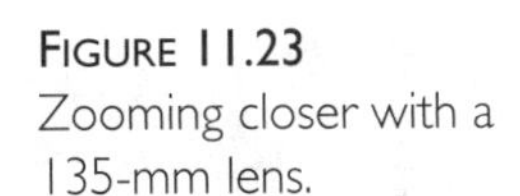

FIGURE 11.23
Zooming closer with a 135-mm lens.

Unlock the target. Your new camera view should be similar to Figure 11.22.

## MODIFYING THE CAMERA PARAMETERS

16. Select the camera again and then open the Modify command panel.
17. Let's take a closer look at the objects on the table. Set the lens size to 135 mm. Save the scene and perform a test render. The view should now show a close-up of the moon globe on the table, as shown in Figure 11.23.
    Close the Render window to continue.
18. Now change the lens to 28 mm, save the scene, and test render. The view should now show more of the scene, giving a wider view, as shown in Figure 11.24.
    Close the Render window.
19. Return the lens size to the standard 50 mm and save your scene as CH11A.MAX.

## ADDING LIGHTS

You are now going to add two light types to your scene.

20. Perform a test rendering of the Camera viewport using the Quick Render tool. Because you have already set the Render settings during the test stage, you will

FIGURE 11.24
Widening the view with a 28-mm lens.

FIGURE 11.25
Rendered image of Camera viewport with default lighting.

not need to change them at this point. Your test rendering should look similar to Figure 11.25. The rendered image shows the scene with default lighting. As soon as you add your first light, the default lighting is turned off.

Close the Render window.

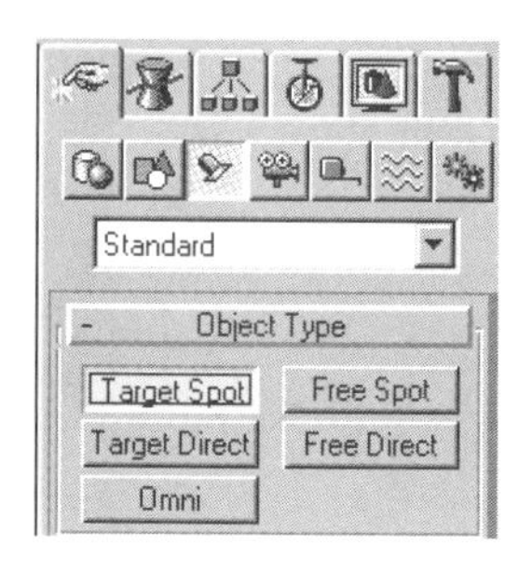


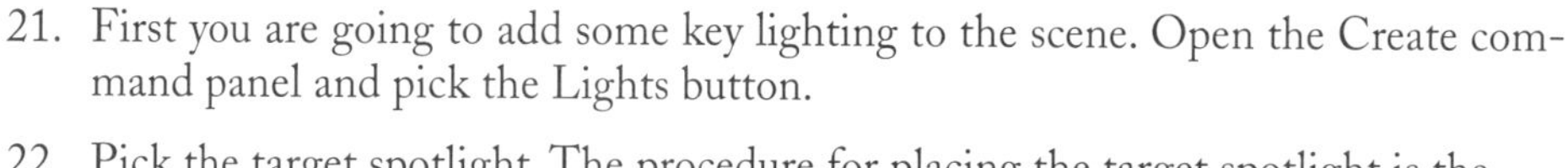

21. First you are going to add some key lighting to the scene. Open the Create command panel and pick the Lights button.
22. Pick the target spotlight. The procedure for placing the target spotlight is the same as for placing a Target Camera. Refer to Figure 11.26 for the final position of the spotlight and its target. You will first need to place the spotlight in the Top viewport and drag to locate the target. Then, you will have to use the Move transform to reposition the height of both the spotlight and target. Proceed to do this while referring to Figure 11.26 for the position and Figure 11.27 for the parameters.
23. Save your scene and test-render the scene again using the Quick Render tool. It should look like Figure 11.28. Note how everything is dark except for the area on which the spotlight shines. What is needed is some fill light to give some background lighting.

    Close the Render window.

FIGURE 11.26
Viewports showing the placement of the spotlight and target.

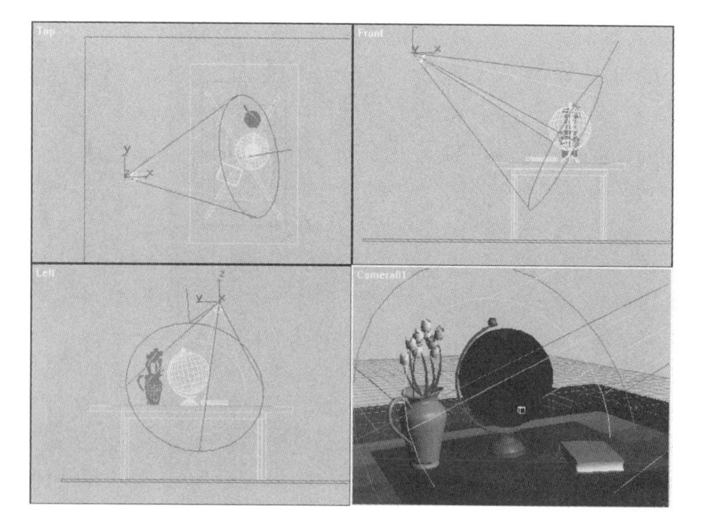

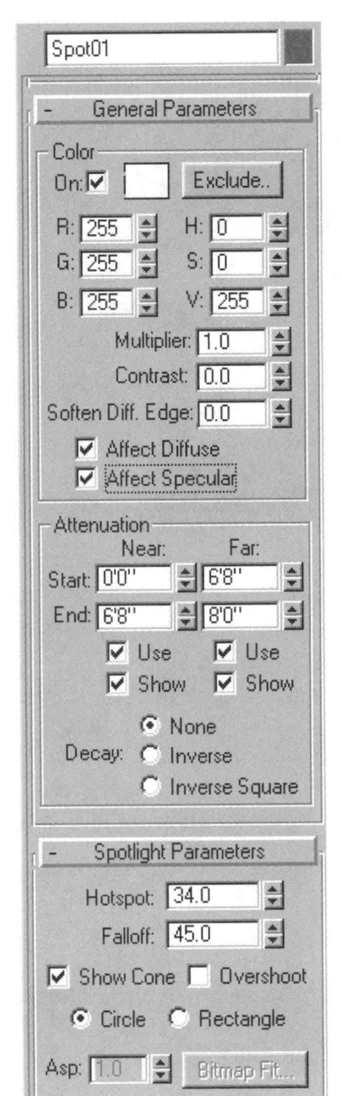


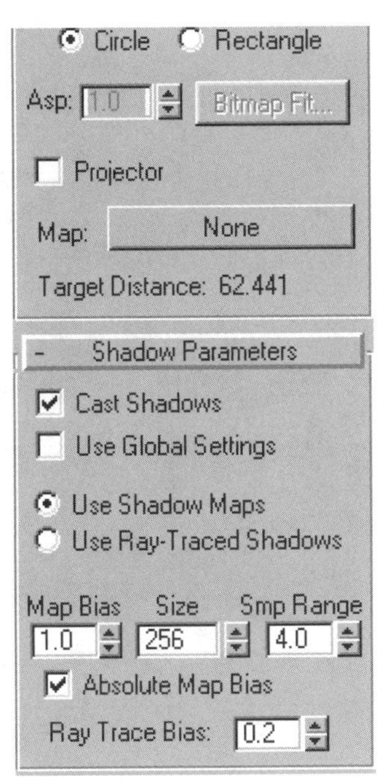


FIGURE 11.27
Spotlight parameters.

FIGURE 11.28
Rendered image with only one spotlight.

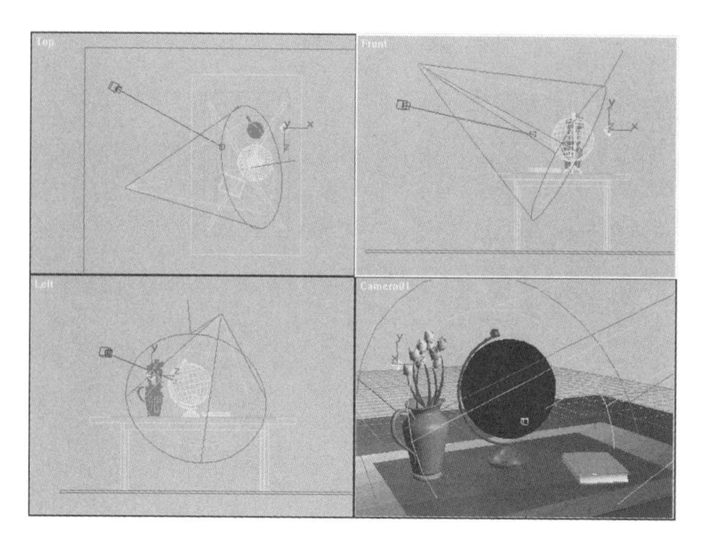

FIGURE 11.29
Placement of omni light to be used as fill light.

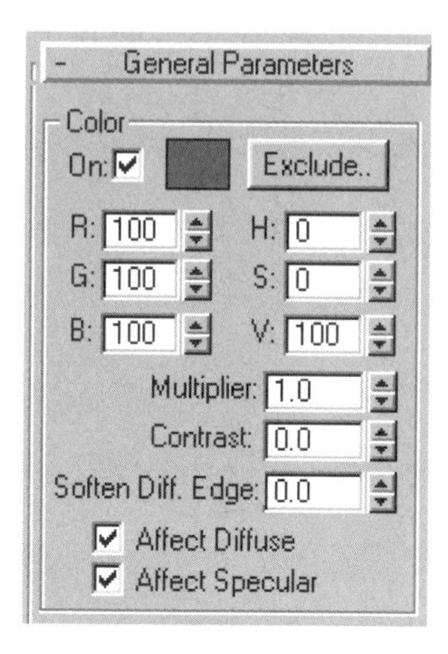


FIGURE 11.30
Omni light parameters.

24. Choose the Omni light and place it in the Top viewport as shown in Figure 11.29. You will have to use the Move transform to change its location in the Front viewport. Refer to Figures 11.29 and 11.30 for the omni light's position in the other viewports and the creation parameters.
25. Save your scene, test-render the scene again, and see the results, as shown in Figure 11.31. More of the scene is now visible, blending in the spotlight.
    Close the Render window.

## RENDERING AND SAVING THE FINAL IMAGE

Now that you have positioned the camera and placed the lights, it is time to produce the final presentation rendering and save it to a file. For the test images the size was set to 320 × 240; now you are going to increase the size to 640 × 480. If

FIGURE 11.31
Rendered image with added fill light.

your computer is capable of larger image sizes, you can save another image at an even higher size. However, remain with the 640 × 480 size for the initial rendering for this stage.

26. Make sure the Camera viewport is active and select the Render Scene tool to display the Render dialog.
27. Change the Output size to 640 × 480 and then pick the Files button. You should be presented with a Files dialog similar to the one shown in Figure 11.32. Set your file type to .BMP and enter the file name as C11IA.BMP (Chapter 11, Image A). OK out of this dialog and then pick the Render button.

    If you still have the Virtual Frame Buffer checked, the image should first appear on your screen and then be written to disk. The final image should be similar to Figure 11.31 except for its larger size and finer detail.
28. Save your scene to disk as CH11A.MAX.
29. Close the Render widow and test to see if you have saved the image to disk. Select the File/View File pull-down menu item and search for your file (C11IA.BMP). See Figure 11.33. Highlight the file and then pick the OK button. Your image should reappear on the screen. If you couldn't find the file or it didn't appear, you will have to perform Steps 26 and 27 again.

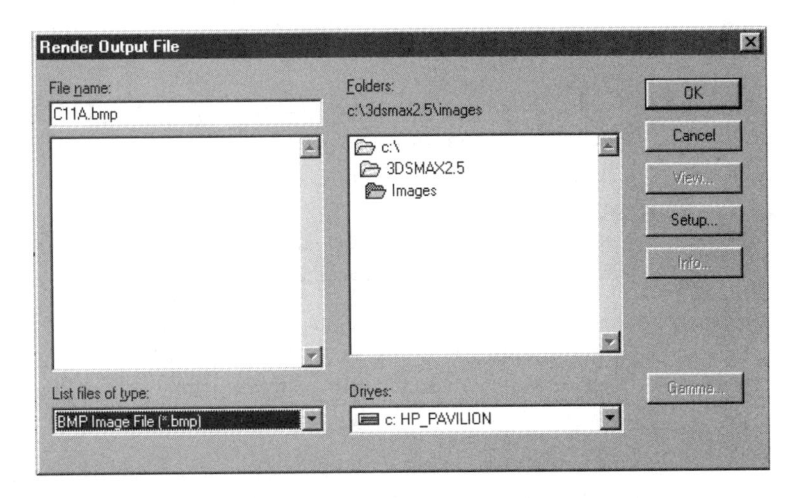


FIGURE 11.32
Files dialog.

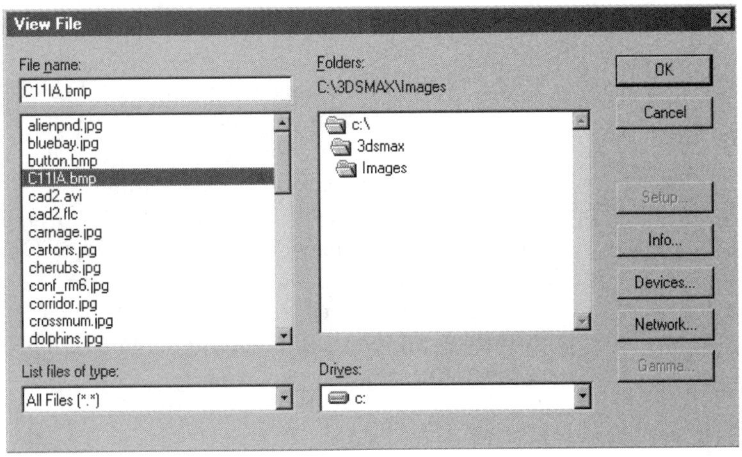

FIGURE 11.33
View File dialog.

## QUESTIONS AND ASSIGNMENTS

### ? QUESTIONS

1. What is the importance of using cameras?
2. Explain the difference between the two camera types.
3. What effect does the use of a Camera viewport have on the navigation buttons?
4. Explain the usefulness of transforms on the placement of a Free Camera object.
5. After reviewing the creation parameters for lights, which ones have the Attenuation settings?
6. Explain the two shadow casting procedures.
7. What effect does ambient light have on a scene?
8. Explain the three types of light objects.
9. Why might you want to render an image at a smaller size than your system is capable of? (The answer to this is contained in the lab.)
10. What are the file formats to which you can save a rendered still image?
11. What are the file formats to which you can save rendered animated images?

### ASSIGNMENTS

1. Experiment with the camera options. Open the file CH11A.MAX created in the lab. Using the Modify command panel, go through the various stock lenses and observe the results each time. Do any distort the view? If yes, can you identify why?

   Alternate changing the value in the Lens and FOV boxes and observe how they affect each other. Save the file as CH11B.MAX.
2. Experiment with adding cameras. Open the file CH11A.MAX created in the lab. Try adding more cameras and different locations in the scene. Then activate a viewport and switch to the different camera views by right-clicking on the viewport label. Save the file as CH11C.MAX.
3. Experiment with camera clipping planes. Open the file CH11A.MAX created in the lab. Using the Modify command panel, select the camera, and experiment with the Clipping Planes parameters by temporarily hiding objects from view. Save the file as CH11D.MAX.
4. Experiment with light options. Open the file CH11A.MAX created in the lab. Perform the following to test the effects:
   a. Turn off shadow casting for the lights in the scene and render to see the results. (Turn them back on before continuing.)
   b. Render the scene using shadow-mapped shadows (light parameter) and then render the same scene with ray-traced shadows. Did you see any difference? You may have to increase the sample range for the shadow-mapped shadows to soften the shadow edge.
   c. Try turning off the shadow casting of individual objects in the scene and render to see the results.

d. Note the current setting of the ambient light. Increase the intensity of the ambient light in stages and render the scene to see the effect. (Return the ambient light setting to its initial setting before continuing.)

Save the file as CH11E.MAX.

5. Experiment with Render settings. Open the file CH11A.MAX created in the lab. To speed up the rendering process during experimental or test stages it is often useful to turn off different rendering features. Use the Render Scene dialog each time to perform the following to test the results:
   a. Open the Max Default Scanline A-Buffer rollout and turn off (uncheck) the Mapping box and render the scene.
   b. Open the Max Default Scanline A-Buffer rollout and turn off (uncheck) the Shadows box and render the scene.
   c. Open the Max Default Scanline A-Buffer rollout and turn on (check) the Force Wireframe box and render the scene.

# A New Coat of Paint: Materials Creation and Applications

## 12.1 INTRODUCTION

To make your 3D objects as realistic as possible, you need to add materials. A material can be as simple as a color or as complex as a compound material with a variety of bitmap images. This chapter introduces you to the material basics and explains the procedure required in the Materials Editor to apply and create your own materials. Some of the special effects using materials are also discussed.

## 12.2 MATERIAL BASICS

When you first create an object, there are no materials assigned to it. It basically has a blank surface material taking on a single color type. A material is a property that can be assigned to a single surface of an object or the entire object. It controls how the surface is rendered and affects light behavior, color reflection, and finally the application and depiction of bitmap images on the surfaces. This section reviews these concepts.

### Color and Light

A material can affect how light is reflected or absorbed. It determines whether it will be shiny or duff, rough or smooth. This is controlled by three main color components: Ambient, Diffuse, and Specular. Figure 12.1 shows a rendered sphere indicating the different color components. 3D Studio MAX refers to these as Basic parameters.

FIGURE 12.1
Rendered sphere showing color components.

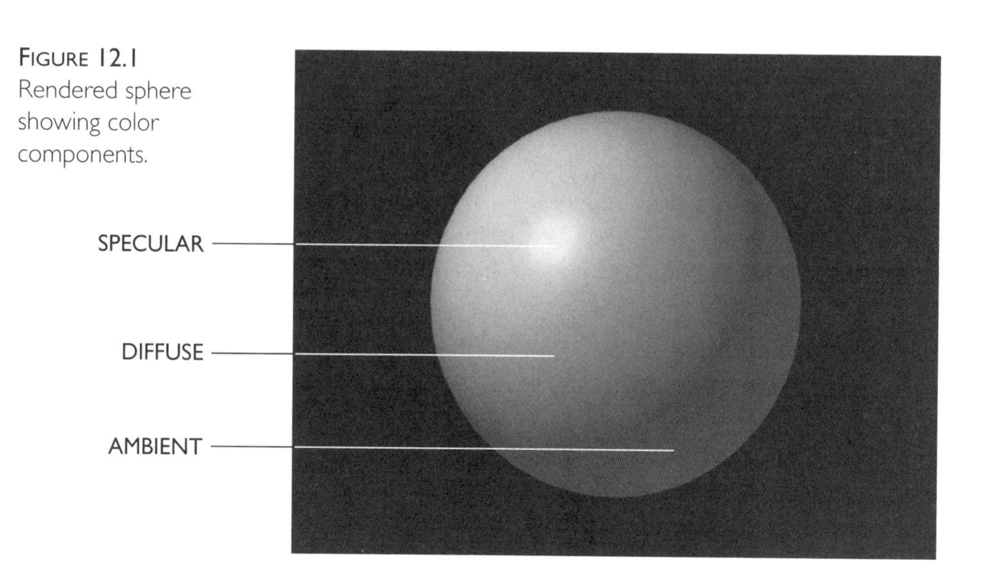


**Ambient**
: The color of the object that is in shadow. It is the part of the object that reflects the ambient light and not any direct light being shone upon the object. You should set this to a dark color with a small amount of the diffuse color.

**Diffuse**
: The color of the object in direct lighting and the main color of the object. You should set this to the desired color of the material.

**Specular**
: The color of an object where light is reflected directly at the viewer. It is the bright spot of light referred to as the highlight. You should set this to a bright color, often a pale yellow for sunlight or white for indoor lighting.

You have individual control of each of these color areas on the object. Also, there are further basic parameters that control the rendering: Shininess, Shininess Strength, Self-Illumination, and Opacity.

**Shininess**
: A percentage value that increases or decreases the size of the highlight. At maximum value (100%) the highlight is very small because the surface is extremely shiny. A small value makes the highlight larger because the surface is not as shiny.

**Shininess Strength**
: Controls the intensity of the highlight. At 0% there is no highlight; at 100% the highlight is strongest.

**Self-Illumination**
: Makes a material glow. It works by replacing the ambient color with the diffuse color and, in effect, removing the shadow areas. At 100% there is no ambient color.

**Opacity**
: Makes a material appear transparent. By reducing the value, an object that uses the material will appear transparent. To change the color of light that passes through a transparent object, a filter color is used.

FIGURE 12.2
Shiny, matte, and glossy surface finishes.

## Light and Material Types

The following describes some guidelines in the creation of materials used for different purposes.

### Shininess of Different Materials

If a material must have a very shiny finish, it should have a high shininess value as well as a high shininess strength. This combination makes the material highly reflective. If the material should have a matte finish, then it must have low shininess and shininess strength values. Sometimes materials have glossy finishes that reflect a lot of light but do not have distinct highlight points. If this is the case, the material must have a low shininess value with a medium-to-high shininess strength. Figure 12.2 shows the three surface finishes: shiny, matte, and glossy.

### Natural Materials

Predominantly natural materials have a matte surface with little or no specular color. See Figure 12.3. The colors used to define ambient diffuse should be those found in nature,

FIGURE 12.3
Natural, manufactured, and metallic materials.

with the ambient color having the same Hue but a darker Value. The specular color should have the same Hue as the diffuse but have a higher Value and a lower Saturation.

### Manufactured Materials

Manufactured materials often have colors that do not match those in nature and very often have very shiny or reflective surface finishes. See Figure 12.3. Because of this, there is a wider range of colors to choose from for ambient and diffuse settings. The specular color should be close to white.

### Metallic Materials

Even though metal is a natural element, it takes on manufactured properties when it is polished (Figure 12.3). When rendering metal materials, the ambient color covers a greater area because of the high reflectiveness of polished metal. Also, there is a special Shading type setting for metal material called, appropriately, Metal. When this is chosen, the Specular color is set automatically by the program and is greyed out (not selectable). Explanation of this concept follows.

## Shading Type

Each material has a *shading type*. It controls the manner in which the material is shaded during rendering. There are four shading types: Constant, Phong, Blinn, and Metal.

**Constant**
Causes each face of a surface to be rendered with a single color intensity. The edges between each face are visible and not smoothed.

**Phong**
Causes edges between faces to be smoothed by calculating each pixel. This is the normal setting for most materials.

**Blinn**
Renders materials in the same manner as Phong but with the added feature of showing rounder highlights.

**Metal**
Used to realistically render polished metal.

## Materials and Mapping

The addition of maps to materials allows you to add greater detail and realism to an object without having to increase the complexity of the object. Simply put, maps are bitmap images that are applied to the surface of the object. How they affect the surface depends on how they are applied and their intensity. A higher value causes the map to have more of an effect on the object. You can use more than one method of map application on a single material. The following are the different ways in which a map can be applied. Figure 12.4 illustrates the application methods. Part A shows the original basic material. The table on which the vase is sitting has an automatic reflection material of the flat mirror type.

**Diffuse**
Applies the map to the diffuse (and usually the ambient) color component. It appears as if the map is painted on the surface.

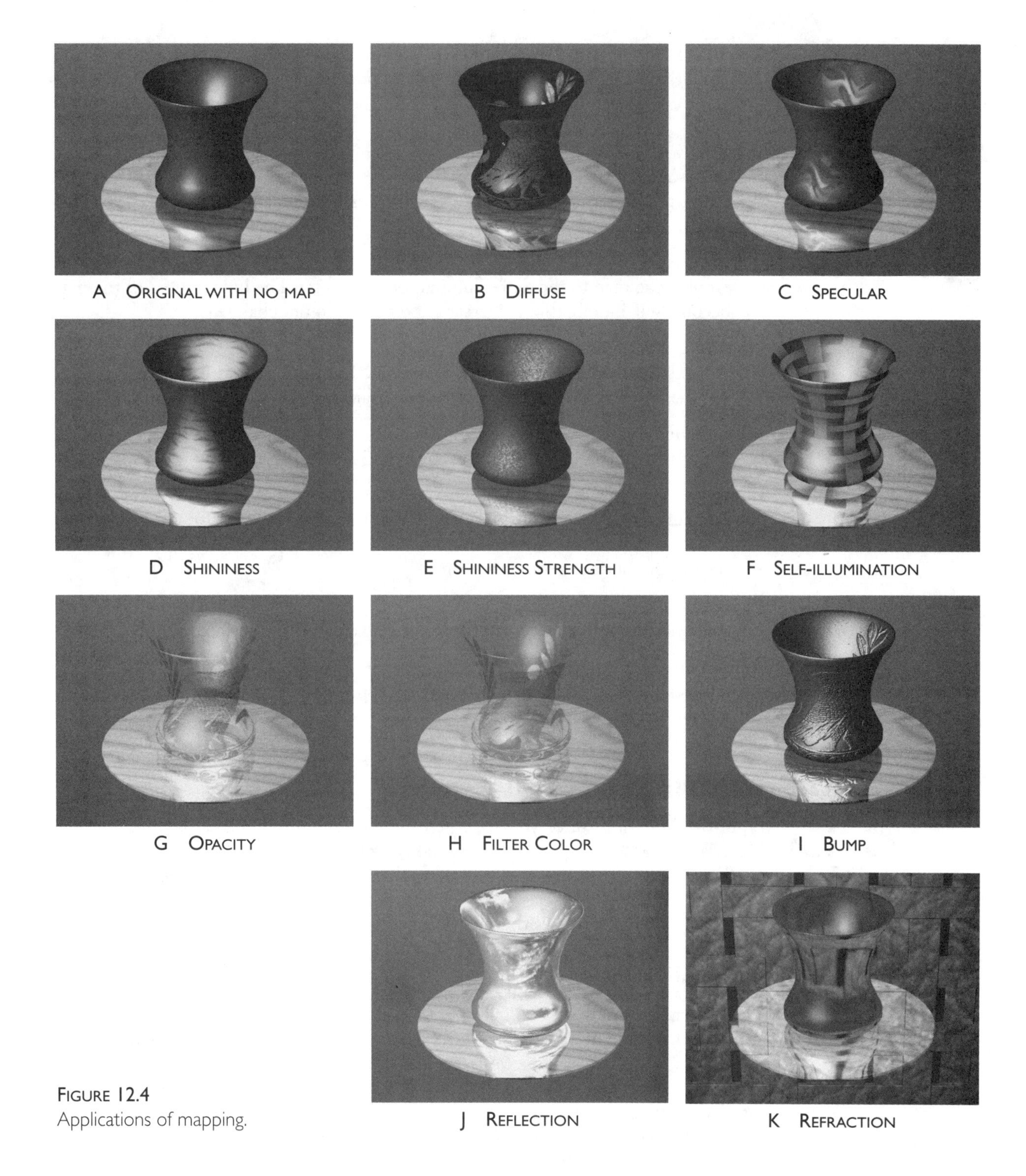


FIGURE 12.4
Applications of mapping.

**Specular**
Applies the map to the specular color component.

**Shininess**
Applies the map to the shininess color component.

**Shininess Strength**
Alters the intensity of the surface's highlights based on the intensity of the map's pixels.

**Self-Illumination**
Applies the map to the Self-Illumination parameter. The lighter areas of the map become self-illuminating, whereas darker areas do not change.

**Opacity**
Applies the map to the Opacity parameter. The lighter areas of the map remain opaque, whereas the darker areas become transparent.

**Filter color**
Alters the filter color of a transparent material based on the map's color.

**Bump**
Applies the map to surface-in a sculpting effect. Lighter areas of the map appear to be raised from the surface, whereas darker areas appear closer to the surface of the original surface geometry.

**Reflection**
Applies the map so that it appears to be reflected off the surface.

**Refraction**
Applies the map so that the background appears to be refracted through the surface or object.

## 12.3 MATERIAL EDITOR DIALOG

From the Material Editor you select, create, test, and apply materials. Selecting the Material Editor tool displays the Material Editor dialog shown in Figure 12.5.

Each material is given a unique name that is then applied to a selected object or surface in the scene.

The following discusses the various areas of the dialog and how to use them.

### Material Preview

The Material Preview area contains six visible preview slots that are used to preview and test different material selections before they are applied to actual objects. (Depending on your system, you can use the panning hand to see more preview slots.) To make a slot active, pick on the slot. A white border will surround the slot, signifying that it is active; its name will appear in the material name field. To copy the settings of one color slot to another, use the pick-and-drag method.

Once you have activated a preview slot, you can select, modify, or apply the material in the slot. The following Tool buttons explain the procedure.

### Tool Buttons

There are main tool buttons that surround the Material Preview slots. The horizontal buttons are used to manage the materials with such choices as selection and application. The vertical buttons mainly control how the materials are displayed in the preview slots. The following describes each one and its purpose. Shown first are the horizontal buttons, followed by the vertical.

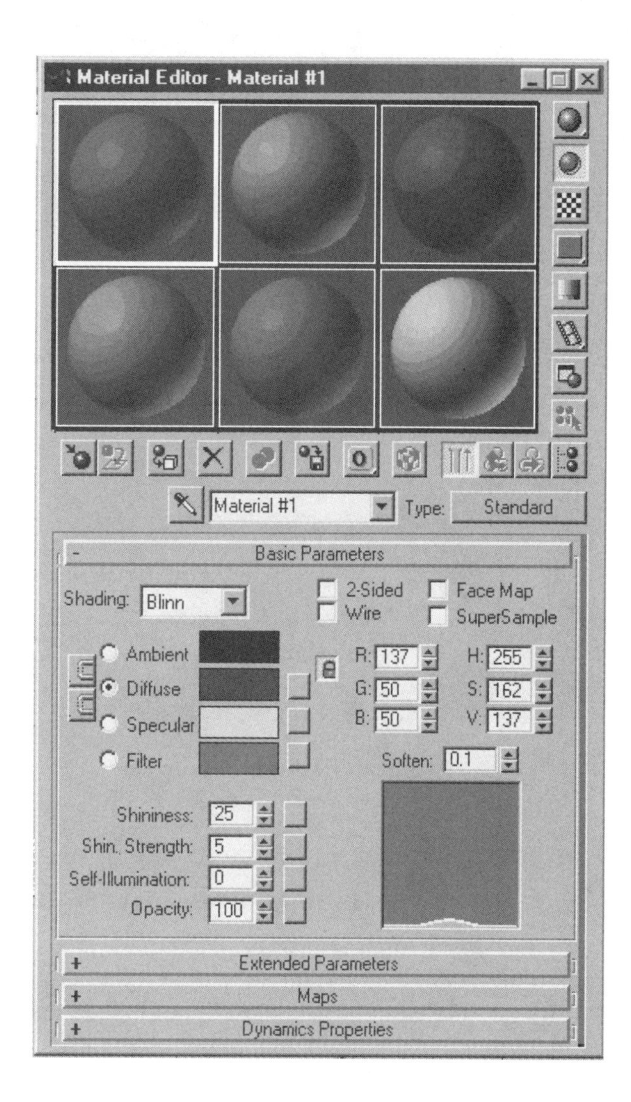


FIGURE 12.5
Material Editor dialog.

## Horizontal Tools: Material Manager

**Get Material**

Brings up the Material Browser used to select and save materials. You can select a previously created material from a library. This is the easiest way to start using materials. It is explained in detail later.

**Put Material**

Replaces a material in the scene by its updated version in the Material Editor.

**Assign Material**

Assigns the active material to a selected object in the scene. *Note:* When you assign a material to an object, the material becomes hot. This means if you change the material, it is automatically updated on the objects in the scene that use that material.

**Reset Map/Mtl**

Clears any previous map or material settings.

**Make Material Copy**

Copies a material from one preview slot to another.

**Put to Library**
Saves the active material to the current material library. You still have to save the library file itself to retain the material for later use. This is explained in Section 12.4.

**Material Effects Channel**
Used to assign channel for video posting. Should be left at 0 unless video posting.

**Show Map**
Shows mapped material in the viewport but turns off all other maps.

**Show End Result**
Shows the end result of maps. To see an individual map, this must be turned off.

**Go To Parent**
Goes to parent material when maps are used.

**Go To Sibling**
Goes to sibling map when maps are used.

**Material/Map Navigator**
Displays a dialog so that the location of an assigned map can be found.

### Vertical Tools: Material Display

**Sample Type**
Changes the shape of the object in the preview slots. You have your choice of a sphere, cube, or cylinder. This button is selectable only if the Scanline Render option is active. The default is Quick Renderer, which doesn't support different sample types.

**Backlight**
When active, renders sample objects as if some background light were shining upon them. It is useful when testing metallic materials.

**Background**
Displays a colored background and is useful when testing semi-transparent materials.

**Sample UV Tiling**
Adjusts the number of tiled bitmap images upon the sample object.

**Video Color Check**
Checks the validity of the colors used for video output.

**Make Preview**
Creates or plays a preview animation file.

**Options**
Displays the Material Editor Options dialog, which is used to adjust such items as ambient light and Renderer type, as mentioned in the Sample Type section.

**Select By Material**
Used to select objects that have materials assigned.

## Basic Parameters

The Basic Parameters area controls the color elements of the objects. See Figure 12.6. Most of these elements were discussed in Section 12.2 under Color and Light. The items not mentioned are explained next.

**2-Sided**
Causes the material to be applied to both sides of a surface.

**Wire**
Causes the object that uses the material to be displayed as a wireframe.

**Face Map**
Causes bitmap images to be applied to each individual face instead of the whole object or surface.

**Highlight**
The graphic box shown displays a curve to show the effect of the Shininess settings. The Soften box softens the highlight spot.

The small buttons beside the various color elements are used to apply bitmaps to any of the elements.

## Extended Parameters

Depending on the material type, a selection of extended parameters is available, including wire size to control the size of the wires used in a wireframe material. Refer to Figure 12.7.

## Maps

The Maps area is used to control the maps that are applied to various elements of the material. You can control whether they are on or off, the amount, and the

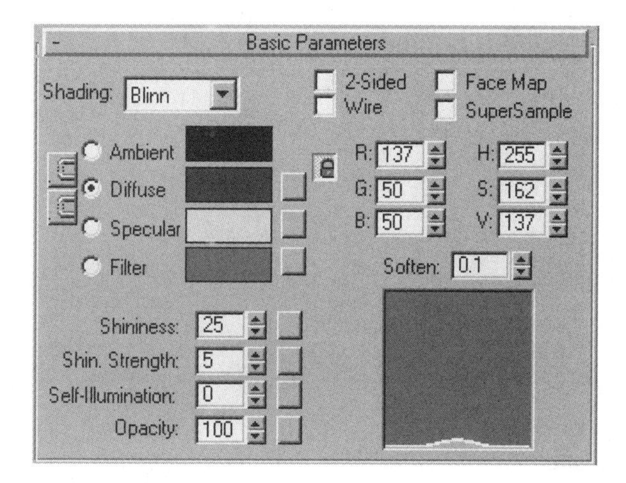


FIGURE 12.6
Basic Parameters of Material Editor dialog.

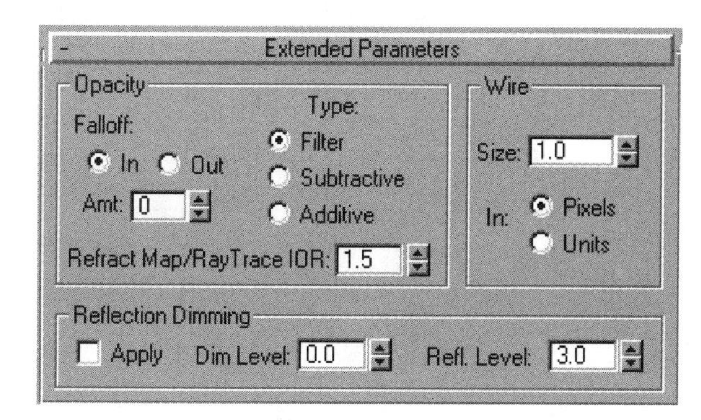


FIGURE 12.7
Extended parameters.

name. Figure 12.8 shows a sample of the Maps rollout. When you pick on the name area, you are presented with the Material/Map Browser to select a map to apply to the particular element. The application of maps is explained in Section 12.6.

## 12.4 MATERIAL/MAP BROWSER

The Material/Map Browser is used for a variety of tasks. It is used, for instance, to select materials or maps from a library, save materials to the library, and open different libraries. Figure 12.9 shows the dialog. The following describes the different areas.

The area to the right is used to display either the names of the materials and maps or a sample view of the material. Along the top of the display area are buttons that let you choose the type of material list to display and delete materials from the current library. Figure 12.10 shows a partial material list using View Small icons and View Large icons.

**Browse From**

Selects the location of materials from which to browse. The Material Library lists the materials in the current open library file that contain previously stored materi-

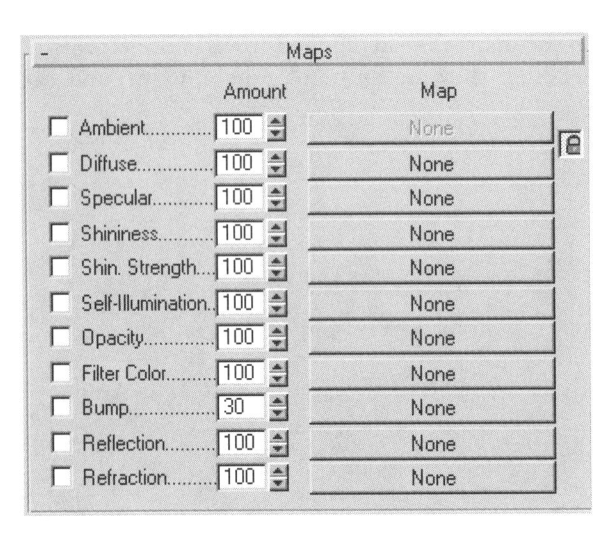


FIGURE 12.8
Maps rollout.

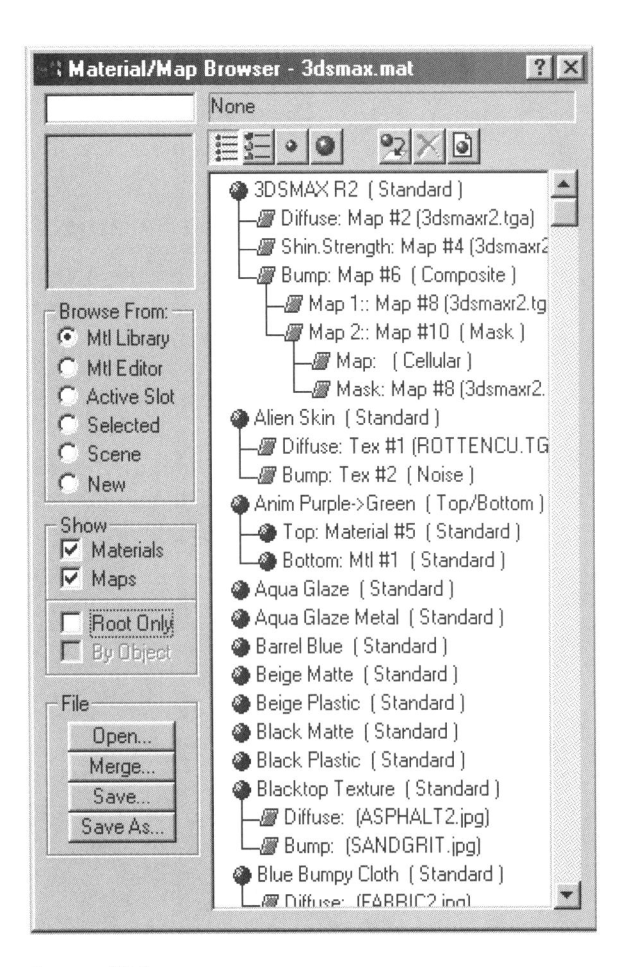


FIGURE 12.9
Material/Map Browser dialog (showing the material list in text form).

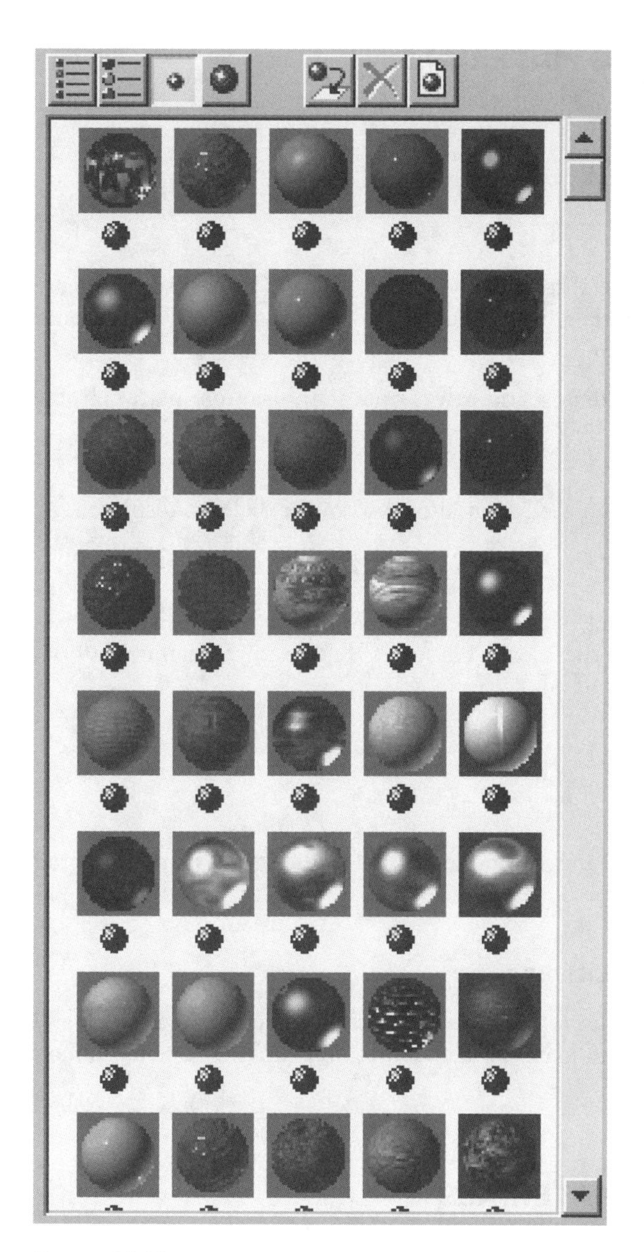

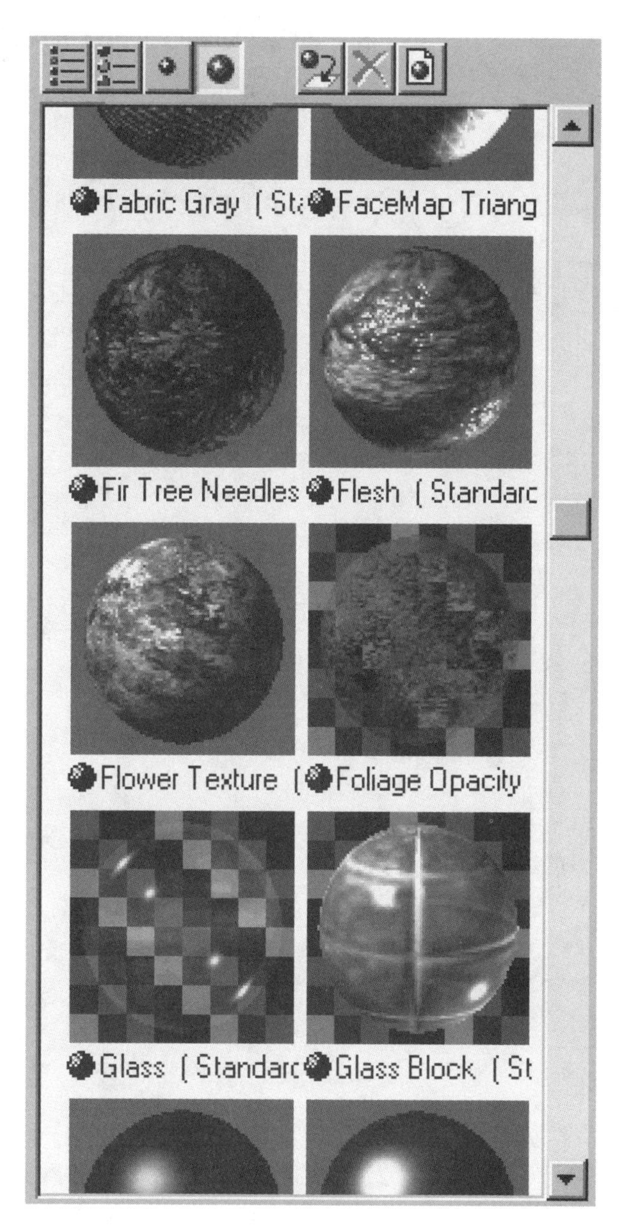


FIGURE 12.10
View Small icons and View Large icons.

als; Material Editor lists the materials contained in the sample boxes; Selected lists the materials of selected objects; Scene lists materials already used in the current scene; and New lists the material options for creating a new material.

**Show**
Controls the display of special material properties.

**File**
Opens a new material library, saves the current one, or saves the current library as a new file.

## 12.5 APPLYING AND SAVING MATERIALS

This section outlines the procedure necessary to manipulate materials, such as applying them to objects or adding them to a library.

### Applying Materials

1. Select the object(s) or surface(s) to which you wish to apply a material. If you are going to use mapped materials, you should have previously applied mapping coordinates to the objects.

2. Open the Material Editor dialog and select one of the sample material preview slots.

3. Pick the Get Material tool and the Material/Map Browser dialog is displayed.

4. Open the desired library and pick the desired material from the list. You can also select a material from the scene. Choose OK to return to the Material Editor dialog.

5. Pick the Put Material tool and the material will be assigned to the selected objects.

### Adding Materials to the Library

To add a material to the current library, activate the desired material preview slot and pick the Put to Library tool. The material is added to the currently opened library and saved to the library on disk.

## 12.6 CREATION OF BASIC MATERIALS AND MAPPED MATERIALS

To create a basic material that does not use a map is a simple process that involves identifying the material type and then adjusting the color component. The procedure is outlined as follows:

1. Open the Material Editor.
2. Select one of the preview slots.
3. Pick on the material name box and fill in a unique name for the material.
4. Pick the Type button. The Material/Map browser will appear. You can select a previously created material or select from the New material list. For this procedure pick the Standard material type from the New list. The preview slot will then show a grey material.
5. Use the color components such as Diffuse and Specular to set the color.

6. Use the other modifiers such as Shininess or Shininess Strength to adjust the highlights.
7. Save the material in the library or apply it to an object.

## Creation of Mapped Materials

The creation of mapped materials is a little more detailed. It involves the first five steps of the creation of the basic material; in addition, it involves assigning bitmaps to different-color components or other areas such as Bump or Reflection. Figure 12.11 shows the Maps rollout, where each component to which a map can be applied is listed.

The following procedure adds a map to the Diffuse component:

1. Open the Maps rollout and in the case of Diffuse map, make sure the lock is on.
2. Check the box of the desired components, such as Diffuse.
3. Set the Amount level. This controls how strong the display of the map is. For example, if you set the Diffuse Amount to a small value, such as 20, 80% of the diffuse color will show through the bitmap. If you set the value to 100, none of the diffuse color will show through; 100% of the bitmap is visible.
4. Pick the Map button beside the desired component and the Material/Map Browser dialog appears.
5. Check the New box, pick Bitmap from the list of map types, and then pick OK.
6. The Material Editor will reappear. The overall Material parameters will be replaced with the Map parameters for the bitmap selected, and the material name will be replaced with a name for the Map, such as Tex#1. You can give this a new name to identify its unique properties.
7. In the Bitmap parameters, select the button labeled with the filename of the bitmap. You will then be presented with the Select Bitmap Image File dialog. You can search through your disk for any appropriate image file, even animation files such as FLC or AVI. You will not be able to see the animations until you render your current animation.

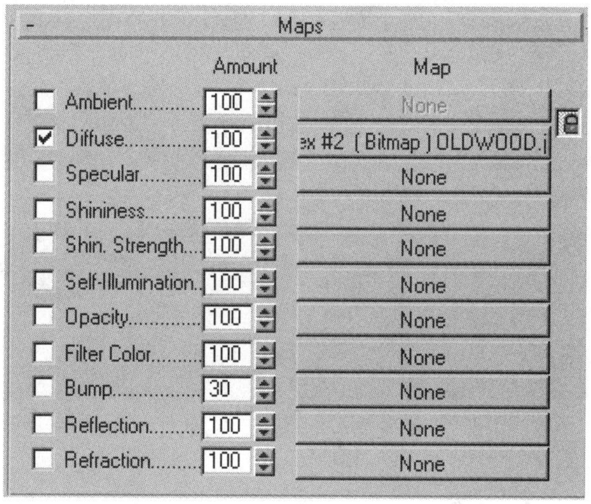

FIGURE 12.11
Maps rollout.

Maps

| | Amount | Map |
|---|---|---|
| Ambient | 100 | None |
| ☑ Diffuse | 100 | ex #2 ( Bitmap ) OLDWOOD.j |
| Specular | 100 | None |
| Shininess | 100 | None |
| Shin. Strength | 100 | None |
| Self-Illumination | 100 | None |
| Opacity | 100 | None |
| Filter Color | 100 | None |
| Bump | 30 | None |
| Reflection | 100 | None |
| Refraction | 100 | None |

## LIGHTS! CAMERA! ACTION!

### Copying Maps

When using the Map rollout, you can copy maps by using the pick-and-drag method.

8. Once you have selected the image file, you can adjust the parameters controlling the placement of the image in the Coordinate rollout.
9. To return to the parent material, either pick on the material name box and highlight the parent material name or pick the Go to Parent tool.
10. To edit the map parameters again, pick the map name in the box beside the appropriate component, such as Diffuse.

### Map Types

There are a variety of map types that you can use in a material. The bitmap is the simplest, but there are other more complex ones. Figure 12.12 shows some of these types.

FIGURE 12.12
Map types: (A) original, (B) checker, (C) marble, (D) flat mirror, (E) gradient, (F) noise.

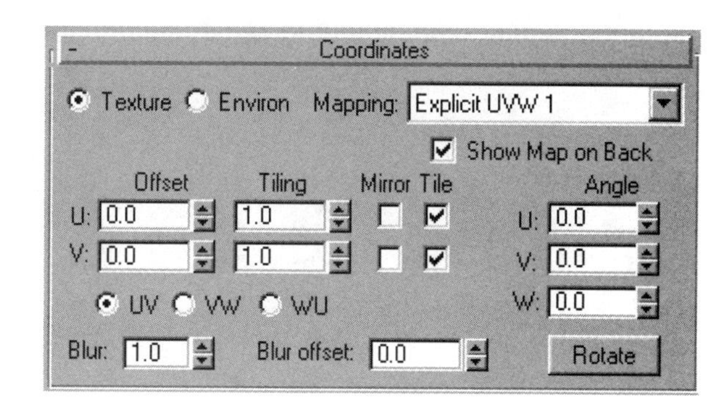


FIGURE 12.13
Coordinates rollout.

## Map Coordinates Rollout

The Map Coordinates rollout controls the placement and position of a map in the material. Refer to Figure 12.13.

**Texture**
Applies the map as a texture over the entire object. It is the default setting.

**Eviron Mapping**
Used to apply the map in different forms, such as spherical and screen.

**Offset**
Two values, U and V, that cause the map to be repositioned on the material.

**Tiling**
Two values, U and V, that cause the map to be duplicated over the material.

**Mirror**
Two boxes, U and V, that cause the map to be mirrored in either axis.

**Tile**
Two boxes, U and V, that control on which axes the tiling takes place. If the Tile and Mirror boxes are not checked, the map takes on the properties of a decal, whose placement can be adjusted with the Offset values.

**Angle**
Causes the map to be rotated.

***LIGHTS! CAMERA! ACTION!*** 

### Displaying a Mapped Material in a Viewport

You can display a mapped material assigned to an object in a viewport by picking the Show Map button. This button is selectable only if you are working on a map's parameters. To do this, select the map button for the material component.

FIGURE 12.14
Noise rollout.

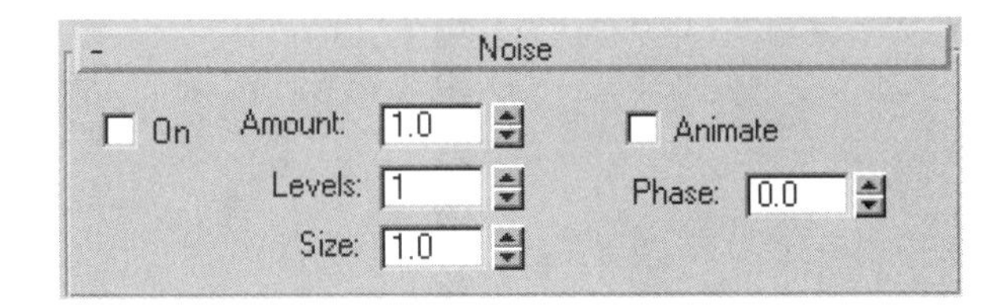


**Blur and Blur Offset**
Cause the map to be blurred and define the direction of the blur.

**UV, VW, WU**
Radio buttons that control which 2D plane is used for mapping. The default is the UV plane. The W coordinate is at right angles to the UV plane.

### Map Noise Rollout

The Map Noise rollout causes random noise to appear on the material. See Figure 12.14.

**Amount**
The strength of the fractal function.

**Levels**
The number of times the function is applied.

**Size**
The scale of the noise function relative to the geometry.

**Phase**
Shifts the starting point.

### Material Types

The previous information discussed the standard material type. There are other types used for the creation of more complex material. The different types of materials are: Multi/Sub-Object, Top/Bottom, Double Sided, Blend, and Matte/Shadow.

Multi/Sub-Object is used to assign more than one material to the same object. Top/Bottom is used to assign two materials, where one is rendered on an object's top faces and the other on the bottom faces. Double Sided is used to assign one material to the outside and another material to the inside of an object. Blend combines two materials together, and Matte/Shadow is used to create matte objects to use with environment maps.

## 12.7 OBJECT MAPPING COORDINATES

To use mapped materials on an object, the object must have mapping coordinates. If the object is a standard one, such as a box or sphere, you can apply automatic mapping coordinates. However, if you create a new complex object or want to modify the mapping on a standard, you need to adjust the mapping parameters. To do this you

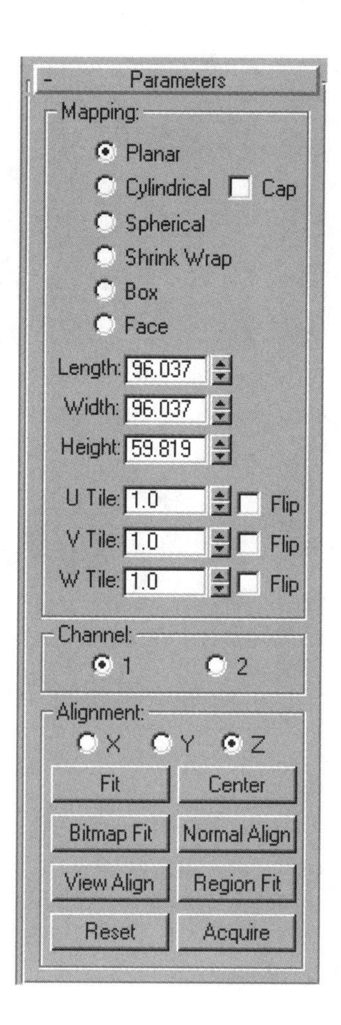


FIGURE 12.15
UVW Mapping parameters.

first select the object and then open the Modify command panel and apply a UVW Map modifier. This gives you control over the mapping on the selected object. Figure 12.15 shows the parameters for applying mapping coordinates.

## Mapping Projection

There are five different types of mapping projection methods: planar, cylindrical, spherical, shrink-wrap, and box. You decide which type to apply based on the shape of your object. Figure 12.16 shows the six different methods applied to objects.

**Planar**
: Projects the map from a single plane similar to projecting a slide.

**Cylindrical**
: Projects the map from a cylinder that wraps around the object. With this type of projection you have the option to cap the object as well. With cap on, additional maps are projected on the top and bottom of the object. Without capping, the top and bottom faces are radially streaked with the map.

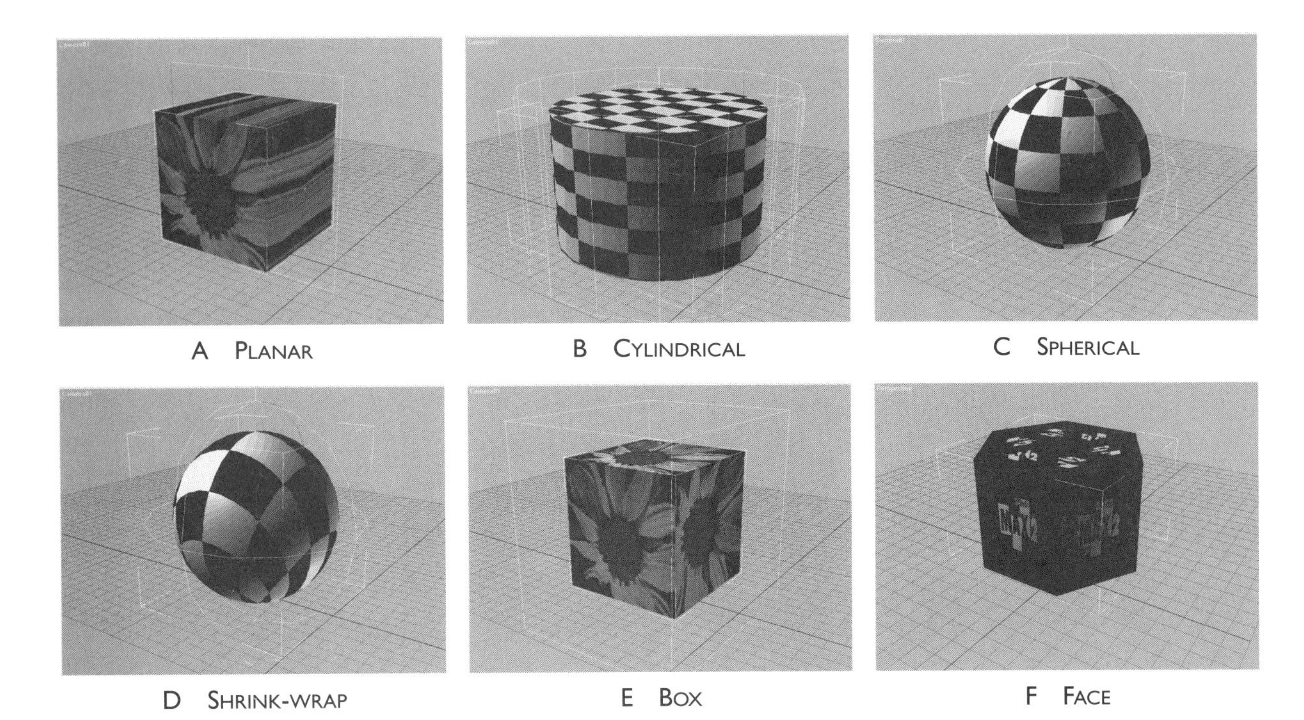


FIGURE 12.16
Different mapping methods.

**Spherical**
Surrounds the object with the map. With this method there is a seam and singularities at the top and bottom of the sphere, where the edges of the image meet.

**Shrink-Wrap**
Uses spherical mapping but truncates the corners of the map and joins them all at a single pole. This is useful when you want to hide the singularity.

**Box**
Projects the map from six sides, where each side has an identical image of the map.

**Face**
Applies mapping coordinates to selected faces.

The Tile settings are used to set the number of images projected in the U, V, and W directions.

## Orientation and the UVW Map Gizmo

To alter the orientation of the projection of the mapping coordinate, you simply transform the gizmo for the projection modifier. Figure 12.17 shows the activation of the gizmo subobject. Once activated you can move and rotate the gizmo around the object. The gizmo appears as a wireframe shape, signifying the type of projection,

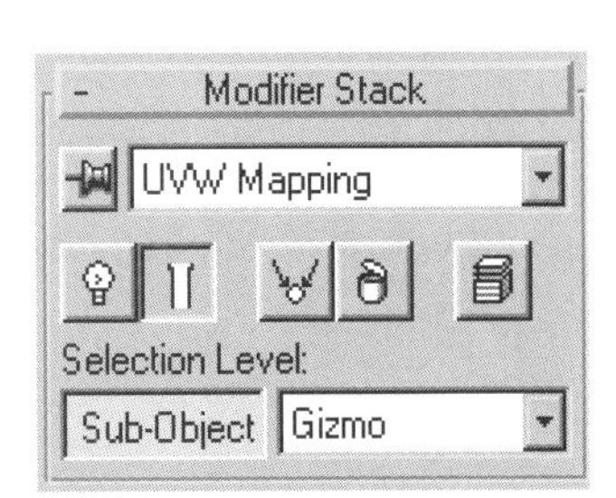


FIGURE 12.17
Gizmo activation.

such as a rectangle for planar or a cylinder for cylindrical. Scaling the gizmo can affect the overall mapped image.

A short yellow line sticking out of the gizmo identifies orientation of the gizmo, and a green edge indicates the right side of the map. On cylindrical and spherical mapping, a green line at the right edge indicates where the right and left edge meet, creating the seam.

### Alignment Controls

The buttons in the lower area of the Parameters rollout are used to control the gizmo's size, position, and orientation.

**Fit**
Centers the gizmo on the object and matches the size of the object.

**Center**
Moves the gizmo, centering it on the object.

**Bitmap Fit**
Sizes the gizmo to an image that you select.

**Normal Align**
Aligns the gizmo to a face of the object that you indicate.

**Reset**
Centers and fits the gizmo to the object, and resets its values and the UVW Map.

**Acquire**
Acquires the gizmo settings from an object you select.

## 12.8 MAPPING TO CREATE SPECIAL EFFECTS

Applying maps to certain components of a material can achieve some interesting special effects. The following are the procedures for creating some of these effects using mapped materials. Figure 12.18 shows the various special effects discussed in this section.

### Partial Glow

The Self-Illumination component of a material causes the material to be unaffected by lights in the scene, giving the effect that the object glows by its own light. If you apply a map to the Self-Illumination component, the lighter areas of the map will self-illuminate, whereas the darker areas will not be affected by self-illumination.

### Partial Transparency

The Opacity component of a material makes the material become transparent. Using a map in the Opacity component will give it a partially transparent effect. The lighter areas of the map render as opaque, and the darker areas render as transparent.

If you assign the same map to the Shininess component, highlights will not show up in the transparent areas of the object.

### Bumpy Objects

The Bump component under the material's Maps rollout will simulate changes in the objects surface without actually modeling it. The lighter (whiter) areas of the map

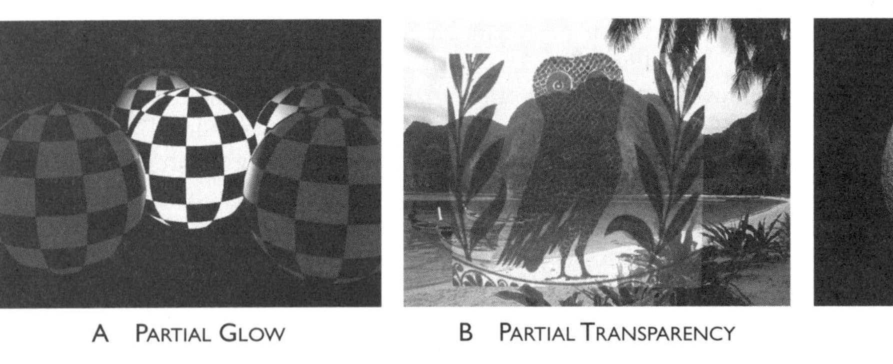

A Partial Glow B Partial Transparency C Bumpy Objects

D Simulated Reflections E Automatic Reflections

Figure 12.18
Special effects with mapping.

will appear raised, whereas the darker (blacker) areas will appear to be lower. This gives a three-dimensional effect to a surface that is actually smooth. This is useful for quickly creating the appearance of relief without complicated modeling.

### Simulated Reflections

You can add maps to the Reflection components of the Map rollout to simulate the reflection effect without time-consuming rendering of the actual reflections. The map image is reflected or refracted on the object, not the actual scene. To produce true automatic reflected images, you need to use a special map type called Reflect/Refract.

### Automatic Reflections

To create automatic reflections of a scene, the Reflect/Refract is required. The Reflect/Refract map type is used for curved surfaces, whereas the Flat Mirror map type is used for flat surfaces such as tabletops, as explained next. The following is the procedure for creating reflective material for curved objects.

1. Pick the Reflection map button and the Material/Map Browser is displayed.
2. Select New in the Browse From: area, and pick the Reflect/Refract material.
3. You will be presented with parameters as follows:

**Size**
Adjusts the resolution of the reflected image in percentages. The default is 100% resolution. A smaller value decreases resolution but improves rendering time.

**Blur**
Blur is used to soften the jagged edges of an image. The range between 0.5 and 2.0 seems to be most effective.

**Render**

This area is used when rendering animations. You can set it so the reflection is rendered in the first frame and not animated, or you can set in which frames you want the reflection to change.

4. Apply the material to the object.
5. To see reflections you need to position light so that it will be bounced off of the objects to be reflected and strike the reflecting surface.

### Flat-Surface Reflections

Flat-surface reflections are accomplished using the Flat Mirror material type. This material type can only be applied to coplanar (on the same plane) surfaces of an object. You can apply a mirror material to one face of an object or you can create a Multi/Sub-Object material. This type of material allows you to apply different materials to the same object. Each subobject material is given a number; the surfaces of an object are given individual material ID numbers. By matching the subobject material number with the material ID number of the surface, you can apply individual materials to individual surfaces. For example, a box has six surfaces (sides); each one is given a different material ID number. If you create a Multi/Sub-Object material that has six different materials you can assign each one to a different side. One of those sides could be a Flat Mirror material type. The application of Flat Mirror materials is demonstrated in the lab at the end of this chapter.

### Animated Materials

Just as you can apply bitmap images to material components, you can also apply animation files to material components. Instead of picking a BMP or JPG, you can select an FLC or AVI. If you render a still image, you will see the first frame of the animation applied to the object. If you render a complete animation, you will see the animated material run through its animation on the object. If the animated material sequence is shorter than the animation, the sequence will be repeated.

When you have added an animation file to a material component, you can adjust when the animation starts, how fast it plays, and what the end condition will be. These are controlled using the Time rollout of the map parameter.

## 12.9 SUMMARY

The application of materials to objects dramatically increases their realism. The creation of materials involves the manipulation of color elements to control how light is reflected. To further enhance a material's properties, bitmap images can be applied to the various material components. This can save time in the modeling of the object by replacing a complex surface with a bitmap image of the surface. A variety of special effects can be created through the use of maps; the creation and application of materials is done through the Material Editor dialog. Materials you create can be stored in material libraries for later retrieval and application.

# LAB 12.A

## Material Creation and Application

### Purpose

This lab reviews the basics of material creation and application. You will create a variety of material types and practice the manipulation of their various parameters. Once you have created some different materials, you will recall a previously created scene and learn how to apply the materials under different circumstances.

This lab requires the use of a scene that has already been created. It is called MXMAT.MAX and is contained on the CD-ROM included with this textbook.

### Objectives

You will be able to

- Create different material types.
- Adjust the color elements and parameters for different effects.
- Apply the materials to different objects.
- Adjust the mapping coordinates for different objects.

### Procedure

1. With this lab you are going to use a scene that has already been created.

   Open the file called MXMAT.MAX and immediately save the file as CH12A.MAX. This way you retain the original file if you need to refer to it again. Remember to save your scene periodically, so that if something happens, you won't lose your work.

2. The following should be the current state of the prompt line buttons:

| BUTTON | STATE | PURPOSE |
|---|---|---|
| Region Selection | Window Selection | Limits selection of objects totally contained within a window. |
| 2D Snap | OFF | Allows unlimited cursor movement in 2D. |
| Angle Snap | ON | Limits angular movement to set intervals. |
| Percent Snap | ON | Limits percent scaling to set intervals. |

### TEST RENDERING

3. Perform a test rendering of the Camera viewport at the size of 320 × 240. It should look like Figure 12.19. Note that every object is rendered in a flat color. No materials have been added. Also note the dark shadows created using the ray-traced method. The purpose of this will be evident in step 26.

   Close the Rendered image window before continuing.

FIGURE 12.19
Test rendering.

## BASIC MATERIAL CREATION

To begin you are going to create a basic material that requires no mapping. It will be a very shiny red material that you will apply to the ball in the scene.

4. Open the Material Editor and activate the first material review slot.

5. Open the Material/Map Browser, set the Browse From to Material Library, and use the File Open button. Search for the material library named MOTION2.MAT. This library comes on the CD-ROM included with this textbook and should have already been copied onto your computer in the 3D Studio MAX library subdirectory.
6. Close the Material/Map Browser and return to the Material Editor.
7. Pick in the Material name box and enter the name of your material. Call it Red-shiny.
8. Pick the Type button next to the name. When the Material/Map Browser appears, check that Browse From is set to New and then pick Standard as the material type. Pick OK to return to the Material Editor.

   The preview slot should now contain a basic grey material. Figure 12.20 shows the current settings of the Material Editor.
9. Now you are going to turn the material red. Make sure that the radio button to the left of the Diffuse color component is checked and then pick the color box to the right of the Diffuse. Set Hue to 255, Saturation to 255, and Value to 230. You should see a bright red color.
10. Normally, the Ambient color component is very dark with a slight amount of diffuse color. Check the Ambient radio button.

    Pick and drag the Diffuse color box so that the arrow points to the Ambient color box and release the button. Pick the Copy button.

    Pick the Ambient color box and set the Value to 70 to darken the red. The sample slot should show a red ball with dark red ambient shadow.

    Close the Color Selection dialog.

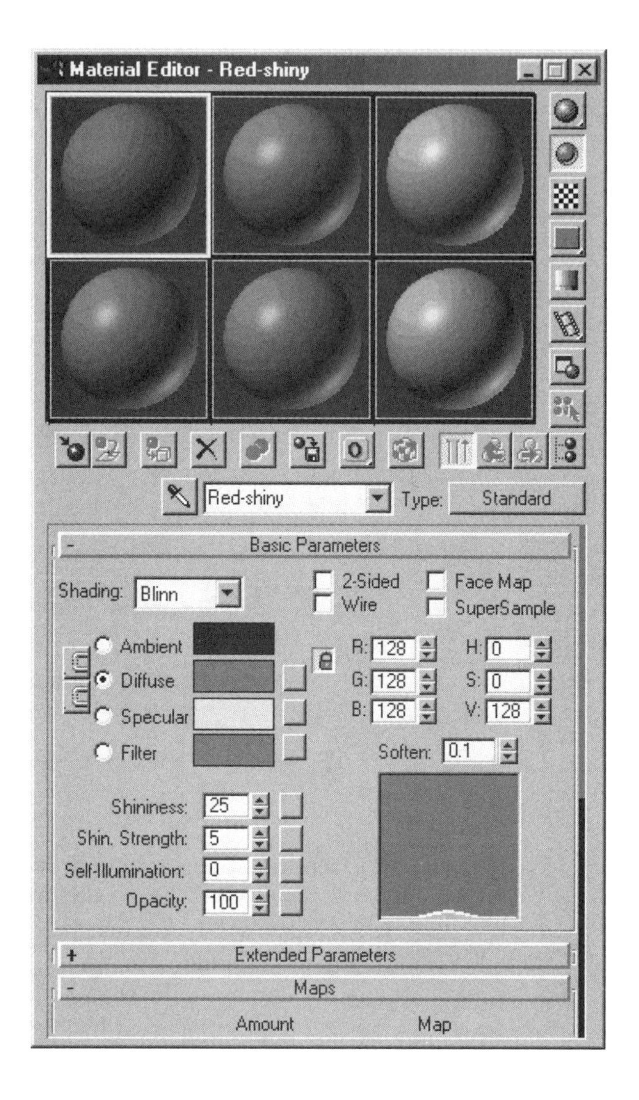


FIGURE 12.20
Current settings of the Material Editor.

## ADJUSTING COMPONENTS

11. To make the material have very shiny properties, you need to adjust the shininess components. Set the Shininess value to 70 and the Shininess Strength to 100. Note how the white highlight spot becomes smaller and whiter. This is how light is reflected off of a very shiny surface.

## APPLICATION OF BASIC MATERIAL

12. Select the blue ball from the camera scene and then pick the Assign Material to Selection button.
13. Save the scene and test render the Camera viewport to see the results. Close the rendered image window before continuing.

## ADJUSTING OBJECT MAPPING COORDINATES

To see how to adjust object mapping coordinates, you are going to apply a previously created material to the floor and then adjust the floor's mapping parameters to get the desired effect.

14. Activate the second material preview slot and pick the Get Material from the MOTION2.MAT library. From the list, select the Blue-Checker material and return to the Material Editor.
15. Select the Floor and pick the Assign Material to Selection button.
16. Test render the Camera viewport. Note how the checker pattern is very large. You are going to reduce its size. Close the rendered image window before continuing.
17. To make the pattern smaller you are going to adjust the UVM Mapping coordinates of the Floor object. With the floor still selected, open the Modifier command panel.
18. Pick the UVW Map modifier. Change both the U tile and V tile from 1.0 to 4.0. This means the map will be tiled four times across the object instead of once.
19. Close the Modify command panel by picking the Create tab.
20. Save the scene and test-render the Camera viewport. You should now see more checkers across the floor. Figure 12.21 shows the smaller checker pattern. Close the rendered image window before continuing.

## CREATION OF A TRANSPARENT MATERIAL

You are now going to create a smoky glass material to be applied to the bowl.

21. Activate the third material preview slot.
22. Pick in the Material name box and enter the name of your material. Call it Smoky-glass.
23. Pick the Type button next to the name. When the Material/Map Browser appears, check that Browse From is set to New and then pick Standard as the material type. Close the browser and return to the Material Editor.

    The preview slot should now contain a basic grey material.

24. Now let's make the material slightly transparent. Turn on Background to show the colored checkers behind the preview object. This makes it easier to see transparencies.

    Set the Opacity component value to 70. This makes the material 30% transparent. You should be able to see the checkered background through the preview object.

FIGURE 12.21
Small checker pattern.

FIGURE 12.22
Rendering showing smoky-glass bowl.

25. Select the bowl and then assign the material to it.
26. Save the scene and test-render the Camera viewport. You should be able to see the red ball, plain orange (it appears green), and checkered floor through the smoky glass bowl. Figure 12.22 shows the bowl with the smoky-glass material applied. Note how the bowl shadow is now lighter because of the bowl's transparency. This works only with Ray-Traced shadows.

    Close the rendered image window before continuing.

## CREATING A MIRROR MATERIAL

You are going to create a mirror face on one of the faces of the Wall object. To do this you need to create a material that contains submaterials. First you need to change the material ID of the face of the wall.

27. Select the Wall and open the Modify command panel. This time pick the Edit Mesh Select modifier. Turn on the Sub-Object level and pick Face from the pop-up list. You now need to select only the face of the wall that is going to be the mirror. Pick the surface that faces toward the bowl.

    In the Top viewport select the face by windowing (make sure the window selection button is active) around it or you can pick in the center of the wall in the Front viewport. Only the front face should turn red.
28. Pan down the parameters until you see the Material ID number for that face. Enter 7 for that face as shown in Figure 12.23, part A.
29. Pan up to the Modifiers heading until you see the More... button. Pick it and you will be presented with the entire list of modifiers. Highlight *Material* and pick OK. This will give you the parameters to adjust the material ID. Under the parameters for Material, enter 7 for the Material ID as shown in Figure 12.23, part B.
30. In the Material Editor, activate the fourth material preview slot.
31. Pick in the Material Name box and enter the name of your material. Call it Wall-mirror.
32. Pick the Type button next to the name. When the Material/Map Browser appears, check that Browser From is set to New and pick Standard as the material type. The material slot should contain a basic grey material.

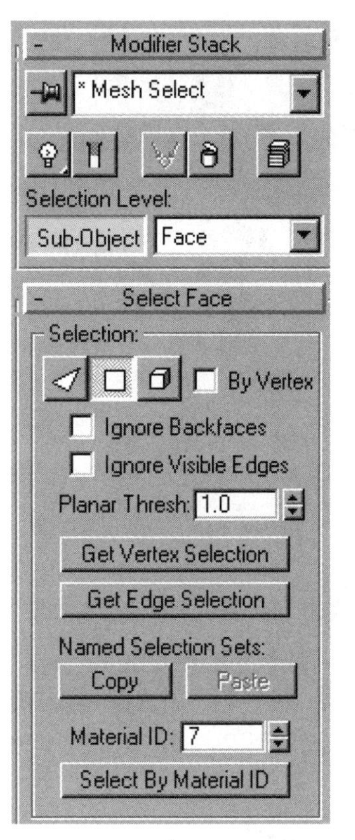


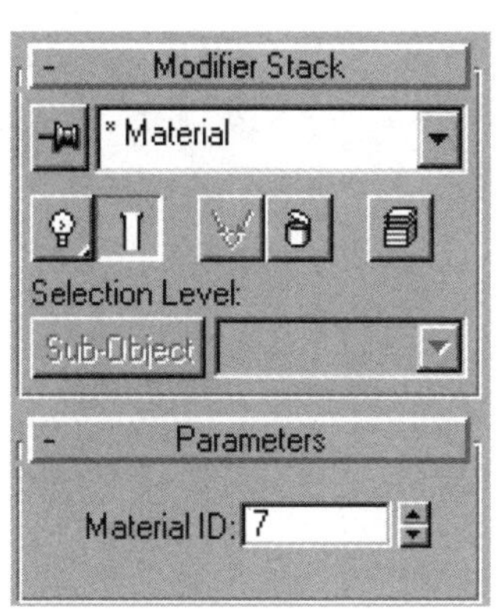


FIGURE 12.23
Modifying Material ID of front face.

33. Open the Maps rollout for this material, check the Reflection component box, set the reflection number to 100, and pick the Map button beside this component.
34. From the new material list, select Flat Mirror and OK it. Under the Flat Mirror Parameters, check the Apply to Faces with ID box and enter 7 for the ID number as shown in Figure 12.24, part B.

35. Return to the Parent material Wall-mirror by picking on the Go to Parent button. You may need to pick this twice.
36. With the wall still selected, assign the material to it.
37. Save the scene and test-render the Camera viewport. The results should be similar to Figure 12.25. The other objects should be reflected in the mirror wall. Close the rendered image window before continuing.

## ADDING A BUMP MATERIAL

You are going to add a material that uses the bump component to the orange that sits in the bowl. The bump effect will make the orange appear to have an irregular surface, even though it was created with a smooth surface.

38. Activate the fifth material preview slot.
39. Open the Material/Map Browser and select the Orange-fruit from the MOTION2.MAT library. It should appear in the fifth material preview slot.

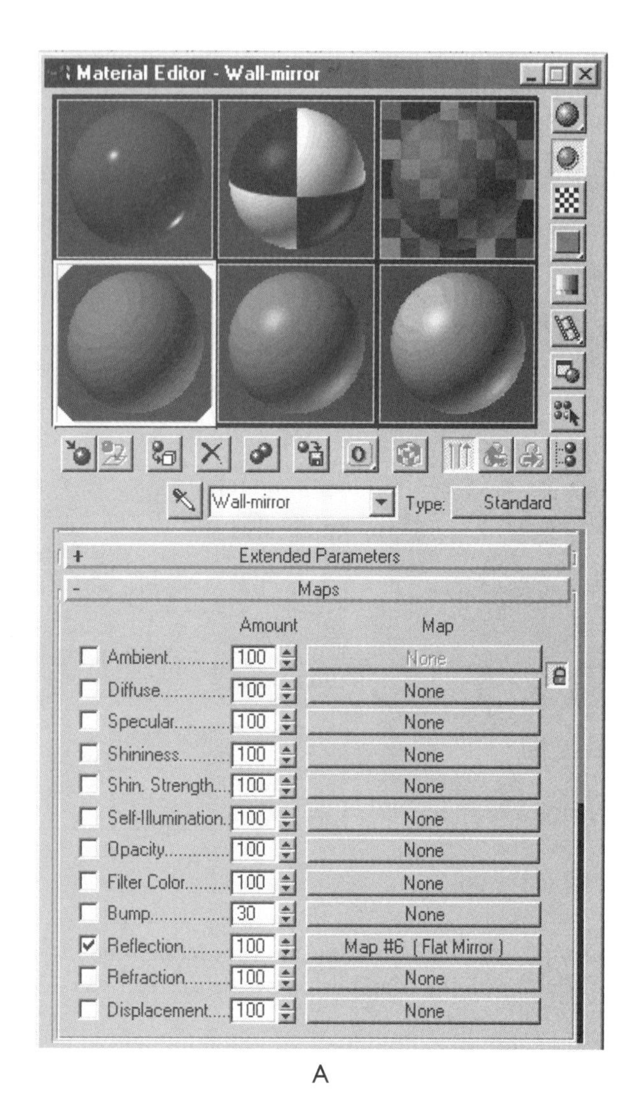


A

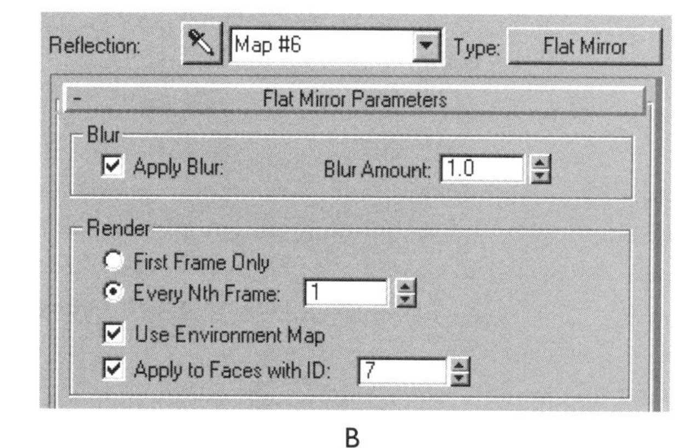


B

FIGURE 12.24
Creating a Flat-Mirror material and assigning it to faces with Material ID 7.

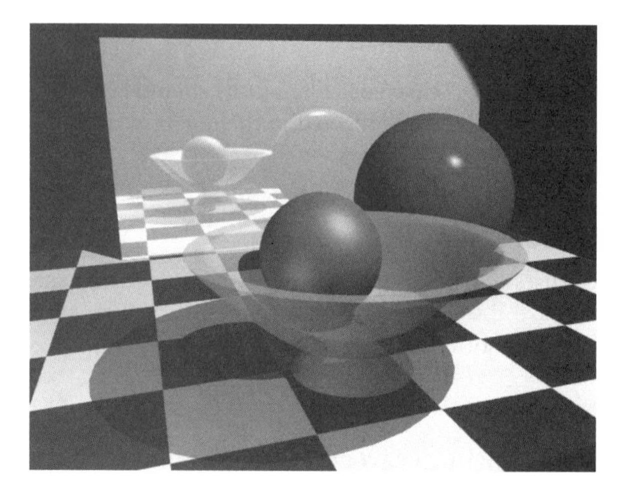

FIGURE 12.25
Rendering showing mirror wall.

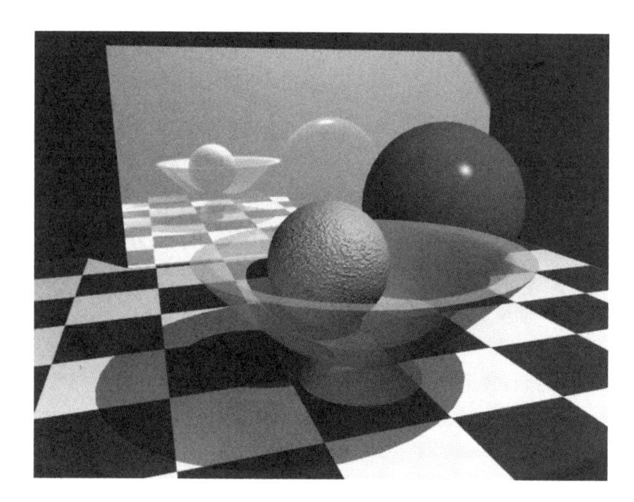

FIGURE 12.26
Rendering with bumpy orange-fruit material.

40. Select the green Orange object in the bowl and assign the material to it.
41. Save the scene and render at a size of 640 × 480. The image should be similar to Figure 12.26. The bumps on the orange should be evident.
42. Look at the Maps rollout for Orange-fruit material and notice the Bump component. It uses a bit map image of sand to give the bumpy effect. Try changing the bump value and re-render the scene to see the effect. A smaller value gives less bump.

## QUESTIONS AND ASSIGNMENTS

### QUESTIONS

1. Explain the three main color components of a material.
2. What are the effects of the Shininess and Shininess Strength components on a material?
3. Why would you add a bitmap image to a material?
4. How are materials displayed in the Material Editor?
5. Explain the function of the Material/Map Browser.
6. Briefly explain the steps to create and apply a material to an object.
7. How are bitmap images added to a material?
8. What are the five methods of mapping projection?
9. What is the function of the UVW Map Gizmo?
10. What is the limiting criterion of the Flat Mirror mapping type?

### ASSIGNMENTS

1. Experiment with automatic reflection. Open the file CH12A.MAX created in the lab.

   Using the Red-shiny material, add the Reflect/Refract map type to the Reflection component and render the scene. See how the various objects are reflected in the ball. Look in the mirror and see the reflection of the ball. What can you see there?

   Using the Smoky-glass material, add the Reflect/Refract map type to the Reflection component and render the scene. The bowl now reflects the floor, the orange, and the ball, as well as the mirror, making it more realistic in appearance.

   You have probably noticed that the rendering time has increased due to the addition of the automatic reflection of the ball and bowl. Save the file as CH12B.MAX.

2. Experiment with self-illumination. Open the file CH12A.MAX created in the lab.

   Using the Orange-fruit material, increase the self-illumination component to 100 and render the scene. Note how the orange appears to glow. However, the orange does not cast any real light. To do this you must add an omni light placed in the center of the orange. Add an omni light to the orange. You may have to adjust the intensity of the omni light so that it doesn't overwhelm the scene. Save the file as CH12C.MAX.

3. Experiment with bump maps. Open the file CH12A.MAX created in the lab.

   Using the different map images, add maps to the bump component of the Red-shiny material. Render the scene in each case to see the results. How do the different images affect the appearance of the bump? Try matching the diffuse map image with the Bump map image. This can give the best bump effect. However, if you use 100% for the diffuse image, you will lose the basic color components. Save the scene as CH12D.MAX.

4. Experiment with different mapping types. Open the file CH12A.MAX created in the lab.

   Using the Red-shiny material, add the following mapping types individually to the Diffuse component of the material: Checker, Marble, Gradient, and Noise. Render the scene for each mapping type and try adjusting their parameters for some interesting effects.

# Let's Get Moving: Animation

## 13.1 INTRODUCTION

You can animate almost every element within 3D Studio MAX. This chapter explains the concepts behind animation and the tools at your disposal to aid in performing animated actions. Once you have an understanding of the principles, you can apply them to the various elements of the program to achieve an amazing array of animation effects. How you apply the principles is limited only by your imagination.

## 13.2 ANIMATION BASICS

When we are shown a series of pictures in rapid succession with minute changes in each picture, we perceive that motion is taking place. Animation is based on this perception.

### Keyframes

3D Studio MAX refers to each picture in a series of pictures as a frame. Each frame in the animation contains some change in the scene. Because it would be very time consuming to make every change in every frame, the program uses keyframes within an animation. These are special frames where a key activity is performed.

Think of a car traveling across a bridge. To animate this, you start with the car at one end of the bridge. At the end of the sequence of frames the car will be at the other end of the bridge. If you had to move the car a small amount of distance in each frame, it would take a long time to create the entire series of frames. Instead, you establish the first frame, the frame where the car begins, as a keyframe. Then you go to last frame, set it as a keyframe, and move the car to its final position in this frame. 3D Studio MAX does the rest; it automatically moves the car in each frame along the desired path from its starting position to the position you designated in the last keyframe. See Figure 13.1. You can create as convoluted a path as you desire and have the car or object follow it. Although it takes complex maneuvering to achieve a complex animation, the basic process of keyframing is straightforward.

## Frames and Time

To start animating, you need to establish a time frame within which the animation happens. This can be a number of frames or a length of time. Figure 13.2 shows the Time Configuration dialog accessed from the Time Configuration tool.

You have your choice of different frame rates and the manner in which the time is displayed. For the beginner it is easiest to set the frame rate to NTSC (National Television Standards Committee). This sets the frame rate to 30 FPS (frames per second) automatically. It also makes manipulation easier at first if you set the time display to Frames instead of a time increment. Using these settings you can calculate the time length of the movie by taking the length of the animation in frames and dividing by 30. Later on, when you are more comfortable with the process, you may want to set the display to actual time increments.

In the Animation section of the dialog, you need to set the length of the entire animation. You can also specify the active segment of the animation using the start-

FIGURE 13.1
Start keyframes, end keyframes, and automatically created frames in between.

> **LIGHTS! CAMERA! ACTION!** 
>
> ### Active Time Segments
>
> When working on a long animation with many frames, it can be easier to limit the number of frames to only the ones on which you are currently working. This is achieved by using the Start and Stop section of the Time Configuration dialog. You can set different time segments at any point in the process.

time and end-time boxes. This sets the block of time or number of frames on which you wish to work. Because the start time, end time, and length are interrelated, adjusting any one of them will affect the other two.

## Animate Button

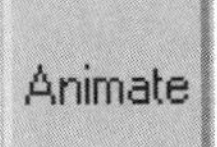


The animate button is the key to performing animated changes to a scene. To use it, you simply move to the desired frame, turn on the button (turning it red), and make the change to the scene, whether using a transform such as move or a modifier to change the appearance of an object. A keyframe is then generated for that object, at that time, using that particular alteration or parameter. Every time you make a change with the Animate button on, a new keyframe is created. To keep track of all the keyframes you create, there is a Track View dialog that stores all your objects and keyframes in a visual manner.

FIGURE 13.2
Time Configuration dialog.

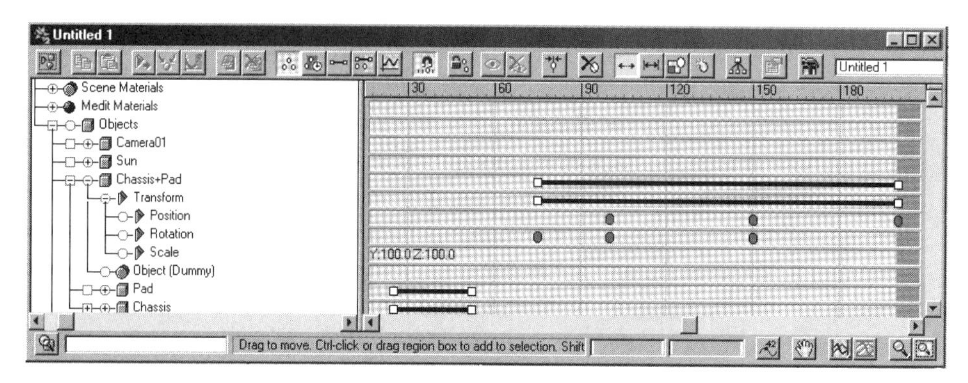


FIGURE 13.3
Track View dialog.

## Track View

To display the Track View dialog, select the Track View tool at the top right of the screen. Figure 13.3 shows the dialog. The list along the left is referred to as the *hierarchy list*. It shows the interrelationships of all the objects in the scene as well as any key changes you make to the objects. Along the right is the edit window. This shows the key dots (keyframes) and the ranges between them. You will find that you can animate almost every element of 3D Studio MAX. The Track View can help you determine if something can be animated. If the object or parameter is shown in the Track View, then it can be animated. More details on this are given in Section 13.3.

## Time Control Buttons

At the lower right of the screen are the Time Control buttons. These buttons are used to move through the animation or play it.

Note in particular the Key tool. It affects the action of the Previous and Next Frame buttons. If it is not active, the buttons move backward and forward one frame at a time. If the Key is active, the buttons move backward and forward to the next transform key.

Also note the current time field. It is the white box that contains a frame number, which represents the current frame. You can enter this box and set the desired current frame or you can use the time slider that runs above the time control buttons. You can pick and drag on the slider to change the current frame.

# 13.3 TRACK VIEW DETAILS

The Track View dialog is used to monitor and modify the timing of your entire scene. Whenever you create or transform an object, it is recorded in the Track View. As you make keyframes you will see that they are added to the Track View as key dots. In this way you can make changes to a key, such as moving it to a new location. Look back at Figure 13.3; it shows the various elements of the Track View dialog.

## Hierarchy List

The left side of the Track View displays the hierarchy list. This lists contains every element about your scene. Use this list to highlight items you wish to alter, copy, or paste. Its operation is similar to the Windows environment. You can expand or collapse the list as required. The following is a description of the various icons used in the list.

### Main Branches

**World**
Contains the five main branches. It is the root of the scene hierarchy.

**Sound**
Contains items for loading and synchronizing a single sound file.

**Environment**
Controls the background and scene environmental effects.

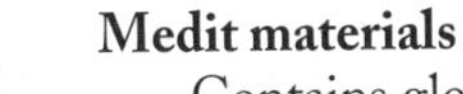

**Medit materials**
Contains global material definitions.

**Scene materials**
Contains definitions for all materials in the scene.

**Objects**
Contains the branches for all the objects in the scene.

### Subbranches and Icons

**Material**
Indicates a material either in a scene or assigned to an object.

**Map**
Indicates map definitions.

**Object**
Indicates an object.

**Container**
Contains various items to organize complex items.

**Modifier**
Indicates modifiers and space warp bindings

**Controller**
Indicates controllers, which contain the animation values.

**Circle icons**
Expands and collapses tracks for parameters and modifiers below them.

**Square icons**
Expands and collapses linked children of an object.

## Hierarchy Filter

You can use the Filters dialog to simplify the display of hierarchies. Figure 13.4 shows the dialog. You can decide which elements you want to see. If you right-click on the Filters tool, you will be presented with a pop-up menu with the same items as the dialog.

## Edit Window

The right side of the Track View dialog contains the Edit window. This window is used to change the values and timing of your animation. Key dots and range bars will appear in this window when you start to animate objects or items in the scene. They rest on tracks associated with the hierarchy list. One track goes with one item in the list.

Key dots represent the location of the keyframe of an item. You will notice start and stop key dots. Range bars encompass a series of key dots. They indicate the range of time over which the animation takes place. By picking and dragging these elements, you can reposition or copy them.

You can display certain elements in the window using the Track View edit modes. The following is a description of these modes:

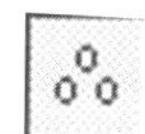

**Edit Keys**
Displays only the animation key dots and range bars.

**Edit Time**
Displays key dots and range bars in the background.

**Edit Ranges**
Displays all tracks as range bars.

**Position Ranges**
Displays key dots and superimposes range bars over the key dots.

FIGURE 13.4
Filters dialog.

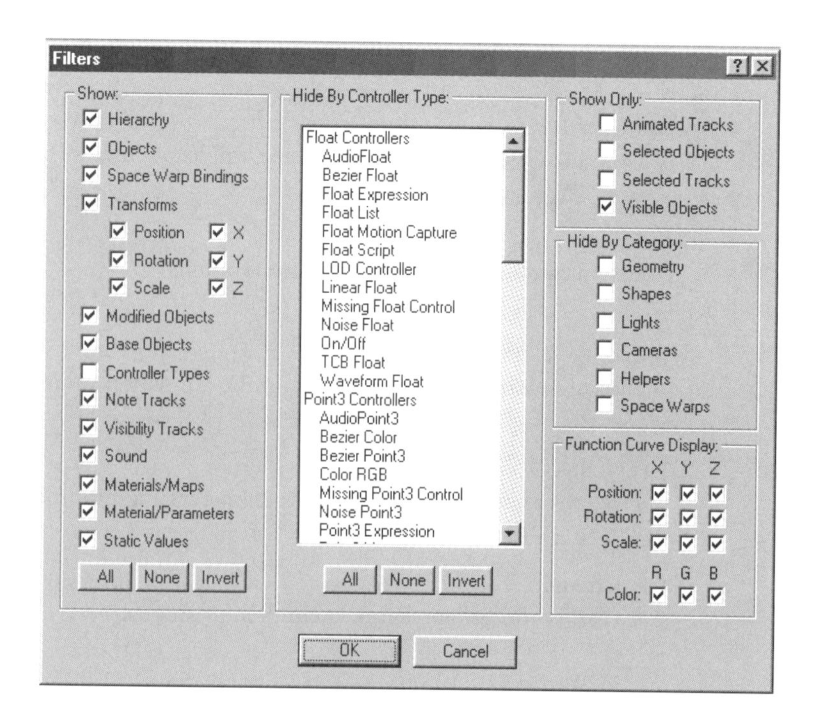

**Function Curves**
Charts a controller's change of value over time as curves.

## 13.4 USING THE EDIT WINDOW

Most of motion animation can take place using the object transforms. Simply by moving to the desired frame and using the animate button, you can move, rotate, or scale any object in your scene. However, when you want to alter the time when certain animations take place, you need to use the Edit window of the Track View. The Edit window contains horizontal tracks for every object or material used in your scene. When you animate some aspect of an object, a key dot and range bar are created along the tracks. To make changes to an animation you need to alter the keys or ranges displayed in the Edit window. The following describes the methods for selecting keys and ranges and how to modify them.

### Selecting Keys and Range Bars

The selection of keys is similar to the selection of objects in a scene. You pick the key to select it. If you hold down the CTRL key, you can add or remove keys from the selection. You can also use the region method of dragging a window around several keys.

To select keys you need to be in the Edit Keys mode and identify the transform type using the following buttons:

**Move**
Used to select and move keys.

**Slide**
Used to select and slide keys.

**Scale**
Used to select and scale keys.

**Snap Frames**
The movement of the cursor snaps to frame increments when this button is active.

Range bars are normally altered by picking and dragging to reposition them.

### Adding, Deleting, and Cloning Keys

When the Add Keys button is active, you can click in an animation track to add a key.

To delete a key, select it and pick the Delete Keys button.

To clone a key, simply press the SHIFT key while using either the Move or Scale Keys buttons. This works only along a key's own track.

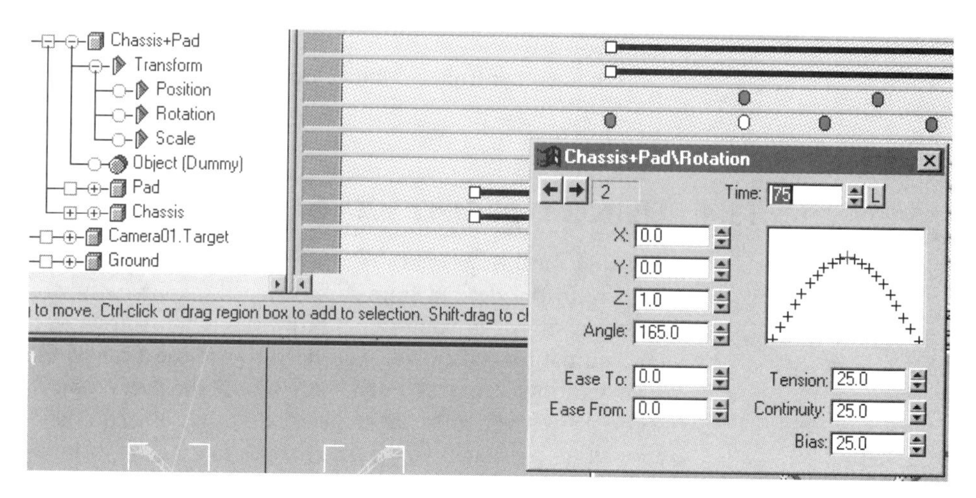


FIGURE 13.5
Properties dialog of a key dot.

You can also use the Motion panel to add and delete Transform keys. To use this panel, select the object and open the panel. You can then use the Delete or Create keys for position, rotation, or scale.

## Aligning Keys

You can align keys on different tracks to the same current frame. The following is the procedure:

1. Set the current frame.
2. Make sure the Edit Keys mode is active.
3. Using one of the Transform keys, select one or more keys.
4. Pick the Align Keys button, and the leftmost selected key in each track will align with the current frame.

## Changing Animation Values

The Properties button is used to change animation values. The type of track you are on changes the type of properties dialog that appears. If you are on a track with keys, you will get a dialog similar to Figure 13.5. If you are on a track with parametric controllers, you will get a dialog similar to Figure 13.6. To display the properties of a particular key, select the key and then pick the Properties button or right-click on the dot.

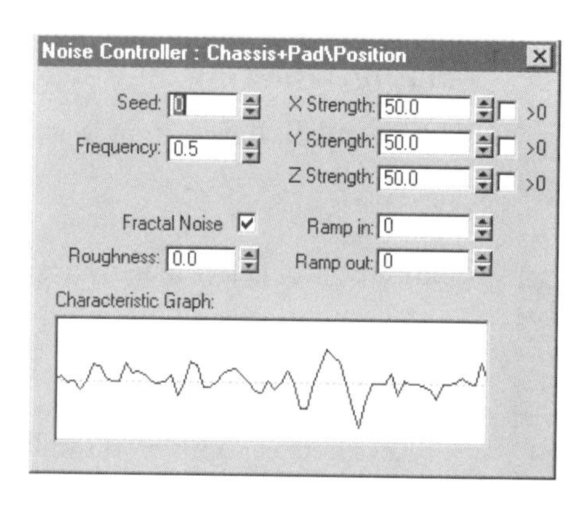


FIGURE 13.6
Properties dialog for a controller track.

## 13.5 MODIFYING TIME ELEMENTS

When you are working on an animation, you may find yourself wanting to extend a section of animation or clip out a portion. This is accomplished with the use of the Edit Time mode. When you have activated it, the tools at the top of the Track View window will change to display tools associated with time. With the Edit Time mode active you can select, delete, cut, copy, paste, reverse, and scale blocks of time, as well as reduce the number of keys in a time block. You can select multiple items in the hierarchy list to perform time edits all at once. The following are some of the time tools.

**Select Time**
Used to highlight blocks of time along a track. When the tool is active, pick and drag along a track to create a block of time.

**Delete Time**
Removes a highlighted block of time.

**Insert Time**
Inserts or removes time along a track. To insert time, activate the tool and pick and drag to the right in the desired track. If you drag to the left it will remove time from the track.

**Scale Time**
Increases or decreases a block of time. To use, activate the tool, select a block of time, and then drag in the right (increases) or left (decreases) directions.

**Time Clipboard**
Cuts, copies, and pastes with the clipboard tools.

**Reverse Time**
Reverses the time of a highlighted block of time. All actions included in the time block will be reversed.

**Reduce Keys**
Reduces the number of keys in a highlighted block of time. Used when there are numerous keys that have little differences between them.

## 13.6 CONTROLLERS

Whenever you animate some element in a scene, a controller is assigned. The controller controls the behavior of the Animation key. It contains the parameters that tell 3D Studio MAX what to do with the animated item at that key point, such as follow a straight path from one point to another or use a Bezier curve. 3D Studio MAX assigns a default controller type, but you can change the type of controller used on any key point.

### Track View Access

You can access the controllers from the Track View, selecting them from the hierarchy list (green arrow icon) and graphically viewing the settings in the Edit Window, as shown in Figure 13.7. You use the Filters tool to display the controllers in the hierarchy list.

To change a controller, highlight the item in the list and pick the Assign Controller tool. You will be presented with a list of choices for that particular item. The list changes depending on the item selected.

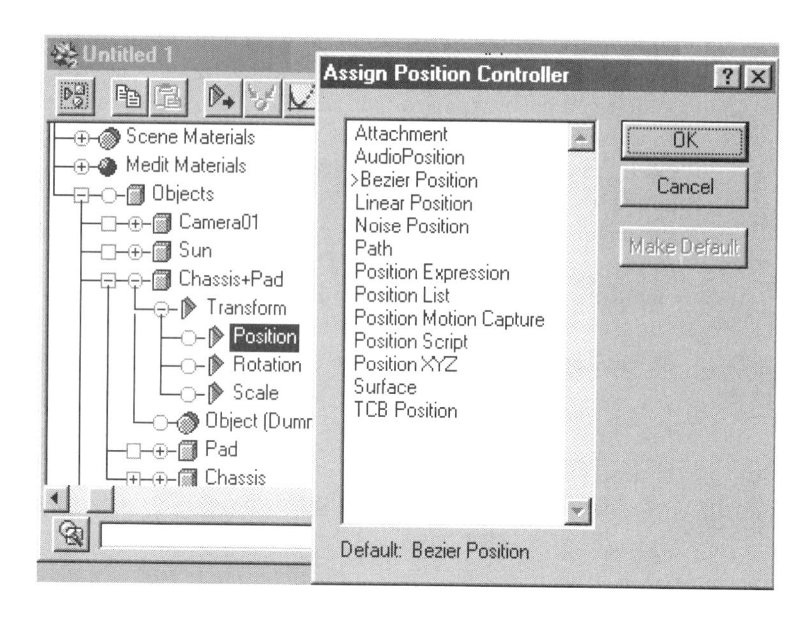


FIGURE 13.7
Accessing controllers from the Track View.

To graphically view the controller's properties in the Edit window, use the Function Curves button.

### Motion Panel Access

You can also access the controllers from the Motion panel, as shown in Figure 13.8, after you have selected an object. Use the Assign Controllers rollout to view and change the controllers.

### Path Position Controller

One of the most common changes to a controller is to change the transform position controller so that it uses a path created by you. The following is the procedure for doing this:

1. Create the spline path.
2. Select the object you want to follow the path.
3. Open the Motion panel and open the Assign Controller rollout.

**LIGHTS! CAMERA! ACTION!**

#### Displaying Move Transforms as a Path

When you animate movement of an object, a trajectory path is created and you can see this path on the screen using the Display command panel. Under Display Optimizations, there is a Trajectory box. Select the desired object and then turn on its Trajectory box. A blue dashed line will appear showing the movement path of the object.

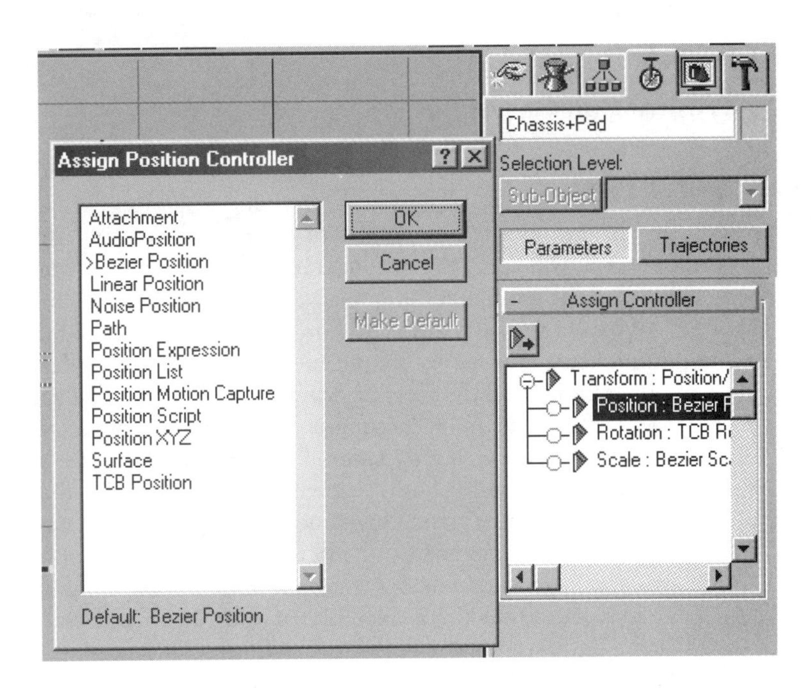


FIGURE 13.8
Accessing controllers through the Motion panel.

4. Highlight Position from the hierarchy list, pick the Assign Controller tool, and select Path from the list.
5. Under the Path Parameters rollout, activate the Pick Path button and pick the path.

## 13.7 SUMMARY

Almost any element of a scene in 3D Studio MAX can be animated. Most often it is as simple as turning on the Animate button at the appropriate frame and making the change. To make more complex changes, especially those that involve timing, the Track View dialog is required. It displays the hierarchy list of all the objects in the scene, along with their track bars and key dots showing exactly when and where an animated sequence takes place. By manipulating track bars and key dots you can alter when and where changes take place. 3D Studio MAX also gives you control over the behavior of different types of animation, with the use of controllers, allowing you to fine-tune your animation.

# LAB 13.A

## Animation Basics

### Purpose

This lab reviews the principles of animation by using transforms on objects in a scene. You will apply the various transforms at different frames and create a final rendering of the sequences.

This lab is a little different than the rest in that it contains two simultaneous procedures using two scenes: simple and complex. The complex scene contains a detailed model of a hovercraft, showing windows and doors. The simple scene is of the same hovercraft, but the model is composed only of basic box shapes.

The purpose of the two scenes is to allow you to use either the simple scene or the complex scene (or both) to practice the same animation techniques. The difference lies in the final rendering time of the animation. The simple scene takes about 25 minutes to render using a Pentium 100 with 32 Mb of RAM. The complex scene takes about 3 hours to render using the same level of computer.

Depending on the availability of your computer, you may want to follow the lab for both scenes but perform the final rendering only for the simple scene. In any case, a sample rendered animation file of the detailed scene is contained on the CD-ROM.

This lab requires the use of two scenes that have already been created. The simple scene is called MXANIM1.MAX, and the complex scene is called MXANIM2. Both are contained on the CD-ROM included with this textbook.

### Objectives

You will be able to

- Set the time length of the animation in frames.
- Animate the three transforms: scale, rotate, and move.
- Adjust the tracks of the different transforms using the Track View dialog.
- Render the animation sequence.
- Adjust the mapping coordinates for different objects.

### Procedure

1. With this lab you are going to use either of the two scenes that have already been created. You can follow the lab with the simple scene (MXANIM1) and then use the complex scene (MXANIM2). The lab is identical for both scenes. Two sets of figures have been created, one for the simple scene, one for the complex.

   Open one of the hovercraft files. If you open the simple file called MXANIM1.MAX, save the file as CH13A.MAX. If you open the complex file called MXANIM2.MAX, save the file as CH13B.MAX.

   This way you retain the original file if you need to refer to it again. Remember to periodically save your scene, so that if something happens, you won't lose your work.

2. The following should be the current state of the prompt line buttons:

| BUTTON | STATE | PURPOSE |
|---|---|---|
| Region Selection | Window Selection | Limits selection of objects totally contained within a window. |
| 2D Snap | OFF | Allows unlimited cursor movement in 2D. |
| Angle Snap | ON | Limits angular movement to set intervals. |
| Percent Snap | ON | Limits percent scaling to set intervals. |

## STAGES OF ANIMATION

The rest of the lab is divided into the various animation stages. To make it easier to follow, those stages are explained here, before you start. Figure 13.9 shows keyframes for the simple version and Figure 13.10 shows them for the complex version. The figures for the rest of the lab will use the complex model.

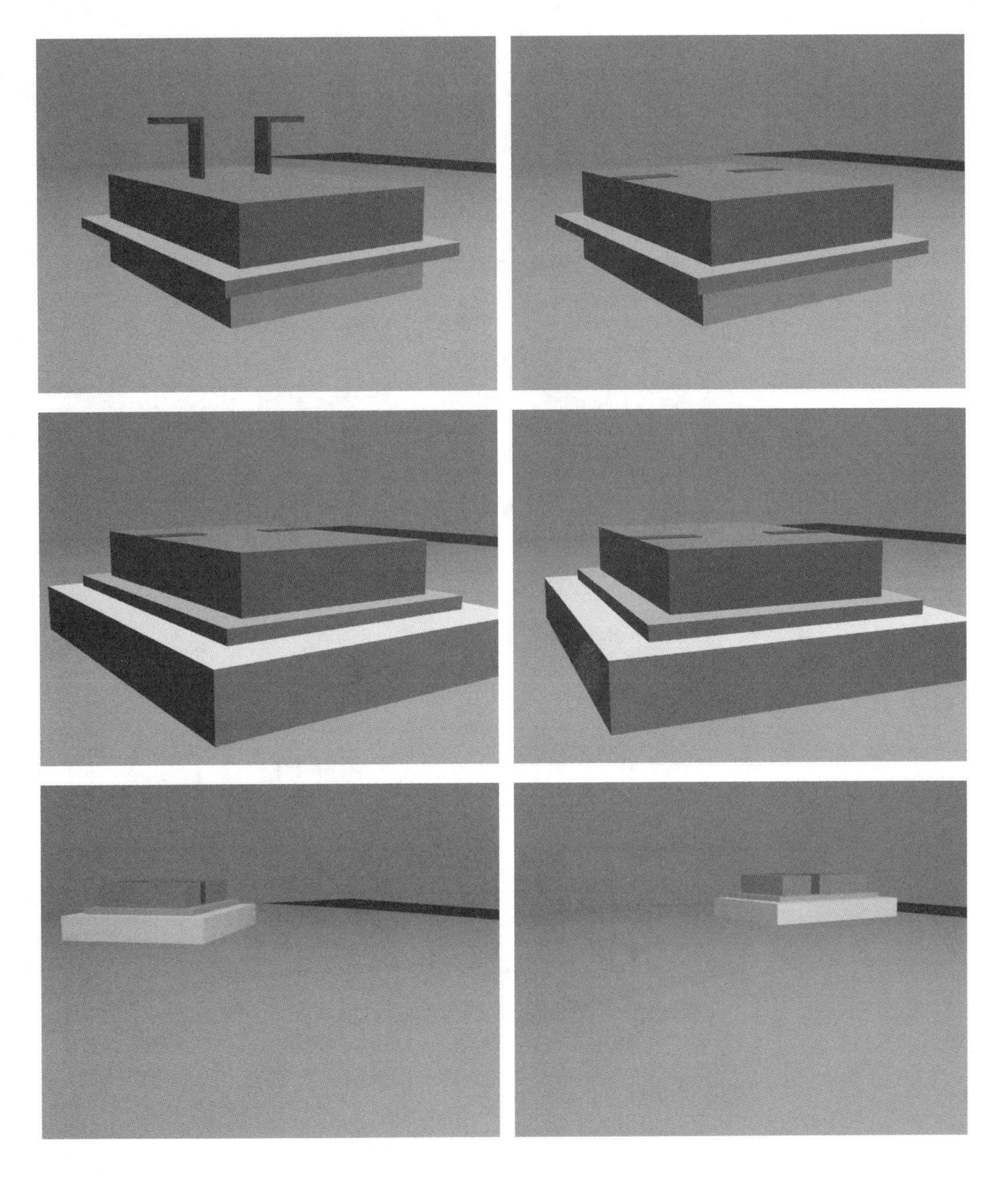

FIGURE 13.9
Keyframes rendered for simple scene.

FIGURE 13.10
Keyframes rendered for complex scene.

## Stages

**Close Doors**

The two doors to the hovercraft start out open 90° and rotate into a closed position.

**Inflate Pad and Raise Chassis**

The rubber Pad lies under the Chassis. The Pad inflates, with the Chassis rising with it.

**Rotate Chassis+Pad**

The hovercraft turns left 165°.

**Move Chassis+Pad**

The hovercraft travels along the ground away from the camera.

**Rotate Chassis+Pad**

The hovercraft turns right 110°.

**Move Chassis+Pad**

The Chassis and Pad travel across the ground in view of the camera from left to right.

## SET FRAMES AND OPEN GROUPS

3. To set up the animation, you need to establish an initial length. This can be changed at any time. Open the Time Configuration dialog, as shown in Figure 13.11, and set the length of the animation to 150 frames. Close the dialog when you are finished.

4. The complete model of the hovercraft is assembled as groups of objects. You need to open these groups to get access to the doors and other parts.

   Select the entire hovercraft using the Select Object tool. The complete model should turn white, because all the parts are grouped together. The group is named Chassis+Pad.

   Use the Group/Open pull-down menu item to open the group so that you can get access to the parts inside. Usually the group is deselected when you do this.

   In the Left viewport, select the top of the hovercraft. This is the Chassis group. Open this group using the Group/Open pull-down menu item.

   Now you will have access to the doors.

## CLOSE DOORS

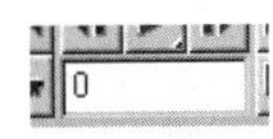


5. You are going to animate the closing of the doors using the Rotate transform at frame 25. Figure 13.12 shows a view of the rotated doors.

   Select the field box for the frame number. It should be initially 0. Enter 25 for the frame number.

6. Turn on the Animate button. This button needs to be on (red) when any transforms are to be animated. Remember to have this on during the other transforms. You also need to be in the desired frame before you use the transform.

FIGURE 13.11
Time Configuration dialog.

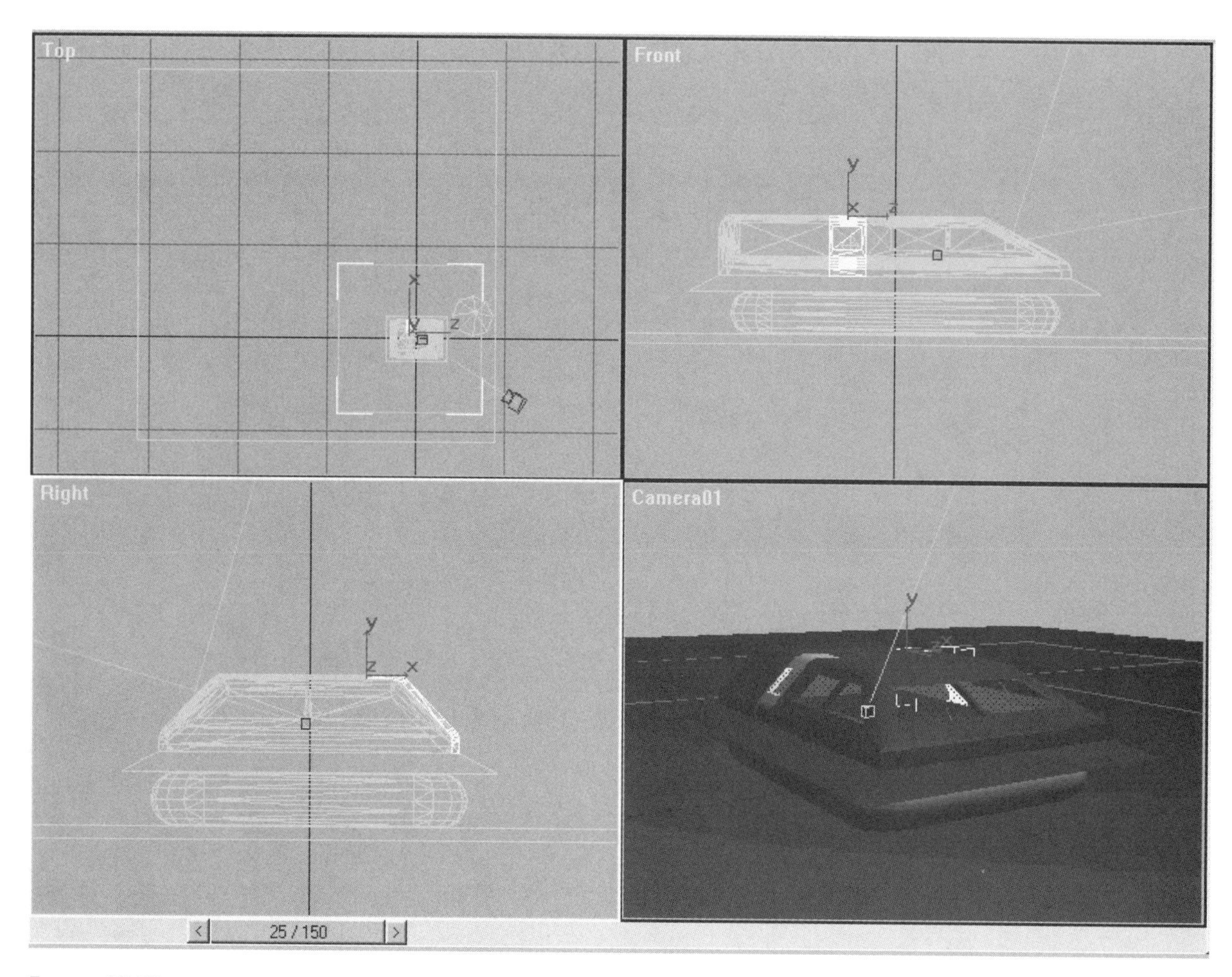


FIGURE 13.12
Doors closed.

7. Using the Rotate transform, select one of the doors in the Left viewport, and rotate it so that it closes. Repeat for the other door.
8. With one of the doors still selected, use the Group/Close pull-down menu item to close the Chassis group. This assembles the doors and other parts together as one group, making it easier to manipulate.

9. Test the animated sequence by activating the Camera viewport and then picking the Play button. You should see the doors close from frame 0 to 25. Nothing happens yet beyond frame 25. Stop the animation when you are ready to continue.

## INFLATE PAD AND RAISE CHASSIS

10. The Pad lies under the Chassis. You are going to use the Scale transform to inflate the Pad. You are also going to raise the Chassis using the Move transform so that it sits on the Pad. This will occur at frame 50.

    Select the field box for the frame number and enter 50 for the frame number.

11. Using the Scale transform, select the Pad in the Left viewport and scale it up by 140%. The Animate button is still turned on.

12. Using the Move transform, select the Chassis in the Left viewport and move it up so that it sits on the Pad. You may want to restrict the axis movement to the Y axis. Figure 13.13 shows an illustration of the scaled Pad and moved Chassis.
13. Test the animation sequence using the Play button in the Camera port. Note how the Pad inflates and the Chassis raises at the same time as the doors close. In this animation we want the doors to close first; then we want the Pad to inflate and Chassis to rise. To make a change in the timing, you will need to use the Track View dialog.

## ADJUSTING TIMING WITH TRACK VIEW

14. Open the Track View dialog and refer to Figure 13.14, showing the key dots and tracks for the transforms. To access the tracks for the Scale transform of the Pad and the Move transform of the Chassis, you need to expand the trees. The following are the steps to follow:
    a. Pick on the Objects square/plus box to expand the tracks for the various groups.
    b. Pick on the Chassis+Pad square/plus box to expand the tracks for that group.
    c. Pick the square/plus box for the Chassis.
    d. Pick the round/plus box for the Pad and the Chassis
    e. Pick the Transform round/plus boxes for both the Pad and the Chassis. You should now be able to access the keys for the transforms.

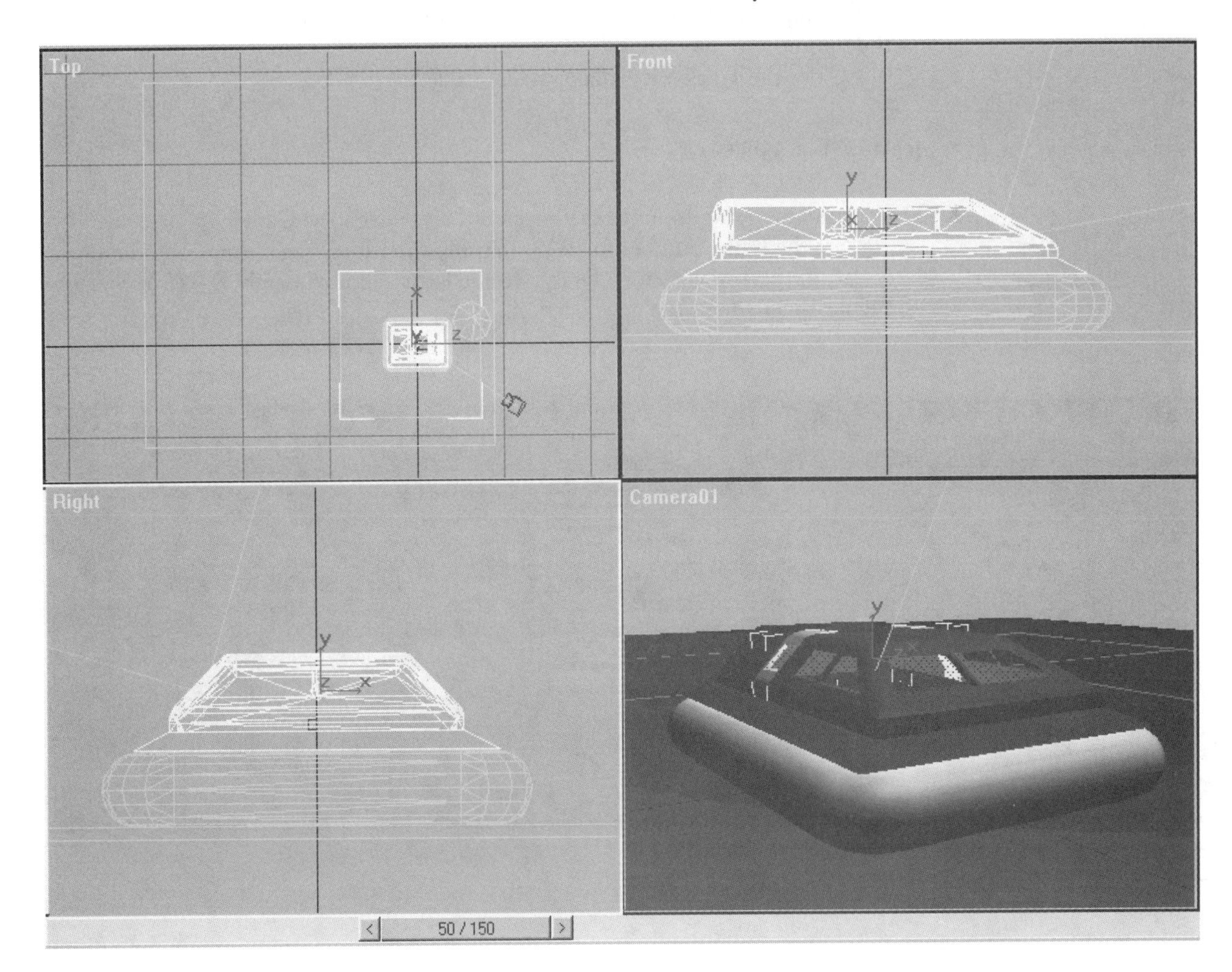


FIGURE 13.13
Inflated Pad and raised Chassis.

15. With the Edit Keys, Snap Frames, and Move Keys tools active, pick on the Pad Scale start key (turning it white) and move it from frame 0 to frame 25. Now pick on the Chassis Move start key and move it from frame 0 to 25. Figure 13.14 shows the final locations.

    Close the Track View dialog to continue.

## ROTATE CHASSIS+PAD

16. Using the Rotate Transform, you are going to rotate the Chassis+Pad group 165° at frame 75. You will need to use the Track View to move the start of the rotate to Frame 50.

    First, select the field box for the frame number and enter 75 for the frame number.
17. Select the Chassis and use the Group/Close pull-down menu item to close the entire hovercraft group. Now when you make use of the transforms they will apply to the entire hovercraft.
18. Use the Rotate transform to select the hovercraft (Chassis+Pad) in the Top viewport and rotate it 165°. Figure 13.15 shows the outcome.
19. As before, you are going to have to adjust the keyframe timing for the Rotate transform. This time it will be for the Chassis+Pad group object. Figure 13.16 shows the expanded track. Move your start key dot to frame 50, as shown in the figure.

    Close the Track View dialog to continue.

## MOVE CHASSIS+PAD

20. You are now going to move the hovercraft away from the Camera.

    Set the frame number to 100 and, using the Move transform, select the hovercraft in the Top viewport. Drag it to the left to approximately X: -16 Y: 5 Z: 0. Figure 13.17 shows the new location.

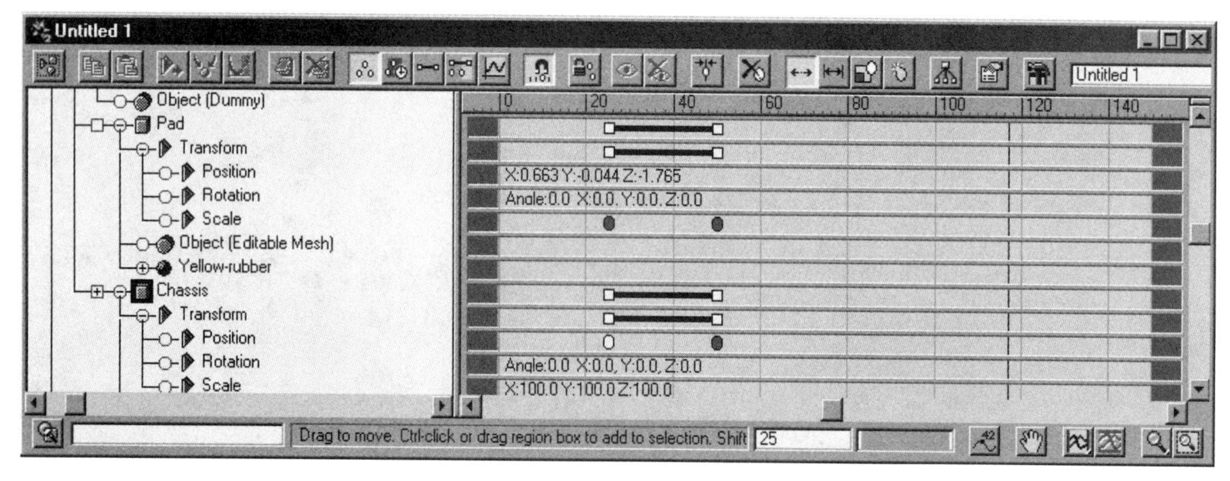


FIGURE 13.14
Track View showing moved Transform start keys.

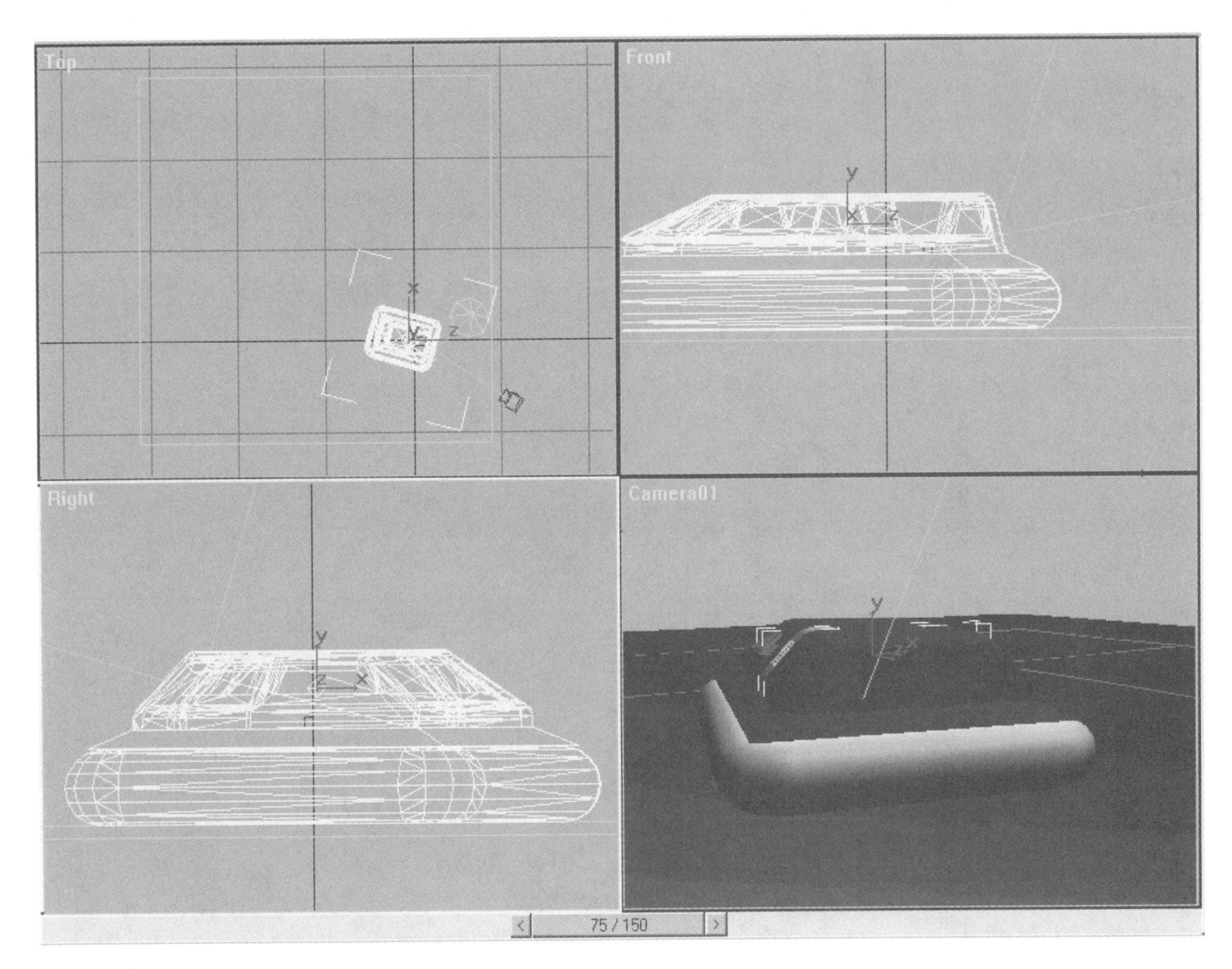


FIGURE 13.15
Rotated hovercraft.

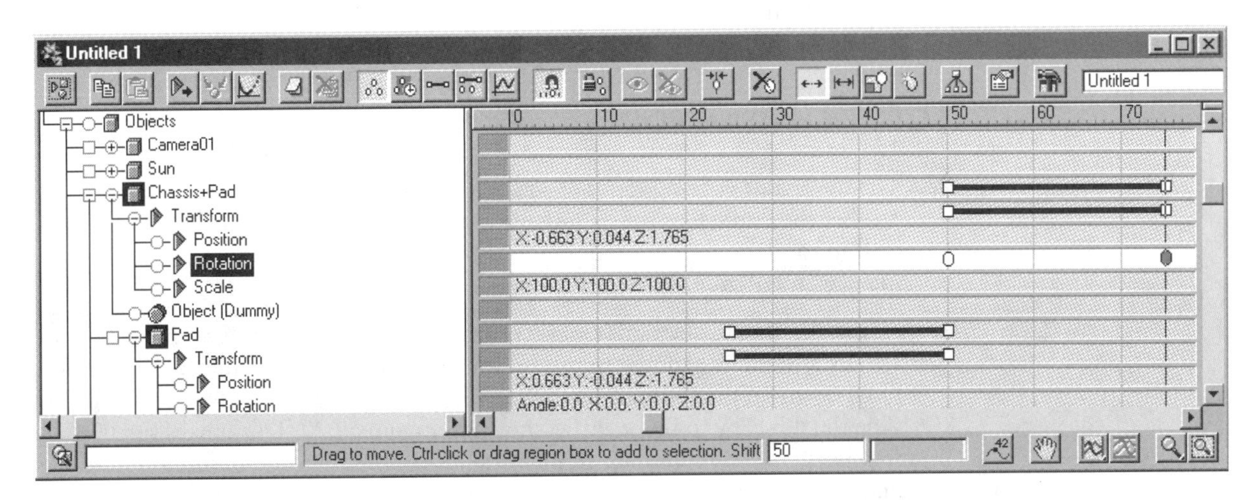


FIGURE 13.16
Track View showing Rotate track.

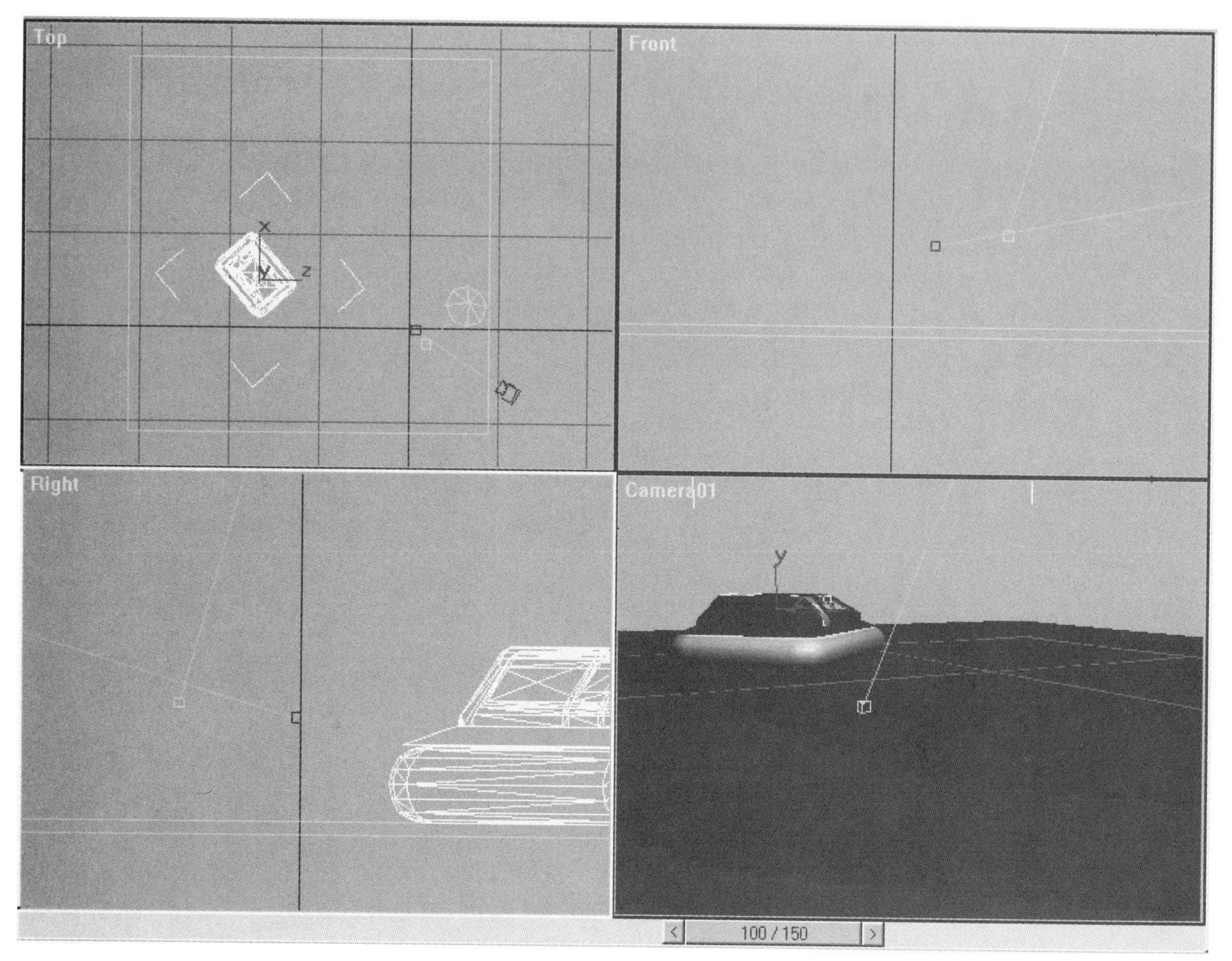


FIGURE 13.17
New hovercraft location.

21. Adjust the keyframe timing using the Track View. The start key dot of the Move transform should be moved to frame 75 as shown in Figure 13.18.
    Close the Track View dialog to continue.

## ROTATE CHASSIS+PAD

22. The hovercraft is going to rotate again to move in another direction.
    Set the frame number to 110; using the Rotate transform, select the hovercraft in the Top viewport and rotate it approximately -10°. Figure 13.19 shows the new orientation.
23. Adjust the Rotate keyframe timing using the Track View. Because there is already a Rotate key dot at frame 75, you are going to have to make a copy of it. Hold down on the Shift keyboard key while picking the dot at frame 75 and slide the dot copy to frame 90, as shown in Figure 13.20. This makes sure the rotation value stays constant from frame 75 until 90, when it starts to change until frame 110.
    Close the Track View dialog to continue.

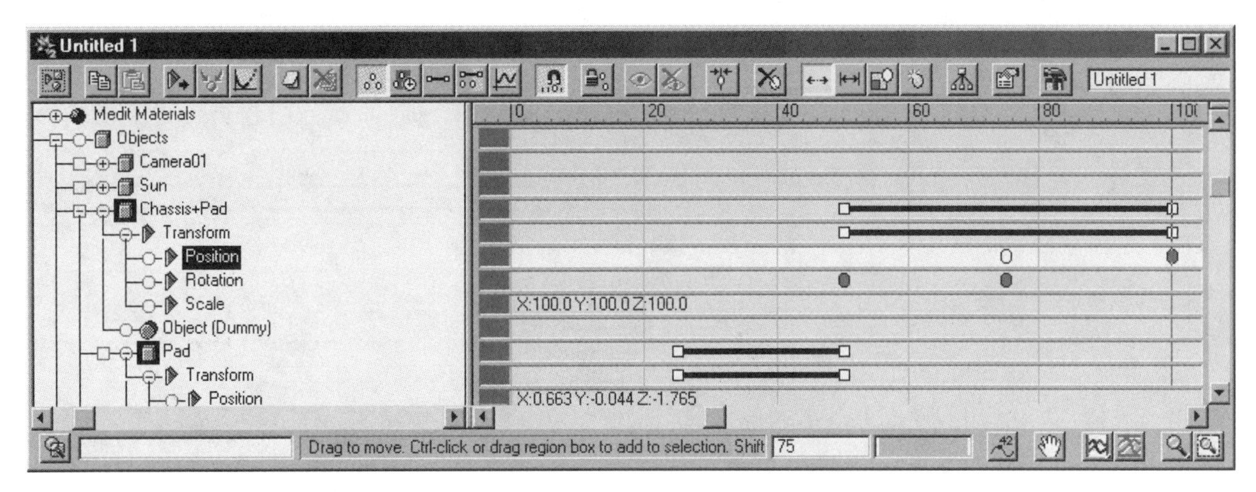


FIGURE 13.18
Track View showing Move track.

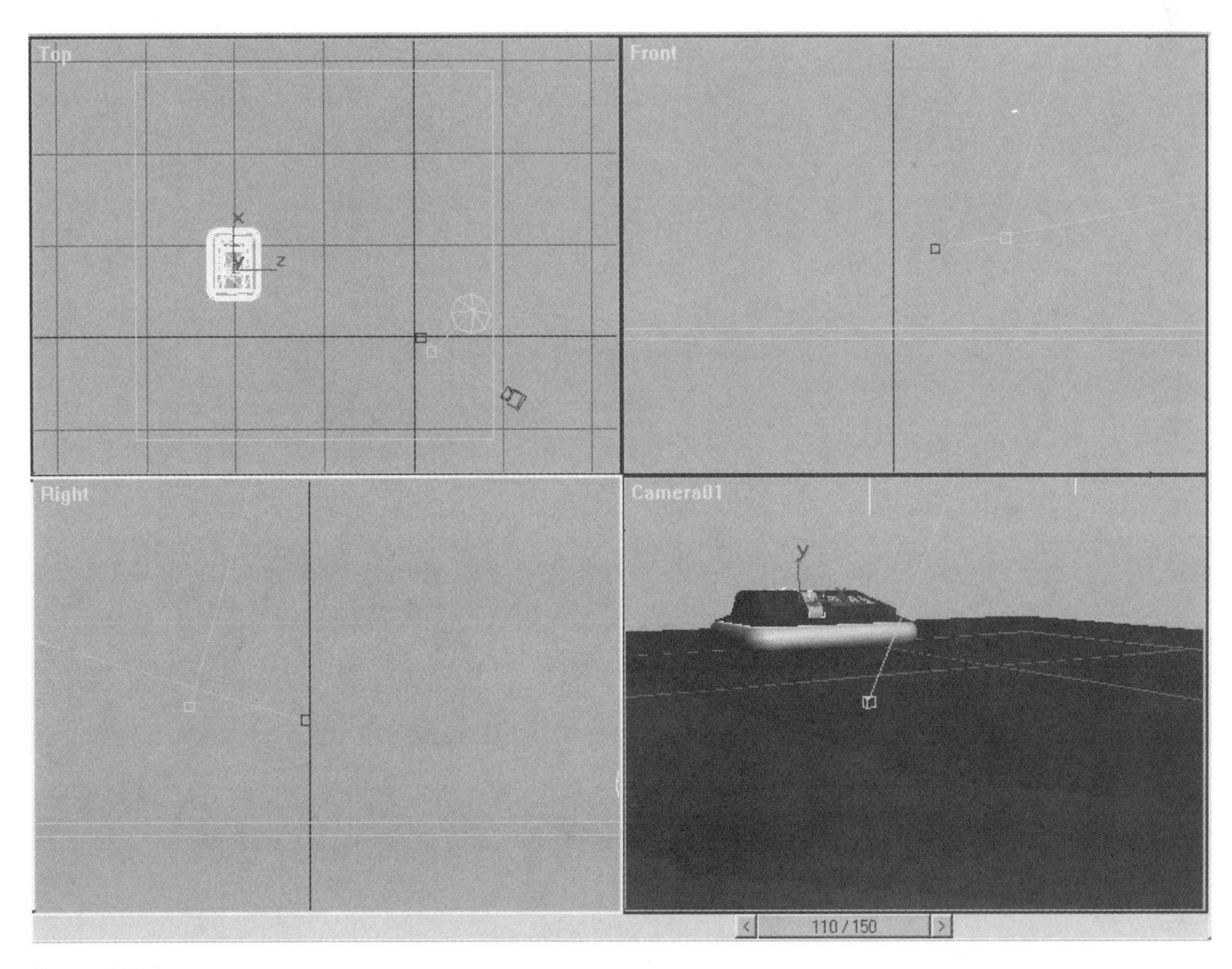


FIGURE 13.19
New hovercraft orientation.

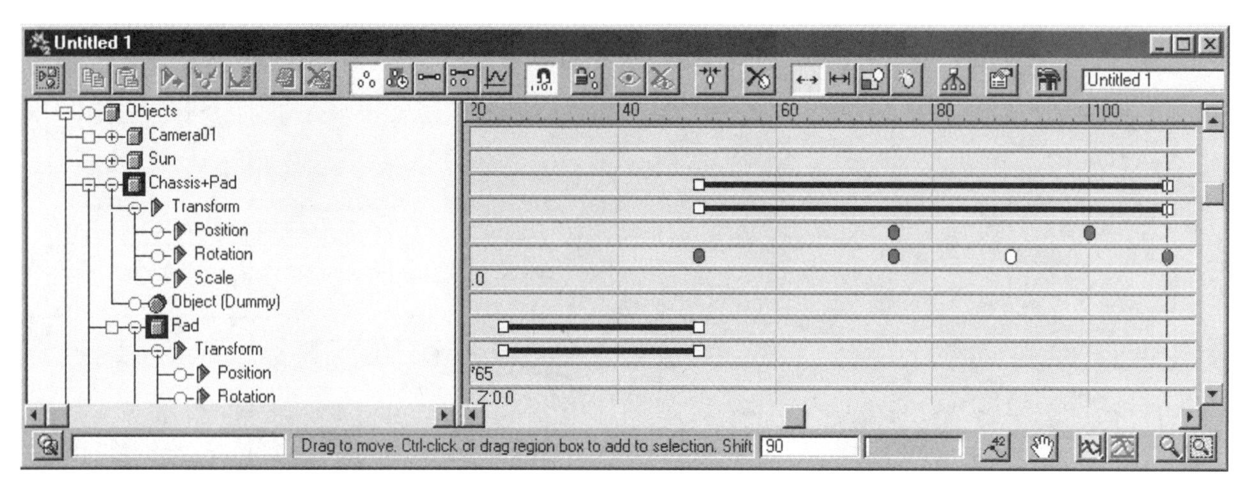


FIGURE 13.20
Track View showing Rotate track.

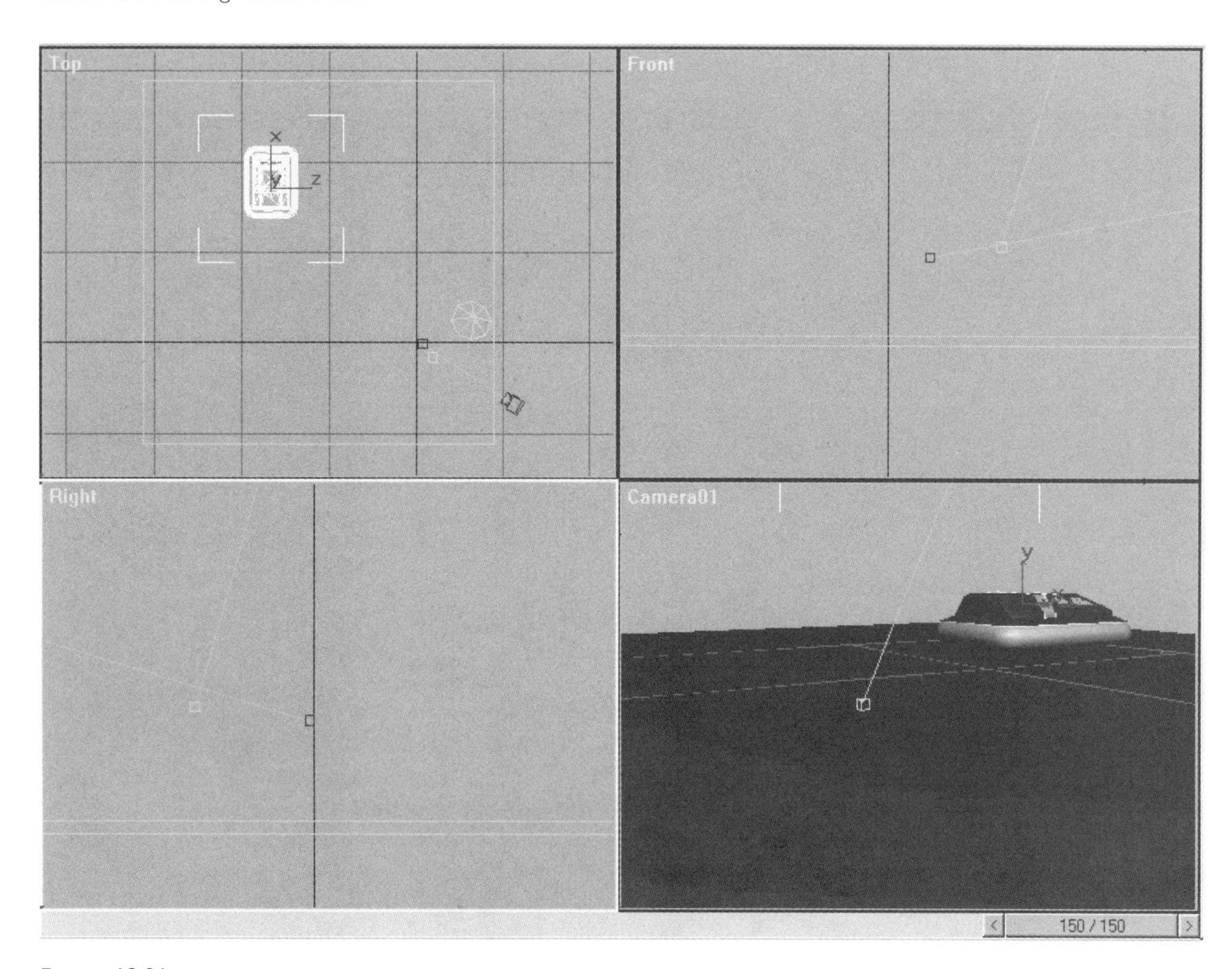


FIGURE 13.21
New location of hovercraft.

## MOVE CHASSIS+PAD

24. The hovercraft is now going to move across the view of the camera.
    Set the Frame number to 150; using the Move transform, select the hovercraft in the Top viewport and drag it to approximately X: 0 Y: 12 Z: 0. Refer to Figure 13.21.
25. Because the hovercraft is always in motion, there is no need to adjust the timing of the last move transform. Turn off the animate button.
26. Test the animation in the Camera viewport. It may look a little choppy, depending on the speed of your computer.

## FINAL RENDERED ANIMATION

27. The last step is to render the complete animation and have it saved to disk. Open the Render Scene dialog and refer to Figure 13.22 for the settings. For this lab, you are going use a resolution of 640 × 480 and save the file as a HOVER.FLC. You could save it as an AVI, but the file size would be much larger. However, it is up to you. You should also note that the Virtual Frame Buffer box is not checked. This means that the rendering will not be shown on the screen. This will save a little on the rendering time, and you will be able to see the animation when it is complete.
    If you render the simple scene it should take approximately 21 minutes using a Pentium II 350 with 96 Mb of RAM. The complex scene will take up to 1 hour 20 minutes using the same level of computer.
28. To replay the animation, select the File/View File pull-down menu item. You will be presented with a dialog to choose your file type (FLC) and the location of the file.

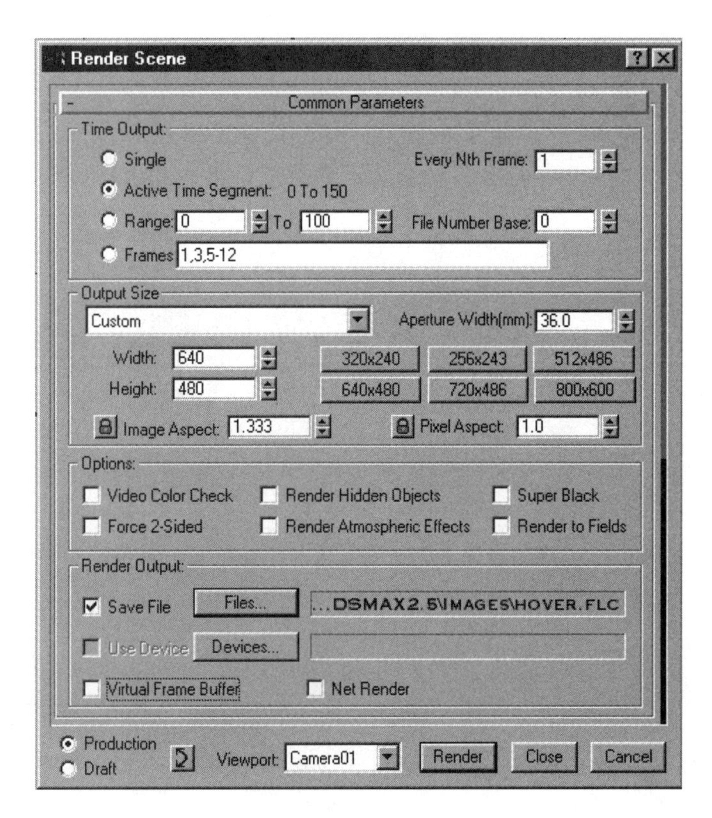


FIGURE 13.22
Render Scene dialog.

## QUESTIONS AND ASSIGNMENTS

### QUESTIONS

1. Explain the function of keyframes.
2. List the four types of Frame Rates shown in the Time Configuration dialog.
3. How do you set the active segment of an animation?
4. Explain the function of the Animate button.
5. How do you play or move through an animation sequence on the screen?
6. What is the purpose of the Track View?
7. What is the hierarchy list?
8. What function does the Edit window perform?
9. Explain the function of controllers.
10. What are the two methods of accessing controllers?

### ASSIGNMENTS

1. Experiment with controllers. Start a new scene called CH13C.MAX.
   a. Create a small box shape in the lower-left corner of the Top viewport. The height should be less than the width.
   b. Using the Time Configuration dialog, set the length of the animation to 50 frames and go to frame 25.
   c. Turn on the Animate button and move the box straight up along the Y axis in the Top viewport.
   d. Move to frame 50. With the Animate button on, move the box straight along the X axis to the right side of the Top viewport.
   e. In the Top viewport, play the animation. Note how the box moves in an arc, not a straight line. This is because a Bezier Position controller was assigned automatically.
   f. Select the box and turn on Trajectory in the Display command panel. You should be able to see a blue dashed line representing the curved trajectory of the box.
   g. With the box still selected, open the Motion command panel and open the Assign Controller rollout. Highlight the Bezier Position controller in the hierarchy list and pick on the Assign Controller button.
   h. From the Replace Position Controller dialog, highlight Linear Position and OK it. Note how the blue dashed trajectory line is now composed of straight lines. Play the animation in the Top viewport. The box now moves along straight lines.

      Save the scene as CH13C.MAX.

2. Experiment with the active-time segment. Open the animation scene created in this chapter (CH13A or CH13B).
   a. Activate the Camera viewport. Using the Time Configuration dialog, set the start time to 50 and the end time to 100.
   b. Play the animation. Note how only frames 50 to 100 of the animation are shown. You can set any segment of time by using the start and end frame

locations. This is useful for isolating smaller sections of a longer animation.

c. Open the Track View to see how setting an active segment affects the display of tracks.

# Follow the Leader: Hierarchy Linking and Inverse Kinematics

## 14.1 INTRODUCTION

When creating animated sequences, you will find the need to link objects together to form an interdependent relationship referred to as *hierarchy linking*. This chapter explains the concepts and procedures behind this linking. It also introduces you to the method of linking referred to as inverse kinematics. Using these techniques you can create complex links between objects so that when one object changes, it will have an effect on a series of objects linked together. This can save time and create realistic movements of linked components.

## 14.2 HIERARCHY LINKING

Hierarchy linking is the linking of two or more objects to form parent-child relationships. In this way, transformations applied to a parent are also transmitted to the child. By using this method of linking you can form complex relationships with many objects.

For instance, consider the flight of a flock of geese. They fly in V-formation, all following the lead goose. To animate this movement, you could link all the other geese to the lead goose. Wherever you move the lead (parent) goose—up or down, left or right—the other geese (children) would follow.

With hierarchy linking, the child objects of the link have no effect on the parent. In the case of the geese, if you moved a child goose out of formation, it would have no effect on the other children geese or the parent goose.

One common application of hierarchy linking in 3D Studio MAX is to link the target of a camera to an object in the scene. When you move the object, the camera continues to point at the object. Figure 14.1 shows a camera target linked to an object. The series of frames shows how the camera follows the object.

## Definitions

To understand hierarchy linking and its application you should know some of the definitions that 3D Studio MAX uses. These are related to a family tree.

**Parent**
: An object that controls one or more children. The children may be parents of other children.

**Child**
: An object that is controlled by its parent.

**Ancestors**
: The parent and all the parent's parents.

**Descendants**
: The children and all the children's children.

FIGURE 14.1
Camera target linked to object as it moves.

**Root**
A single parent object that is superior to all other objects in the hierarchy.

**Subtree**
All the descendants of the selected parent.

**Branch**
The path through the hierarchy from a parent to a single descendant.

**Leaf**
The last child in a branch that has no children.

**Link**
The invisible connection between a parent and its child.

**Pivot**
The local center and coordinate system for each object. A link connects the pivot of the child to the pivot of the parent.

## 14.3 LINKING AND UNLINKING OBJECTS

The process of linking one object to another is this simple series of steps:

1. Activate the Link tool.
2. Position the cursor over the desired child object. The cursor will change to the Make Link cursor if the object is acceptable as a child. Pick it and drag the cursor.
3. Move the cursor over the desired parent. The Make Link cursor will appear if the object is acceptable as a parent. Release the cursor and the link is formed.

4. To unlink a child object, select the child object and pick the Unlink tool.

If you are going to link many objects together in a complex hierarchy, you should plan out the tree before you start so that you can keep track of the relationships.

### Viewing Links with Track View

The Track View, described in Section 13.3, can be used to view the links between parents and children. Figure 14.2 shows the hierarchy link tree.

**LIGHTS! CAMERA! ACTION!** 

**Linking Order**

A good rule of thumb for determining the order in which you link objects is to begin by designating the object that moves the least as the parent and constructing the rest of the links from that point. The last (leaf) object is usually the one that moves the most.

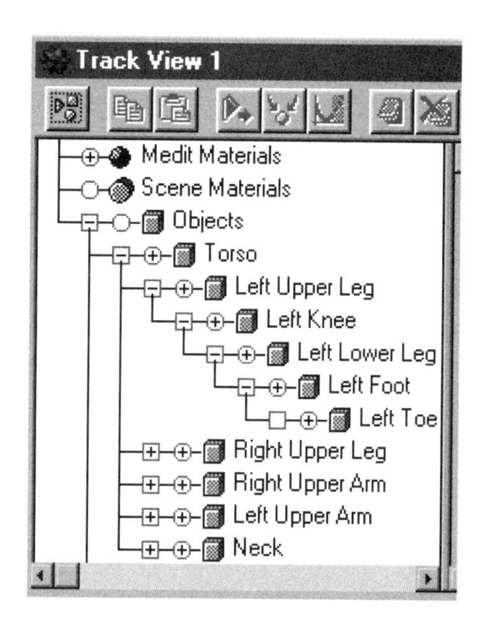


FIGURE 14.2
Track View showing hierarchy links.

## Hierarchy Command Panel

You can control the behavior of a link with the use of the Hierarchy command panel accessed through the Hierarchy tab. Figure 14.3 shows the command panel.

If you pick the Pivot button, you are presented with parameters that affect the pivot point of a selected object. The Adjust Pivot rollout allows you to alter the pivot point of any selected object. The Adjust Transform rollout allows you to transform a parent object without affecting its children.

If you pick the Link Info button, you are presented with parameters that can be used to restrict the application of transforms to a child object.

The IK button is used for Inverse Kinematics, which is explained in Section 14.5, Joints and Parameters.

## Using Dummy Helper Objects

A dummy helper object is a box that will not render in a scene. For more information see Section 6.4 on helpers. The dummy helper is to be used as a parent object that other objects can be linked to. It can be used to add complex motion to an already active object. For instance, you may require a sled to slide back and forth across the snow as it goes down a slope. The following procedure uses a dummy object:

1. Create the sled and create the dummy helper object.
2. Link the sled (child) to the dummy (parent).
3. With the Animate button on, move the sled back and forth along the same axis (X axis) over the sequence of frames.
4. In the last frame of the sequence, with the Animate button on, move the dummy object down the slope (Y and Z axes).
5. When you run the animation, the sled will move back and forth in a zigzag pattern as it follows the dummy down the slope.
6. When you render the animation, you will not see the dummy object.

You can link several dummy objects to form very complex maneuvers by combining simple movements of the dummies.

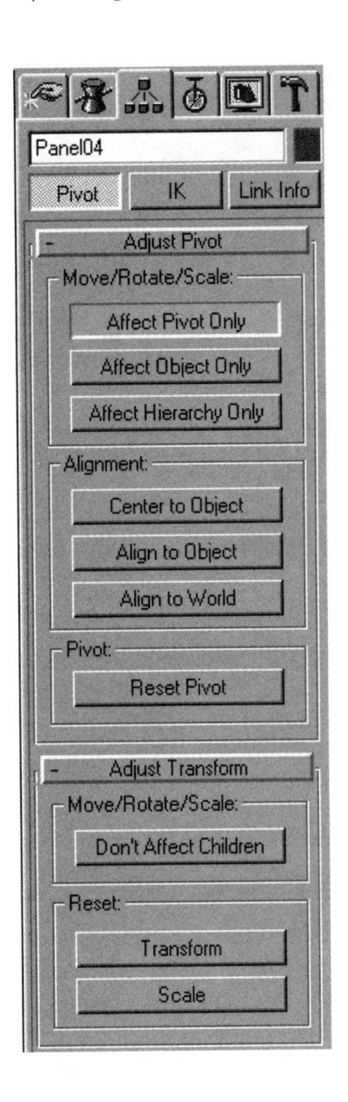


FIGURE 14.3 Hierarchy command panel.

## 14.4 INTRODUCTION TO INVERSE KINEMATICS

In Section 14.3 you learned how to link objects together to form a hierarchy where the parent controls all the children. This is referred to as forward kinematics. Inverse kinematics work on the principle that you move the child and the parent follows.

For instance, think of moving your hand. As you move your hand, your lower arm and upper arm follow, each pivoting about a joint, whether it is the wrist, elbow, or shoulder. This movement can be thought of as inverse kinematics. The desired final position of the hand controls the movement of the other limbs. Each joint has certain physical restraints. You can rotate the hand back only to a certain degree on the wrist before it stops.

This is the same procedure you apply using 3D Studio MAX. You create the link the same way as in forward kinematics. Then you determine where the link or joint will be between two objects, the type of link, and the restraining parameters. In effect you are creating real-world connections and movements.

### Definitions

The following definitions will help you understand the principles and procedures required to use inverse kinematics:

**Joints**

Joints control how the link between the parent and child behaves. There are three broad categories: Object pivot point, Joint parameters, and Parent pivot point. Object pivot point defines where the joint motion is applied. Joint parameters adjust items such as direction and constraints on movement. Parent pivot point defines the origin from which joint constraints are measured.

**Chains**

The chain represents the single branch (path) from the child until it reaches the root, or terminator, for the chain. Inverse kinematics uses the chain to determine how all the objects behave in relation to each other.

**End Effector**

The selected child at the end of the chain is referred to as the end effector.

**Terminators**

Terminators are used to set the end of a chain before it reaches the root object. This is used to stop movement up the branch.

**Bound Objects**

Bound objects are objects bound to other objects outside the hierarchy. They are used so that objects in a hierarchy can follow the movement of other objects. Think of the animation of a baseball player throwing a ball. The ball is not part of the hand, but you want the hand to follow the ball as the ball is thrown.

## 14.5 JOINTS AND PARAMETERS

There are three types of joints: Sliding, Rotational, and Path. Sliding controls movement along each of the three axes. Rotational controls rotation in the three axes. Path controls the movement along a selected path. Sliding and Rotation are based on using the standard Move and Rotate transforms.

To set the type of joint you want, select the child object and use the Hierarchy command panel, turning on the IK button, as shown in Figure 14.4. You are presented with four different parameter rollouts: Inverse Kinematics, Object Parameters, Sliding Joints, and Rotational Joints. The Path rollout does not become visible until you assign a path controller to the object, as explained in Section 13.6. Once you have decided on the type of joint, activate the desired axes of the joint and set the limits.

### *LIGHTS! CAMERA! ACTION!*

#### Joint Limits and Inverse Kinematics

The joint limits are not functional until you turn on the Inverse Kinematic tool. When it is off, you can move the linked objects any way you wish. When the tool is on, limits are in effect.

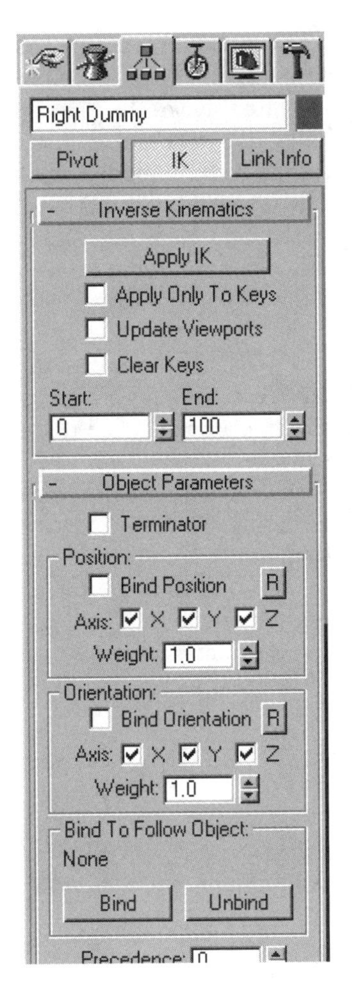


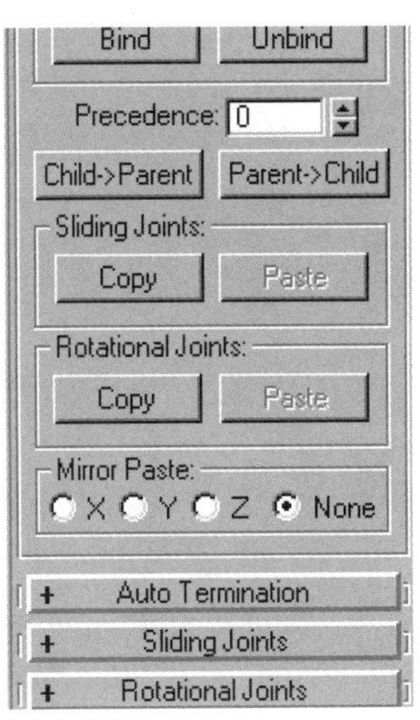


FIGURE 14.4
Hierarchy command panel with IK active.

## Pivot Points and Axes

The child object's rotation or sliding joint occurs at its pivot point. You may need to use the Pivot Section of the Hierarchy command panel to adjust its location. The parent object's pivot point is used as the reference location for the axes and the start point for the sliding joint.

## Rotational Joint Example

In this example, you want to rotate a parking lot barrier arm up and down 90°. Figure 14.5 shows a parking lot entrance barrier. The barrier arm is the child and the mech-

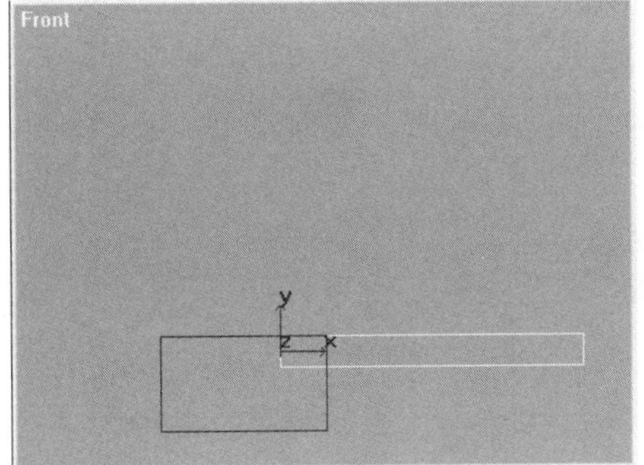


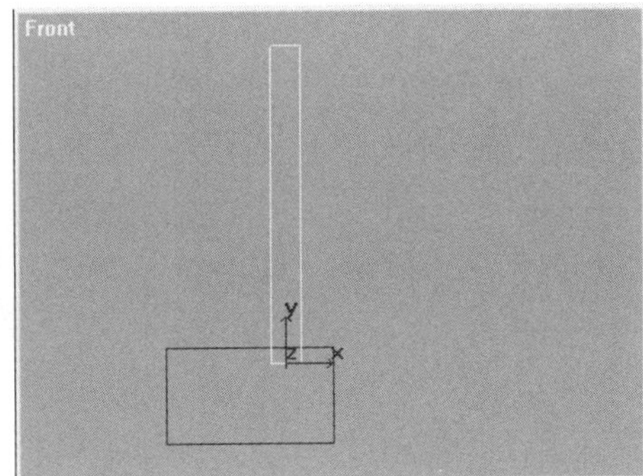


FIGURE 14.5
Parking lot barrier arm.

anism box is the parent. Two facts need to be considered first: The pivot point used for movement is the child's pivot point, and the axes from which the measurements are taken are those of the parent.

Refer now to Figure 14.6, which shows the Rotational Joints rollout for the selected child object (barrier arm).

When you check the Active box for a particular axis, the child object can move only in that axis. Remember that this represents the axis of the parent.

When you check the Limited box, the rotation is limited to a number of degrees set in the From and To boxes. Even though the rotation pivots around the child's pivot point, the axes are measured from the parent object, so you may have to test which axis to limit, depending on the orientation of the parent object.

The Ease box causes a joint to resist motion as it approaches the From and To limits. The Damping value (0.0 to 1.0) is used to apply resistance to overall motion along an axis.

*Note:* The parent object's axes must be limited as well if you want it to be stationary during kinematic movement.

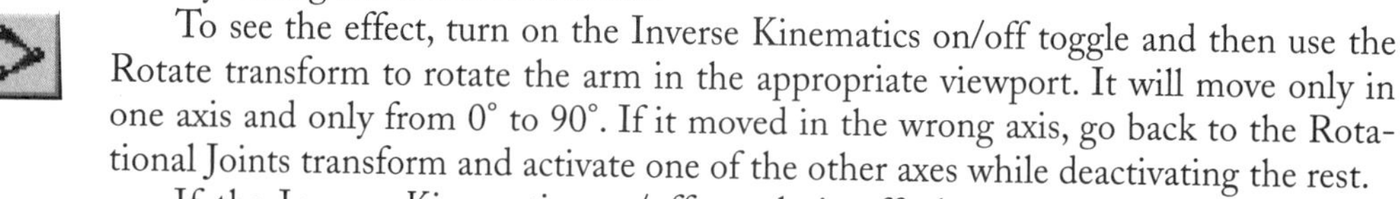

To see the effect, turn on the Inverse Kinematics on/off toggle and then use the Rotate transform to rotate the arm in the appropriate viewport. It will move only in one axis and only from 0° to 90°. If it moved in the wrong axis, go back to the Rotational Joints transform and activate one of the other axes while deactivating the rest.

If the Inverse Kinematics on/off toggle is off, there are no restraints on the object.

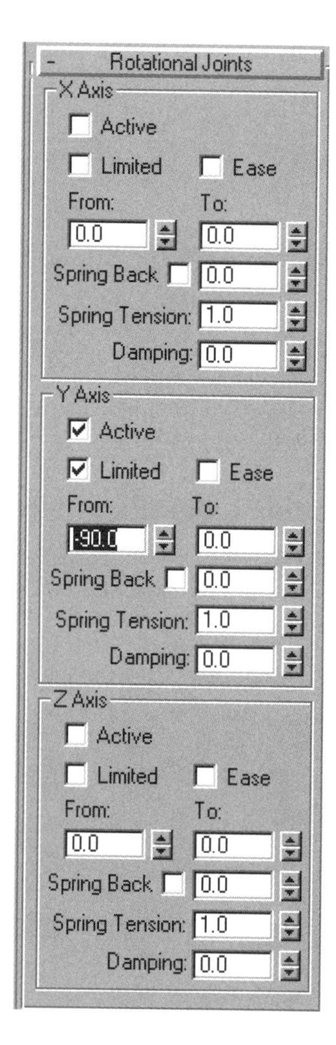


FIGURE 14.6 Rotational Joints rollout.

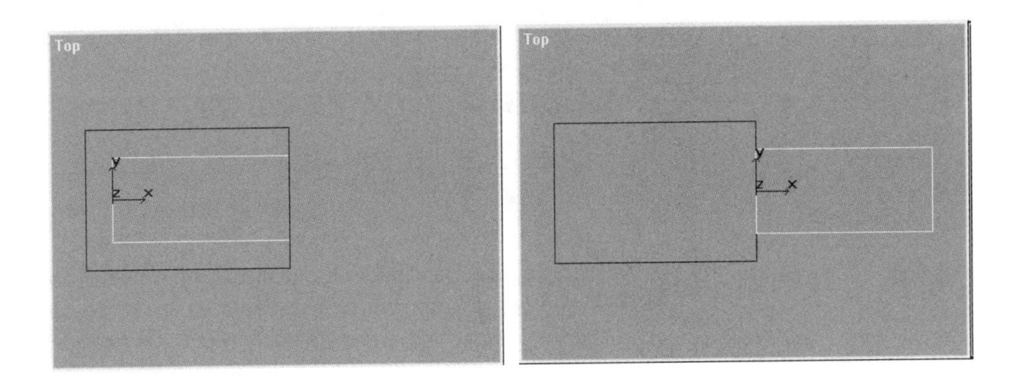


FIGURE 14.7
Sliding panel cover.

## Sliding Joint Example

In this example you want a panel cover to slide open and stop before it slides off the box. Figure 14.7 shows the sliding panel cover and box. The cover is the child and the box is the parent. As in the previous example, you select the child and then open the IK portion of the Hierarchy command panel. Make sure that the axes of Rotational Joints rollout are all inactive. Then, set the axes for the Sliding Joints rollout, as shown in Figure 14.8. You limit the movement along the axis so that the cover cannot slide off the box. The value represents the actual movement from the pivot point of the parent in relation to the pivot point of the child. To test the settings, activate the Inverse Kinematics on/off toggle and try sliding the cover back and forth in the appropriate viewport.

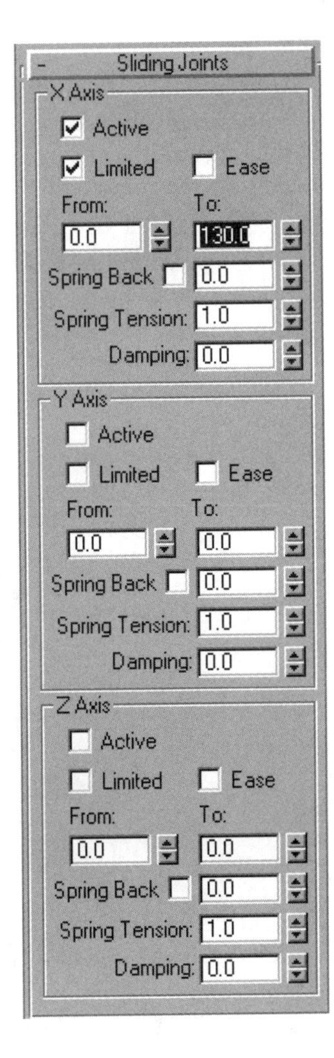


FIGURE 14.8
Sliding Joints rollout.

## LIGHTS! CAMERA! ACTION!

### Setting Joints

When setting the axis limits of joints, try to have your objects aligned along the axis of the world system first. This makes it easier to control the limits. Once this is done you can move the objects into any orientation.

### Setting Joint Precedence

In order to have objects move realistically at different joint locations, you may need to adjust the joint preference. This determines which objects move first along a kinematic chain. Figure 14.9 shows the Object Parameters rollout. The two buttons Child>Parent and Parent>Child determine the direction in which the precedence takes place. These buttons set the precedence values automatically, but you can set them yourself. High values are calculated first; low values are done last.

## 14.6 SUMMARY

When one object's movement affects another in an animation sequence, you should use a form of hierarchy linking. If it is a simple link where one object is following another, then forward kinematics is used. However, if a series of objects are related to each other and one moves, they all move within certain limitations; this is when inverse kinematics is required.

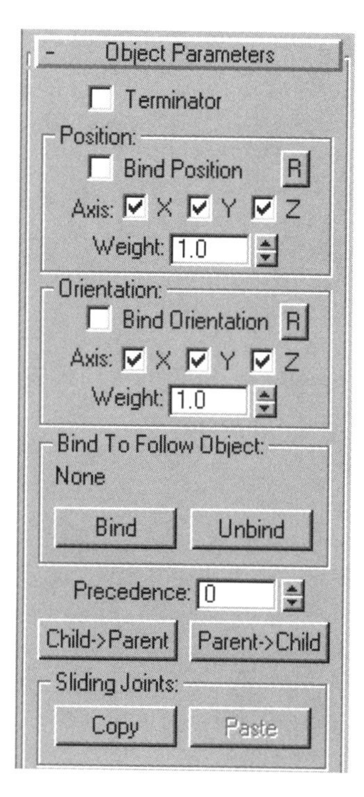


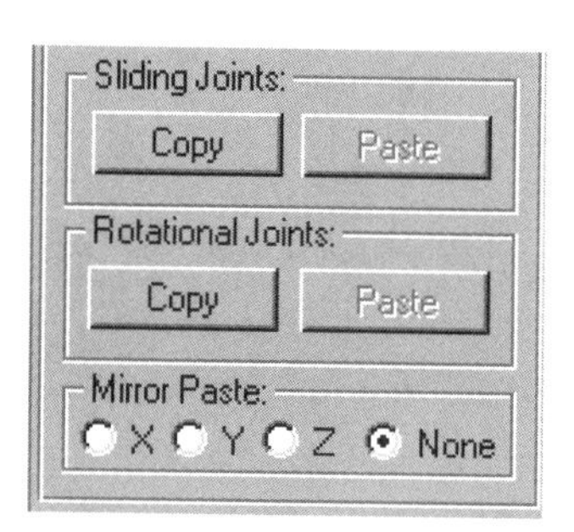


FIGURE 14.9
Object Parameters.

# LAB 14.A

## Hierarchy Linking and Basics of Inverse Kinematics

### Purpose

This lab introduces you to the application of hierarchy linking and the use of inverse kinematics.

There are two sections in the lab. The first section uses a scene already created called MXKIN.MAX. It depicts a shuttle on the launch pad. In this scene you will use simple hierarchy linking to create the animation. The second section of the lab uses a scene already created called MXIK.MAX. It depicts a multipaneled door in a large doorway. In this scene you will make use of inverse kinematics to produce the animation sequence.

Both these scenes are contained on the CD-ROM that is supplied with this textbook.

### Objectives

You will be able to

- Use hierarchy linking to link a camera target with an object.
- Use hierarchy linking to link several objects together.
- Use inverse kinematics to control the movement of objects.
- Bind an object to a dummy helper object.
- Use applied kinematics to calculate an IK.

### Procedure

1. Open the first file, MXKIN.MAX, and save the file as CH14A.MAX. This way you retain the original file if you need to refer to it again. Remember to periodically save your scene, so that if something happens, you won't lose your work.
2. The following should be the current state of the prompt line buttons

| BUTTON | STATE | PURPOSE |
|---|---|---|
| Region Selection | Window Selection | Limits selection of objects totally contained within a window. |
| 2D Snap | OFF | Allows unlimited cursor movement in 2D. |
| Angle Snap | ON | Limits angular movement to set intervals. |
| Percent Snap | ON | Limits percent scaling to set intervals. |

## TEST PLAY

3. The scene you have just loaded displays a shuttle craft on the launchpad. Currently the camera points at the shuttle. Using the Play button, play the animation in the Camera viewport. The sequence should look similar to the sample frames shown in Figure 14.10.

   Notice how the camera points in one direction only and the shuttle takes off and rises out of the scene.

## HIERARCHY LINKING

4. Now you are going to link the camera target to the shuttle so that when the shuttle launches, the camera will follow it as it rises into the sky.

   In the Back viewport, zoom in close so that you can see the blue box that represents the camera target.

   Using the Select and Link tool, pick and drag the target box. The icon will change to the Hierarchy Link icon. Drag the icon onto the shuttle and release. The shuttle flashes white to signify that it is the object to which you linked the target box. The camera target should now be linked to the shuttle.

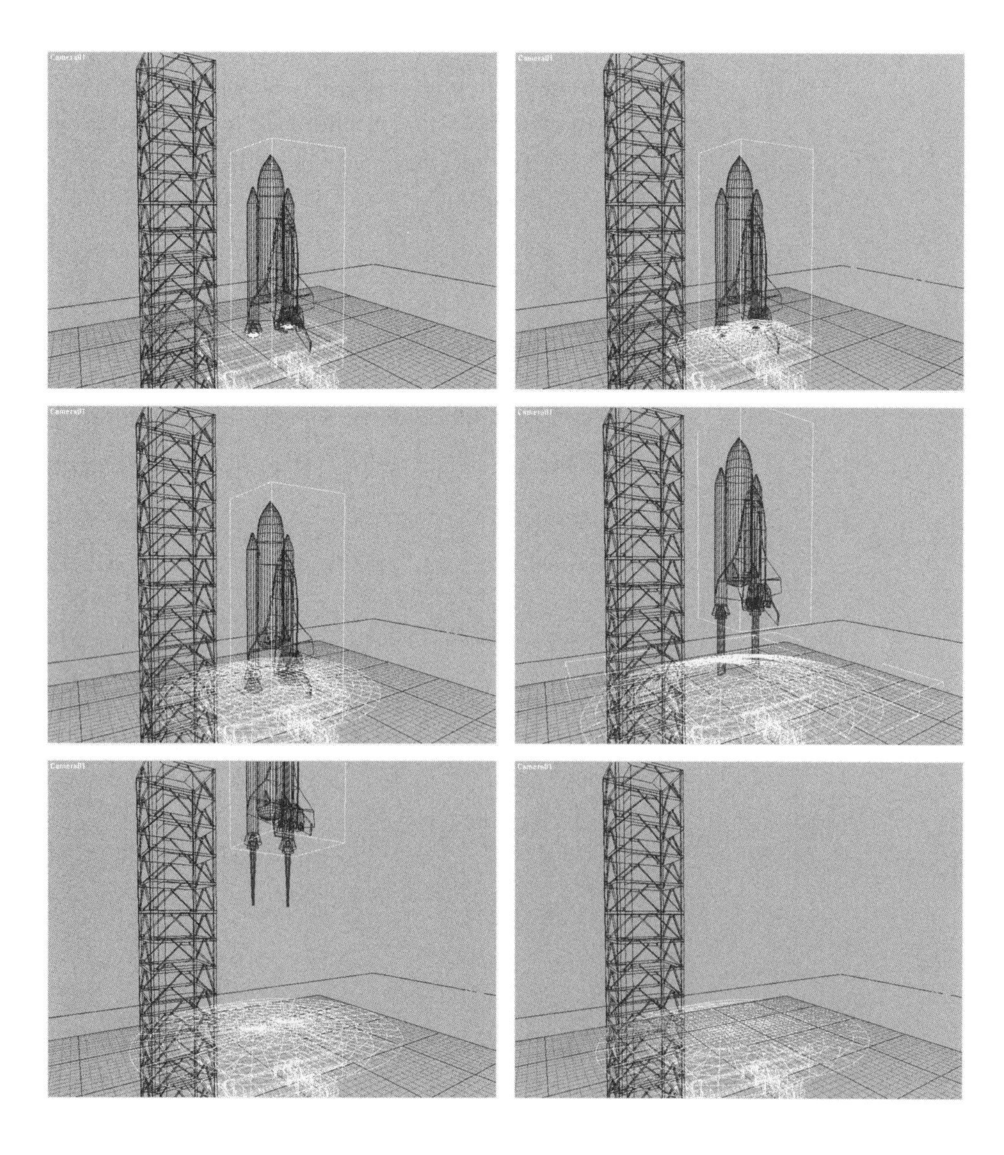

FIGURE 14.10
Sample frames with stationary camera.

## TEST PLAY

5. Test-play the Camera viewport again. This time the camera should follow the shuttle as it takes off and rises. Figure 14.11 shows some sample frames of the animation.

## RENDERING

6. If you wish, you can render the animation. It takes about 32 minutes to render at a resolution of 640 × 480 using a Pentium II 350 with 96 MB RAM. Save the rendered animation file as SHUTTLE.FLC. Figure 14.12 shows some sample frames of the rendered animation.
7. Save the file.

## FORWARD KINEMATICS

8. Open the second scene, called MXIK.MAX, and save it as CH14B.MAX. Check the state of the buttons, as mentioned in step 2.

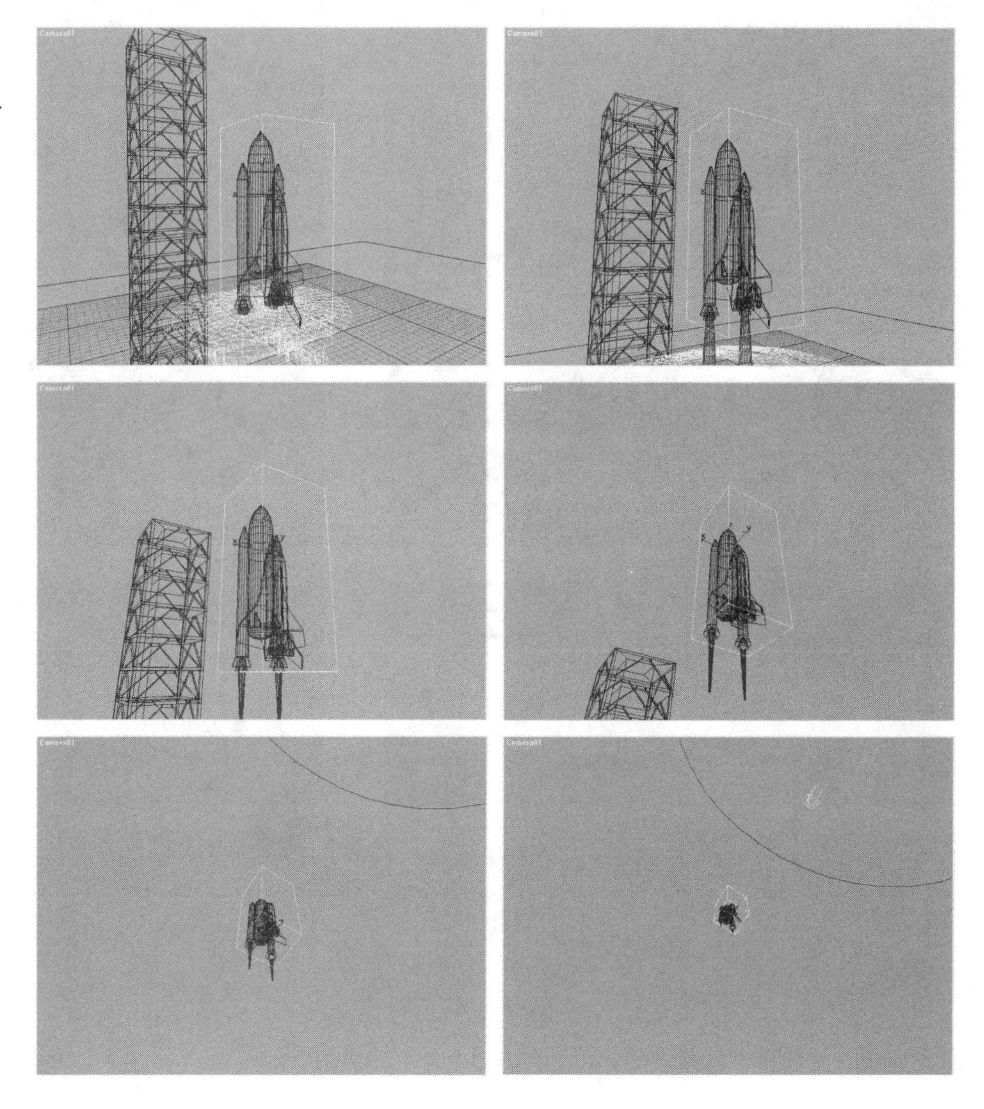

FIGURE 14.11
Sample frames with animated camera target.

FIGURE 14.12
Sample rendered frames.

In this scene there are four panels that represent a multipanel door. They are called Panel01, Panel02, Panel03, Panel04. Currently they are not linked to each other. That is the first procedure you need to perform.

9. In the Left viewport, zoom in on the four panels, as shown in Figure 14.13. Using the Select and Link tool, link the panels in the following order: Panel04 to Panel03, Panel03 to Panel02, Panel02 to Panel 01, and Panel01 to the wall. Panel04 is on the left, and Panel01 is on the right.

   *Note:* Take care when linking and watch that the proper panel flashes to signify the link. If you link incorrectly, you can unlink or use the Undo to undo the last link.

10. Save the file and select the Edit/Hold pull-down menu item. This will save the original locations of the door panels.

11. Test the links by moving each panel in turn from 4 to 1 to see the effect.

    Panel04 should move separately on its own. Panel03 should move Panel04 and itself. Panel02 should move Panel04, Panel03, and itself. Panel01 should move Panel04, Panel03, Panel02, and itself.

    This is forward kinematics with the parent controlling the child. Now you are going to use inverse kinematics so that when you close (move down) Panel04, the other panels will follow in a sliding motion.

12. Select the Edit/Fetch pull-down menu item to restore the location of the doors. If this doesn't work, open your file CH14A.MAX again and continue.

## INVERSE KINEMATICS

13. In the Left viewport, zoom in on the four panels again.

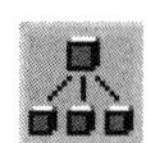

14. Select Panel04, open the Hierarchy command panel, pick the IK button, and pick the Child>Parent button. This will set the joint precedence. The panel should look similar to Figure 14.14.

15. Pan down the panel until you see the Rotational Joints rollout. Uncheck the Active boxes for all three axes. This action stops the panel from rotating.

16. Open the Sliding Joints rollout and match the settings with Figure 14.15. The X axis is limited to no movement. The Y axis limits the movement from 0.125 to 0.125. This is used to place the panel in reference to the pivot point of its parent panel. The pivot point is 0.125 units away along the Y axis. Now refer to the Z axis. This is where the sliding movement will take place. It is limited to move only -1 unit. That is how far the panel will slide down until it stops.

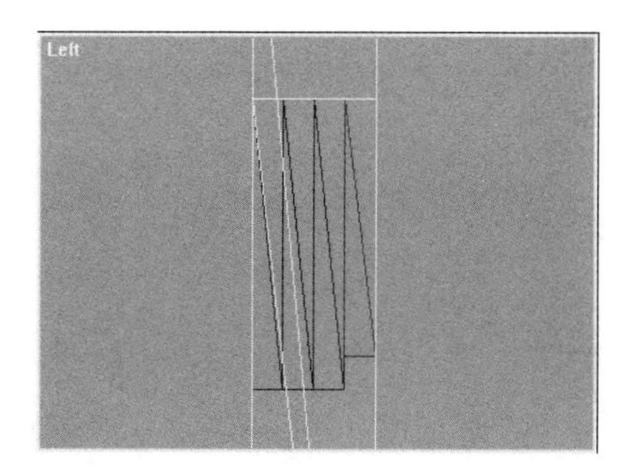


FIGURE 14.13
Close-up of door panels.

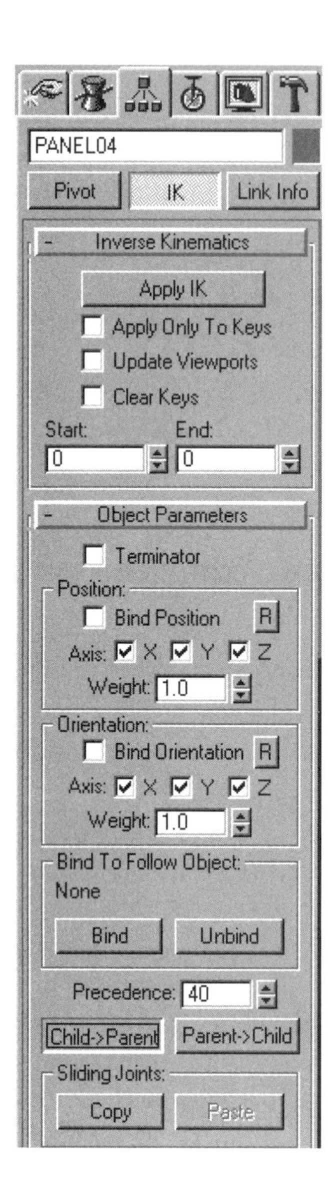


FIGURE 14.14
Hierarchy command panel with IK open.

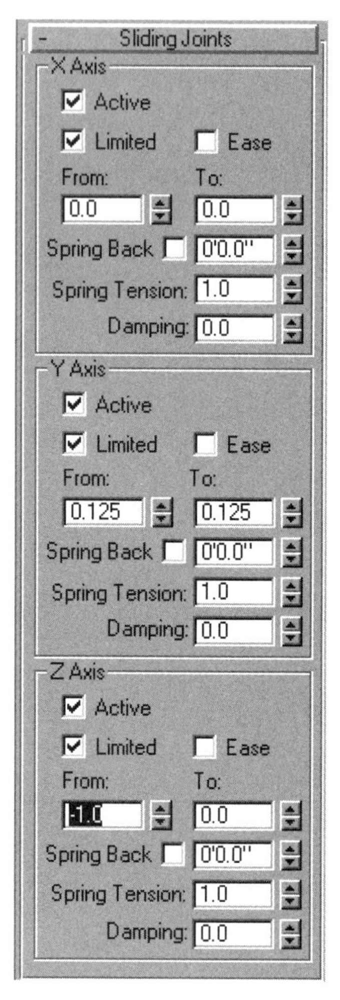


FIGURE 14.15
Sliding Joints parameters for Panel04 and Panel03.

17. Select Panel03 and perform the settings outlined in steps 15 and 16.
18. Select Panel02 and perform step 15. Open the Sliding Joints rollout and match the settings with Figure 14.16.
19. Select Panel01 and repeat step 15. Open the Sliding Joints rollout and match the settings with Figure 14.17. This panel is to stay stationary with the wall.
20. Select the wall. Make sure that there are no active axes for sliding or rotation. The wall is to be stationary as well.

## TESTING INVERSE KINEMATICS

21. Using the Time Configuration button, set the length of the animation to 50 frames and move to frame 25. Turn on the Animation button.
22. Save the file and select the Edit/Hold pull-down menu item. This will save the original locations of the door panels.

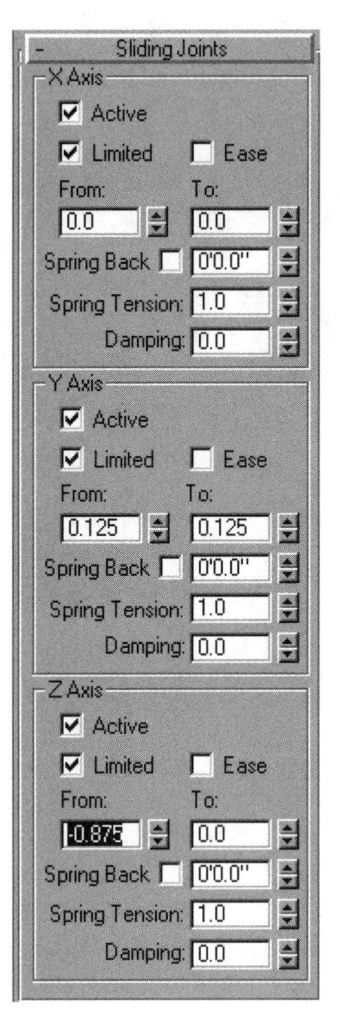


FIGURE 14.16
Sliding Joints parameters for Panel02.

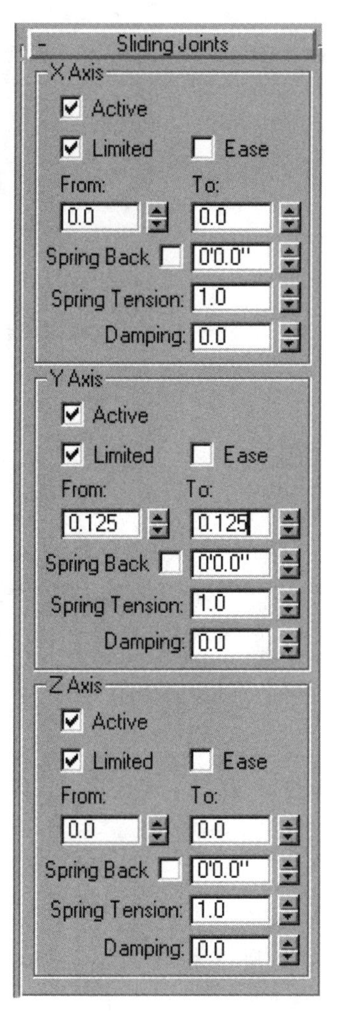


FIGURE 14.17
Sliding Joints parameters for Panel01.

23. Turn on the Inverse Kinematics toggle.
24. In the Left viewport, select Panel04 and lock it.
25. Zoom out in the Left viewport so that you can see the entire wall.
26. Using the Move transform, pick on Panel04 and drag it to the base of the floor. You may find that the panel lags behind and does not move immediately. Continue to drag until you see movement. The final position should look similar to Figure 14.18.
27. Turn off the Animate button, play the animation in the Perspective viewport, and watch the behavior of the panels. They should move at the same time to their limits, with Panel04 touching the floor and the other panels stacked upward.

    However, in this lab we want the panels to move in sequence instead of together. Panel04 should move first, then Panel03, and so on. To do this involves the binding of Panel04 to a dummy object outside the link.

## BINDING AND APPLIED IK

28. Use the Edit/Fetch pull-down menu item to undo the animated movement.

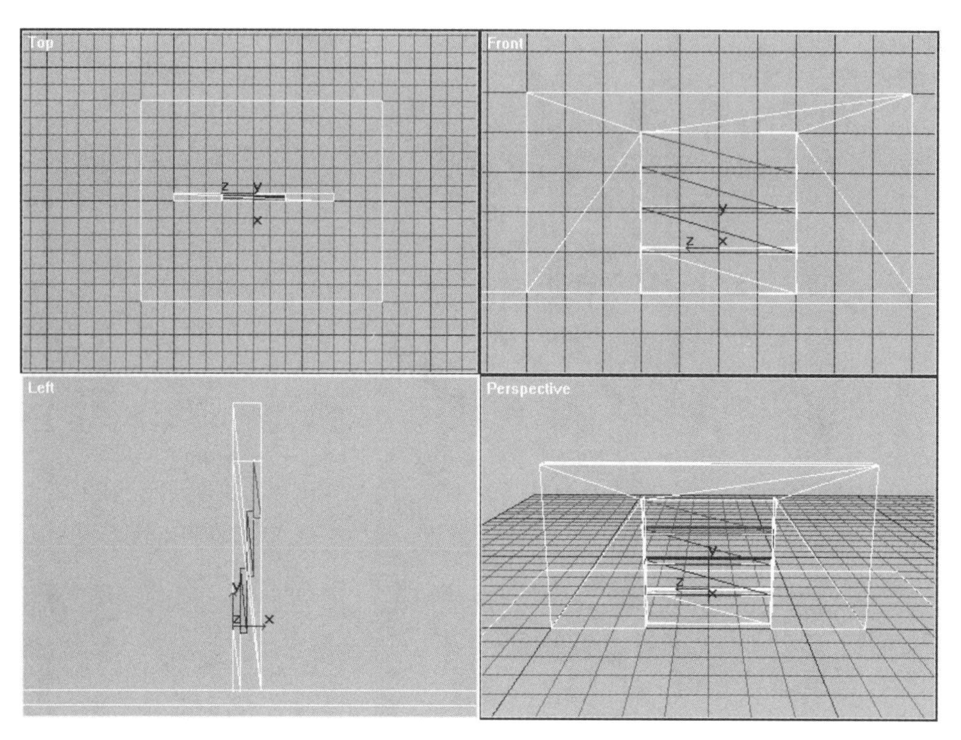


FIGURE 14.18
Final position of panels using inverse kinematics.

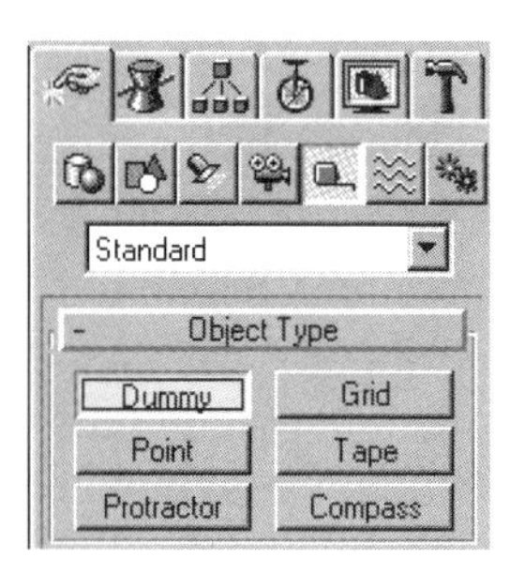


29. Create a Dummy Helper object, as shown in Figure 14.19. It should sit in line with the top of Panel04. The size of the box is not important. You will probably need to use the Move transform to place the dummy box in its proper position.

30. Select Panel04 and open IK on the Hierarchy command panel.

31. Expand the Object parameters rollout, check the Bind Position box, and turn on the Bind button.

    Pick Panel04 again, drag the icon to the dummy object, and release. The name of the dummy object will appear above the Bind button.

32. Zoom out in the Left viewport so that you can see the entire wall and turn off the Inverse Kinematics tool button.

33. Go to frame 25 and turn on the Animate button.

34. Using Move transform, move the dummy box to below the floor, as shown in Figure 14.20. You may want to use the Limit to Y tool, located in the Main toolbar at the top of the screen, to force the box to move only along the Y axis.

35. Turn off the Animate button.

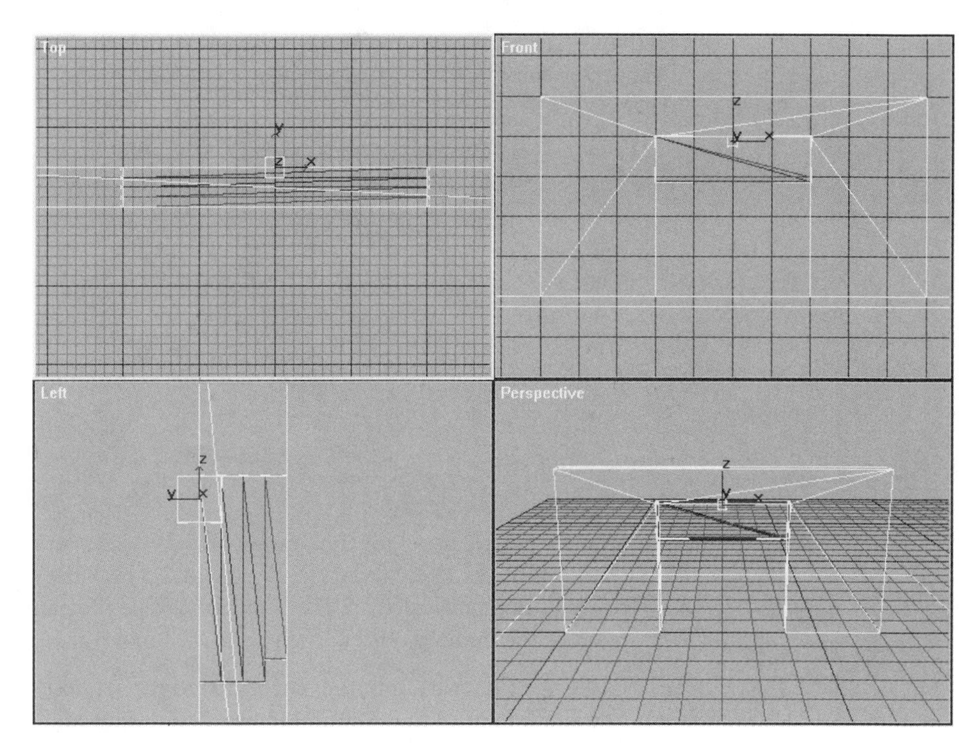


FIGURE 14.19
Creation of dummy object.

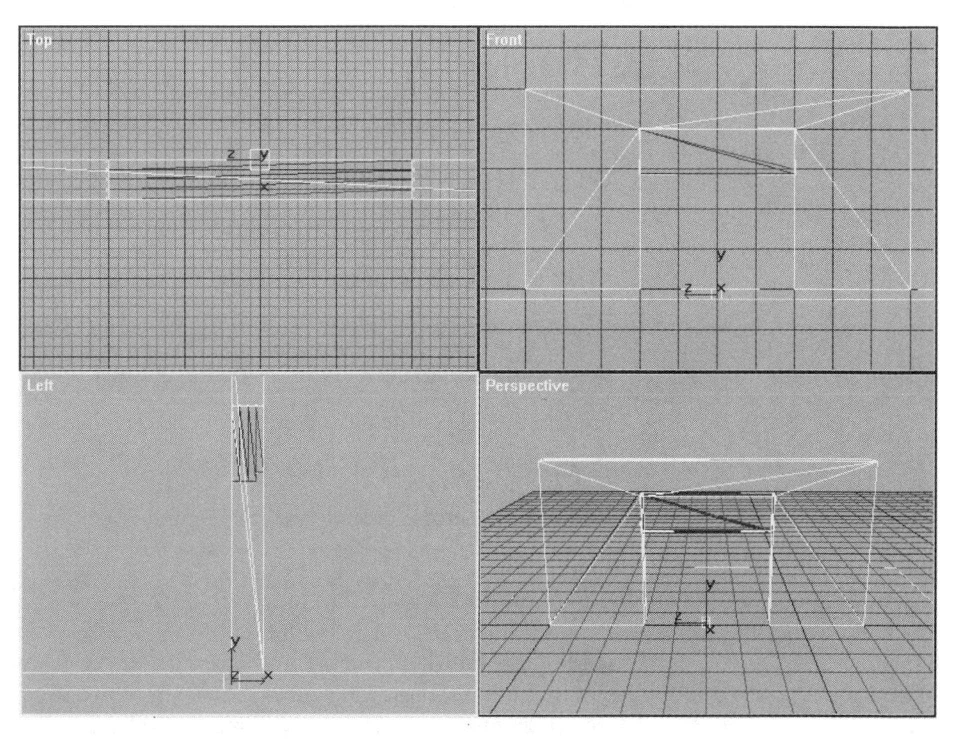


FIGURE 14.20
Dummy box's new position.

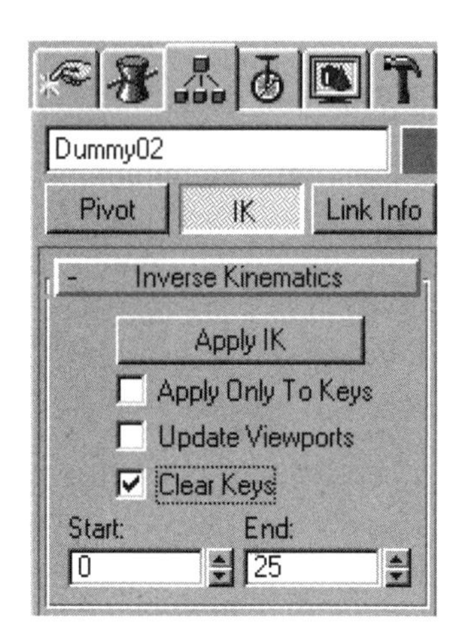


FIGURE 14.21
IK panel for dummy object.

36. Refer to the IK panel for the dummy object. Make sure the Start and End boxes are set to 0 and 25, as shown in Figure 14.21. Pick the Apply IK button. The program will now calculate the placement of all the panels based on the movement of the dummy object. Each panel will move in sequential order.
37. Using the Play button in the perspective viewport, test the animation sequence. You should notice that Panel04 moves first, followed by Panel03, and so on.

## QUESTIONS AND ASSIGNMENTS

### QUESTIONS

1. Define *hierarchy linking.*
2. What is a branch, and what is the significance of the leaf on the branch?
3. How do you link an object with another object?
4. What is the purpose of the Hierarchy command panel?
5. What function can a dummy helper object perform in hierarchy linking?
6. What is the difference between forward and inverse kinematics?
7. Explain the role of the pivot point of a child and the parent in inverse kinematics.
8. Explain the two types of joints.
9. How do you set the precedence of the joints?

### ASSIGNMENTS

1. Open CH14B.MAX created in the lab. Using the dummy object, continue with the animation so that the panels open from frame 26 to frame 50. You will need to follow steps 31 to 34, but this time you will animate the movement of the dummy object in frame 50 and apply IK for frames from 26 to 50.
   Save the scene as CH14C.MAX.
2. Create a robotic arm using forward kinematics.
3. Create a robotic arm using inverse kinematics.

# PART SIX

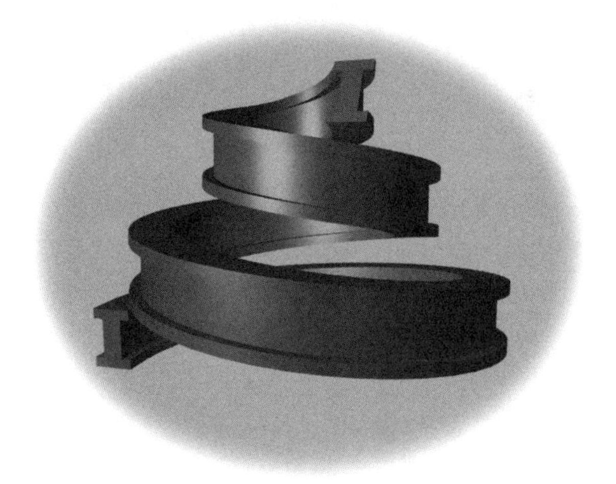

# Practical Applications

# Still Life: Working with Light and Shadow

## 15.1 INTRODUCTION

The effective lighting of a scene adds realism to the final rendering. The contrast between light and shadow makes the objects stand out and appear more three-dimensional. It also adds atmosphere to the scene. Creating the proper lighting for a scene can take a large proportion of the total time it takes to compose the scene. Although it can be as simple as placing one light source to give a desired effect, more often more than one light is needed to create the effect you want. Sometimes you have to simulate, or "fake," light to compensate for the inadequacies of computer-generated light.

The purpose of this project is to allow you to experiment with various types of lighting to understand their effects on a scene. You will make use of an interior scene already created, adjusting the various lights already contained in the scene to see how they behave. You will create still rendered images of the various composed lighting scenes. This will give you a better understanding of the effect of light and shadow.

## 15.2 SCENE COMPOSITION

The first step in this project is to review the scene. You need to go over the various elements that will provide better manipulation of the lighting as you go along.

### Opening the Scene

Open the scene MXLIGHT.MAX. If you have followed the procedure outlined in Appendix A, the file is already installed on your system. If you didn't, you will need to open the file from the CD-ROM that came with this text.

Save the scene as CH15A.MAX so that you can retain the original scene.

## Test Rendering

Once the scene is loaded, activate the camera viewport labeled OVERVIEW and perform a test rendering. Start with the largest image your system will allow. This lets you look over the scene. The rendering makes use of an omni light so that you can see most of the objects in the scene.

Refer to Figure 15.1 and your screen. The scene is composed of a round table in a small room. The room is not complete, but it does have a window and a doorway as well as a floor and a ceiling. An oil lamp, a vase, a single flower, and a picture of a cat in a frame sit on the table. A light fixture hangs from the ceiling.

The oil lamp is composed of several objects, all held together in a group. Included in the group is a flame object that is currently hidden. During this process of lighting the scene, you will have to open the group to unhide the flame object.

## Main Objects

The following are the names of the main objects in the scene, including cameras and lights.

**Groups**

Flower-BrownEye01

Table-Round

Oil-Lamp

Cat-Picture

**Individual Objects**

Vase

Flame (part of Oil-Lamp group); hidden

**Cameras**

Close-up (Target Camera)

Overview (Target Camera)

**Lights**

Light-Flame (Omni Light)

FIGURE 15.1
Overview of lighting project scene.

Light-Ceiling (Target Spotlight)

Light-Sun (Directional Light)

Light-Sun-Accent (Omni Light)

Light-Moon (Directional Light)

Light-Test (Omni Light)

### Project Stages

The project is separated into four lighting stages: Indoor Light, Lamp Light, Sun Light, and Moon Light. By referring to the names of light objects listed previously, you can see how the lights have been named in reference to the lighting stages. The three light types—omni, spot, and directional—have been used for different effects in the lighting stages. In this way you will be able to see how their behavior affects the final rendering.

Remember to use the Hold command just before you perform any operation about which you are not certain. Then you can restore the previous settings with the use of the Fetch command. Also, it is good form to always save your scene file just before performing a rendering. You never know when your computer system may crash, but during a rendering it is commonplace for this to happen.

## 15.3 INDOOR LIGHT

The first lighting stage uses a target spotlight concealed in a ceiling lighting fixture named Light-Ceiling. It is going to simulate an indoor ceiling light turned on at night. Using a special option of the spotlight, it will also act as an omni light, thereby limiting the number of lights required to light an area.

#### Camera View

1. Activate the camera viewport and change the view to Close-Up by right-clicking on the viewport label and picking Views from the pop-up menu. The two cameras will be listed: Overview and Close-up. Pick Close-up.

   The camera viewport should now display a close-up of the table and the items sitting on it, as shown in Figure 15.2.

FIGURE 15.2
Close-up camera view.

### Turning Off the Light-Test

2. In this project you will be turning lights on and off to create the different effects. The Overview scene was lit with the use of an omni light named Light-Test. This was used to light the scene generally so that all the objects could be seen. You need to turn this light off before accessing the other lights. If you didn't, you would get conflicting light sources, ruining the rendering.

Using the Select By Name tool, select the Light-Test object. Open the Modify command panel. Under General Parameters you will find an On box. When the box is checked the light will be used in the scene. Uncheck the box so that the Light-Test will not affect the scene.

### Turning On the Light-Ceiling

3. The light at the ceiling is named Light-Ceiling and is a spotlight. A spotlight is used because it can cast shadows, whereas an omni light can't. You cannot select it because it is part of the Fixture group that is composed of the objects that make up the light fixture. To access the light object, you need to open the Fixture group.

Using the Select By Name tool, select the Fixture object. From the Group pull-down menu, select the Open command. This opens the group to allow access to individual objects in the group.

Now that the group is open, you can use the Select By Name tool to select the Light-Ceiling object. Do so.

The Modify panel should now be displaying the parameters for the Light-Ceiling object. If it isn't, make sure the object is selected and the panel is open.

Turn the light on by checking the On box under General Parameters.

Also notice the color of the light shown in the General Parameters. It is set to pure white light to represent the artificial light of an incandescent lightbulb. By adjusting the V value of the HSV, you can create the effect of a dimmer control on the ceiling light. For this step it is set to 255 for maximum brightness.

Look for the light in the Top, Front, and Left viewports. Because it is selected, it should appear as a white cone inside the ceiling fixture.

### Initial Rendering with Light-Ceiling

4. Use the Render Scene tool and render the Close-Up camera viewport. The resulting figure should look similar to Figure 15.3. The table and objects on it are

FIGURE 15.3
Initial rendering using Light-Ceiling.

FIGURE 15.4
Rendering using Light-Ceiling with Overshoot.

lit nicely, and shadows are cast from the objects. This gives a realistic-looking picture of that area. However, the rest of the room is still too dark, because the spotlight is restricted to shine in a tight area to form distinct shadows.

5. To alleviate the problem of lighting the rest of the room, you are going to modify a parameter of the spotlight. The spotlight is capable of doing double duty, as a spotlight and an omni light. Refer to the Modify panel for the Light-Ceiling and look under Spotlight Parameters. You should see the Overshoot box. When this is turned on, the spotlight will act like a spotlight in the area specified by the hotspot and falloff and like an omni light for the areas beyond.

   Make sure the Overshoot box is checked.

**Rendering with Light-Ceiling Overshoot On**

6. Use the Render Scene tool and render the Close-Up camera viewport. You may want to save the image to a file at this time. The resulting figure should be similar to Figure 15.4. Now the rest of the room is brightly lit, along with the table and its objects. You can see the reflection of the walls and the window in the table top, adding more realism to the image.

   Using the Overshoot method is a quick and easy way of limiting shadows to particular areas while still illuminating the rest of the scene.

7. Use the Select By Name tool to select the Light-Ceiling object. In the Modify panel uncheck the On box to turn the light off.

8. With the Light-Ceiling object still selected (highlighted), use the Close command from the Group pull-down menu to close the Fixture group.

9. Save your scene file.

## 15.4 LAMPLIGHT

You are now going to adjust the Light-Flame object. It is the light that is part of the Oil-Lamp group. It is going to simulate the glow of the oil lamp in a dark room. To add to the rendering, you are going to reveal the Flame object that is also part of the Oil-Lamp group. The Flame object is hidden for the scenes when the lamp is not lit.

1. First select the Oil-Lamp object and use the Open command from the Group pull-down menu to allow access to objects that are part of the Oil-Lamp group.
2. Using the Select By Name tool, select the Light-Flame object. This is an omni light. The omni light is useful for creating a radiating glow, effectively simulating a flame. The drawback is that it does not cast shadows. For this close-up scene, that is not a problem.
3. Using the Modify panel, make sure the On box is checked for the Light-Flame object.

   Look for the light in the Top, Front, and Left viewports. Because it is selected, it should appear as a white faceted shape, inside the oil lamp.

### Initial Rendering of Lamp Light

4. Using the Render Scene tool, render the Close-Up camera viewport. The resulting image should look similar to Figure 15.5 showing the objects on the table revealed in the glow of white light from the lamp. Notice the use of Attenuation. This is the process of limiting how far the light is cast. In this case, the range is 1 ft 2 in. to 1 ft 8 in. This gives the effect of the limited number of lumens cast by the Oil-Lamp. It is not nearly as bright as a 100W lightbulb. You could adjust Attenuation values to give the effect of turning up or down the flame of the lamp, thereby reducing or increasing the area the light reaches. That brings us to the next point. Look at the rendering again. Notice that there is no flame. It currently is a hidden object.

### Revealing the Flame object

5. The display of the Flame object has been set to hide it. To unhide it, open the Display Panel. Make sure no object is selected by using the Select Object tool and picking in open space in the viewport. This will give you access to the Hide by Selection parameters.

   Pick the Unhide By Name button. You will be presented with a list showing the objects that are currently hidden.

   Select Flame from the list and pick the Unhide button. The Flame object should now be displayed in the scene. You may not be able to see it, depending how far away the view is. Activate the Left viewport and try zooming in on the Oil-Lamp to see if you can see the flame object.

FIGURE 15.5
Initial rendering using Light-Flame.

### Adjusting the Light-Flame

6. There is one final adjustment you need to make to the Light-Flame object before you render the scene. The initial rendering you performed using the Light-Flame was with pure white light. This was good for the artificial light of the lightbulb but not so realistic for a flame light. You are going to add some color to the lamp light.

   Use the Select By Name tool to select the Light-Flame object. Open the Modify panel and refer to the General Parameters of the Light-Flame. You are going to adjust the HSV settings.

   First make sure V is set to 255, S to 128, and, finally, H to 41. This will give a yellow cast to the flame light.

### Rendering with Yellow Light-Flame and Flame Showing

7. Use the Render Scene tool and render the Close-Up camera viewport. You may want to save the image to a file at this time. The resulting figure should look similar to Figure 15.6. You can now see that the flame of the lamp and the light cast have a yellow hue. The use of colored light is very effective in simulating different lighting types and conditions.
8. With the Light-Flame still selected and the Modify panel open, uncheck the On box so that the light is turned off.
9. You also need to hide the Flame object. To do this you are going to learn another special technique. Because the Flame is part of a group, you cannot just select it and hide it. Only a closed group can be hidden by selection. If we close the Oil-Lamp group and hide, all the objects comprising the lamp will hide. To get only the flame to hide, you first need to hide everything and then unhide everything except the Flame.

   Make sure nothing in the scene is selected. Open the Display panel and pick the Hide Unselected button. Everything in the scene should hide.

   Now, pick the Unhide by Name button and a list of the all the objects in the scene should appear.

   While holding down on the CTRL key, select and highlight the Flame object. Pick the Invert button. This has the effect of unhighlighting the Flame object and highlighting the rest.

**FIGURE 15.6** Rendering using Light-Flame.

Pick the Unhide button and all the objects should reappear, except the Flame.

10. Save your scene file.

## 15.5 SUNLIGHT

You are now going to simulate a bright sunny day with sunlight streaming through the window. This scene requires a Directional light object called Light-Sun to act as the sun. There is also going to be an additional omni light called Light-Sun-Accent.

1. Using the Select By Name tool, select the Light-Sun object and turn it on using the Modify panel.

   Look for the light in the Top, Front, and Left viewports. Because it is selected, it should appear as a white arrow shape, outside the room pointing in.

### Initial Rendering of Light-Sun

2. Using the Render Scene tool, render the Close-Up camera viewport. The resulting image should look similar to Figure 15.7, which shows the objects on the table revealed by light shining through the window. However, the light is not very strong. It looks more like pale moonlight than bright sunlight.

### Adjusting the Intensity of the Light-Sun

3. Refer to the Modify panel for the Light-Sun. The V value of HSV is set at the highest. This is the strongest value for that color. However, look under that and you see a setting called Multiplier. This setting has the effect of multiplying the HSV light intensity.

   Set the Multiplier value to 3 and render the camera view again. The result should look like Figure 15.8.

   The light is much stronger now, showing brightly where it strikes surfaces. But the edges are too fuzzy and indistinct. This is because the rendering was done with Shadow Maps. Shadow Maps are great when you want soft shadows. But for bright sun you would normally want hard-edged shadows. For this you need Ray-Traced shadows. This takes longer to render but is more detailed. Its also has the added effect of creating shadows of glass, such as the glass cover on the Oil-Lamp.

FIGURE 15.7
Initial rendering using Light-Sun.

FIGURE 15.8
Rendering using adjusted Light-Sun with multiplier.

### Creating Ray-Traced Shadows

4. Go to the bottom of the panel under Shadow Parameters and check the Use Ray-Traced Shadows button. Render the camera view again. The new results should be similar to Figure 15.9.

   The shadow edges are now distinct. When looking closely at the shadows cast by the Oil-Lamp, you can see that some light passes through the glass giving the shadow a transparent look.

### Adding Color and Accent Lighting

5. The last step before the final rendering of the sunlight scene is to add some color to the sunlight and add some accent lighting. Sunlight isn't usually pure white. As with the oil lamp, you are going to add some yellow to it. You will not add as much as in the case of the oil lamp, but a hint of yellow represents early morning light.

   With the Light-Sun still selected and the Modify panel open, go to the General Parameters section and enter the following values for the HSV settings: V 255, S 60, and H 45.

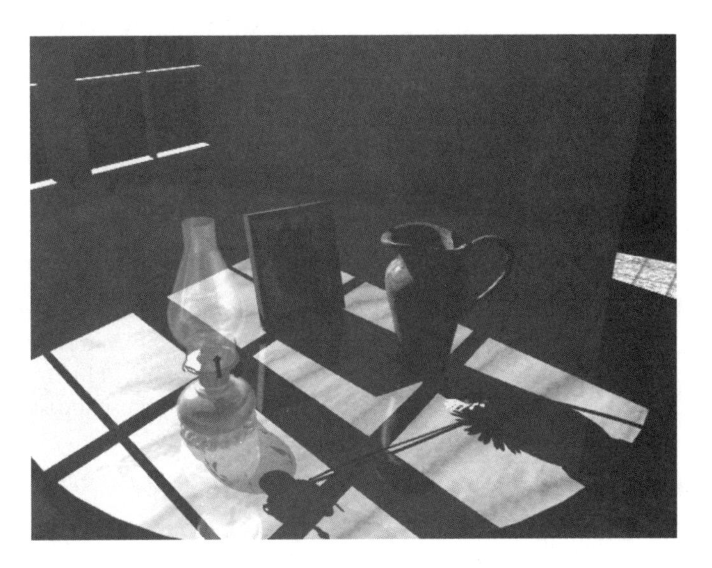

FIGURE 15.9
Rendering using adjusted Light-Sun with Ray-Traced shadows.

FIGURE 15.10
Final Light-Sun rendering.

6. Even though the sunlight is bright and shines strongly through the window, the rest of the room is too dark. There is no radiosity effect. Radiosity happens from light reflected off surfaces to illuminate an area. Currently 3D Studio MAX does not have the capability to do this.

    Using the Select By Name tool, select the Light-Sun-Accent object. Open the Modify panel for the object. Make sure that the On box is checked. Notice that the omni light's color is set to complement the Light-Sun's color. This will simulate the sunlight being reflected and illuminating the room.

    Look for the light in the Top, Front, and Left viewports. Because it is selected, it should appear as a white, faceted shape inside the room.

7. Render the camera viewport for a final rendering. You may want to save the image to a file at this time. The results should look similar to Figure 15.10.
8. Save your scene file.

## 15.6 MOONLIGHT

The last stage of this project is to simulate moonlight. The light itself behaves much the same as the sunlight but has a different color and softer shadows This scene requires a Directional light object called Light-Moon to act as the moon.

1. Using the Select By Name tool, select the Light-Moon object and turn it on using the Modify panel.

    Look for the light in the Top, Front, and Left viewports. Because it is selected, it should appear as a white arrow shape outside the room pointing in.

### Initial Rendering of Light-Moon

2. Using the Render Scene tool, render the Close-Up camera viewport. The resulting image should look similar to Figure 15.11, which shows the objects on the table revealed by pale light shining through the window. In this case shadow maps were used because indistinct shadows are wanted to give an ethereal atmosphere to the image.

FIGURE 15.11
Initial rendering using Light-Moon.

**Adjusting the Color of Light-Moon**

3. To add to the atmosphere of the scene, you are going to change the color of the Light-Moon from white to blue. This will give a cooler feel to the light.

   In the General Parameters of the Light-Moon, change the settings for HSV to V 255, S 141, and H 148.

   Render the scene again. You may want to save the image to a file as the final rendering for the moonlight.

4. Save your scene file.

## 15.7 GLASS'S EFFECT ON LIGHT

One last item you may want to check is the effect of glass on the passage of light. The two objects Winglas1 and Winglas2 have been hidden throughout this project. They represent the planes of glass for the windows. They have glass material properties assigned to them. Unhide them, render the sunlight scene again, and observe the results.

FIGURE 15.12
Final rendering of Light-Moon with blue light.

# Architectural Presentation: Camera Techniques

## 16.1 INTRODUCTION

There are various ways to present an architectural model to a client using 3D Studio MAX, from showing various still images depicting different views to creating an animated presentation. In either case it involves the selection and placement of a camera. For stills, a Target Camera is used to focus on a particular area. For animated flybys, a Free Camera can be used.

The purpose of this project is to allow you to experiment with different applications of cameras. You will use a scene of several city blocks that holds a number of simplified buildings. The focus of the scene is a convention center. The simulated purpose is to create images of the city scene that present the convention center. Contained within the scene are a number of cameras in various positions. By accessing and manipulating these cameras you will gain a better understanding on how to *shoot* an architectural city scene.

## 16.2 SCENE COMPOSITION

The first step in this project is to review the scene. You need to examine the various elements that comprise each camera scene that forms the project.

### Opening the Scene

Open the scene MXCITY.MAX. If you followed the procedure outlined in Appendix A, the file is already installed on your system. If you didn't, you will need to open the file from the CD-ROM that came with this text.

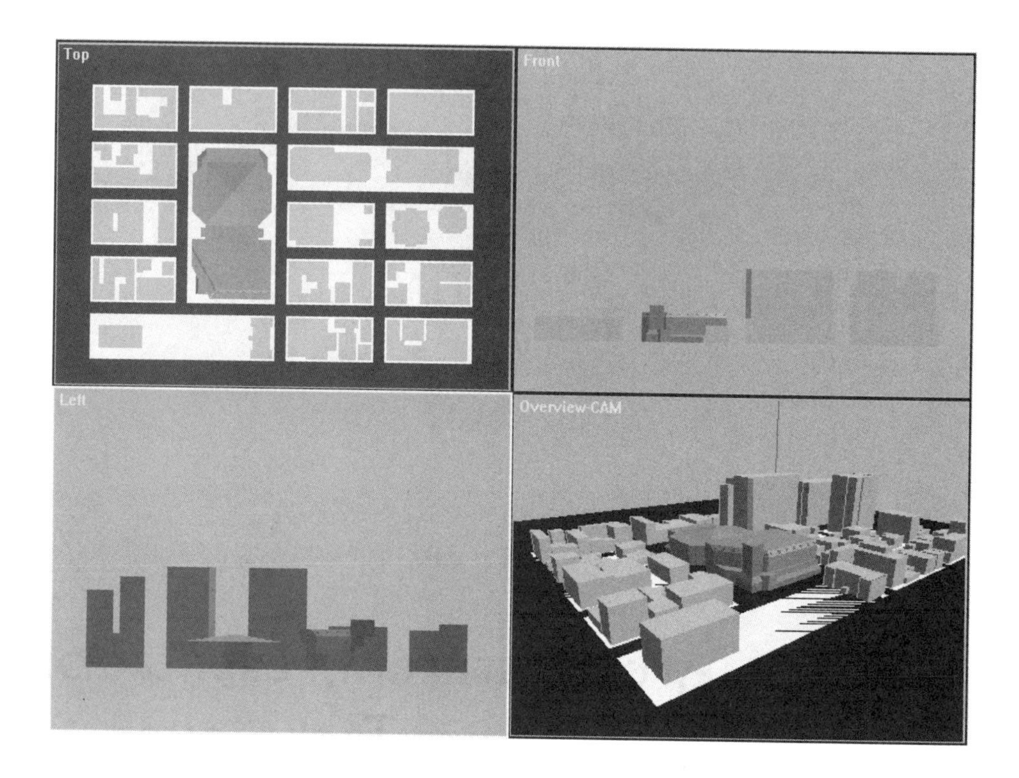


FIGURE 16.1
Four viewports

Save the scene as CH16A.MAX so that you can retain the original scene.

The screen should show four viewports depicting the Top, Front, Left and Overview camera view. All are in wireframe. Go to each viewport in turn, and by right-clicking on the viewport label, set each to show Smooth+Highlight. This will give you better orientation later when you will be using animated cameras. Your screen should look similar to Figure 16.1.

## Test Rendering

Activate the camera viewport labeled Overview and perform a test rendering. Start with the largest image your system will allow. This lets you look over the scene. The rendering makes use of an omni light so that you can see most of the objects in the scene.

Refer to Figure 16.2 and your screen. The scene is composed of a number of city blocks. Most of the buildings are simplified. In the approximate middle is the convention center. It is composed of two sections, with one section of the structure used for hotel conventions and the other used as an exhibition hall. There are two glass canopies at the exhibition end, with one long glass canopy at the side of the hotel. There is also a glass tower at the corner of the center that is the architectural focus of the building.

This building is not to be used to teach you how to design a commercial building but as a vehicle to practice camera techniques. As such, there is minimal detail and no special application of materials. You may want to add materials to the convention center and simplified buildings after you have completed the project to enhance the images and animations.

In the CD Rom file, a variety of cameras are already created and hidden, as are path shapes that will be used to animate camera movement. You will reveal these as you proceed through the project.

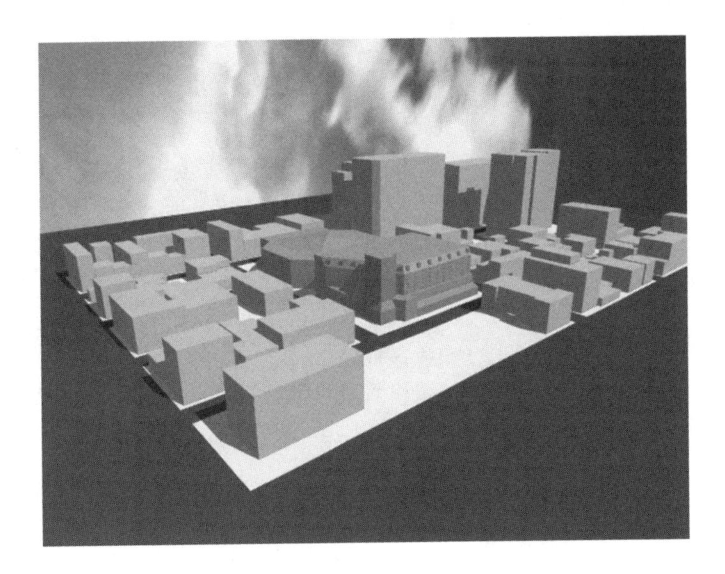

FIGURE 16.2
Overview of camera project scene.

## Main Objects

The following are the names of the main objects in the scene, including cameras and lights.

**Groups**

Buildings

Center-Convention

**Individual Objects**

Asphalt

Sky-BackDrop

Walkways

**Shapes**

AroundView-PATH (Circle)

CarView-PATH (Bezier Spline)

JetView-PATH (Bezier Spline)

**Cameras**

AerialView-CAM (Target Camera)

AroundView-CAM (Target Camera)

CarView-CAM (Free Camera)

JetView-CAM (Free Camera)

Overview-CAM(Target Camera)

RoofView-CAM (Target Camera); not created

TowerView-CAM (Target Camera)

**Lights**

Sun (Directional Light)

### Project Stages

The project is separated into six camera stages: Aerial View, Tower View, Roof View, Around View, Car View, and Jet View. By referring to the names of camera objects listed previously, you can see how the stages have been named in reference to the cameras. Two camera types, Target and Free, have been used for different effects. In this way you will be able to see how their behavior affects the view displayed.

Remember to use the Hold command just before you perform any operation about which you are unsure. Then you can restore the previous settings with the use of the Fetch command. It is also good form to always save your scene file just before performing a rendering. You never know when your computer system may crash, but during rendering is a likely place for it to happen.

## 16.3 AERIAL VIEW

The first stage makes use of a camera to generate an aerial view. Refer to the Top viewport. It shows an orthographic view looking down on the city. Because it is an orthographic view, everything appears flat. You do not get any impression of depth. This is one of the reasons to use a camera to create a view. It gives you control over creating a perspective view. It this case a Target Camera will be used. A Target Camera allows you to position the camera and point it at a target.

#### Camera View

1. Activate the overview viewport and change the view to Close-Up by right-clicking on the viewport label and picking Views from the pop-up menu. There are a number of cameras listed. These will be used throughout the project. For this step, pick AerialView-CAM.

   The camera viewport should now display an aerial view, as shown in Figure 16.3. However, the view is too close.

#### Adjusting the Camera Lens

2. To get the proper view, you need to adjust the lens size of the camera. Before you can do this, you need to reveal the hidden camera.

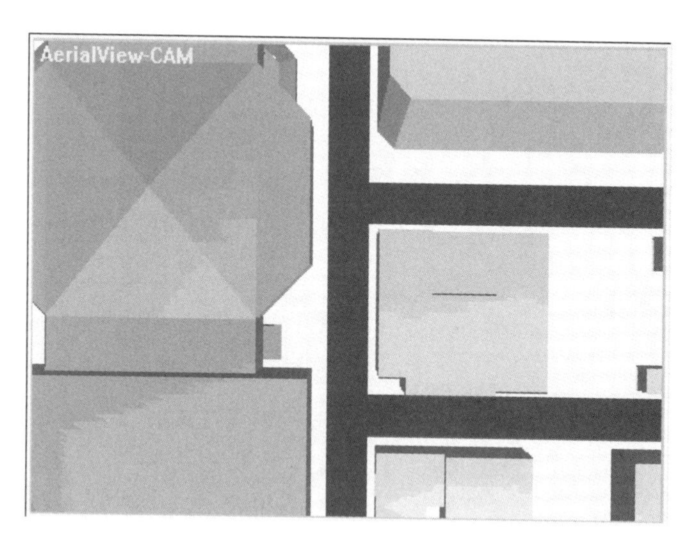


FIGURE 16.3
Aerial camera view.

Open the Display Panel. Make sure no object is selected by using the Select Object tool and picking in open space in the viewport. This will give you access to the Hide by Selection parameters.

Pick the Unhide By Name button. You will be presented with a list showing the objects that are currently hidden.

While holding down on the CTRL key, select AerialView-CAM and AerialView.Target from the list and pick the Unhide button. The camera and target object should now be displayed in the scene.

In the Front viewport, you can see the camera above the city pointing down to the target that is at city level.

3. Using the Select By Name tool, select the AerialView-CAM object. Open the Modify command panel. Look in the Parameters rollout for the camera. You should see the lens size in a box. By default it is set at 50 mm. Below this are nine stock lens buttons, as shown in Figure 16.4.
4. Pick on the 15-mm button. This is the widest stock wide-angle lens, and gives it a wide view of the city. Look back and forth from the Top viewport to the camera viewport. You can see how the camera viewport gives you the feel of being above the city. With the added perspective, you can tell the buildings have height.
5. Now you want to tighten the view a bit. The 15-mm lens shows too much outside the city area. Pick the 20-mm stock lens. This is still wide-angle, but it brings the view in so that you don't see so much of the area outside the city.
6. Perform a rendering of the camera view. You may want to save the image as a file. Your rendering should be similar to Figure 16.5. Notice the shadows of the buildings.
7. Using the Display panel, hide the AerialView-CAM by selecting it and then picking the Hide Selected button.
8. Save your scene file.

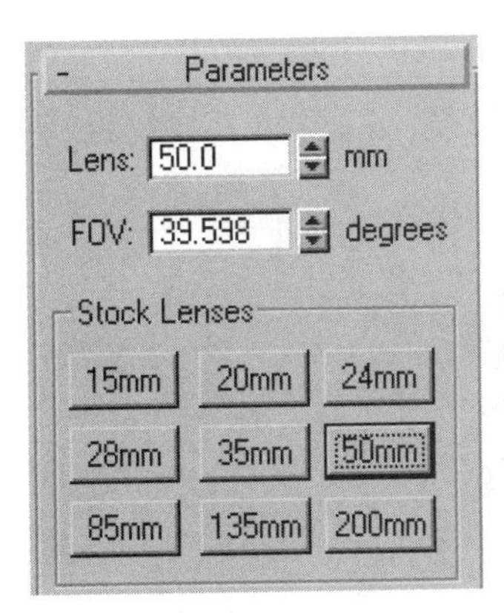


**FIGURE 16.4**
Lens parameters.

**FIGURE 16.5**
Rendered Aerial view with 20-mm lens.

As a rule of thumb, the 50-mm lens is the standard lens. It displays an unenhanced view; it is neither wide-angle nor telephoto (zoom). Lenses below 50 mm are considered wide-angle, showing more of an area. Lenses above 50 mm are telephoto, or zoom, lenses and are used to show a closer view of an area. By using different lens sizes, you can display large areas of a scene or focus in on specific areas, all without moving the camera.

## 16.4 TOWER VIEW

This next stage again uses a target camera. Its center of interest is going to be the entrance tower on the convention center. The view to be depicted is of a pedestrian on the sidewalk looking up at the tower. Like the camera before, this one is hidden and must be revealed to modify it.

### Revealing the Camera and Target

1. Using the Display panel, pick the Unhide By Name button and highlight TowerView-CAM and TowerView.Target. Unhide these two objects. You should be able to see the camera symbol in the Top and Front viewports.
2. Replace AerialView-CAM with TowerView-CAM in the camera viewport by right-clicking on the viewport label, picking Views and then selecting the name from the list. The view should look similar to Figure 16.6. As in the case of the initial aerial view, a 50-mm lens was used and is too close. You do not get the full effect of the tower.

### Adjusting the Lens Size

3. Using what you have learned so far, adjust the lens of the TowerView-CAM to get a view similar to Figure 16.7. Figure 16.7 is a rendered image. When you have adjusted the lens of the camera to the desired view, render the view and save it to a file.
4. Using the Display panel, hide the TowerView-CAM by selecting it and then picking the Hide Selected button.
5. Save your scene file.

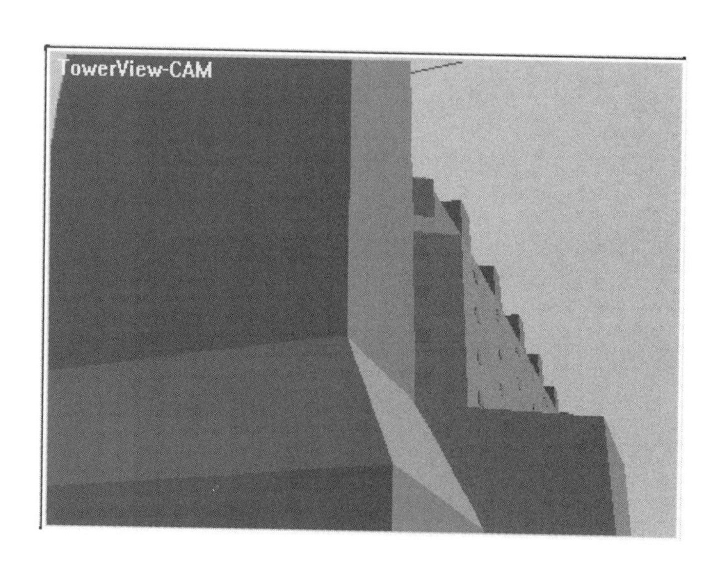


FIGURE 16.6
Tower view.

FIGURE 16.7
Rendered image of proper tower view.

## 16.5 ROOF VIEW

In this stage you are going to create a camera that is going to be on the roof of an adjacent building. The building is higher than the convention center, so the camera is looking down on the exhibition building. From what you have learned in Chapter 11 and this chapter, you should be able to place the camera, direct the view, and choose the proper lens.

### Placing the Camera

1. Refer to Figure 16.8. It shows a close-up view in the top, back, and left viewports. The camera viewport displays the view created by the camera you are about to create.

FIGURE 16.8
Close-up viewports.

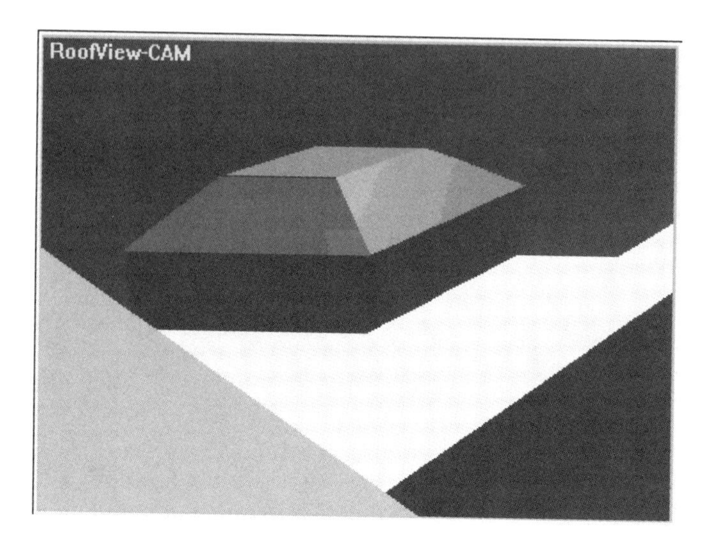


FIGURE 16.9
Close-up view of solarium.

2. Create a target camera called RoofView-CAM. If you look at the top view of the center, the camera is on the roof of the building that is in the upper left, across the street from the exhibition part of the center. The exhibition part is the upper part of the convention center in the top view.

   The target of the camera should be near the glass solarium of the exhibition building, as shown in the top view.

   The initial lens setting is 15 mm, displaying a view similar to the RoofView-CAM shown in Figure 16.8.

### Adjusting the Lens for Different Views

3. Once you have placed the camera and target so that you have a view similar to the camera view in Figure 16.8, you are going to adjust the lens to give different views.

   Figure 16.9 shows the first view, a close-up view of the solarium. To get this view you should not have to move the camera, only change the lens size.

4. Now adjust the lens size so that more of the exhibition building is displayed, as shown in Figure 16.10.

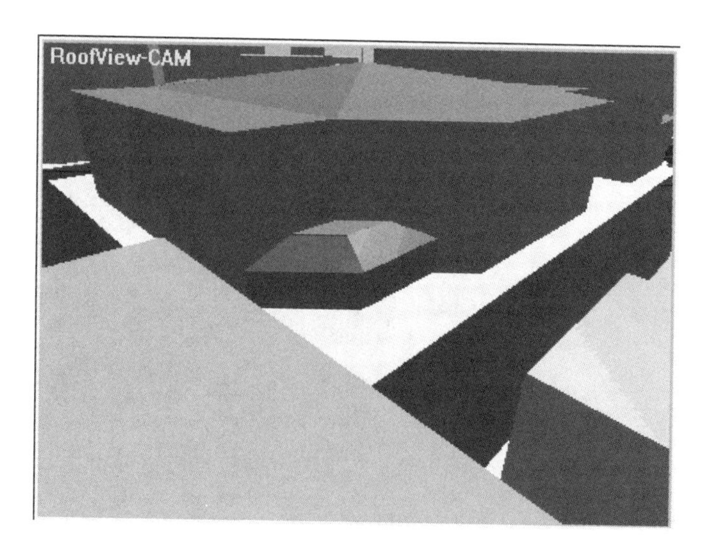


FIGURE 16.10
Overview of exhibition building.

5. Using the Display panel, hide the RoofView-CAM by selecting it and then picking the Hide Selected button.
6. Save your scene file.

At this point you should have a good understanding of the application of cameras to generate a still image. The next stage is to apply camera movement to present the convention center.

## 16.6 AROUND VIEW

In this stage of the project you are going to animate a camera so that it revolves around a selected area. The purpose is to create an animated presentation that shows off the convention center from different angles. To do this a path is required. In this case it is a simple circle spline that lies above the convention center. You are going to change the position controller of the camera from a linear form to a path. This means that the camera will move along the path over a series of frames.

### Revealing the Camera and Path

1. Using the Display panel, pick the Unhide By Name button and highlight AroundView-CAM, AroundView–Target, and AroundView-PATH. Unhide these three objects. You should be able to see the camera symbol and circular path in all the viewports. If you can't, use the zoom commands so that you are able to see the camera and the path.
2. Replace RoofView-CAM with AroundView-CAM in the camera viewport by right-clicking on the viewport label, picking Views, and then selecting the name from the list. The screen should look similar to Figure 16.11.

FIGURE 16.11
Around view.

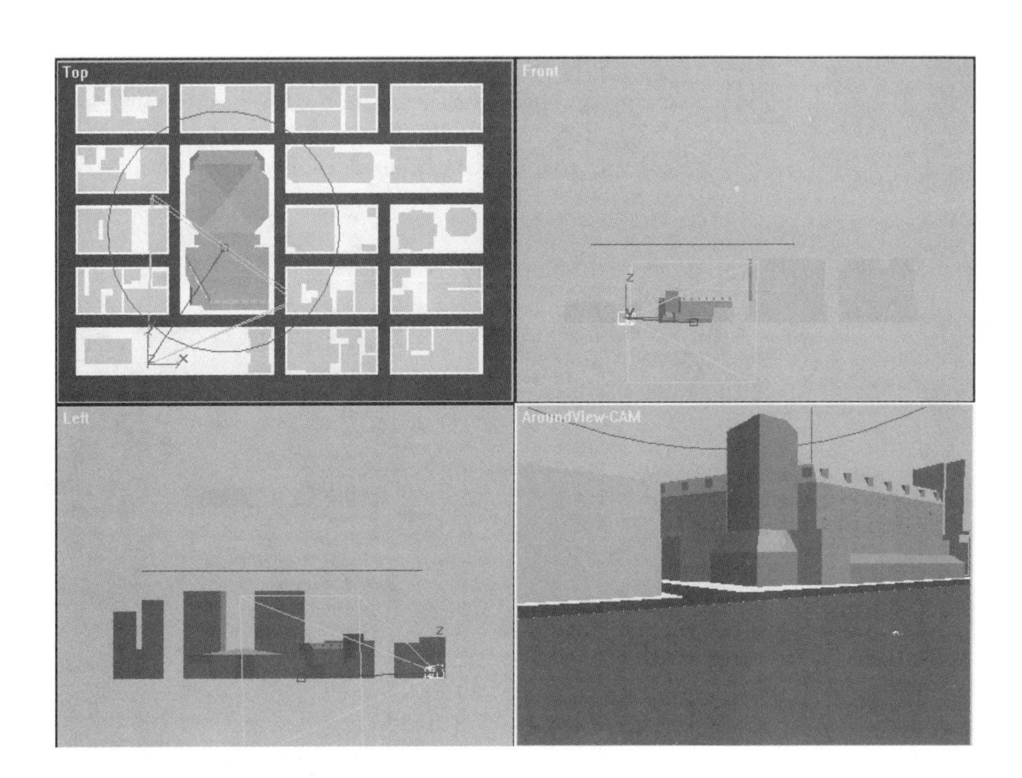

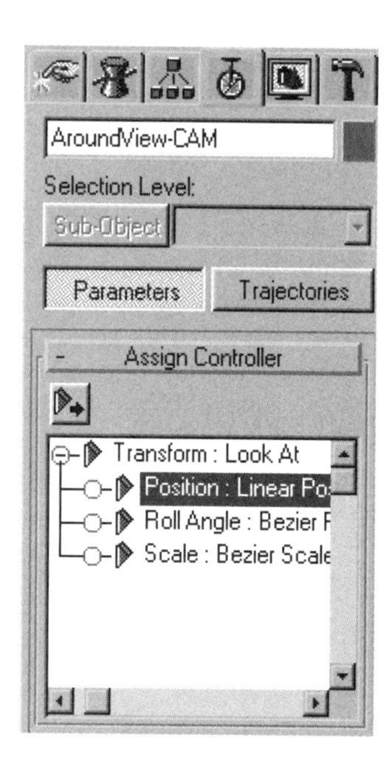


FIGURE 16.12
Assign the Controller rollout for the AroundView-CAM.

### Changing the Position Controller

3. At this point the camera is free to move anywhere in the scene because its position controller is set to linear. What you are going to do is modify the controller so that the camera uses a path to determine its position.
   Using the Select By Name tool, select the AroundView-CAM object.

4. Open the Motion command panel and open the Assign Controller rollout.
   Highlight the Position: Linear Position controller, as shown in Figure 16.12.

5. Pick the Assign Controller button. The Replace Position Controller dialog will appear. Highlight Path from the list, as shown in Figure 16.13, and pick OK.
   Refer back to the Motion command panel and you will see that new Parameter rollouts have been added. Pan down until you can see the Path Parameters rollout.

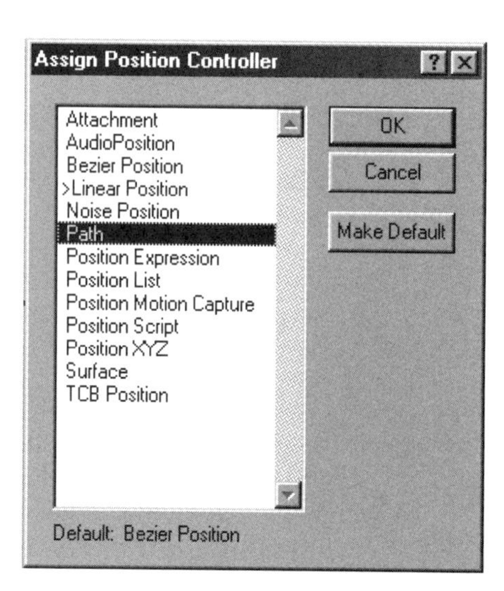


FIGURE 16.13
Replace Position Controller dialog.

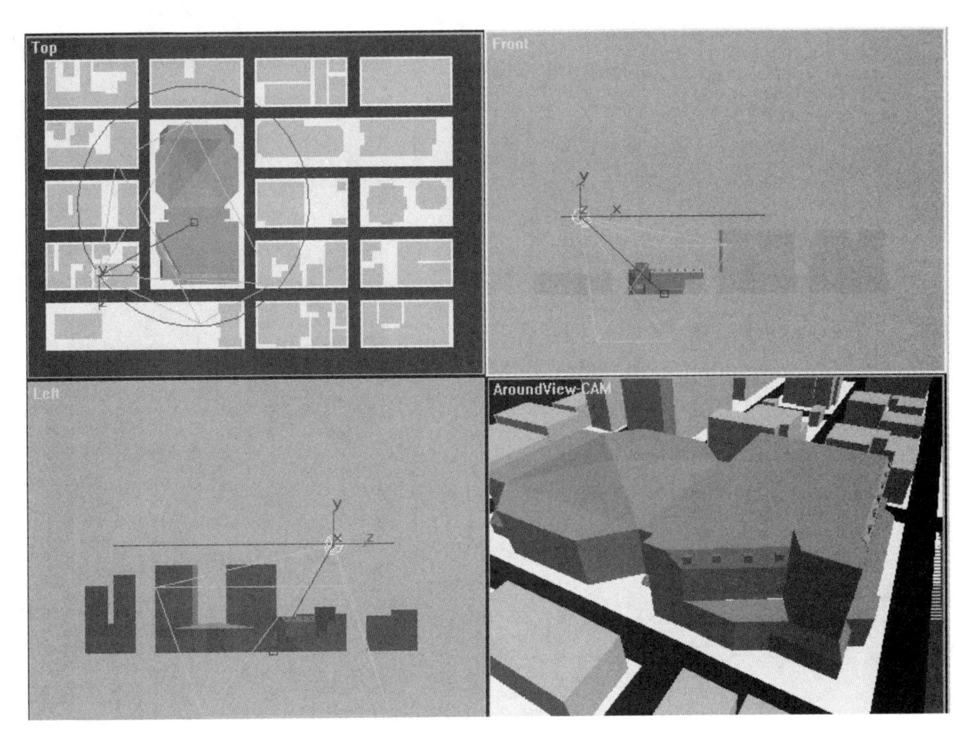

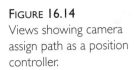

FIGURE 16.14
Views showing camera assign path as a position controller.

6. Select the Pick Path button from the Path Parameters. It will turn green, signifying it is active. While it is active, pick the circle path in the Front viewport. The camera view should immediately change to look similar to Figure 16.14.

   Notice the position of the camera on the circle. Its location is defined by a key vertex, on the circle spline, referred to as the *first vertex*. You can modify the spline and make a new vertex the first vertex or you can use the Rotation transform to rotate the circle.

**Testing the Animation**

7. To test the animation at this stage, activate the camera viewport and pick the Next Frame tool. The view should move to the next frame. Slowly pick the Next Frame tool several times in a row and watch the other viewports. You should be able to see the camera symbol move around the circle and at the same time, the camera should display the matching view.

**Creating a Preview**

8. It is often useful to create a preview of the animation just to see the behavior of the camera.

   Select the Make Preview command from the Rendering pull-down menu. You should be presented with a Make Preview dialog, as shown in Figure 16.15.

   Check to make sure your settings match those in the figure and then pick the Create button. The preview frames will appear one at a time as the entire file is created. Once it is done it goes into play mode, allowing you to play the preview. Do so. Close the windows once you have seen enough.

   For this animation only 100 frames were used. For an actual presentation you would probably want more.

9. Save your scene file and hide the camera, target, and path.

**Creating the Final Animation**

10. You are now going to create a final animation of the camera moving around the convention center. This may take some time, so be prepared for the wait. Render-

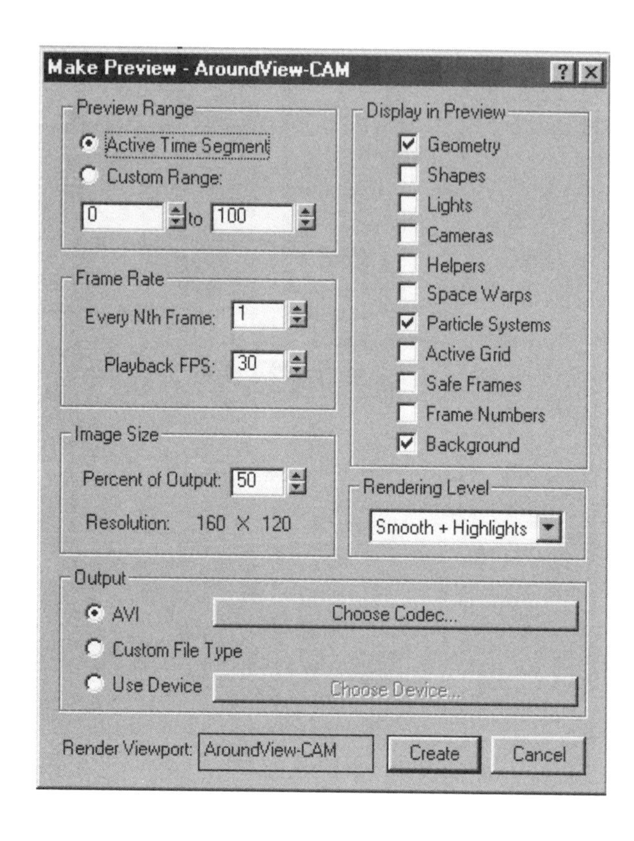


FIGURE 16.15
Make Preview dialog.

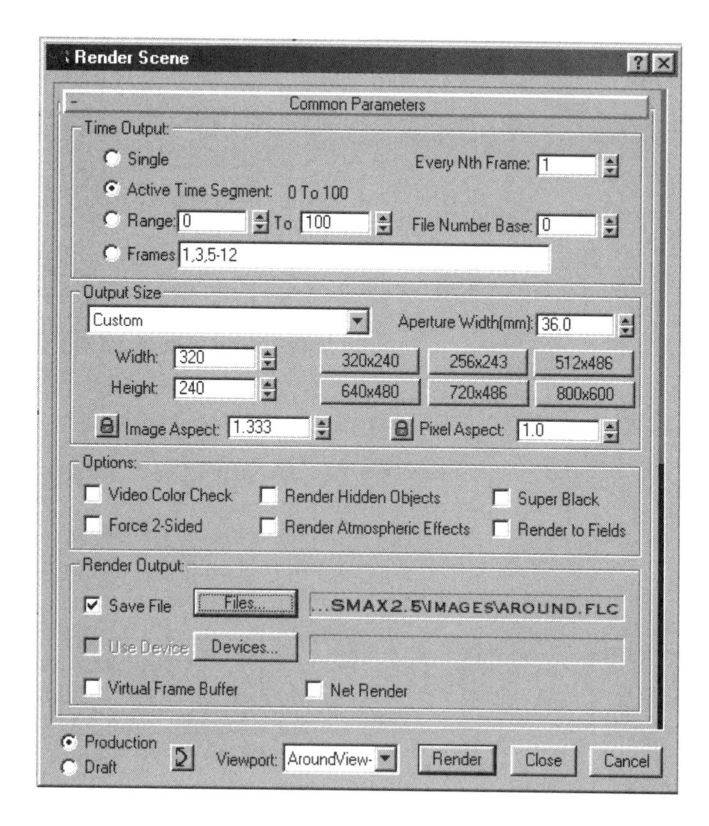


FIGURE 16.16
Render Scene dialog box.

ing, with shadow casting off, a 320 × 240 image using a Pentium II 350 Mhz system with 96 MB of RAM takes about 6 minutes.

Pick the Render Scene tool and refer to Figure 16.16 for the settings. Where you save your file and what file type you choose is up to you.

11. Using the View File command from the File pull-down menu, play your final animation.

## 16.7 CAR VIEW

The next two stages are used to show you what can be done by having a camera follow a path. In the last section, the camera moved around a path but stayed focused on one spot. In this stage and the next, a Free Camera will be used. A Free Camera has no target and is basically free to point to where it wants. The purpose of this is to have the camera follow a path and point wherever the path goes. The other added element is the ability of the camera to bank, which is the movement an airplane makes when it leans into a turn.

In this stage you are going to modify a camera attached to a path so that it follows the path. The path runs along several streets at ground level, simulating a car driving quickly down the street.

**Revealing the Camera and Path**

1. Using the Display panel, pick the Unhide By Name button and highlight CarView-CAM and CarView-PATH. Unhide these two objects. Because it is a Free Camera, there is no target object. You should be able to see the camera symbol and the winding path in all the viewports. If you can't, use the Zoom commands so that you are able to see the camera and the path.
2. Replace AroundView-CAM with CarView-CAM in the camera viewport by right-clicking on the viewport label, picking Views, and then selecting the name from the list. The screen should look similar to Figure 16.17.

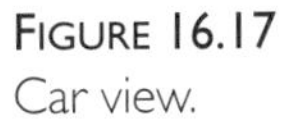

FIGURE 16.17
Car view.

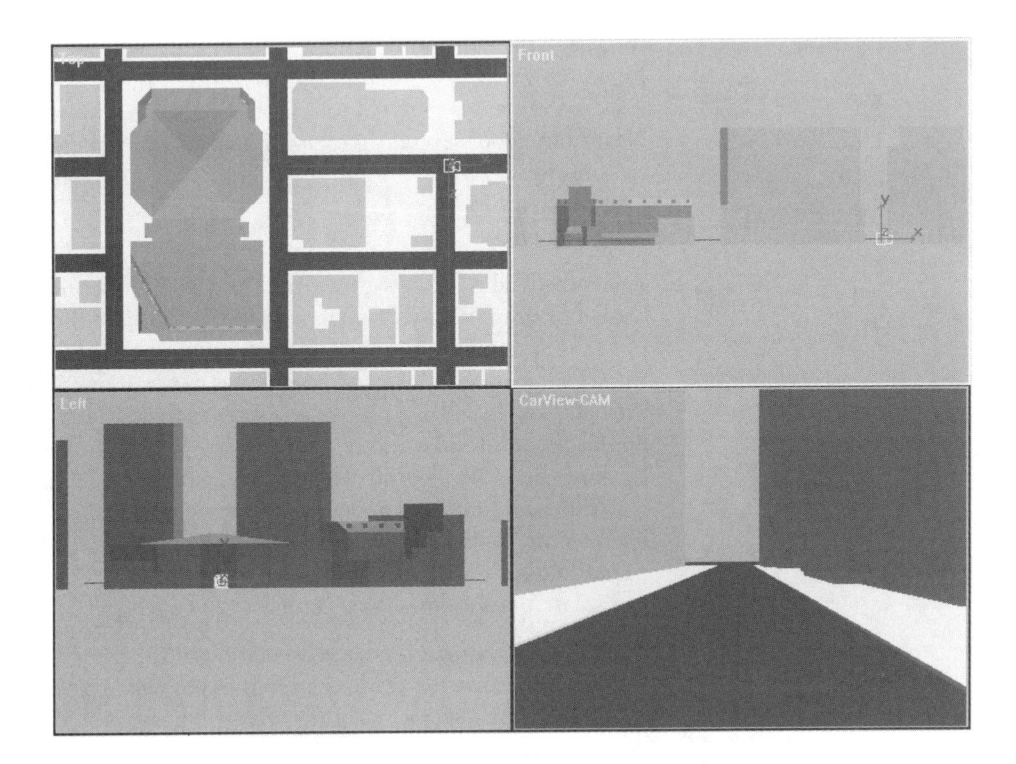

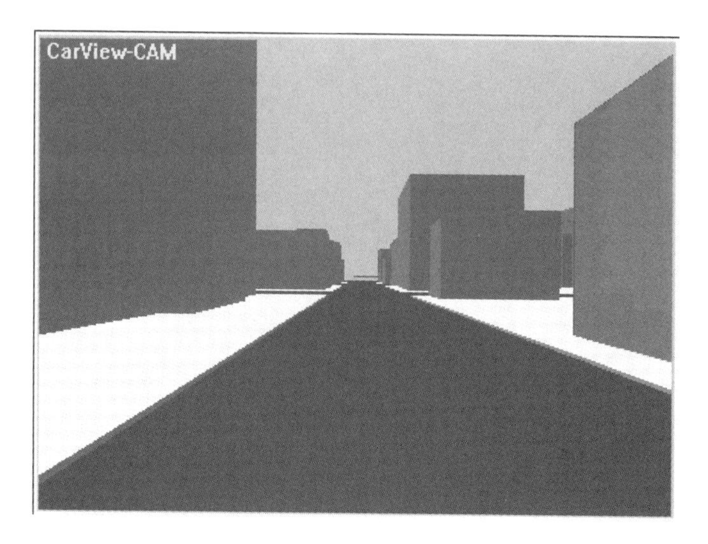


FIGURE 16.18
Camera following the path.

Look at the direction in which the camera is pointing in the Top viewport. It is actually pointing away from the path. The path is the red line winding through the streets.

3. Try picking the Next Frame tool and watch the progress of the camera and the resulting view. It points in the wrong direction. You can't see where you're going, only where you've been. Let's remedy that.

   Return to frame 0.

### Camera Follows Path

4. Using the Select By Name tool, select the CarView-CAM object.

5. Open the Motion command panel and open the Assign Controller rollout. The camera has its position controller already assigned to the path.

   Pan down to the Path Parameters rollout. Notice the Follow check box. When you check this box, the camera is forced to follow the path it is assigned to. Check the box and watch the camera and the view. It should look similar to Figure 16.18.

   The camera is now pointing in the right direction along the path. Try the Next Frame tool several times and watch the movement of the camera and the camera view.

### Creating a Preview

6. Select the Make Preview command from the Rendering pull-down menu. You should be presented with a Make Preview dialog, as shown in Figure 16.19.

   Check to make sure your settings match those in the figure and then pick the Create button. This preview is going to use 10 FPS (frames per second). The preview frames will appear one at a time as the entire file is created. Once it is done, it goes into play mode, allowing you to play the preview. Do so. You can see how the camera points wherever the path goes. At the street corners, the path is rounded so that the camera has to swing around the corner and then correct itself before continuing straight down the street. This simulates the movement of a speeding car trying to negotiate sharp corners.

   Close the windows once you have seen enough.

7. You can create a final rendered animation of the car view if you like. You may want to customize the number of frames per second using the Time Configuration tool in the lower right of the screen. Setting it at 10 to 15 FPS should give

FIGURE 16.19
Make Preview dialog.

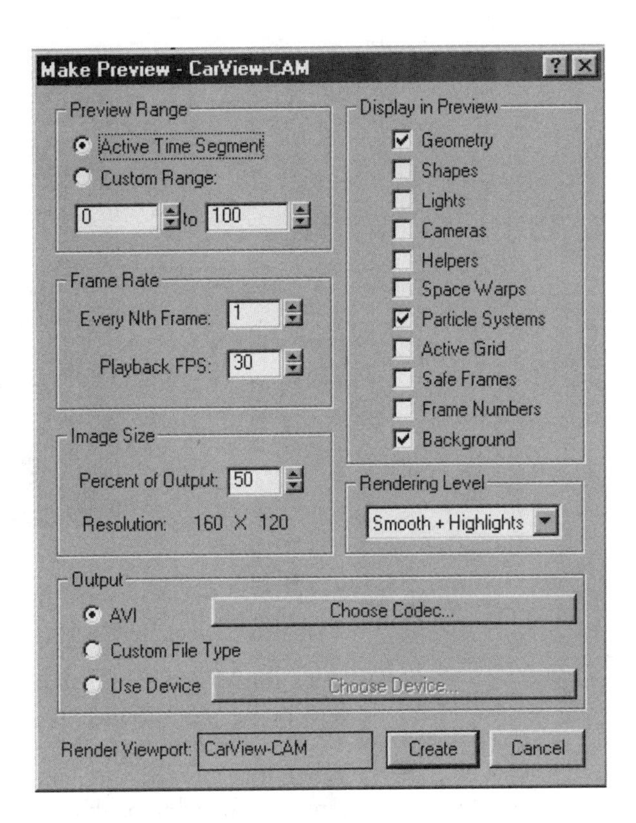


you plenty of movement without having to increase the number of frames in the entire animation.

8. Save your scene file and hide the camera and path.

## 16.8 JET VIEW

In this stage the camera is going to simulate a jet zooming over the cityscape. It is similar to the car view in that it uses a path for the camera to follow. However, in this stage the path starts out above the buildings, passes over them, and loops between them. To aid in the simulation of the movement of a jet, you will activate *follow* and *banking* as well.

### Revealing the Camera and Path

1. Using the Display panel, pick the Unhide By Name button and highlight JetView-CAM and JetView-PATH. Unhide these two objects. Because it is a Free Camera there is no target object. You should be able to see the camera symbol and winding path in all the viewports. If you can't, use the Zoom commands so that you are able to see the camera and the path.

2. Replace CarView-CAM with JetView-CAM in the camera viewport by right-clicking on the viewport label, picking Views, and then selecting the name from the list. The camera is already set to follow the path.

3. Pick the Next Frame tool slowly several times in succession until the camera and view turn around the corner. Notice how the movement is flat, as if the jet can turn without banking.

   Go to frame 24, as shown in Figure 16.20. This frame represents the jet coming out of a sharp turn. To simulate real life, the jet would be banking at this point to achieve the turn. Let's fix that.

FIGURE 16.20
Jet view without banking.

### Camera Banking

4. Using the Select By Name tool, select the JetView-CAM object.
5. Open the Motion command panel and open the Assign Controller rollout. The camera has its position controller already assigned to the path.

   Pan down to the Path Parameters rollout. Make sure that Follow is checked. When it is checked, the Bank box is available. When you check this box, the camera is forced to bank around corners in the path to which it is assigned. Check the box and set the Bank Amount to 10. Bank Amount controls the degree of twist the camera performs. For slow, mild turns, a low number would be used. For this project a high number is used to simulate a fast, sharp turn.

   Now refer to your camera view or Figure 16.21. Notice the twisted camera view. This is the simulated banking of the camera in a sharp turn. Try using the Next Frame tool several times in succession and watch how the camera banks back and forth, depending on the direction of the turn.
6. Save your scene file.

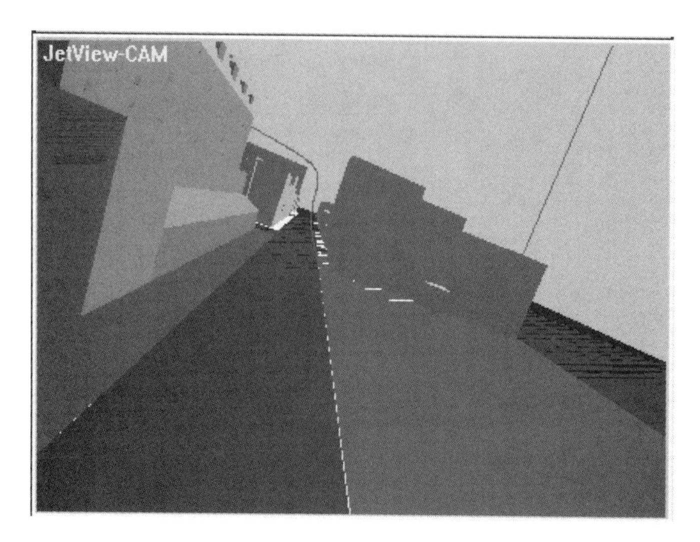

FIGURE 16.21
Jet view with banking added.

### Preview and Final Rendering

7. Create a preview of the jet animation. Remember to use 10 FPS. Play the preview several times so that you can see how the camera twists when banking.
8. You may want to create a final rendering of the jet view. Experiment with the number of frames per second to get the feel of the speed of the jet.

## 16.9 BANKING AND THE CAR VIEW

One last item with which you may want to experiment is to add banking to the camera used for the car view. This could simulate a car riding up on two wheels as it careens around a corner at high speeds. Try it out to see the effect.

CHAPTER 17

# Artist's Exhibition: Applying Bitmaps

## 17.1 INTRODUCTION

The application of a bitmap image to surfaces in a scene is an efficient method for adding realism without having to perform sophisticated modeling. Bitmaps can be used in a variety of ways. They can be used to add surface textures, pasted signs, projected images, or pictures.

The purpose of this project is to introduce you to a variety of application methods for using bitmap images. A scene of an art gallery has already been created for your use. During the project you will apply paintings to canvases, pick out frame materials, hang the paintings, experiment with material types on a sculpture, project images simulating a slide projector, and paint the ceiling.

## 17.2 SCENE COMPOSITION

The first step in this project is to review the scene and to review the various elements that will provide effective lighting as you furnish your gallery.

### Opening the Scene

Open the scene MXART.MAX. If you followed the procedure outlined in Appendix A, the file is already installed on your system. If you didn't, you will need to open the file from the CD-ROM that came with this text.

Save the scene as CH17A.MAX so that you can retain the original scene.

The screen should show four viewports, depicting the Top, Front, Left, and CAM-Overview. Your screen should look similar to Figure 17.1.

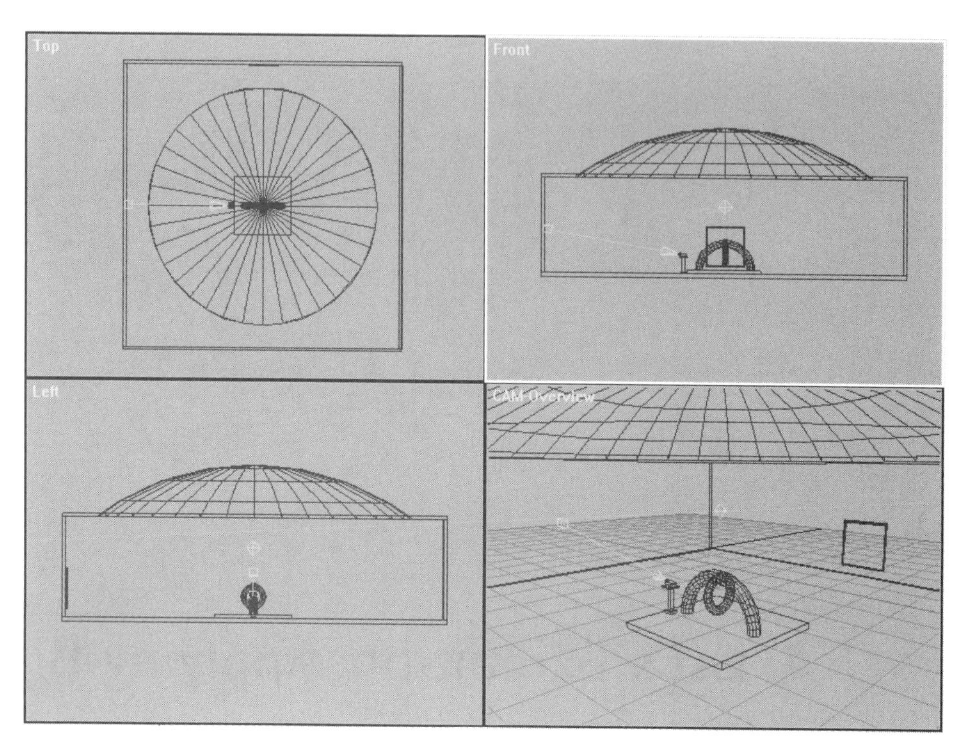


FIGURE 17.1
Four viewports.

## Test Rendering

Activate the camera viewport labeled CAM-Overview and perform a test rendering. Start with the largest image your system will allow in order to view the scene in as much detail as possible. This rendering uses an omni light so that you can see most of the objects in the scene.

Refer to Figure 17.2 and your screen. The scene is composed of a large gallery room. There is one painting hung on the north wall, which has been placed to show you an example of what you will be doing in a later step. If you select the painting, you will see it has been given the name of the painter, Monet. The gallery has a domed roof. You will paint it during the project. A sculpture sits in the center of the

FIGURE 17.2
Overview of the gallery.

room and appears to be made of white plaster. Later you will assign different materials to the sculpture for a variety of effects. A slide projector, sitting on a pedestal, points toward the west wall. It projects only a white light at this stage. You will modify the light so that it projects a bitmap image.

Upon opening the file, there are a variety of cameras already created and hidden. They point toward various features in the gallery. There is one camera pointing toward each wall, one that focuses on the sculpture, and one that points at the ceiling. These cameras have been established so that you can display any point in the room.

Practice switching the camera viewport to show the different views and perform a test rendering of each.

## Main Objects

The following are the names of the main objects in the scene, including cameras and lights.

**Groups**

Monet10x10

Pedestal

Projector

**Individual Objects**

Arch

Platform

Ring

Roof-Curve

**Cameras (Hidden)**

CAM-Overview (Target Camera)

CAM-North (Target Camera)

CAM-South (Target Camera)

CAM-East (Target Camera)

CAM-West (Target Camera)

CAM-Roof (Target Camera)

CAM-Roof-Gaze (Target Camera)

CAM-Person (Target Camera)

CAM-Projector (Target Camera)

CAM-Sculpture (Target Camera)

**Lights**

Accent-Light (Omni Light)

Spot-Projector (Target Spotlight)

Spot-Sculpture (Target Spotlight)

### Project Stages

The project is separated into six stages: painting template, creating a painting, placing a painting, painting the ceiling, sculpture medium, and slide projector. Each stage involves some aspect of using a bitmap image, such as applying or enhancing.

## 17.3 PAINTING TEMPLATE

The first stage is to set up a painting template that can be used to display any painting image. There are three files, MXPA, MXPB, MXPC. They represent three different canvas sizes:

MXPA 10 ft high x 10 ft wide
MXPB 8 ft high x 6 ft wide
MXPC 4 ft high x 3 ft wide

Recall each file and save it as a new file so that you retain the original.

1. Open MXPA and save it as MXP10X10.
   Open MXPB and save it as MXP8X6.
   Open MXPC and save it as MXP4X3.

### Standard Canvas Material

To apply the different paintings, you need to create a standard canvas material and apply it to the canvas. Once this is done, you can make a few simple changes to create any new painting. If you need a refresher on materials, refer to Chapter 12.

2. Open MXP10X10. It contains two objects: Canvas-10x10 and Frame-10x10 contained in the group object FC-10x10.
   Select the group object FC-10x10 and open it using the Group/Open pull-down menu item.
   Select the Canvas-10x10 object.

3. Open that Material Editor dialog by using the Material Editor tool and activate the first material review slot.
   Pick in the Material name box and enter the name of your material. Call it Canvas.
   Pick the Type button next to the name. When the Material/Map Browser appears, check that Browse From is set to New and then pick Standard as the material type. Close the browser and return to the Material Editor.
   The preview slot should now contain a basic grey material.

4. Open the Maps rollout and pick on the None button across from the Diffuse heading. When the Material/Map Browser appears, check that Browse From is set to New and then pick Bitmap as the map type. Close the browser and return to the Material Editor.
   A new rollout will appear: Bitmap Parameters. In this rollout, pick the blank button below the Bitmap heading. You will be presented with the Select Bitmap Image file dialog. Make sure you are in the directory that contains the map files for 3D Studio MAX. It is usually called C:\3DSMAX\Maps. If you followed the procedure outlined in Appendix A of this book, the image files from the CD-ROM should have been copied to this subdirectory. Set List Files of Type: to *.GIF. Scroll down until you find the one called STANDARD.GIF. This will be used as a sample painting map. Select it and OK to close the dialog. The map is now part of the material. Figure 17.3 shows the material in the preview slot and the map listed in the Maps rollout.

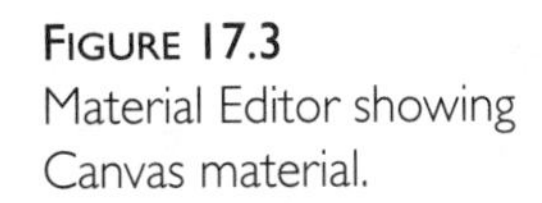

FIGURE 17.3
Material Editor showing Canvas material.

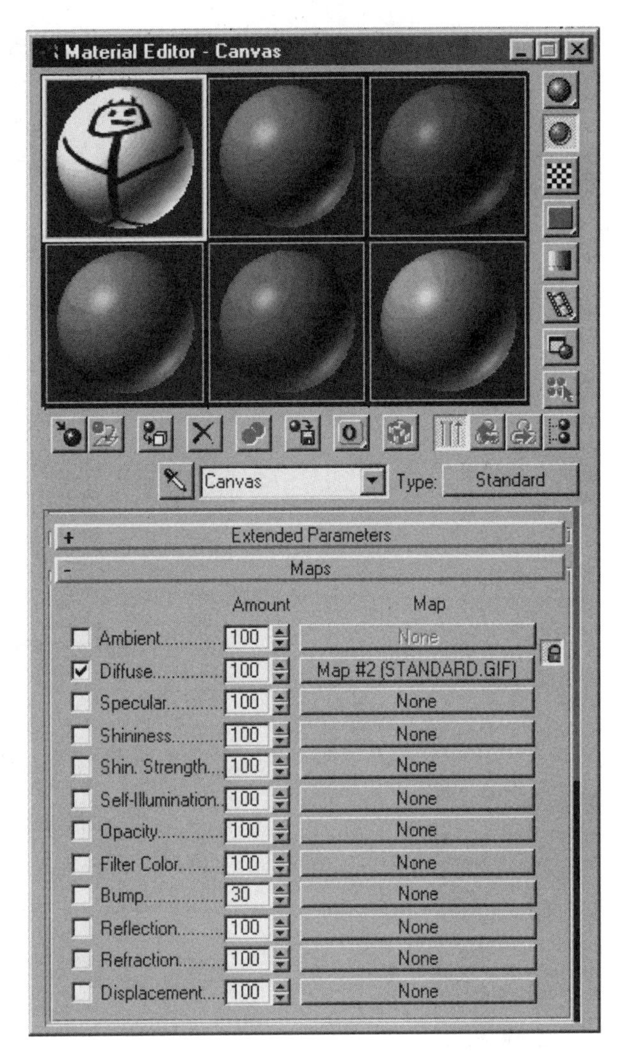

Select the Go to Parent tool to display the parameters for the Canvas material.

With the Canvas-10x10 object still selected, pick the Assign Material to Selection tool. The material Canvas should now be assigned to the Canvas-10x10 object.

5. Activate the next material preview box in the Material Editor dialog and pick the Get Material tool. When the Material/Map Browser appears, check that Browse From is set to Material Library, and use the File Open button. Search for the material library named MOTION2.MAT. This library comes on the CD-ROM included with this textbook and should have already been copied onto your computer in the 3D Studio MAX maps subdirectory.
6. Scroll down the material types until you find Wood-Frame. Select it and close the browser and return to the Material Editor.

   The preview slot should now contain a wood material, as shown in Figure 17.4.
7. With the Material Editor still displayed, select the Frame-10x10 object and then use the Assign Material tool to assign the wood material to the frame.
8. Close the group using the Group/Close pull-down menu item. *Note:* One of the items in the group must be selected to be able to close the group.

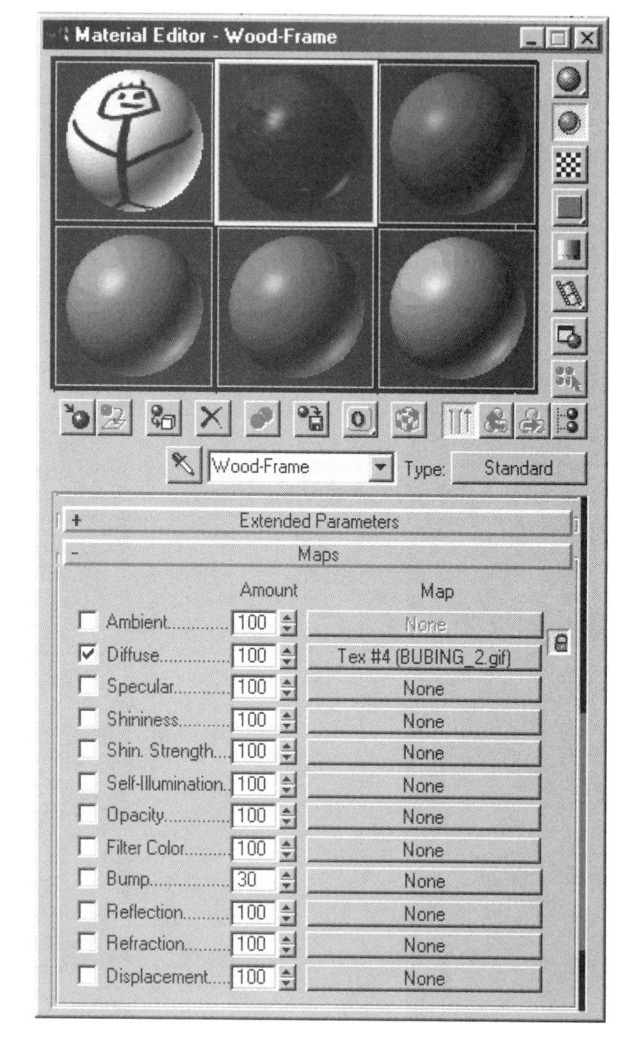


FIGURE 17.4
Material Editor dialog showing wood frame material.

FIGURE 17.5
Maps applied to canvas and frame.

9. Save the file and perform a test rendering of the Perspective viewport. The rendered image should look similar to Figure 17.5.
10. Repeat steps 2 to 8 for the other two painting sizes.

## 17.4 CREATING A PAINTING

In this section you will take one of the standard frame\canvas files, add a specific painting to the canvas, and then save it under the painter's name.

1. Open the standard frame\canvas file MXP10X10.
2. Select the FC-10x10 object and open the group. Select the Canvas-10x10 object.
3. Open the Material Editor dialog and activate the material preview that contains the Canvas material.
4. Change the name of the Canvas material to DALI. This represents the name of the painter.
5. Open the Maps rollout and pick on the Standard.Gif map button across from the Diffuse heading. The Bitmap Parameters rollout will appear.

Pick on the Standard.Gif button and the Select Bitmap Image File dialog will appear, listing the various bitmap files. Set List Files of Type: to *.JPG. Scroll down the list until you see DALI.JPG. Select it and OK to close the dialog.

Pick the Return to Parent tool. This takes you back to the DALI material, as shown in Figure 17.6.

6. Use the Assign Material tool to assign the material to the Canvas-10x10 object.
7. Close the Group and save the file as MXDALI.MAX.
8. Perform a test rendering of the Perspective viewport. It should look similar to Figure 17.7.
9. You can create a series of paintings in different sizes and by different artists just by following the previous steps. The following is a list of artists and their associated bitmap files.

| Bitmap File | Artist and Origins |
|---|---|
| BOTTICEL.JPG | Sandro Botticelli, Italian renaissance |
| BRUEGEL.JPG | Pieter Brueghel, Dutch exteriors |
| C&I.JPG | Currier and Ives, American lithographs |
| CARAVAGG.JPG | Caravaggio, Italian Counter-Reformation |
| CEZANNE.JPG | Paul Cezanne, French modern |

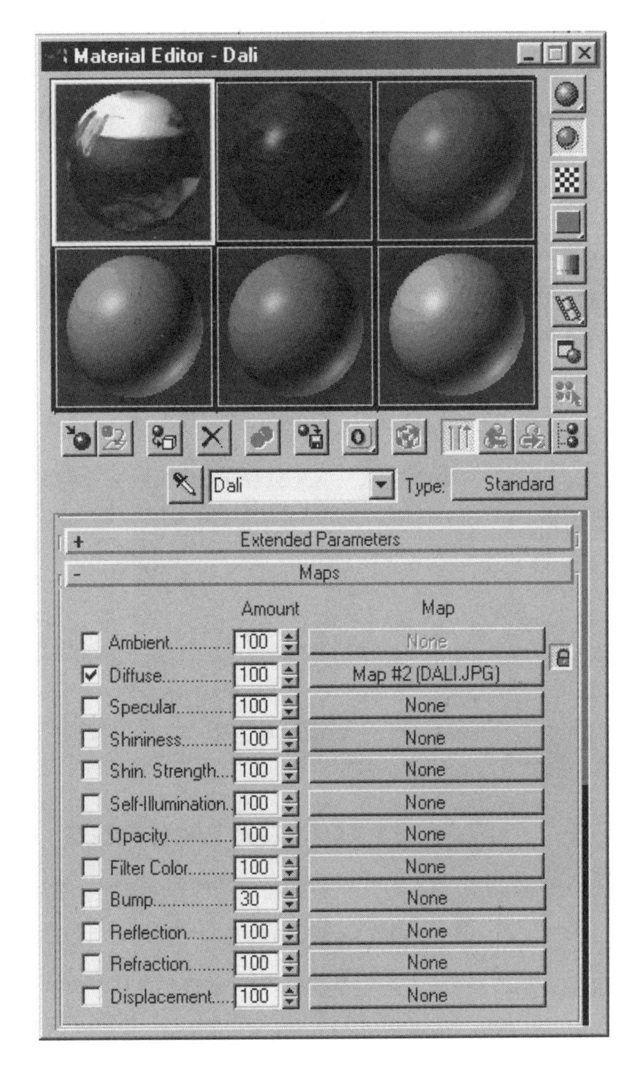


FIGURE 17.6
Material Editor dialog showing DALI material.

FIGURE 17.7
Rendered Dali painting.

| | |
|---|---|
| DALI.JPG | Salvador Dali, Spanish surrealist |
| DAVINCI.JPG | Leonardo da Vinci, Italian renaissance |
| DEGAS.JPG | Degas, French impressionist |
| EYCK.JPG | Jan van Eyck, Flemish renaissance |
| GAINSB.JPG | Thomas Gainsborough, English portraits |
| GOYA.JPG | Francisco Goya, Spanish politico |
| GRECO.JPG | El Greco, Spanish landscape and social conscience painter |
| HOLBEIN.JPG | Hans Holbein, German |
| JACKSON.JPG | A. Y. Jackson, Canadian landscape |
| KADIN.JPG | Wassily Kandinsky, Russian abstract |
| MATISSE.JPG | Henri Matisse, French *Fauve* |
| MICHEL.JPG | Michelangelo, Italian painter and sculptor |
| MONDRIAN.JPG | Piet Mondrian, Dutch founder of Mondrian style |
| MONET.JPG | Monet, French impressionist |
| MUNCH.JPG | Edvard Munch, Norwegian expressionist |
| OKEEF.JPG | Georgia O'Keeffe, American abstract |
| PICASSO.JPG | Pablo Picasso, Spanish cubist |
| POLLACK.JPG | Jackson Pollack, American abstract expressionist |
| RAPHAEL.JPG | Raphael, Italian renaissance |
| REMBRANT.JPG | Rembrant, Dutch baroque |
| RENOIR.JPG | Pierre-Auguste Renoir, French impressionist |
| TOULOUSE.JPG | Henri de Toulouse-Lautrec, French post-impressionist |
| TURNER.JPG | Joseph Turner, English landscape |
| VANGOGH.JPG | Vincent van Gogh, abstract expressionist |
| WHISTLER.JPG | James Whistler, American modern |
| YUAN.JPG | Ma Yuan, Chinese landscape |

## 17.5 PLACING A PAINTING

In this stage you are going to place a painting on one of the walls of the gallery.

1. Open the gallery file, CH17A.MAX.
2. Display the view of a person looking at the painting on the north wall in the camera viewport by right-clicking the viewport label, picking Views, and picking

CAM-Person from the list. The painting should be off to the left, leaving room for you to add your Dali painting.

3. In the Front viewport, zoom in on the painting, displaying it on the left and leaving room to insert your painting. The viewports should look similar to Figure 17.8.
4. Make sure the Front viewport is active.

   To bring in another file, you need to select the File/Merge pull-down menu item. Find and pick the MXDALI.MAX file. This is the painting file you saved earlier.

   When the Merge dialog appears, pick on the All and OK buttons. This will bring all the objects of the MXDALI file into the current file.

   The painting appears at 0,0,0 and is highlighted white. Lock it.
5. In the Top viewport, move the painting into position. In the Front viewport, adjust the height. You may have to zoom in on the Top viewport to get the right placement on the wall. The final position should look similar to Figure 17.9.
6. Save your file and perform a test rendering of the CAM-Person viewport. It should look similar to Figure 17.10.
7. At this stage you can add more paintings to walls of the gallery. The only limitation is that you must leave the east wall blank for its slide projected image. Remember to save your file when you are finished adding paintings.

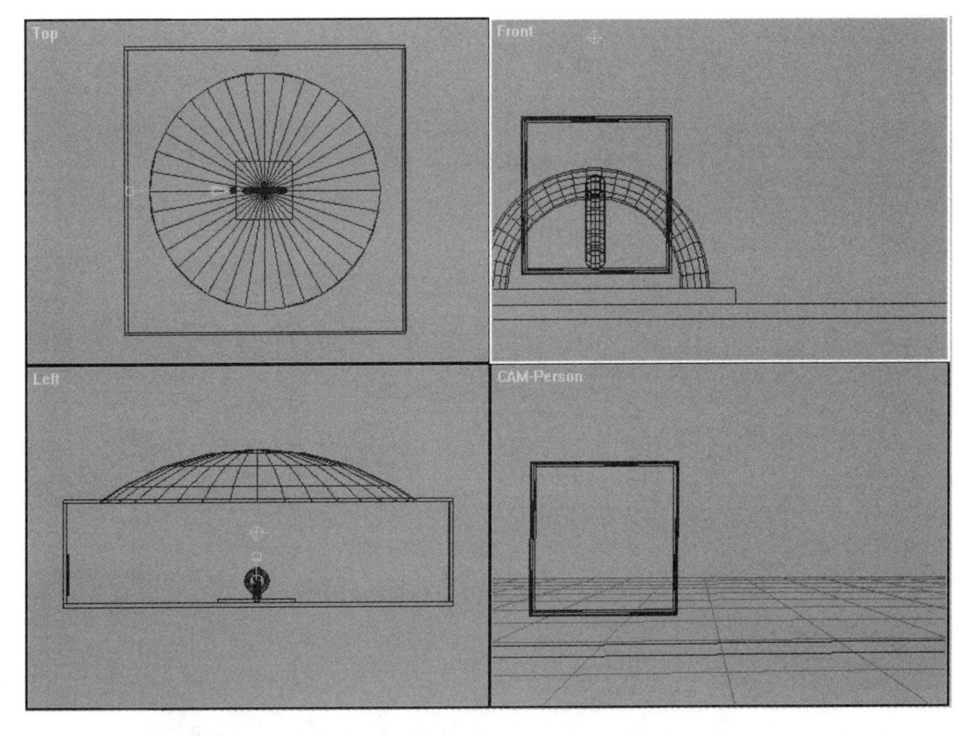


FIGURE 17.8
Viewports showing close-up of north wall painting.

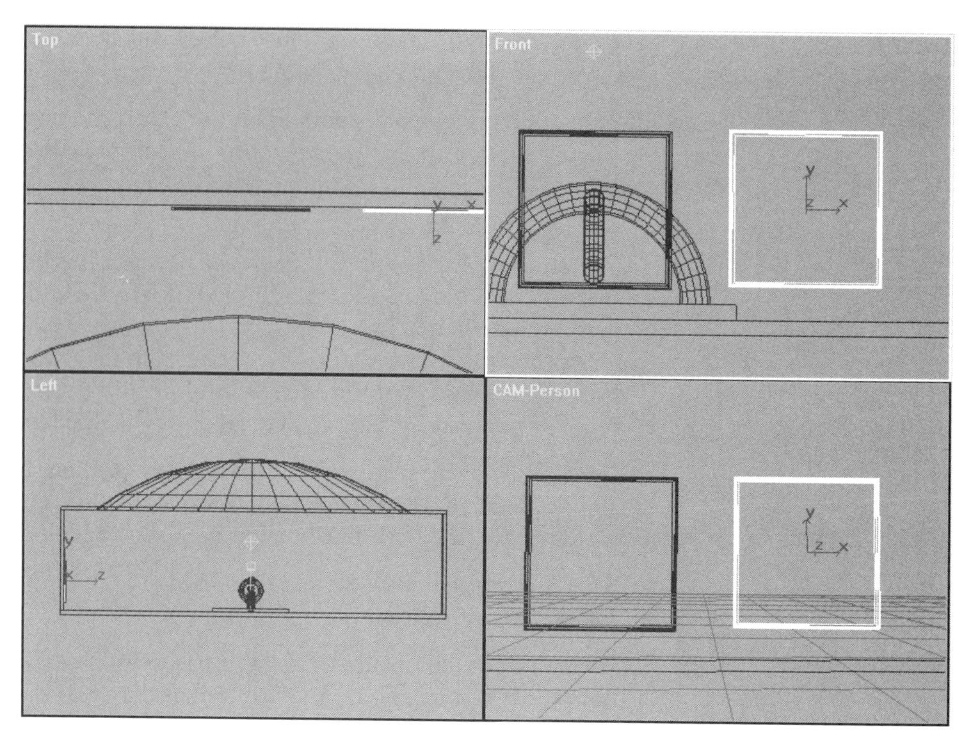


FIGURE 17.9
Viewports showing the location of the new painting.

FIGURE 17.10
Rendering of CAM-Person.

## 17.6 PAINTING THE CEILING

In this stage you are going to add a painting to the ceiling. This is a partial image of Michelangelo's painting on the ceiling of the Sistine Chapel. He painted the ceiling with various mosaics by laying on his back, in severe pain, almost going blind in the process. Your application is going to be much easier.

1. Select the object called Roof-Curve. This object represents the dome roof of the gallery.
2. Open the Material Editor, activate the first material preview box, and pick the Get Material tool. When the Material/Map Browser appears, check that Browse

From is set to Material Library, and use the File Open button. Search for the material library named MOTION2.MAT. From the list of materials, select Michel and OK it.

3. Assign the material Michel to the Roof-Curve object and close the Material Editor.
4. Display a roof view in the camera viewport by right-clicking the viewport label, picking Views, and then picking CAM-Roof from the list.
5. Render the CAM-Roof viewport. The image should look similar to Figure 17.11.
6. The next step is to turn the image 90°. Open the Material Editor again and activate the Michel material.

   Open the Maps rollout and pick on the Michel.Jpg map button. When the Bitmap Parameters appear, enter 90 in the Angle box, as shown in Figure 17.12.
7. Render the camera viewport again. It should now look like Figure 17.13.
8. Change the camera viewport to display the CAM-Roof-Gaze view. This is a view looking at the roof from an angle so that you can also see the floor and walls.
9. Render the CAM-Roof-Gaze viewport. It should appear similar to Figure 17.14.

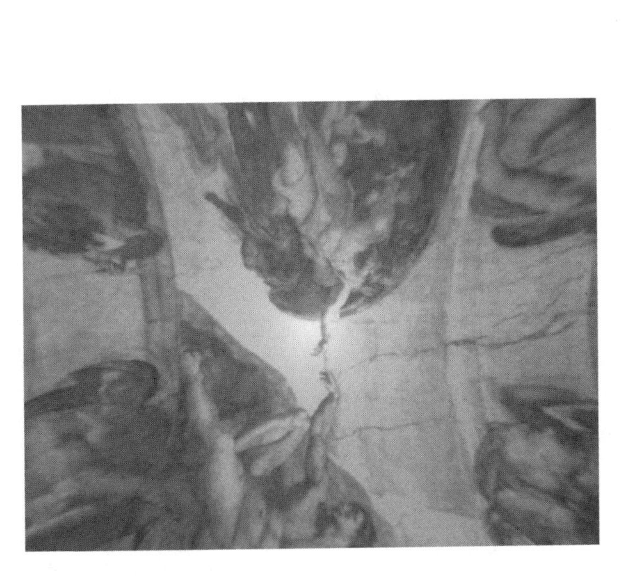

FIGURE 17.11
Painting on the ceiling.

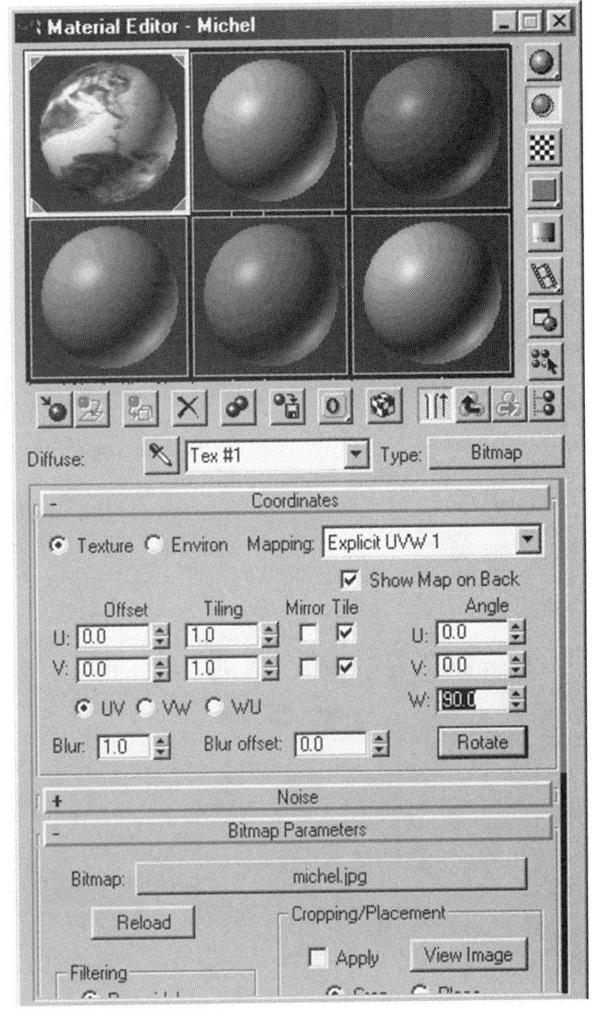


FIGURE 17.12
Bitmap parameters showing rotation angle.

FIGURE 17.13
Rendered image showing image rotated 90°.

FIGURE 17.14
Rendered image of roof, walls, and floor.

## 17.7 SCULPTURE MEDIUM

In this stage, you are going to experiment with different materials to change the medium of the sculpture. The sculpture is composed of three objects: Arch, Ring, and Platform. You will assign different materials for each.

1. Activate the camera viewport and display the CAM-Sculpture view.
2. Activate the Front viewport and zoom in on the sculpture.
3. Select the Platform and open the Material Editor.
4. Activate the second material review slot and pick the Get Material tool.

   When the Material/Map Browser is displayed, set the Browse From to Material Library, and use the File Open button. Search for the material library named MOTION2.MAT. From the list of materials, select Platform and OK it.

   Activate the third material review slot and pick the Get Material tool.

   When the Material/Map Browser is displayed, select Arch-Fire from the list and OK it.

   Activate the fourth material review slot and pick the Get Material tool.

   When the Material/Map Browser is displayed, select Ring-Water from the list and OK it.

   Figure 17.15 shows that the Arch-Fire material is made of two materials: top and bottom. If you pick on the Yellow-Glow button, you will see it has a Self-Illumination of 90. This gives a glow to the yellow.

   Figure 17.16 shows that the Ring-Water material uses bitmap images. If you look under the Basic parameters for the material, you will see it has an opacity of 70. This gives the material some transparency, so that you can see through it.
5. Assign the material Platform to the Platform object and close the Material Editor.

   Assign the material Arch-Fire to the Arch object and close the Material Editor.

   Assign the material Ring-Water to the Ring object and close the Material Editor.
6. Save the file and activate the CAM-Sculpture viewport and render the scene. It should appear as shown in Figure 17.17.
7. Experiment with assigning different materials to the sculpture to see the rendered effect.

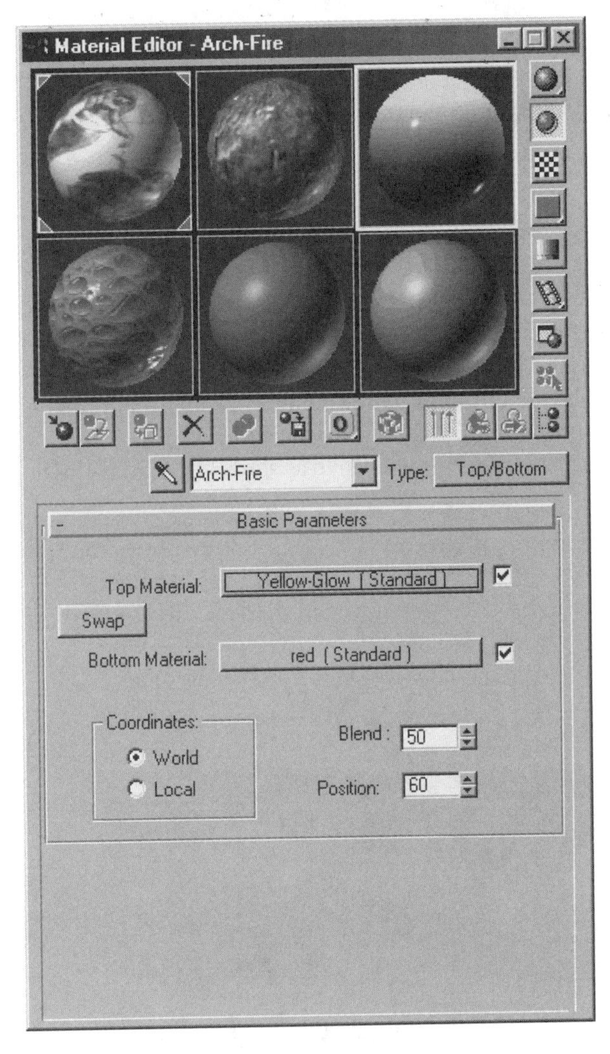


FIGURE 17.15
Arch-Fire material.

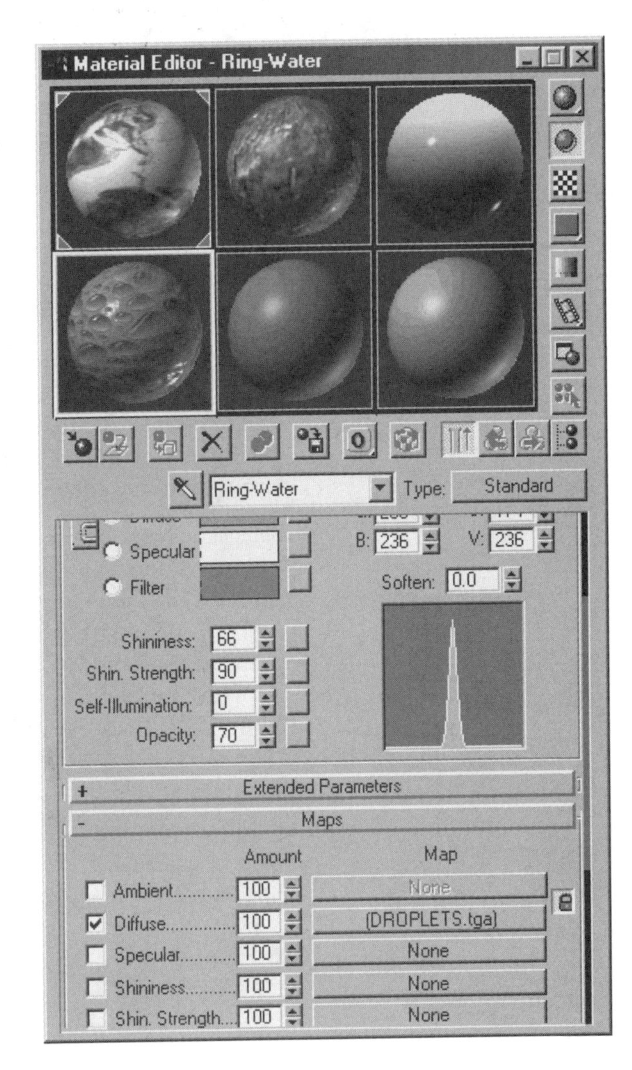


FIGURE 17.16
Ring-Water material.

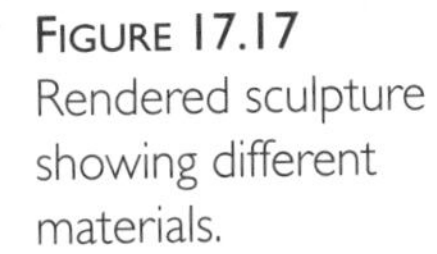
FIGURE 17.17
Rendered sculpture showing different materials.

## 17.8 SLIDE PROJECTOR

In this stage, you are going to assign a bitmap image to a spotlight. The spotlight will be used as a projector, projecting an image on the east wall.

1. Activate the camera viewport and display the CAM-Projector view.
2. Select the Projector object and open the group. The light is contained within it.
3. Open the Display panel and uncheck Lights under the Hide by category. This will allow you to select the projector light.
4. Open the Material Editor and activate the fifth material preview slot. Name this material: Projector. Use the Type: Standard button to create a new material of the standard type. The material slot should show a grey material. Under the Maps parameters, pick the blank button opposite the Diffuse heading. Create a new bitmap and find the file MONET.JPG for the bitmap as shown in Figure 17.18.
5. Select the Spot-Projector light object and open the Modify panel.

   Scroll down until you see the Spotlight parameters. Check the Projector box and pick the None button beside Map:. When the Material/Map Browser appears, check Mtl Editor in the Browse From area and then pick MONET.JPG from the list. Check Copy and pick OK.

   Now, in the Spotlight Parameters, the projector button has the label MODET.JPG as shown in Figure 17.19.

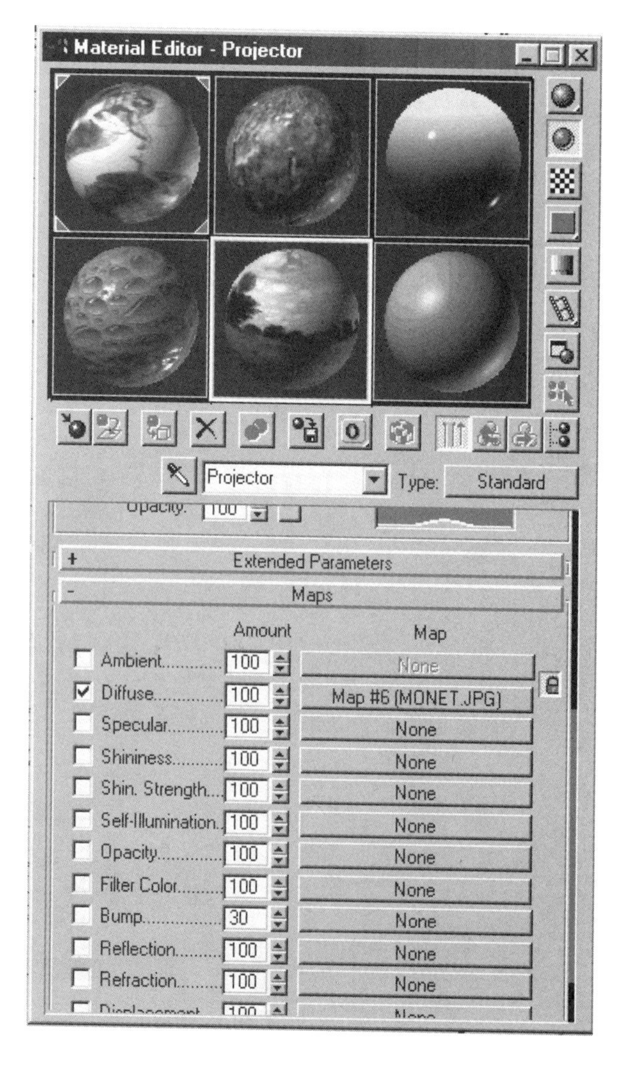


FIGURE 17.18
Material Editor showing the Projector material using the bitmap Monet.jpg.

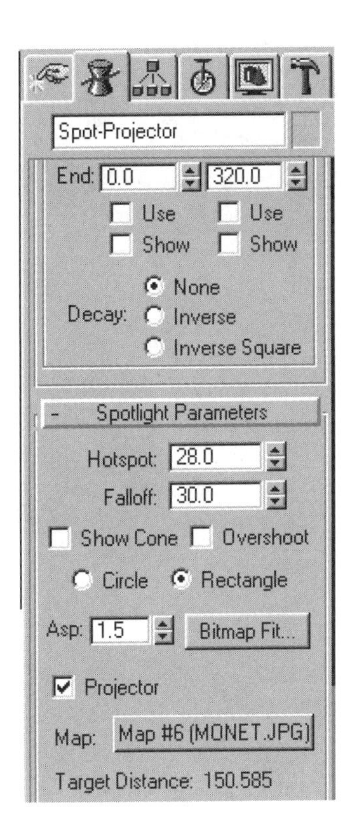


FIGURE 17.19
Spotlight parameters showing the projector map set to Monet.jpg.

6. Select Accent-Light and open the Modify panel. Under General parameters, set V from 180 to 100. This dims the light in the gallery so that you can see the projected light better.
7. Select Spot-Sculpture. In the Modify panel, under General parameters, Uncheck the On box. This turns the light off.
8. Save your file and render the CAM-Projector viewport. The image should look similar to Figure 17.20.

You may want to create an animated sequence of someone strolling through the gallery, looking at the various paintings and sculpture. Animation is discussed in Chapter 13. And to add some more realism, you could add a door to the gallery by creating a box for the door and using a Boolean operation to create the opening. This is discussed in Chapter 9.

FIGURE 17.20
Rendered image showing projected bitmap.

# Mechanical Motion: Hierarchical Linking

## 18.1 INTRODUCTION

When mechanisms move, whether they are human bodies or robotic assemblers, their component parts move in relation to each other. This form of relationship is referred to as hierarchical linking. When one component moves, it has an effect on the next component attached to it.

The purpose of this project is to allow you to experiment with forming hierarchical links and producing accurate motion in an animation. A scene of an assembly-line robot has already been created for the purpose of linking and animating.

## 18.2 SCENE COMPOSITION

The first step in this project is to review the scene in order to review the various elements involved in the linking process.

### Opening the Scene

Open the scene MXROBOT.MAX. If you followed the procedure outlined in Appendix A, the file is already installed on your system. If you didn't, you will need to open the file from the CD–ROM that came with this text.

Save the scene as CH18A.MAX so that you can retain the original scene.

The screen should show four viewports, depicting the Top, Front, Left and Overview camera view. All are in wireframe except for the camera viewport. Your screen should look similar to Figure 18.1.

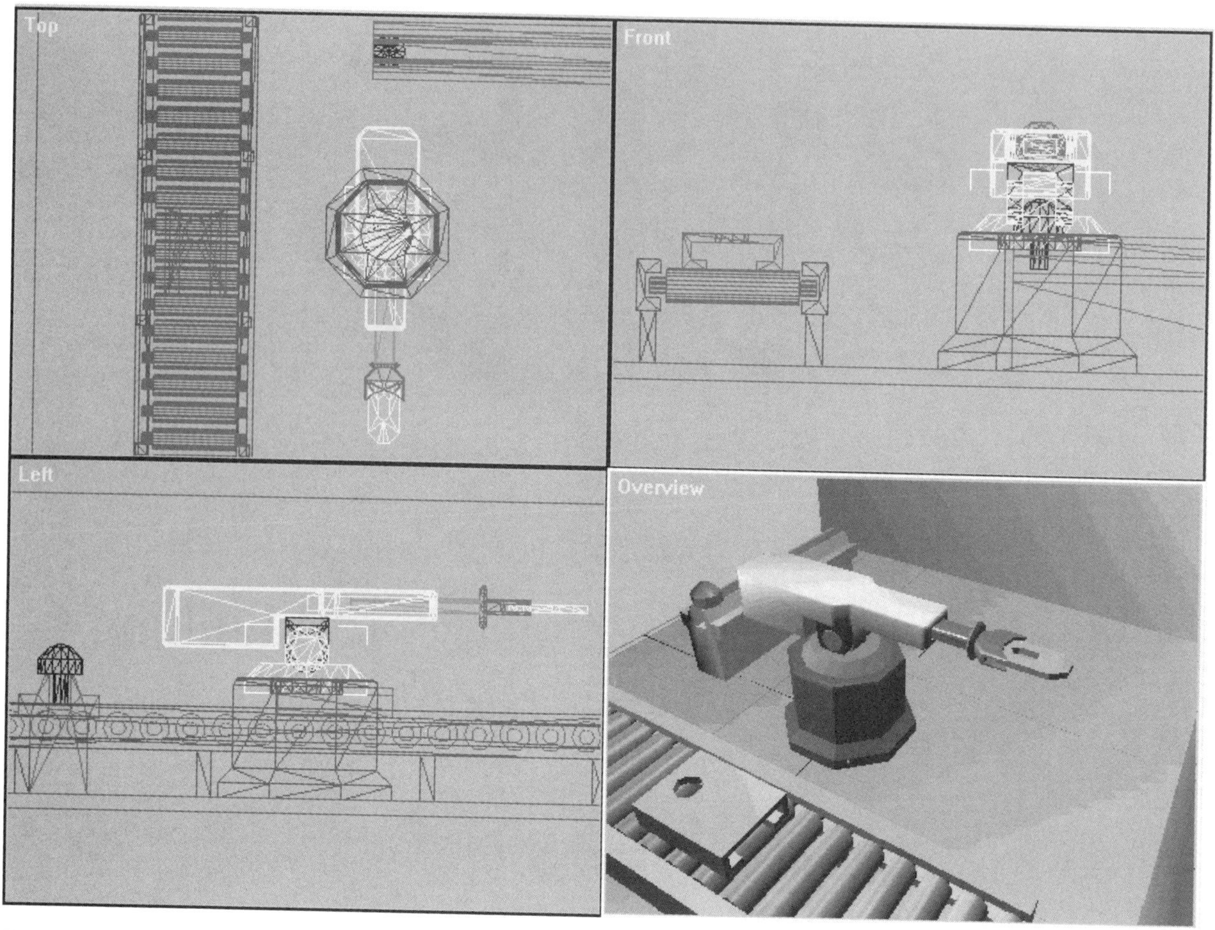


FIGURE 18.1
Four viewports.

## Component Identification

Figure 18.2 identifies the major components of the scene.

## Test Rendering

Activate the camera viewport labeled Overview and change it to the Close-Up camera view. Perform a test rendering on the Close-Up viewport. Start with the largest image your system will allow to get a detailed picture of the scene. The rendering makes use of two spotlights so that you can see most of the objects in the scene. This is the view that will be used to create the final rendered animation.

Refer to Figure 18.3 and your screen.

## Main Objects

The following are the names of the main objects in the scene, including cameras and lights.

**Groups**

Conveyor

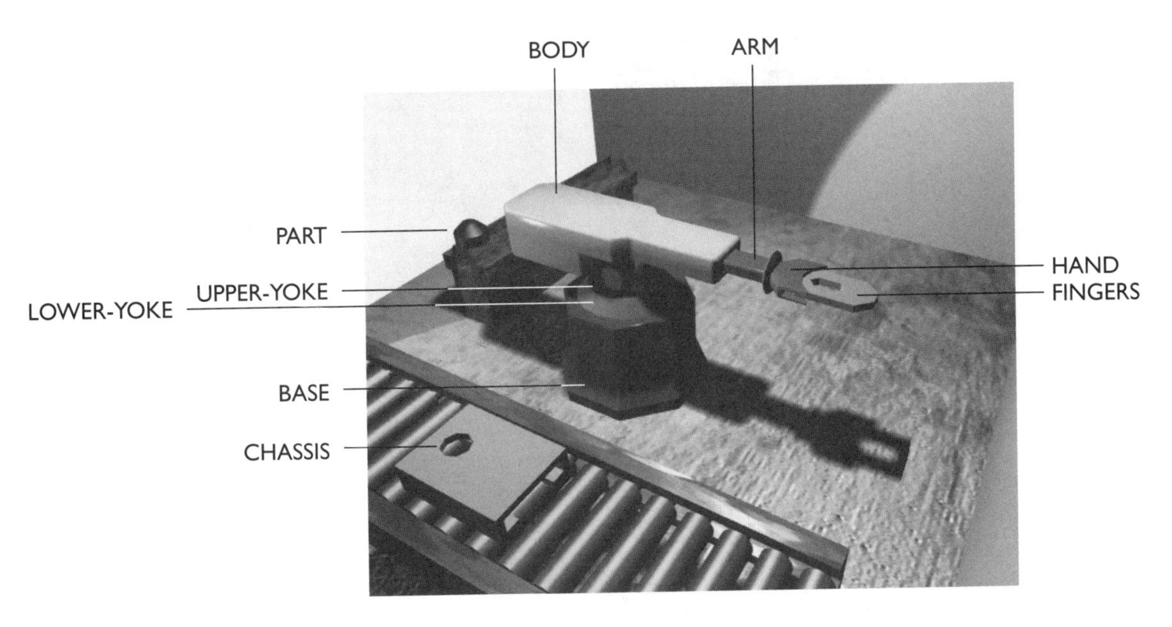


FIGURE 18.2
Overview with component identification.

**Individual Objects**

Finger-Left

Finger-Right

Hand

Arm

Body

Upper-Yoke

Lower-Yoke

Base

Part

Chassis

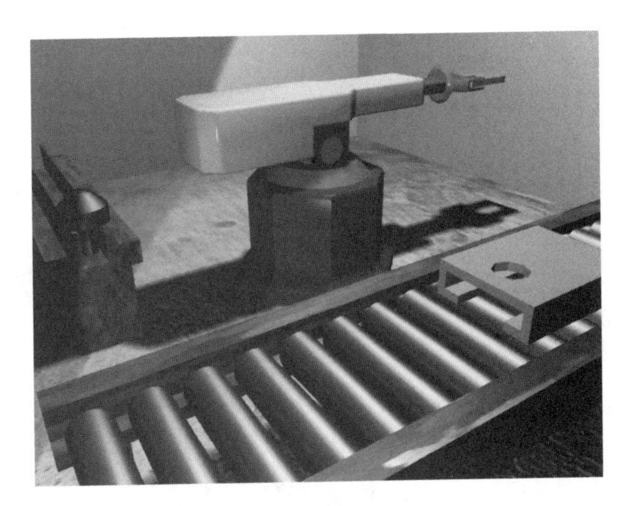

FIGURE 18.3
Rendered close-up of motion project scene.

**Cameras**

Overview (Target Camera)

Close-Up (Target Camera)

**Lights**

Spot01 (Target Spot)

Spot02 (Target Spot)

## Project Stages

The project is separated into three stages: hierarchy linking, adding precision movement and animation, and rendering the animation.

Remember to use the Hold command just before you perform any operation you are not sure of. Then you can restore the previous settings with the use of the Fetch command. Also, it is good form to save your scene file just before performing a rendering. You never know when your computer system may crash, but during rendering is a likely place for it to happen.

## 18.3 HIERARCHY LINKING

### Displaying Track View Dialog

1. Before you start linking objects to one another, take a look at the Track View dialog that shows the hierarchy of the objects in the scene.

   Pick the Track View tool and the Track View dialog will be displayed, similar to Part A of Figure 18.4. You can see that no object is connected to any other. This will change when the linking is done.

   Close the Track View dialog.

### Linking Procedure

2. The procedure for linking one object to another is quite simple, but you must be careful always to link the child to the parent. The following is the procedure for linking the child (Finger-Left) to the parent (Hand).
   a. Pick the Select Object tool, turning it on.
   b. Pick the Select by Name tool, highlight the child object (Finger-Left), and pick the Select button. The object will be highlighted white.

   c. Pick the Select and Link tool so that it is now on.
   d. Pick the Select by Name tool, highlight the parent object (Hand), and pick the Link button. The parent object will blink white to show which one you have picked.

   The Finger-Left is now linked to the Hand. If you make a mistake and link a child to the wrong parent, just pick the Unlink Selection tool.

3. Pick the Track View tool again to display the Track View dialog. You should notice that Finger-Left is not visible on the list. Go down the list until you find the Hand object. Pick the plus-square box to reveal the objects linked to the hand. The Finger-Left should be there, as shown in Part B of Figure 18.4.

   Close the Track View dialog.

   As you link objects to one another, they will be *buried* deeper and deeper, until only the Base is visible. This is the root object. After linking all the

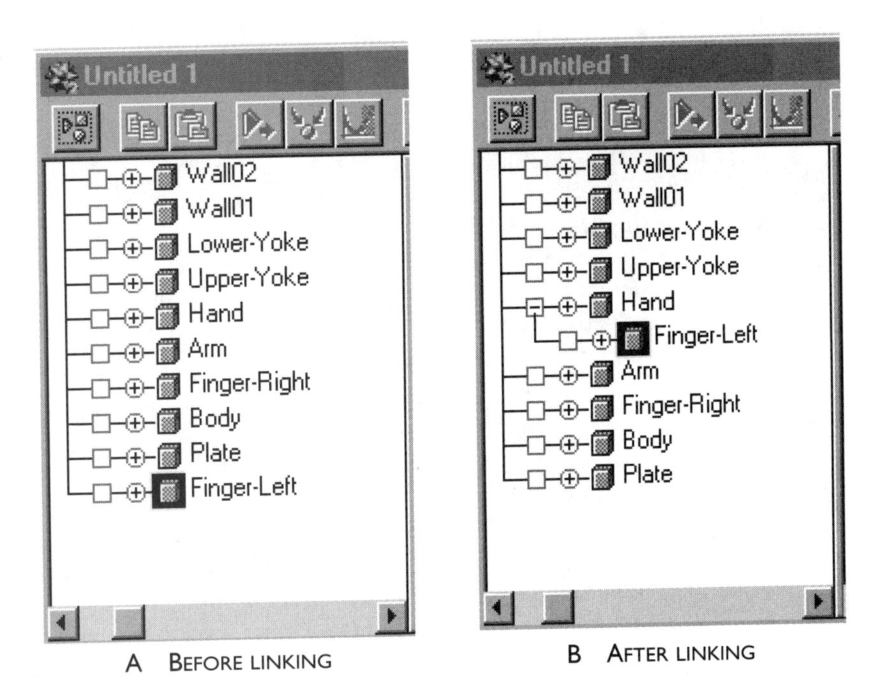


A BEFORE LINKING B AFTER LINKING

FIGURE 18.4
Track View dialog showing hierarchy before and after linking.

objects, you can reveal the link order by picking the plus-square box for each object. You start with the root (Base) and go through until you reach the leaf (Finger-Left).

4. Repeat (a)–(d) of step 2 for the following links:

| **Child—Link to—Parent** | |
|---|---|
| Finger-Right | Hand |
| Hand | Arm |
| Arm | Body |
| Body | Upper-Yoke |
| Upper-Yoke | Lower-Yoke |
| Lower-Yoke | Base |

5. Save your scene.

### Testing the Hierarchy Link

6. Now that all the objects are linked, you are going to test out the links. First, select the Edit/Hold pull-down menu command to protect the current state of your scene.
7. Turn on the Inverse Kinematics tool.
8. Use the Select by Name tool, select the Hand, and lock the selection.
9. Turn on the Move transform and pick and drag on the Hand in the Top viewport.

   Move the cursor and watch the behavior of the linked objects. They all should be rotating at the same time. This is because as you move the Hand, the objects linked to the Hand move as well.

   Pick any location on the screen. Now try the Move transform in the Left viewport. The objects rotate in all directions. They are rotating because the rotation joint parameter is assigned automatically to a newly linked object. You are going to correct this next.

10. Use the Edit/Fetch pull-down menu command to restore the objects to their original positions.

**Setting Joints and Limits**

The objects that make up the robot each need to have joint limits applied. These limits control their movement and stop them from swinging wildly about, as you experienced in step 9. You are going to start with the fingers and move down the hierarchy until you reach the base.

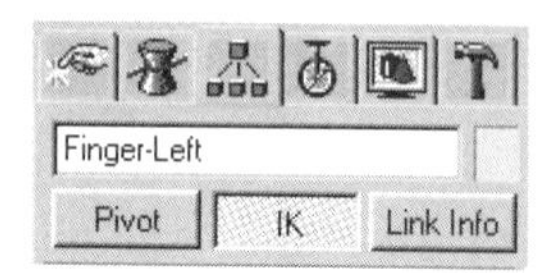


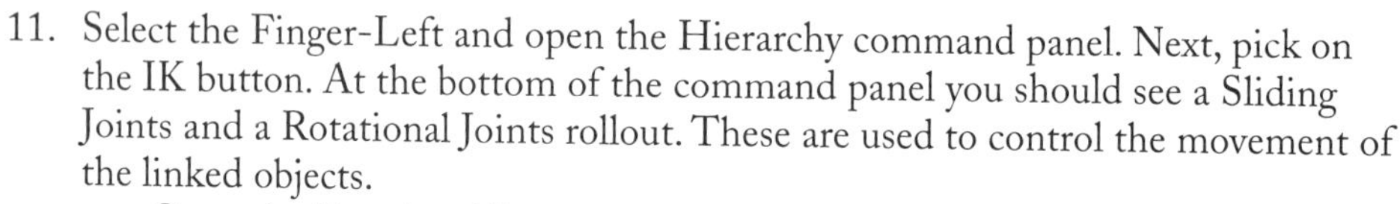

11. Select the Finger-Left and open the Hierarchy command panel. Next, pick on the IK button. At the bottom of the command panel you should see a Sliding Joints and a Rotational Joints rollout. These are used to control the movement of the linked objects.

    Open the Rotational Joints rollout. Notice how all the Active boxes are checked. This is what caused the objects to rotate earlier when using the Move transform. Uncheck all three of these boxes.

    Open the Sliding Joints rollout. Check only the Active box for the Y axis. This will limit the sliding of the Finger-Left to only one axis. Now, check the Limited box. This allows you to limit the amount of movement along the axis. Enter 0.75 in the From box and 2.5 in the To box. See Figure 18.5.

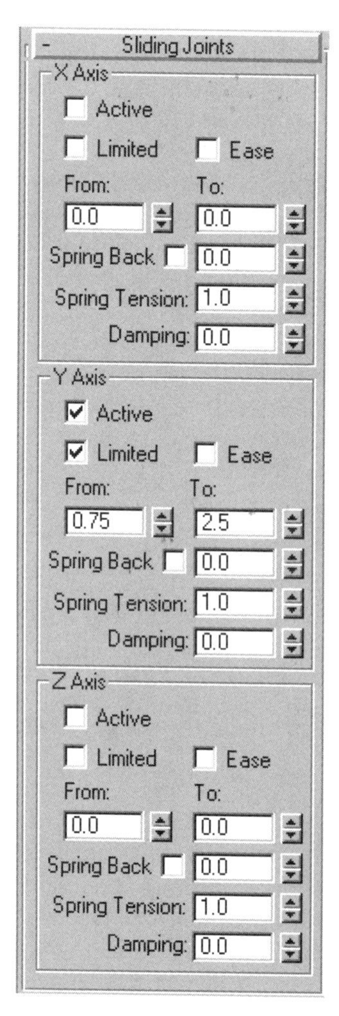


FIGURE 18.5
Sliding Joints parameters for Finger-Left.

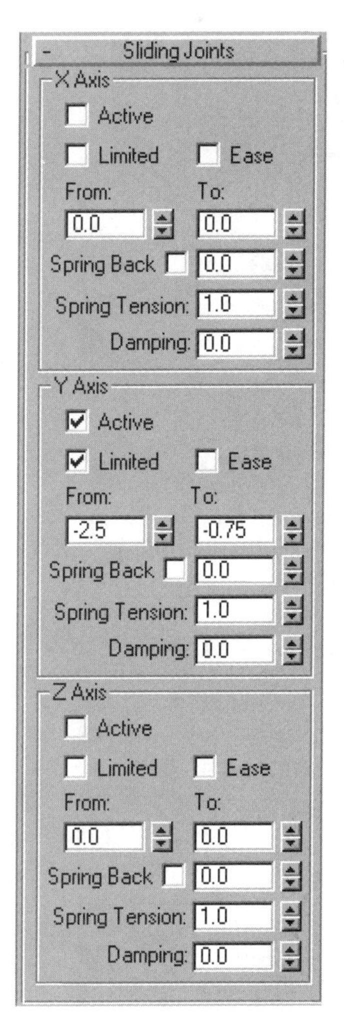


FIGURE 18.6
Sliding Joints parameters for Finger-Right.

12. Select the Finger-Right. Uncheck the Active boxes in the Rotational Joints rollout. Check only the Y axis in the Sliding Joints rollout. Check the Limited box and enter -2.5 in the From box and -0.75 in the To box. See Figure 18.6.
13. Select the Hand. Uncheck the Active boxes in both the Rotation Joints rollout and the Sliding Joints rollout. This causes the Hand to stay fixed to the arm and move with it. Later on you may want to experiment by allowing the X axis rotation, but for now none of the axes should be active.
14. Select the Arm. Uncheck the Active boxes in the Rotational Joints rollout. Check only the X axis in the Sliding Joints rollout. Check the Limited box and enter -12.0 in the From box and -6.0 in the To box. See Figure 18.7.
15. Select the Body. Uncheck the Active boxes in both the Rotation Joints rollout and the Sliding Joints rollout. As with the Hand, this causes the Body to stay fixed to the Lower-Yoke and move with it.
16. Select the Upper-Yoke. This time uncheck the Active boxes in the Sliding Joints rollout. Check only the Y axis in the Rotational Joints rollout. Check the Limited box and enter -20.0 in the From box and 0.0 in the To box. This allows the Upper-Yoke to rotate downward 20°. See Figure 18.8.
17. Select the Lower-Yoke. Uncheck the Active boxes in the Sliding Joints rollout. Check only the Z axis in the Rotational Joints rollout. Check the Lim-

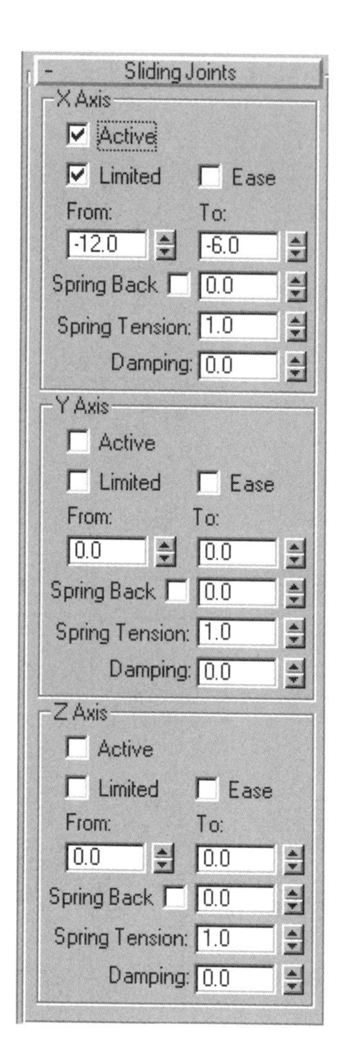


FIGURE 18.7
Sliding Joints parameters for Arm.

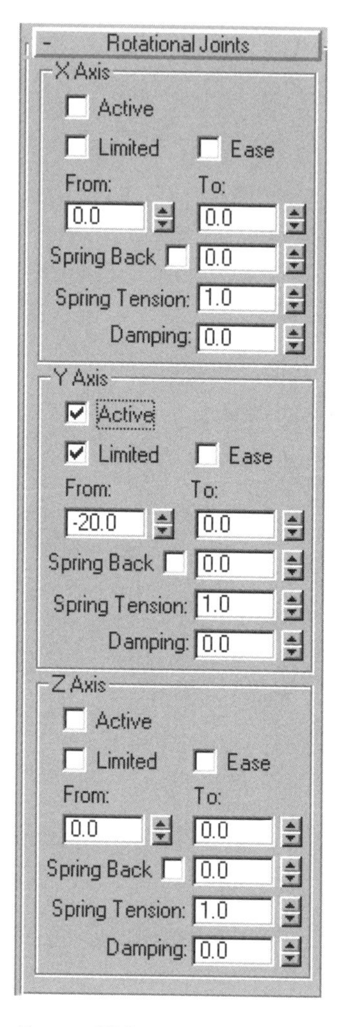


FIGURE 18.8
Rotational Joints parameters for Upper-Yoke.

ited box and enter -100.0 in the From box and 100.0 in the To box. This allows the Lower-Yoke to pivot around the base −100° to +100°. See Figure 18.9.

18. The last step is to make sure the base remains fixed. Select the Base and uncheck the Active boxes in both the Rotational Joints rollout and the Sliding Joints rollout.
19. Save your scene.

### Testing the Joint Limits

20. Select the Edit/Hold pull-down menu command to protect the current state of your scene.
21. Turn on the Inverse Kinematics tool.

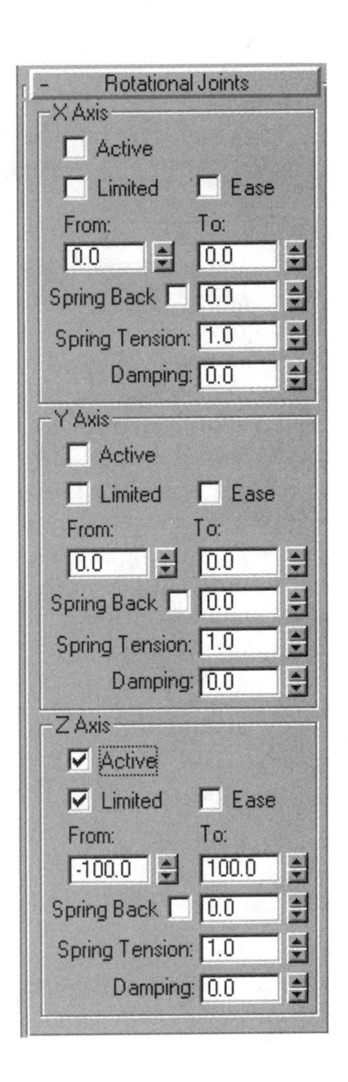


FIGURE 18.9
Rotational Joints parameters for Lower-Yoke.

22. Use the Select by Name tool; select the Hand and lock the selection.
23. Turn on the Move transform and pick and drag the Hand in the Top viewport.

    Move the cursor and watch the behavior of all the linked objects. Instead of all rotating at the same time, the appropriate movement takes place. The arm slides in and out and the Lower Yoke rotates around the base, with the other objects moving with them.

    Pick any location on the screen. Now try the Move transform in the Left viewport. You can see the Upper-Yoke rotates up with the other objects with it.

    The purpose of joint parameters is to cause objects to move in a controlled fashion.
24. Use the Edit/Fetch pull-down menu command to restore the objects to their original positions.
25. Save your scene.

## 18.4 ADDING PRECISION MOVEMENT AND ANIMATION

The next procedure animates the movement of the robot. The robot will move from its original position to grab a Part in its fingers. It will transport the Part and insert it into the hole in the Chassis. Once it has done that, it will return to its original position.

To perform this kind of precision movement, you will be using the Transform Type-in dialog box for movement and the Angle Snap Toggle for rotation.

Whenever you animate an object using transforms, the Transform keys are added to the Track View. The key that represents the transform end position is placed at the frame where you performed the current transform. The transform then takes place from the last key until the current frame key. In this animation you will want the one object's transform to start after another object's transform is finished. If you were to perform all the transforms and then run the animation, all the objects would start moving or rotating at once, because all the start keys begin at Frame 0.

To alleviate this problem, each step is broken into three parts: A, B, and C. In Part A, you perform the transform. In Part B, you assign a motion controller to make sure the robot behaves in a linear, mechanical fashion. In Part C, you copy the last Transform key to just after the end key used in the previous movement. This is done in the Track View dialog just after you perform the transform. In this way, a movement will occur, followed directly by the next one, in sequential order. However, some movements will occur at the same time, such as the fingers closing together or the part moving with the robot.

For the first several steps, the procedure is detailed. After you have performed several transforms, assigned the controller, adjusted the tracks, and have become comfortable with the procedure, the steps are abbreviated.

1. Make sure that the Inverse Kinematic tool is turned off.
2. Make sure the Angle Snap tool, located at the bottom of the screen, is on.

3. Pick the Time Configuration tool and set the length of the animation to 175 frames, as shown in Figure 18.10.

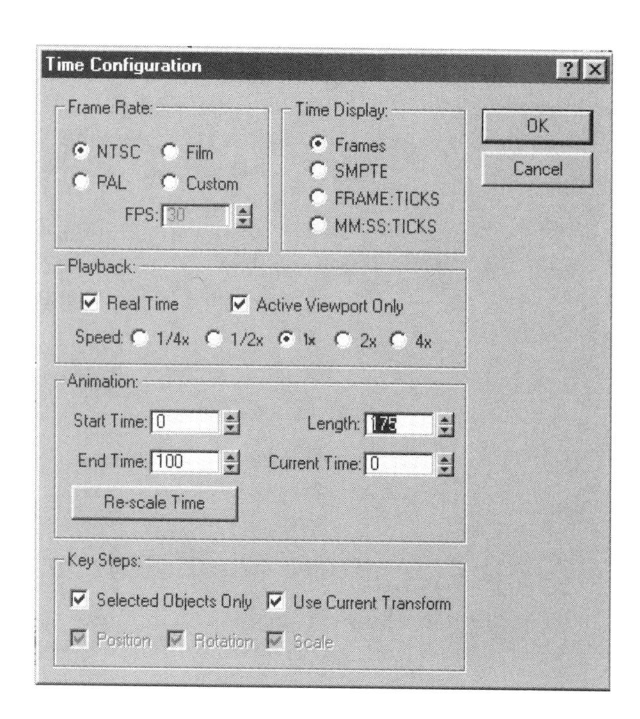


FIGURE 18.10 Time Configuration dialog.

### Robot Swing

4. The robot is going to swing clockwise on the Lower-Yoke from its original position to locate itself above the part, as shown in Figure 18.11.

   Select the Edit/Hold pull-down menu item to store the current state of the animation. If you make a mistake, you can use the Edit/Fetch command to restore it to the last step and start again. Save your scene.

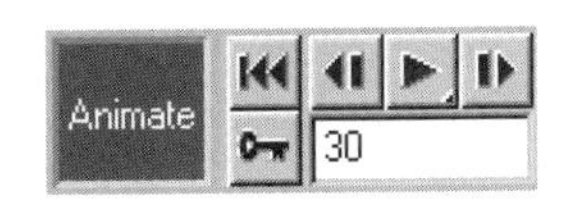


#### Part A Movement

Make sure the Frame is set to 30 and the Animate button is on (red).

Select the Lower-Yoke using the Select by Name tool and lock it.

Activate the Top viewport and turn on the Rotate transform.

Set the Reference Coordinate System to Local and turn on the Restrict to Z tool.

In the Top viewport, pick and drag near the Lower-Yoke until the Z coordinate on the status line reads -180°. Release the pick button. The new position of the robot should look like Figure 18.11.

Turn off the Animate button (grey).

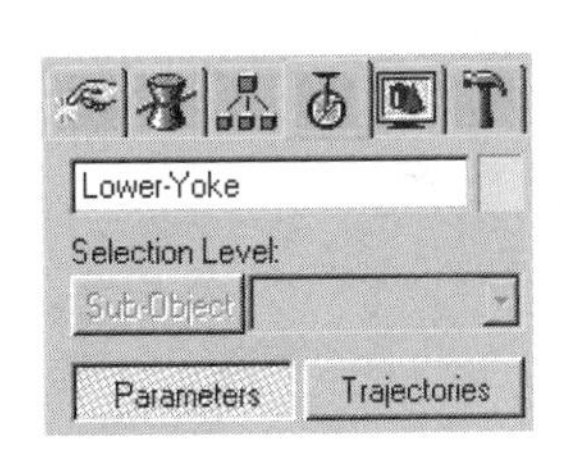


#### Part B Assign Motion Controller

Open the Motion command panel and make sure the Parameters button is on. Open the Assign Controller rollout and highlight Rotation in the white transform list box. Pick the Assign Controller tool above the box. The Replace Rotation Control dialog will appear. Highlight Linear Rotation and pick OK. Refer to Figure 18.12 for the final setting.

#### Part C Adjust Track

Because this is the first movement, its keys do not have to be adjusted.

Test the animation by picking the Play tool. When you have seen enough, stop the animation.

Unlock the selection of the Lower-Yoke.

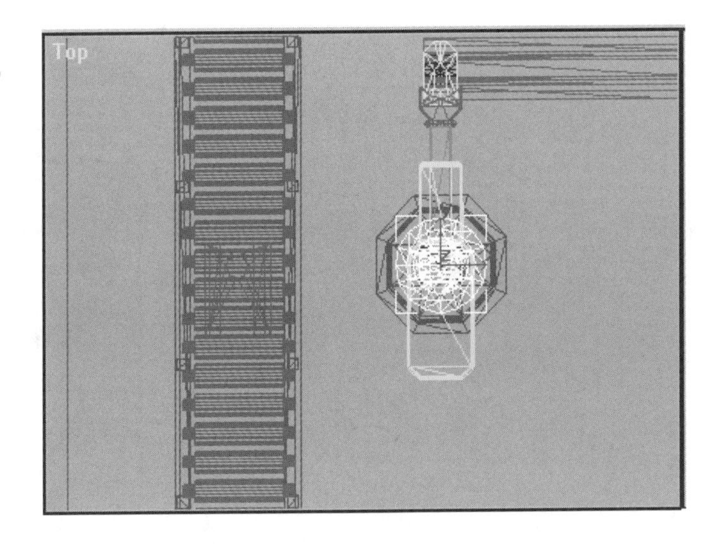


FIGURE 18.11
Robot swung 180° into new position.

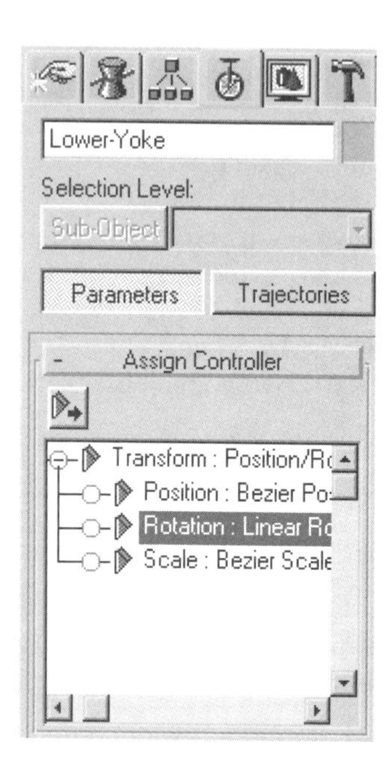


FIGURE 18.12
Controller set to linear rotation.

### Arm Slide

5. The arm will slide in to align with the part, as shown in Figure 18.13.
   Select the Edit/Hold pull-down menu item and save your scene.

#### Part A Movement

Make sure the Frame is set to 40 and the Animate button is on (red).

Select the Arm using the Select by Name tool and lock it.

Activate the Top viewport and turn on the Move transform.

Set the Reference Coordinate System to Local and turn on the Restrict to X tool.

Select the Tools/Transform Type-In pull-down menu item. The dialog should appear. Enter 1.0 in the Offset:Screen X box. This will cause the arm to slide a distance of 1. Refer to Figure 18.13 for the new position.

Turn off the Animate button (grey) and close the Transform Type-In dialog.

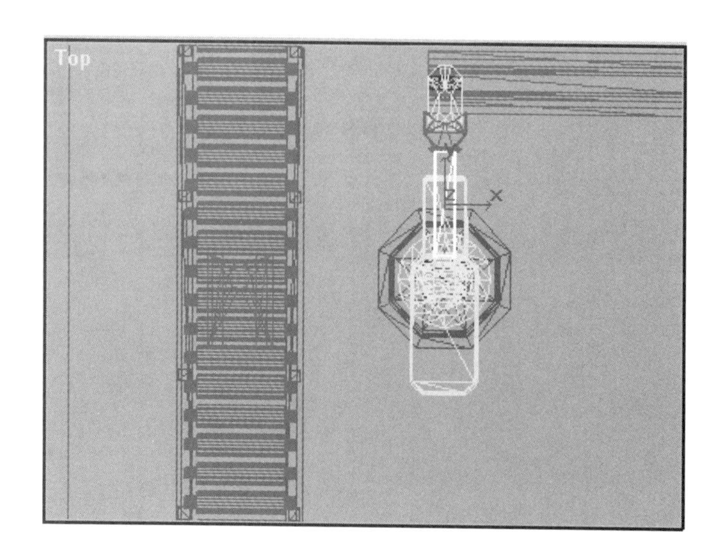


FIGURE 18.13
Arm sliding in to align with part.

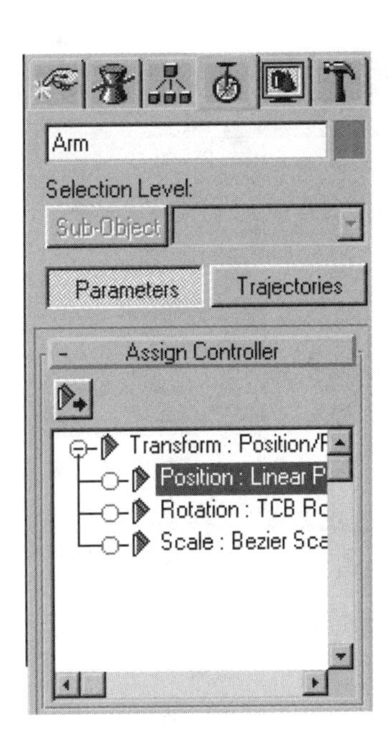


FIGURE 18.14
Controller set to linear position.

**Part B Assign Motion Controller**

Open the Motion command panel and make sure the Parameters button is on. Open the Assign Controller rollout and highlight Position in the white transform list box. Pick the Assign Controller tool above the box. The Replace Position Control dialog will appear. Highlight Linear Position and pick OK. Figure 18.14 shows the final setting.

**Part C Adjust Track**

Pick the Track View tool to display the dialog, as shown in Figure 18.15. Scroll down and open the tracks until you see the Arm.

The Start key of the position transform for the Arm is at Frame 0. It must be copied to Frame 31. With the Move Keys tool on, hold the Shift key and pick and drag the Position Key from Frame 0 to Frame 31. Refer to Figure 18.15 for the original position and Figure 18.16 for the new position.

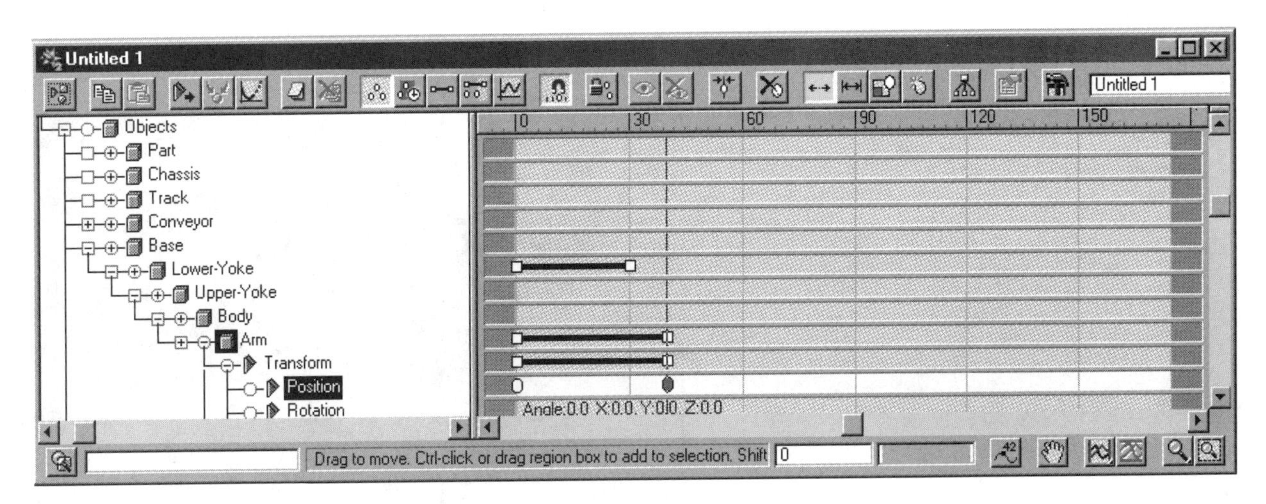


FIGURE 18.15
Track View showing the original position of the start key.

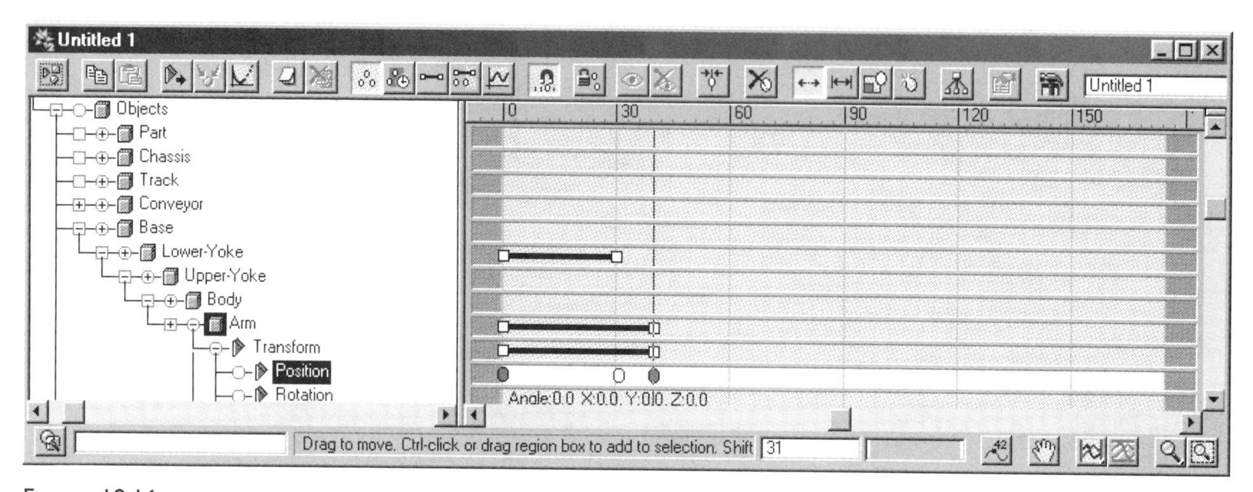


FIGURE 18.16
Track View showing the copied position of the start key.

Close the Track View dialog, activate the Top viewport, and test the animation.

Unlock the selection of the Arm.

### Fingers Open

6. The fingers will slide open, as shown in Figure 18.17.
   Select the Edit/Hold pull-down menu item and save your scene.

**Part A Movement**

Frame = 50 — Animate = On
Top viewport = Active
Select Finger-Right — Move transform = On
Reference Coordinate System = Local — Restrict to Y = On
Tools/Transform Type-In = Open — Offset:Screen Y box = -1.75 *Enter*
Select Finger-Left
Edit/Transform Type-In = Open — Offset:Screen Y box = 1.75 *Enter*
Turn off the Animate button (grey) and close the Transform Type-In dialog.

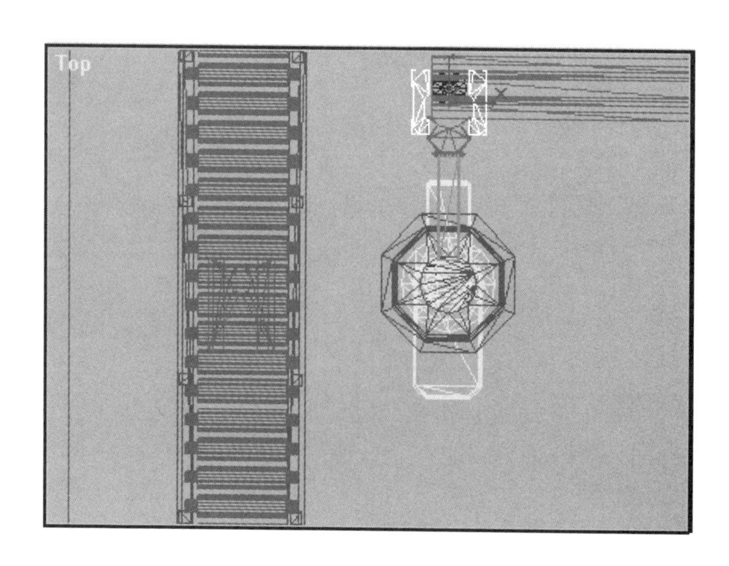


FIGURE 18.17
Fingers sliding open.

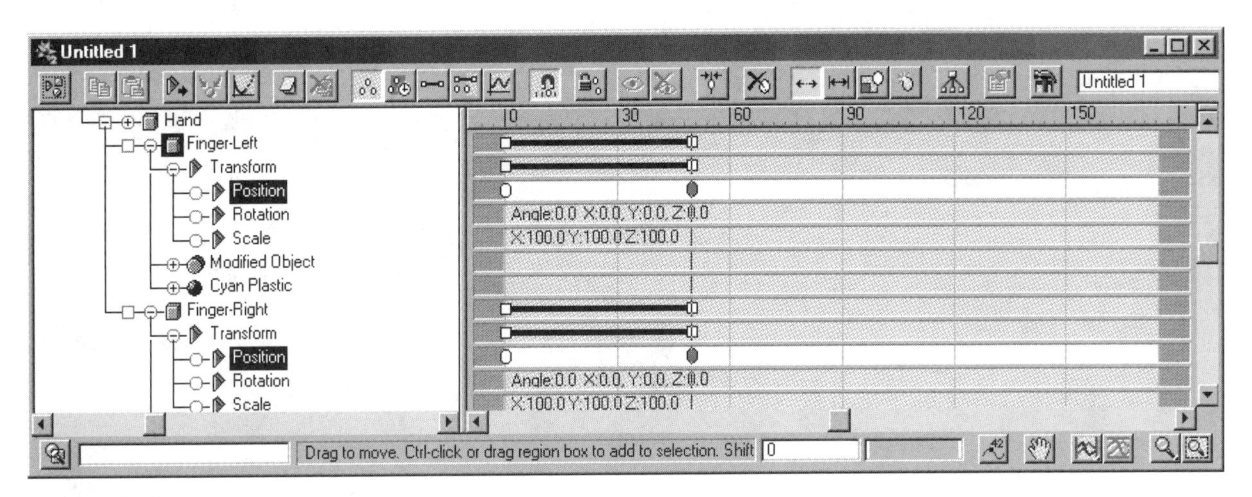

FIGURE 18.18
Track View showing Fingers start keys in the original position.

**Part B Assign Motion Controller**
Motion panel = Open
Assign Controller rollout = Open
Parameters button = On
Transform Position = Set to Linear
Repeat for both Fingers.

**Part C Adjust Track**
Track View dialog = Displayed

Position Key = copy key from 0 to 41 for both Fingers

Refer to Figures 18.18 and 18.19 for before and after key locations.

Close the Track View dialog, activate the Top viewport, and test the animation.

## Robot Lowers

7. The robot will pivot on the Upper-Yoke and lower itself until the Fingers are around the Part, as shown in Figure 18.20.
   Select the Edit/Hold pull-down menu item and save your scene.

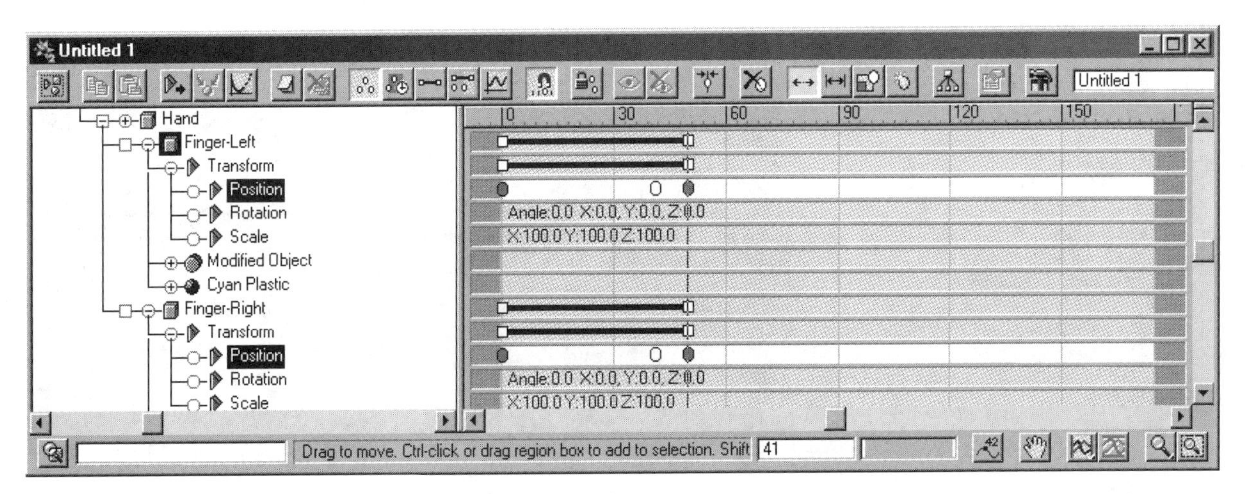

FIGURE 18.19
Track View showing Fingers start keys in the copied position.

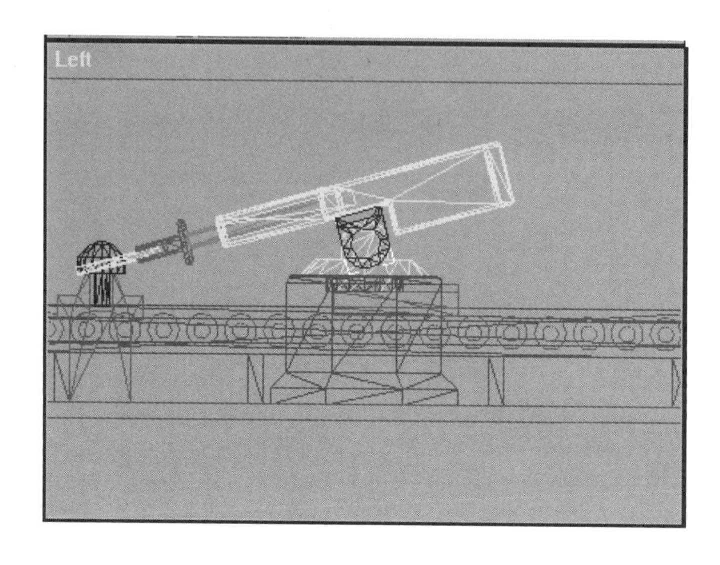


FIGURE 18.20
Left viewport showing the robot lowering to meet the Part.

**Part A Movement**

Frame = 65
Animate = On
Left viewport = Active
Select Upper-Yoke
Rotate transform = On
Reference Coordinate System = Local
Restrict to Y = On
Pick and Drag in Left Viewport until coordinate Y reads -15°
Turn off the Animate button (grey).

**Part B Assign Motion Controller**

Motion panel = Open
Parameters button = On
Assign Controller rollout = Open
Transform Rotation = Set to Linear

**Part C Adjust Track**

Track View dialog = Displayed

Rotation Key = Copy from 0 to 51 for Upper-Yoke

Figures 18.21 and 18.22 show before and after key locations.

Close the Track View dialog, activate the Left viewport, and test the animation.

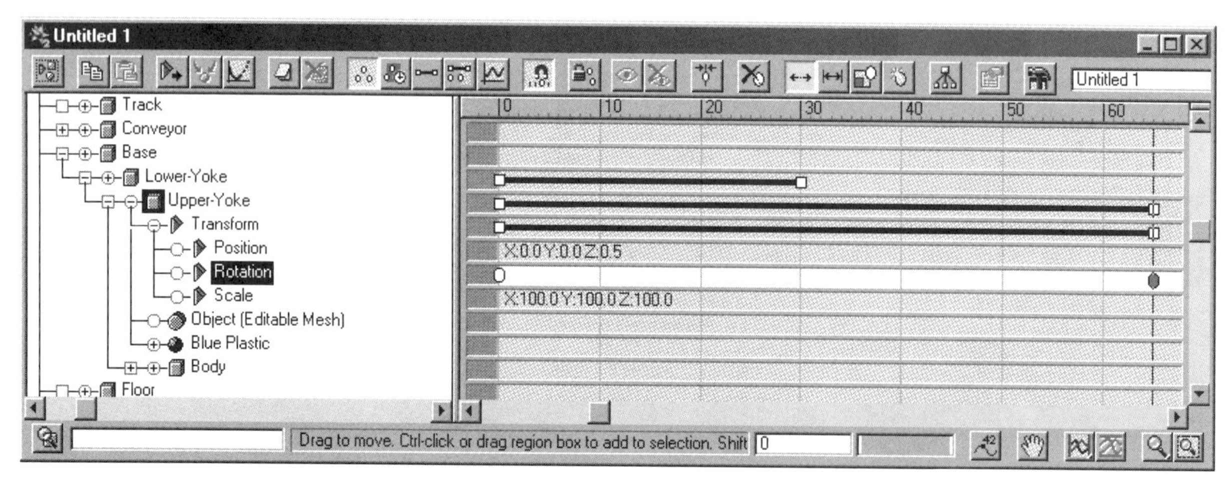


FIGURE 18.21
Track View showing Upper-Yoke key in the original position.

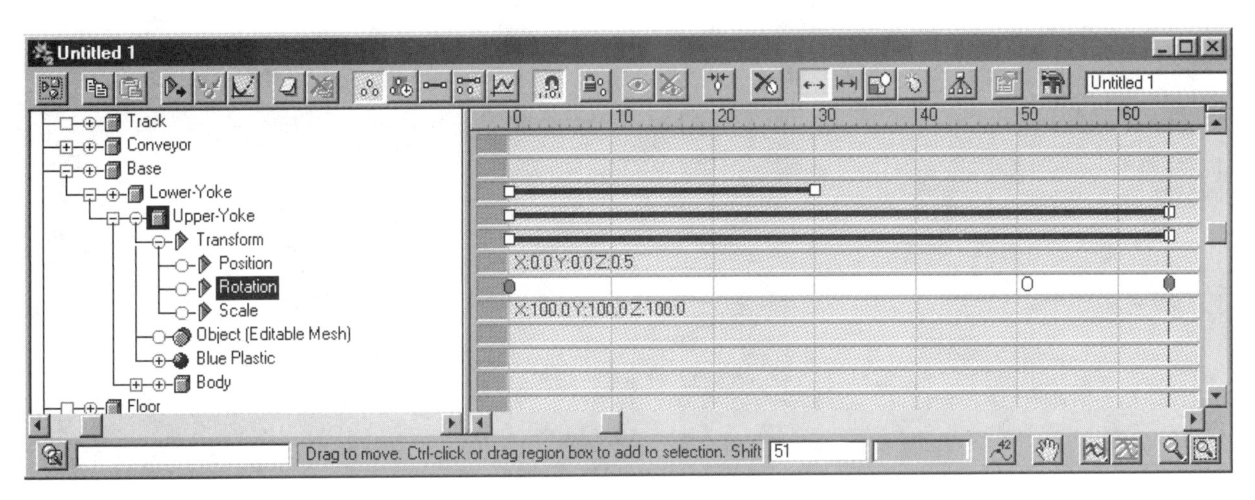


FIGURE 18.22
Track View showing Upper-Yoke key in the copied position.

**Fingers Close on Part**

8. The Fingers will slide closed to touch the Part, as shown in Figure 18.23. Select the Edit/Hold pull-down menu item and save your scene.

**Part A Movement**

| | |
|---|---|
| Frame = 75 | Animate = On |
| Top viewport = Active | |
| Select Finger-Right | Move transform = On |
| Reference Coordinate System = Local | Restrict to Y = On |
| Tools/Transform Type-In = Open | Offset:Screen Y box = 0.25 *Enter* |
| Select Finger-Left | |
| Tools/Transform Type-In = Open | Offset:Screen Y box = -0.25 *Enter* |

Turn off the Animate button (grey) and close the Transform Type-In dialog.

**Part B Assign Motion Controller**

This step is not required because it was done earlier.

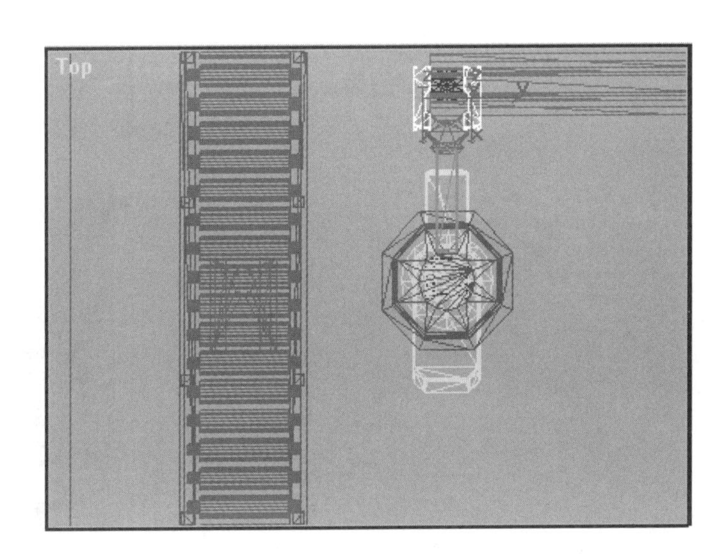


FIGURE 18.23
Fingers sliding to close on Part.

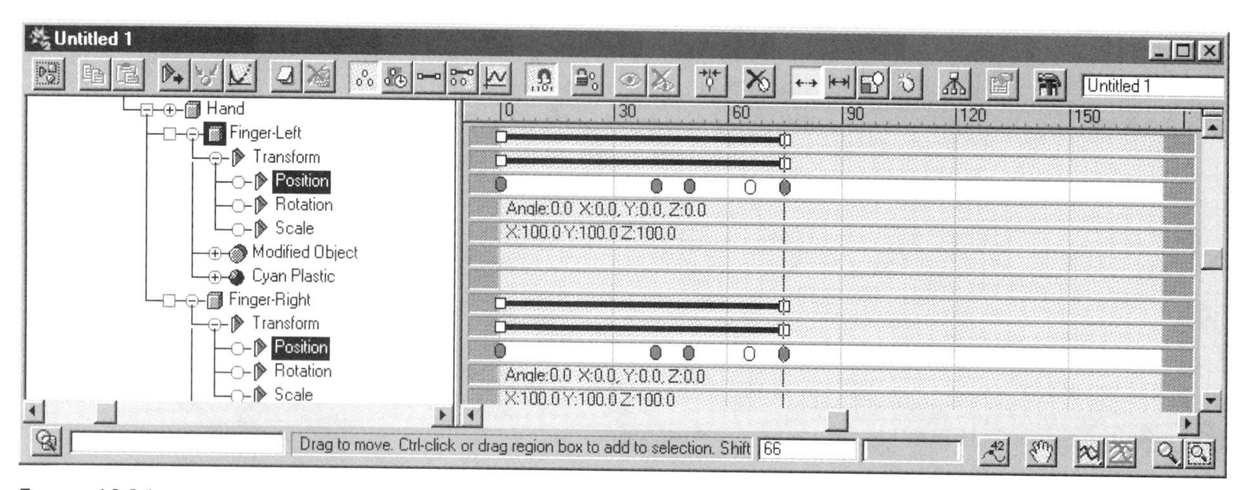


FIGURE 18.24
Track View showing Fingers keys in copied positions.

**Part C Adjust Track**
Track View dialog = Displayed

Position Key = Copy from 50 to 66 for both Fingers

Refer to Figure 18.24 for copied key locations.

Close the Track View dialog, activate the Top viewport, and test the animation.

### Robot Swing with Part

9. The robot will swing counterclockwise on the Lower-Yoke, bringing the Part with it, until it is clear of the track that held the Part, as shown in Figure 18.25.
   Select the Edit/Hold pull-down menu item and save your scene.

**Part A Movement**
Frame = 85 Animate = On

Top viewport = Active

Select Lower-Yoke and Part together (use CTRL key while picking)

Rotate transform = On

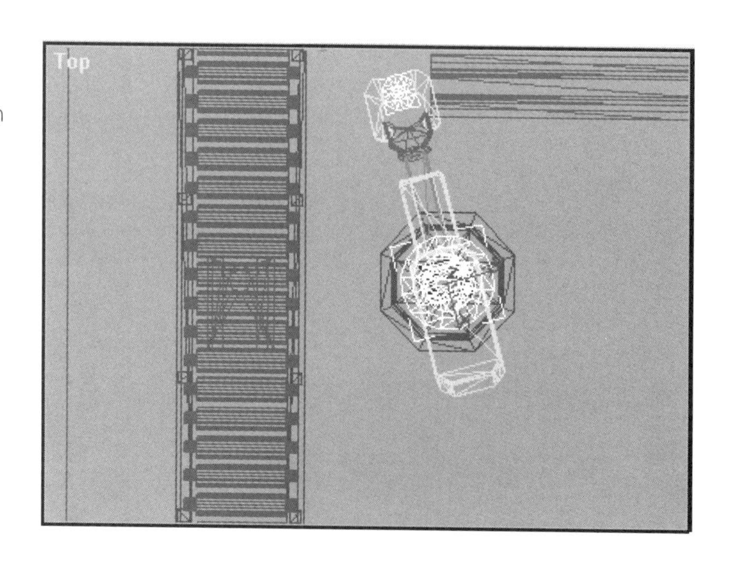


FIGURE 18.25
Top viewport showing the robot swinging with the Part.

Reference Coordinate System = Pick (pick Lower-Yoke in Left viewport)

Restrict to Z = On

Pick and Drag in Top viewport until coordinate Z reads +15°.

Turn off the Animate button (grey).

**Part B Assign Motion Controller**
Select Part object only

Motion panel = Open — Parameters button = On

Assign Controller rollout = Open — Transform Rotation = Set to Linear

Transform Position = Set to Linear

**Part C Adjust Track**
Track View dialog = Displayed

Rotation Key = Copy from 30 to 76 for Lower-Yoke

Rotation Key = Copy from 0 to 76 for Part

Refer to Figure 18.26 for the Lower-Yoke copied key location.

Close the Track View dialog, activate the Top viewport, and test the animation.

**Robot Raises with Part**

10. The robot will pivot upward on the Upper-Yoke, raising the Part, as shown in Figure 18.27.
    Select the Edit/Hold pull-down menu item and save your scene.

**Part A Movement**
Frame = 95 — Animate = On
Left viewport = Active
Select Upper-Yoke and Part together — Rotate transform = On
Reference Coordinate System = Pick (pick Upper-Yoke in Left viewport)
Restrict to Y = On
Pick and Drag in Left Viewport until coordinate Y reads +15°.
Turn off the Animate button (grey).

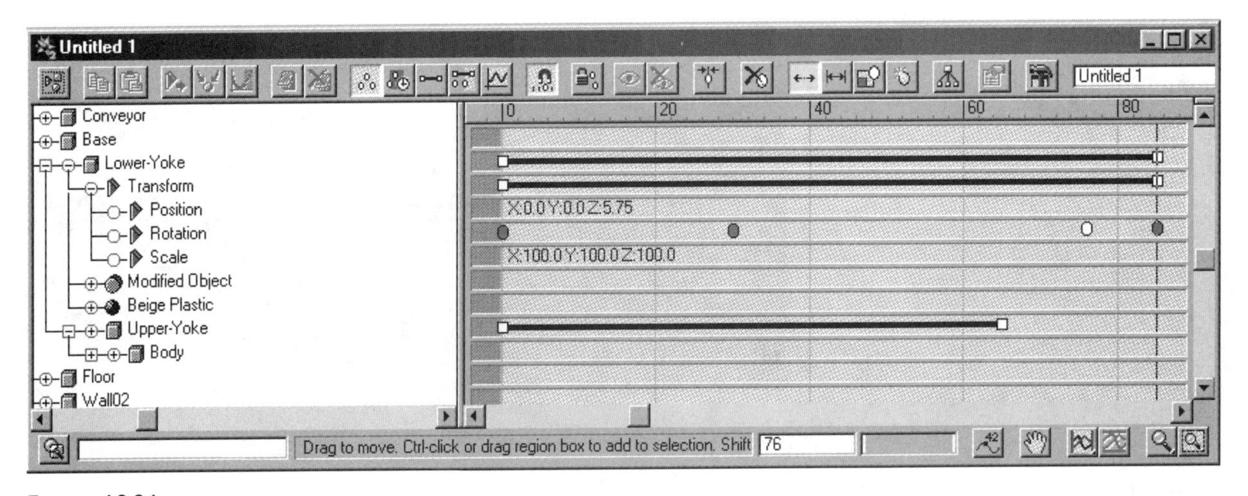


FIGURE 18.26
Track View showing Lower-Yoke key in copied position.

FIGURE 18.27
Left viewport showing the robot raising with the Part.

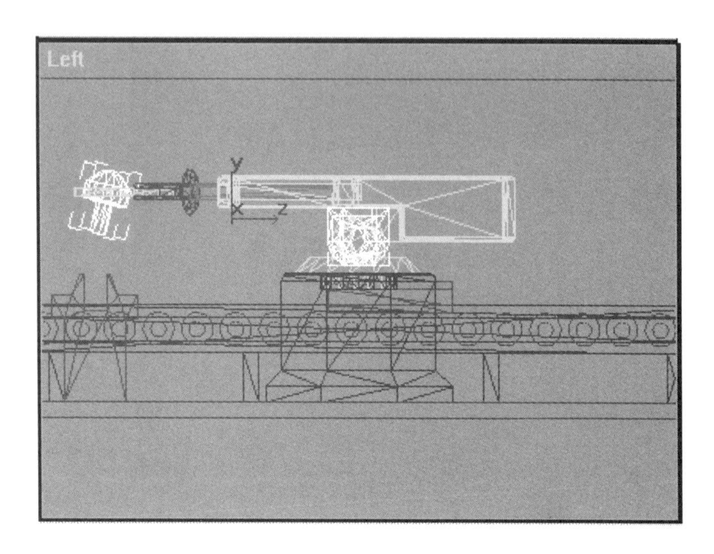


**Part B Assign Motion Controller**
This step is not required.

**Part C Adjust Track**
Track View dialog = Displayed

Rotation Key = Copy from 65 to 86 for Upper-Yoke

Rotation Key = Copy from 85 to 86 for Part

Refer to Figure 18.28 for Upper-Yoke key locations.

Close the Track View dialog, activate the Left viewport, and test the animation.

## Robot Swings Over Chassis

11. The robot will swing counterclockwise on the Lower Yoke until the Part is over the hole in the Chassis, as shown in Figure 18.29.
    Select the Edit/Hold pull-down menu item and save your scene.

**Part A Movement**
Frame = 110 Animate = On
Top viewport = Active

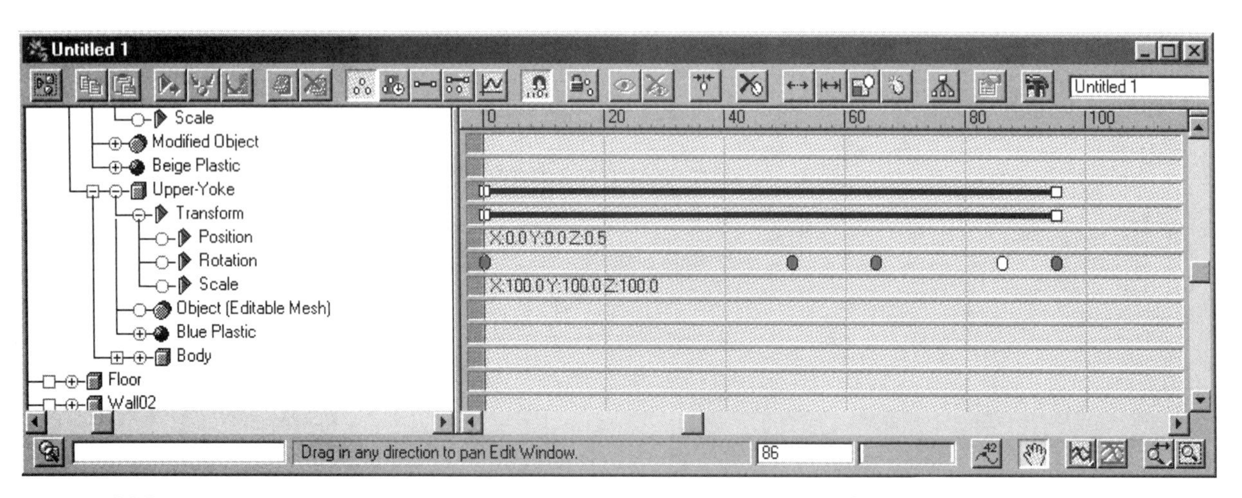


FIGURE 18.28
Track View showing Upper-Yoke key in copied position.

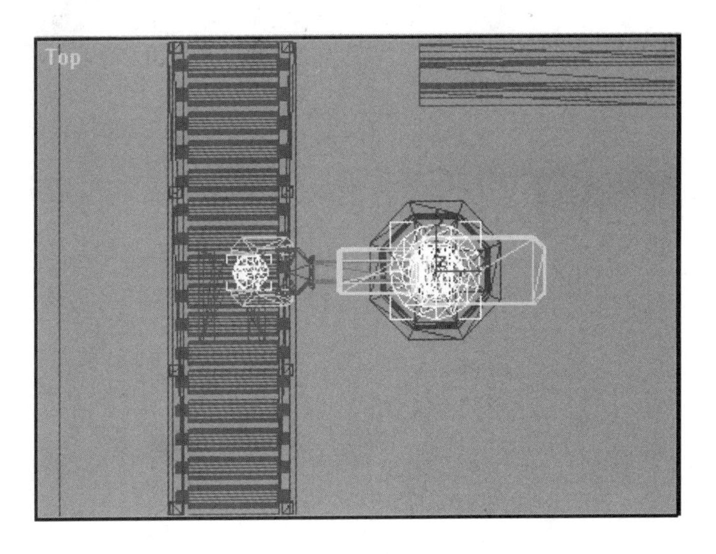

FIGURE 18.29
Top viewport showing robot swinging (with Part) over Chassis.

Select Lower-Yoke and Part together  Rotate transform = On
Reference Coordinate System = Pick (pick Lower-Yoke in Top viewport)
Restrict to Z = On
Pick and Drag in Top viewport until coordinate Z reads +75°.
Turn off the Animate button (grey).

**Part B Assign Motion Controller**
This step is not required.

**Part C Adjust Track**
Track View dialog = Displayed

Rotation Key = Copy from 85 to 96 for Lower-Yoke

Rotation Key = Copy from 95 to 96 for Part

Close the Track View dialog, activate the Top viewport, and test the animation.

**Arm and Part Slide Over Chassis**

12. The arm will slide out so that the Part is aligned with the hole, as shown in Figure 18.30.

    Select the Edit/Hold pull-down menu item and save your scene.

**Part A Movement**
Frame = 120  Animate = On
Top viewport = Active
Select Arm and Part  Move transform = On
Reference Coordinate System = View  Restrict to X = On
Tools/Transform Type-In = Open  Offset:Screen X box = -1.0 *Enter*
Turn off the Animate button (grey) and close the Transform Type-In dialog.

**Part B Assign Motion Controller**
This step is not required.

**Part C Adjust Track**
Track View dialog = Displayed

Position Key = Copy from 40 to 111 for Arm

Position Key = Copy from 0 to 111 for Part

Close the Track View dialog, activate the Top viewport, and test the animation.

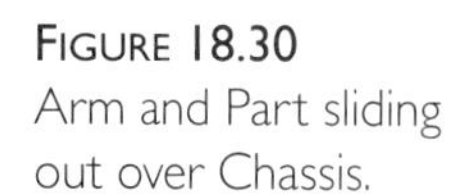

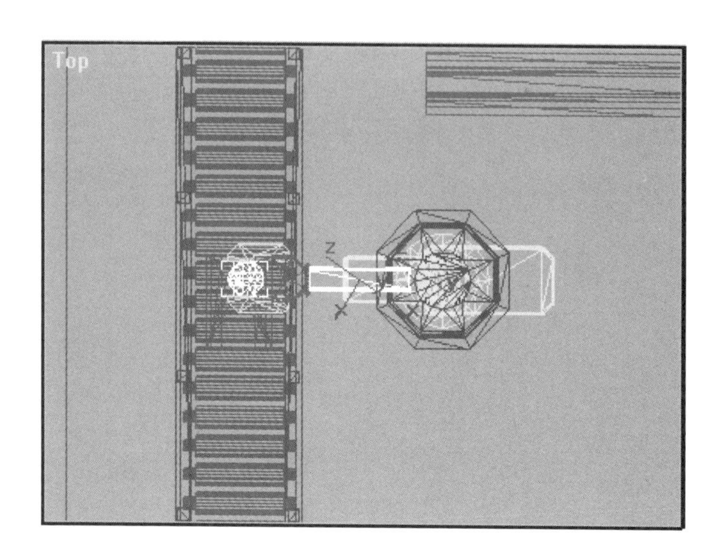


FIGURE 18.30
Arm and Part sliding out over Chassis.

**Upper-Yoke and Part Lower to Chassis**

13. The robot will pivot on the Upper-Yoke, lowering the Part into the hole, as shown in Figure 18.31.

    Select the Edit/Hold pull-down menu item and save your scene.

    **Part A Movement**
    Frame = 130 Animate = On
    Front viewport = Active
    Select Upper-Yoke and Part together Rotate transform = On
    Reference Coordinate System = Pick Upper-Yoke from list
    Restrict to Y = On
    Pick and Drag in Front Viewport until coordinate Y reads -15°.
    Turn off the Animate button (grey).

    **Part B Assign Motion Controller**
    This step is not required.

    **Part C Adjust Track**
    Track View dialog = Displayed

    Rotation Key = Copy from 95 to 121 for Upper-Yoke

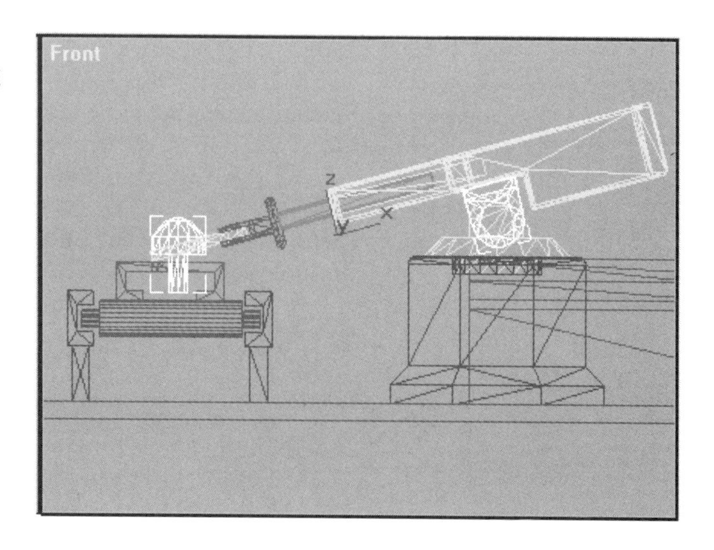


FIGURE 18.31
Front viewport showing robot lowering with Part.

Rotation Key = Copy from 110 to 121 for Part

Close the Track View dialog, activate the Front viewport, and test the animation.

### Fingers Open, Releasing Part

14. The fingers slide open to release the Part, as shown in Figure 18.32. Select the Edit/Hold pull-down menu item and save your scene.

**Part A Movement**

| | |
|---|---|
| Frame = 140 | Animate = On |
| Top viewport = Active | |
| Select Finger-Right | Move transform = On |
| Reference Coordinate System = Local | Restrict to Y = On |
| Tools/Transform Type-In = Open | Offset:Screen Y box = -0.25 *Enter* |
| Select Finger-Left | |
| Tools/Transform Type-In = Open | Offset:Screen Y box = 0.25 *Enter* |

Turn off the Animate button (grey) and close the Transform Type-In dialog.

**Part B Assign Motion Controller**

This step is not required.

**Part C Adjust Track**

Track View dialog = Displayed

Position Key = Copy from 75 to 131 for both Fingers

Close the Track View dialog, activate the Top viewport, and test the animation.

### Robot Raises without Part

15. The robot will raise by pivoting on the Upper-Yoke, as shown in Figure 18.33. Select the Edit/Hold pull-down menu item and save your scene.

**Part A Movement**

| | |
|---|---|
| Frame = 150 | Animate = On |
| Front viewport = Active | |
| Select Upper-Yoke | Rotate transform = On |
| Reference Coordinate System = Local | Restrict to Y = On |

Pick and Drag in Front viewport until coordinate Y reads +15°.

Turn off the Animate button (grey).

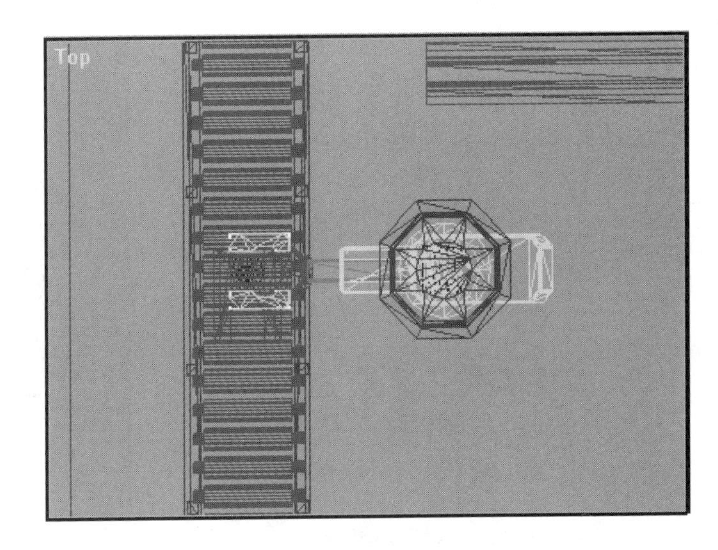


FIGURE 18.32
Fingers sliding to open to release Part.

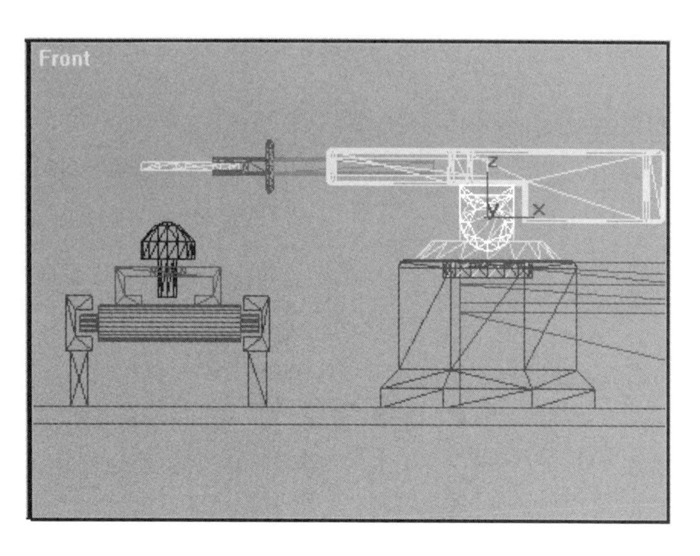


FIGURE 18.33
Front viewport showing robot raising without Part.

**Part B Assign Motion Controller**
This step is not required.

**Part C Adjust Track**
Track View dialog = Displayed

Rotation Key = Copy from 130 to 141 for Upper-Yoke

Close the Track View dialog, activate the Left viewport, and test the animation.

### Robot Returning to Start Position

16. The robot will swing counterclockwise on the Lower Yoke, returning to its starting position, as shown in Figure 18.34.
    Select the Edit/Hold pull-down menu item and save your scene.

**Part A Movement**

| | |
|---|---|
| Frame = 165 | Animate = On |
| Top viewport = Active | |
| Select Lower-Yoke | Rotate transform = On |
| Reference Coordinate System = Local | Restrict to Z = On |

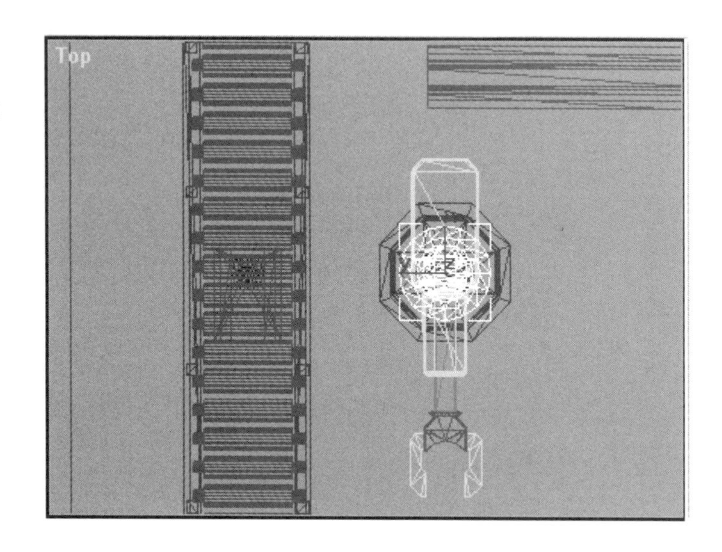


FIGURE 18.34
Top viewport, showing robot swinging to start position.

Pick and Drag in Top viewport until coordinate Z reads +90°.
Turn off the Animate button (grey).

**Part B Assign Motion Controller**
This step is not required.

**Part C Adjust Track**
Track View dialog = Displayed

Rotation Key = Copy from 110 to 151 for Lower-Yoke

Close the Track View dialog, activate the Top viewport, and test the animation.

**Fingers Close to Start Position**

17. The Fingers will close to return to their original positions, as shown in Figure 18.35. Select the Edit/Hold pull-down menu item and save your scene.

**Part A Movement**

| | |
|---|---|
| Frame = 175 | Animate = On |
| Top viewport = Active | |
| Select Finger-Right | Move transform = On |
| Reference Coordinate System = Local | Restrict to Y = On |
| Tools/Transform Type-In = Open | Offset:Screen Y box = 1.75 *Enter* |
| Select Finger-Left | |
| Tools/Transform Type-In = Open | Offset:Screen Y box = -1.75 *Enter* |

Turn off the Animate button (grey) and close the Transform Type-In dialog.

**Part B Assign Motion Controller**
This step is not required.

**Part C Adjust Track**
Track View dialog = Displayed

Position Key = Copy from 140 to 166 for both Fingers

Close the Track View dialog, activate the Top viewport, and test the animation.

Save your scene.

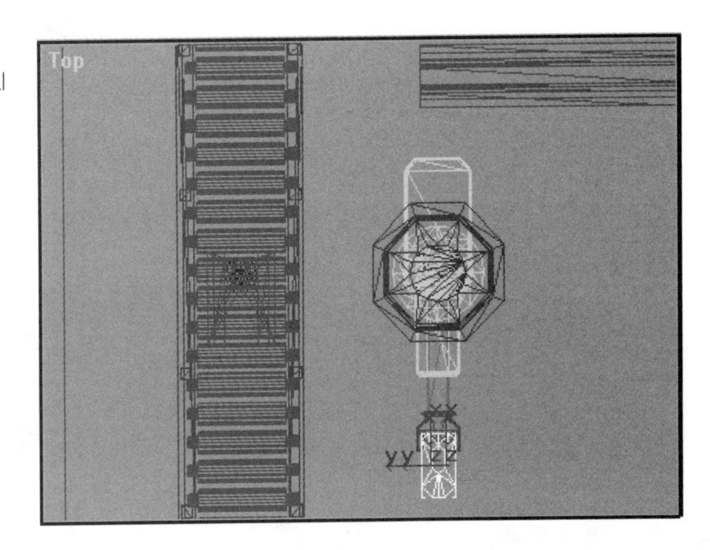


FIGURE 18.35
Fingers sliding to original start position.

## 18.5 RENDERING THE ANIMATION

The last process in this project is to render the animation. This may take awhile, so you had better plan for it (1 hr 15 min using a PII 350 MHz with 96 MB RAM).

1. Open the Render Scene dialog and adjust the settings, as shown in Figure 18.36. Save the rendered animation as MXROBOT. You can save it as an FLC or AVI. The choice is yours. The FLC file is smaller in size, whereas the AVI file can easily be used in other programs.
   Render the animation.
2. Once the animation has been rendered, use the File/View File pull-down menu item. Find your file and play it. You may have to switch subdirectories.

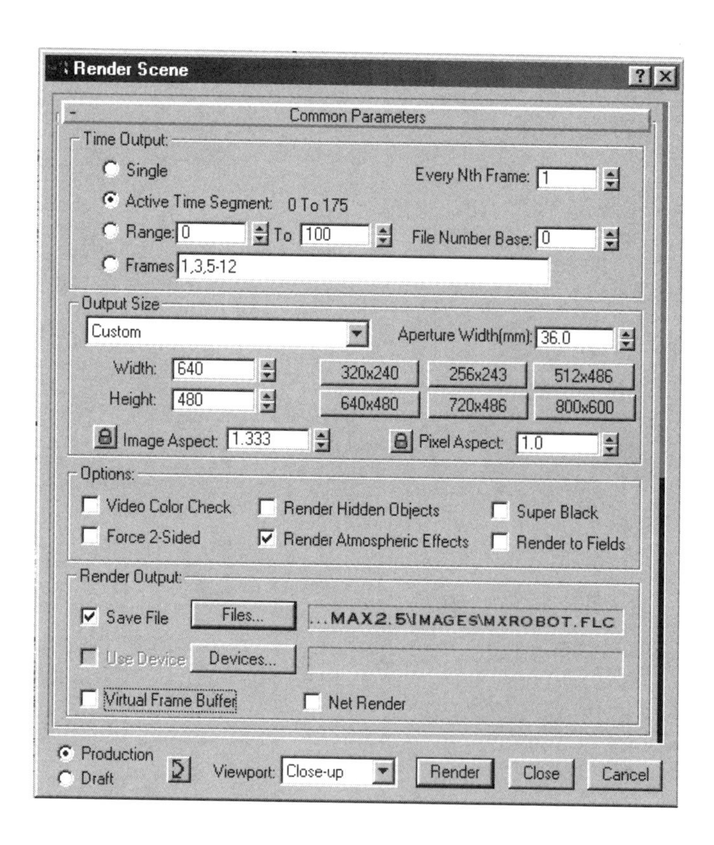


FIGURE 18.36
Render Scene dialog.

# Appendices

# Installing the CD-ROM Files

## ORGANIZATION OF CD-ROM

The CD-ROM is separated into five directories:

| Directory | Description |
|---|---|
| ANIMATED | Animation files that can be viewed inside 3D Studio MAX using the File/View File pull-down menu item. These can be viewed directly from the CD-ROM. Chapter 2 shows three still images of each animation. |
| MAPS | Bitmap image files that should be copied into 3D Studio Max's Maps subdirectory: C:\3DSMAX2.5\MAPS. Some of the files are duplicates of those supplied with 3D Studio MAX. They are there to ensure that you have the necessary files with which to perform the labs and projects.<br>Also contained in this directory is the material library file called MOTION2.MAT. This should be copied into 3D Studio MAX's Library subdirectory: C:\3DSMAX2.5\ MATLIBS. |
| SCENES | Scene files that are used in the labs. All the files start with MX and have the extension .MAX. These should be copied into the 3D Studio MAX Scenes subdirectory: C:\3DSMAX2.5\SCENES. |
| IMAGES | Rendered color image files of figures used in the textbook. |
| PROJECTS | Still Images and Animation files that illustrate completed labs or projects. You can refer to them if you want to see the outcome of a still rendering or an animation for a lab or project. |

## INSTALLING FILES

### Maps

The Maps directory on the CD-ROM contains all the bitmap images and material libraries that are required to perform the labs and projects. You need to copy all the files in the MAPS directory on the CD-ROM into the Maps subdirectory of 3D Studio MAX, which is normally called C:\3DSMAX2.5\MAPS. However, you should check your system for the location of the subdirectory and copy the files into it. Remember to copy MOTION2.MAT to the material library subdirectory C:\3DSMAX2.5\MATLIBS.

### Scenes

The Scenes directory on the CD-ROM contains all the scene files that are required to perform the labs and projects. You need to copy all the files from the SCENES directory on the CD-ROM into the Scenes subdirectory of 3D Studio Max, which is normally called C:\3DSMAX2.5\SCENES. However, you should check your system for the location of the subdirectory and copy the files into it.

# Importing and Exporting Files

## IMPORTING FILES

The standard 3D Studio MAX has the capability of importing the following file types:

| File Type | File Extension |
|---|---|
| 3D Studio Mesh | *.3DS or *.PRJ |
| 3D Studio Shape | *.SHP |
| Adobe Illustrator | *.AI |
| AutoCAD | *.DWG |
| AutoCAD | *.DXF |
| VRML | *.WRL or *.WRZ |
| SteroLitho | *.STL |

To import a file, use the File/Import pull-down menu item from within 3D Studio MAX.

## EXPORTING FILES

The Standard 3D Studio MAX has the capability of exporting to the following file types:

| File Type | File Extension |
|---|---|
| 3D Studio Mesh | *.3DS |
| AutoCAD | *.DWG |
| AutoCAD | *.DXF |
| ASC File | *.ASC |

| | |
|---|---|
| ASCII Scene | *.ASE |
| SteroLitho | *.STL |
| VRML 1.0/VRBL | *.WRL |
| VRML97 | *.WRL |

To export to a different file type, use the File/Export pull-down menu item from within 3D Studio MAX.

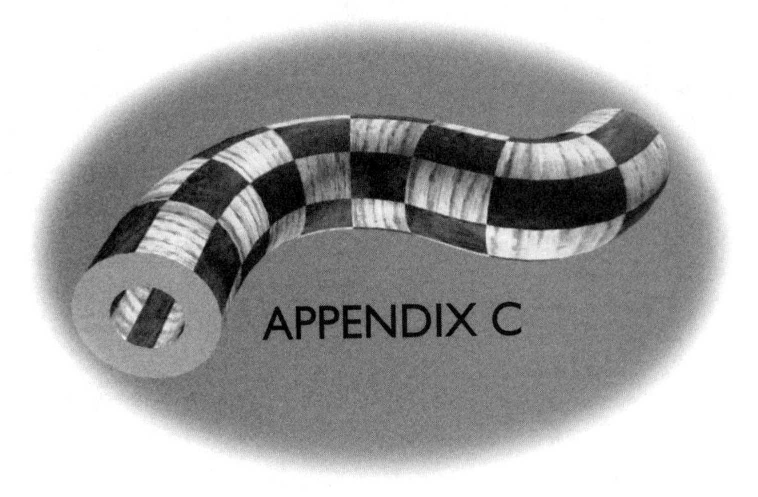


# Video Post

## INTRODUCTION

Video Post is used to manipulate the final animations and still images to achieve combinations and effects. It can be thought of as the postproduction phase. You can take several animations and combine them; you can insert still images and add transitional effects at the beginning, in between, or at the end of combined files; you can even change the size of the output image or animation.

This appendix reviews the basics of using the Video Post dialog.

## THE VIDEO POST DIALOG

The Video Post dialog is very similar to the Track View dialog. Figure C.1 shows the Video Post dialog and the following list of main elements.

**Toolbar**
Running along the top are the various tools used to save, add, or modify events.

**Queue**
Along the left side is the event hierarchy, or queue. As you add or manage events, they appear in this area, showing various links or relationships to each other.

**Edit Window**
On the right of the dialog is the Edit window. This displays the range bars, which represent the length of frames over which the events occur.

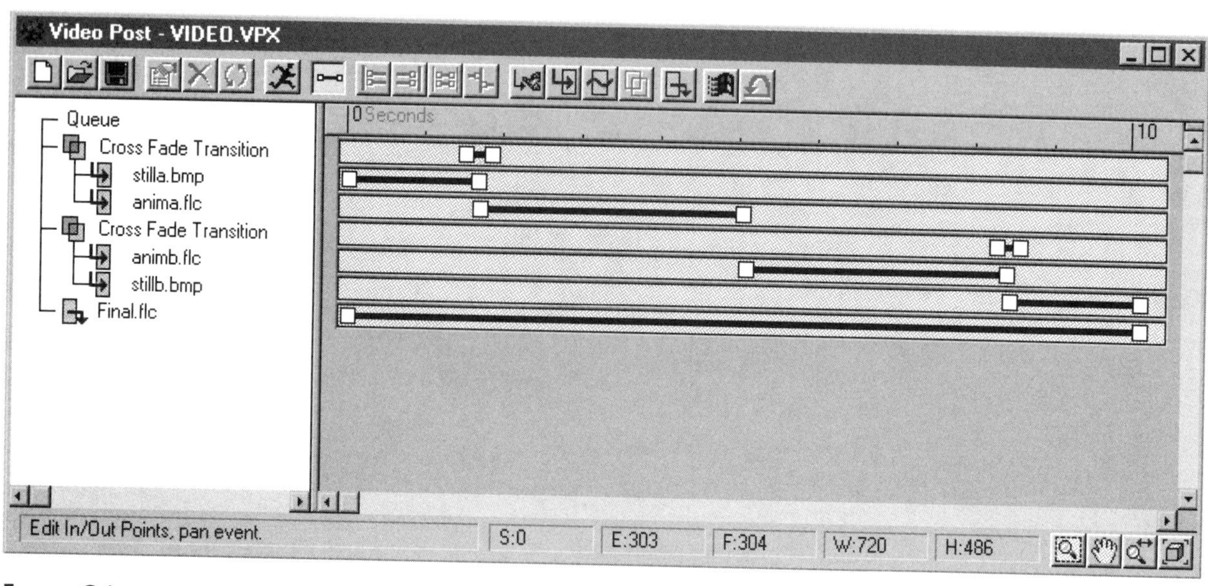


FIGURE C.1
Video Post dialog.

**Status Line**

Running along the bottom is the status line, displaying the following information:

S: Start frame
E: End frame
F: Total number of frames in output video
W: Width of frame in output video
H: Height of frame in output video

The tools used to navigate the Edit window are also located here.

## TOOLBAR

The tool bar is separated into six groups of related tools.

### File Buttons

The File buttons create a new Video Post file, open an existing file, or save the current data. The file has the extension .VPX.

### Edit Buttons

The Edit buttons edit the current event, delete events, or swap two events positioned in the queue.

### Execute Button

The Execute buton is used to execute the events in the cue to create an animation or image.

*Note:* You must have included an Output event to save the resulting animation or image to disk.

### Edit Range Bar Button

The Edit Range Bar button is used to edit the range bar. When a bar is active, you can drag it or move its endpoints.

### Align and Abut Tools

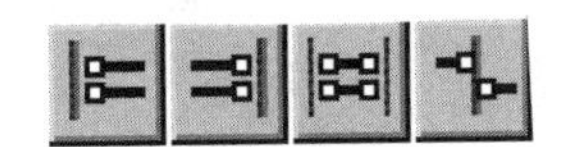

The Align and Abut buttons are used to adjust the endpoints of two or more ranges so that they either align or abut each other.

### Event Buttons

The Event buttons add input and output events to the queue.

The **Scene** events button adds a view of the current 3DS MAX scene or animation to the final video.

The **Image Input** events button adds still images or animations to the final video. You can select from a directory list of previous image or animation files.

The **Image Filter** events button adds processing to an image. It can be used to change the appearance of an image or to make a transition between two events.

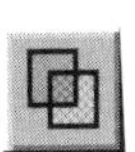

The **Image Layer** events button is used to combine two images.

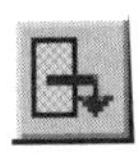

The **Image Output** events button is used to send the result of the executed events in the queue to either an external device or a saved file. You can use this event to change the size of the output image or animation. This event must be included in the queue to save and execute a sequence to disk.

The **External** events button adds an external program to the queue usually used to process an image.

The **Loop** events button causes other events to repeat over time.

### Adding and Executing Events

This section explains the procedure for creating a sample output video file by combining two animation files. The following is a list of the sequence of events. Following this is the procedure for setting up the queue and executing it to create a new animation file.

### Sequence of Events

1. A still image (STILLA) is displayed for 50 frames. This represents an introduction image that could contain the name of the animation and a list of credits.
2. A transition occurs between the still image and the next animation file.
3. Animation file (ANIMA) runs for its entire length of 100 frames.
4. Animation file (ANIMB) runs for its entire length of 100 frames.
5. A transition occurs between the final animation (ANIMB) and a still image.
6. A still image (STILLB) is displayed at the end of the animation for 50 frames. This could display information signifying the end of the video.

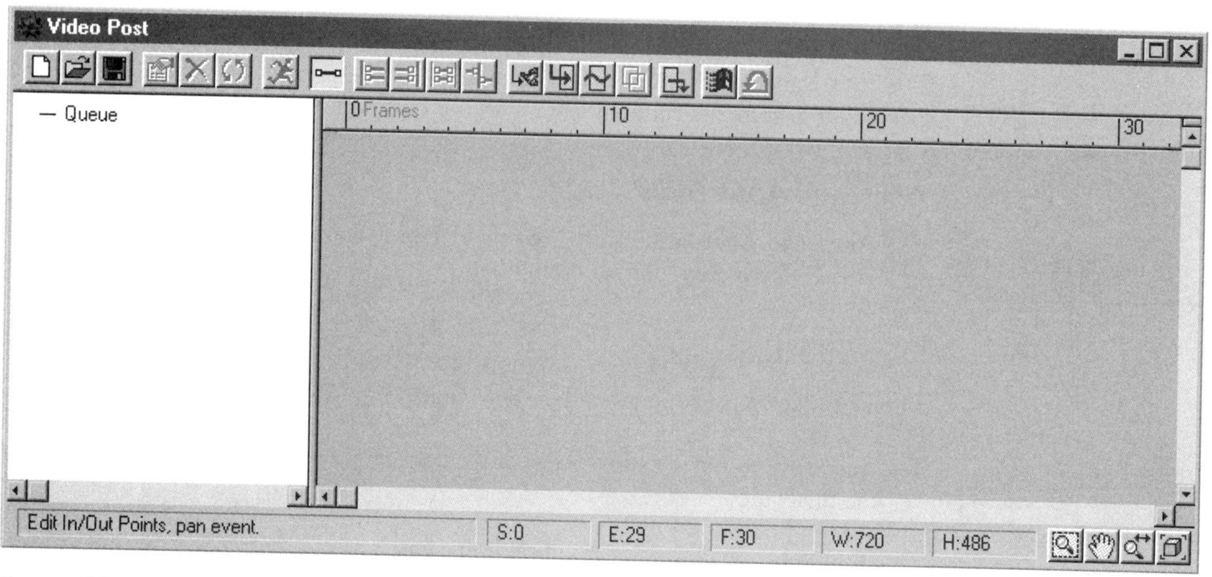


FIGURE C.2
Video Post dialog with no events added.

## Video Post Procedure

1. Display the Video Post dialog, as shown in Figure C.2, using the Rendering/Video Post pull-down menu item.

### Adding an Event

2. Pick the Add Image Input Event button; dialog similar to Figure C.3 is displayed. This is used to select the file to be added to the queue as well as to set the length of the event.

   In the Image Input area, pick the Files button, and dialog similar to Figure C.4 is displayed. Scroll through until you find the desired file, in this case STILLA.BMP. Highlight and OK it.

   Once back in the Add Image Event dialog, set the VP End Time to 50 frames. This will be the length of time the image is displayed. Refer to Figure C.5, OK to close the dialog, and return to the Video Post dialog. You should see that the event has appeared, as shown in Figure C.6. You may need to perform a Zoom Extents (found in the lower-right corner of the dialog) to see the entire bar.

FIGURE C.3
Add Image Input Event dialog.

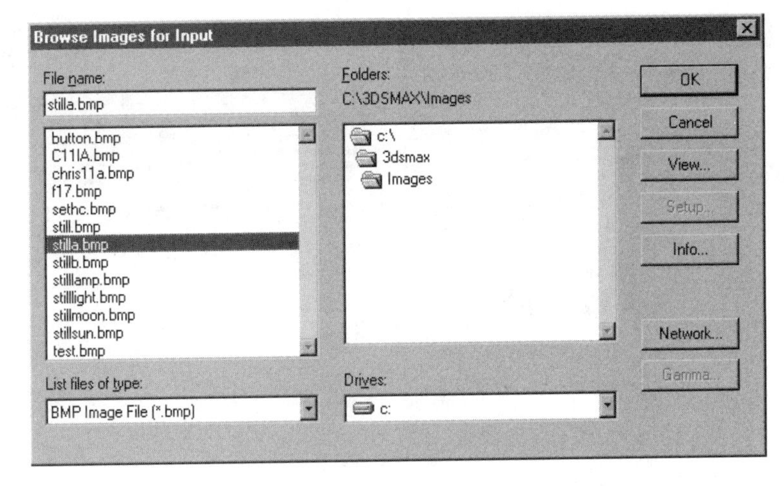


FIGURE C.4
Browse Images for Input dialog.

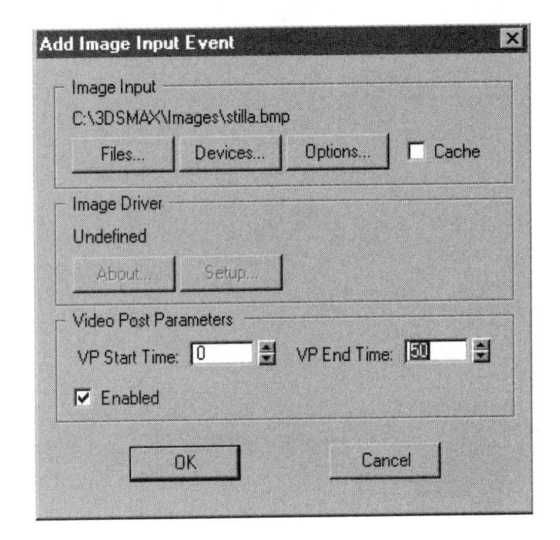


FIGURE C.5
Add Image Input Event dialog showing selected file and length of event.

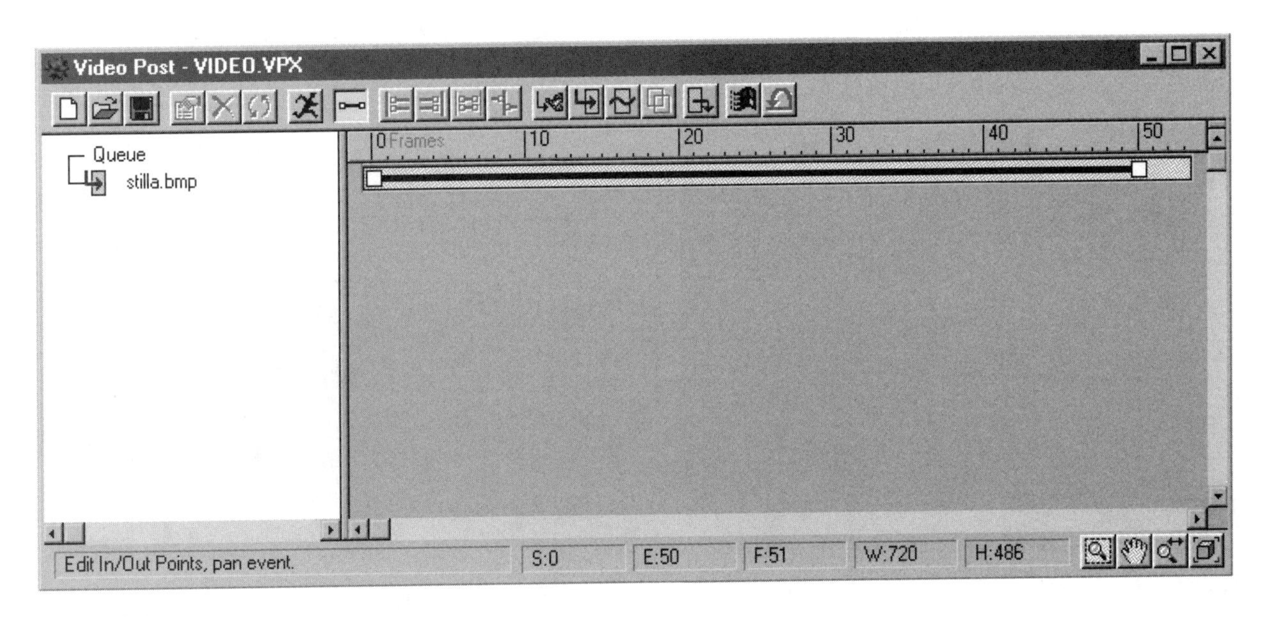


FIGURE C.6
Video Post dialog showing added event.

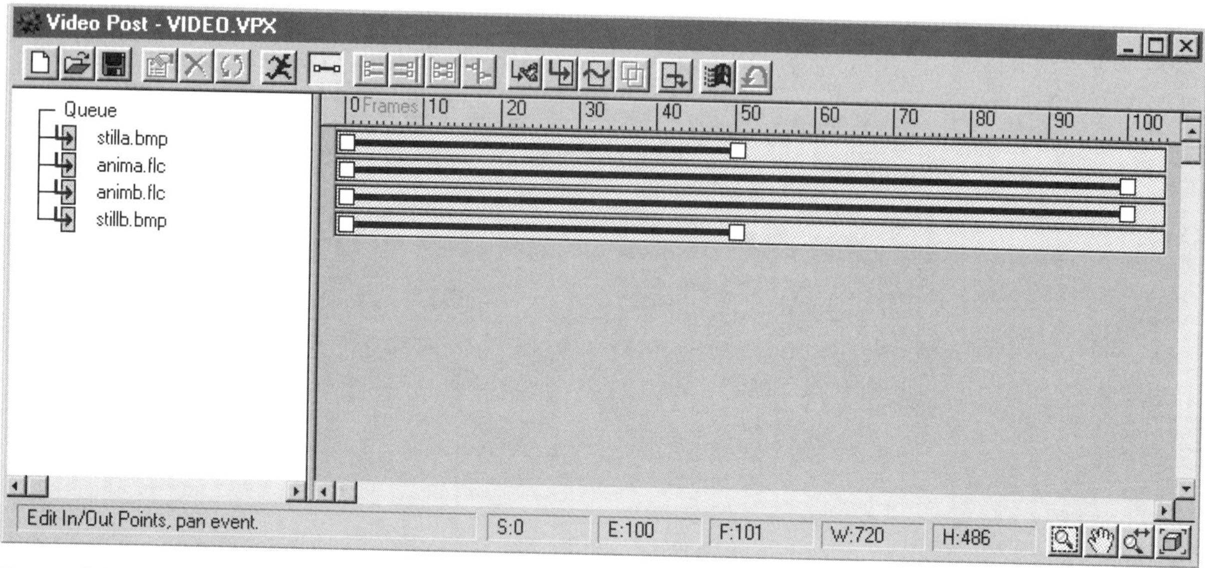


FIGURE C.7
Video Post dialog showing additional events.

3. Add any additional events, in this case: ANIMA.FLC, ANIMB.FLC, and STILLB.BMP. Refer to Figure C.7. Note how they all start at the same time. This is easily remedied.

### Moving the Bars

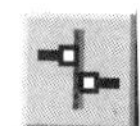

4. Highlight all the bars by holding down the CTRL key while picking the names or the bars. Once they are all highlighted, pick the Abut Selected button. Refer to Figure C.8, showing that the bars now start after each other.

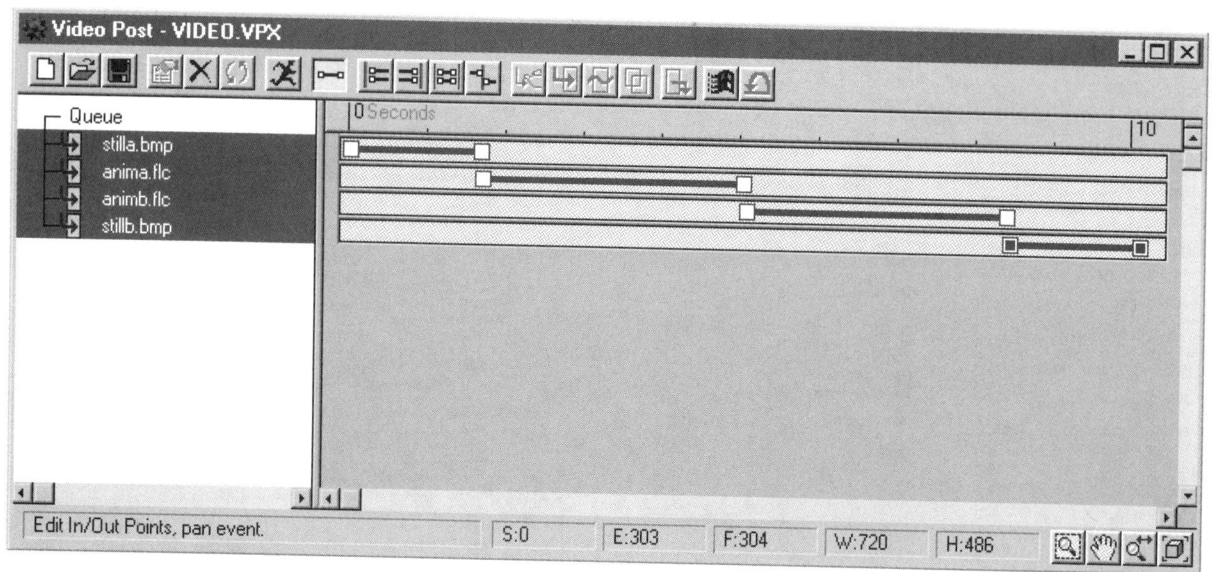


FIGURE C.8
Video Post dialog showing events starting one after another.

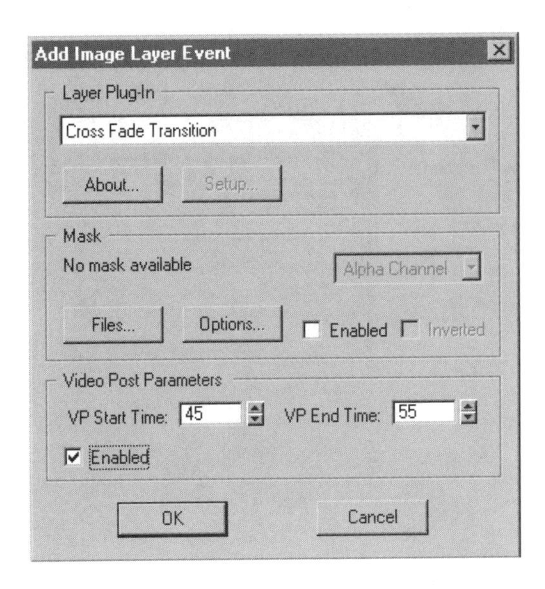


FIGURE C.9
Add Image Layer Event dialog.

### Adding a Transition

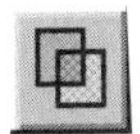

5. To cause a transition between two images, you need to add an Image Layer Event.

   Highlight the two events, pick the Add Image Layer Event, and a dialog appears similar to Figure C.9. Select a Layer Plug-in, such as Cross Fade Transition, and then enter the VP Start Time and VP End Time. The start and end times must overlap the two files. This decides when the transition will occur. Figure C.9 shows the dialog and Figure C.10 shows the addition of the event linking the still image and animation.

6. Add any other filters required. Refer to Figure C.11 showing the other filter linking ANIMB and STILLB.

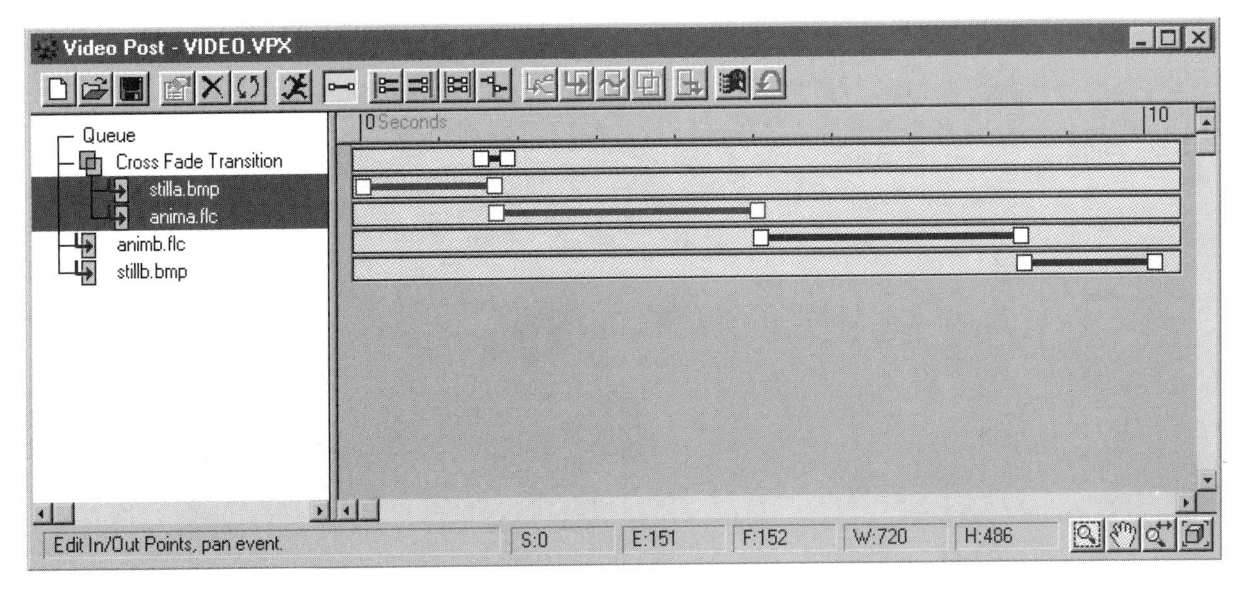


FIGURE C.10
Video Post dialog showing transition-linked events.

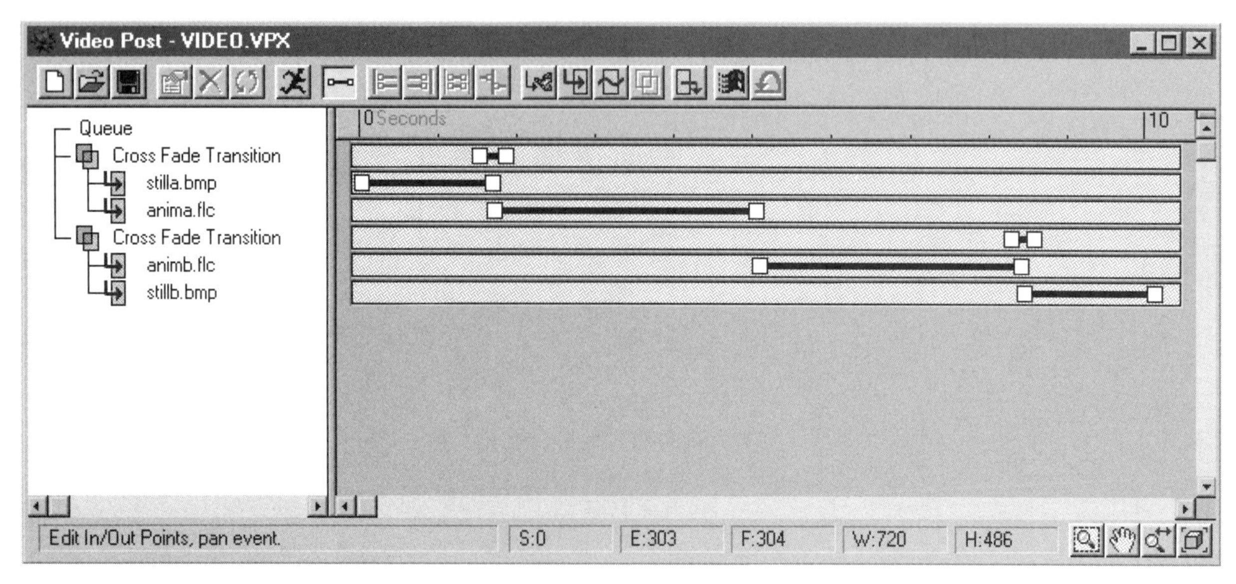


FIGURE C.11
Video Post dialog showing added transition-linked event.

### Adding an Output Event

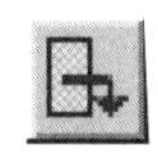

7. Lastly, you need an output event.

   Pick the Add Image Output Event. The dialog appears as shown in Figure C.12. Use the Files button to name the final animation, in this case FINAL.FLC. This additional output event is added to the queue, as shown in Figure C.13.

### Executing the Events

8. The final step is to execute the events in the queue.

   Pick the Execute Sequence button and the dialog shown in Figure C.14 appears. Using this dialog, you can make changes to the output file, such as Output Size. Once the execution is complete, you can use the File/View File pull-down menu item in 3D Studio MAX to display the composite animation (FINAL.FLC).

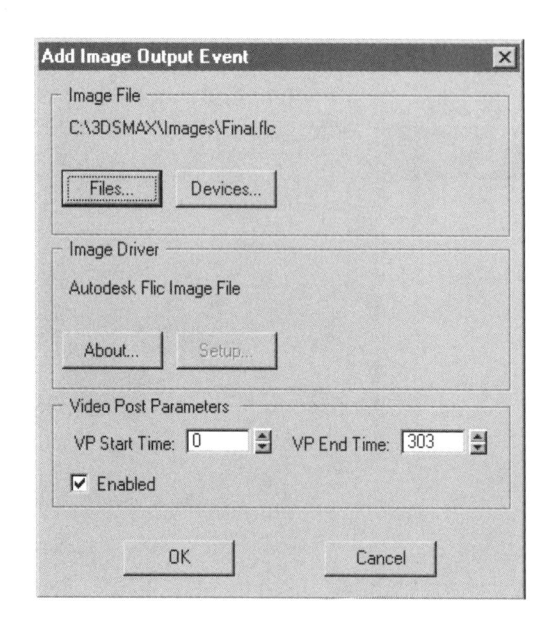


FIGURE C.12
Add Image Output Event dialog.

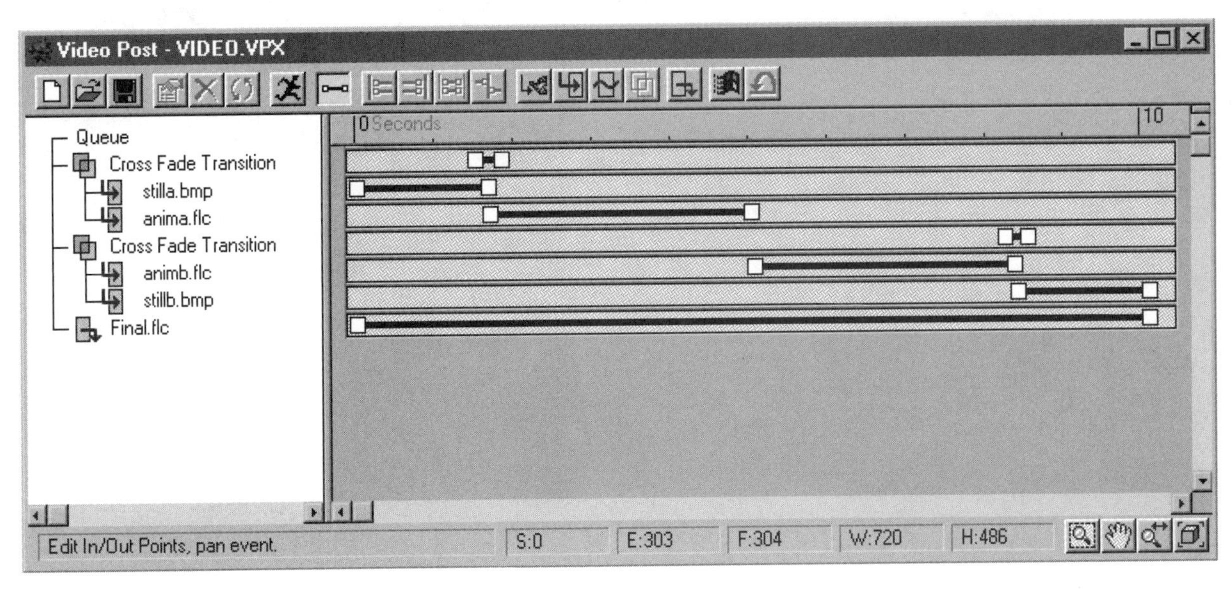


FIGURE C.13
Video Post dialog showing output event.

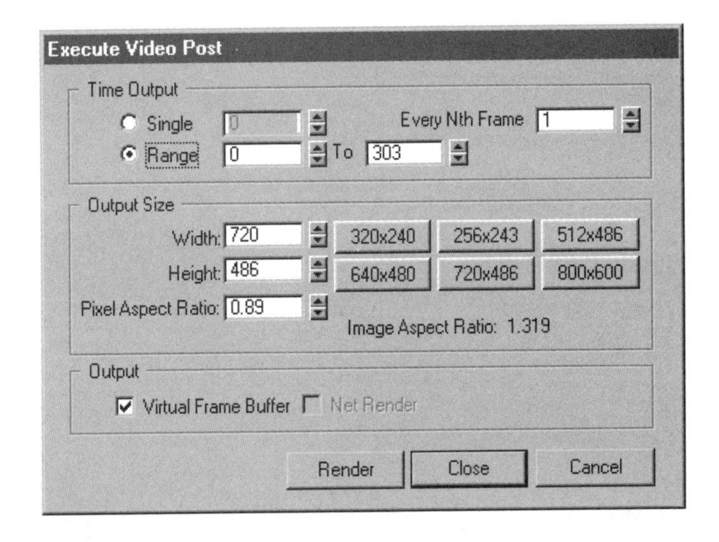


FIGURE C.14
Execute Video Post dialog.

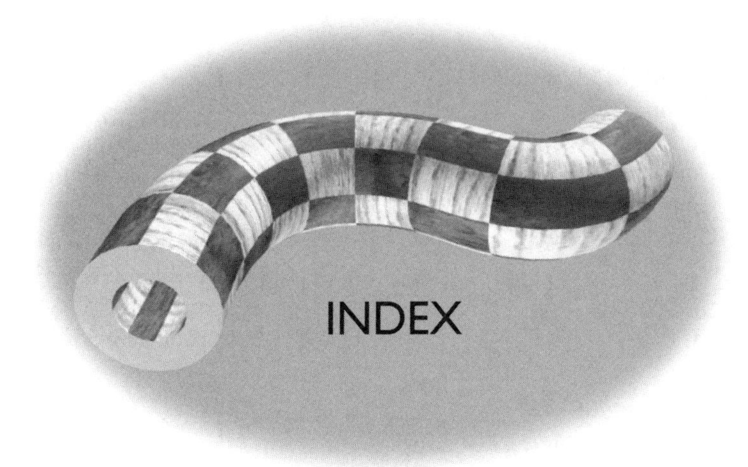
INDEX

## M



## N



## O

## W